A COMPANION TO ECONOMIC FORECASTING

Blackwell Companions to Contemporary Economics

The *Blackwell Companions to Contemporary Economics* are reference volumes accessible to serious students and yet also containing up-to-date material from recognized experts in their particular fields. These volumes focus on basic bread-and-butter issues in economics as well as popular contemporary topics often not covered in textbooks. Coverage avoids the overly technical, is concise, clear, and comprehensive. Each Companion features an introductory essay by the editor, extensive bibliographical reference sections, and an index.

A Companion to Theoretical Econometrics edited by Badi H. Baltagi
A Companion to Economic Forecasting edited by Michael P. Clements and David F. Hendry

A Companion to Economic Forecasting

Edited by

MICHAEL P. CLEMENTS AND
DAVID F. HENDRY

First published 2002

2 4 6 8 10 9 7 5 3 1

Blackwell Publishers Inc.
350 Main Street
Malden, Massachusetts 02148
U.S.A.

Blackwell Publishers Ltd
108 Cowley Road
Oxford OX4 1JF
U.K.

Library of Congress Cataloging-in-Publication Data has been applied for.

ISBN 0-631-21569-7 (hardback)

British Library Cataloguing in Publication Data

A CIP catalogue record for this book is available from the British Library.

Typeset in 10/12pt Book Antique
by Graphicraft Limited, Hong Kong
Printed in Great Britain by TJ International, Padstow, Cornwall

This book is printed on acid-free paper.

To:
Peter & Doreen; Carolyn, Anna & William
and
Bob & Rena

Contents

List of Contributors

R.J. Bhansali, University of Liverpool

Gonzalo Camba-Mendez, European Central Bank, and the National Institute of Economic and Social Research

Michael P. Clements, University of Warwick

Øyvind Eitrheim, Norges Bank

Neil R. Ericsson, Federal Reserve Board

Robert Fildes, Lancaster University

Philip Hans Franses, Erasmus University Rotterdam

David I. Harvey, Loughborough University

David F. Hendry, Nuffield College Oxford

Tore Anders Husebø, Norges Bank

George Kapetanios, Bank of England

Stefan Lundbergh, Skandia Asset Management

Helmut Lütkepohl, Humboldt Universität zu Berlin

Roberto S. Mariano, University of Pennsylvania

Michael W. McCracken, University of Missouri-Columbia

Terence C. Mills, Loughborough University

Paul Newbold, University of Nottingham

Ragnar Nymoen, University of Oslo

Dilek Önkal-Atay, Bilkent University

Keith Ord, Georgetown University

Denise R. Osborn, University of Manchester

Richard Paap, Erasmus University Rotterdam

Adrian R. Pagan, Australian National University

Diego J. Pedregal, Universidad de Castilla-La Mancha

M. Hashem Pesaran, University of Cambridge

Andrew C. Pollock, Glasgow Caledonian University

Tommaso Proietti, Università di Udine

John Robertson, Federal Reserve Bank of Atlanta

Spyros Skouras, Santa Fe Institute

Richard J. Smith, University of Bristol
Herman O. Stekler, George Washington University
Anthony S. Tay, National University of Singapore
Timo Teräsvirta, Stockholm School of Economics
Mary E. Thomson, Glasgow Caledonian Business School
Ruey S. Tsay, University of Chicago
Kenneth F. Wallis, University of Warwick
Martin R. Weale, National Institute of Economic and Social Research
Kenneth D. West, University of Wisconsin
Peter C. Young, Lancaster University

Preface

This book provides an accessible and comprehensive explanation of the art and science of macroeconomic forecasting. The various chapters have each been prepared by experts on their topic, with the common objective of describing the range of models, methods, and approaches to economic forecasting. There are contributions across the full breadth of the subject, bringing together in a single volume a range of contrasting approaches and views. Forecasting is a practical venture, and many of the chapters are aimed at practitioners and nonspecialists, although recent – more technical – advances are also covered.

In the last decade of the twentieth century, economic forecasting became the focus of intensive research from many different perspectives. The fruits of these labors include new developments or improvements in the following areas: statistical models and techniques for generating forecasts; ways of understanding the reasons for forecast failure in macroeconomics; ways of comparing and evaluating the relative merits of rival forecasts; ways of producing, and evaluating, more complete descriptions of the likely outcomes, reflecting a growing disenchantment with point forecasts; and a closer integration between the producers of forecasts and the requirements of consumers; to name but a few. Considerable progress has been made in a number of areas, such as in our *understanding* of why things sometimes go wrong, but much remains to be done on improving forecast accuracy before the transmogrification of the ugly duckling into the beautiful swan is complete.

Central to our attempt to assimilate the diverse findings into a coherent whole, which offers a comprehensive, state-of-the-art guide to the field, is an overview chapter. The overview poses ten questions about economic forecasting as a framework for organizing the following chapters: What is a forecast? What can be forecast? How confident can we be in forecasts? How is forecasting done generally? How is forecasting done by economists? How can one measure the success or failure of forecasts? How does one analyze the properties of forecasting methods? What special data features matter most? What are the main problems? Do these problems have potential solutions? What is the future of economic forecasting? The chapters offer answers to most of these questions, albeit that some are – deservedly – accorded much more attention than others.

MICHAEL P. CLEMENTS
Reader in Economics
Department of Economics
University of Warwick

DAVID F. HENDRY
Professor
Department of Economics
Oxford University
Fellow of Nuffield College

Acknowledgments

We are indebted to many colleagues and friends for their comments, discussions, and criticisms of our ideas, over the years. In particular, we wish to thank: Anindya Banerjee, Gunnar Bårdsen, Julia Campos, Jurgen Doornik, Rob Engle, Rebecca Emerson, Neil Ericsson, Tony Espasa, Clive Granger, Eilev Jansen, Søren Johansen, Katarina Juselius, Hans-Martin Krolzig, Massimiliano Marcellino, John Muellbauer, Grayham Mizon, Bent Nielsen, Jean-François Richard, Neil Shephard, Jeremy Smith, Nick Taylor, Timo Teräsvirta, and Ken Wallis. We are also very grateful to Jurgen Doornik for his immense help in organizing the styles and computing background, especially the use of his excellent OxEdit and indexing programs.

Our own research has been generously financed by the United Kingdom Economic and Social Research Council, and we are delighted to acknowledge our gratitude for their sustained level of support over the last decade, through the funding of *The Econometrics of Economic Policy*, (R000233447), *The Econometrics of Macroeconomic Forecasting*, (L116251015), and *Modelling, Forecasting and Policy in the Evolving Macro-economy* (L138251009). MPC records his gratitude to the Department of Economics, University of Warwick, for his appointment as Research Fellow in Economics, and DFH is greatly indebted to the support of Nuffield College, Oxford.

Information on corrections will be placed on the Web page: http://www.nuff.ox.ac.uk/users/hendry/

Scientific Word (TCI Software Research, New Mexico), in combination with MikTeX, and DVIPS, eased the writing of the book in LaTeX.

Michael P. Clements and David F. Hendry, December 2000

CHAPTER ONE

An Overview of Economic Forecasting

Michael P. Clements and David F. Hendry

1.1. INTRODUCTION

The chapters of this *Companion* address a wide range of issues and approaches to economic forecasting. We overview its material in terms of 11 key questions that might fruitfully be asked of any practical venture, but here specifically concern forecasting.[1]

1 What is a forecast?
2 What can be forecast?
3 How confident can we be in forecasts?
4 How is forecasting done generally?
5 How is forecasting done by economists?
6 How can one measure the success or failure of forecasts?
7 How does one analyze the properties of forecasting methods?
8 What special data features matter most?
9 What are the main problems?
10 Do these problems have potential solutions?
11 What is the future of economic forecasting?

Some of these questions can be dealt with quickly and are not specifically addressed by any of the contributors, while others provide the subject matter for several chapters. Moreover, several chapters relate to a number of the questions. To set the scene, the first part of this overview provides preliminary remarks in response to each question. The second part of the overview then summarizes each chapter in relation to these 11 questions. It is hoped that organizing the *Companion* in this way will be helpful to the nonspecialist reader. The questions we ask, and the answers that are provided here, require no foreknowledge of the subject, and should allow the reader to dip in at will, without approaching the material in any particular order.

1.1.1. What is a forecast?

A forecast is any statement about the future. Such statements may be well founded, or lack any sound basis; they may be accurate or inaccurate on any given occasion, or on average; precise or imprecise; and model-based or informal. Forecasts are produced by methods as diverse as well-tested systems of hundreds of econometrically-estimated equations, through to methods which have scarcely any observable basis (such as forecasts of the 2003 Derby winner made on 31 December 2000 – before the entrants are even known). Thus, forecasting is potentially a vast subject. Historically, almost every conceivable method has been tried, with the legacy that there are in excess of 36 different words in English for the activity of "foretelling," in a broad sense, what the future might bring forth.

1.1.2. What can be forecast?

Since it is merely a statement about the future, anything can be forecast, ranging from next month's rate of consumer price inflation, tomorrow's weather patterns, the average rise in sea levels by the end of the third millennium, through the earth's population at the same date, to the value of the Dow Jones index at the start of 2010. We are not claiming that the resulting forecasts are necessarily *useful* in any sense: consider, for example, a forecast that the first Extra Terrestrial to land on Earth will be six meters tall, blue, and will arrive in New York on July 4th, 2276 to celebrate the quincentenary of the U.S.A. Even if such a claim were to prove correct, it would be of no value for the next 250 years; and of course, it is anyway essentially certain to be incorrect.

1.1.3. How confident can we be in forecasts?

Clearly, our confidence will depend on how well-based the forecasts are. Mere guesses should not inspire great confidence; forecasts from well-tested approaches may be viewed more hopefully. Unfortunately, even the latter is not enough. The trouble is that the future is uncertain. There are two distinct senses in which this applies, expressed by Maxine Singer in her "Thoughts of a Nonmillenarian" (*Bulletin of the American Academy of Arts and Sciences*, 1997, **51**, 2, p. 39) as:

> Because of the things we don't know [that] we don't know, the future is largely unpredictable. But some developments can be anticipated, or at least imagined, on the basis of existing knowledge.

Little can be done in advance about uncertainty stemming from "things we don't know we don't know." However, the apparent randomness of outcomes within the realms we do understand, which we will call "measurable uncertainty," can often be usefully communicated to the user of a forecast. This usually takes the form of a forecast interval around a "point" forecast, the latter then being viewed as the central tendency, or "most likely" outcome. For example, the statement that "the moon is *exactly* 5,000 miles away" is very precise (but wholly inaccurate), and taken literally would be associated with a forecast interval of length zero. On the other hand, the statement that "the moon lies between 1,000 and 1 billion miles away" is correct, but very imprecise, having a huge forecast interval. More sophisticated presentations of measurable uncertainty include density forecasts; namely, estimates of the probability distribution of the possible future outcomes. The Bank of England tries to present its *Inflation Report* forecasts in this last form, using a "fan chart" where uncertainty fans out into the future in ever wider bands of lighter color (unfortunately, they chose red for the inflation forecasts and green for output, so these were called "rivers of blood" and "rivers of bile" respectively: see Coyle (2001) for an amusing discussion.

1.1.4.   How is forecasting done generally?

There are many ways of making forecasts. These include formal model-based statistical analyses, statistical analyses not based on parametric models, informal "back-of-the-envelope" calculations, simple extrapolations, "leading indicators," "chartist" approaches, "informed judgment," tossing a coin, guessing, and "hunches." It is difficult to judge the frequency with which each of these methods is used in practice, but most occur regularly in our everyday lives. In earlier times, tea leaves, entrails, movements of the stars, etc., all were tried – without great success so far as we can ascertain – but some (such as astrology) remain in use today. This book, for better or worse, will focus on formal statistical approaches.

1.1.5.   How is forecasting done by economists?

In economics, methods of forecasting include:

1 guessing, "rules of thumb," or "informal models";
2 expert judgment;
3 extrapolation;
4 leading indicators;
5 surveys;
6 time-series models; and
7 econometric systems.

Guessing and related methods only rely on luck. While that may be a minimal assumption compared to the other methods we will discuss, guessing is not generally a useful method: "good" guesses are often reported, and bad ones quietly ignored; and the uncertainty attaching to each guess is usually impossible to evaluate in advance. If many individuals guess, some will be "right" by chance, but that hardly justifies the approach (otherwise economists will start producing thousands of forecasts and claiming success whenever any one of them is accurate).

Expert judgment is usually part of a forecasting approach, but lacks validation when it is the sole component, even if at any point in time, some "oracle" manages to have forecasted accurately. Unfortunately, systematic success proves elusive even to experts, and no one can predict which oracle will be successful next (note the recent advice to ignore past performance when choosing a fund manager!).

Extrapolation is fine so long as the tendencies persist, but that is itself doubtful: the telling feature is that different extrapolators are used at different points in time. Moreover, forecasts are most useful when they predict changes in tendencies, which extrapolative methods are likely to miss. Many a person has bought shares, or a house, at the peak of a boom. . . .

Forecasting based on *leading indicators* requires a stable relationship between the variables that "lead" and the variables that are "led." When the reasons for the lead are clear, as with orders preceding production, then the indicators may be useful, but otherwise are liable to give misleading information. Even for such "obvious" leading indicators as housing starts leading to completed dwellings, the record is poor (because the delay can narrow and widen dramatically in housing market booms and busts – or with very severe weather).

Surveys of consumers and businesses can be informative about future events, but rely on plans being realized. Again we see "many a slip twixt cup and lip": adverse changes in the business "climate" can induce radical revisions to plans, since it is less costly to revise a plan than the actuality.

Time-series models which describe the historical patterns of data are popular forecasting methods, and have often been found to be competitive relative to econometric systems of equations (particularly in their multivariate forms). These are the work-horse of the forecasting industry, and several chapters below explain and analyze variants thereof. But like all other methods, they focus on "measurable uncertainty."

Econometric systems of equations are the main tool in economic forecasting. These comprise equations which seek to "model" the behavior of discernible groups of economic agents (consumers, producers, workers, investors, etc.) assuming a considerable degree of rationality – moderated by historical experience. The advantages to economists of using formal econometric systems of national economies are to consolidate existing empirical and theoretical knowledge of how economies function, provide a framework for a progressive research strategy leading to increased understanding over time, help to explain their own failures, as well as provide forecasts and policy advice. Econometric and time-series models are the primary methods of forecasting in economics, but "judgment," "indicators," and even "guesses" may modify the resulting forecasts.

1.1.6.   How can one measure the success or failure of forecasts?

A forecast might reasonably be judged "successful" if it was close to the outcome, but that judgment depends on how "close" is measured. Reconsider our example of "guessing" the distance to the moon: it is apparent that accuracy and precision are two dimensions along which forecasts may be judged. To the layman, a very precise forecast that is highly inaccurate might be thought undesirable, as might an accurate but very imprecise forecast: and experts concur – the "gold standard" is an accurate and precise forecast. Failure is easier to discern: a forecast is a failure if it is inaccurate by an amount that is large relative to its claimed precision. Thus, forecasters are squeezed between wanting accurate and precise forecasts, yet not claiming so much precision that they regularly fail.

The notion of "unbiasedness," whereby forecasts are centered on outcomes, is used in technical analyses to measure accuracy; whereas that of small variance, so only a narrow range of outcomes is compatible with the forecast statement, measures precision. In principle, in any specific instance, the costs attached to bias and variance will depend on the purposes to which the forecast is to be put, via the costs of any actions taken on the basis of the forecast. Such costs define the "loss function," though in practice, the loss function may not be explicitly stated. When (squared) bias and variance are combined one-for-one, we obtain the commonly-reported mean square forecast error (MSFE).

Unfortunately, no unique measure of a "winner" is possible in a forecasting competition involving either multi-period or multi-variable forecasts, which are the norm in economics – forecasting say unemployment and inflation up to two years ahead for a "misery index." Surprisingly, that claim remains true even when the metric for "closeness" (such as MSFE) is agreed. Figure 1.1 illustrates the problem. The forecast in the top-left panel (denoted a) is awful for the levels of the series shown, but is accurate for the growth rates (top-right panel); conversely, forecast b (lower-left panel) is fine for the levels, but dreadful for growth (lower-right panel). Thus, one must decide on which aspect it is important to be close before any choice between methods is possible. Worse still, MSFE itself is not an obvious criterion: a stockbroker probably does not care how good or bad a model is on MSFE if it is the best for making money. Indeed, errors on the sign of a price change may be much more important to her than mistakes with a large magnitude, but the correct sign.

To explore the difficulty of judging the winner of a forecasting competition further, consider two friends passing time while waiting at a bus-stop. Sue challenges Peter to forecast the behavior of a student who is standing inside the bus shelter: every 30 seconds they will both write in their diary a forecast for the next 30 seconds as to whether or not the student will have left. Sue realizes that she

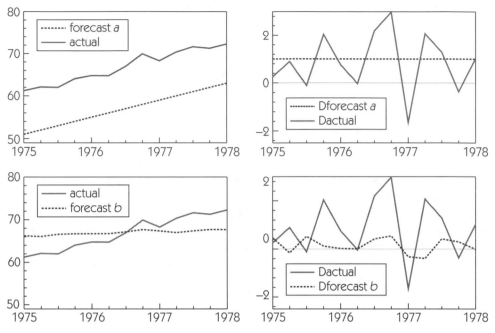

Figure 1.1   Which wins: forecasts of levels or growth?

will only ever make a single mistake if she adopts the following strategy: always forecast that the current state will persist. When the student is there, she forecasts he will still be there in 30 seconds' time; and when he has left, she simply writes that. Thus, in the 5 minutes' wait before the student departs, Sue is correct 10 times, then wrong once, but thereafter correct for ever. Peter, however, is an economist, so he uses a "causal model": students stand at bus stops to get on buses. Thus, if no bus approaches, Peter forecasts the student will stay; but when a bus appears, he forecasts the student will board the bus. Unfortunately, four different buses come by, and the student remains stubbornly at the bus stop – then his girlfriend appears on her motor bike, the student climbs on, and they go away. Peter is wrong four times in the 5 minutes, and if he stuck to his causal model, wrong ever after since the student never got on a bus! Sue wins easily: or does she?

Substitute the phrase "the volcano will not explode" for "will remain at the bus stop," and the vacuous nature of Sue's forecast is clear, even if she did appear to win. On any reasonable loss function, the ability to *anticipate* a volcanic eruption, however imperfectly – which her "no-change" forecast is inherently unable to do – should score highly. The appearance of winning is dependent on agreeing a particular "metric," whereas only awarding a "win" for correctly forecasting the specific event could yield a different winner (of course, that in turn leads to the problem of "forecasting eight of the last three recessions". . .).

In addition to bias and variance considerations, point forecasts are often judged on criteria such as the efficient use of information. Also, forecasts often include forecast intervals, and sometimes of the complete density of outcomes, so these are required to be "well calibrated." Because it is seldom the case that only a single forecast exists of any economic phenomenon of interest, rival forecasts are often available to allow comparisons of one against the other, *ex post*. A natural focus of attention is then whether a combination of one or more forecasts is better than any one forecast alone, or whether one forecast contains all the useful information in another (so that it *encompasses* that forecast). We may wish to test whether, given a particular loss function, one forecast is statistically better than another, and further, whether allowing for the uncertainty inherent in the estimates of a model's parameters affects the inferences made.

1.1.7. How does one analyze the properties of forecasting methods?

The properties of forecasting methods can be investigated in both empirical and artificial settings, using mathematical analysis and computer-intensive numerical methods. For example, we could try the ideas discussed just above for measuring the success or failure of forecasts by testing combinations of forecasting models for encompassing. Forecasting methods can also be compared by Monte Carlo (or stochastic simulation), where an investigator generates artificial "data" on which the models are compared in repeated trials, to calculate how well such methods perform in a controlled environment of their own choosing. However, the empirical relevance of such results depends on whether or not the artificial data "mimic" the relevant properties of the "real world," so may be open to doubt. This method of analysis is most useful when we know the large-sample behavior of statistics of interest for the forecasting methods (say, MSFEs), and wish to investigate the usefulness of these asymptotic results for samples of the size typically available to the applied researcher. This is an example of one of the earliest uses of Monte Carlo in econometrics, namely calculating the small-sample distributions of estimators and tests whose asymptotic behavior is known.

Empirical comparisons, in the form of forecasting competitions, typically look at the performance of different methods for many time series. Because the data-generating process is not under the investigator's control, and will only be imperfectly known, the results of forecast comparisons for any one series could turn on idiosyncratic features of the series, so limit their general applicability. For this reason, many series are compared, and often series are selected which share certain characteristics, with the caveat that the results might only be expected to hold for other series with those characteristics. This highlights a "circularity problem": until we know how empirical economic data are generated, we cannot know the appropriate framework for developing or analyzing methods, so cannot actually know how well they should perform.

1.1.8.   What special data features matter most?

Many economic and financial time series possess a number of special features, including, in various combinations: seasonality, business-cycle fluctuations, trend growth, successive dependence, and changing variability. More generally, data in economics is often "nonstationary," namely, has changing means and variances over time. These special data features are potentially important for a number of reasons. Failure to allow for such specific characteristics (say, seasonality) may result in inferior forecasts of aspects of interest (say, turning points, or the underlying trend) especially if, as some recent research suggests, these characteristics are inherently interlinked. More positively, certain of these characteristics may themselves be the focus of attention in the forecasting exercise. For example, one may wish to forecast a business-cycle characteristic, such as the next recession, and be otherwise uninterested in the level, or rate of growth, of the series. For both these reasons, models have been developed which attempt to capture special features, and as will become apparent, many different approaches have been proposed.

Provided that "nonstationary" can be modeled, or incorporated in a systematic way into a forecasting method, having changing means and variances over time is unproblematic. Thus, so-called "unit-root" nonstationary (which leads to trending variances) has been the focus of much research, partly because solutions were clear, although important generalizations were in fact discovered (see, for example, Hendry and Juselius (2000), and Doornik, Hendry, and Nielsen (1998), for recent surveys). However, some other sources of change, particularly in means, have not yielded to modeling as yet; and what "we don't know we don't know" simply cannot be included in any model.

1.1.9.   What are the main problems?

One of the main problems with forecasting in economics is that economies evolve over time and are subject to intermittent, and sometimes large, unanticipated shocks. Economic evolution has its sources in scientific discoveries and inventions, which lead to technical progress. This becomes embodied in physical and human capital, and provides the engine for sustained growth in real output. In addition, structural breaks may be precipitated by changes in legislation, sudden switches in economic policy, or political turmoil (examples of breaks relevant to the U.K. include the abolition of exchange controls, the introduction of interest-bearing checking accounts, privatization, the introduction of several radically different monetary-policy regimes, and the steep rises in fuel prices in the 1970s). Thus, erstwhile stable relationships between economic variables are subject to change, and if used to provide forecasts at such times, can result in large and persistent forecast errors.

Moreover, the empirical econometric models used to understand and forecast processes as complicated as national economies are far from perfect representations of behavior. Forecasters may only be dimly aware of what changes are afoot, and even when developments can be envisaged, may find it hard to quantify their likely impacts (for example, the effects of building society demutualizations on consumers' spending in the 1990s). These difficulties entail that economic forecasting is fraught with problems, and in practice, forecast failure – a significant deterioration in forecast performance relative to the anticipated outcome – is common.

Econometric forecasting models are systems of relationships between variables such as GNP, inflation, exchange rates, etc. Their equations are then estimated from available data, mainly aggregate time series. Such models may be viewed as having three main components: deterministic terms introduced to capture averages and steady growth (represented here by intercepts and linear trends, which take the values 1, 1, 1, . . . ; and 1, 2, 3, . . . respectively), and whose future values are known; observed stochastic variables with unknown future values (like consumers' expenditure, prices, etc.); and unobserved errors, all of whose values (past, present, and future) are unknown (though perhaps estimable in the context of a model). The relationships between any of these three components could be inappropriately formulated, inaccurately estimated, or change in unanticipated ways. Each of the resulting nine types of mistake *could* induce poor forecast performance, either from inaccurate (that is, biased), or imprecise (that is, high variance) forecasts. However, it transpires that systematic forecast failure is most likely to depend on the behavior of the deterministic terms, and in particular on unanticipated changes in their values. Such deterministic shifts may reflect changes elsewhere in the economy, interacting with an incomplete or incorrect model specification.

1.1.10. Do these problems have potential solutions?

Forecast intervals seek to measure forecast uncertainty, but can only reflect the "known uncertainties" – deriving from model estimation, assuming future shocks resemble the past – whereas unanticipated deterministic shifts occur intermittently in economics. As we have already stressed, since we don't know what we don't know, it is difficult to account for this "unknown uncertainty."

A simple example may make this clear. Suppose that the variable we wish to forecast is in fact generated by the following equation:

$$Y_t = \delta + \phi Y_{t-1} + a_t, \tag{1.1}$$

where $\{a_t\}$ is a sequence of independent and normally distributed random variables with mean zero, and variance σ_a^2, written $\{a_t\} \sim \text{IN}[0, \sigma_a^2]$. At period T, we know that the value the variable will take next period (in $T + 1$) will be $y_{T+1} = \delta + \phi y_T$ *plus* the realized value of some random shock.[2] Here, we know the distribution of that shock, so we know that Y_{T+1} will be normally distributed around a mean of $\delta + \phi y_T$ with variance σ_a^2. Thus, we can construct intervals for our central projection ($y_{T+1|T} = \delta + \phi y_T$). These will take the form of probability statements that the outcome will fall in certain intervals, say:

$$\Pr(Y_{T+1} \in \{y_{T+1|T} \pm z_{\frac{\alpha}{2}} \sigma_a\}) = 1 - \alpha,$$

where $z_{\frac{\alpha}{2}}$ is the value such that the probability that a standard normal variate is smaller is $\alpha/2$. This interval states that if we were able to witness R realizations of $\{Y_{T+1}\}$, then on $(1 - \alpha) \times R$ of them, the actual outcome would fall within $\pm z_{\frac{\alpha}{2}} \sigma_a$ of the central projection. Since the degree of uncertainty in our point forecast is known *exactly*, wherein lies the problem?

First, in practice we will never know the values of the parameters of the model, $\{\delta, \phi, \sigma_a^2\}$ so these will have to be replaced by estimates. However, the additional uncertainty this step imparts is a form of "known uncertainty": we know it will arise, and it can be taken into account; see, for example, Clements and Hendry (1998, ch. 4), and the survey of bootstrap techniques in Clements and Taylor (2001). Second, the form of the model cannot be known for certain: there may be further lagged responses than those included in (1.1), or the logs of the variables may be needed rather than the levels, and so on. Uncertainty that may arise from the model specification not being known is less easy to handle: see for example, Chatfield (1993), Chatfield (1995), and Draper (1995). The third major problem, though, is when the future ceases to resemble the past, and this change is unknown to the forecaster. Suppose $\{a_t\} \sim \text{IN}[\mu, \tilde{\sigma}_a^2]$ for $t > T$, say, where either $\mu \neq 0$ and/or $\tilde{\sigma}_a^2 \neq \sigma_a^2$. Notice that $\mu \neq 0$ is equivalent to a shift in δ to $\delta + \mu$. Of course, there is no good reason to suppose that the form of the distribution of the shocks also remains unchanged. The shift in the mean will affect the accuracy of our predictions, and the change in the variance of the disturbances means that we will either over- or under-estimate the uncertainty surrounding the point forecasts. The shift in the error distribution will induce incorrect density forecasts.

Nevertheless, there are ways of avoiding systematic forecast failure in economies that are subject to sudden, unanticipated, large shifts. When shocks are unanticipated, it would take a magician to conjure ways of avoiding large errors in forecasts announced *before* such shocks have occurred. Rather, given an inability to forecast the shock, adaptation is required once a shock has occurred, to avoid a sequence of poor forecasts. Some models adapt more quickly than others. We cannot explain the precise nature of all the relevant models in this introduction, but note, for example, that shifts in the means of stationary combinations of variables appear to be a key cause of mis-prediction in the widely-used "vector equilibrium-correction mechanism" class of model, whereas vector autoregressions in first (and even second differences) are more robust to deterministic shifts, and adapt to the changed environment. Even when a given model type does not itself adjust rapidly, devices exist to speed that process: for example, so-called "intercept corrections" can be used to "set a model back on track" and thereby attenuate systematic failure. Thus, some solutions exist for at least part of the problem.

To illustrate these, suppose that in (1.1), the intercept δ changes to $\delta + \mu$ at $T + 1$, and for simplicity, $\phi = 0$, so the process is

$$Y_t = \delta + \mu 1_{(t>T)} + a_t, \tag{1.2}$$

where $1_{(t>T)}$ takes the value 1 when $t > T$ and zero otherwise. Forecasting period $T + 2$ at time $T + 1$, without realizing the mean had changed, we would on average make an error of μ, whereas if we used a "random walk predictor," namely $\tilde{y}_{T+2|T+1} = y_{T+1}$, the average error is zero! Alternatively, suppose we revise our forecast of $T + 2$ by the amount by which we were wrong in predicting period $T + 1$, then the average error is again zero. But the cost of improved accuracy is reduced precision. It is simple to show that a confidence interval which would contain the actual outcome $(1 - \alpha) \times 100\%$ of the time would be approximately $\{\tilde{y}_{T+2|T+1} \pm z_{\frac{\alpha}{2}} 2\sigma_a\}$, which is twice as large as for a one-step-ahead prediction using the correct model in the absence of the mean shift.

Effort is also being devoted to studying "early warning" signals. Such methods seek to anticipate change by observing it elsewhere in "leading regions" (California, say), or at a higher frequency (such as in weekly data, when the usual frequency is quarterly). However, logical problems begin to arise in a social science. First, say, the IMF could predict the onset of currency crises, then remedial action would prevent the forecasted outcome from materializing (this is rather like a car mechanic replacing brakes suspected of likely failure, so that failure does not eventuate). Second, say *you* could forecast a crisis, and kept it secret – apart from being believed by a small group of financial backers – then you could create a money machine: your actions might alter the outcome from what was originally predicted, but might equally induce a "self-fulfilling prophecy," creating a crisis where none would otherwise occur. Thus, there are limits, albeit wide, to what we may ever hope to forecast.

1.1.11. What is the future of economic forecasting?

To succeed simultaneously in forecasting competitions and in the policy arena, econometric models will have to mimic the adaptability of the best forecasting devices, while retaining their foundations in economic analysis. Despite a relatively poor track record to date, and the many problems that economic forecasts from econometric systems confront, these models offer a vehicle for understanding, and learning from, failures, as well as consolidating our growing knowledge of economic behavior. Moreover, a close interaction between theory and evidence is essential for a successful economic science. Consequently, econometric systems provide the best long-run hope for successful forecasting, especially as suitable methods are developed to improve their robustness to unanticipated breaks.

We have highlighted many difficulties in our introduction: what we have been less able to do is emphasize the tremendous progress achieved in understanding the properties of forecasting models, methods, and measures. Economic forecasting used to be the orphan of the discipline: "those who could, did; those who couldn't, forecast." Its poor track record tainted the messengers and analysts, as well as the models. However, the 1990s saw a resurgence of interest in the theory and practice of economic forecasting that continues as we write. This *Companion* describes the outcomes of much of that intellectual endeavor, and points to a bright future – at least for those who study economic forecasting.

1.2.   A REVIEW OF THE *COMPANION* CONTENTS

What can be forecast? And how confident can we be in our forecasts?

The chapters by Neil Ericsson on forecast uncertainty, and the survey on density forecasting in economics and finance by Anthony Tay and Ken Wallis, can be viewed as a response to "how confident can we be in our forecasts?"

Neil Ericsson discusses the sources of both predictable and unpredictable forecast uncertainty in empirical economic modeling. The key features of predictable uncertainty are illustrated by several analytic models, and with empirical models of the U.S. trade account and U.K. inflation and real income.

Anthony Tay and Ken Wallis present a survey of density forecasting in macroeconomics and finance, and cover the production, presentation, and evaluation of density forecasts. A density forecast is an estimate of the probability distribution of the possible future values of the variable.

How is forecasting done generally?

The chapters by Diego Pedregal and Peter Young, and by Tommaso Proietti, exposit general statistical approaches to modeling time series. The techniques, models, and methods discussed are applicable to observations recorded at equally-spaced intervals of time, and have been employed in many disciplines outside economics. Diego Pedregal and Peter Young's chapter is a "multi-disciplinary overview of the current state-of-the-art" of statistical approaches to modeling time series. From the numerous statistical approaches available, they focus on the unobserved components approach, which they favor for the modeling and forecasting of nonstationary data. The practical usefulness is demonstrated with two detailed empirical examples.

The chapter by Tommaso Proietti also considers unobserved components models. He discusses the specification of models for the major components: models for trend, cycle, and seasonal components, as well as recent developments concerning multivariate extensions of the models, and technical aspects concerning the specification of initial conditions for estimation. Illustrations of forecasting Italian GDP and U.S. auto sales series show the efficacy of the approach relative to Box–Jenkins time-series models.

How is forecasting done by economists?

As one might anticipate, a wide variety of models and methods are used. In contrast to the statistical, model-based approaches surveyed by Pedregal and Young, and Proietti, Dilek Önkal-Atay, Mary Thomson, and Andrew Pollock discuss judgmental forecasting. They note that judgment may enter the forecasting exercise at many levels, from the choice of the variables to include, to the adjustment of model predictions for new information. The term judgmental forecasting refers to "the incorporation of forecasters' opinions and experience into the prediction process," and so covers a wide variety of situations. They review the factors that affect the accuracy of judgmental forecasts, studies that have sought to compare the accuracy of judgmental and model-based forecasts, and judgmental adjustments and the combination of the two types of forecast. They discuss why forecast users sometimes prefer judgmental forecasts, irrespective of their accuracy.

Adrian Pagan and John Robertson discuss how forecasting is done in central banks with a view to informing the setting of macroeconomic monetary policy. From their account of the approaches adopted in a number of central banks, it becomes apparent that there is a good deal of diversity. An important dimension is the extent to which formal methods are preferred to expert systems. They conjecture as to why the specific banks they consider align themselves as they do.

Helmut Lütkepohl exposits modeling and forecasting with cointegrated vector autoregressive-moving average (VARMA) processes. VAR models have been popular in empirical macroeconomic research and in forecasting since Sims (1980) and Doan, Litterman, and Sims (1984), and VARMA models can be viewed as the natural multivariate successors to the univariate models of Box and Jenkins (1976). The moving-average component of the multivariate models has often been ignored in empirical applications, but Lütkepohl provides a comprehensive and clear treatment of the more general model, and shows how the results specialize for the more familiar VAR models. It is important to allow for cointegration in models of this sort because of the existence of long-run relationships between some economic variables; see, for example, Engle and Granger (1987) and Johansen (1995).

The chapter by Raj Bhansali on multi-step forecasting warns that the standard approach to prediction is only optimal when the model coincides with the data generating process. In general, more accurate predictions may result by selecting a new model and/or reestimating the model parameters separately for each forecast horizon of interest.

How can one measure the success or failure of forecasts?

Herman Stekler surveys the literature on testing the rationality and efficiency of individuals' forecasts, and reports on applications to inflation and output-growth forecasts in both the U.S. and U.K. He conjectures as to why some forecasts are not rational, and draws out the connections between some tests of rationality, and tests of forecast encompassing and combination. He concludes that we do not know why "irrational" forecasts appear to have been made at some times but not others, but that some systematic errors may result from fundamental changes in market structure or in the economy which could not be foreseen, so the resulting errors could not in some sense be reasonably avoided, although there is little evidence on this.

Hashem Pesaran and Spyros Skouras provide an overview of quantitative and qualitative methods for evaluating forecasts when there exists *a priori* information regarding the use to which the forecasts will be put. They contrast the decision-based approach to the evaluation and comparison of forecasts with purely statistical approaches, and show how such an approach can provide a unifying theme for recent developments in the forecast-evaluation literature – namely the use of generalized cost-of-error functions, probability event, and density forecast evaluation and the evaluation of market-timing skills. The problem of testing the "equivalence" of two forecast distributions in a decision-based context is also addressed briefly.

The motivation for the chapter by Paul Newbold and David Harvey on forecast combination and encompassing is that two or more forecasts of the same phenomenon may sometimes be available. Empirically, it is often the case that a combination of the forecasts is preferable to any individual forecast, as might seem reasonable when the forecasts draw on different sources of information. One forecast is said to encompass another when the optimal combination of the two assigns zero weight to the second forecast.

Roberto Mariano considers ways in which *tests* of models' out-of-sample performance can be constructed. This goes beyond the *comparison* of models' forecasts, by attempting to determine whether differences in performance are significant once the stochastic nature of the problem is taken into account. Early efforts toward the construction of appropriate statistical tests of forecast accuracy made a number of stringent assumptions concerning the properties of the forecast errors and loss functions that belied their usefulness, though recent contributions relax these conditions.

Even so, these tests of a model's out-of-sample predictive accuracy often proceed as if the parameters of the models from which the forecasts come are known. Michael McCracken and Kenneth West show that parameter estimation uncertainty can affect the construction of asymptotically-valid tests of predictive ability. They explain the circumstances in which the impact of parameter estimation uncertainty needs to be allowed for in making inference on predictive ability, and suggest how this can be done.

How do we analyze the properties of forecasting methods?

Robert Fildes and Keith Ord review the role of forecasting competitions in improving forecasting practice and research. They consider what has been learnt from the major competitions over the past 30 years. They first describe the components of a competition and the criteria for making comparisons across competing methods. The principal competitions are then reviewed, along with the criticisms that have been levelled against them. They argue that it is possible to draw valid conclusions about the performance of different methods, based upon the evidence provided by forecasting competitions.

Øyvind Eitrheim, Tore Anders Husebø, and Ragnar Nymoen report on empirical forecast accuracy comparisons between models that feature equilibrium-correction mechanisms, and models in differences (or growth rates), in the context of inflation targeting. As they note, one- or two-year-ahead forecasts of inflation are a vital input to monetary policy decision-making in countries which have adopted inflation targeting. They show that rival models of the inflation process have different forecasting properties over a period that covers a change in regime in the Norwegian economy, and that models in differences are in some instances preferable.

The third contribution on comparing forecasting methods is by Gonzalo Camba-Mendez, George Kapetanios, Martin Weale, and Richard Smith, who consider the forecasting performance of leading indicators for predicting industrial production in four major European countries. They present a way of evaluating the forecasting ability of composite leading indicator variables of industrial economic activity, and apply it to the four European countries.

What special data features matter most?

Seasonality is an important feature of many economic and financial time series. Traditionally, seasonality has often been viewed as being essentially fixed over time, and a "nuisance" that masks the underlying movements in the original series. As such, researchers interested in, say, the long-run properties of economic time series, have felt justified in analyzing seasonally-adjusted data, although as Denise Osborn notes, seasonality may be viewed as exhibiting a type of unit-root behavior, which has consequences for the long-run properties of the series. Her chapter looks at the issues concerned with whether seasonal patterns exhibit unit roots or are deterministic. Philip Hans Franses and Richard Paap consider forecasting univariate seasonal time-series data using periodic autoregressive models. Periodic models allow the parameters of the model to vary with the season. They discuss a concept of integration that arises in such models, and the appropriate treatment of deterministic terms. They provide an empirical comparison of the out-of-sample forecast performance of a number of models of seasonality for quarterly U.K. consumption series.

There has been much recent interest in time-series models that are able to capture perceived asymmetries in the phases of business-cycle fluctuations in activity. Ruey Tsay provides a general review of nonlinear time-series models and forecasting. He discusses testing for nonlinearity, modeling procedures, and forecasting for some nonlinear time-series models, and illustrates with a number of empirical applications. This is an area of on-going intensive research activity, and Tsay's chapter offers the reader the opportunity to gain a better understanding of nonlinear models and an appreciation of their applications.

Stefan Lundbergh and Timo Teräsvirta focus on a particular class of nonlinear time-series model – smooth transition autoregressive (STAR) models. They discuss modeling procedures, techniques for obtaining multi-period predictions, and the generation and display of forecast densities. For an empirical example, they estimate and forecast STAR models for two quarterly unemployment series.

Terence Mills reviews a number of the special features possessed by many financial time series, such as that price changes (or returns) may be largely uncorrelated, but that the conditional variances of price changes are likely to be forecastable. His chapter covers the long-memory or long-range dependence thought to be a feature of some financial time series, the "fat-tailedness" of the unconditional distributions of returns, nonlinear models of returns, trading rules, calendar effects, and forecasting returns using other variables, and equilibrium-correction models of returns. He conjectures that future developments in the econometric analysis of financial time series will continue to exploit the explosion in computer power of the last decade, focusing on nonlinear models and computer-intensive evaluation techniques such as the bootstrap. Both linear and nonlinear multivariate cointegration techniques are expected to become more widespread.

What are the main problems?
Do these have potential solutions?

Clements and Hendry argue that the main problems that afflict economic forecasting arise from "the things we don't know we don't know," and of these, shifts in deterministic terms might be the most pernicious. Other possible sources of forecast errors – such as misspecifying the stochastic components or uncertainty due to estimating their parameters – are likely to be less important. Potential solutions such as updating the models parameters, differencing to exploit the rapid adaptability of a random walk process, "intercept corrections," and modeling the intercept shifts are briefly reviewed by Clements and Hendry. Øyvind Eitrheim, Tore Anders Husebø, and Ragnar Nymoen consider whether "differencing," that is, using forecasts from models in the first differences of the variables, may yield better forecasts than models with fully articulated long-run solutions in the presence of possible nonconstancies.

In general, the relative efficacy of these methods will depend on the nature and frequency of the shifts. When a time series exhibits a sudden change in mean over the sample period, one possible course of action is to include appropriate dummy variables (impulse or shift, depending on whether the change is immediately reversed) to capture the effects of outliers or "one-off" factors, without which the model may not be constant over the past. This strategy is popular in econometric modeling. However, to the extent that these "one-off" factors could not have been foreseen *ex ante* and may recur, the model standard error is an under-estimate of the true uncertainty inherent in explaining the dependent variable, and prediction intervals may be similarly misleading.

The nonlinear time-series models reviewed by Ruey Tsay, and Stefan Lundbergh and Timo Teräsvirta, arguably offer a more accurate picture of the uncertainty surrounding the model predictions, because they explicitly build into the probabilistic structure of the model the possibility that further regime changes may occur. For example, if one regime change of a particular type was observed historically in the last 30 years, then the model could be set up in such a way that a typical sample of 30 years generated by the model would include one such episode of that type. However, unless the shifts are regular and to some extent predictable, the best that one might be able to do is to rapidly adapt to the changed circumstances following the break, to prevent sequences of large errors of the same sign occurring. A similar point relates to the unobserved component, or structural time-series, models reviewed by Diego Pedregal and Peter Young, and by Tommaso Proietti. These models would appear to be most useful when there is *gradual* change in, say, the slope and level of the trend.

General treatments of economic forecasting are provided by, in roughly increasing order of difficulty, Hendry and Ericsson (2001), Diebold (1998), Allen and Fildes (2001), Whitley (1994), Box and Jenkins (1976), Granger and Newbold (1986), Harvey (1989), Clements and Hendry (1998), Clements and Hendry (1999), Hackl and Westlund (1991), and Engle and White (1999).

Acknowledgments

Financial support from the U.K. Economic and Social Research Council under grant L138251009 is gratefully acknowledged by both authors.

Notes

1   This chapter is based on Hendry (2001).
2   Lower case letters denote realizations of the random variables given by the upper case letter. $y_{T+1|T}$ is used to denote the forecast of period $T + 1$ made at time T.

References

Allen, P.G. and R.A. Fildes (2001). Econometric forecasting strategies and techniques. In J.S. Armstrong (ed.), *Principles of Forecasting: A Handbook for Researchers and Practitioners*. Kluwer Academic Press, USA.

Box, G.E.P. and G.M. Jenkins (1976). *Time Series Analysis, Forecasting and Control*. San Francisco: Holden-Day. First published, 1970.

Chatfield, C. (1993). Calculating interval forecasts. *Journal of Business and Economic Statistics*, 11, 121–35.

Chatfield, C. (1995). Model uncertainty, data mining and statistical inference. *Journal of the Royal Statistical Society*, A 158, 419–66. With discussion.

Clements, M.P. and D.F. Hendry (1998). *Forecasting Economic Time Series*. Cambridge: Cambridge University Press.

Clements, M.P. and D.F. Hendry (1999). *Forecasting Non-stationary Economic Time Series*. Cambridge, Mass.: MIT Press.

Clements, M.P. and N. Taylor (2001). Bootstrapping prediction intervals for autoregressive models. *International Journal of Forecasting*. 17, 247–67.

Coyle, D. (2001). Making sense of published economic forecasts. In D.F. Hendry and N.R. Ericsson (eds.), *Understanding Economic Forecasts*, pp. 54–67. Cambridge, Mass.: MIT Press.

Diebold, F.X. (1998). *Elements of Forecasting*. Cincinnati: South-Western College Publishing.

Doan, T., R. Litterman, and C.A. Sims (1984). Forecasting and conditional projection using realistic prior distributions. *Econometric Reviews*, 3, 1–100.

Doornik, J.A., D.F. Hendry, and B. Nielsen (1998). Inference in cointegrated models: U.K. M1 revisited. *Journal of Economic Surveys*, 12, 533–72.

Draper, D. (1995). Assessment and propagation of model uncertainty. *Journal of the Royal Statistical Society*, B 57, 45–97. With discussion.

Engle, R.F. and C.W.J. Granger (1987). Cointegration and error correction: Representation, estimation and testing. *Econometrica*, 55, 251–76.

Engle, R.F. and H. White (eds.) (1999). *Cointegration, Causality and Forecasting*. Oxford: Oxford University Press.

Granger, C.W.J. and P. Newbold (1986). *Forecasting Economic Time Series*, 2nd edn. New York: Academic Press.

Hackl, P. and A.H. Westlund (eds.) (1991). *Economic Structural Change, Analysis and Forecasting*. Berlin: Springer-Verlag.

Harvey, A.C. (1989). *Forecasting, Structural Time Series Models and the Kalman Filter*. Cambridge: Cambridge University Press.

Hendry, D.F. (2001). How economists forecast. In D.F. Hendry and N.R. Ericsson (eds.), *Understanding Economic Forecasts*. Cambridge, MA.: MIT Press, 15–41.

Hendry, D.F. and N.R. Ericsson (eds.) (2001). *Understanding Economic Forecasts*. Cambridge, MA: MIT Press.

Hendry, D.F. and K. Juselius (2000). Explaining cointegration analysis: Part I. *Energy Journal*, 21, 1–42.

Johansen, S. (1995). *Likelihood-based Inference in Cointegrated Vector Autoregressive Models*. Oxford: Oxford University Press.

Sims, C.A. (1980). Macroeconomics and reality. *Econometrica*, 48, 1–48. Reprinted in Granger, C.W.J. (ed.) (1990). *Modeling Economic Series*. Oxford: Clarendon Press.

Whitley, J.D. (1994). *A Course in Macroeconomic Modeling and Forecasting*. London: Harvester Wheatsheaf.

CHAPTER TWO

Predictable Uncertainty in Economic Forecasting

Neil R. Ericsson

2.1. INTRODUCTION

Forecasts of economic variables play a prominent role in business decision-making, government policy analysis, and economic research. Forecasts often are model-based, with forecasts from an estimated model being constructed as the model's fitted values over a sample not used in estimation. Forecasts typically differ from the realized outcomes, with discrepancies between forecasts and outcomes reflecting forecast uncertainty. Depending upon the degree of forecast uncertainty, forecasts may range from being highly informative to utterly useless for the tasks at hand.

Measures of forecast uncertainty have numerous uses in economic practice. For instance, prior to the realization of outcomes, a measure of forecast uncertainty provides an assessment of the "expected" or predicted uncertainty of the forecast errors, helping to qualify the forecasts themselves and to give a picture of the expected range of likely outcomes. That is, a measure of forecast uncertainty helps distinguish between numerical accuracy and statistical accuracy in forecasts. Information about forecast uncertainty is important in addition to the forecast itself. Also, once outcomes are known, the corresponding forecast errors and the anticipated forecast uncertainty can be used to evaluate the models from which the forecasts were generated.

Thus, this chapter considers forecast uncertainty in econometric modeling, analyzing at a general level the sources of uncertainty present in economic forecasting. At the outset, a distinction is made between predictable uncertainty and unpredictable uncertainty, with the focus of the chapter being on the former. Key features of predictable forecast uncertainty are illustrated by several analytic models, including static and dynamic models, and single-equation and multiple-equation models. Empirical models of the U.S. trade balance, U.K. inflation, and U.K. real national income clarify the issues involved.

This chapter is organized as follows. Section 2.2 reviews a taxonomy for the sources of forecast uncertainty, partitioning those sources into ones that generate predictable uncertainty and ones that generate unpredictable uncertainty. This section then sketches a framework for analyzing economic forecasts. Combined, the taxonomy and the framework guide the choice of models examined in subsequent sections. Sections 2.3 and 2.4 analyze the properties of predictable uncertainty associated with forecasts from single-equation and multiple-equation models respectively. These sections highlight how predictable forecast uncertainty is affected by the forecast horizon and by the type of forecast model – whether static or dynamic, and whether a single equation or a system. Section 2.5 considers various uses of predictable forecast uncertainty in economic modeling. Section 2.6 concludes.

Some preliminary comments will aid following the presentation below. This chapter presupposes an understanding of "how economists forecast" on the level of the discussions in Granger (1989) and Hendry and Ericsson (2001). For the most part, the current chapter restricts itself to time series and econometric models as the tools for forecasting itself, where these models are assumed to be well-specified. Clements and Hendry (1998), Clements and Hendry (1999), and Ericsson and Marquez (1998) consider some of the generalizations required and implications for situations in which the empirical forecast model is misspecified and for which that misspecification is important. Wallis (2000) *inter alia* discusses various ways of characterizing forecast uncertainty in macroeconomic modeling. Finally – and at a very practical level – figures, which are central to the chapter's examples, typically appear as panels of graphs, with each graph designated by a suffix *a*, *b*, *c*, . . . , row by row.

2.2. MODEL-BASED FORECASTS AND FORECAST ERRORS

This section summarizes a taxonomy of forecast errors (section 2.2.1) and a framework for analyzing economic forecasts (section 2.2.2). Together, these set the stage for discussing predictable uncertainty in economic forecasting (sections 2.3, 2.4, and 2.5).

2.2.1. A taxonomy of forecast uncertainty

This subsection examines the determinants of forecast uncertainty, drawing on a taxonomy for the sources of model-based forecast error in Clements and Hendry (1998, ch. 7.3, especially table 7.1).[1] Table 2.1 summarizes Clements and Hendry's taxonomy, partitioning the sources into "what we know that we don't know" (items 1(a)–1(b)) and "what we *don't* know that we don't know" (items 2(a)–2(c)), to paraphrase Maxine Singer (1997, p. 38). In practice, all of the listed sources are important when analyzing forecast uncertainty.

Items 1(a) and 1(b) are predictable in the sense that the degree of uncertainty arising from them can be anticipated and even calculated. Item 1(a) – the cumulation of future shocks to the economy – captures the uncertainty inherent to future events. It contains shocks that would be expected to occur, given the model used in forecasting. Item 1(b) results in "estimation uncertainty," which is due to using coefficient estimates in forecasting, rather than the underlying parameter values.

By contrast, items 2(a), 2(b), and 2(c) are unpredictable and unanticipated. If their extent and nature were known, they could be incorporated into the model and they – or at least the uncertainty that they create – would be predictable and predicted. Interactions between the three sources of unpredictable uncertainty can be particularly important; see Clements and Hendry (1998, 1999). The current chapter focuses on the two sources of *predictable* uncertainty, and primarily on inherent uncertainty – item 1(a). That said, the sources of unpredictable uncertainty are central to evaluating empirical models; see section 2.5 below.

At a more prosaic level, forecast uncertainty depends upon the variable being forecast, the type of model used for forecasting, the information available for constructing forecasts, and the economic process actually determining the variable being forecast. On the first, some variables may be inherently more difficult to forecast than others. For instance, imports and exports each might be highly predictable, and good models might exist for forecasting them. The trade balance – that is, the value of exports minus imports – might be quite difficult to forecast. In particular, by being the difference between two relatively large quantities (exports and imports), the trade balance is itself a relatively small quantity, whereas its forecast error reflects the forecast errors of both imports and exports. As another example, forecasting the level of the exchange rate might be relatively easy, in that the exchange rate in (say) a month's time is likely to be close to today's exchange rate. That said, forecasting the change in the exchange rate over the next month could be quite difficult. So, the particular variables being forecast and the transformations applied to those variables can affect the degree of forecast uncertainty present.

Second, forecast uncertainty depends upon the model that is being used for forecasting. Some models may simply be better for forecasting than others. Also, the particular form of the model determines what the predictable forecast uncertainty is, as distinct from the *actual* forecast uncertainty that arises. As table 2.1 clarifies, that distinction exists because a model is a simplified characterization of the economy, not a reproduction of the economy. Sometimes that characterization is a good one, and sometimes it is not.

Third, forecast uncertainty depends upon the information available for constructing the forecasts. This aspect is closely tied to the design of the forecast model. More information would seem to be beneficial for forecasting, and it is so in some situations. That said, when the model is misspecified and there are structural breaks in the data, use of additional information can actually increase forecast uncertainty; see Clements and Hendry (1999, ch. 2).

Fourth, the underlying process generating the data plays a role in determining forecast uncertainty, such as by placing limits on the minimum forecast uncertainty obtainable from a model. That distinguishes between the predictable

Table 2.1 A taxonomy of the sources of model-based forecast error

1 Sources of predictable uncertainty –
   "what we know that we don't know":
   (a) cumulation of future errors ("shocks") to the economy
   (b) inaccuracies in estimates of the forecast model's parameters

2 Sources of unpredictable uncertainty –
   "what we *don't* know that we don't know":
   (a) currently unknown future changes in the economy's structure
   (b) misspecification of the forecast model
   (c) mis-measurement of the base-period data

---

forecast uncertainty – that is, the forecast uncertainty anticipated, given the model – and the actual forecast uncertainty, which is the uncertainty arising from the combination of the model with the actual behavior of the economic data.

To consider the role of these and other aspects of forecasts *per se*, the next subsection draws on Ericsson and Marquez's (1998) framework for economic forecasting.

2.2.2. A framework for interpreting forecasts

Ericsson and Marquez (1998) divide the mechanics of forecasting into three parts:

1 *design*, in which the characteristics of the forecasts and the relationship(s) of interest are specified;
2 *evaluation*, wherein the forecasts and their characteristics are calculated; and
3 *post-evaluation analysis*, in which the forecasts are presented.

The current chapter employs all three aspects. That said, design is most relevant to the pedagogical approach taken in subsequent sections because forecast design specifies the relationship of interest for generating the forecasts and the characteristics of the forecasts being examined. Table 2.2 lists some details of forecast design.

Design itself is subject to a tripartite division: the relationship of interest, the data generation process (DGP), and characteristics of the forecast. The relationship of interest may be classified by its dimension (single equation versus multiple equations), completeness (subsystem versus full system), temporal form (static versus dynamic), and distributional assumptions (for the error, for the coefficient estimates, and for the initial conditions). The underlying DGP may also be described in a similar fashion. The characteristics of the forecast include its dimension (scalar versus vector), the set of forecasts examined (subset versus full set), the forecast horizon (one step ahead versus multiple steps ahead), and the distributional property of interest (such as the forecast's mean, bias, variance, and

Table 2.2 Some issues in designing economic forecasts

Relationship of interest, and DGP	Characteristics of the forecast
Dimension	Dimension
single equation	scalar
multiple equations	vector
Completeness	Forecasts examined
subsystem	subset
full system	full set
Temporal form	Forecast horizon
static	one step ahead
dynamic	multiple steps ahead
Distributions	Distributional property
error	mean (and bias)
coefficient estimates	variance (and MSFE)
initial conditions	other

mean square forecast error). These characteristics roughly parallel those for the relationship of interest and the DGP. However, even for similar categories, the classifications need not match: for example, a relationship might be a multiple-equation complete system, while the forecast of interest is scalar.

Each combination of characteristics for the relationship of interest, the DGP, and the forecasts may imply different properties for the associated predictable uncertainty. Even the limited classification in table 2.2 entails 13,824 (= $(2^3 \cdot 3)^3$) possible combinations. Extensive analysis of these combinations is not feasible, nor is it necessary. Rather, a small set of combinations serves to highlight essential interactions between the various characteristics. Table 2.3 lists the five models examined in sections 2.3 and 2.4 below: three single-equation models (one static, one dynamic, and one mixed), and two dynamic systems (one very specific, and

Table 2.3 A guide to the models examined

Model class (relationship of interest)	Model
Static single equation	M_1: $y_t = bz_t + u_t$
Dynamic single equation	M_2: $y_t = by_{t-1} + u_t$
(Generalized) dynamic single equation	M_3: $y_t = b_1 y_{t-1} + b_2 z_t + u_t$
Simple dynamic system	M_4: $\begin{cases} y_t = bz_t + u_t \\ z_t = cy_{t-1} + v_t \end{cases}$
(Generalized) dynamic system	M_5: $\mathbf{x_t} = \mathbf{B}\mathbf{x_{t-1}} + \mathbf{w_t}$

the other general). Three issues listed in table 2.2 (dimension, completeness, and temporal form) characterize these models.

Evaluation is the process of generating forecasts and calculating their characteristics, such as their variances. For some models, evaluation is analytic. However, even for relatively simple models, exact analytic results are not available, so calculation of forecasts and their characteristics may involve numerical integration, analytic approximations, Monte Carlo simulation, or bootstrapping. See Ericsson and Marquez (1998) for a summary.

Post-evaluation analysis concerns the presentation of the forecasts and their characteristics, once calculated. Tables and graphs are common modes – graphs are used extensively below. Sometimes, the properties of forecasts are summarized through a statistic, as in the Chow (1960) statistic and the forecast-encompassing statistic; see Chong and Hendry (1986) on the latter. The purposes of the particular forecasting endeavor often govern the structure of post-evaluation analysis.

Before proceeding, a few comments are in order. First, the models considered are kept very simple for expositional reasons. Even so, many features of their forecasts' predictable uncertainty are characteristic of much more general models. Second, and relatedly, analytic techniques exist for examining forecast uncertainty from general linear models, and numerical techniques are available for nonlinear models if analytic solutions are unknown. Third, in order to simplify the analysis of predictable uncertainty, the econometric model underlying the relationship of interest is typically assumed to be the DGP. That said, section 2.5 necessarily distinguishes between the DGP and the model when interpreting tests for the latter's constancy. Finally, the taxonomy in table 2.1 and the framework above delineate the models in table 2.3 and their forecasts' properties, which are the focus of the remaining sections.

2.3. PREDICTABLE UNCERTAINTY FOR STATIC AND DYNAMIC SINGLE-EQUATION MODELS

This section calculates analytically and numerically the predictable forecast uncertainty for some specific static and dynamic single-equation models. The aim is to characterize how various features listed in table 2.2 affect predictable forecast uncertainty. Thus, this section focuses on the effects of static versus dynamic specifications, of forecast horizon, of parameter values, and of estimation uncertainty. The subsequent section (section 2.4) examines forecasting from a system of equations. Straightforward results follow from simple assumptions, such as univariate or bivariate DGPs, single-equation or two-equation models, first-order dynamics (at most), stationarity, and ergodicity. Many – but not all – results carry through or generalize naturally under weaker restrictions.

Section 2.3.1 considers a simple static model, section 2.3.2 a simple dynamic model, and section 2.3.3 compares and contrasts these results, with further evidence from an application to forecasting U.K. net national income. Each example proceeds pedagogically with the specification of the model, the forecasts, the forecast errors, and the forecast errors' properties.

2.3.1. A static single equation

This subsection describes the model, model-based forecasts, forecast errors, and their properties for a simple static single-equation model. This model serves as a benchmark for comparison with other models, and it creates a template for the analysis of other models. Chow (1960) discusses forecasts from this model in detail.

This first model (denoted M_1) is a static single equation:

$$M_1: y_t = bz_t + u_t \quad u_t \sim \text{NI}(0, \sigma^2) \quad t = 1, \ldots, T, T + 1, \ldots, T + H, \qquad (2.1)$$

where y_t is the dependent variable; z_t is an exogenous variable; b is an unknown coefficient; u_t is an error term, assumed to be independently and normally distributed with a zero mean and a variance σ^2; t is the time subscript; and the estimation and forecast periods are $[1, T]$ and $[T + 1, T + H]$ respectively, implying T observations for estimation and H observations being forecast.

Several types of model-based forecasts are feasible from (2.1), each with specific implications for the properties of the corresponding forecasts and forecast errors. For expositional convenience, consider the forecasts based on least squares estimation of the coefficient b in model M_1:

$$\hat{y}_t = \hat{b}z_t \quad t = T + 1, \ldots, T + H, \qquad (2.2)$$

where $\hat{y}_t$ is the forecast of y_t, and $\hat{b}$ is the least squares estimator of b, distributed as $\text{N}(b, \sigma^2(\sum_{t=1}^{T}z_t^2)^{-1})$. To highlight the distinction between the estimation period $[1, T]$ and the forecast period $[T + 1, T + H]$, it is helpful to rewrite (2.2) with a different time subscript:

$$\hat{y}_{T+h} = \hat{b}z_{T+h} \quad h = 1, \ldots, H, \qquad (2.3)$$

where h indexes the forecast horizon.

The forecast $\hat{y}_{T+h}$ in (2.3) assumes that z_{T+h} is known. That is, in period T, the value of z at period $T + h$ (that is, h periods into the future) is known. While this assumption is sensible for deterministic variables such as an intercept and a linear trend, it is unjustified for many variables, particularly when $h > 1$. Section 2.3.2 explores that issue further, with $z_t = y_{t-1}$.

The forecast error e_{T+h} is the difference between the outcome y_{T+h} and its forecast $\hat{y}_{T+h}$:

$$\begin{aligned} e_{T+h} &= y_{T+h} - \hat{y}_{T+h} \\ &= (bz_{T+h} + u_{T+h}) - \hat{b}z_{T+h} \\ &= u_{T+h} + (b - \hat{b})z_{T+h} \quad h = 1, \ldots, H, \end{aligned} \qquad (2.4)$$

where the second line of (2.4) uses the definitions of y_{T+h} and $\hat{y}_{T+h}$ from (2.1) and (2.3) respectively, and the third line rearranges terms. So, from (2.4), the forecast error e_{T+h} is comprised of the (unknown) future shock u_{T+h}, and $(b - \hat{b})z_{T+h}$, which is the error in forecasting that arises from estimating rather than knowing the coefficient b. These are the components 1(a) and 1(b) in table 2.1, with the two components together representing "what we know that we don't know" about the future outcome y_{T+h}.

Many measures exist for summarizing properties of a forecast and its corresponding forecast error, including the bias of the forecast, the variance of the forecast error, and the mean square forecast error (MSFE), which is a common summary measure of a forecast error's properties. The MSFE is defined as the mean of the squared forecast error, for example, $E(e_{T+h}^2)$ for the forecast error e_{T+h} in (2.4). In general, the whole distribution of outcomes is of interest when considering forecast uncertainty. However, the primary measure of forecast uncertainty in economics is the MSFE, which simplifies to the variance of the forecast error when the forecast is unbiased. The variance and MSFE capture important aspects of forecast uncertainty and so are considered in much of the discussion below. Still, they have substantive limitations as measures of forecast uncertainty; see Clements and Hendry (1993) and chapter 11 by Pesaran and Skouras for detailed analyses.

For the static model (2.1), the forecast error (2.4) has easily derivable properties. In fact, its distribution is normal:

$$e_{T+h} \sim N(0, \sigma^2[1 + z_{T+h}^2(\textstyle\sum_{t=1}^{T} z_t^2)^{-1}]) \quad h = 1, \ldots, H, \tag{2.5}$$

as follows immediately from normality and independence of $\{u_t\}$, and hence the normality and independence of u_{T+h} and $\hat{b}$. Further results depend on the nature of z_t. For the simple case where z_t is an intercept (that is, $z_t = 1$), then (2.5) simplifies:

$$e_{T+h} \sim N(0, \sigma^2[1 + (1/T)]) \quad h = 1, \ldots, H. \tag{2.6}$$

Because the forecast $\hat{y}_{T+h}$ in (2.3) is unbiased for the outcome y_{T+h}, the variance of e_{T+h} is also the MSFE.

Figure 2.1a (the upper left graph in figure 2.1) plots the MSFE for $b = 0.5$ as a function of the forecast horizon h, where the units are in terms of σ^2. Figure 2.1a contains two calculations of the MSFE. The first is the variance in (2.6) for a large estimation sample (that is, $T = \infty$) and so is denoted the asymptotic MSFE ("no estimation uncertainty"). From (2.6), the asymptotic MSFE equals σ^2 for all forecast horizons: hence it is a flat line at unity in the graph. The second MSFE is the variance in (2.6) for a specific estimation sample (here, $T = 5$) and so is denoted the finite sample MSFE ("with estimation uncertainty").[2] From (2.6), it numerically equals $1.20\sigma^2$.

In summary, for a static model with only an intercept, the predictable uncertainty as measured by the MSFE is constant across forecast horizons. The MSFE decreases as the estimation sample increases, tending to a positive value (the asymptotic MSFE) for a large estimation sample. For static regression models in general, the asymptotic MSFE is invariant to the forecast horizon; in finite samples, it may depend on both h and T through the component involving estimation uncertainty.

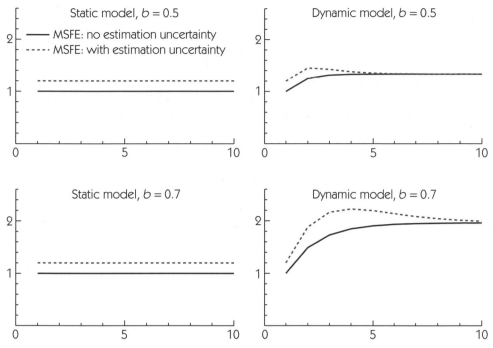

Figure 2.1 Asymptotic and finite sample mean square forecast errors (MSFEs) for static and dynamic models with coefficient values of $b = 0.5$ and $b = 0.7$

2.3.2. A dynamic single equation

This subsection describes the model, model-based forecasts, and forecast errors for a simple dynamic model – specifically, for a univariate first-order autoregressive model. This model has been extensively studied analytically, numerically, and empirically in the statistical, econometric, and economic literature; see Orcutt and Winokur (1969), Hoque, Magnus, and Pesaran (1988), and Clements and Hendry (1998, ch. 4) *inter alia* on the model's forecast properties. This model highlights the effects of dynamics on forecasts, and many of its forecasts' properties generalize readily to systems of dynamic equations with multiple lags; see section 2.4.

The first-order autoregressive model (denoted M_2) is:

$$M_2: y_t = by_{t-1} + u_t \quad u_t \sim NI(0, \sigma^2) \quad t = 1, \ldots, T, T + 1, \ldots, T + H, \quad (2.7)$$

where b is now the unknown coefficient on the lagged dependent variable y_{t-1}. The variable z_t in model M_1 is now y_{t-1}, but the properties of the error term u_t and the notation are otherwise as in model M_1 (section 2.3.1). For expositional convenience, it is assumed that $|b| < 1$ and that $y_0 \sim N(0, \sigma^2/(1 - b^2))$.[3]

The forecasts considered are those based on least squares estimation of the coefficient b in model M_2:

$$\hat{y}_t = \hat{b}y_{t-1} \quad t = T + 1, \ldots, T + H, \tag{2.8}$$

where $\hat{b}$ is the least squares estimator of the coefficient b, and is approximately distributed as $N(b, (1 - b^2)/T)$. As with (2.2), equation (2.8) may be re-indexed, resulting in the following sequence of one-step-ahead forecasts:

$$\hat{y}_{T+h} = \hat{b}y_{T+h-1} \quad h = 1, \ldots, H. \tag{2.9}$$

Equation (2.9) may be written more explicitly as

$$
\begin{aligned}
\hat{y}_{T+1} &= \hat{b}y_T \\
\hat{y}_{T+2} &= \hat{b}y_{T+1} \\
&\vdots \\
\hat{y}_{T+h} &= \hat{b}y_{T+h-1} \\
&\vdots \\
\hat{y}_{T+H-1} &= \hat{b}y_{T+H-2} \\
\hat{y}_{T+H} &= \hat{b}y_{T+H-1}.
\end{aligned}
\tag{2.10}
$$

Equation (2.10) highlights a complication when forecasting from dynamic models: the one-period-ahead forecast $\hat{y}_{T+1}$ is easily constructed because y_T is known, but forecasts at longer horizons depend upon future (unknown) outcomes of y. The usual approach is to replace those future outcomes by their forecasts – but see chapter 4 by Pedregal and Young for alternatives. Thus, the forecast $\hat{y}_{T+2}$ becomes $\hat{b} \cdot (\hat{b}y_T)$ and, more generally, the h-period-ahead forecast $\hat{y}_{T+h}$ is

$$\hat{y}_{T+h} = \hat{b}^h y_T \quad h = 1, \ldots, H. \tag{2.11}$$

The forecast error e_{T+h} is the difference between the outcome y_{T+h} and its forecast $\hat{y}_{T+h}$, as in the first line of (2.4), but the analytics differ from (2.4). To calculate the forecast error, it is helpful first to derive y_{T+h} in terms of the observed y_{T+i} (for $i < h$) and the unobserved future shocks $\{u_{T+1}, u_{T+2}, \ldots, u_{T+h}\}$. By repeated substitution from (2.7), y_{T+h} is

$$
\begin{aligned}
y_{T+h} &= by_{T+h-1} + u_{T+h} \\
&= b \cdot (by_{T+h-2} + u_{T+h-1}) + u_{T+h} \\
&\vdots \\
&= b^h y_T + \sum_{i=0}^{h-1} b^i u_{T+h-i}.
\end{aligned}
\tag{2.12}
$$

Thus, the forecast error e_{T+h} is

$$e_{T+h} = y_{T+h} - \hat{y}_{T+h}$$

$$= (b^h y_T + \sum_{i=0}^{h-1} b^i u_{T+h-i}) - \hat{b}^h y_T$$

$$= \sum_{i=0}^{h-1} b^i u_{T+h-i} + (b^h - \hat{b}^h) y_T \qquad h = 1, \dots, H. \tag{2.13}$$

As with the static model, the dynamic model's forecast error depends upon future shocks to the economy and upon estimating rather than knowing the coefficient b. The static and dynamic forecast errors do differ in the form of their dependence on those two components, as comparison of (2.4) and (2.13) clarifies. First, the forecast error of the static model depends on the future shock in period $T + h$ alone, whereas the dynamic model's forecast error contains a weighted cumulation of shocks from period $T + 1$ through period $T + h$. Second, the static model's forecast error depends on the simple difference between the coefficient b and its estimate $\hat{b}$. The dynamic model's forecast error depends upon the difference between powers of b and $\hat{b}$. For the one-period-ahead forecast, the dynamic model's forecast error is $u_{T+1} + (b - \hat{b}) y_T$, paralleling the static model's forecast error of $u_{T+1} + (b - \hat{b}) z_{T+1}$. At other horizons, forecasts errors from the two types of models differ in detail, even while each has the two components 1(a) and 1(b) from table 2.1.

From (2.13), the properties of the dynamic model's forecast errors depend upon the distribution of $\sum_{i=0}^{h-1} b^i u_{T+h-i}$ and $(b^h - \hat{b}^h)$, and upon the initial condition for forecasting, that is, y_T. While $\sum_{i=0}^{h-1} b^i u_{T+h-i}$ is visually the most complex of the three terms, its distribution is the most straightforward, as the future shocks $\{u_{T+h-i}\}$ are normally distributed and serially independent. The mean of $\sum_{i=0}^{h-1} b^i u_{T+h-i}$ is zero, and its variance is the sum of the variances of its components:

$$\text{var}(\sum_{i=0}^{h-1} b^i u_{T+h-i}) = \text{var}(u_{T+h}) + \text{var}(b u_{T+h-1}) + \cdots + \text{var}(b^{h-1} u_{T+1})$$

$$= \sigma^2 + b^2 \sigma^2 + \cdots + b^{2(h-1)} \sigma^2$$

$$= \sigma^2 \left(\frac{1 - b^{2h}}{1 - b^2} \right). \tag{2.14}$$

The exact distribution of the forecast errors is complicated by the nonlinearity $\hat{b}^h$ and by the dependence of $\hat{b}$ on y_T. However, under one standard set of approximations, $(b^h - \hat{b}^h)$ is distributed as $N(0, [(hb^{h-1})^2(1 - b^2)/T])$, the variable y_T has its unconditional distribution $N(0, [\sigma^2/(1 - b^2)])$, and the term $(b^h - \hat{b}^h)$ and y_T are independently distributed. Using these approximations, the forecast error from the dynamic model has a mean of (approximately) zero and a variance (approximately) equal to:

$$\sigma^2 \left(\frac{1 - b^{2h}}{1 - b^2} \right) + \frac{\sigma^2 (hb^{h-1})^2}{T}, \tag{2.15}$$

which is also its (approximate) finite sample MSFE. The first term in (2.15) is the asymptotic MSFE in (2.14). The second term captures the complicated dependence of $(b^h - \hat{b}^h)y_T$ on four factors: the forecast horizon h, the autoregressive coefficient b, the estimation sample size T, and the equation error variance σ^2.

Figure 2.1b plots the asymptotic MSFE in (2.14) as a function of the forecast horizon h. From (2.14), the asymptotic MSFE equals σ^2 for $h = 1$, $\sigma^2 + b^2\sigma^2$ for $h = 2$, $\sigma^2 + b^2\sigma^2 + b^4\sigma^2$ for $h = 3$, and so on, tending to $\sigma^2/(1 - b^2)$ for large h. In figure 2.1b, $b = 0.5$, so these values are σ^2, $1.25\sigma^2$, $1.31\sigma^2$, and so on, tending to $1.33\sigma^2$. The (asymptotic) predictable uncertainty increases as the forecast horizon increases; and that predictable uncertainty is bounded over all forecast horizons.

Figure 2.1b also plots the (approximate) finite sample MSFE in (2.15). This MSFE is larger than (or at least as large as) the asymptotic MSFE: estimation uncertainty adds to the inherent uncertainty from the future shocks, as for the static model. The finite sample MSFE is also bounded over all forecast horizons. As figure 2.1b demonstrates, the finite sample MSFE need not increase monotonically in the forecast horizon: as h increases, the finite sample MSFE may decrease as well as increase. The explanation for this nonmonotonicity turns on the term $\sigma^2(hb^{h-1})^2/T$ in (2.15). That term has a complicated dependence on the forecast horizon h, but in any case is always positive for nonzero b and tends to zero as h becomes large. For economic and policy analysis, nonmonotonicity in the MSFE can be worrying: the forecast horizons of greatest economic or policy interest may have the greatest (predictable) uncertainty; see Chong and Hendry (1986).

To summarize, for a dynamic first-order autoregressive model, the predictable uncertainty as measured by the MSFE tends to increase in the forecast horizon, although estimation uncertainty may induce nonmonotonicity. As with the MSFE from the static model, the dynamic model's MSFE decreases as the estimation sample increases, tending to a positive value (the asymptotic MSFE) for a large estimation sample. The MSFEs from dynamic and static models differ most notably through their dependence (or lack thereof) on the forecast horizon. The following subsection, along with section 2.4, examines this issue in greater detail.

2.3.3.   A comparison

This subsection compares the predictive uncertainty from the static and dynamic models in the two previous subsections, focusing on the roles of coefficient estimation and the forecast horizon. To highlight the latter, two empirical models of U.K. net national income are examined.

Figures 2.1a and 2.1b plotted the MSFEs for the static and dynamic models, evaluated at a specific value of the regression parameter b: $b = 0.5$. Figures 2.1c and 2.1d plot the comparable graphs for a different value of b: $b = 0.7$. For the static model (figure 2.1c), both the asymptotic and finite sample MSFEs remain unchanged. In fact, the MSFEs for the static model are invariant to b, as (2.5) and (2.6) imply. For the dynamic model (figure 2.1d), both the asymptotic and finite sample MSFEs have altered. Each increases more rapidly at small forecast horizons; and they tend to a larger MSFE for large h: to $1.96\sigma^2$, rather than to $1.33\sigma^2$. For multi-period-ahead forecasts at a given horizon h, both the asymptotic and finite sample MSFEs increase in the coefficient b, as follows from the sum in the second line of (2.14) and from the second term in (2.15).

Thus, the static nature of the static model over the estimation (in-sample) period carries through to the (predictable) properties of its forecasts and forecast errors. Time dependence characterizes the nature of the dynamic model, both in sample and over the forecast period. These results show that characteristics of forecasts are model *dependent*. Somewhat surprisingly, characteristics of forecasts are relatively data *independent*.

To illustrate these results, the remainder of this subsection considers two models – one static and the other dynamic – that generalize or expand upon the models in sections 2.3.1 and 2.3.2. The first is a regression model with an intercept and linear trend, and the second is a random walk model with drift. Both have played important roles in statistical and economic modeling; see Box and Jenkins (1970), Hendry, Pagan, and Sargan (1984), Hendry (1995, ch. 7), and Clements and Hendry (2001) *inter alia*. For ease of exposition, uncertainty from coefficient estimation is ignored.

The first model is a static model with both an intercept and a linear trend:

$$M_1^*: y_t = b_1 + b_2 t + u_t \quad u_t \sim NI(0, \sigma^2) \quad t = 1, \ldots, T, T + 1, \ldots, T + H, \quad (2.16)$$

where b_1 is the intercept and b_2 is the coefficient on the trend t. The forecasts are:

$$\hat{y}_{T+h} = b_1 + b_2 \cdot (T + h) \quad h = 1, \ldots, H, \quad (2.17)$$

so the forecast errors are

$$e_{T+h} = u_{T+h} \quad h = 1, \ldots, H, \quad (2.18)$$

and the MSFE is

$$var(e_{T+h}) = \sigma^2 \quad h = 1, \ldots, H. \quad (2.19)$$

As in the simpler static model with only an intercept, the (asymptotic) MSFE does not depend upon the forecast horizon h.

The MSFE in (2.19) is the "predicted" MSFE, in that σ^2 is the value of the MSFE, assuming that model M_1^* in (2.16) is the DGP. With some distributional assumptions about u, the predicted MSFE can provide the basis for calculating confidence intervals for the forecasts in (2.17), as is common in many econometrics software packages. In general, the predicted MSFE differs from the actual MSFE, as when the assumed model is not the DGP; see Clements and Hendry (2001).

To illustrate the properties of the predicted MSFE empirically, consider modeling real net national income in the United Kingdom over 1970–1993 and forecasting it through 2010. The data are from Ericsson, Hendry, and Prestwich (1998), and the model is (2.16), where y is the logarithm of real net national income. Figure 2.2a shows the results from estimating this model and forecasting from it. The left half of figure 2.2a plots actual income and the fitted values of income from the estimated model over 1970–1993. The right half of figure 2.2a plots the model's forecasts through 2010. The vertical bars around those forecasts represent the

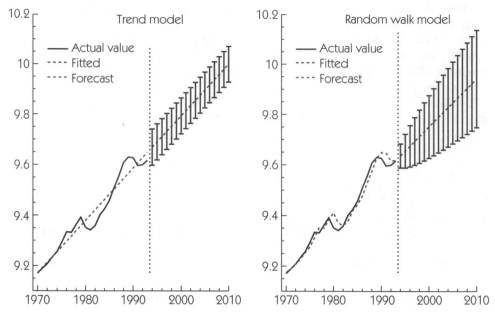

Figure 2.2   Actual, fitted, and forecast values from the trend and random walk models of annual real net national income for the United Kingdom (in logs), with 95% confidence intervals for the forecasts

anticipated 95 percent confidence intervals for income, which are roughly $\pm 2\hat{\sigma}$ (namely, plus-or-minus twice the estimated equation standard error). While this model for income does include a trend, that trend is deterministic, implying that its future values are known, as well as its current and past values. So, in essence, this model is static, and the anticipated forecast uncertainty is constant across different forecast horizons.

The second model is a random walk with an intercept:

$$\text{M}_2^*: y_t = a + y_{t-1} + u_t \quad u_t \sim \text{NI}(0, \sigma^2) \quad t = 1, \ldots, T, T+1, \ldots, T+H, \quad (2.20)$$

where a is the intercept, and the coefficient on the lagged dependent variable is constrained to equal unity.

Following (2.11), (2.13), and the first two lines of (2.14), the h-step-ahead forecasts are

$$\hat{y}_{T+h} = ah + y_T \quad h = 1, \ldots, H, \quad (2.21)$$

the forecast errors are

$$e_{T+h} = \sum_{i=0}^{h-1} u_{T+h-i} \quad h = 1, \ldots, H, \quad (2.22)$$

and the MSFE is

$$\mathrm{var}(e_{T+h}) = h\sigma^2 \quad h = 1, \ldots, H. \tag{2.23}$$

The predicted MSFE increases in the forecast horizon h, and in fact increases linearly in h, and without bound. The predicted MSFE in (2.23) assumes that model M_2^* in (2.20) is the DGP.

Figure 2.2b plots the actual, fitted, and forecast values from this random walk model of income, using the same sample periods for estimation and forecasting as with the static model in figure 2.2a. The confidence intervals for the random walk forecasts in figure 2.2b increase very substantially as the forecast horizon itself increases, contrasting with confidence intervals of fixed width in figure 2.2a.

Figures 2.2a and 2.2b portray two very different patterns for the anticipated (or predicted) forecast uncertainty, and their comparison illustrates how model choice can affect those patterns. Exactly the same series is being modeled and forecast in figures 2.2a and 2.2b: only the models themselves differ. More generally, static models often imply predicted forecast uncertainty that is time invariant or nearly so, whereas dynamic models generally imply time-dependent predicted forecast uncertainty, often increasing in the forecast horizon.

Models M_1 and M_2 present static and dynamic relationships as black and white, but in practice a whole spectrum of models exists with both static and dynamic aspects. The simplest example is

$$M_3: y_t = b_1 y_{t-1} + b_2 z_t + u_t, \tag{2.24}$$

where b_1 and b_2 are the coefficients of lagged y and current z. Model M_3 includes models M_1 and M_2 as special cases with $b_1 = 0$ and $b_2 = 0$ respectively. When b_1 and b_2 are both nonzero, model M_3 has both dynamic and static features. Analytic examination of model M_3's predictable forecast uncertainty is feasible but reveals relatively little beyond what has been seen from models M_1 and M_2 separately.

This section has considered models and forecasts of individual variables only, and not of sets of variables. Yet, economics typically is about relationships between variables, where those variables may interact with each other, either contemporaneously, or at a lag, or both. The next section thus turns to system forecasts and their associated predictable uncertainty. In the language of table 2.2, the issues are the dimension and completeness of the relationship of interest and of the forecast.

2.4.   PREDICTABLE UNCERTAINTY FOR SYSTEMS

In section 2.3.1 above, future values of the exogenous variable z were assumed to be known when forecasting y. This assumption is sensible for deterministic variables such as an intercept or a linear trend. However, for most economic variables, the variables themselves would need to be forecast when forecasting y. Doing so leads directly to forecasting from systems of equations. This section first considers a simple but historically important two-variable system (section

2.4.1) and then turns to a vector autoregressive model (or VAR, section 2.4.2), which is the basis for much empirical forecasting in economics. As in section 2.3, the focus is on the inherent predictable uncertainty. The predictable uncertainty from estimation is calculable, both analytically and numerically, but it provides less direct insight due to the increased complexity of the models.

2.4.1. A simple dynamic system

The static model in (2.1) expresses y_t in terms of z_t and a disturbance u_t. This subsection augments that model with an equation for z_t itself, so that forecasts of y can be constructed from forecasts of z when the future values of z are unknown.

Many possible models exist for z_t. One plausible determinant of z_t is y_{t-1}: that is, y Granger-causes z. See Granger (1969) for the development of the concept of Granger causality, and Hendry and Mizon (1999) for reasons why Granger causality is so prevalent in economic data.

Thus, it is of interest to consider model M_4:

$$M_4: \begin{cases} y_t = bz_t + u_t \\ z_t = cy_{t-1} + v_t \end{cases} \quad \begin{bmatrix} u_t \\ v_t \end{bmatrix} \sim NI\left(\begin{bmatrix} 0 \\ 0 \end{bmatrix}, \begin{bmatrix} \sigma^2 & 0 \\ 0 & \omega^2 \end{bmatrix} \right), \quad (2.25)$$

where c is the coefficient on lagged y in the equation for z; and v_t is the disturbance in that equation. The two disturbances $(u_t : v_t)$ are assumed to be normally and independently distributed, having mean zero and (respectively) variances σ^2 and ω^2. The covariance between u_t and v_t is zero: that is, the equation for y is a conditional model of y_t given z_t, and b is the coefficient implied by that conditioning; see Ericsson (1992a) for an introductory exposition on conditioning and (relatedly) exogeneity. These assumptions about normality and conditioning are convenient, but are not central to the properties of the forecasts.

In economics, (2.25) is known as a cobweb model, which may characterize a market with lags in the production process, as of agricultural commodities. In the cobweb model, y and z are interpreted as the logs of price and quantity, respectively. Denoting those logs as p and q, (2.25) becomes:

$$M_4^*: \begin{cases} p_t = bq_t + u_t \\ q_t = cp_{t-1} + v_t \end{cases} \quad \begin{bmatrix} u_t \\ v_t \end{bmatrix} \sim NI\left(\begin{bmatrix} 0 \\ 0 \end{bmatrix}, \begin{bmatrix} \sigma^2 & 0 \\ 0 & \omega^2 \end{bmatrix} \right). \quad (2.26)$$

The cobweb model (2.26) has the following interpretation. The equation for p_t is derived from a demand equation: the price p_t clears the market for a given quantity q_t supplied. The value $1/b$ is the price elasticity of demand. The equation for q_t is a supply equation, capturing (for instance) how much farmers decide to produce this year (q_t), depending upon the price that they were able to obtain in the previous year (p_{t-1}). The value c is the price elasticity of supply. See Tinbergen (1931) and Suits (1955) for pivotal contributions on the cobweb model, and Henderson and Quandt (1971, pp. 142–5) for an exposition.

Forecasting from the cobweb model generalizes on the mechanism for forecasting from the first-order autoregressive model in section 2.3.2, so we revert to the $(y : z)$ notation in (2.25). Ignoring estimation, the forecasts derive from (2.25) without the disturbances, whose future values are by definition unknown:

$$\begin{cases} \hat{y}_{T+h} = bz_{T+h} \\ \hat{z}_{T+h} = cy_{T+h-1} \end{cases} \quad h = 1, \ldots, H. \tag{2.27}$$

Equation (2.27) may be written more explicitly as

$$\begin{bmatrix} \hat{y}_{T+1} \\ \hat{z}_{T+1} \end{bmatrix} = \begin{bmatrix} bz_{T+1} \\ cy_T \end{bmatrix}$$

$$\begin{bmatrix} \hat{y}_{T+2} \\ \hat{z}_{T+2} \end{bmatrix} = \begin{bmatrix} bz_{T+2} \\ cy_{T+1} \end{bmatrix}$$

$$\vdots$$

$$\begin{bmatrix} \hat{y}_{T+h} \\ \hat{z}_{T+h} \end{bmatrix} = \begin{bmatrix} bz_{T+h} \\ cy_{T+h-1} \end{bmatrix}$$

$$\vdots$$

$$\begin{bmatrix} \hat{y}_{T+H-1} \\ \hat{z}_{T+H-1} \end{bmatrix} = \begin{bmatrix} bz_{T+H-1} \\ cy_{T+H-2} \end{bmatrix}$$

$$\begin{bmatrix} \hat{y}_{T+H} \\ \hat{z}_{T+H} \end{bmatrix} = \begin{bmatrix} bz_{T+H} \\ cy_{T+H-1} \end{bmatrix}. \tag{2.28}$$

Formally, (2.28) parallels (2.10), with the former delineating pairs of forecasts at a given horizon h, rather than a single forecast at each horizon. All variables except y_T on the right-hand side of (2.28) are dated in the future and hence unknown, so an implementable forecasting algorithm is still required.

Consider generating the forecasts for y first. Substituting the second equation of (2.27) into the first obtains

$$\hat{y}_{T+h} = bcy_{T+h-1} \quad h = 1, \ldots, H, \tag{2.29}$$

which is identical to (2.9), except that the autoregressive coefficient is bc, rather than b itself. All H forecasts for y can be generated from (2.29), employing the approach in section 2.3.2. The H forecasts for z follow immediately from the second line in (2.27):

$$\hat{z}_{T+h} = cy_{T+h-1} \quad h = 1, \ldots, H, \tag{2.30}$$

using cy_T as the forecast for z_{T+1}, and $c\hat{y}_{T+h-1}$ (that is, with a forecast of y) as the forecast for z_{T+h} for $h > 1$.

For (2.25), the forecasts for y and z were conveniently solved for y in terms of its own lag, and then for z in terms of lagged y. Expositionally, this is clearly convenient. However, for more complicated models, a generic approach is usually taken. Specifically, the one-period-ahead ($h = 1$) forecasts for both y and z are derived, as from the first block of rows in (2.28). The two-period-ahead ($h = 2$) forecasts are calculated, using the one-period-ahead forecasts. The remaining forecasts of y and z are then solved in this stepwise fashion, period by period.

2.4.2. A generalized dynamic system

The approach to forecasting in section 2.4.1 suggests a generic formulation for forecasting from dynamic systems. The current subsection discusses that formulation and summarizes the properties of predictable uncertainty from such systems.

In section 2.4.1, the model M_4 in (2.25) describes y as a function of contemporaneously dated z. By contrast, the forecasting equation for y, in (2.29), solves for y in terms of its lags by substitution with the forecasting equation for z. A similar substitution can be applied to the *model* for y, that is, to the first line of (2.25). Substituting the second line of (2.25) into the first obtains

$$y_t = bcy_{t-1} + (u_t + bv_t)$$
$$= b^*y_{t-1} + u^*_t, \tag{2.31}$$

where $b^* = bc$, $u^*_t = u_t + bv_t$, and b^* and u^*_t are the reduced form coefficient and disturbance of the equation for y. Combining (2.31) with the equation for z in (2.25) produces a system for $(y_t : z_t)$ that depends on only their lags and a pair of disturbances:

$$M_4^{rf}: \begin{cases} y_t = b^*y_{t-1} + u^*_t \\ z_t = cy_{t-1} + v_t \end{cases} \quad \begin{bmatrix} u^*_t \\ v_t \end{bmatrix} \sim NI\left(\begin{bmatrix} 0 \\ 0 \end{bmatrix}, \begin{bmatrix} \sigma^2 + b^2\omega^2 & b\omega^2 \\ b\omega^2 & \omega^2 \end{bmatrix} \right), \tag{2.32}$$

where the "rf" in M_4^{rf} indicates that the model is a reduced form. This model can be rewritten in matrix form:

$$\begin{bmatrix} y_t \\ z_t \end{bmatrix} = \begin{bmatrix} b^* & 0 \\ c & 0 \end{bmatrix} \begin{bmatrix} y_{t-1} \\ z_{t-1} \end{bmatrix} + \begin{bmatrix} u^*_t \\ v_t \end{bmatrix} \quad \begin{bmatrix} u^*_t \\ v_t \end{bmatrix} \sim NI\left(\begin{bmatrix} 0 \\ 0 \end{bmatrix}, \begin{bmatrix} \sigma^2 + b^2\omega^2 & b\omega^2 \\ b\omega^2 & \omega^2 \end{bmatrix} \right). \tag{2.33}$$

Equation (2.33) can be written symbolically in the form

$$M_5 : x_t = Bx_{t-1} + w_t \quad w_t \sim NI(0, \Omega), \tag{2.34}$$

where bold characters denote vectors or matrices, as required:

$$\mathbf{x_t} = \begin{bmatrix} y_t \\ z_t \end{bmatrix},$$

$$\mathbf{B} = \begin{bmatrix} b^* & 0 \\ c & 0 \end{bmatrix},$$

$$\mathbf{w_t} = \begin{bmatrix} u_t^* \\ v_t \end{bmatrix}, \text{ and}$$

$$\Omega = \begin{bmatrix} \sigma^2 + b^2\omega^2 & b\omega^2 \\ b\omega^2 & \omega^2 \end{bmatrix}. \tag{2.35}$$

Equation (2.34) is the system analog of the first-order univariate autoregressive model in equation (2.7), and the algebra for constructing forecasts from (2.7) generalizes directly to constructing forecasts from (2.34); see Clements and Hendry (1998).

Equation (2.34) provides a remarkably general framework for forecasting, hence its designation as a separate model – model M_5. The elements in the feedback matrix $\mathbf{B}$ may take a wide range of values, and the covariance matrix Ω need be only symmetric, positive semidefinite. Equation (2.34) includes models with multiple lags, as those lags may be "stacked" in $\mathbf{x_t}$, with a given lag of a variable (in $\mathbf{x_t}$) equal to (and defined as) the first lag of that variable with one shorter lag (that is, in $\mathbf{x_{t-1}}$) plus a disturbance that is identically zero. Equation (2.34) also may include an intercept (that is, a variable equal to just its own lag, and with a starting value of unity) and a linear trend (that is, a variable equal to its own lag plus an intercept). More generally, (2.34) may include exogenous variables whose future values are known through similar deterministic relations. Alternatively, (2.34) may be viewed as a special case of a dynamic system with exogenous variables, when those exogenous variables are restricted to have coefficients of zero. These two complementary views reflect the two generic systems for forecasting examined in the literature; see Baillie (1979) and Schmidt (1974), who derive and discuss the properties of forecast errors from these two systems. Clements and Hendry (1998, 1999) review properties of forecasts from systems and provide extensions; Watson (1994) summarizes general properties of VARs.

Several features characterize the predictable uncertainty associated with forecasts using the univariate first-order autoregressive model (2.7). Those features also characterize the predictable uncertainty associated with forecasts using the vector autoregressive model (2.34). Specifically, the MSFE depends upon the forecast horizon h and the feedback matrix $\mathbf{B}$. The asymptotic MSFE increases in h, and the finite sample MSFE may decrease in h.

Some complications are specific to systems. For instance, linear transformations of $\mathbf{x}$ may change the associated predictable uncertainty. Forecast errors for y and z in (2.25) may each have a high degree of predictable uncertainty, yet those for $y - z$ may have little (predictable) uncertainty, as when y and z are strongly cointegrated, with cointegrating vector $(+1 : -1)$. Conversely, y and z may be highly predictable, whereas $y - z$ may be very uncertain, as with the trade balance, which is constructed from the difference between exports and imports. See Campos (1992) and Clements and Hendry (1998) for extensive discussions on transformations of forecasts, and some empirical applications.

2.5. USES OF CALCULATED PREDICTABLE UNCERTAINTY

Calculations of predictable uncertainty serve important roles, both statistically and economically. This section illustrates these roles through a few examples, including forecast confidence intervals, tests of constancy, and fan charts in policy.

Statistically, calculations of predictable uncertainty are the basis for forecast confidence intervals, and for tests of a model's constancy over time. Prior to the realization of outcomes, confidence intervals provide an assessment of "expected" or predicted forecast uncertainty, helping to qualify the forecasts themselves and to give a picture of the expected range of likely outcomes. That is, information about forecast uncertainty is important in addition to the forecast itself.

In section 2.3.3, the confidence intervals in figure 2.2 for both the trend model and the random walk model were obtained from formulas for the associated predictable uncertainty. Even in more complicated models, predictable uncertainty still may be computed, as in Marquez and Ericsson (1993), who examine the one-period- and multiple-period-ahead forecasts from various nonlinear, multiple-equation models of the U.S. trade balance. Figure 2.3 plots the forecasts,

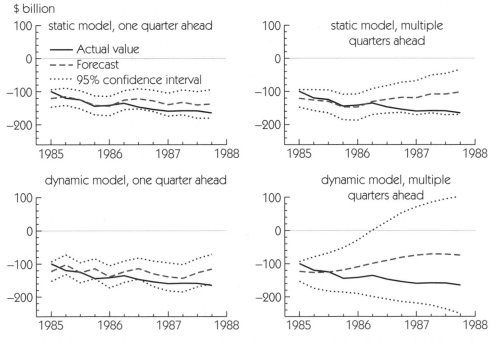

Figure 2.3 Actual and forecast values from two models of the real U.S. trade balance, both one quarter and multiple quarters ahead, with 95% confidence intervals for the forecasts

outcomes, and 95 percent forecast confidence intervals for two of their models, both one quarter ahead and multiple quarters ahead.[4] The forecast period is 1985Q1–1987Q4. For the first, near-static model, the width of the confidence interval varies only slightly with the forecast horizon. For the second, highly dynamic model, the confidence interval depends strongly upon the forecast horizon, with much greater forecast uncertainty at longer horizons. The multi-period-ahead confidence intervals for these two models parallel in character the confidence intervals in figure 2.2 for the trend and random walk models. In particular, the fan shape of the confidence intervals for the second trade model and the random walk model suggests the very dynamic nature of the variables being forecast and of the models being used to forecast it.

Predictable forecast uncertainty also can help evaluate the models from which the forecasts were generated. For instance, if the forecast errors lie well outside the range that was anticipated, that indicates specification problems with the model. Predictable forecast uncertainty thus permits assessing how important *unpredictable* forecast uncertainty is in contributing to the realized forecast error – that is, in determining the empirical role of items 2(a)–2(c) in the forecast error taxonomy of table 2.1. Specifically, items 2(a)–2(c) reflect discrepancies between the model used for forecasting and the actual behavior of the economy, with item 2(a) typically being primarily responsible for forecast failure in econometric models.

Formal statistical analysis of model-based forecasts in light of predictable forecast uncertainty – through tests of parameter constancy – has been central to evaluating and improving empirical economic models. Chow (1960) provides the initial development of these evaluation techniques, building on Fisher (1922), with Hansen (1992a, 1992b) and Andrews (1993) constructing constancy tests with an unknown breakpoint. Goldfeld (1973, 1976), Judd and Scadding (1982), and Baba, Hendry, and Starr (1992) examine constancy tests in their central role in modeling the demand for money. At a more general level, constancy tests are key to evaluating the Lucas (1976) critique, with constancy tests providing the primary empirical basis for refuting the Lucas critique; see Hendry (1988), Engle and Hendry (1993), Ericsson and Irons (1995), and Hendry (2000). Predictable forecast uncertainty is also central to calculating forecast encompassing test statistics; see Chong and Hendry (1986), Granger (1989), Ericsson (1992b), Ericsson and Marquez (1993), and West (1996).

Even as a statistical tool, measures of predictable forecast uncertainty have immediate economic implications. For instance, if the forecast uncertainty for a certain variable is viewed as being considerable, insurance might be desirable as a mechanism for protecting against untoward outcomes; and different types of insurance might be available. Also, forecast uncertainty is inherent to many economic activities, such as business investment, with the possibility of large successes often being an attraction of such investment. Forecast uncertainty is ubiquitous in economics, and many consequences follow from the presence and extent of that uncertainty.

Predictable forecast uncertainty has recently taken a visible role in the economic policy arena – in the Bank of England's "fan charts." For the last few

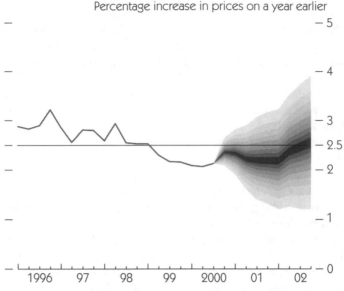

Percentage increase in prices on a year earlier

Figure 2.4   The Bank of England's November 2000 fan chart for
projections of RPIX inflation

years, the Bank of England has published its assessment of (predictable) forecast
uncertainty through fan charts for its forecasts of both inflation and GDP growth;
see the Bank of England (2000, overview and section 6). Figure 2.4 reproduces the
Bank's fan chart (their chart 6.2, on p. 64) for its November 2000 forecast of
inflation. The Bank describes this graph as follows:

> The fan chart depicting the probability distribution for inflation is rather like a
> contour map. At any given point during the forecast period, the depth of shading
> represents the height of the probability density function over a range of outcomes
> for inflation. The darkest band includes the central (single most likely) projection
> and covers 10% of the probability. Each successive pair of bands is drawn to cover a
> further 10% of the probability, until 90% of the probability distribution is covered.
> The bands widen as the time horizon is extended, indicating increasing uncertainty
> about outcomes. (Bank of England, 2000, chart 6.2, p. 64)

This fan chart summarizes the Bank's predicted or anticipated probability distribution of inflation outcomes. The Bank of England (2000, chart 6.4, p. 66) also
publishes the density function corresponding to that distribution, which appears
in figure 2.5. From figure 2.5, the Bank's 90 percent confidence interval for annual
inflation in the 12 months 2002Q1–2002Q4 is from about 1.2 percent to 3.9 percent, as indicated by the shaded area in the graph. Outcomes for inflation could
occur outside that range, but the probability of those outcomes is believed to be
relatively small.

Improvements to the Bank's fan charts may be feasible; see Wallis (1999).
In the future, economists also could examine whether the Bank of England's

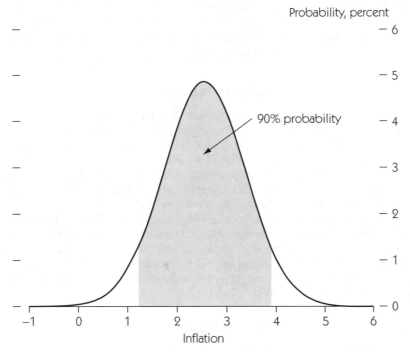

Figure 2.5 The November 2000 projection by the Bank of England for the probability density of RPIX inflation in the year to 2002Q4

published confidence bands reflect what happened in the data, or if those bands were too narrow or too wide. Such an analysis could benefit the construction of future monetary policy. Thus, the statistical and economic aspects of predictable uncertainty are often closely intertwined.

2.6. CONCLUSIONS

Forecast uncertainty reflects the dispersion of possible outcomes relative to the forecast being made. Forecast uncertainty arises both from "what we don't know that we don't know" and from "what we know that we don't know." In econometric models, forecast uncertainty from the latter – predictable forecast uncertainty – can be calculated numerically. Forecast uncertainty also depends upon the variable being forecast, the type of model used for forecasting, the economic process actually determining the variable being forecast, and the forecast horizon.

Calculation of predictable forecast uncertainty has numerous uses in economic practice. First, prior to the realization of outcomes, it helps in qualifying the forecasts themselves and in giving a picture of the expected range of likely outcomes. Information about forecast uncertainty is important in addition to the forecast itself, as with the Bank of England's fan charts. Measures of forecast uncertainty also provide economists with a tool for assessing the importance of unmodeled features of the economy, both directly through the calculated forecast uncertainty, and indirectly through comparison of that calculated uncertainty with the realized distribution of forecast errors.

Acknowledgments

The author is a staff economist in the Division of International Finance, Board of Governors of the Federal Reserve System, Washington, DC 20551 U.S.A., and may be reached on the Internet at ericsson@frb.gov. The views in this chapter are solely the responsibility of the author and should not be interpreted as reflecting the views of the Board of Governors of the Federal Reserve System or of any other person associated with the Federal Reserve System. I am grateful to Julia Campos, Mike Clements, Clive Granger, David Hendry, Jaime Marquez, and Hayden Smith for helpful discussions and comments; to Jurgen Doornik for providing me with a beta-test copy of GiveWin Version 2.00; and to the Bank of England for permission to reprint the fan chart and density function in figures 2.4 and 2.5. All numerical results were obtained with PcGive Professional Version 9: see Doornik and Hendry (1996). Data and output listings for this chapter's empirical results are available from the author and at www.federalreserve.gov/pubs/ifdp/2000/695/default.htm on the WorldWide Web.

Notes

1   Strictly speaking, "forecast uncertainty" should be called "forecast error uncertainty," as the forecast error is what is uncertain, not the forecast. However, following common usage in the literature, and for brevity's sake, the phrase "forecast uncertainty" is used throughout this chapter.
2   While a sample size of $T = 5$ seems very small, it may not be so in this context, where only a single parameter is estimated. In unrestricted vector autoregressive models and autoregressive distributed lag models, the number of estimated parameters per equation is commonly 10 percent to 30 percent of the sample size – similar to the percentage here.
3   These assumptions imply that y_t is integrated of order zero and ergodic. See Banerjee, Dolado, Galbraith, and Hendry (1993) for details.
4   In the notation of Marquez and Ericsson (1993), the models are Models M1 and M5.

References

Andrews, D.W.K. (1993). Tests for parameter instability and structural change with unknown change point. *Econometrica*, 61(4), 821–56.

Baba, Y., D.F. Hendry, and R.M. Starr (1992). The demand for M1 in the U.S.A., 1960–1988. *Review of Economic Studies*, 59(1), 25–61.

Baillie, R.T. (1979). Asymptotic prediction mean squared error for vector autoregressive models. *Biometrika*, 66(3), 675–8.

Banerjee, A., J.J. Dolado, J.W. Galbraith, and D.F. Hendry (1993). *Co-integration, Error Correction, and the Econometric Analysis of Non-stationary Data*. Oxford: Oxford University Press.

Bank of England (2000). *Inflation Report: November 2000*. London: Bank of England.

Box, G.E.P. and G.M. Jenkins (1970). *Time Series Analysis: Forecasting and Control*. San Francisco: Holden-Day.

Campos, J. (1992). Confidence intervals for linear combinations of forecasts from dynamic econometric models. *Journal of Policy Modeling*, 14(4), 535–60.

Chong, Y.Y. and D.F. Hendry (1986). Econometric evaluation of linear macro-economic models. *Review of Economic Studies*, 53(4), 671–90.

Chow, G.C. (1960). Tests of equality between sets of coefficients in two linear regressions. *Econometrica*, 28(3), 591–605.

Clements, M.P. and D.F. Hendry (1993). On the limitations of comparing mean square forecast errors. *Journal of Forecasting*, 12(8), 617–37. With discussion and reply.

Clements, M.P. and D.F. Hendry (1998). *Forecasting Economic Time Series*. Cambridge, England: Cambridge University Press.

Clements, M.P. and D.F. Hendry (1999). *Forecasting Non-stationary Economic Time Series*. Cambridge, Massachusetts: MIT Press.

Clements, M.P. and D.F. Hendry (2001). Forecasting with difference-stationary and trend-stationary models. *Econometrics Journal*, 4(1), S1–S19.

Doornik, J.A. and D.F. Hendry (1996). *PcGive Professional 9.0 for Windows*. London: International Thomson Business Press.

Engle, R.F. and D.F. Hendry (1993). Testing super exogeneity and invariance in regression models. *Journal of Econometrics*, 56(1/2), 119–39.

Ericsson, N.R. (1992a). Cointegration, exogeneity, and policy analysis: An overview. *Journal of Policy Modeling*, 14(3), 251–80.

Ericsson, N.R. (1992b). Parameter constancy, mean square forecast errors, and measuring forecast performance: An exposition, extensions, and illustration. *Journal of Policy Modeling*, 14(4), 465–95.

Ericsson, N.R., D.F. Hendry, and K.M. Prestwich (1998). The demand for broad money in the United Kingdom, 1878–1993. *Scandinavian Journal of Economics*, 100(1), 289–324. With discussion.

Ericsson, N.R. and J.S. Irons (1995). The Lucas critique in practice: Theory without measurement. In K.D. Hoover (ed.), *Macroeconometrics: Developments, Tensions, and Prospects*, Boston, Massachusetts: Kluwer Academic Publishers, chapter 8, 263–312. With discussion.

Ericsson, N.R. and J. Marquez (1993). Encompassing the forecasts of U.S. trade balance models. *Review of Economics and Statistics*, 75(1), 19–31.

Ericsson, N.R. and J. Marquez (1998). A framework for economic forecasting. *Econometrics Journal*, 1(1), C228–C266.

Fisher, R.A. (1922). The goodness of fit of regression formulae, and the distribution of regression coefficients. *Journal of the Royal Statistical Society*, 85(4), 597–612.

Goldfeld, S.M. (1973). The demand for money revisited. *Brookings Papers on Economic Activity*, 1973(3), 577–638. With discussion.

Goldfeld, S.M. (1976). The case of the missing money. *Brookings Papers on Economic Activity*, 1976(3), 683–730. With discussion.

Granger, C.W.J. (1969). Investigating causal relations by econometric models and cross-spectral methods. *Econometrica*, 37(3), 424–38.

Granger, C.W.J. (1989). *Forecasting in Business and Economics*, 2nd edn. Boston, Massachusetts: Academic Press.

Hansen, B.E. (1992a). Testing for parameter instability in linear models. *Journal of Policy Modeling*, 14(4), 517–33.

Hansen, B.E. (1992b). Tests for parameter instability in regressions with I(1) processes. *Journal of Business and Economic Statistics*, 10(3), 321–35.

Henderson, J.M. and R.E. Quandt (1971). *Microeconomic Theory: A Mathematical Approach*. New York: McGraw-Hill.

Hendry, D.F. (1988). The encompassing implications of feedback versus feedforward mechanisms in econometrics. *Oxford Economic Papers*, 40(1), 132–49.

Hendry, D.F. (1995). *Dynamic Econometrics*. Oxford: Oxford University Press.

Hendry, D.F. (2000). Forecast failure, expectations formation, and the Lucas critique. Mimeo, Nuffield College, Oxford.

Hendry, D.F. and N.R. Ericsson (eds.) (2001). *Understanding Economic Forecasts*. Cambridge, MA: MIT Press.

Hendry, D.F. and G.E. Mizon (1999). The pervasiveness of Granger causality in econometrics. In R.F. Engle and H. White (eds.), *Cointegration, Causality, and Forecasting: A Festschrift in Honour of Clive W.J. Granger*, chapter 5, pp. 102–34. Oxford: Oxford University Press.

Hendry, D.F., A. Pagan, and J.D. Sargan (1984). Dynamic specification. In Z. Griliches and M.D. Intriligator (eds.), *Handbook of Econometrics*, volume 2, chapter 18, pp. 1023–1100. Amsterdam: North-Holland.

Hoque, A., J.R. Magnus, and B. Pesaran (1988). The exact multi-period mean-square forecast error for the first-order autoregressive model. *Journal of Econometrics*, 39(3), 327–46.

Judd, J.P. and J.L. Scadding (1982). The search for a stable money demand function: A survey of the post-1973 literature. *Journal of Economic Literature*, 20(3), 993–1023.

Lucas, Jr., R.E. (1976). Econometric policy evaluation: A critique. In K. Brunner and A.H. Meltzer (eds.), *The Phillips Curve and Labor Markets*. North-Holland, Amsterdam, 19–46. Carnegie-Rochester Conference Series on Public Policy, volume 1, *Journal of Monetary Economics*, Supplement. With discussion.

Marquez, J. and N.R. Ericsson (1993). Evaluating forecasts of the U.S. trade balance. In R.C. Bryant, P. Hooper, and C.L. Mann (eds.), *Evaluating Policy Regimes: New Research in Empirical Macroeconomics*. Washington, D.C.: Brookings Institution, chapter 14, 671–732.

Orcutt, G.H. and H.S. Winokur, Jr. (1969). First order autoregression: Inference, estimation, and prediction. *Econometrica*, 37(1), 1–14.

Schmidt, P. (1974). The asymptotic distribution of forecasts in the dynamic simulation of an econometric model. *Econometrica*, 42(2), 303–9.

Singer, M. (1997). Thoughts of a nonmillenarian. *Bulletin of the American Academy of Arts and Sciences*, 51(2), 36–51.

Suits, D.B. (1955). An econometric model of the watermelon market. *American Journal of Agricultural Economics* (formerly the *Journal of Farm Economics*), 37(2), 237–51.

Tinbergen, J. (1931). Ein ßchiffbauzyklus? *Weltwirtschaftliches Archiv*, 34, 152–64. Reprinted as "A Shipbuilding Cycle?" in L.H. Klaassen, L.M. Koyck, and H.J. Witteveen (eds.) (1959). *Jan Tinbergen: Selected Papers*. Amsterdam: North-Holland, 1–14.

Wallis, K.F. (1999). Asymmetric density forecasts of inflation and the Bank of England's fan chart. *National Institute Economic Review*, 167, 106–12.

Wallis, K.F. (2000). Macroeconometric modelling. In M. Gudmundsson, T.T. Herbertsson, and G. Zoega (eds.) *Macroeconomic Policy: Iceland in an Era of Global Integration*. Reykjavik: University of Iceland Press, 399–414.

Watson, M.W. (1994). Vector autoregressions and cointegration. In R.F. Engle and D.L. McFadden (eds.), *Handbook of Econometrics*, vol. 4. Amsterdam: North-Holland, chapter 47, 2843–915.

West, K.D. (1996). Asymptotic inference about predictive ability. *Econometrica*, 64(5), 1067–84.

CHAPTER THREE

Density Forecasting: A Survey

Anthony S. Tay and Kenneth F. Wallis

3.1. INTRODUCTION

A density forecast of the realization of a random variable at some future time is an estimate of the probability distribution of the possible future values of that variable. It thus provides a complete description of the uncertainty associated with a forecast, and stands in contrast to a point forecast, which by itself contains no description of the associated uncertainty. Intermediate between these two extremes is an interval forecast, which specifies the probability that the actual outcome will fall within a stated interval. To report a forecast interval represents a first response by point forecasters to criticism of their silence on the subject of uncertainty, and this practice is becoming more common in macroeconomic forecasting. This field also contains several examples of density forecasts, and these feature as a more direct object of attention in the fields of finance and risk management. This chapter presents a selective survey of the use of density forecasts, and discusses some issues concerning their construction, presentation, and evaluation.

A density forecast is, of course, implicit in the standard construction and interpretation of a symmetric forecast interval. This is usually given as a band of plus or minus one or two standard errors around the point forecast, and the associated statement of a probability of 68 percent or 95 percent respectively rests on an assumption of a normal or Gaussian distribution. Sometimes the use of Student's t-distribution is suggested, having in mind that the variance of the forecast error must be estimated, or the departure from normality caused by the more general parameter estimation problem may be acknowledged, nevertheless such calculations typically rest on a model with normally distributed innovations. These methods seem to assume that the normal distribution is "too good not to be true," in the classic phrase of Anscombe (1967). This was a position of which he was critical, however, instead advocating the use of nonnormal distributions: the complete sentence reads "the disposition of present-day statistical theorists to suppose that all 'error' distributions are exactly normal can be ascribed to their ontological perception that normality is too good not to be true" (Anscombe, 1967, p. 16). His advice has been taken to heart in much of the density forecasting literature, where a wide range of functional forms and nonparametric empirical methods appears, as discussed below.

A density forecasting problem can be placed in a decision theoretic environment by a direct generalization of the point forecasting problem, as described by Diebold, Gunther, and Tay (1998). Suppose that the forecast user has a loss function $L(a(p(y)), y)$ which depends on the action $a(\cdot)$ chosen in the light of the density forecast $p(y)$ and on the realization of the forecast variable. Choosing an action a^* to minimize expected loss calculated as if the density forecast $p(y)$ is correct implies that

$$a^*(p(y)) = \underset{a \in A}{\text{argmin}} \int L(a, y)p(y)dy,$$

where A denotes all possible choices that the forecast user might make. The choice a^* incurs loss $L(a^*, y)$, which is a random variable whose expected value with respect to the true density $f(y)$ is

$$E[L(a^*, y)] = \int L(a^*, y)f(y)dy,$$

and a "better" density forecast is one with lower expected loss. However, there is even less literature on explicit decision problems and their associated loss functions for density forecasts than for point forecasts, where it is in any event very scarce. Here the standard treatment takes the action to be the choice of a point forecast $\hat{y}$, with the loss function a simple nonnegative function of the error $(y - \hat{y})$, taking the value zero for zero error. Different loss functions may lead to different optimal point forecasts, particularly if $f(y)$ is not symmetric. A corresponding body of results is only just beginning to emerge in the density forecasting case. The problem of evaluating density forecasts *ex post* is considered below, with some discussion of the problem of evaluation under general loss functions, following discussion of a range of applications in macroeconomics and finance.

The general setting of this chapter is the time-series forecasting problem, rather than other prediction problems discussed by Aitchison and Dunsmore (1975), for example, under the heading of statistical prediction analysis. In both cases an essential feature of the characterization is the pair of experiments e and f. "From the information which we gain from a performance of e, the *informative* experiment, we wish to make some reasoned statement concerning the performance of f, the *future* experiment" (1975, p. 1). The experiments are linked by the indexing parameter of the probability models for e and f, and a feature of all the problems Aitchison and Dunsmore consider is that, for a given index, the experiments *e* and *f* are independent. This excludes the time-series forecasting problem, in which *e* records a realization to date of some stochastic process of which *f* is a continuation. Our focus on the time-series forecasting problem in turn tends to exclude a range of prediction problems where Bayesian techniques have found application.

The chapter proceeds as follows. Section 3.2 discusses the use of density forecasts in macroeconomics and finance. Section 3.3 considers some issues concerning the interpretation and presentation of density forecasts, and the available techniques for evaluating density forecasts are reviewed in section 3.4. Section 3.5 contains conclusions.

3.2. DENSITY FORECASTS IN MACROECONOMICS AND FINANCE

3.2.1. Applications in macroeconomics

The longest-running series of density forecasts in macroeconomics dates back to 1968, when the Business and Economic Statistics Section of the American Statistical Association (ASA) and the National Bureau of Economic Research (NBER) jointly initiated a quarterly survey of macroeconomic forecasters in the United States, known as the ASA–NBER survey; Zarnowitz (1969) describes its original objectives. Later the Federal Reserve Bank of Philadelphia assumed responsibility for the survey, and the name was changed to the Survey of Professional Forecasters (see Croushore, 1993). Most of the questions ask for point forecasts, for a range of variables and forecast horizons, but density forecasts are also requested for inflation and output growth. In each case a number of intervals, or bins, in which the future value of the variable might fall are provided, and each forecaster is asked to report their associated forecast probabilities. The density forecast is thus represented as a histogram, on a preassigned grid. These are averaged over respondents, and the mean probability distributions are published. A recent example of a density forecast of inflation is shown in table 3.1. There are numerous interesting issues associated with the compilation and reporting of such forecasts, including the combination of individual responses by simple averaging and the potential usefulness of measures such as the standard errors of the mean probabilities. These are familiar topics in point forecasting, whose extension to density forecasting has scarcely begun to be considered.

In the United Kingdom the history is much shorter. When the Treasury established its Panel of Independent Forecasters (the "seven wise men") in late 1992, one of the present authors suggested that the panel members be asked to report density forecasts for inflation and growth, using the same questions as the U.S. Survey of Professional Forecasters, in addition to their point forecasts. It was some time before this suggestion was adopted, and only one set of density forecasts was published before the panel, by now the "six wise people," was dissolved on the change of government in May 1997. In February 1996 the Bank of England had begun to publish average survey responses of density forecasts of inflation in its quarterly *Inflation Report*, along the lines of the U.S. survey, but in

Table 3.1 Density forecasts of U.S. inflation: mean probability (of 28 forecasters) attached to possible percent changes in GDP price index, 1998–9

Inflation rate (%)	Probability (%)
8.0 or more	0.07
7.0 to 7.9	0.11
6.0 to 6.9	0.14
5.0 to 5.9	0.25
4.0 to 4.9	1.21
3.0 to 3.9	8.96
2.0 to 2.9	20.00
1.0 to 1.9	49.54
0.0 to 0.9	17.89
Will decline	1.82

Source: Philadelphia Fed., *Survey of Professional Forecasters*, 20 November 1998 (http://www.phil.frb.org/econ/spf/spfq498.pdf).

Table 3.2 Density forecasts of U.K. inflation: probability of indicated annual RPIX inflation rate, percent, 1997Q4

	KB	TC	GD	PM	BR	MW
8.0 or more	0	0	0	0	0	1
7.0 to 7.9	0	0	0	0	0	1
6.0 to 6.9	1	0	1	0	0	4
5.0 to 5.9	4	2	2	0	1	8
4.0 to 4.9	8	7	8	0	6	13
3.0 to 3.9	22	32	16	5	22	18
2.0 to 2.9	55	50	40	30	35	19
1.0 to 1.9	10	9	25	40	26	16
0.0 to 0.9	0	0	6	20	9	11
Will decline	0	0	2	5	1	9

Source: Panel of Independent Forecasters, November 1996 Report (London: HM Treasury). The panel members are Kate Barker, Tim Congdon, Gavin Davies, Patrick Minford, Bridget Rosewell, and Martin Weale.

contrast the panel published the individual responses; in any case this was not difficult, since there were only six. These are shown, for one-year-ahead inflation (in the Retail Prices Index excluding mortgage interest payments, RPIX), in table 3.2. It is seen that the first five density forecasts are much less dispersed than the sixth, and round numbers catch the eye, with modal probabilities 55 percent,

50 percent, 40 percent, 40 percent, and 35 percent, coincidentally declining with the alphabet. Such rounding is commonly observed in reported probabilities with a strong subjective element. In contrast, the probabilities in the sixth column of table 3.2 are known to be calculated assuming a normal distribution. The forecast is based on that published in the *National Institute Economic Review* (Martin Weale being the Institute's Director), which since February 1996 has included a density forecast of inflation and growth alongside its long-established macroeconomic point forecasts. The forecasts are based on a macroeconometric model, subject to the forecaster's residual adjustments, as usual, and analysis of past forecast errors cannot reject the hypothesis that they are normally distributed (Poulizac, Weale, and Young, 1996). This analysis also cannot reject the hypothesis that past forecasts are unbiased, so the normal density forecast is centered on the point forecast, with variance equal to that of the errors in past forecasts at the same horizon (over 1983–95). Historical forecast errors are an appropriate starting point for this calculation since they incorporate a range of possible sources of error including model error, but projecting the variance forward is itself a forecasting problem and, as with point forecasts, failures may occur due to structural breaks. In this case an obvious change is the introduction of a monetary policy regime of inflation targeting, so the past may not be a good guide to future behavior, as anticipated by Poulizac et al. In these circumstances the first five forecasters are clearly much less uncertain about future inflation, which in the event stood at 2.7 percent at the end of 1997.

An alternative way of calibrating a model-based density forecast is through stochastic simulation of the model in the new policy environment, as discussed in a companion article on the National Institute model by Blake (1996), although this does not include the effects of model uncertainty. Stochastic simulation methods are required to calculate empirical distributions of estimated outcomes from large-scale macroeconometric models, because these are typically nonlinear in variables and analytic methods are not available. The underlying pseudo-random error terms are usually generated assuming a normal distribution, a test of the normality of residuals being a standard diagnostic test during the specification of the econometric equations. Often these equations are log-linear, or include more complex forms such as the constant elasticity of substitution (CES) function, whereas definitions and accounting identities are linear, involving products or ratios if variables appear in both real and nominal terms. The result is that the predictive densities are nonnormal but of unknown form, and they are simply reported graphically or numerically. Even with linear models stochastic simulation methods may be advantageous whenever it is desired to take account of uncertainty due not only to the model's random error terms but also to coefficient estimation error, errors in projecting exogenous variables, and so forth. For a vector autoregressive model of interest rates, money, prices, and output Kling and Bessler (1989) present density forecasts calculated by stochastic simulation with respect to model errors and sampling errors in regression coefficients, also taking account of nonconstant residual variances. We return to this example in section 3.4 below.

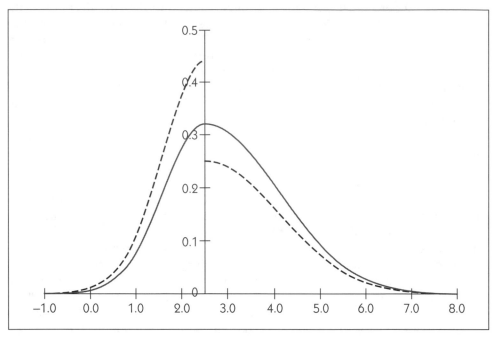

Figure 3.1 The probability density function of the two-piece normal distribution. Dashed line, two halves of normal distributions with $\mu = 2.5$, $\sigma_1 = 0.902$ (left) and $\sigma_2 = 1.592$ (right); solid line, the two-piece normal distribution

A density forecast of inflation represented analytically by a specific nonnormal probability distribution has been published by the Bank of England in its quarterly *Inflation Report* since February 1996 (see http://www.bankofengland.co.uk/Links/setframe.html). The chosen distribution is the two-piece normal distribution, whose probability density function, with parameters μ, σ_1 and σ_2, is

$$f(y) = \begin{cases} A \exp\left[-(y - \mu)^2/2\sigma_1^2\right] & y \le \mu, \\ A \exp\left[-(y - \mu)^2/2\sigma_2^2\right] & y \ge \mu, \end{cases}$$

where $A = (\sqrt{2\pi}(\sigma_1 + \sigma_2)/2)^{-1}$ (John, 1982; Johnson, Kotz, and Balakrishnan, 1994). It is formed by taking two halves of normal distributions with parameters (μ, σ_1) and (μ, σ_2) respectively and scaling them to give the common value $f(\mu)$ as above. Figure 3.1 uses the parameter values corresponding to the eight-quarter-ahead forecast published in the August 1997 *Inflation Report*, also used for illustrative purposes by Britton, Fisher, and Whitley (1998) and Wallis (1999). With $\sigma_2 > \sigma_1$ this has positive skewness, which can be seen algebraically by noting that the mean is

$$E(Y) = \mu + \sqrt{\frac{2}{\pi}} (\sigma_2 - \sigma_1)$$

and so exceeds the mode, μ, if $\sigma_2 > \sigma_1$, or that the third moment about the mean is a positive multiple of $(\sigma_2 - \sigma_1)$. The coefficient of kurtosis exceeds 3 whenever $\sigma_1 \neq \sigma_2$, so the distribution is leptokurtic. It is a convenient way of representing departures from the symmetry of the normal distribution since probability calculations can still be based on standard normal tables, with suitable scaling; however, it has no convenient multivariate generalization.

The density forecast describes the subjective assessment of inflationary pressures by the Bank's Monetary Policy Committee, and although the prevailing level of uncertainty is initially assessed with reference to past forecast errors, the final calibration of the distribution represents the Committee's judgment, the degree of skewness in particular exhibiting their view of the balance of risks on the "upside" and "downside" of the forecast (Britton et al., 1998). This approach to the construction of a density forecast is closer to Bayesian elicitation methods, although the extent to which the Committee's procedures reflect the common approach in the general field of probability assessment of basing elicitation procedures on quantiles is not known. It nevertheless stands in contrast to the National Institute's approach of superimposing a data-based normal distribution on a point forecast. It should be noted, however, that the conventional null hypothesis of normality would be unlikely to be rejected in this approach if the degree of asymmetry in the example in figure 3.1 were to apply in practice. For these parameter values, one would expect to require a sample of almost 200 observations before the conventional asymptotic $\chi^2(2)$ statistic would reject normality at the 5 percent level; even the more powerful likelihood ratio test given by Kimber (1985) for the null hypothesis that $\sigma_1 = \sigma_2$ in the two-piece normal distribution would be expected to require a sample of 115 to reject in this case. Samples of this size are rare in macroeconomic forecasting, and in any event there is no presumption in the Bank of England's forecasts that the balance of risks is constant over time.

In addition to constructing macroeconomic density forecasts to assist in setting their policy instruments, monetary policy-makers also use financial market forecasts, to which we now turn. In particular, density forecasts of future interest rates and exchange rates can be extracted from sets of prices of traded options and futures contracts as discussed below. These then assist the interpretation of market sentiment and provide a check on the credibility of policy.

3.2.2. Applications in finance

In finance, much effort has been put into generating forecasts with a complete characterization of the uncertainty associated with asset and portfolio returns, recognizing that the normal distribution is inadequate for this purpose. Tests of normality typically rely on third and fourth moments, rejecting the null hypothesis of normality if there is significant skewness and/or excess kurtosis, and many empirical studies have found nonnormal higher moments in the (unconditional) distributions of stock returns, interest rates, and other financial data series. An early example is Fama (1965), who reports evidence of excess kurtosis in the unconditional distribution of daily returns of stocks listed in the Dow Jones Industrial Average. Many studies have since attempted to model this excess kurtosis, and also asymmetries in the distribution of asset returns, although the early studies tended not to deal with forecasts *per se*. The models proposed considered returns to be iid processes and should be viewed as attempts to explain the unconditional distribution of asset returns rather than to develop forecasting models; nevertheless, they do reflect an increasing awareness that such asymmetries should carry over to forecasts of asset returns.

There are several motivations for an interest in more complete and accurate probability statements. A leading example is the issue of risk management, with which the concept of density forecasting is intimately related. The business of risk management has in recent years developed into an important industry, with density forecasts regularly issued by J.P. Morgan, Reuters, and Bloomberg, among others. The basic idea of such systems is to allow the user to generate density forecasts of the change in the value of customized portfolios over a particular holding period. The focus of these forecast densities is typically the nth percentile of the distribution, embodied in a measure commonly known as Value-at-Risk (VaR); the portfolio is forecasted to lose a value greater or equal to its VaR over the specified period with probability $n/100$. It is clear that departures from normality in the portfolio returns will adversely affect the usefulness of VaR estimates if the assumption of normality is inappropriately used in generating the forecast. In particular, the presence of excess kurtosis implies that the Gaussian-based VaR of a portfolio will be underestimated, and much effort has gone into developing accurate density forecasts that can overcome this difficulty in the context of VaR analysis. Such measurements are also of concern to regulators, the Capital Adequacy Directive of the Bank for International Settlements, for example, requiring a bank to hold risk capital adequate to cover losses on its trading portfolio over a ten-day holding period on 99 percent of occasions. This example indicates that it may be only a single quantile of the distribution that is of interest, moreover one located in its extreme tail, and some methods, discussed below, focus directly on these aspects of the problem. The presence of nonnormal higher moments in financial data also has implications for numerous other issues in addition to risk management, including asset pricing, portfolio diversification, and options pricing. For example, Simkowitz and Beedles (1978) demonstrate that the degree of skewness preference among investors will affect the extent to which they diversify. The higher the degree of skewness, the fewer assets the investor would hold since diversification reduces the amount of skewness in the portfolio. Cotner (1991) provides some evidence that asymmetries affect options prices. The presence of skew in asset returns will also play an important role in developing hedging strategies.

MODELING AND FORECASTING VOLATILITY, SKEW, AND KURTOSIS

Density forecasting in finance can be viewed as beginning with the literature that aims to model and forecast volatility. The ARCH model of Engle (1982) models the conditional variance as a linear function of squares of past observations, and thus delivers forecasts with time-varying conditional variances. A Generalized ARCH(1, 1) process includes the lagged conditional variance and can be written (with zero mean) as

$$y_t = e_t h_t^{1/2}$$

$$h_t = \omega + \alpha y_{t-1}^2 + \beta h_{t-1},$$

where the standardized residual e_t is distributed identically and independently with some zero-mean unit-variance density $f(e_t)$. ARCH models imply larger kurtosis in the unconditional distribution than the normal distribution, although the commonly used conditionally Gaussian varieties deliver symmetric density forecasts, which is unsatisfactory given evidence of asymmetries in asset returns. The excess kurtosis generated by conditionally Gaussian models was also found to be insufficient to explain the degree of leptokurtosis in many financial time series. The literature on ARCH models and its applications is enormous, and we do not attempt to review that literature here, nor the related literature on stochastic volatility models. For a good review of ARCH models, see Bollerslev, Engle, and Nelson (1994) and, in a more general context, Pagan (1996). Our focus on density forecasting directs attention toward higher-order moments.

GARCH models can produce skewed and leptokurtic conditional forecasts – many do – and they do so by incorporating skew and kurtosis directly into the distribution of the standardized residuals of GARCH processes. A leading example is the t-distributed GARCH model of Bollerslev (1987) which directly incorporates excess kurtosis in the conditional forecasts by specifying a Student's t-distribution for the standardized residuals. The t-distribution with v degrees of freedom has kurtosis $3(v - 2)/(v - 4)$, $v > 4$, which approaches 3 from above as v increases. Estimation and inference is often conducted in terms of the reciprocal $1/v$, since the interesting null hypothesis is often $1/v = 0$, namely normality.

Some applications have attempted to model the densities of the standardized residuals by using asymptotic expansions, instead of assuming fully parameterized functional forms. Lee and Tse (1991) model the standardized residuals as a Gram–Charlier type distribution; an application to the one- and two-month interbank rates of the Singapore Asian Dollar Market reveals evidence of excess kurtosis in the residuals of an ARCH-M regression, but not of skew. Baillie and Bollerslev (1992) use asymptotic expansions to obtain multi-step-ahead predictions from a GARCH process, which are nonnormal even if the one-step-ahead conditional prediction densities are normal; they approximate the quantiles of these forecast densities using Cornish–Fisher asymptotic expansions. Another approach to producing density forecasts, along similar lines, uses nonparametric procedures to model the density of the standardized residual. An example is the semiparametric ARCH approach of Engle and Gonzalez-Rivera (1991) which specifies the variable of interest as a GARCH process and exploits the fact that quasi-maximum likelihood estimation can deliver consistent estimates of the GARCH parameters. The standardized residuals from this step are then estimated nonparametrically using the discrete maximum penalized likelihood estimation technique. An application to daily stock returns for the sample period 1962 to 1988 showed that skewness is an important feature of stock returns, while an analysis of daily returns to the £/U.S.$ exchange rate produced evidence of less pronounced skew. Other nonparametric approaches, including bootstrap methods, can be combined with parametric GARCH models in a similar manner.

The idea of accommodating higher moment effects by developing sophisticated distributional specifications, parametric or otherwise, for the standardized residuals of a GARCH model nevertheless does not allow the higher moments to be time-varying in general. For instance, the forecasts delivered by a conditional normal GARCH model will always deliver a conditional density forecast with kurtosis equal to 3. Asymmetric GARCH models, such as the Exponential GARCH model of Nelson (1991), allow negative and positive shocks to affect the conditional variance asymmetrically, but still deliver density forecasts that are symmetric if the distribution of the standardized residuals is so specified. The possibility of forecasting higher moments is something worth exploring, and while there are some studies that pertain to the forecastability of higher moments, the evidence is mixed. Singleton and Wingender (1986) find considerable skewness in the distribution of the monthly returns of common stocks from 1961 to 1980, but also find that this skewness did not persist – that is, stocks that displayed skewness in one period did not always remain skewed in future periods – and using the Spearman rank order correlation test they provide evidence that the skew in the distribution of stock returns is not predictable. However, they base their study on the standardized third central moment. This measure is known to be very sensitive to outliers, so the results they obtain may be due to a few anomalous observations. Alles and Kling (1994) consider the distributions of daily returns on the NYSE (Jul. 1962 to Dec. 1989), AMEX (Jul. 1962 to Dec. 1989) and NASDAQ (Dec. 1972 to Dec. 1989) market indices. Across four-year-long sample periods, they find that the skew varies in direction and size from period to period. No attempt is made to relate current skew to the returns' observed history, although there is evidence that the skew in the distribution of the returns varies according to the business cycle. Their analysis is also based on the standardized third central moment. An analysis of bond returns (market value-weighted indices of long- and medium-term Treasury bonds) shows that the degree of skew in these series is generally less than for stock indices.

Rare examples of the modeling of the dependence of higher-order moments on the past are the studies by Gallant, Hsieh, and Tauchen (1991) and Hansen (1994), again from contrasting points of view. Gallant et al. apply their semi nonparametric approach to density estimation, based on a series expansion about the Gaussian density which in effect makes the density a polynomial in the past history of returns; the application deals with daily pound/dollar exchange rates. Hansen notes that the method needs very large data sets to achieve good precision, and prefers a model that is fully – yet in contrast parsimoniously – parameterized. His ARCD (autoregressive conditional density) model uses a novel "skewed Student's t" conditional distribution with an additional skewness parameter. This skewness parameter, along with the kurtosis (degrees of freedom) and other parameters of the model, are allowed to depend on the lagged error terms. Application of the model to the monthly excess holding yield on U.S. Treasury securities (allowing only for time-varying kurtosis) and to the U.S.$/ Swiss Franc exchange rate (allowing for both time-varying kurtosis and skew) produces evidence of time-varying higher moments in the data. It would be of interest to see if other distributions can be effectively applied to the question of the predictability of distributional shape, perhaps using measures of asymmetry and elongation that are known to be more resistant to the influence of outliers.

DENSITY FORECASTS FROM OPTIONS PRICES

A recent development is the derivation of density forecasts from the information about market participants' perceptions of the underlying asset price distribution contained in option market data. Soderlind and Svensson (1997) describe how methods of extracting information about market expectations from asset prices for monetary policy purposes have developed from the estimation of expected means of future interest rates and exchange rates from forward rates to estimation of their complete densities from traded options prices. The risk-management motivation noted above has also driven applications in finance, as deeper markets and new instruments have provided relevant data. The starting point is the derivation by Breeden and Litzenberger (1978) of a relationship between the risk-neutral density of the price of the underlying asset and the pricing function of European (exercised only at the maturity date) call options. For example, the classic Black–Scholes option pricing model implies a lognormal risk-neutral density function. Once markets were established and became sufficiently active, empirical applications followed. Thus Fackler and King's (1990) analysis of implied density forecasts of U.S. agricultural commodity prices followed the initiation of trading in commodity option futures in 1984, while Jackwerth and Rubinstein's (1996) data on options on the S & P 500 index start on April 2, 1986, the date the Chicago Board Options Exchange switched from American (exercised at any time up to the maturity date) to European options. Bahra (1996, 1997) analyzes the risk-neutral density functions of short-term sterling and Deutschemark interest rates implied by options traded on the London International Financial Futures and Options Exchange (LIFFE), which launched options trading in 1985.

Observed differences between market prices and the prices implied by the Black–Scholes model have led to variations in the model's assumptions and the use of distributions other than the lognormal for the underlying asset price. In particular, the estimated volatility of the underlying asset's return varies with the exercise or strike price, contrary to the Black–Scholes model – the so-called "volatility smile" – which calls for distributions with fatter tails than the lognormal and possibly a different degree of skewness. More general functional forms that have been employed include a mixture of lognormals (Bahra, 1996; Melick and Thomas, 1997; Soderlind and Svensson, 1997) and the generalized beta (Aparicio and Hodges, 1998); Ait-Sahalia and Lo (1998) develop a nonparametric approach to estimating the density. Jackwerth (1999) reviews the various methods, noting that the results tend to be rather similar unless only a very few option prices are available. It should also be noted, as several authors do, that the risk-neutral densities coincide with the "true" densities only in the absence of risk premia, and Soderlind (2000) considers how measures of risk premia might be used to adjust estimated risk-neutral densities.

Value-at-Risk and extreme quantiles

In the VaR context, as in macroeconomics, stochastic simulation methods are a means of generating nonnormal density forecasts. This approach develops a density forecast by simulating possible future paths of the various components of the portfolio of interest, based on models of those components with parameters estimated from past realizations of the corresponding variable. These various sample paths are combined into a sample path of the portfolio and a density forecast is then obtained from repeated simulations. Early implementations of this approach assumed price changes to be iid Gaussian, so that the portfolio return is also normally distributed. Later examples employ mixtures, jump diffusions, and models with conditional dynamics in the second moments, which would generate nonnormal distributions. Duffie and Pan (1997) and Dowd (1998) present comprehensive summaries of the issues and methods in generating VaRs.

The focus of attention in VaR analysis is often an extreme quantile of the distribution. However, the methods described above usually perform better near the center of the data than at the extreme tails, where data are scarce. This has motivated the introduction of methods based on extreme value theory to improve the estimation of the tail of the distribution (see McNeil and Frey, 2000, and references therein). The oldest problems connected with extreme values arise from floods. The relevant distribution theory has developed as a branch of the theory of order statistics, and some important results on the distribution of extremes apply irrespective of the original distribution from which the full random sample is taken. Many applications have used the Pareto distribution, named for Pareto's observation that in many populations the proportion whose income exceeded a given level y was well approximated by $ky^{-\alpha}$ for some real k and $\alpha > 0$, modified by the subsequent recognition that this approximation was only acceptable for large values of y. If the question of interest is the existence of moments, then attention focuses on the estimation of the tail index α (see Pagan, 1996, for example).

It can be argued that the development of extreme value methods beyond the limitations of the assumptions of iid sampling and Pareto-type tails is important for the theory's relevance to financial applications (see, for example, Diebold, Schuermann, and Stroughair, 1998). McNeil and Frey (2000) extend existing methods by considering the conditional distribution of asset returns and the generalized Pareto distribution function for the upper tail of the standardized residuals. This is

$$F(y) = \begin{cases} 1 - (1 + \xi y/\beta)^{-1/\xi} & \xi \neq 0, \\ 1 - \exp(-y/\beta) & \xi = 0, \end{cases}$$

where $\beta > 0$, with support $y \geq 0$ when $\xi \geq 0$ and $0 \leq y \leq -\beta/\xi$ when $\xi < 0$. The case $\xi > 0$ corresponds to heavy-tailed distributions whose tails decay like power functions, including the Pareto, Student's t, Cauchy, and Burr distributions, while $\xi = 0$ corresponds to the distributions such as the normal, lognormal, exponential, and gamma, whose tails decay exponentially. The case $\xi < 0$ includes distributions like the uniform and beta, with finite upper bound.

The quantile regression methods of Koenker and Bassett (1978) represent an alternative, robust approach to the estimation of conditional quantile functions. These methods estimate forecasting relationships at a particular quantile of the conditional distribution of y by choosing estimates of its parameters as the solution to the minimization problem

$$\min_\beta \left[\sum_{t \in \{t: y_t \geq x_t\beta\}} \theta | y_t - x_t\beta | + \sum_{t \in \{t: y_t < x_t\beta\}} (1-\theta) | y_t - x_t\beta | \right],$$

where θ is the desired quantile. The minimization problem is solved by a linear programming algorithm; the case $\theta = 0.5$ gives the usual least absolute error estimator. Koenker and Zhao (1996) extend these ideas to the ARCH setting, noting that quantiles are readily interpretable in semiparametric location-scale models and are easier to estimate robustly than moments. Thus, moving outside the Gaussian context, they focus on models for conditional scale rather than conditional variance. In an earlier application, Granger, White, and Kamstra (1989) use quantile regression to combine several quantile estimates, in the course of constructing forecast intervals which vary over time thanks to ARCH effects. In a general time-series forecasting context, Taylor and Bunn (1999) apply quantile regression techniques to obtain quantiles of multi-step-ahead forecast densities as functions of the lead time.

3.3. PRESENTATION OF DENSITY FORECASTS

No matter how density forecasts are generated, it is important to pay attention to their presentation. The way density forecasts are presented and communicated may hide some features of the forecasts, and emphasize others. Inappropriate presentation of forecasts will reduce the forecasts' usefulness for certain forecast users, and worse, may be misleading or misinterpreted, resulting in improper use of the forecasts. Presentation of forecasts tends, however, to be given limited coverage in discussions of forecasting, and we highlight some aspects of this important issue.

In forecasting, different users have different concerns (or loss functions, formally) and so may be interested in different aspects of the forecast. In the context of point forecasts, for instance, it is known that if the relevant loss function is symmetric then the optimal point predictor is the conditional mean, but that this is not true for general loss functions, as noted by Granger (1969) and Christoffersen and Diebold (1997). Producers of forecasts need to understand the concerns of the target audience (the particular set of forecast users) and present the appropriate point forecast, as a user with asymmetric loss who bases a decision on a conditional mean point forecast will make a sub-optimal decision. In principle, the use of density forecasts overcomes this problem: density forecasts are relevant to all forecast users since they are a complete description of the uncertainty associated with the forecast of a variable. In practice, however, the question of how to present density forecasts without losing vital information remains.

The notion of finding the most appropriate way of presenting density forecasts is very much in the spirit of exploratory data analysis where the concern is how best to summarize graphically the information contained in a sample of data (see Tukey, 1977). In forecasting, the same problem arises because different features of the forecast are of interest to different users, and the presentation of the forecast should highlight the appropriate features. For example, if a forecast user is interested in possible asymmetries in the future distribution of the forecast variable, a plot of the density estimate with an appropriate symmetric density superimposed may be more helpful than the presentation of the forecast by itself.

It is sometimes feasible to present the analytic form of the density forecasts, but these are available only if standard distributions are used, and in any event the features of the forecast may not be immediately obvious from algebraic expressions. A more common way of presenting density forecasts is by plotting the density estimate. This would usually be the case for forecasts obtained from semiparametric approaches to density forecasting discussed above, or if the forecast is obtained via simulation methods and the density estimate computed using kernel methods such as those described by Silverman (1986). Graphical presentations are useful – asymmetries in the forecasts are often easily picked out, and the normal distribution (the symmetric distribution taken by convention as having "neutral elongation") can be imposed to highlight the presence of asymmetries or excess kurtosis in the data to the user. It is often helpful to discretize the density, perhaps by presenting it as a histogram, graphically or in tabular form, indeed this is how density forecasts are elicited in the Survey of Professional Forecasters, as noted above. Table 3.1 gives an example. When a complete density is available, the conventional discretization is based on quantiles, so that forecast intervals are reported, again as a graph or a table, for a regular sequence of coverage probabilities, in contrast to the reporting of probabilities for a regular sequence of intervals, as in the histogram case. On the other hand, a particular interval may be a focus of attention. In a monetary policy regime of inflation targeting, for example, the objective of policy is sometimes expressed as a target range for inflation, whereupon it is of interest to report the forecast probability that the future outcome will fall in the target range.

In real-time forecasting, a sequence of forecasts for a number of future periods from a fixed origin (the "present") is often presented as a time-series plot. The central forecast may be shown as a continuation of the plot of actual data recently observed, and limits may be attached, either as standard error bands or quantiles, becoming wider as the forecast horizon increases. As Thompson and Miller (1986) note, "typically forecasts and limits are graphed as dark lines on a white background, which tends to make the point forecast the focal point of the display."

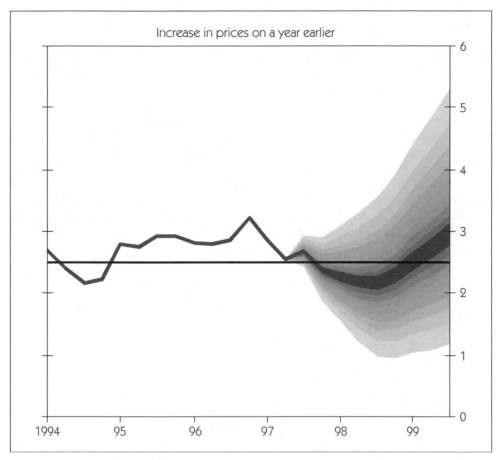

Figure 3.2 The August 1997 *Inflation Report* forecast

They argue for and illustrate the use of selective shading of quantiles, as "a deliberate attempt to draw attention away from point forecasts and toward the *uncertainty* in forecasting" (1986, p. 431, emphasis in original). In presenting its density forecasts of inflation the Bank of England takes this argument a stage further, by replacing a point forecast by a central 10 percent interval. The altern- ative presentation of a recent Bank forecast by Wallis (1999), based on conven- tional percentiles, is shown in figure 3.2. The density forecast is represented graphically as a set of forecast intervals covering 10 percent, 20 percent, . . . , 90 percent of the probability distribution, of lighter shades for the outer bands; equivalently the boundaries of the bands are the 5th, 10th, . . . , 95th percentiles (excluding the 50th). This is done for inflation forecasts one to eight quarters ahead, and since the dispersion increases and the intervals "fan out" as the forecast horizon increases, the result has become known as the "fan chart."

The Bank of England's preferred presentation of the fan chart is based on the shortest intervals for the assigned probabilities, which differ from the "central" intervals used in figure 3.2 whenever the density is asymmetric: in particular they converge on the mode, rather than the median, as the coverage is reduced. Moreover, the tail probabilities for the shortest intervals are not only unequal, they are not reported, leaving open the possibility of misinterpretation by a user who assumes them to be equal. Comparison of the two can be illuminated by reference to a loss function, which provides a rare example of the use of a loss function beyond the point forecast context, albeit to the interval forecast problem rather than the complete density forecast. To construct an optimal or minimum cost forecast interval (a, b) it is first assumed that there is a cost proportional to the length of the interval which is incurred irrespective of the outcome, and the distinction between the two cases arises from the assumption about the additional cost associated with a mistake, that is, the interval not containing the outcome. If this has an all-or-nothing form, being zero if the interval contains the outcome and a positive constant otherwise, then the optimal interval satisfies $f(a)$ $= f(b)$, and this "equal height" property is also a property of the interval with shortest length $b - a$ for given coverage. If, however, the cost of a mistake is proportional to the amount by which the outcome lies outside the interval, then the optimal interval is the central interval with equal tail probabilities (see Wallis, 1999, for derivations). We find the all-or-nothing loss function's indifference to the actual magnitude of error unrealistic. A preference for the alternative is implicit in the practice of the overwhelming majority of statisticians of summarizing densities by presenting selected percentiles.

While a density forecast can be seen as an acknowledgment of the uncertainty in a point forecast, it is itself uncertain, and this second level of uncertainty is of more than casual interest if the density forecast is the direct object of attention, as in several of the finance applications discussed above. How this might be described and reported is beginning to receive attention. For parametric approaches that treat the underlying distributional assumptions as correct the effect of parameter estimation error can be estimated via an appropriate covariance matrix and reported as a point-by-point confidence interval for the density forecast: Soderlind and Svensson (1997) plot an example for an options-based implied risk-neutral density. For approaches based on simulation methods, not only the point estimate of the density but also a sampling standard error or robust alternative measures of dispersion could likewise be reported.

Finally, we note that the problem of reporting results and communicating with "remote clients" has been a concern of Bayesian statisticians at least since Hildreth (1963) characterized users in this way. With the increasing use of simulation methods in economic forecasting, many forecasts will be available in the form of a sample from the predictive distribution, and these simulations could be used by various forecast users to generate estimates of specific features appropriate to their individual purposes. In this connection, the proposal by Geweke (1997) to exploit modern computation, communication and information storage and retrieval capabilities to facilitate Bayesian communication also merits attention by density forecasters.

3.4. EVALUATION AND CALIBRATION

Given a series of forecasts over a period of time, we consider the question of how to assess forecasting performance *ex post*. Evaluation of the quality of the forecasts may be of interest for its own sake, or may be explicitly directed toward improvement of future performance. For point forecasts, there is a large literature on the *ex post* evaluation of *ex ante* forecasts, and a range of techniques has been developed, recently surveyed by Wallis (1995) and Diebold and Lopez (1996). The evaluation of interval forecasts has a much newer literature (Christoffersen, 1998; Taylor, 1999), as does the evaluation of density forecasts, which is our present concern.

One strand of the literature on point forecasts comprises descriptive accounts of forecasts and forecast errors in specific episodes of particular interest, often business cycle turning points. For example, Wallis (1989) reviews several accounts of macroeconomic forecast performance during the recessions of the 1970s. It is striking that many studies of the performance of options-based densities adopt the same approach, describing the behavior of the implied probability distributions before and after such events as the U.S. stock market crash of October 1987 (Jackwerth and Rubinstein, 1996), the Persian Gulf crisis of 1990–91 (Melick and Thomas, 1997), the crisis in the European exchange rate mechanism around 16 September 1992 – "black Wednesday" – (Malz, 1996) together with the following month's announcement of a new monetary policy framework in the United Kingdom (Soderlind, 2000) and, at a more mundane level, announcements of economic news and shifts in official interest rates (Bahra, 1996). Agreement with other sources of information validates the estimated distributions – they "are consistent with the market commentary at the time" (Melick and Thomas) or are "validated by recent market developments" (Bahra) – and they can also supplement accounts of the events as they unfolded – "the market clearly believed that U.K. monetary policy was in big trouble"; later "this took the market by some surprise" (Soderlind). Interesting, indeed entertaining, as these accounts are, they provide little systematic information on such questions as the comparative performance of different models or methods, and one suspects that here, as in other areas of forecasting, they will gradually be replaced by more formal analyses.

It is often argued that forecasts should be evaluated in an explicit decision context; that is, in terms of the economic consequences that would have resulted from using the forecasts to solve a sequence of decision problems. The incorporation of a specific loss function into the evaluation process would focus attention on the features of interest to the forecast user, perhaps also showing the optimality of a particular forecast. In macroeconomic forecasting this does not happen, given the difficulty of specifying a realistic loss function and the absence of a well-defined user. In finance there is usually a more obvious profit-and-loss criterion, and there is a long tradition of forecast evaluation in the context of investment performance. This extends to volatility models (West, Edison, and Cho, 1993, for example) but not yet to density forecasts. Here there are relatively few results based on explicit loss functions, as noted above. The basic result that a "correct" forecast is optimal regardless of the form of the loss function is extended from point forecasts to event probability forecasts by Granger and Pesaran (1996) and to density forecasts by Diebold, Gunther, and Tay (1998). The latter authors also show that there is no ranking of sub-optimal density forecasts that holds for all loss functions. The problem of the choice of forecast would require the use of loss functions defined over the distance between forecast and actual densities. Instead, the general objective of density forecasters is to get close to the correct density in some sense, and practical evaluations are based on the same idea.

Statistical evaluations of real-time density forecasts have recently begun to appear, although the key device, the probability integral transform, has a long history. The literature usually cites Rosenblatt (1952) for the basic result, and the approach features in several expositions from different points of view, such as Dawid (1984) and Cooke (1991). For a sample of n one-step-ahead forecasts and the corresponding outcomes, the probability integral transform of the realized variables with respect to the forecast densities is

$$z_t = \int_{-\infty}^{y_t} p_t(u)du$$

$$= P_t(y_t), \quad t = 1, \ldots, n,$$

where $P_t(\cdot)$ is the forecast distribution function. If $P_t(\cdot)$ is "correct," then the z_t are independent uniform U[0, 1] variates. The independence property is obvious in the case of iid forecasts, and also extends to the case of time dependent density forecasts, as when the forecasts comprise a sequence of conditional densities, provided that the forecasts are based on an information set that contains the past history of the forecast variable (Diebold, Gunther, and Tay, 1998). The question then is whether the z_t sequence "looks like" a random sample from U[0, 1] (Dawid, 1984, quotation marks in original); that is, whether the forecasts are "well calibrated." Deviations from uniform iid will indicate that the forecasts have failed to capture some aspect of the underlying data generating process. Serial correlation in the z_t sequence (in squares, third powers, etc.) would indicate poorly modeled dynamics, whereas nonuniformity may indicate improper distributional assumptions, or poorly captured dynamics, or both. Diebold, Hahn, and Tay (1999) show that if the true conditional density belongs to a location-scale family, and the forecaster issues location-scale density forecasts with correctly specified location and scale, the z_t sequence will continue to bear the iid property but will no longer be uniform if the wrong location-scale density is used. Extensions to multi-step-ahead forecasts are awaited.

The uniformity of the probability integral transforms is usually evaluated by plotting the empirical distribution function and comparing with a 45° line, whereas some authors find an estimate of the density easier to check visually for departures from uniformity. Formal tests of goodness of fit can be employed, such as that based on Kolmogorov's D_n-statistic, the maximum absolute difference between the empirical distribution function and the null hypothesis uniform distribution function. The distribution theory for D_n rests on an assumption of random sampling, however, whereas the hypothesis of interest is the joint hypothesis of iid uniformity, and little is known about the impact on critical values of D_n of departures from independence. Diebold, Gunther, and Tay (1998) also consider the conditional dynamics of the density forecasts by examining the correlograms of the levels and powers of the probability integral transforms, and present an application to density forecasts of daily S & P 500 returns. Diebold, Tay, and Wallis (1999) add resampling procedures to the toolkit in the course of an evaluation of the Survey of Professional Forecasters' density forecasts of inflation. These authors supplement formal tests with a graphical approach, in an exploratory spirit, so that the evaluation process might be informative about the direction in which a forecasting model could be improved. Extensions to the multivariate case are considered by Diebold, Hahn, and Tay (1999) and Clements and Smith (2000). Both approaches are based on a decomposition of multivariate forecasts into univariate conditionals. The first paper evaluates a bivariate forecasting model of high-frequency exchange rates, and the latter paper uses density forecast performance to compare linear models with nonlinear forecasting models of output growth and unemployment.

Clements and Smith use forecast densities to discriminate between competing models, in place of standard measures such as mean square forecast errors. To see how forecast densities can discriminate between competing models, consider the simple example of comparing two zero-mean volatility models differing only in distributional assumptions. The conditional mean forecasts generated by both models are identical (zero), as are their mean square forecast errors. The forecast densities, on the other hand, would be different in general, and the probability integral transform would highlight these differences. Clements and Smith find that while standard means of comparing models suggest that nonlinear models offer no improvement over linear models, evaluation techniques that consider the entire forecast density are able to discriminate between the two: in their example the nonlinear models they consider (self-exciting threshold autoregressive models) outperform the linear models, being better able to predict higher-order moments.

If a given model or systematic forecasting method is found to produce poorly calibrated forecasts over an early time period, it may be possible to use the results of this initial evaluation to improve subsequent forecasts. Dawid (1984) speaks of "tuning" the system to provide better calibrated forecasts; other authors speak of "de-biasing" or "recalibrating" the later forecasts. Given an estimate $\hat{Q}(z)$ of an empirical distribution function whose graph does not look like a 45° line, the recalibrated forecast distribution function is

$$P^*(y) = \hat{Q}[P(y)].$$

Specifying $\hat{Q}(\cdot)$ is not straightforward. Kling and Bessler (1989) estimate it as a piecewise linear function in the course of a recalibration of their VAR-based density forecasts of interest rates, money, prices, and output. Fackler and King (1990) fit a beta distribution to the empirical distribution of the z's to recalibrate option-based density forecasts of prices in agricultural commodity markets, initially based on a lognormal assumption. The beta distribution contains the uniform distribution as a special case, and so admits the possibility of a likelihood ratio test. Diebold, Hahn, and Tay (1999) again provide a multivariate extension and recalibrate a series of bivariate Gaussian density forecasts of high-frequency exchange rate returns based on an exponential smoothing approach to estimation of the conditional variances and covariances of the returns. These examples all illustrate a further way of generalizing distributional assumptions away from normality.

3.5.   Conclusions

The interest in and use of density forecasts has increased in recent years. As in other areas of quantitative economics, advances in statistical methodology, the greater availability of relevant data, and increases in computing power have all played a part. Public discussion of macroeconomic point forecasts too often treats them as exact, and to acknowledge explicitly that they are not, perhaps by publishing a density forecast, can only improve the policy debate. In finance density forecasts are used more directly for specific assessments of risk, where mistakes have obvious commercial consequences. In our discussion of the construction, presentation and evaluation of density forecasts the need to keep in mind the loss function of the forecast user is always present in principle, but in practice this rarely features explicitly in the literature. Perhaps this is one direction in which to look for future developments. The commercial consequences of risk assessments can be expressed as a loss function, whose formulation might be extended to illuminate the specification and evaluation of density forecasts. Even when this is done, however, it will be important to have methods of communication that can accommodate users with a variety of loss functions.

Other future developments in density forecasting might be identified with reference to the literature on point forecasts. Both forecasts are usually model-based, and model improvements are often motivated by the need to improve forecasts; a particular issue identified above relates to the predictability of higher moments. The evaluation of density forecasts is at a comparatively rudimentary stage, and issues that merit attention are the optimal revision of fixed-event forecasts, the comparative evaluation of forecasts, and evaluation of multi-step-ahead density forecasts. (Clements and Smith (2000) consider one- and two-step-ahead forecasts.) Combinations of forecasts sometimes form part of comparative evaluations and sometimes are of interest for their own sake, and the literature on combining point forecasts that springs from Bates and Granger (1969) has reached interval forecasts but not yet density forecasts. Finally we note that, while a density forecast provides a representation of the uncertainty in a point forecast, its own uncertainty should also be acknowledged and quantified. How this second level of uncertainty might in turn be described and the description subsequently evaluated has scarcely begun to be considered. A future survey of this area has much to look forward to.

Acknowledgments

This chapter first appeared as an article with the same title in *Journal of Forecasting*, 19, (2000), 235–54. The helpful comments and suggestions of Frank Diebold, Stewart Hodges, and two anonymous referees are gratefully acknowledged. Subsequent editorial changes have been made following suggestions from the editors of this volume. Responsibility for errors remains with the authors.

References

Ait-Sahalia, Y. and A. Lo (1998). Nonparametric estimation of state-price densities implicit in financial asset prices. *Journal of Finance*, 53, 499–547.

Aitchison, J. and I.R. Dunsmore (1975). *Statistical Prediction Analysis*. Cambridge: Cambridge University Press.

Alles, L.A. and J.L. Kling (1994). Regularities in the variation of skewness in asset returns. *Journal of Financial Research*, 17, 427–38.

Anscombe, F.J. (1967). Topics in the investigation of linear relations fitted by the method of least squares (with discussion). *Journal of the Royal Statistical Society* B, 29, 1–52.

Aparicio, S.D. and S.D. Hodges (1998). Implied risk-neutral distribution: a comparison of estimation methods. Preprint 98/95, Financial Options Research Centre, University of Warwick.

Bahra, B. (1996). Probability distributions of future asset prices implied by option prices. *Bank of England Quarterly Bulletin*, 36, 299–311.

Bahra, B. (1997). Implied risk-neutral probability density functions from option prices: theory and application. Working Paper No. 66, London: Bank of England.

Baillie, R.T. and T. Bollerslev (1992). Prediction in dynamic models with time dependent conditional variances. *Journal of Econometrics*, 52, 91–114.

Bates, J.M. and C.W.J. Granger (1969). The combination of forecasts. *Operations Research Quarterly*, 20, 451–68.

Blake, A.P. (1996). Forecast error bounds by stochastic simulation. *National Institute Economic Review*, 156, 72–9.

Bollerslev, T. (1987). A conditionally heteroskedastic time series model for speculative prices and rates of return. *Review of Economics and Statistics*, 69, 542–6.

Bollerslev, T., R.F. Engle and D. Nelson (1994). ARCH models. In R.F. Engle and D. McFadden (eds.), *Handbook of Econometrics 4*. Amsterdam: Elsevier.

Breeden, D.T. and R.H. Litzenberger (1978). Prices of state-contingent claims implicit in options prices. *Journal of Business*, 51, 621–51.

Britton, E., P.G. Fisher, and J.D. Whitley (1998). The *Inflation Report* projections: understanding the fan chart. *Bank of England Quarterly Bulletin*, 38, 30–7.

Christoffersen, P.F. (1998). Evaluating interval forecasts. *International Economic Review*, 39, 841–62.

Christoffersen, P.F. and F.X. Diebold (1997). Optimal prediction under asymmetric loss. *Econometric Theory*, 13, 808–17.

Clements, M.P. and J. Smith (2000). Evaluating the forecast densities of linear and nonlinear models: applications to output growth and unemployment. *Journal of Forecasting*, 19, 255–76.

Cooke, R.M. (1991). *Experts in Uncertainty: Opinion and Subjective Probability in Science*. Oxford: Oxford University Press.

Cotner, J.S. (1991). Index option pricing: do investors pay for skewness. *Journal of Futures Markets*, 11, 1–8.

Croushore, D. (1993). Introducing: The Survey of Professional Forecasters. *Business Review,* Federal Reserve Bank of Philadelphia, November/December 1993, 3–15.

Dawid, A.P. (1984). Statistical theory, the prequential approach. *Journal of the Royal Statistical Society* A, 147, 278–90.

Diebold, F.X. and J.A. Lopez (1996). Forecast evaluation and combination. In G.S. Maddala and C.R. Rao (eds.), *Handbook of Statistics 14: Statistical Methods in Finance.* Amsterdam: North-Holland.

Diebold, F.X., T.A. Gunther and A.S. Tay (1998). Evaluating density forecasts with applications to financial risk management. *International Economic Review,* 39, 863–83.

Diebold, F.X., J. Hahn, and A.S. Tay (1999). Multivariate density forecast evaluation and calibration in financial risk management: high-frequency returns on foreign exchange. *Review of Economics and Statistics,* 81, 661–73.

Diebold, F.X., T. Schuermann, and J.D. Stroughair (1998). Pitfalls and opportunities in the use of extreme value theory in risk management. In A.N. Refenes, A.N. Burgess, and J.D. Moody (eds.), *Advances in Computational Finance.* Amsterdam: Kluwer.

Diebold, F.X., A.S. Tay, and K.F. Wallis (1999). Evaluating density forecasts of inflation: the Survey of Professional Forecasters. In R.F. Engle and H. White (eds.), *Cointegration, Causality, and Forecasting: A Festschrift in Honour of Clive W.J. Granger.* Oxford: Oxford University Press.

Dowd, K. (1998). *Beyond Value at Risk: The New Science of Risk Management.* Chichester: John Wiley.

Duffie, D. and J. Pan (1997). An overview of Value at Risk. *Journal of Derivatives,* 4(3), 7–49.

Engle, R.F. (1982). Autoregressive conditional heteroscedasticity with estimates of the variance of United Kingdom inflation. *Econometrica,* 50, 987–1008.

Engle, R.F. and G. González-Rivera (1991). Semiparametric ARCH models. *Journal of Business and Economic Statistics,* 9: 345–59.

Fackler, P.L. and R.P. King (1990). Calibration of options-based probability assessments in agricultural commodity markets. *American Journal of Agricultural Economics,* 72, 73–83.

Fama, E.F. (1965). The behavior of stock market prices. *Journal of Business,* 38, 34–105.

Gallant, R., D.A. Hsieh, and G. Tauchen (1991). On fitting a recalcitrant series: the pound/dollar exchange rate 1974–83. In W.A. Barnett, J. Powell, and G. Tauchen (eds.), *Nonparametric and Semiparametric Methods in Econometrics and Statistics: Proceedings of the Fifth International Symposium in Economic Theory and Econometrics.* Cambridge: Cambridge University Press.

Geweke, J. (1997). Posterior simulators in econometrics. In D.M. Kreps and K.F. Wallis (eds.), *Advances in Economics and Econometrics: Theory and Applications Vol. III.* Cambridge: Cambridge University Press.

Granger, C.W.J. (1969). Prediction with a generalized cost of error function. *Operational Research Quarterly,* 20, 199–207.

Granger, C.W.J. and M.H. Pesaran (1996). A decision theoretic approach to forecast evaluation. Discussion Paper 96-23, Department of Economics, University of California, San Diego.

Granger, C.W.J., H. White, and M. Kamstra (1989). Interval forecasting: an analysis based on ARCH-quantile estimators. *Journal of Econometrics,* 40, 87–96.

Hansen, B.E. (1994). Autoregressive conditional density estimation. *International Economic Review,* 35, 705–30.

Hildreth, C. (1963). Bayesian statisticians and remote clients. *Econometrica,* 31, 422–38.

Jackwerth, J.C. (1999). Option implied risk-neutral distributions and implied binomial trees: a literature review. *Journal of Derivatives,* 7, 66–82.

Jackwerth, J.C. and M. Rubinstein (1996). Recovering probability distributions from option prices. *Journal of Finance*, 51, 1611–31.

John, S. (1982). The three-parameter two-piece normal family of distributions and its fitting. *Communications in Statistics – Theory and Methods*, 11, 879–85.

Johnson, N., S. Kotz and N. Balakrishnan (1994). *Continuous Univariate Distributions*, 2nd edn, vol. 1. New York: Wiley.

Kimber, A.C. (1985). Methods for the two-piece normal distribution. *Communications in Statistics – Theory and Methods*, 14, 235–45.

Kling, J.L. and D.A. Bessler (1989). Calibration-based predictive distributions: an application of prequential analysis to interest rates, money, prices and output. *Journal of Business*, 62, 477–99.

Koenker, R. and G. Bassett (1978). Regression quantiles. *Econometrica*, 46, 33–50.

Koenker, R. and Q. Zhao (1996). Conditional quantile estimation and inference for ARCH models. *Econometric Theory*, 12, 793–813.

Lee, T.K.Y. and Y.K. Tse (1991). Term structure of interest rates in the Singapore Asian dollar market. *Journal of Applied Econometrics*, 6, 143–52.

Malz, A.M. (1996). Using option prices to estimate realignment probabilities in the European monetary system: the case of sterling-mark. *Journal of International Money and Finance*, 15: 717–48

McNeil, A.J. and R. Frey (2000). Estimation of tail-related risk measures for heteroscedastic financial time series: an extreme value approach. *Journal of Empirical Finance*, 7, 271–300.

Melick, W.R. and C.P. Thomas (1997). Recovering an asset's implied PDF from option prices: an application to crude oil during the Gulf crisis. *Journal of Financial and Quantitative Analysis*, 32, 91–115.

Nelson, D.B. (1991). Conditional heteroskedasticity in asset returns. a new approach. *Econometrica*, 59, 347–70.

Pagan, A.R. (1996). The econometrics of financial markets. *Journal of Empirical Finance*, 3, 15–102.

Poulizac, D., M.R. Weale, and G. Young (1996). The performance of National Institute economic forecasts. *National Institute Economic Review*, 156, 55–62.

Rosenblatt, M. (1952). Remarks on a multivariate transformation. *Annals of Mathematical Statistics*, 23, 470–72.

Simkowitz, M.A. and W.L. Beedles (1978). Diversification in a three-moment world. *Journal of Finance*, 33, 288–92.

Singleton, J.F. and J. Wingender (1986). Skewness persistence in common stock returns. *Journal of Financial and Quantitative Analysis*, 21, 335–41.

Silverman, B.W. (1986). *Density Estimation for Statistics and Data Analysis*. New York: Chapman and Hall.

Soderlind, P. (2000). Market expectations in the U.K. before and after the ERM crisis. *Economica*, 67, 1–18.

Soderlind P. and L.E.O. Svensson (1997). New techniques to extract market expectations from financial instruments. *Journal of Monetary Economics*, 40, 383–429.

Taylor, J.W. (1999). Evaluating volatility and interval forecasts. *Journal of Forecasting*, 18, 111–28.

Taylor, J.W. and D.W. Bunn (1999). A quantile regression approach to generating prediction intervals. *Management Science*, 45, 225–37.

Thompson, P.A. and R.B. Miller (1986). Sampling the future: a Bayesian approach to forecasting from univariate time series models. *Journal of Business and Economic Statistics*, 4, 427–36.

Tukey, J.W. (1977). *Exploratory Data Analysis*. Reading, Mass: Addison-Wesley.

Wallis, K.F. (1989). Macroeconomic forecasting: a survey. *Economic Journal*, 99, 28–61.

Wallis, K.F. (1995). Large-scale macroeconometric modeling. In M.H. Pesaran and M.R. Wickens (eds.), *Handbook of Applied Econometrics*. Oxford: Blackwell.

Wallis, K.F. (1999). Asymmetric density forecasts of inflation and the Bank of England's fan chart. *National Institute Economic Review*, 167, 106–12.

West, K.D., H.J. Edison, and D. Cho (1993). A utility-based comparison of some models of exchange rate volatility. *Journal of International Economics*, 35, 23–45.

Zarnowitz, V. (1969). The new ASA-NBER survey of forecasts by economic statisticians. *American Statistician*, 23, 12–16.

CHAPTER FOUR

Statistical Approaches to Modeling and Forecasting Time Series

Diego J. Pedregal and Peter C. Young

4.1. INTRODUCTION

There are numerous statistical approaches to forecasting, from simple, regression-based methods to optimal statistical procedures formulated in stochastic state-space terms. Since it would be impossible to review all these methods here, the present chapter tries to distill, from this large mixture of models and methods, those that the authors feel have most significance in theoretical and practical terms within the specific context of economic forecasting.

Most of the statistical forecasting methods referred to in the chapter are model-based, in the sense that the forecasting operation is carried out subsequent to the statistical identification and estimation of a suitable (usually stochastic) mathematical model based on the available time-series data. Consequently, in the subsequent subsections, the differentiation between forecasting methods is based largely on the type of model used to characterize the data. The forecasting procedures themselves are simply devices for utilizing the model to project its output forward into the future in stochastic terms, normally through the evolution of the mean and standard error bands associated with forecast distributions.

4.1.1. "Classical" regression methods

One of the best known statistical approaches to forecasting derives from classical regression analysis. This approach has been used by most scientific disciplines and has served as the basis for a wide range of subsequent developments in forecasting. It has been applied to time-series and cross-sectional data; and it is useful not only in forecasting applications but also in the "structural analysis" of economic time series.

The standard regression model consists of a linear specification that relates one endogenous variable (also called the dependent variable, output, or regressand) to a number of unmodeled variables (independent variables, inputs, or regressors). The unknowns in this model are the parameters associated with the regressors and these are estimated by a variety of methods, depending on the particular setting of the model: for example, *Least Squares* (LS), *Generalized Least Squares* (GLS), *Instrumental Variable* (IV) methods, or *Maximum Likelihood* (ML) optimization.

When regression analysis was first applied in a time-series context, a number of extensions were necessary as a consequence of particular features in the data. The basic regression model, coupled with these extensions, constitutes the material for standard courses in econometrics all over the world and is well documented in a number of standard textbooks written in a wide range of languages (the number of references here would be immense but, for an econometric treatment, see for example Judge et al., 1985; Johnston, 1963, 1984; Intriligator et al., 1996; Greene, 1998).

There are a number of problems associated with the regression-based approach to forecasting, many of them shared with more sophisticated methods. Multicollinearity (correlation amongst regressors) does not affect the forecasting power of the model, in principle, but can affect its identifiability, the precision of estimators and the subsequent quality of the inference obtained from the model. Other problems arise when the exogenous or input variables are stochastic, so that the statistical inference has to rely on asymptotic results, in contrast to the situation when these variables are deterministic. Another common dilemma in economic applications is the *errors-in-variables* problem, where the regressors are measured in the presence of noise. This results in LS estimates of the regression parameters that are asymptotically biased and inconsistent to a degree dependent on the noise level. Paradoxically, the forecasts obtained from such models are not necessarily biased but they are normally inefficient (Johnston, 1963). The Instrumental Variable (IV) method can provide consistent (and in some cases optimal) estimates of the parameters in this *errors-in-variables* situation, provided that appropriate instruments can be found. A variety of IV approaches have been suggested in both the econometric (for example, any of the texts referred to above) and systems (for example, Young, 1984, and the references therein) literatures, although most of these are associated with the more sophisticated time-series models discussed later.

Other extensions to the basic regression model are necessary to overcome difficulties that arise from particular features of the data, such as heteroskedasticity and autocorrelation; problems that may be solved by extending the model and estimating it by GLS, ML, or optimal IV methods. Even so, the solution in practical situations may not be that easy because these problems have to be detected and the specific forms of heteroskedasticity or autocorrelation identified in some way before the final model can be estimated satisfactorily. Also, a number of other extensions are necessary in order to make the models both more realistic and more comprehensive. In the analysis of time series, for example, it is usual to find dynamic specifications and nonlinearity in the model. As a result, the regression model is automatically converted into one that has stochastic regressors, lagged dependent variables, and/or nonlinear relationships.

Finally, econometricians quickly realized the limitations of single-equation regression models in economic data analysis and forecasting, and devised methods for extending the models into a multivariable or vector form: for example, *Seemingly Unrelated REgressions* (SURE; Zellner, 1962) and *Simultaneous Equations Models* (SEM; for example, see any of the econometrics texts referred above). The latter have been popular and used extensively by statistical agencies all over the world in their efforts at constructing macroeconometric models for forecasting purposes. It is worth noting that, despite the theoretical worries about estimating these multi-equation models separately, equation by equation, this has remained a common strategy, mainly due to the nonlinear complexities of the models, dynamical specifications, nonspherical properties of the residuals, and the shortage of data.

4.1.2. "Modern" time-series methods

In contrast to "classical" regression analysis, the more recent approaches to forecasting based on modern methods of time-series analysis allow inherently for the specification of dynamic relationships and automatically handle the statistical consequences of this. They began with a consideration of simple, univariate series, stimulated by the discovery that such models were not only simpler to estimate, but they could often produce forecasts that compared well with, and often outperformed, those generated by the large and expensive macroeconometric models. And univariate models do not, of course, require the concurrent modeling and forecasting of additional endogenous or exogenous variables, since the forecast relies entirely on the past history of the time series itself.

Some of the earliest and simplest univariate options are those based on forms of *Exponential Smoothing* (ES) methods that were introduced by Holt (1957) and Winters (1960) but, because of their practical utility and success, are still used today (see, for example, Brown, 1963; Abraham and Ledolter, 1983). Different versions of these ES forecasting procedures are available, but the general idea is the synthesis of forecasting functions on the basis of discounted past observations. These apparently *ad hoc* methods can, however, be justified and unified by reference to both the univariate *AutoRegressive Integrated Moving Average* (ARIMA) model and alternative *Unobserved Component* (UC) models.

Although there were a number of important contributions dealing with the ARIMA class of models prior to 1970, that year marked the beginning of the popularization of this model and its associated forecasting methodology, with the publication of Box and Jenkins' most influential book *Time-Series Analysis, Forecasting and Control* (1970, 1976; see also Box et al., 1994). Indeed, the influence of this monograph has been so great that it is considered by some authors to mark the beginning of modern econometric time-series developments. As in the case of regression analysis, this methodology has served as the basis of innumerable developments and extensions since 1970, as the number of published books on the subject clearly demonstrate (see, for example, Harvey, 1981; Abraham and Ledolter, 1983; Chatfield, 1984; Granger and Newbold, 1986; Diggle, 1990; Mills, 1990; Wei, 1990; Hamilton, 1994; Diebold, 1998; etc.).

There have been a number of extensions of the simple ARIMA models within the univariate context. These include nonlinear models, such as *Conditional Heteroskedasticity* models (ARCH, GARCH, etc.) and *Threshold AR* models (TAR, STAR, SETAR, etc.). Excellent reviews of these and other nonlinear models are given in Tong (1990) and Granger and Teräsvirta (1993) (see also the chapters by Mills, Ljungberg and Teräsvirta, and Tsay in this volume). Also within the univariate context are *AR Fractional Integrated MA* (ARFIMA) models (for example Baillie and King, 1996), in which the integration order is not necessarily an integer number, as assumed in ARIMA models. This latter model has become a popular type of "long-memory" model.

The most obvious extension of univariate time-series models is the addition of explanatory input (exogenous) variables or "leading indicators." These input-output models are sometimes termed "Systems" or "Control" models because they allow for the inclusion of control input effects. They include the simple but somewhat limited *AR model with eXogenous inputs* (ARX), the *AutoRegressive Moving Average model with eXogenous variables* (ARMAX), and the *Transfer Function* (TF) model with ARMA noise. They have all proven useful in practice over the past 30 years and derive from research in both the time-series and systems literatures (for example, Box and Jenkins, 1970, 1976; Box et al., 1994; Ljung and Söderstrom, 1983; Young, 1984). These types of models have also formed the basis for some successful methods of intervention analysis and outlier detection. They are also closely related, and in some cases identical to, the *Distributed Lag* (DL) models of econometrics. The DL models differ mainly in terms of their historical development and disciplinary setting. They were developed mainly by econometricians within a regression context, rather than by time-series and systems analysts within a more overtly stochastic, dynamic context.

It is interesting to note that all of the linear input–output models subsume linear regression models as a particular static case: that is, the equilibrium solutions of TF models provide the static characteristics of the models and relate the outputs to the inputs by a regression-like relationship. However, it is important not to consider them in simple regression terms, since they have an inherently different stochastic nature which needs to be taken into consideration when devising statistical identification and estimation strategies.

The input–output models discussed so far are all linear in stochastic, dynamic terms. Given the importance of nonlinear relationships in many practical situations, it is not surprising that more recent research has extended these models to include nonstationary and nonlinear mechanisms. Of note in this context is the *Time Variable Parameter* (TVP) or *Dynamic Linear Model* (DLM) (for example, West and Harrison, 1989; Ljung and Söderstrom, 1983; Young, 1984, 1999a) with the time variable parameters estimated recursively; the *Nonlinear AutoRegressive Moving Average eXogenous variables* (NARMAX) model (for example, Chen and Billings, 1989); and, most recently, the *State Dependent Parameter* (SDP) nonlinear model (Young, 1993, 1999b). In effect, the SDP model is a nonparametric model, since the parameters are related to the state variables of the model, and so it can be compared with other nonparametric approaches such as the *Generalized Additive Model* (GAM) of Hastie and Tibshirani (1990), although the GAM is normally only used for static modeling.

Other nonlinear models have appeared in the systems and signal-processing literature, including the popular (but largely nonstatistical) *Neural Network* (NN) models (see, for example, the special issue of the *Journal of Forecasting* on the application of NN to electricity load demand forecasting, November 1996, Vol. 15, No. 6). Apparently, NN models have been successful in financial forecasting, due to the availability of the large data sets that are usually necessary for their estimation. It is important to realize, however, that NN models simply represent another class of nonlinear model, notable mainly for its generality and the rather misleading analogy with neural processes in the brain (which is completely unproven). However, this generality is obtained at a cost: in addition to their limitations in a statistical sense, NN models are often excessively over-parameterized and, probably in consequence, the promised forecasting performance is often rather better than that actually produced in practice.

Yet another way of considering nonlinear time-series modeling is the *Nonlinear Dynamic Systems* approach, which includes aspects of chaos theory. Here, until recently, the emphasis has been on the capacity of nonlinear deterministic dynamic systems to produce behavior that resembles some aspects of stochastic systems. Although chaotic models are interesting in principle, they have attracted little attention in economics compared with other types of analysis. This is probably due to the belief that the economic system is inherently stochastic rather than chaotic. As in the environmental sciences, there is also a continuing debate about the practical relevance of chaotic systems. While there is no doubt that the theory behind, and analysis of, chaotic time series is interesting, there are still very few measured time series obtained from natural or economic systems that appear to exhibit chaotic behavior. As a result, their practical relevance in economics and environmental science has still to be established.

One important extension of the univariate models is to multivariate or Vector AR and ARMA models (VAR; VARMA), as introduced by Quenouille (1957) and Tiao and Box (1981), and described in the book by Lütkepohl (1991; see also chapter 8 by Lütkepohl in this volume). Sims (1980) commended the use of VAR models in econometric modeling, in part as a criticism of the *a priori* constraints imposed by economic theory on more traditional economic models. Often, VAR is preferred instead of VARMA because any VARMA model can be expressed as an equivalent (although parametrically less efficient) VAR model and, in addition, the estimation methods are simpler in the latter case. In particular, estimation of the VAR model can be carried out separately equation-by-equation using linear LS methods, without any loss of efficiency. Versions of these models with exogenous input variables have also been developed (that is, VARMAX and VARX models).

4.1.3. The Unobserved Components (UC) model

Another time-series approach that has developed in parallel with the previous methodologies and, indeed, can subsume some of them straightforwardly, is the *Unobserved Components* (UC) model, also known in the econometrics literature as the *Structural Model* (SM), as discussed by Thomas Proietti in chapter 5 of this volume. These models are based on a decomposition of the time series into simple components (sometimes also called "stylized facts"). These components are normally recognizable visually both in a temporal plot of the series and in its spectral analysis. They normally include: a low-frequency stochastic trend; a (possibly damped) periodic cycle; a seasonal component defined at fundamental and associated harmonic frequencies; and an irregular component, normally considered as a zero mean, serially uncorrelated sequence of random variables (white noise).

The UC approach can be divided roughly into three groups. First, there are *ad hoc* methods that are not model-based, of which the most important is the X-11 model and its subsequent extensions, X11-ARIMA, X12, and X12 ARIMA (for example, Shiskin et al., 1967; Dagum, 1980, 1988; Findley et al., 1992, 1996). Second, there are those methods that are based directly on the UC model and take a variety of forms depending upon the nature of the stochastic models used to define the components (for example, Harrison and Stevens, 1976; Jakeman and Young, 1984; Young, 1984, 1994; Harvey, 1989; West and Harrison, 1989; Young et al., 1989; Ng and Young, 1990; Koopman et al., 1995; Pole et al., 1995; Young et al., 1999). Finally, there are *Reduced Form* models, in which the UC model components are inferred from other models, most notably the Box–Jenkins ARIMA type (for example, Burman, 1980; Hillmer et al., 1983; Maravall and Gómez, 1998).

The main differences among these groups relate to the way the models for the components are specified and the type of analysis each strategy allows:

- The *ad hoc* approaches do not use explicit models for the components, but exploit a number of centralized moving-average filters for extracting the components. The results of this analysis are not normally used for forecasting at all but they are de rigueur in government departments all over the world for performing off-line analysis and seasonal adjustment.
- In the *reduced form* models, the components are obtained as an identification process in which a number of arbitrary constraints have to be imposed on the model to achieve the existence and uniqueness of the component decomposition. Normally, these models are used only for signal extraction with the forecasting option based on the "mother" ARIMA model used in the analysis.
- In the main UC (or structural) models, the components are specified directly by the user based on a variety of component modeling options available in

the associated software and ensuring that the complete model is identifiable from the available time-series data. These models can be used for forecasting, backcasting, and signal extraction (including seasonal adjustment); and they can handle "messy" time series that are affected by missing data, outliers, sudden level shifts, etc.

In other words, the *structural form* UC models represent complete time-series analysis and forecasting tools; while in either the *reduced form* or *ad hoc* methods, the UC components are used simply as sub-models for signal extraction, normally without the option of forecasting. Reflecting their perceived importance in a forecasting and signal extraction context, many extensions of UC models have been developed. For instance, new models for trend and seasonal components have been introduced, some of which are discussed in later sections of this chapter, including a facility to allow for the modulation of one periodic component by another (Young and Pedregal, 1997a); the introduction of nonlinear and transfer function components (for example, Young, 1994); and the use of vector models including phenomena such as cointegration (Harvey and Koopman, 1997; West and Harrison, 1989).

4.1.4. Other methods

Two other important topics of research that are beyond the scope of this chapter are *Nonparametric* and *Bayesian* statistical methods. Nonparametric methods, mentioned briefly above, allow for more flexible formulations of the regression and time-series models; while the Bayesian methodology provides an alternative way of formulating models for time-series analysis and forecasting, in which the *a priori* perceptions of the researcher can be included in a formal manner. These *a priori* assumptions, normally in the form of prior probability distributions, are combined with the information extracted from the time-series data, to produce the *a posteriori* distribution, which then constitutes the basis for analysis and forecasting.

This Bayesian approach to stochastic modeling and forecasting has been used to develop alternative Bayesian-inspired methods for almost all the modeling strategies mentioned previously. Indeed, as we shall see, UC models normally exploit recursive state estimation algorithms (for example, the Kalman filter: Kalman, 1960) that are the very embodiment of Bayesian estimation. However, now that the desktop computer is almost a miniature super-computer, able to break the gigaflop barrier, the Bayesian approach can utilize Monte Carlo Simulation methods to handle non-Gaussian distributions. Perhaps the ultimate Bayesian approaches to modeling time series available at this time are those based on *Markov Chain Monte Carlo* methods (for example, Gamerman, 1997). However, these are demanding in computational terms; they are rather difficult to assimilate and require experienced analysts; and they have yet to be tested within a forecasting context.

For the moment, at least, it appears to us that recursively updated (adaptive), Gaussian UC models provide the most powerful and accessible approach to time-series modeling and forecasting (see Young, 2001a). In particular, the latest UC models that include state-dependent parameter components, and so can handle non-Gaussian phenomena, appear to be flexible and hold great promise.

4.1.5.   Special issues

There are three other important issues related to the above modeling procedures that should be mentioned: *exogeneity*, *causality*, and the treatment of *nonstationarity*.

Exogeneity is an important question when estimating models with input or exogenous variables, mainly because problems of inconsistency and loss of efficiency may occur if endogenous variables are treated as exogenous. However, different concepts of exogeneity are relevant, depending on the objectives of the study. For statistical inference, *weak exogeneity* is sufficient; while *strong exogeneity* is necessary for forecasting; and *superexogeneity* is the key concept for a correct analysis of simulation and control. This topic has been treated in Engle et al. (1983) and Ericsson (1992), among others. In addition, a number of exogeneity tests have been proposed in the literature (for example Wu, 1973; Hausman, 1978; Engle, 1984; Engle and Hendry, 1989).

Causality is an important topic in all science disciplines, but it is often rather difficult to demonstrate in many economic relationships, partly because economic data can be ambiguous and the underlying relationships can be obscured by considerable noise effects. Furthermore, in contrast to some other scientific disciplines, it is virtually impossible to conduct planned experiments that might help to remove these ambiguities. In consequence, inputs may not be *sufficiently exciting* to make the model parameters identifiable from the data; or they may not be *persistently exciting* and so cannot ensure consistency (see, for example, Young, 1984). Other studies of these problems can be found in Granger (1969), Sims (1972), and Geweke et al. (1983). Despite their importance, however, we believe they are considered insufficiently in the practical modeling and forecasting of economic time series.

Nonstationarity is also important, since many economic time series are nonstationary in the simplest sense; namely that the first two statistical moments (mean and variance) often change over the observation interval. The major approaches to this problem are: differencing and/or nonlinear transformations of the data prior to analysis; intervention analysis; modeling trends and changes in variance overtly by UC models; and cointegration analysis.

- Differencing is a method popularized by Box and Jenkins (1970, 1976) and widely used for removing nonstationarity in the mean, despite the fact that it often introduces undesirable side effects. These include the attenuation of information at, or in the vicinity of, zero frequency (which is important for long-term analysis); and the (sometimes major) decrease in the signal-to-noise ratio arising from the amplification of the high-frequency noise effects. Because of these distortions, explicit modeling of the nonstationary part of the series is better than removing it by differencing. Prior nonlinear processing, such as logarithmic or Box–Cox transformation, can help to remove nonstationarity in the variance of a time series. However, it is often advantageous to first identify the form of the nonlinearity (for example, by nonparametric methods) before utilizing standard transforms such as these.

- Rather than removing nonstationarity in the mean prior to estimation, UC modeling involves explicit (normally stochastic) modeling and estimation of the trend, together with other components that are important in the analysis of the time series. Modeling changes in variance can also be accommodated in UC models (see, for example, West and Harrison, 1989; Young and Pedregal, 1996; Young et al., 1999) although this is not very common. Also, cointegration constraints on trends can be introduced into UC models (see below; also Harvey and Koopman, 1997).

- The concept of cointegration was introduced by Granger (1981) and considered in depth through a number of papers (see, for example, Engle and Granger, 1987; Phillips, 1991). It has had wide influence in modern econometrics, as the number of books and papers published on the topic demonstrate. The basic idea behind cointegration is that a linear combination of two nonstationary I(1) variables can be stationary I(0), revealing that, although the two series both have trend behavior, they tend to drift together and can be analyzed with this in mind. The normal analysis of this kind is the use of an *Equilibrium Correction Model* (ECM)[1] for the series that takes explicit account of the long run relationships between the trends. This topic has received a great deal of attention and Vector Error or Equilibrium Correction Models (VECM) are now available for modeling and forecasting. In the opinion of the present authors, the main difficulty of this ECM analysis is that it relies on a number of rather low power statistical tests (Dickey and Fuller, 1979; Perron, 1990; Johansen, 1988; Osborn et al., 1988). Alternative modeling strategies are available for nonstationary data that do not use the standard cointegration assumptions and solutions but are similarly motivated: for instance, in Young and Pedregal (1999b), two related nonstationary variables (private capital investment and government spending) are converted to stationarity when divided by a third (GNP).

Of course, it has to be stressed that nonstationarity is not limited to temporal changes in the first two moments (mean and variance). In general, as we discuss later, *all* of the parameters in the system model may change over time, so that the system can be nonstationary in this much wider sense, with potential changes in the complete system dynamics and all of the statistical moments.

4.1.6. Unification of the methods

The difference between what we have called the *classical* and *modern* approaches to forecasting is much less than it was perceived to be some years ago. Indeed, the differences now are mostly due to the theoretical setting of the analyses, rather than the nature of the procedures utilized to carry them out. In the *classical* approaches, the theoretical basis of the model leads to the imposition of constraints on the specification of the model. In the *modern*, data-based methods, such constraints are mostly imposed by the nature of the data itself, as revealed by the analysis. In the end, however, analysis using both approaches should reproduce similar results. In other words, if the constraints imposed by theory are correct, both models may often be equivalent. The difficulty, of course, lies in ensuring that the theoretical speculation is, indeed, correct.

This unified point of view has been explicitly reflected in some methodologies that try to bring together the background theory and the empirical objective modeling approaches. This is the case, for instance, in the *Structural Econometric Modeling Time-Series Analysis* strategy (SEMTSA; Zellner and Palm, 1974; Wallis, 1977; Zellner, 1979) and the econometric methodology associated with the London School of Economics (LSE; for example, Sargan, 1964; Davidson et al., 1978; Hendry and Wallis, 1984; etc.). A somewhat similar idea, although exploiting rather different analytic and numerical procedures, is the Data-Based-Mechanistic (DBM) modeling approach (for example, Young, 1998, 1999a,b,c, 2001a,b and the references, therein) proposed largely within the context of the environmental sciences, but applied also to macroeconomic data (Young and Pedregal, 1997b; 1999b).

To exemplify the connection between *classical* and *modern* approaches to forecasting, let us consider the following example that shows that any regression model may be expressed as an alternative TF; and, conversely, that any TF may be expressed in regression terms. Consider the model

$$y_t = \mathbf{u}_t \beta + \frac{\vartheta(L)}{\phi(L)} a_t,$$

where y_t is an endogenous variable; $\mathbf{u}_t$ is a set of variables that may contain present and past values of the exogenous variables (denoted by u_{it}, $i = 1, 2, \ldots, m$) and/or endogenous variables; β is a set of *structural* or *deep* parameters; $\vartheta(L) = (1 + \vartheta_1 L + \vartheta_2 L^2 + \ldots + \vartheta_q L^q)$ and $\phi(L) = (1 + \phi_1 L + \phi_2 L^2 + \ldots + \phi_p L^p)$ are polynomials in the backward-shift or lag operator L (that is, $L^k y_t = y_{t-k}$); and a_t is a zero mean, serially uncorrelated (white noise) variable. With suitable manipulation and definition of variables, a time series that can be modeled in these terms can also characterized by the following multiple Transfer Function (TF) model:

$$y_t = \sum_{i=1}^{m} \frac{\omega_i(L)}{\delta_i(L)} u_{it} + \frac{\vartheta(L)}{\phi(L)} a_t,$$

where now $\omega_i(L)$ and $\delta_i(L)$ are a set of additional polynomials in the backward shift operator affecting each one of the inputs u_{it}. The only difference between these two models is that, in the first, the lag structure would normally be suggested by economic theory; while, in the second, such structure would be identified from the data using systems methods.

Naturally, this example could be extended to multivariable (vector) models, although then some complications arise because of the inherent complexity of multivariable dynamic relationships. One of the most general models from an econometric standpoint is the SEM mentioned previously; that is,

$$\mathbf{A}(L)\mathbf{y}_t + \mathbf{B}(L)\mathbf{u}_t = \frac{\boldsymbol{\vartheta}(L)}{\phi(L)}\mathbf{a}_t \quad E(\mathbf{a}_t\mathbf{a}_t') = \Sigma,$$

where now all the polynomials and matrices are defined in appropriate multivariable, vector terms. One counterpart in time-series modeling terms is the VARMAX model; that is,

$$\mathbf{A}^*(L)\mathbf{y}_t + \mathbf{B}^*(L)\mathbf{u}_t = \boldsymbol{\vartheta}^*(L)\mathbf{a}_t \quad E(\mathbf{a}_t\mathbf{a}_t') = \Sigma.$$

Again, the models differ mainly in the way they are specified: in the case of the SEM, by reference to theory and standard identification tools; and in the case of the VARMAX model by direct identification from the data. However, there is another important difference between these models: in the SEM, contemporaneous relations are introduced explicitly in the definition $\mathbf{A}(L)$, whereas this is not a feature of the VARMAX model. Indeed, in econometric terms, the VARMAX is considered as the reduced form of the SEM. Thus by manipulating the SEM model we obtain the reduced form,

$$\phi(L)\mathbf{A}(L)\mathbf{y}_t + \phi(L)\mathbf{B}(L)\mathbf{u}_t = \boldsymbol{\vartheta}(L)\mathbf{a}_t \quad E(\mathbf{a}_t\mathbf{a}_t') = \Sigma,$$

where $\phi(L)\mathbf{A}(L) = \mathbf{A}^*(L)$; $\phi(L)\mathbf{B}(L) = \mathbf{B}^*(L)$; and $\boldsymbol{\vartheta}(L) = \boldsymbol{\vartheta}^*(L)$ represents a large set of equations that links the *structural* and the *reduced form* parameters. As in the univariate situation, both of these models, if applied rigorously to the same data set, should yield equivalent results *provided that the constraints imposed by theory in the SEM model are correct.* However, while the VARMAX model would be immediately useful in forecasting terms, the SEM model would have difficulty in this regard if it included the specification of contemporaneous relations and one would use the restricted reduced form implied by the SEM.

Probably the most elegant way of further unifying the various models discussed above is to consider them within the context of the stochastic state-space formulation (see, for example, Young, 1984; Aoki, 1990; Harvey, 1989 and many others), particularly if the objective of the stochastic modeling is forecasting and signal extraction. This modeling concept, imported into economics mainly from the earlier developments in modern control theory, provides a powerful framework in which any linear univariate or multivariate dynamic system can be accommodated. In particular, all the linear systems discussed above, as well as many of the nonlinear ones, can be written in SS form. Moreover, this formulation of the stochastic modeling and forecasting problem suggests many interesting and exciting new possibilities when applied to nonstationary and nonlinear systems. Some of these are discussed in the subsequent sections of this chapter, largely within the specific context of UC models, where the SS concepts are most obviously applicable.

4.2.   State-Space Models

The discrete-time, stochastic *State Equations* reflect all the dynamic behavior of the system by relating the current value of the states to their past values, as well as to the deterministic and stochastic inputs; while the *Observation Equations* define how the state variables are related to the observed data. There are a number of different formulations of these vector-matrix equations, but the one favored here is as follows:

$$\text{State equations:} \qquad \mathbf{x}_t = \mathbf{A}_t\mathbf{x}_{t-1} + \mathbf{B}_t\mathbf{u}_{t-1} + \mathbf{G}_t\boldsymbol{\eta}_{t-1} \quad (i)$$

$$\text{Observation equations:} \quad \mathbf{y}_t = \mathbf{H}_t\mathbf{x}_t + \mathbf{D}_t\mathbf{u}_t + \mathbf{e}_t \qquad\qquad (ii) \qquad\qquad (4.1)$$

where $\mathbf{y}_t$ is the N-dimensional vector of observed variables; $\mathbf{x}_t$ is an n-dimensional stochastic state vector; $\mathbf{u}_t$ is a k-dimensional vector of deterministic input (exogenous) variables; $\boldsymbol{\eta}_t$ is an n-dimensional vector of (normally assumed Gaussian) system disturbances, that is zero-mean white-noise inputs with covariance matrix $\mathbf{Q}_t$; and $\mathbf{e}_t$ is a N-dimensional vector of zero-mean white-noise variables (measurement noise: again usually assumed to be Gaussian) with covariance matrix $\mathbf{R}_t$. In general, the vector $\mathbf{e}_t$ is assumed to be independent of $\boldsymbol{\eta}_t$, and these two noise vectors are independent of the initial state vector $\mathbf{x}_0$. $\mathbf{A}_t$, $\mathbf{B}_t$, $\mathbf{D}_t$, $\mathbf{G}_t$, and $\mathbf{H}_t$ are, respectively, the $n \times n$, $n \times k$, $N \times k$, $n \times n$, and $N \times n$ system matrices, some elements of which are known and others need to be estimated.

The main reason for formulating the system model in discrete-time SS terms is to facilitate the process of recursive state estimation by exploiting the power of the Kalman Filter (KF: Kalman, 1960). When Kalman developed the filter, he assumed that the form and parameters $(\mathbf{A}_t, \mathbf{B}_t, \mathbf{G}_t, \mathbf{Q}_t)$ of the state equations, which are used to compute the stochastic evolution of the state variables, are known exactly; and that the observation equations, through the parameters $\mathbf{H}_t$, $\mathbf{D}_t$, $\mathbf{R}_t$, simply define the relationship between the observation vector and the state vector. As we have stressed here by the inclusion of the t subscript, all the parameters in the SS equations can vary with time, so that the KF is able to handle nonstationarity in its widest sense, as mentioned in section 4.1.3.[2] However, Kalman assumed that, normally, $\mathbf{H}_t$ and $\mathbf{D}_t$ would be defined quite simply by a set of constant parameters (often zeros and ones), since this seemed more natural within the systems context of the 1960s.

In the present UC context, we turn this original formulation on its head: the observation equation is used primarily to define the dynamics of the system and the state equations define the evolution of changing parameters (surrogate states) that appear in the observation equations and are assumed to evolve stochastically over time, usually in a fairly simple manner. Here, for clarity of exposition, the observation equations (4.1)(*ii*) are expressed as a multivariate Unobserved Components model of the following form:

$$\mathbf{y}_t = \mathbf{T}_t + \mathbf{C}_t + \mathbf{S}_t + f(\mathbf{u}_t) + \mathbf{N}_t + \mathbf{e}_t, \qquad\qquad (4.2)$$

where $\mathbf{T}_t$ is a set of trend components for each observed variable; $\mathbf{C}_t$ is a cyclical component, that is with a period longer than one year; $\mathbf{S}_t$ is a seasonal component or cycle of one year period; $f(\mathbf{u}_t)$ is a set of linear or nonlinear relations between the outputs and certain inputs; $\mathbf{N}_t$ is a vector of colored ARMA noise; and $\mathbf{e}_t$ is the same vector white-noise sequence as above. In this formulation $\mathbf{C}_t$ and $\mathbf{S}_t$ may represent cyclical components of any period needed, for example in electricity demand (see later) they are replaced by annual, weekly, and daily cycles. As we shall see later, the state equations (4.1)(i) simply define the stochastic evolution of the components in (4.2), often in the form of simple stochastic equations that allow the parameters to evolve over time in order to handle nonstationarity in the model (4.2).

This apparently simple model is a general formulation for the analysis of time series: it subsumes most of the univariate, single equation, and multivariate models presented in the introduction as particular cases; as illustrated, in part, by the examples discussed later. The reader should be aware, however, that the model is presented in this form simply for completeness. In the majority of applications, the complete model in (4.2) will underlie the model used but will rarely, if ever, be required in this complete form. Indeed, important identification problems may arise amongst the components should the complete model be used and the components not be defined appropriately. For example, an ARMA model for the $\mathbf{N}_t$ component, including unit or seasonal roots, will conflict severely with any trend and seasonal components. Also, the identification of full multivariable vector models is a complex question that must be exercised with care and can cause many practical difficulties. Although multivariable formulations of the UC model (4.2) above have been produced (for example, Harvey, 1989; Harvey and Koopman, 1997; West and Harrison, 1989), we believe that there is still a long way to go before a general, comprehensive and practical methodology is developed for multivariable UC models. This is an important topic for future research and so, in the following sections, we consider only the case of a scalar observation equation in a single output variable y_t.

4.2.1. State estimation

Given the model in equation (4.1), and (normally) under the assumption of Gaussian stochastic disturbances, the estimation problem consists of finding the first and second order moments (mean and covariance) of the state vector, conditional on all of the time-series data. The general tools that allow us to perform this operation within the stochastic SS framework are, as mentioned previously, the *Kalman Filter* (KF, Kalman, 1960), which provides the recursive state estimation and forecasting framework; and the *Fixed Interval Smoothing* (FIS, Bryson and Ho, 1969) algorithms, which allow for recursive signal extraction, interpolation, and seasonal adjustment.

For a data set of N observations, the KF algorithm runs forward in time and yields a "filtered" estimate $\hat{\mathbf{x}}_{t|t}$ of the state vector $\mathbf{x}_t$ at every sample t, based on the time-series data up to sample t. The FIS algorithm, in contrast, is applied subsequent to the filtering pass and runs backwards in time, producing a "smoothed" estimate $\hat{\mathbf{x}}_{t|N}$ of $\mathbf{x}_t$ which, at every sample t, is based on all N observations of the data. This means that, as more information is used in the latter estimate, its Mean Square Error cannot be greater than the former. As these algorithms are discussed in detail in other references (including some of those already cited), we will not pursue the topic further (see, for example, Young, 1984; Harvey, 1989; Ng and Young, 1990; Young et al., 1999).

It is well known that these KF/FIS algorithms allow for a number of useful operations when dealing with real data; operations that are not normally available in other forecasting/signal extraction algorithms. If missing data anywhere within, or immediately outside, the data set are detected, then the filtering and smoothing algorithms simply replace the missing samples by their expectations, based on the SS model and the data. In this way, the KF would produce multiple-step-ahead forecasts, while FIS can provide interpolations and backcasts of the series. The off-line FIS algorithm is particularly useful for interpolation, signal extraction, seasonal adjustment and lag-free TVP estimation. Also, it is useful in "variance intervention" (for example, Young and Ng, 1989) and related, more complex, methods for handling sudden changes in the trend level.

Despite the generality and advantages of the KF and FIS algorithms, there are other popular algorithms for the estimation of the state vector. As we have pointed out previously (Young and Pedregal, 1999a), the Bayesian approach interprets the KF and FIS recursive algorithms in terms of Bayes theory (Bryson and Ho, 1969; West and Harrison, 1989); while the classical Wiener–Kolmogorov–Whittle filter is still used in some approaches to signal extraction (for example, Maravall and Gómez, 1998), despite its asymptotic formulation and consequent disadvantages in comparison with the KF/FIS estimation. Furthermore, a number of deterministic optimization methods have been proposed for signal extraction. These deterministic methods are considered from a variety of different standpoints such as: "regularization" (for example, Akaike, 1980; Hodrick and Prescott, 1980, 1997; Jakeman and Young, 1984; Young, 1991); "smoothing splines" (for example, Wahba, 1990); "smoothing kernels" (for example, Wand and Jones, 1995); "pseudosplines" (Hastie, 1996); and "wavelet" methods (for example, Daubechies, 1988). The relationship of these approaches to the KF/FIS methodology is discussed in detail by Young and Pedregal (1999a).

4.2.2. Optimization of hyperparameters

The application of the recursive KF/FIS algorithms requires knowledge of all the system matrices $\mathbf{A}_t$, $\mathbf{B}_t$, $\mathbf{D}_t$, $\mathbf{G}_t$, and $\mathbf{H}_t$, together with the noise covariance matrices $\mathbf{Q}_t$ and $\mathbf{R}_t$. In the present UC context, we restrict all of these vector-matrices, except for $\mathbf{H}_t$ which needs to be time dependent (since it includes the model components that are functions of time) to have time-invariant parameters (that is they become $\mathbf{A}$, $\mathbf{B}$, $\mathbf{D}$, $\mathbf{G}$, and $\mathbf{H}$). Depending on the particular structure of the model, there will be a number of elements in these matrices that are known *a priori* (usually zeros and ones). Normally, however, there will be some unknown elements, usually called *hyperparameters*, that must be estimated in some manner.

There are a number of ways of handling this hyperparameter estimation problem, but the approach based on Maximum Likelihood (ML) optimization in the time domain is most common. Assuming that all the disturbances in the state-space form are normally distributed, the log-likelihood function can be computed using the KF via "prediction error decomposition" (Schweppe, 1965; Harvey, 1989). For the general SS model in equation (4.1), this function is

$$\log L = -\frac{NT}{2} \log 2\pi - \frac{1}{2} \sum_{t=1}^{T} \log |\mathbf{F}_t| - \frac{1}{2} \sum_{t=1}^{T} \mathbf{v}_t' \mathbf{F}_t^{-1} \mathbf{v}_t, \qquad (4.3)$$

where N is the number of observations; $\mathbf{v}_t$ is the vector of one-step-ahead errors or innovations; and $\mathbf{F}_t$ is the covariance matrix of $\mathbf{v}_t$. These two measures are computed directly by the KF algorithm; in particular,

$$\mathbf{v}_t = \mathbf{y}_t - \mathbf{H}_t \hat{\mathbf{x}}_{t|t-1} - \mathbf{D}\mathbf{u}_t,$$

$$\mathbf{F}_t = \mathbf{H}_t \mathbf{P}_{t|t-1} \mathbf{H}_t' + \mathbf{R},$$

where $\hat{\mathbf{x}}_{t|t-1}$ and $\mathbf{P}_{t|t-1}$ are the one-step-ahead forecast of the state vector and its covariance matrix (also computed by the KF), respectively. The normalized innovations vector (that is, the innovations for each observation equation divided by the associated time-varying standard error) is an important measure in the evaluation of SS models, since, in the optimal situation, it should constitute a Gaussian white-noise vector.

When maximizing (4.3) a number of issues must be taken into account (see, for example, Harvey, 1989; Koopman et al., 1995). First, the gradient and Hessian are necessary to find the optimum by numerical procedures and these can be evaluated either analytically or numerically (with the standard errors of the estimates also computed from the Hessian). Second, it is usual to maximize the concentrated likelihood, instead of the function above. This concentrated likelihood is a function of the hyperparameters known as *Noise Variance Ratios* (NVR) in the systems literature (for example, Ng and Young, 1990), or signal/noise *q-ratios* in the statistics/econometrics literature (for example, Koopman et al., 1995). Finally, as in most time-series analysis, the problem of defining initial conditions needs to be resolved. The easiest and most popular solution to this problem is by defining *diffuse priors*; for example, zero values for the initial state vector and large values for the diagonal elements of its covariance matrix. More theoretical solutions are possible, however, such as the incorporation of the initial conditional distribution into the likelihood function to yield the *exact likelihood function*. This is useful for short length time-series (see, for example, De Jong, 1988, 1991) but is not necessary when the database is more extensive.

There is no doubt that ML has theoretical and practical advantages. Its optimal properties are well-known and, in the above form, it is generally applicable if Gaussian assumptions are valid. But ML in the time domain is not the only estimation method available. Other methods are: (i) ML in the frequency domain (Harvey, 1989; pages 191–204: this is based on equation (4.3) formulated in the frequency domain using a Fourier transform); (ii) other frequency domain methods (Ng and Young, 1990; Young et al., 1999); (iii) optimization of the one- or multiple-step-ahead prediction errors; (iv) combinations of all the previous methods (Young and Pedregal, 1998); (v) Bayesian approaches (West and Harrison, 1989); and (vi) estimation methods based on the *reduced* ARIMA form (these are only applicable to univariate UC models: see, for example, Hillmer et al., 1983; Maravall and Gómez, 1998). Another very popular method is the Expectation and Maximization (EM) algorithm (Dempster et al., 1977).

These other approaches have been developed because the ML optimization procedure has some disadvantages. In its usual form, for example, it is heavily dependent on the length of the series and dimension of the model, since the recursive algorithms must be used to compute the ML function at each iteration in the numerical optimization. Also, there may be some problems when the theoretical hypotheses, on which it is based, do not hold well. For instance, it is well-known (see, for example, Young et al., 1999) that the likelihood surface can be flat around its optimum, making the optimization inefficient at times and even impossible in some cases. Consequently, these models usually have to be (unnecessarily) constrained when estimated by ML: see the discussion on this topic in Young et al. (YFD, 1999).

The latter reference suggests an alternative frequency-domain method for hyperparameter optimization that appears to be superior to ML, particularly for higher-dimensional models. In particular, the optimum is much better defined and computation times are much less than those required for equivalent ML optimization. Indeed, ML often fails to converge in these higher-dimensional situations, and convergence may only be achieved if several harmonics in the seasonal components are constrained to have the same hyperparameters. Paradoxically, therefore, the YFD method can produce solutions that are even better in likelihood terms than the constrained versions of the same model estimated directly by ML (see Young et al., 1999).

Given the pros and cons of different optimization methods, it is possible to improve model optimization and estimation by combining methods for different parts of the model so that each part is estimated by the best available method. This is the approach suggested in the DBM approach to modeling where frequency and time-domain objective functions are sometimes used concurrently within iterative estimation algorithms.

Most of the methods mentioned above have been implemented in statistical packages available commercially: the multi-platform CAPTAIN Time-Series Analysis and Forecasting Toolbox in Matlab (and its predecessor, the MS-DOS based microCAPTAIN program) provides an array of time-series analysis and forecasting tools, including UC models optimized in the time and frequency domains (information available at http://cres1.lancs.ac.uk/captain/); univariate and multivariable UC models optimized by ML are available in the STAMP program (Koopman et al., 1995; the Windows version 6.02 is now available); a Bayesian approach to UC models is implemented in BATS (Pole et al., 1995); and SEATS (complemented by the companion program TRAMO) is a software package for the reduced form decomposition of time-series (Maravall and Gómez,

1998). Of course, no one optimization and estimation method will outperform the rest in all situations, and all have their own particular advantages and disadvantages. Consequently, as is often the case, the user's experience and knowledge is essential in selecting the best option for each application.

4.3.   TYPICAL UC MODELS

In this section we consider the likely components of a typical, but fairly comprehensive, UC model of the form given in equation (4.2). The components below exemplify the kind that would need to be specified and identified in a UC model in order to meet particular data and user requirements.

The components described here are: low-frequency trends or slowly variable regression parameters modeled by a family of random walk models; seasonal and cyclic periodic components, including an interesting new type in which one cyclic component is modulated by another at a different frequency; and inputs entering the UC relationship through Transfer Function (TF) models. Also, canonical SS forms associated with vector processes are presented. Illustrative practical examples using these components in scalar dependent variable models are described in section 4.4.

4.3.1.   Trend components

There are a number of possibilities available in the literature for modeling a trend or slowly time variable parameter (TVP). One commonly used formulation is the following Generalized Random Walk (GRW) model. This is one of the simplest stochastic representations of trend/TVP behavior and it takes the form of equation (4.1) with the following matrix definitions:

$$\mathbf{A} = \begin{bmatrix} \alpha & \beta \\ 0 & \gamma \end{bmatrix}; \quad \mathbf{G} = \begin{bmatrix} \delta & 0 \\ 0 & \tau \end{bmatrix}; \quad \mathbf{H} = [1 \quad 0]; \quad \mathbf{B} = 0; \quad \mathbf{D} = 0. \tag{4.4}$$

Here, the state vector $\mathbf{x}_t$ is two-dimensional (x_{1t} is the trend itself and x_{2t} is a second state variable, generally considered as the "slope" or derivative of the trend; see below); and α, β, γ, δ and τ are constant parameters, constrained by the user or estimated. This model includes as special cases the Random Walk (RW: $\alpha = 1$; $\beta = \gamma = 0$; $\delta = 1$; $\tau = 0$); the AR(1) process (AR(1): $0 < \alpha < 1$; $\beta = \gamma = 0$; $\delta = 1$; $\tau = 0$); the Smoothed Random Walk (SRW: $0 < \alpha < 1$; $\beta = \gamma = 1$; $\delta = 0$; $\tau = 1$); the Integrated Random Walk (IRW: $\alpha = \beta = \gamma = 1$; $\delta = 0$; $\tau = 1$); the Local Linear Trend (LLT: $\alpha = \beta = \gamma = 1$; $\delta = 1$; $\tau = 1$); and the Damped Trend (DT: $\alpha = \beta = 1$; $0 < \gamma < 1$; $\delta = 1$; $\tau = 1$). The RW process is the most widely used model for trend/TVP modeling. The IRW is also particularly useful in practice, since trends estimated in this manner (by FIS) have the properties of a cubic spline. In the IRW, x_{1t} and x_{2t} can be interpreted as level and slope variables associated with the variations of the trend, with the random disturbance entering only via the second state equation.

4.3.2. Dynamic Linear Regression (DLR) components

The Dynamic[3] Linear Regression (DLR) is a generalization of the standard linear regression model to allow the regression parameters to vary over time. Considering, for simplicity, the case of a single unknown TVP, equation (4.2) in the DLR case simplifies to

$$y_t = u_t b_t + e_t,$$

where b_t is the TVP and u_t is the regression variable. This can also be considered as a static input–output process, with the output y_t related to the input u_t by the TVP b_t. As such, it can be considered as a special static example of the TF model component considered later. The most obvious SS setting in this case is the following, which is a simple modification of (4.4):

$$\mathbf{A} = \begin{bmatrix} \alpha & \beta \\ 0 & \gamma \end{bmatrix}; \quad \mathbf{G} = \begin{bmatrix} \delta & 0 \\ 0 & \tau \end{bmatrix}; \quad \mathbf{H} = [u_t \quad 0]; \quad \mathbf{B} = 0; \quad \mathbf{D} = 0. \tag{4.5}$$

As in (4.4), particular values for parameters α, β, γ, δ, and τ are set depending on the type of variation selected for the TVP. In practical examples, however, the simple RW (that is, $\alpha = 1$; $\beta = \gamma = 0$; $\delta = 1$; $\tau = 0$) is sufficient to represent a wide range of slow temporal variation in the parameter b_t. In this model, there is only one hyperparameter to estimate; namely the associated NVR (see section 4.2.2). This directly controls the degree of smoothness of the variations in the parameter: the smaller the NVR, the smoother the parametric variation. Moreover, if this NVR is constrained to zero (that is, the variance of the associated system noise is zero, so the parameter cannot vary), then the standard constant parameter linear regression model is obtained.

Models of this DLR type with more than one regression variable (or regressor) are obtained by appropriate block concatenation of the system matrices in (4.5). Other interesting extensions of this model are: the *Dynamic AutoRegression* (DAR) model, in which the regression variables are simply the past values of the output; the *Dynamic Harmonic Regression* (DHR) model, described later; and the *Dynamic AutoRegressive eXogenous Variables* (DARX) model. A detailed description of these models and their practical utility is given in Young (1999a).

4.3.3. Seasonal and cyclic components

Both of these components can be treated in the same way from a modeling standpoint, since they both reflect sustained or damped periodic behavior in the time series. The difference between them lies only in the period considered: "seasonal" is often reserved for the annual cycle; "cyclic" refers either to periodic behavior at other frequencies (diurnal, weekly, etc.), or quasi-oscillatory behavior (the economic cycle, the El Niño cycle, etc.). A number of different stochastic models have been suggested to characterize such behavior.

MODEL 1:　DUMMY SEASONALITY (HARVEY, 1989)

This is a linear regression with or without TVPs, in which the inputs are deterministic dummy variables. For a time series with a seasonal period s, for instance, such dummy variables are

$$u_{jt} = \begin{cases} 1, & t = j, j + s, j + 2s, \ldots \\ 0, & t \neq j, j + s, j + 2s, \ldots \quad j = 1, 2, \ldots, s - 1. \\ -1, & t = s, 2s, 3s, \ldots \end{cases}$$

MODEL 2:　DYNAMIC HARMONIC REGRESSION (DHR: YOUNG ET AL., 1999)

Once again, this model is represented by a linear regression with TVPs, but this time the input (regression) variables are deterministic trigonometric functions in the fundamental frequency of the identified periodicity and its harmonics (as identified from the sample spectrum: for example, the AR spectrum with order identified by the Akaike Information Criterion (AIC); or some other sample spectrum, such as the periodogram). Thus, the regression variables are defined as

$$\mathbf{u}_{jt} = [cos\,(\omega_j t) \quad sin\,(\omega_j t)],$$

with

$$\omega_j = \frac{2\pi j}{s} \quad j = 1, 2, \ldots, \left[\frac{s}{2}\right]$$

and $[s/2] = s/2$ for even s; $[s/2] = (s - 1)/2$ for odd s. Note that setting $\omega_0 = 0$ reduces $\mathbf{u}_{0t}$ to a matrix of ones and zeros, implying that GRW trends are naturally accommodated within a DHR context. The rigidity introduced by the deterministic functions is compensated by the modulating TVPs that give the model great flexibility, making it capable of representing many different types of periodic behavior with time-varying amplitude and phase.

MODEL 3:　TRIGONOMETRIC CYCLE OR SEASONAL (HARVEY, 1989; WEST AND HARRISON, 1989)

The main difference relative to model 2 is that the periodic behavior is introduced via the state equations rather than being included in the observation equation. In particular,

$$\mathbf{A}_j = \rho \begin{bmatrix} cos\,(\omega_j t) & sin\,(\omega_j t) \\ -sin\,(\omega_j t) & cos\,(\omega_j t) \end{bmatrix}; \quad \mathbf{G}_j = \begin{bmatrix} 1 & 0 \\ 0 & 1 \end{bmatrix}; \quad \mathbf{H}_j = [1 \quad 0]; \quad \mathbf{B} = 0; \quad \mathbf{D} = 0,$$

where the ω_j are defined as above, and the matrices $\mathbf{A}$, $\mathbf{G}$, and $\mathbf{H}_t$ in equation (4.1) are obtained by block concatenation of the respective $\mathbf{A}_j$, $\mathbf{G}_j$, and $\mathbf{H}_{jt}$, for $j = 1$,

$2, \ldots, [s/2]$. The damping coefficient $0 < \rho < 1$ allows for the periodic behavior to decay over time: if $\rho = 1$, the cycle is undamped and the periodicity is sustained, so the effect is then similar to the DHR model with RW parameters.

Model 4: Modulated Cycle or Seasonal Components (Young and Pedregal, 1997a)

As can be seen in the previous paragraphs, different formulations of periodic components models are possible, including the periodic behavior either in the state equations or in the observation equation. Such duality allows for a mixture of periodic behaviors by combining state and observation equations that have periodic components simultaneously at different frequencies. Such a model introduces multiplicative cycles since, in the observation equation, periodic functions of a given frequency are multiplied by parameters defined by the state equations that are themselves periodic functions of a different frequency. This is known as "modulation" in the signal-processing literature, and such modulated cycles have been exploited extensively in the electricity demand forecasting example discussed later.

4.3.4. Other type of components

Model 1: Transfer Function (TF) models

For simplicity of presentation, we will consider once more the simplest SISO version of the TF model with a pure time delay d; that is,

$$f(u_t) = \frac{\omega(L)}{\delta(L)} u_{t-d},$$

where $\omega(L) = (\omega_0 + \omega_1 L + \omega_2 L^2 + \ldots + \omega_p L^p)$ and $\delta(L) = (1 + \delta_1 L + \delta_2 L^2 + \ldots + \delta_p L^p)$ are both polynomials in the backward shift operator of the same order. One canonical SS form of such a model is the following:

$$\mathbf{A} = \begin{bmatrix} -\delta_1 & 1 & 0 & \ldots & 0 \\ -\delta_2 & 0 & 1 & \ldots & 0 \\ \vdots & \vdots & \vdots & \ddots & \vdots \\ -\delta_{p-1} & 0 & 0 & \ldots & 1 \\ -\delta_p & 0 & 0 & \ldots & 0 \end{bmatrix}; \ \mathbf{G} = 0; \ \mathbf{H}_t = [1 \quad 0 \quad \ldots \quad 0]; \ \mathbf{B} = \begin{bmatrix} \omega_1 \\ \omega_2 \\ \vdots \\ \omega_p \end{bmatrix}; \ \mathbf{D} = 0.$$

Models with different orders in the numerator and denominator can be specified easily by constraining to zero the appropriate trailing coefficients.

Of course, there is no unique SS description of a TF model and other SS forms may have greater physical (here economic) significance. Nor is this the only way of incorporating TF components in UC models. One alternative approach, which we prefer, is to apply the optimal SRIV instrumental variable method of TF model identification and estimation (Young, 1984 and the references therein) directly to the time-series data. Then, if there are other components (for example, seasonal or cyclical), it is possible to utilize a backfitting algorithm to estimate these, in addition to the TF components (this approach is used in a later example). Having estimated the model in this UC form, however, the TF model will normally be converted into a suitable SS form, within the UC model, for forecasting and signal extraction purposes.

MODEL 2: VECTOR ARMA

In order to consider this model in SS form, it is convenient to assume that the sum of the colored noise and the white noise component in equation (4.2) constitutes a Vector ARMA process with the same white noise input; that is,

$$\mathbf{N}_t + \mathbf{e}_t = \frac{\Theta(L)}{\Phi(L)} \mathbf{e}_t,$$

where

$$\Theta(L) = (\mathbf{I} + \Theta_1 L + \ldots + \Theta_p L^p),\ \Phi(L) = (\mathbf{I} + \Phi_1 L + \ldots + \Phi_p L^p)$$

are both multivariate polynomials in the backward shift operator of the same order; the Φ_j and Θ_j, $j = 1, 2, \ldots, p$ are $N \times N$ coefficient matrices; and $\mathbf{I}$ is an Nth order identity matrix. One canonical SS form of this model is:

$$\mathbf{A} = \begin{bmatrix} -\Phi_1 & \mathbf{I} & 0 & \ldots & 0 \\ -\Phi_2 & 0 & \mathbf{I} & \ldots & 0 \\ \vdots & \vdots & \vdots & \ddots & \vdots \\ -\Phi_{p-1} & 0 & 0 & \ldots & \mathbf{I} \\ -\Phi_p & 0 & 0 & \ldots & 0 \end{bmatrix}; \mathbf{G} = \begin{bmatrix} \Theta_1 - \Phi_1 \\ \Theta_2 - \Phi_2 \\ \vdots \\ \Theta_p - \Phi_p \end{bmatrix}; \mathbf{H}_t = [\mathbf{I}\ \ 0\ \ \ldots\ \ 0]; \mathbf{B} = 0; \mathbf{D} = 0.$$

Models with polynomials of different orders can be implemented by constraining to zero the corresponding parameters. In the same way, multiplicative polynomials (typical of seasonal ARMA models, as in Box and Jenkins, 1970, 1976) can be converted into this form by convoluting the polynomials in an appropriate manner and transforming the model into one of this form with a higher order. Special cases of this formulation are univariate ARMA, AR, MA, and vector AR (VAR) and MA models.

MODEL 3: STATIC RELATIONSHIPS

Static relationships between the outputs and a set of deterministic inputs may also be introduced via matrix $\mathbf{D}$, which has been constrained to zero in all previous discussion. Setting $\mathbf{B} = 0$ in equation (4.1) and selecting appropriate inputs, all the dynamics of the model can be specified independently of the relations with the inputs. In this way, any of the models discussed above can be expanded to include the instantaneous effect of exogenous inputs. Some interesting options are static Linear Regression; ARX; ARMAX; UC models of any type discussed above with inputs added; and multivariate versions of all these models. SS versions of SURE, SEM, and VECM models are also possible.

To summarize, the process of UC model formulation and identification involves several stages. In the initial formulation of the model, a subset of the components relevant to the time-series data being analyzed are selected in an identifiable form and used to develop an initial, comprehensive UC model. This is a straight-forward operation, involving the assembly of all the component system matrices into an aggregate SS form by block concatenation of all the matrices for the individual components or parts of the model. Normally, this is facilitated by the software being used, which will carry out this aspect of the model formulation, following the user's selection of components, or a specific "library" UC model form that has been found to have wide application potential (for example, Harvey's *Basic Structural Model*, BSM; or the DHR model). The hyperparameters in this model are then optimized in the manner described above (see also the later examples); and, finally, the KF/FIS estimation is performed. Statistical diagnostic testing is then imperative and, on the basis of this, the model may need to be modified until a satisfactorily formulated, final UC model structure is identified and estimated. This model then forms the basis for forecasting and signal extrac-tion using the KF/FIS algorithms.

4.4. PRACTICAL EXAMPLES

In this section, we consider two examples that typify the use of UC models in time-series analysis and forecasting. The first concerns electricity demand in the U.K. In this case, the series is rapidly sampled (thus exhibiting complex periodic behavior) and the UC model makes use of both modulated cycles and nonlinear input terms. The second example concerns bed occupancy in a U.K. hospital and illustrates the use of a UC model containing an input component entering through a transfer function. This is a difficult example, but it illustrates the importance of the UC analysis in defining the limitations of data and specifying future data requirements.

Many other interesting examples are not included in this chapter, but are documented in several papers. One of these is the well-known Airline Passenger series: here, our analysis (Young et al., 1999) reveals longer-term cyclic charac-teristics of the series, not previously taken into account. A second example con-cerns the modeling and forecasting of macroeconomic data: in particular, the level of unemployment in the U.S. between 1948 and 1998, based on the changes in government spending and private capital investment. The analysis produces some interesting (and perhaps surprising) results about the behavior of the U.S. economy over this long period (Young, 1994; Young and Pedregal, 1997b; 1999b). A third example is the analysis and forecasting of hourly telephone calls received by the Customer Service Centres of Barclaycard plc over three years. This example, as in the example discussed in the next section, is a case of rapidly sampled data in which periodical components at different frequencies are superimposed. Other examples are concerned with environmental forecasting; for example, river flow forecasting and flood warning (for example, Lees et al., 1994).

4.4.1. Rapidly-sampled data: Electricity demand forecasting

There are an increasing number of areas in which rapidly-sampled data are available (for example, weekly, daily, hourly, etc.). There seem to be two main problems with this type of data. First, the length of the series necessary to achieve a sufficient representation of the data must be large (compared, for example, with monthly-sampled data). Second, the number and complexity of the modes of behavior present in the data are important. In particular, the number of parameters necessary to achieve a reasonable representation of such series would be excessive if the methods developed for less rapidly-sampled series were used without modification. Consequently, some simplifying assumptions and proced-ures are necessary in order to achieve acceptable results.

Electricity demand forecasting is one application that exhibits these problems. Here, several years of half-hourly data are often available and the daily periodic components are modulated by weekly and annual cycles, together with long-run trends and nonlinear influences from inputs such as climate variables. Given this inherent complexity, the number of modeling possibilities is large, as the wealth of literature on this topic suggests. In the area of electricity demand alone, there are already a large number of approaches (see, for example, Young and Pedregal, 1998, and references therein).

The particular series come from a British electrical company transformer. Figure 4.1 shows four weeks of four-hourly electricity load-data series for two seasons of the year. The data reveal all the typical features commonly found in most energy demand series: even by eye, for instance, it is easy to recognize strong daily and weekly patterns. The daily pattern is different for some days (especially weekends), and it also changes according to the season of the year. Other features, not obvious in the figure, are also present in the series: for ex-ample, an annual cycle (due mainly to the temperature effects), outliers, bank and public holidays, missing data, etc.

In this example, we will show how the univariate DHR model may be used to model and forecast four-hourly demand data. The univariate model in this case is as follows:

$$y_t = T_t + W_t + D_t + e_t,$$

where y_t is the observed four-hourly electricity demand; T_t is a trend or low frequency component; W_t is a weekly component; D_t is a daily component; and e_t is the irregular component. The trend component actually accounts for the annual cycle, which could be estimated as a separate component, if desired. However, while this component may be interesting in signal extraction terms, it is not so important in the context of the project that originated this example, where forecasting in the short term (up to one week ahead) was the main objective.

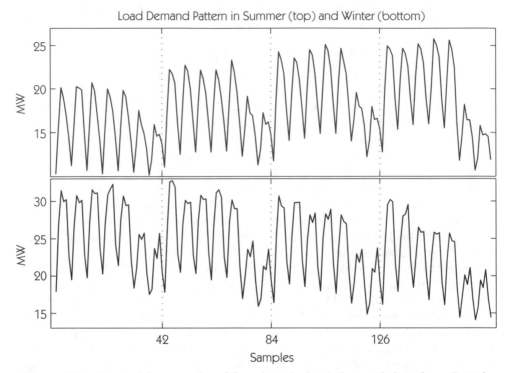

Figure 4.1 Typical four weeks of four-hourly load demand data for a British
company transformer in summer (top plot) and winter (bottom plot)

The identification stage in the frequency domain is presented in figure 4.2
(solid line), where the AR spectrum shows peaks of similar height disposed
symmetrically around all the daily periods (6, 3, and 2 samples/cycle (s/c)), with
some distortion due to the long spectral effect of the trend. This is precisely the
type of spectral behavior that is typical of modulated cycle and seasonal components; see Young and Pedregal (1998) for details.

Because of these modulation phenomena, the specific form of the model used
in this case includes the fundamental daily periodic component and its harmonics (6, 3, and 2 s/c) modulated by the weekly period harmonics (namely, 42,
21, and 14 s/c). Coherent with this formulation, the weekly cycle is specified as a
standard additive DHR model, including the fundamental period and two harmonics (as above), each with TVP parameters characterized by the RW-type model.
An IRW trend is then added to model the long-term behavior of the series. In this
way, all the spectral peaks that appear in figure 4.2 are recovered by some term
in the modified DHR model.

Estimation in the frequency domain is straightforward, mainly because of the
good definition of the spectral peaks. The fit in the frequency domain is presented in figure 4.2, where the fitted spectrum is shown as the dashed line. The
estimated components for four weeks of data are shown in figure 4.3. All of these

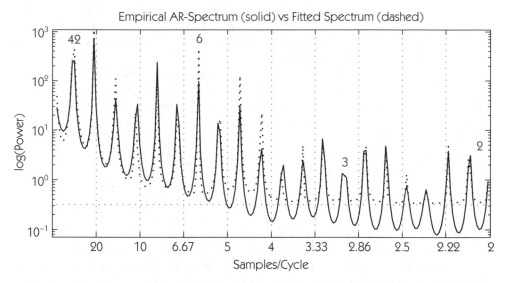

Figure 4.2 Typical empirical AR-Spectrum (solid) and fit (dashed) of DHR model that includes modulated cycles

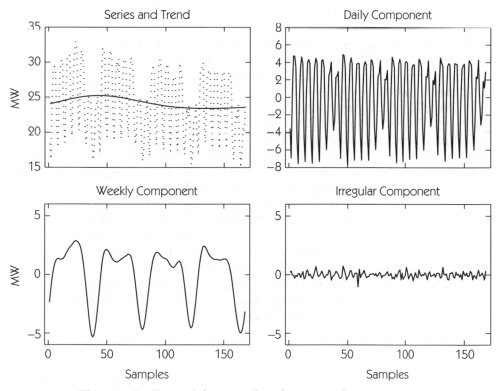

Figure 4.3 Typical four weeks of estimated components

possess the properties assumed: the trend evolves smoothly in time; the daily component exhibits the differences between days of the week; the modulating weekly component is as expected; and the irregular component is small compared with the rest of the components.

In order to produce more material for comparison, rival models were estimated. An extension of the "airline model" to four-hourly data with three multiplicative polynomials was estimated. This ARIMA model was one of the options used by the electrical company to produce hourly forecasts of the demand. However, in the case of four-hourly data, the autocorrelation coefficients for the residuals up to order four were significantly different from zero. Therefore, the ARIMA model finally used in the comparisons was:

$$(1 - L)(1 - L^6)(1 - L^{42})\phi(L)y_t = (1 + \theta L)(1 + \theta_6 L^6) (1 + \theta_{42}L^{42})a_t,$$

with $\phi(L) = (1 + \phi_1 L + \phi_2 L^2 + \phi_3 L^3 + \phi_4 L^4)$. This model was estimated by ML.

In order to evaluate the forecasting performance of the model, the following experiment was carried out. The model was estimated using a rectangular window of 20 weeks, moving on one day at each iteration and producing forecasts up to one week ahead. This procedure was repeated for one year of data. Restricting the length of the window to 20 weeks reduces the computational burden of this comprehensive evaluation, and is quite appropriate since the longest period of the components in the model is weekly, and this is still estimated on the basis of 20 full cycles.

Figure 4.4 shows a forecast comparison of three models based on the MAPE: a naive model, in which the last observed week is considered the forecast for the next week (dashed dot); the ARIMA model considered above (dotted); and the DHR model (solid). The upper plot shows the mean of the *Mean Absolute Prediction Error* (MAPE) for forecast horizons from four hours up to one week ahead; while the lower plot shows the standard deviation counterparts. It is clear that the UC model produces better aggregate results than either the naive or ARIMA models. Both ARIMA and UC are much better than the naive model for short forecast horizons, implying that both models are doing much more than simply replacing the forecasts by the latest week. However, only the UC is superior for longer horizons, up to one week. Similar comments apply to the standard error of the MAPE.

Finally, it should be noted that the basic UC–DHR model outlined above has been extended to allow for multi-rate modeling and nonlinear input effects. In the multi-rate case, several models are estimated at different sampling intervals and then combined together to produce the forecasts at the required frequency. The nonlinear inputs account for the effects on the electricity demand of a chill factor, identified as a nonlinear combination of temperature, relative humidity, and wind speed. Full details of these extensions are given in Young and Pedregal (1998).

4.4.2. Bed occupancy at some hospitals in the U.K.

This example illustrates the use of UC models that include exogenous input variables, whose effect enters through Transfer Function (TF) relationships. As far as

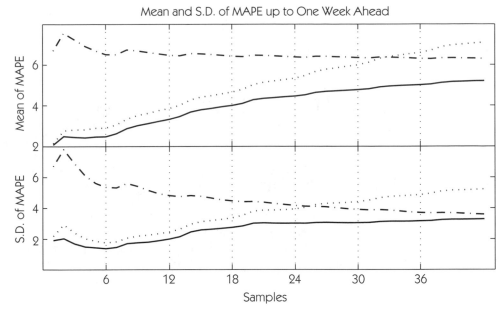

Figure 4.4   Mean (top plot) and standard deviation (bottom plot) of MAPE
of true one-week-ahead forecasts evaluated on repeated forecasts along
one year of data for three models: modulated DHR (solid); ARIMA (dotted);
and naive (dashed dot)

we are aware, although this possibility has been contemplated in other UC
methodologies, no practical implementation and examples have been reported.
The example concerns the modeling and forecasting of beds occupied daily at
several hospitals in the U.K. The original project had the objective of building a
system to provide 21-day-ahead forecasts, where the forecasts should lie within a
10 percent error band about the actual figures of bed occupancy.

One example of the hospital series is shown in figure 4.5, where all the typical
features are clearly discernible. The series consists of a 1251 measurements of the
daily bed occupancy from April 1, 1994 until September 2, 1997, plotted on an
annual basis. The dotted vertical lines show the beginning of each month starting
in September. The different years of data have been represented in ascending
order with a constant added to the data each year in order to add clarity to the
figure, that is the series in the bottom panel corresponds to the data from 4/1/94
to 8/31/94; while the series in the top panel corresponds to the data from 9/1/96
to 8/31/97.

The most evident feature of the data in figure 4.5 is the upward trend and the
volatile changes that occur about this trend. This volatility is present throughout the series and is enhanced by a number of sudden changes of behavior, such
as peaks and troughs at different, irregularly-spaced locations, as well as outlier
effects. The most important visible outliers are the large and, we presume,
expected changes in the behavior of the series around Christmas every year. In

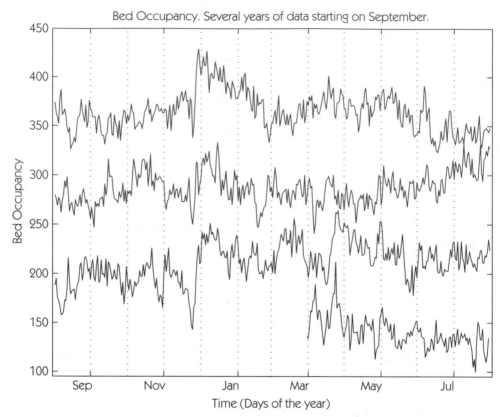

Figure 4.5   The bed occupancy data presented on an annual basis. The series at the bottom corresponds to the data from 4/1/94 to 8/31/94, while the series on top corresponds to the data from 9/1/96 to 8/31/97. Constants have been added to each year in order to add clarity to the figure

particular, there is a significant reduction in bed occupancy around Christmas Day. This is followed by a large, sudden increase, and then a subsequent exponential-like decay with a relatively long time constant. In addition to this, there is an Easter effect, which is fairly clear in years 1994–1996 (Good Friday occurred on 4/1/94, 4/14/95, and 4/5/96 respectively), but it is not apparent in 1997 (3/28/97). This suggests that the Easter effect, as estimated over the period 1994–1996, will not assist much in forecasting over 1997 without the help of additional information that explains the reason for its volatility.

It is also clear that the series is characterized by other, fairly abrupt and apparently unpredictable, changes in level that are not found in all years: see, for example, September, February, and especially July, where the volatility in 1997 has no precedent at all in previous years. Although apparently very irregular, not all the volatility in the series is unpredictable. In particular, AR spectral analysis reveals a weekly component and a much less important monthly component.

The weekly component is very well defined by a decreasing level of occupation as the week progresses, with two peaks on Mondays and Fridays, respectively; and two minima on Wednesdays and Saturdays.

A possible UC model that accounts for all the features of the above data is the following:

$$y_t = T_t + S_t + f(\mathbf{u}_t) + e_t,$$

with the usual definitions. Here $f(\mathbf{u}_t)$ is a term that recovers the influence of either the Christmas and Easter effects by means of linear Transfer Function (TF) models. The seasonal component consists predominantly of the weekly cycle. The ill-defined monthly cycle was omitted from the analysis because it led to no improvement in forecasting terms over the historical data.

The complete optimization of the above UC model requires concurrent estimation of the periodic and exogenous variable components. This is achieved by an iterative procedure known as backfitting, in which the frequency domain optimization is combined with an optimal recursive Instrumental Variable (RIV) algorithm, as mentioned previously. At each iteration, the TF parameters are estimated by the RIV methods conditional on the previously estimated parameters for the trend and seasonal components; and these components are then estimated, in turn, in the frequency domain conditional on the TF model estimates. After a few iterations (three in this case), convergence is achieved and the whole set of unconditional parameter estimates is obtained.

Figure 4.6 shows the estimated components obtained in this manner for one year of data starting on June 1, 1995 (only one year is shown to avoid confusion in the plots). The "trend-plus-outlier" effects (Christmas and Easter) evolve smoothly through the series, as expected. The weekly component is quite regular (with some very smooth changes in amplitude at some points). As pointed out previously, it is notable that the amplitude of this component is smaller than that of the irregular component (plotted at the same scale to facilitate comparison), indicating the extreme difficulty of the forecasting exercise in this case. Finally, the plot at the bottom of figure 4.6 shows that the Christmas and Easter effects are quite important in comparison with the other, more regular, periodic components; and that their inclusion in the model (particularly the effects at Christmas) is essential to the analysis and forecasting of the bed occupancy data.

The model has been tested for consistency and forecasting performance by a thorough evaluation study, as in the previous example. Here, one whole year of 21-step-ahead forecasts were produced, starting on August 11, 1996; and this was continued, adding one daily observation and reestimating all the parameters in the model at each step, right through to the end of the data. The resulting large set of multi-step-ahead forecasts were then compared with the actual bed occupancy values, and the RMSE's of the forecasts were computed.

For most of the year, the model fulfils the requirements of the study (78.4 percent of the time forecast errors were within the 10 percent error band). By months, the mean percentages of fulfilment are (starting in September): 86.82; 96,46; 100; 97.38; 93.85; 96.91; 80.18; 97.46; 96.77; 70.50; 96.46. This reveals that the

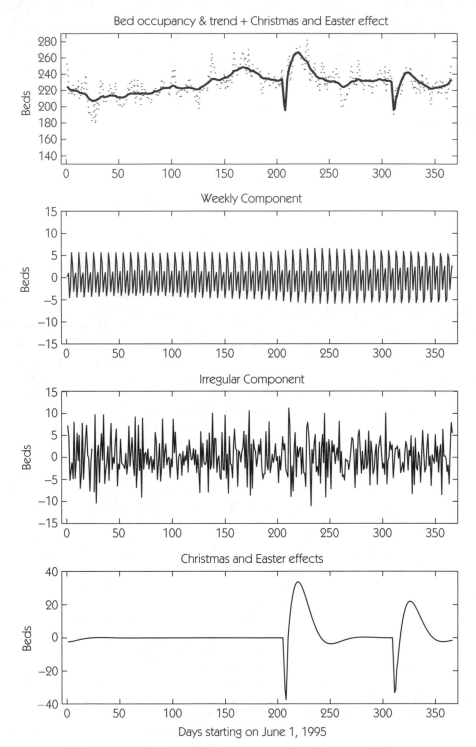

Figure 4.6   Estimated components for one year of data
starting on June 1, 1995

situations where the forecasting model does not perform so well are located mainly in September, March, and July. Referring to figure 4.5, the reason why the model is not fulfilling the objectives in these particular months is quite clear. At these times, the series is much more volatile, mainly because of sudden and unpredictable (from the bed occupancy series alone) jumps in level. Note, however, that the Christmas effect, which is quite well modeled from the historical data, is predicted by the incorporation of the TF intervention terms.

It must be stressed that, in a day-to-day application of this UC model, the performance of the model would be better than that described above. This is because the unpredictable daily events could be incorporated into the model by a user who had prior knowledge of the system and could quickly correct for these unforeseen (and therefore un-modelable) events, on-line. Since we had no information on this behavior in formulating the model, however, we were not able to include it in the analysis. Nevertheless, given the flexibility of the model, should any additional variables or information relating to such sudden and unforeseen events become available, it can be incorporated quite easily. This would not require any radical change in the methodological approach and it should improve the forecasting performance over these difficult periods. Of course, the degree of improvement would depend upon the quality of the information.

Similar conclusions to the above arise if we consider the monthly means of the RMSE's (quoted in percentage error terms) shown in table 4.1 for different forecasting horizons. As might be expected, the worst forecast months are September, March, and July. Although large, these RMSEs are quite acceptable given the volatile nature of the bed occupancy series. Certainly, the model discussed here

Table 4.1 Monthly average of the RMSE for different forecast horizons of bed occupancy at a hospital in the U.K.

	1-step	7-step	14-step	21-step
September	3.4483	5.3744	6.4375	6.6848
October	3.3027	5.2275	5.2388	5.1765
November	2.9939	3.6258	3.8074	4.0260
December	2.3538	3.4429	3.8997	4.4753
January	3.6080	4.5670	4.9401	5.2468
February	2.2277	2.8811	3.4811	4.5253
March	3.6553	5.5688	6.7395	7.1383
April	2.4698	3.6106	4.1868	4.6860
May	2.4530	4.3034	4.4623	4.5493
June	2.9545	3.7358	4.0569	4.5718
July	3.2611	6.6300	7.8970	8.5914
August	3.6458	4.8156	4.4328	4.2501
OVERALL	3.02	4.48	4.97	5.32

provides a worthwhile improvement over the more *ad hoc* forecasting methods currently used in U.K. hospitals.

4.5. Conclusions

This chapter reviews the various approaches to statistical time-series analysis and forecasting currently available to the econometrician and applied systems analyst. Although it is not comprehensive, the main classical and modern approaches to the subject are outlined and then unified within the context of the many developments in stochastic state-space modeling that have taken place over the past two decades. The chapter also presents a more comprehensive review of the *Unobserved Components* (UC) approach to modeling, as well as the state-space based recursive approaches to estimation that underlie the identification and estimation of such models. To some degree, this reflects the predilections of the authors, who come from different disciplinary backgrounds but feel that this approach offers the currently most flexible and sophisticated method of modeling and forecasting nonstationary time series. The efficacy of the approach in practical terms is illustrated by two examples that reflect different problems of modeling and forecasting, and show how the UC methodology is able to tackle these problems in a straightforward and meaningful manner.

Notes

1   Sometimes termed *Error Correction Model.*
2   Note that, because of this, although the system is nominally linear, it can behave in a rather obvious nonlinear-like manner: for example if the model parameters are changing over time, then the same inputs, imposed at different times, will result in different state behavior.
3   The adjective "dynamic" is used here for historical reasons but it can be rather misleading: it derives from the work of Harrison and Steven (1976) on *Dynamic Linear Models* (DLM's) and is simply a device to differentiate the TVP models from their constant parameter relatives. In fact, only the DARX model (see the main text) is really dynamic in a systems sense.

References

Abraham, B. and J. Ledolter (1983). *Statistical Methods for Forecasting*. New York: John Wiley.

Akaike, H. (1980). Seasonal adjustment by a Bayesian modeling. *Journal of Time Series Analysis*, 1, 1–13.

Aoki, M. (1990). *State-Space Modeling of Time Series*. New York: Springer-Verlag.

Baillie, R.T. and M.L. King (1996). Fractional Differencing and Long Memory Processes. Special Issue of *Journal of Econometrics*, 73.

Box, G.E.P. and G.M. Jenkins (1970, 1976). *Time Series Analysis: Forecasting and Control*. San Francisco: Holden-Day.

Box, G.E.P., G.M. Jenkins, and G.C. Reinsel (1994). *Time Series Analysis, Forecasting and Control*. Englewood Cliffs, New Jersey: Prentice Hall International.

Brown, T.G. (1963). *Smoothing, Forecasting and Prediction*. Englewood Cliffs: Prentice Hall.

Bryson, A.E. and Y.C. Ho (1969). *Applied Optimal Control, Optimisation, Estimation and Control*. Waltham: Blaisdell Publising Company.

Burman, J.P. (1980). Seasonal adjustment by signal extraction. *Journal of the Royal Statistical Society A*, 143, part 3, 321–37.

Chatfield, C. (1984). *The Analysis of Time Series: an Introduction*. London: Chapman and Hall.

Chen, S. and S.A. Billings (1989). Representations of non-linear systems – The NARMAX model. *International Journal of Control*, 49, 1013–32.

Dagum, E.B. (1980). The X-11 ARIMA Seasonal adjustment method. Ottawa: Statistics Canada.

Dagum, E.B. (1988). The X-11/88 ARIMA seasonal adjustment method. Ottawa: Statistics Canada.

Daubechies, I. (1988). Orthonormal bases of compactly supported wavelets. *Communications on Pure Applied Mathematics*, 41, 906–66.

Davidson, J., D.F. Hendry, F. Sbra, and S. Yeo (1978). Econometric modeling of the aggregate time-series relationship between consumer's expenditure and income in the U.K. *Economic Journal*, 88, 661–92.

De Jong, P. (1988). The likelihood for a state-space model. *Biometrika*, 75, 1, 165–9.

De Jong, P. (1991). Stable algorithms for the state-space model. *Journal of Time Series Analysis*, 12, 2, 143–57.

Dempster, A.P., N.M. Laird, and D.B. Rubin (1977). Maximum likelihood from incomplete data via the EM algorithm. *Journal of the Royal Statistical Society, Series B*, 39, 1–38.

Dickey, D.A. and W. Fuller (1979). Distribution of the estimators for autoregressive time series with a unit root. *Journal of the American Statistical Association*, 84, 427–31.

Diebold, F. (1998). *Elements of Forecasting*. Cincinnati: South-Western.

Diggle, P.J. (1990). *Time Series: a Biostatistical Introduction*. Oxford: Clarendon Press.

Engle, R.F. (1984). Wald, likelihood ratio and Lagrange multiplier tests in econometrics. In Z. Griliches and M.D. Intriligator (eds.), 775–826.

Engle, R.F. and C.W.J. Granger (1987). Cointegration and error correction: representation, estimation and testing. *Econometrica*, 55, 251–76.

Engle, R.F. and D.F. Hendry (1989). Testing superexogeneity and invariance. Discussion Paper 89–51, Department of Economics. San Diego: University of California.

Engle, R.F., D.F. Hendry and J.F. Richard (1983). Exogeneity. *Econometrica*, 51, 277–304.

Ericsson, N.R. (1992). Cointegration, exogeneity and policy analysis; an overview. *Journal of Policy Modeling*, 14, 251–80.

Findley, D.F., B.C. Monsell, M.C. Otto, W.R. Bell, and M. Pugh (1992). Towards X-12 ARIMA. mimeo, U.S. Bureau of the Census.

Findley, D.F., B.C. Monsell, W.R. Bell, M.C. Otto, and B.C. Chen (1996). New capabilities and methods of the X-12 ARIMA seasonal adjustment program. U.S. Bureau of the Census, mimeo, May 16.

Gamerman, D. (1997). *Markov Chain Monte Carlo*. London: Chapman and Hall.

Geweke, J., R. Meese, and W. Dent (1983). Comparing alternative tests of causality in temporal systems. *Journal of Econometrics*, 21, 161–94.

Granger, C.W.J. (1969). Investigating causal relations by econometric models and cross-spectral models. *Econometrica*, 37, 424–38.

Granger, C.W.J. (1981). Some properties of times series data and their use in econometric model specification. *Journal of Econometrics*, 16, 121–30.

Granger, C.W.J. and P. Newbold (1974). Spurious regression in econometrics. *Journal of Econometrics*, 2, 111–20.

Granger, C.W.J. and P. Newbold (1986). *Forecasting Economic Time Series*, 2nd edn. San Diego: Academic Press.

Granger, C.W.J. and T. Teräsvirta (1993). *Modeling Nonlinear Economic Relationships*. Oxford: Oxford University Press.

Greene, W.H. (1998). *Econometric Analysis*. Prentice Hall.

Hamilton, J.D. (1994). *Time Series Analysis*. Princeton: Princeton University Press.

Harrison, P.J. and C.F. Stevens (1976). Bayesian forecasting. *Journal Royal Statistical Society, Series B*, 38, 205–47.

Harvey, A.C. (1981). *Time Series Models*. New York: Philip Allan.

Harvey, A.C. (1989). *Forecasting Structural Time Series Models and the Kalman Filter*. Cambridge: Cambridge University Press.

Harvey, A.C. and S.J. Koopman (1997). Comments on "Multivariate structural time series models". In C. Heij et al. (eds.), *System Dynamics in Economic and Financial Models*. Chichester: John Wiley.

Hastie, T. (1996). Pseudosplines. *Journal of the Royal Statistical Society, Series B*, 58, 379–96.

Hastie, T.J. and R.J. Tibshirani (1990). *Generalised Additive Models*. London: Chapman & Hall.

Hausman, J.A. (1978). Specification tests in econometrics. *Econometrica*, 46, 1251–70.

Hendry, D.F. and Wallis, K.F. (eds.) (1984). *Onometrics and Quantitative Economics*. Oxford: Basil Blackwell.

Hillmer, S.C., W.R. Bell, and G.C. Tiao (1983). Modeling considerations in the seasonal adjustment of economic time series. In A. Zellner (ed.), *Applied Time Series Analysis of Economic Data*. Washington D.C.: U.S. Dept. of Commerce-Bureau of the Census, 74–100.

Hodrick, T. and E. Prescott (1980). Post-war U.S. business cycles: an empirical investigation. Carnegie Mellon University, manuscript. (1997) *Journal of Money, Credit and Banking*, 29, 1–16.

Holt, C.C. (1957). Forecasting seasonals and trends by exponentially weighted moving averages. ONR Research Memorandum 52. Pittsburgh: Carnegie Institute of Technology.

Intriligator, M.D., Bodkin, and C. Hsiao (1996). *Econometric Models, Techniques and Applications*. Upper Saddle River: Prentice Hall.

Jakeman, A.J. and P.C. Young (1984). Recursive filtering and the inversion of ill-posed causal problems. *Utilitas Mathematica*, 35, 351–76.

Johansen, S. (1988). Statistical analysis of cointegration vectors. *Journal of Economic Dynamics and Control*, 12, 231–54.

Johnston, J. (1963 and 1984). *Econometric Methods*. New York: McGraw Hill.

Judge, G., W.E. Griffiths, R. Carter-Hill and T. Lee (1985). *The Theory and Practice of Econometrics*, 2nd edn. New York: John Wiley.

Kalman, R.E. (1960). A new approach to linear filtering and prediction problems. *ASME Transactions, Journal of Basic Engineering*, 83-D, 95–108.

Koopman, S.J., A.C. Harvey, J.A. Doornik, and N. Shephard (1995). *STAMP 5.0: Structural Time Series Analyser, Modeller and Predictor*. London: Chapman & Hall.

Lees, M., P.C. Young, K.J. Beven, S. Ferguson, and J. Burns (1994). An adaptive flood warning system for the River Nith at Dumfries. In W.R. White and J. Watts (eds.), *River Flood Hydraulics*. Wallingford: Institute of Hydrology.

Ljung, L. and T. Söderstrom (1983). *Theory and Practice of Recursive Estimation*. Cambridge, Massachusetts: MIT Press.

Lütkepohl, H. (1991). *Introduction to Multiple Time Series Analysis*. Berlin: Springer-Verlag.

Maravall, A. and V. Gómez (1998). Programs TRAMO and SEATS, Instructions for the User (Beta Version: June 1998). Madrid: Bank of Spain.

Mills, T. (1990). *Time Series Techniques for Economists*. Cambridge: Cambridge University Press.

Ng, C.N. and P.C. Young (1990). Recursive estimation and forecasting of nonstationary time series. *Journal of Forecasting*, 9, 173–204.

Osborn, D., A. Chui, J. Smith and C. Birchenhall (1988). Seasonality and the order of integration for consumption. *Oxford Bulletin of Economics and Statistics*, 50, 361–77.

Perron, P. (1990). Testing for a unit root in a time series with a changing mean. *Journal of Business and Economic Statistics*, 8, 153–62.

Phillips, P.C.B. (1991). Optimal inference in cointegrated systems. *Econometrica*, 59, 283–306.

Pole, A., M. West, and J. Harrison (1995). *Applied Bayesian Forecasting and Time-Series Analysis*. New York: Chapman & Hall.

Quenouille, M.H. (1957). *The Analysis of Multiple Time Series*. London: Griffin.

Sargan, J.D. (1964). Wages and prices in the U.K.: a study in econometric methodology. In P. Hart et al. (eds.), 25–63.

Schweppe, F. (1965). Evaluation of likelihood function for Gaussian signals. *I.E.E.E. Transaction Information Theory*, 11, 61–70.

Shiskin, J., A. Young, and J.C. Musgrave (1967). The X-11 variant of the Census method II seasonal adjustment program. Technical Paper 15. Washington: Bureau of the Census.

Sims, C.A. (1972). Money, income and causality. *American Economic Review*, 62, 540–52.

Sims, C.A. (1980). Macroeconomics and reality. *Econometrica*, 48, 1–48.

Tiao, G.C. and G.E.P. Box (1981). Modeling multiple time series with applications. *Journal of the American Statistical Asociation*, 76, 802–16.

Tong, H. (1990). *Nonlinear Time Series. A Dynamical System Approach*. Oxford: Oxford University Press.

Wahba, G. (1990). *Spline Models for Observational Data*. Philadelphia: SIAM.

Wallis, K.F. (1977). Multiple time-series analysis and the final form of econometrics models. *Econometrica*, 45, 1481–97.

Wand, M. and C. Jones (1995). *Kernel Smoothing*. London: Chapman and Hall.

Wei, W.W.S. (1990). *Time Series Analysis*. New York: Addison-Wesley.

West, M. and J. Harrison (1989). *Bayesian Forecasting and Dynamic Models*. New York: Springer-Verlag.

Winters, P.R. (1960). Forecasting sales by exponentially weighted moving averages. *Management Science*, 6, 324–42.

Wu, D.M. (1973). Alternative tests of independence between stochastic regressors and disturbances. *Econometrica*, 40, 733–50.

Young, P.C. (1984). *Recursive Estimation and Time Series Analysis*. Berlin: Springer-Verlag.

Young, P.C. (1991). Comments on likelihood and cost as path integrals. *Journal of the Royal Statistical Society, Series B*, 53, 529–31.

Young, P.C. (1993). Time variable and state dependent modeling of nonstationary and nonlinear systems. In T. Subba-Rao (ed.), *Developments in Time Series Analysis*. London: Chapman and Hall.

Young, P.C. (1994). Time-variable parameter and trend estination in nonstationary economic time series. *Journal of Forecasting*, 13, 179–210.

Young, P.C. (1998). Data-based mechanistic modeling of environmental, ecological, economic and engineering systems. *Environmental Modeling and Software*, 13, 105–22.

Young, P.C. (1999a). Nonstationary time-series analysis and forecasting. *Progress in Environmental Science*, 1, 3–48.

Young, P.C. (1999b). Data-based mechanistic modeling, generalised sensitivity and dominant mode analysis. *Computer Physics Communications*, 115, 1–17.

Young, P.C. (1999c). The identification and estimation of nonlinear stochastic systems. In A.I. Mees (ed.), *Nonlinear Dynamics and Statistics*, Boston: Birkhauser.

Young, P.C. (2001a). Data-based mechanistic modeling and validation of rainfall-flow processes. In M.G. Anderson (ed.), *Model Validatio: Perspectives in Hydrological Science*, Chichester: John Wiley, in press.

Young, P.C. (2001b). Stochastic, dynamic modeling and signal processing: time variable and state dependent parameter estimation. In W.J. Fitzgerald, R. Smith, A. Walden, and P.C. Young (eds.), *Nonlinear and Nonstationary Signal Processing*. Cambridge: Cambridge University Press.

Young, P.C. and C.N. Ng (1989). Variance intervention. *Journal of Forecasting*, 8, 399–416.

Young, P.C., C.N. Ng, and P. Armitage (1989). A systems approach to economic forecasting and seasonal adjustment. *International Journal on Computers and Mathematics with Applications*, special issue on System Theoretic Methods in Economic Modeling, 18, 481–501.

Young, P.C. and D.J. Pedregal (1996). Recursive fixed interval smoothing and the evaluation of LIDAR measurements. *Environmetrics*, 7, 417–27.

Young, P.C. and D.J. Pedregal (1997a). Modulated cycles, a new approach to modeling seasonal/cyclical behavior in unobserved components models. Centre for Research on Environmental Systems and Statistics (CRES), Tech. Note No. TR/145, to be submitted for publication.

Young, P.C. and D.J. Pedregal (1997b). Data-based mechanistic modeling. In C. Heij et al. (eds.), *System Dynamics in Economic and Financial models*. Chichester: John Wiley.

Young, P.C. and D.J. Pedregal (1998). A new adaptive approach to forecasting electricity demand (II). Centre for Research on Environmental Systems and Statistics, Lancaster University, Technical Note No. 155, to be submitted for publication.

Young, P.C. and D.J. Pedregal (1999a). Recursive and en-block approaches to signal extraction. *Journal of Applied Statistics*, 26, 103–28.

Young, P.C. and D.J. Pedregal (1999b). Macro-economic relativity: government spending, private investment and unemployment in the USA. *Structural Change and Economic Dynamics*, 10, 359–80.

Young, P.C., D.J. Pedregal, and W. Tych (1999). Dynamic harmonic regression. *Journal of Forecasting*, 18, 369–94.

Zellner, A. (1962). An efficient method of estimating seemingly unrelated regressions and tests for aggregation bias. *Journal of the American Statistical Association*, 57, 348–68.

Zellner, A. (1979). Statistical analysis of econometric models (with discussion). *Journal of the American Statistical Association*, 74, 628–51.

Zellner A. and F. Palm (1974). Time-series analysis and simultaneous equation econometric models. *Journal of Econometrics*, 2, 15–54.

CHAPTER FIVE

Forecasting with Structural Time-Series Models

Tommaso Proietti

5.1.   INTRODUCTION

Structural time-series models are formulated directly in terms of unobserved components, such as trends, cycles, and seasonals, that have a natural interpretation and represent the salient features of the series under investigation.

An explicit link with other approaches such as the ARIMA approach and the regression methodology can usually be made. As far as the former is concerned, linear univariate structural models have a reduced form ARIMA representation, but the latter is subject to restrictions on the parameter space, which play a relevant role for forecasting and signal extraction, providing a sensible way of weighting the available information. Moreover, structural models can easily be extended to handle any frequency of observation (weekly, daily, hourly) and specific features of the series that are difficult to deal with in the ARIMA framework (heteroskedasticity, nonlinearity, non-Gaussianity). From the second standpoint, structural models are set up as regression models in which the explanatory variables are functions of time and the coefficients are allowed to vary over time, thereby encompassing the traditional decomposition of a time series into deterministic components. A thorough presentation of the main ideas and methodological aspects underlying structural time-series models is contained in Harvey (1989); other important references are West and Harrison (1997) and Kitagawa and Gersch (1996).

The material presented in this chapter is organized as follows: the next three sections deal with the specifications of time-series models respectively for the trend, the cycle, and the seasonal component, and how they can be combined into the main univariate structural models; multivariate extensions are discussed in section 5.5. The disturbances driving the different components are assumed independent and this can be viewed as an identification restriction. However, models with correlated disturbances can be specified and they are briefly discussed in section 5.6. Central to the statistical treatment of structural time-series models is the state-space representation (section 5.7). The Kalman filter is an essential tool for inferences about the unobserved components and for evaluation of the likelihood function. The algorithm is presented along with the modifications that have to be introduced in the presence of nonstationary components. Section 5.8 explains how explanatory variables can be included in a structural model. The estimation of the unobserved components based on the full sample of observations is called *smoothing* and is considered in section 5.9.

Structural time-series models are used not only for providing a description of the salient features of the series, but also for forecasting its future values. Forecasting provides the means of projecting the past into the future by attaching suitable weights to the past and current observations of the variable under investigation. It is the topic of section 5.10, where particular attention is paid on the relation with forecasting with *ad hoc* techniques and ARIMA models. Section 5.11 presents some nonlinear and non-Gaussian extensions. Finally, in section 5.12 two illustrations of modeling and forecasting with structural time-series models are provided.

5.2. TREND MODELS

The specification of a time-series model for the trend component varies according to the features displayed by the series under investigation and any prior knowledge. The most elementary structural model deals with a series whose underlying level changes over time, as in the situation depicted in the first panel of figure 5.1. The data generating process can be thought of consisting of a trend, μ_t, evolving according to a random walk, with a superimposed irregular component, ε_t:

$$y_t = \mu_t + \varepsilon_t, \quad t = 1, 2, \ldots, T, \quad \varepsilon_t \sim \mathsf{NID}(0, \sigma_\varepsilon^2),$$

$$\mu_{t+1} = \mu_t + \eta_t, \qquad\qquad\qquad \eta_t \sim \mathsf{NID}(0, \sigma_\eta^2), \qquad (5.1)$$

where NID denotes normally and independently distributed. This is known as the local level model (LLM) and is a straightforward generalization of the constant level model: $y_t = \mu + \varepsilon_t$, arising when $\sigma_\eta^2 = 0$. On the other hand, when $\sigma_\varepsilon^2 = 0$, (1) reduces to a pure random walk and the trend coincides with the observations.

The stationary representation of the LLM model is obtained by taking first differences: $\Delta y_t = \eta_{t-1} + \Delta\varepsilon_t$. It follows immediately that $\mathsf{E}(\Delta y_t) = 0$, and that the autocovariance function of Δy_t, denoted $c(\tau) = \mathsf{E}(\Delta y_t \Delta y_{t-\tau})$, has nonzero values $c(0) = \sigma_\eta^2 + 2\sigma_\varepsilon^2$, $c(1) = -\sigma_\varepsilon^2$, and $c(\tau) = 0$, $\tau > 1$. Thus, the autocorrelation function, $\varrho(\tau) = c(\tau)/c(0)$, exhibits a cut-off at lag one, with $\varrho(1) = -\sigma_\varepsilon^2/(\sigma_\eta^2 + 2\sigma_\varepsilon^2)$ taking values in $[0, -1/2]$. The ARIMA, or reduced form, representation corresponding to (1) is $\Delta y_t = (1 + \theta L)\xi_t$, $\xi_t \sim \mathsf{NID}(0, \sigma^2)$; equating the autocorrelations at

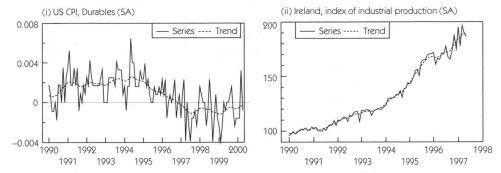

Figure 5.1   (i) U.S. Consumer Price Index for Durables, Seasonally adjusted, monthly growth rates, January 1990–April 2000 (*Source*: Bureau of Labor Statistics). (ii) Index of Industrial Production, Seasonally adjusted, Ireland, January 1990–July 1997 (*Source*: OECD Statistical Compendium). The dotted lines are the smoothed estimates of the trend, see section 5.9 for details.

lag 1 we can express the MA parameter as a function of the signal-to-noise ratio, $q = \sigma_\eta^2 / \sigma_\varepsilon^2$: $\theta = [(q^2 + 4q)^{1/2} - 2 - q]/2$; it can be seen that the MA parameter is constrained to lie in the range $[-1, 0]$.

Consider now the situation depicted in panel (ii) of figure 5.1, concerning the monthly seasonally adjusted index of industrial production for Ireland. The series displays a steady upward movement, suggesting that we have to bring a slope, or a drift, into the model for the trend. A deterministic linear trend model, $\mu_t = \alpha + \beta t$, is likely to be inadequate, but further flexibility can be introduced. The motivation for the extension is as follows: note that such trend would be generated by the recursive formulae $\mu_{t+1} = \mu_t + \beta_t$ and $\beta_{t+1} = \beta_t$, $t = 1, \ldots, T - 1$, respectively, for the level and the slope, with starting values $\mu_0 = \alpha$ and $\beta_0 = \beta$; then, we allow for time variation by introducing random disturbances on the right hand side of the recursive formulae.

The resulting model, known as the *local linear trend model* (LLTM), is written as:

$$y_t \ = \mu_t + \varepsilon_t, \qquad \varepsilon_t \sim \text{NID}(0, \sigma_\varepsilon^2), \quad t = 1, 2, \ldots, T,$$
$$\mu_{t+1} = \mu_t + \beta_t + \eta_t, \quad \eta_t \sim \text{NID}(0, \sigma_\eta^2),$$
$$\beta_{t+1} = \beta_t + \zeta_t, \qquad \zeta_t \sim \text{NID}(0, \sigma_\zeta^2), \tag{5.2}$$

where $\eta_t, \zeta_t, \varepsilon_t$ are independent of one another. For $\sigma_\zeta^2 = 0$ the trend reduces to a random walk with constant drift ($\mu_{t+1} = \mu_t + \beta + \eta_t$), whereas for $\sigma_\eta^2 = 0$ the trend is an integrated random walk ($\Delta^2 \mu_{t+1} = \zeta_{t-1}$). The latter is referred to as a *smoothness prior* specification, as the resulting trend varies very smoothly over time (see Kitagawa and Gersch, 1996, ch. 3, 4, 8, and the references therein); a special case is the Hodrick and Prescott (1997) filter, which fixes $q_\zeta = \sigma_\zeta^2 / \sigma_\varepsilon^2$ to a predetermined value (for example, 1/1600 for quarterly data). Finally, when $\sigma_\eta^2 = \sigma_\zeta^2 = 0$ we fall back on the deterministic linear trend.

The time and frequency domain properties of the LLTM can be ascertained from its stationary representation: $\Delta^2 y_t = \Delta\eta_{t-1} + \zeta_{t-2} + \Delta^2\varepsilon_t$. The autocovariance function of $\Delta^2 y_t$ takes the values $c(0) = 2\sigma_\eta^2 + \sigma_\zeta^2 + 6\sigma_\varepsilon^2$, $c(1) = -\sigma_\eta^2 - 4\sigma_\varepsilon^2$, $c(2) = \sigma_\varepsilon^2$, and $c(\tau) = 0$ for $\tau > 2$. Hence $\varrho(1)$ and $\varrho(2)$ lie respectively in $[-2/3, 0]$ and $[0, 1/6]$, and $\varrho(\tau)$ displays the cut-off at lag 2 that is characteristic of an MA(2) process. Therefore, the reduced form is $y_t \sim ARIMA(0, 2, 2)$, with severe restrictions on the parameter space of the MA parameters.

5.3. Cyclic Models

In economics, the term *business cycle* broadly refers to the recurrent, though not exactly periodic, deviations around the long-term path of the series. A model for the cyclic component should be capable of reproducing commonly acknowledged essential features, such as the presence of strong autocorrelation, determining the recurrence and alternation of phases, and the dampening of the fluctuations, or zero long-run persistence.

A time-series model accounting for these stylized facts can be derived by a stochastic extension of the deterministic cycle model $\psi_t = \alpha \cos \lambda_c t + \alpha^* \sin \lambda_c t$, where λ_c is the angular frequency measured in radians, $\lambda_c \in [0, \pi]$. This defines a perfectly periodic function of time, repeating itself every $\bar{p} = 2\pi/\lambda_c$ time units, where $\bar{p}$ is the period, with constant amplitude $(\alpha^2 + \alpha^{*2})^{1/2}$ and phase $\tan^{-1}(\alpha^*/\alpha)$.

A stochastic cycle can be obtained by letting the coefficients α and α^* follow an AR(1) process with coefficient ρ, $0 \leq \rho \leq 1$, that is responsible for the dampening of the fluctuations: hence, $\alpha_{t+1} = \rho\alpha_t + \tilde{\kappa}_t$, $\alpha_{t+1}^* = \rho\alpha_t^* + \tilde{\kappa}_t^*$, where $\tilde{\kappa}_t$ and $\tilde{\kappa}_t^*$ are mutually independent NID disturbances with zero mean and common variance σ_κ^2.

Equivalently, recognizing that a deterministic cycle can be generated recursively by $\psi_{t+1} = \psi_t \cos \lambda_c + \psi_t^* \sin \lambda_c$ and $\psi_{t+1}^* = -\psi_t \sin \lambda_c + \psi_t^* \cos \lambda_c$, with starting values $\psi_0 = \alpha$ and $\psi_0^* = \alpha^*$, a stochastic cycle is constructed multiplying the right-hand side of these two equations by ρ (*damping factor*), and adding stochastic disturbances in the form of NID sequences, giving:

$$\begin{bmatrix} \psi_{t+1} \\ \psi_{t+1}^* \end{bmatrix} = \rho \begin{bmatrix} \cos \lambda_c & \sin \lambda_c \\ -\sin \lambda_c & \cos \lambda_c \end{bmatrix} \begin{bmatrix} \psi_t \\ \psi_t^* \end{bmatrix} + \begin{bmatrix} \kappa_t \\ \kappa_t^* \end{bmatrix}, \tag{5.3}$$

where again $\kappa_t \sim NID(0, \sigma_\kappa^2)$ and $\kappa_t^* \sim NID(0, \sigma_\kappa^2)$, are mutually independent. The reduced form of (5.3) is the ARMA(2, 1) process:

$$(1 - 2\rho \cos \lambda_c L + \rho^2 L^2)\psi_{t+1} = (1 - \rho \cos \lambda_c L)\kappa_t + \rho \sin \lambda_c L \kappa_t^*;$$

when ρ is strictly less than one the cycle is stationary with $E(\psi_t) = 0$ and $\sigma_\psi^2 = Var(\psi_t) = \sigma_\kappa^2/(1 - \rho^2)$; the autocorrelation at lag τ is $\rho^\tau \cos \lambda_c \tau$. For $\lambda_c \in (0, \pi)$ the roots of the AR polynomial are a pair of complex conjugates with modulus ρ^{-1} and phase λ_c; correspondingly, the spectral density displays a peak at λ_c. When $\lambda_c = 0$, ψ_t collapses to the AR(1) process $\psi_{t+1} = \rho\psi_t + \kappa_t$, whereas in the case $\lambda_c = \pi$, $\psi_{t+1} = -\rho\psi_t + \kappa_t$.

5.4.   SEASONAL MODELS

Seasonal fluctuations account for a major part of the variation of a wide spectrum of economic, social, and environmental phenomena. Hylleberg (1992, p. 4) defines seasonality as "the systematic, although not necessarily regular, intra-year movement caused by the changes of the weather, the calendar, and timing of decisions." A more operational definition is given by Harvey (1989, p. 301) in terms of prediction, as the "part of the series which, when extrapolated, repeats itself over any one-year time period and averages out to zero over such a time period." There are several specifications of a seasonal component, γ_t, satisfying this requirement; nevertheless, the stochastic process for γ_t complying with the above definition is such that that $S(L)\gamma_t \sim MA(q)$ with $q \leq s - 2$, where $S(L) = 1 + L + \ldots + L^{s-1}$ denotes the seasonal summation operator and s the number of seasons in a year (for example, s is equal to 4 and 12 respectively for quarterly and monthly time series).

In the time domain, a fixed seasonal pattern is modeled as $\gamma_t = z_t'\chi$, where $z_t' = [D_{1t}, \ldots, D_{st}]$ is a vector containing the values of s seasonal dummies, D_{jt}, taking value 1 in season j and 0 otherwise, and χ is an $s \times 1$ vector containing the effects associated with the different seasons, which are restricted to sum up to zero in order to enhance identifiability when the level of the series is nonzero. Denoting $i_s = [1, 1, \ldots, 1]'$, an $s \times 1$ vector of ones, the zero sum constraint is expressed as $i_s'\chi = 0$ and ensures that $S(L)\gamma_t = 0$.

A simple way of allowing the seasonal pattern to evolve over time is to let the sum of the seasonal effect be equal to a random disturbance term, that is $S(L)\gamma_t = \omega_t$, $\omega_t \sim \text{NID}(0, \sigma_\omega^2)$; this is referred to as the the *dummy seasonal* model. A richer class of models of stochastic seasonality is derived letting the coefficients χ change over time according to a multivariate random walk:

$$\gamma_t = z_t'\chi_t, \quad \chi_{t+1} = \chi_t + \omega_t, \quad \omega_t \sim \text{NID}(0, \Omega). \tag{5.4}$$

The stochastic counterpart of the zero sum constraint is enforced by $i_s'\Omega = 0_s'$. This implies $i_s'\chi_t = i_s'\chi_{t-1}$, which for $i_s'\chi_0 = 0$ implies in turn that $S(L)\gamma_t$ is a stationary zero mean process. As a matter of fact, by repeated substitution from (5.4) it is possible to show that $S(L)\gamma_t \sim MA(q)$, with $q \leq s - 2$. A special case of (5.4) is the Harrison and Stevens (1976) model, which arises for the specification $\Omega = \sigma_{\omega^*}^2[I_s - (1/s)i_s i_s']$, and is such that $S(L)\gamma_t \sim MA(s - 2)$. As Ω has rank $s - 1$, one of the elements of χ_t is redundant and can be dropped.

In representation (5.4) the disturbances ω_t are season-specific. Proietti (1998) argues that (5.4) can account for seasonal heteroskedasticity in a simple fashion. Moreover, the time-varying periodic cubic spline specification, adopted by Harvey and Koopman (1993) to parsimoniously model daily and weekly seasonality, arises imposing an appropriate reduced rank structure on Ω.

In the frequency domain, a fixed seasonal pattern is modeled by the sum of $[s/2]$ cycles defined at the seasonal frequencies $\lambda_j = 2\pi j/s$, $j = 1, 2, \ldots, [s/2]$, where $[s/2] = s/2$ for s even and $(s - 1)/2$ if s is odd:

$$\gamma_t = \sum_{j=1}^{[s/2]} \gamma_{jt}, \quad \gamma_{jt} = \alpha_j \cos \lambda_j + \alpha_j^* \sin \lambda_j.$$

When s is even the sine term disappears for $j = s/2$, so the number of trigonometric terms is always $s - 1$.

A possible stochastic extension of the trigonometric seasonal model is such that the seasonal effect at time t arises from the combination of $[s/2]$ stochastic cycles formulated as in (5.3), setting $\rho = 1$ to allow for a persistent pattern:

$$\gamma_t = \sum_{j=1}^{[s/2]} \gamma_{jt}, \quad \begin{bmatrix} \gamma_{j,t+1} \\ \gamma_{j,t+1}^* \end{bmatrix} = \begin{bmatrix} \cos \lambda_j & \sin \lambda_j \\ -\sin \lambda_j & \cos \lambda_j \end{bmatrix} \begin{bmatrix} \gamma_{j,t} \\ \gamma_{j,t}^* \end{bmatrix} + \begin{bmatrix} \omega_{j,t} \\ \omega_{j,t}^* \end{bmatrix}. \tag{5.5}$$

For s even, the last component, defined at $\lambda_{s/2} = \pi$, reduces to $\gamma_{\frac{s}{2},t+1} = -\gamma_{\frac{s}{2},t} + \omega_{\frac{s}{2},t}$. The disturbances ω_{jt} and ω_{jt}^* are assumed to be normally and independently distributed with common variance $\sigma_{\omega j}^2$; it is often assumed that the latter is constant across j: $\sigma_{\omega j}^2 = \sigma_{\omega}^2$. In the latter case the trigonometric model can be shown to be equivalent to the Harrison and Stevens model with $\sigma_{\omega^*}^2 = (s/2)\sigma_{\omega}^2$; however, when s is even the equivalence holds if $\sigma_{\omega j}^2 = \sigma_{\omega}^2$, for $j = 1, \ldots, (s-1)/2$, and $\sigma_{\omega_{s/2}}^2 = \sigma_{\omega}^2/2$. The reduced form is $S(L)\gamma_t \sim MA(s-2)$, as can be established by aggregating the $[s/2]$ nonstationary ARMA(2, 1) reduced forms for each γ_{jt}.

A comparison of the various representations of a seasonal component and a discussion of the implications for forecasting are given in Proietti (2000). The model $y_t = \mu_t + \gamma_t + \varepsilon_t$, where μ_t is the local linear trend in (5.2) and γ_t has one of the specifications above, is referred to as the *basic structural model* (BSM). The terminology alludes to the fact that it is successfully fitted to economic time series for which the *airline model*, $\Delta\Delta_s y_t = (1 + \theta L)(1 + \Theta L^s)\xi_t$, with negative MA parameters, is appropriate.

5.5. MULTIVARIATE MODELS

Let us suppose that time-series observations are available on a cross-section of N units and are gathered in the vector $y_t = [y_{1t}, \ldots, y_{it}, \ldots, y_{Nt}]'$. A multivariate structural time-series model for y_t is formulated so that each of the individual time series follows a univariate model, say $y_{it} = \mu_{it} + \psi_{it} + \gamma_{it} + \varepsilon_{it}$, $i = 1, \ldots, N$, and is linked to the other series via the contemporaneous correlation among the disturbances driving the components. This specification is called a *Seemingly Unrelated Time Series Equation* (SUTSE) system; it is tailored for variables that are subject to the same overall environment and are not causally related, although cause and effect relationships can be introduced, for instance, by modeling the short-run dynamics as a stationary vector autoregression.

The most relevant specification issues raised by the multivariate framework are discussed with reference to the multivariate LLM:

$$y_t = \mu_t + \varepsilon_t, \quad t = 1, 2, \dots, T, \quad \varepsilon_t \sim \text{NID}(0, \Sigma_\varepsilon),$$

$$\mu_{t+1} = \mu_t + \eta_t, \qquad\qquad \eta_t \sim \text{NID}(0, \Sigma_\eta), \qquad (5.6)$$

where Σ_ε and Σ_η are $N \times N$ nonnegative definite matrices, and $\text{E}(\varepsilon_t \eta_{t-\tau}) = 0$, $\forall \tau$.

A first special case arises when the covariance matrices of the disturbances are proportional; that is, there exists a scalar q such that $\Sigma_\eta = q\Sigma_\varepsilon$. This restriction is relevant for it leads to a parsimonious model and can be tested as in Fernandez and Harvey (1990); it implies that each component series and any linear combination thereof follow the same time-series process.

Common components arise when the covariance matrices of the relevant disturbances have reduced rank. When rank $(\Sigma_\eta) = K < N$ in (6) we can write $\Sigma_\eta = \Theta D_\eta \Theta'$, where Θ is $N \times K$ with elements $\Theta_{ij} = 0$, $j > i$, $\Theta_{ii} = 1$, and D_η is a diagonal $K \times K$ matrix. The trend component can be then reformulated in terms of a set of K common trends, giving

$$y_t = \Theta \mu_t^\dagger + \mu_\theta + \varepsilon_t, \quad t = 1, 2, \dots, T, \quad \varepsilon_t \sim \text{NID}(0, \Sigma_\varepsilon),$$

$$\mu_{t+1}^\dagger = \mu_t^\dagger + \eta_t^\dagger, \qquad\qquad \eta_t^\dagger \sim \text{NID}(0, D_\eta), \qquad (5.7)$$

where $\mu_\theta = [0_K' \ \bar{\mu}']'$ and $\bar{\mu}$ is an $(N - K) \times 1$ vector. The matrix Θ contains the standardized factor loadings, which can be rotated to enhance interpretation. The important feature of the common trends model is that although each component of y_t is integrated of order 1, $N - K$ linear combinations of y_t are stationary, so the system is cointegrated (Engle and Granger, 1987). In other words, there exists an $(N - K) \times N$ matrix C, with the property $C\Theta = 0$, so that Cy_t is stationary. Further details and extensions to common cycles and common seasonals, along with economic applications, can be found in Harvey and Koopman (1997).

Finally, a *dynamic error component model* is obtained specifying $\Sigma_\varepsilon = \sigma_{\bar{\varepsilon}}^2 ii' + \sigma_{\varepsilon*}^2 I$, $\Sigma_\eta = \sigma_{\bar{\eta}}^2 ii' + \sigma_{\eta*}^2 I$, where i is an $N \times 1$ vector of 1s. Hence, for each component, the correlation between the disturbances in any two units is the same and is accounted for by a time-specific common effect, whereas unit specific effects are mutually independent. Marshall (1992) shows that the model can be transformed to a system of time-series equations consisting of a LLM for the cross-sectional mean, $\bar{y}_t$, and a homogeneous LLM for the $N - 1$ series in deviation form $y_{it} - \bar{y}_t$, $i = 1, \dots, N - 1$.

5.6.   CORRELATED DISTURBANCES

The reader may wonder why the specification of structural models assumes independent disturbances. Actually, this is a restriction which has to be imposed to achieve identifiability; take for instance the LLM (1) and assume $\text{E}(\varepsilon_t \eta_{t-\tau}) = \sigma_{\varepsilon\eta}$ if $\tau = 0$, and zero otherwise; matching the nonzero autocovariances of Δy_t yields a (nonlinear) system of two equations in three unknowns ($\sigma_\varepsilon^2, \sigma_\eta^2, \sigma_{\varepsilon\eta}$) which has infinite solutions. Imposing $\sigma_{\varepsilon\eta} = 0$ gives a unique solution, provided that $c(1)$ is negative. An identifiable model can also be obtained by assuming perfectly correlated disturbances as in Snyder (1985, p. 273), who poses $\eta_t = \alpha \varepsilon_t$.

Thus, structural time-series models usually achieve identification assuming that the disturbances driving the components are independent; this is known to place severe constraints on the ARIMA reduced form parameter space (for instance, in the LLM example above, θ is restricted between -1 and 0, so that only half of the MA parameter range is admissible). It is a matter of debate whether they are overly restrictive and whether they can be meaningfully relaxed assuming correlated disturbances.

Models with correlated components have been considered by Godolphin (1976) with the explicit intention of extending the parameter range yielding decomposable models. Snyder (1985) and Ord, Koehler, and Snyder (1997) propose unobserved components models with only one source of random disturbances, arguing that models with multiple disturbances are unnecessarily complex. Another very popular result, the Beveridge and Nelson (1981) decomposition, is formulated with perfectly correlated disturbances, and is commonly viewed as providing a structural interpretation to *any* ARIMA model (see also section 5.10).

On the contrary, West and Harrison (1997, section 7.3.4) argue against correlated components on the grounds of parsimony in parameterizing a forecasting model, whereas Harvey and Koopman (2000), looking at the implications on the weighting patterns for trend extraction by a local level model, conclude that the scope for such extensions is very limited.

Notice also that the unobserved components have been specified in future form; often (Harvey, 1989; West and Harrison, 1996) the contemporaneous form of the model is used, for example, in the LLM case $y_t = \mu_t^* + \varepsilon_t^*$, $\mu_t^* = \mu_{t-1}^* + \eta_t^*$, with ε_t^* and η_t^* mutually and serially independent. Setting $\mu_t = \mu_{t-1}^*$, we can rewrite the model in future form as $y_t = \mu_t + \varepsilon_t$, $\mu_{t+1} = \mu_t + \eta_t$, where the disturbances $\varepsilon_t = \eta_t^* + \varepsilon_t^*$ and $\eta_t = \eta_t^*$ are now correlated.

5.7. STATISTICAL TREATMENT

The structural time-series models considered in the previous sections are special cases of state-space models (SSM). A SSM consists of a *measurement equation* and a *transition equation*: the former relates the $N \times 1$ vector time series y_t to an $m \times 1$ vector of unobservable components or state vector, α_t:

$$y_t = Z_t \alpha_t + G_t \varepsilon_t, \quad t = 1, 2, \ldots, T, \tag{5.8}$$

where Z_t is an $N \times m$ matrix, G_t is $N \times g$ and ε_t is a $g \times 1$ vector of random disturbances that we assume is $NID(0, I_g)$. The *transition equation* is a dynamic linear model for the states α_t, taking the form of a first order vector autoregression:

$$\alpha_{t+1} = T_t \alpha_t + H_t \varepsilon_t, \tag{5.9}$$

where T_t and H_t are $m \times m$ and $m \times g$ matrices, respectively.

Example 5.7.1: The state-space representation of the LLTM(2) has $\boldsymbol{\alpha}_t = [\mu_t, \beta_t]'$, $\boldsymbol{\varepsilon}_t = [\varepsilon_t/\sigma_\varepsilon, \eta_t/\sigma_\eta, \zeta_t/\sigma_\zeta]'$ (hence $\boldsymbol{\varepsilon}_t$ contains the standardized disturbances), and

$$Z_t = [1 \ \ 0], \quad G_t = [\sigma_\varepsilon \ \ 0 \ \ 0], \quad T_t = \begin{bmatrix} 1 & 1 \\ 0 & 1 \end{bmatrix}, \quad H_t = \begin{bmatrix} 0 & \sigma_\eta & 0 \\ 0 & 0 & \sigma_\zeta \end{bmatrix}.$$

The system matrices, Z_t, G_t, T_t, and H_t, are nonstochastic; that is, they are allowed to vary over time, but in a deterministic fashion, and are functionally related to a set of parameters, $\boldsymbol{\theta}$, which usually will have to be estimated. The SSM is *time invariant* if the system matrices are constant; that is, $Z_t = Z$, $G_t = G$, $T_t = T$ and $H_t = H$, as occurs in example 5.7.1. Moreover, structural time-series models are usually specified in such a way that the measurement and transition equation disturbances are independent, that is $H_t G_t' = 0$; nevertheless, in the derivation of the Kalman filter and smoother we will use the general representation with $H_t G_t'$ not necessarily equal to a zero matrix, since this representation encompasses other structural models with correlated disturbaces (see section 5.6).

The SSM is completed by the specification of initial conditions concerning the distribution of $\boldsymbol{\alpha}_1$: this turns out to be a relevant issue when nonstationary components are present (see section 5.7.2). When the system is time-invariant and $\boldsymbol{\alpha}_t$ is stationary (an instance is provided by the cycle plus irregular model, $y_t = \psi_t + \varepsilon_t$), and the stochastic process governing $\boldsymbol{\alpha}_t$ started in the indefinite past, then $E(\boldsymbol{\alpha}_1) = 0$ and $Var(\boldsymbol{\alpha}_1) = P$, satisfying the matrix equation $P = TPT' + HH'$. Hence, the initial conditions are provided by the unconditional mean and covariance matrix of the state vector. A time-invariant SSM is stationary if the eigenvalues of the transition matrix, T, are inside the unit circle.

5.7.1. The Kalman filter and the prediction error decomposition

The Kalman filter (KF) is a fundamental algorithm for the statistical treatment of a SSM. Under the Gaussian assumption it produces the minimum mean square estimator (MMSE) of the state vector along with its mean square error (MSE) matrix, conditional on past information; this is used to build the one-step-ahead predictor of y_t and its mean square error matrix. Due to the independence of the one-step-ahead prediction errors, the likelihood can be evaluated via the prediction error decomposition.

Denoting $Y_t = \{y_1, \ldots, y_t\}$ the information set available at time t, $\tilde{\boldsymbol{\alpha}}_{t|t-1} = E(\boldsymbol{\alpha}_t | Y_{t-1})$ and $P_{t|t-1} = E[(\boldsymbol{\alpha}_t - \tilde{\boldsymbol{\alpha}}_{t|t-1})(\boldsymbol{\alpha}_t - \tilde{\boldsymbol{\alpha}}_{t|t-1})' | Y_{t-1}]$, the KF for a standard state-space model with initial conditions $\boldsymbol{\alpha}_1 \sim N(\tilde{\boldsymbol{\alpha}}_{1|0}, P_{1|0})$, where $\tilde{\boldsymbol{\alpha}}_{1|0}$ and $P_{1|0}$ are known and finite, consists of the following recursive formulae for $t = 1, \ldots, T$:

$$v_t = y_t - Z_t\tilde{\boldsymbol{\alpha}}_{t|t-1}, \quad F_t = Z_t P_{t|t-1} Z_t' + G_t G_t',$$

$$K_t = (T_t P_{t|t-1} Z_t' + H_t G_t')F_t^{-1},$$

$$\tilde{\boldsymbol{\alpha}}_{t+1|t} = T_t\tilde{\boldsymbol{\alpha}}_{t|t-1} + K_t v_t, \quad P_{t+1|t} = T_t P_{t|t-1} T_t' + H_t H_t' - K_t F_t K_t'. \tag{5.10}$$

As $\tilde{y}_{t|t-1} = E(y_t | Y_{t-1}) = Z_t \tilde{\alpha}_{t|t-1}$, v_t represent the one-step-ahead prediction error, also known as the *innovation* at time t because it represents the part of y_t that cannot be predicted from the past, and F_t is its variance matrix.

A proof of the KF is found in Anderson and Moore (1979) and in the appendix. When the Gaussianity assumption is removed the KF still yields the minimum mean square linear estimator (MMSLE) of the state vector.

For a time-invariant model, the recursions for F_t, K_t and $P_{t+1|t}$ become redundant when the KF has reached a steady state, which occurs if, for some t, $P_{t|t-1} = P$. The conditions under which $\lim_{t\to\infty} P_{t|t-1} = P$ are given in Harvey (1989, sections 3.3.3 and 3.3.4), and, when they are met, the matrix P is the solution of the Riccati equation

$$P = TPT' + HH' - KFK', \tag{5.11}$$

with $K = (TPZ' + HG')F^{-1}$ and $F = ZPZ' + GG'$.

The updated estimates of the state vector, $\tilde{\alpha}_{t|t} = E(\alpha_t | Y_t)$, and their MSE matrix are:

$$\tilde{\alpha}_{t|t} = \tilde{\alpha}_{t|t-1} + P_{t|t-1}Z_t'F_t^{-1}v_t, \quad P_{t|t} = P_{t|t-1} - P_{t|t-1}Z_t'F_t^{-1}Z_tP_{t|t-1}. \tag{5.12}$$

Also, when $H_tG_t' = 0$, the KF recursions for the states can be broken up into an updating step, (5.12), followed by a prediction step:

$$\tilde{\alpha}_{t+1|t} = T_t\tilde{\alpha}_{t|t}, \quad P_{t+1|t} = T_tP_{t|t}T_t' + H_tH_t'. \tag{5.13}$$

As the KF filter provides $y_t | Y_{t-1} \sim NID(\tilde{y}_{t|t-1}, F_t)$, it enables the likelihood function to be written in prediction error decomposition form. Apart from a constant term, the log-likelihood of the observations is computed as follows:

$$L(Y_T; \theta) = \sum_{t=1}^{T} L(y_t | Y_{t-1}; \theta) = -\frac{1}{2}\left(\sum_{t=1}^{T} \ln|F_t| + \sum_{t=1}^{T} v_t'F_t^{-1}v_t\right). \tag{5.14}$$

The likelihood function can be maximized numerically by a quasi-Newton optimization routine. Analytic expressions for the score vector, with respect to the parameters in G_t and H_t (Koopman and Shepard, 1992), and for the information matrix (Harvey, 1989, pp. 140–3) are available. The dimension of the problem can be reduced by concentrating one of the variance parameters out of the likelihood function: if we write $\theta = [\theta^{*\prime}, \sigma^2]'$, and $G_t = \sigma G_t^*$, $H_t = \sigma H_t^*$, $\alpha_1 \sim N(\tilde{\alpha}_{1|0}, \sigma^2 P_{1|0})$ the recursions (5.10), run with G_t and H_t replaced by G_t^* and H_t^*, yield $y_t | Y_{t-1} \sim NID(\tilde{y}_{t|t-1}, \sigma^2 F_t)$. Maximizing the corresponding likelihood with respect to σ^2 gives $\hat{\sigma}^2 = \Sigma v_t'F_t^{-1}v_t/(NT)$ and the concentrated likelihood $L_{\sigma^2}(Y_T; \theta^*)$ $= -0.5[NT(\ln\hat{\sigma}^2 + 1) + \Sigma \ln|F_t|]$.

5.7.2. Initial conditions and nonstationary models[1]

When there are d nonstationary elements in the state vector, we write in general $\alpha_1 = a + B\eta + D\delta$, where a and B are, respectively, an $m \times 1$ known vector and an $m \times (m - d)$ known matrix that may depend on θ, and D is a $m \times d$ selection matrix assigning the appropriate elements of δ to the states. The vectors $\eta \sim N(0, I_N)$ and δ are used to initialize the stationary and nonstationary elements of α_t and are mutually independent and independent of ε_t, $\forall t$. Two assumptions can be made: (i) δ is considered as a fixed, but unknown, vector; (ii) δ is a diffuse random vector, in other words it has an improper distribution with a mean of zero and an arbitrarily large variance matrix: $\delta \sim N(0, \kappa I_d)$, $\kappa \to \infty$. The first assumption is suitable if it is deemed that the transition process (5.9) governing the states has started at time $t = 1$; the second if the process has started in the remote past. For instance, if one of the state components is a random walk, as for LLM model, then its starting value is the cumulative sum of infinite NID disturbances, so its variance will go to infinity. The use of a diffuse prior amounts to leaving the distribution of initial conditions unspecified.

Example 5.7.2: The model $y_t = \mu_t + \gamma_t + \psi_t + \varepsilon_t$, for quarterly data, with the components specified as in (5.2), (5.3) and (5.5), has $\alpha_t = [\mu_t, \beta_t, \gamma_{1t}, \gamma_{1t}^*, \gamma_{2t}, \psi_t, \psi_t^*]'$, $Z = [1, 0, 1, 0, 1, 1, 0]$, $G = [\sigma_\varepsilon, 0, 0, 0, 0]$, $T = \mathrm{diag}\,(T_\mu, T_\gamma, T_\psi)$, where

$$T_\mu = \begin{bmatrix} 1 & 1 \\ 0 & 1 \end{bmatrix}, \quad T_\gamma = \begin{bmatrix} 0 & 1 & 0 \\ -1 & 0 & 0 \\ 0 & 0 & -1 \end{bmatrix}, \quad T_\psi = \rho \begin{bmatrix} \cos \lambda & \sin \lambda \\ -\sin \lambda & \cos \lambda \end{bmatrix},$$

$H = [0 \; \tilde{H}]$, $\tilde{H} = \mathrm{diag}\,(\sigma_\eta, \sigma_\zeta, \sigma_\omega, \sigma_\omega, \sigma_\omega, \sigma_\kappa, \sigma_\kappa)$, and, as regards initial conditions,

$$a = 0, \quad B = \begin{bmatrix} 0 \\ \sigma_\psi I_2 \end{bmatrix}, \quad D = \begin{bmatrix} I_5 \\ 0 \end{bmatrix}.$$

The case when δ is fixed and unknown has been considered by Rosenberg (1973), who shows that it can be concentrated out of the likelihood function. As a matter of fact, the innovations and the conditional mean of the state vector delivered by the the KF with initial conditions $\tilde{\alpha}_{1|0} = a + D\delta$ and $P_{1|0} = BB'$, denoted KF(δ), can be written, respectively, as $v_t = v_t^* - V_t\delta$ and $\tilde{\alpha}_{t+1|t} = \tilde{\alpha}_{t+1|t}^* - A_{t+1|t}\delta$. The starred quantities, v_t^* and $\tilde{\alpha}_{t+1|t}^*$, are produced by the KF run with $\delta = 0$, that is with initial conditions $\tilde{\alpha}_{1|0}^* = a$ and $P_{1|0}^* = BB'$; we denote this filter by KF(0). Note that it produces the matrices F_t^* and $P_{t+1|t}^*$, $t = 1, \ldots T$, which, being invariant to δ, equal the corresponding matrices F_t and $P_{t+1|t}$ produced by KF(δ). The matrices V_t and $A_{t+1|t}$ are generated by the following recursions, that are run in parallel to KF(0):

$$V_t = -Z_t A_{t|t-1}, \quad A_{t+1|t} = T_t A_{t|t-1} + K_t V_t, \quad t = 1, \ldots, T, \qquad (5.15)$$

with initial value $A_{1|0} = -D$. Then, replacing $v_t = v_t^* - V_t\delta$ and $F_t = F_t^*$ into (5.14), yields:

$$L(Y_T;\, \theta,\, \delta) = -\frac{1}{2}\left(\sum_{t=1}^{T} \ln |F_t^*| + \sum_{t=1}^{T} v_t^{*\prime} F_t^{*-1} v_t^* - 2\delta' s_T + \delta' S_T \delta\right), \qquad (5.16)$$

where $s_T = \sum_1^T V_t' F_t^{*-1} v_t^*$ and $S_T = \sum_1^T V_t' F_t^{*-1} V_t$. Hence, the maximum likelihood estimate of δ is $\hat{\delta} = S_T^{-1} s_T$ and the concentrated likelihood is

$$L_\delta(Y_T;\, \theta) = -0.5\left(\sum_{t=1}^{T} \ln |F_t^*| + \sum_{t=1}^{T} v_t^{*\prime} F_t^{*-1} v_t^* - s_T' S_T^{-1} s_T\right), \qquad (5.17)$$

When δ is diffuse, $\delta \sim N(0,\, \kappa I_d)$, $\kappa \to \infty$, the definition of the likelihood needs to be amended; in particular, de Jong (1991) shows that only $L(Y_T;\, \theta,\, \delta) + \frac{d}{2}\ln \kappa$ is a proper likelihood and that its limiting expression for $\kappa \to \infty$ is

$$L_\infty(Y_T;\, \theta) = -\frac{1}{2}\left(\sum \ln |F_t^*| - \ln |S_T| + \sum v_t^{*\prime} F_t^{*-1} v_t^* - s_T' S_T^{-1} s_T\right). \qquad (5.18)$$

Also, the limiting expressions for the mean and variance of δ, conditional on Y_t, are $S_t^{-1} s_t$ and S_t^{-1}, $s_t = \sum_{i=1}^{t} V_i' F_i^{*-1} v_i^*$ and $S_t = \sum_{i=1}^{t} V_i' F_i^{*-1} V_i$, provided that the latter matrix is invertible. All the relevant quantities are available by the run of KF(0), augmented by the recursions (5.15). Furthermore, de Jong shows that the limiting expressions for the innovations, the one-step-ahead prediction of the state vector and the corresponding covariance matrices are

$$v_t = v_t^* - V_t S_{t-1}^{-1} s_{t-1}, \qquad F_t = F_t^* + V_t S_{t-1}^{-1} V_t',$$

$$\tilde{\alpha}_{t|t-1} = \tilde{\alpha}_{t|t-1}^* - A_{t|t-1} S_{t-1}^{-1} s_{t-1}, \qquad P_{t|t-1} = P_{t|t-1}^* + A_{t|t-1} S_{t-1}^{-1} A_{t|t-1}'. \qquad (5.19)$$

Usually, the augmented recursions can be dropped after processing d observations provided that S_d is invertible, in which case $E(\delta|Y_d) = S_d^{-1} s_d$, and a collapse can be made to the standard KF.

The notion of a diffuse likelihood is close to that of a marginal likelihood, being based on a rank $T - d$ linear transformation of the series that eliminates dependence on δ. Comparing (5.18) with (5.17), it turns out that $L_\infty(Y_T;\, \theta)$ differs from $L_\delta(Y_T;\, \theta)$ because of the presence of the term $\ln |S_T|$, which could bear relevant effects on the estimation of θ, especially when the data generating process is close to nonstationarity and noninvertibility. In this situation, as shown by Tunnicliffe-Wilson (1986) and Shephard and Harvey (1990), the latter referring to the estimation of the signal-to-noise ratio for the LLM when the true value is close to zero, the estimators based on (5.18) exhibit better small sample properties.

Recently, Koopman (1997) has provided an exact analytic solution to the initialisation problem that is computationally more efficient than augmenting the KF by the matrix recursions (5.15). His approach entails the derivation of a modified KF, hinging on the fundamental idea, adopted by Ansley and Kohn (1985, 1989), of expressing the KF quantities explicitly in terms of κ and letting $\kappa \to \infty$ to get the exact solution.

A simple illustration is provided with reference to the LLM (5.1), whose state-space space representation has $\alpha_t = \mu_t$, $\boldsymbol{\varepsilon}_t = [\varepsilon_t/\sigma_\varepsilon, \eta_t/\sigma_\eta]'$, $Z = T = 1$, $G = [\sigma_\varepsilon \ 0]$, $H = [0 \ \sigma_\eta]$, and initial conditions $\tilde{\mu}_{1|0} = 0$, $P_{1|0} = \kappa$ (that is, $a = 0$, $B = 0$, and $D = 1$). The run of the KF at time $t = 1$ gives: $v_1 = y_1$, $F_1 = \kappa + \sigma_\varepsilon^2$, $K_1 = \kappa/(\kappa + \sigma_\varepsilon^2)$, $\tilde{\mu}_{2|1} = y_1\kappa/(\kappa + \sigma_\varepsilon^2)$ and $P_{2|1} = \sigma_\varepsilon^2\kappa/(\kappa + \sigma_\varepsilon^2) + \sigma_\eta^2$. Letting $\kappa \to \infty$, we get the limiting expressions $K_1 = 1$, $\tilde{\mu}_{2|1} = y_1$ and $P_{2|1} = \sigma_\varepsilon^2 + \sigma_\eta^2$. Note that $P_{2|1}$ does not depend on κ and $v_2 = y_2 - y_1$ has a proper distribution, $v_2 \sim N(0, F_2)$, with $F_2 = \sigma_\eta^2 + 2\sigma_\varepsilon^2$. In general, the innovations at subsequent times can be written as a linear combination of past and current changes of the series, and therefore have a proper distribution.

Suppressing dependence on $\boldsymbol{\theta} = [\sigma_\varepsilon^2, \sigma_\eta^2]'$, the diffuse log-likelihood is $L(Y_T) + 0.5 \ln \kappa = L(v_1) + 0.5 \ln \kappa + \sum_{t=2}^{T} L(v_t)$, but $L(v_1) + 0.5 \ln \kappa = -0.5 \ln (\kappa/(\kappa + \sigma_\varepsilon^2)) - 0.5y_1^2/(\kappa + \sigma_\varepsilon^2)$ vanishes as $\kappa \to \infty$. Hence the usual KF can be started at $t = 2$ with $\tilde{\mu}_{2|1}$ and $P_{2|1}$ as given. The log-likelihood is computed as in (5.14) with the summation starting at $t = 2$. These calculations confirm the fact that the diffuse likelihood is based on a rank $T - 1$ linear transformation of the series that makes it invariant to δ.

In closing this section, we hint that a simple expedient to obtain an approximation to the diffuse likelihood is to run the standard KF with κ replaced by a large number, such as 10^7. Although this solution is practical, it is theoretically unsatisfactory and prone to numerical inaccuracies.

5.8. EXPLANATORY VARIABLES

Explanatory variables can be brought into the model so as to capture exogenous effects and various types of interventions. If we let X_t and W_t denote fixed and known matrices of dimension $N \times k$ and $m \times k$, respectively, the state-space model is written

$$y_t = Z_t\alpha_t + X_t\boldsymbol{\beta} + G_t\boldsymbol{\varepsilon}_t, \quad \alpha_{t+1} = T_t\alpha_t + W_t\boldsymbol{\beta} + H_t\boldsymbol{\varepsilon}_t. \tag{5.20}$$

When the SSM is stationary, $\boldsymbol{\beta}$ can be estimated by generalized least squares, which amounts to apply the same KF to y_t and each of the explanatory variables in the columns of X_t, and perform a weighted least squares regression (with weights provided by F_t^{-1}); see Harvey (1989, pp. 130–3) for details.

When the SSM is nonstationary (see section 5.7.2), the vector $\boldsymbol{\beta}$ can be incorporated in the vector $\boldsymbol{\delta}$ that is redefined as the $d + k$ vector $\boldsymbol{\delta} = [\boldsymbol{\delta}_\alpha', \boldsymbol{\beta}']'$, with $\boldsymbol{\delta}_\alpha$ being associated to the nonstationary elements in the state vector. The matrix D in this context is the $m \times (k + d)$ matrix $[D_\alpha, 0]$ where the first block is associated with $\boldsymbol{\delta}_\alpha$. The treatment under fixed and diffuse assumption is the same as in the previous subsection, with the matrix recursions (5.15) replaced by

$$V_t = [0, \ X_t] - Z_t A_{t|t-1}, \quad A_{t+1|t} = T_t A_{t|t-1} - [0, \ W_t] + K_t V_t$$

and initialized with $A_{1|0} = -D$.

An alternative equivalent approach consists of inserting $\boldsymbol{\beta}$ in the state vector and redefining the SSM accordingly:

$$y_t = Z_t^\dagger \boldsymbol{\alpha}_t^\dagger + G_t \boldsymbol{\varepsilon}_t, \quad \boldsymbol{\alpha}_{t+1}^\dagger = T_t^\dagger \boldsymbol{\alpha}_t^\dagger + H_t^\dagger \boldsymbol{\varepsilon}_t,$$

where

$$\boldsymbol{\alpha}_t^\dagger = \begin{bmatrix} \boldsymbol{\alpha}_t \\ \boldsymbol{\beta}_t \end{bmatrix}, \quad Z_t^\dagger = [Z_t \quad X_t], \quad T_t^\dagger = \begin{bmatrix} T_t & W_t \\ 0 & I_k \end{bmatrix}, \quad H_t^\dagger = \begin{bmatrix} H_t \\ 0 \end{bmatrix}.$$

5.9.   SMOOTHING

Once the parameters of a structural model have been estimated, interest lies on estimation of the components based on the full sample of observations, Y_T. This operation is referred to as *smoothing* (see Anderson and Moore, 1979, ch. 7, for a comprehensive account of the classic algorithms). The time-series plot of the smoothed components against time is also a valuable diagnostic tool to check if the components extracted provide a suitable representation of the stylized facts concerning the series.

In the Gaussian case smoothing provides the MMSE of $\boldsymbol{\alpha}_t$ using Y_T, $\tilde{a}_{t|T} = \mathsf{E}(\boldsymbol{\alpha}_t|Y_T)$, along with its MSE matrix $P_{t|T} = \mathsf{E}[(\boldsymbol{\alpha}_t - \tilde{a}_{t|T})(\boldsymbol{\alpha}_t - \tilde{a}_{t|T})' | Y_T]$. It can be performed efficiently by the algorithm proposed by de Jong (1989), consisting of the following backwards recursions starting at $t = T$, with initial values $r_T = 0$ and $N_T = 0$:

$$\tilde{\boldsymbol{\alpha}}_{t|T} = \tilde{\boldsymbol{\alpha}}_{t|t-1} + P_{t|t-1} r_{t-1}, \quad P_{t|T} = P_{t|t-1} - P_{t|t-1} N_{t-1} P_{t|t-1},$$
$$r_{t-1} = Z_t' F_t^{-1} v_t + L_t' r_t, \quad N_{t-1} = Z_t' F_t^{-1} Z_t + L_t' N_t L_t, \tag{5.21}$$

where $L_t = T_t - K_t Z_t$. A preliminary forward KF pass is required to store the quantities $\tilde{\boldsymbol{\alpha}}_{t|t-1}, P_{t|t-1}, v_t, F_t$, and K_t. The proof of (5.21) is found in de Jong (1989), who also deals with the modifications under diffuse initial conditions. These involve storage of V_t (5.15) and extra matrix recursions. Alternatively, using the exact initial KF of Koopman (1997), (5.21) still applies for $t = T, \ldots, d + 1$ and a straightforward adjustment can be made for the initial stretch $t = d, \ldots, 1$. When Gaussianity does not hold, the smoother still delivers the MMSLE of $\boldsymbol{\alpha}_t$.

The estimation of the disturbances $\boldsymbol{\varepsilon}_t$ associated with the the various components in a SSM, referred to as *disturbance smoothing*, is built upon the *smoothing errors* (de Jong, 1988) $u_t = F_t^{-1} v_t - K_t' r_t$, with variance $D_t = F_t^{-1} + K_t' N_t K_t$. Koopman (1992) shows that $\tilde{\boldsymbol{\varepsilon}}_{t|T} = \mathsf{E}(\boldsymbol{\varepsilon}_t | Y_t) = G_t' u_t + H_t' r_t$ and $\mathsf{Var}(\tilde{\boldsymbol{\varepsilon}}_{t|T}) = G_t' D_t G_t + H_t' N_t H_t$. The standardized smoothed estimates of the disturbances are known as *auxiliary residuals*. When $H_t G_t' = 0$, the irregular auxiliary residual is $G_t G_t' u_t$, standardized by the square root of the diagonal elements in $G_t G_t' D_t G_t G_t'$, whereas the auxiliary residuals associated with the unobserved components in α_t are the elements of $H_t H_t' r_t$, scaled by the square root of the diagonal elements of $H_t H_t' N_t H_t H_t'$. They provide test statistics for outliers and structural change in the state components (Harvey and Koopman, 1992; de Jong and Penzer, 1998). Unlike the innovations, the auxiliary residuals are serially correlated; Harvey and Koopman (1992) derive their autocorrelation structure and show how they can be employed to form appropriate tests of normality.

5.10. FORECASTING

For a SSM without regression effects, the update of the KF at time t produces $\tilde{\alpha}_{t+1|t}$ and $P_{t+1|t}$, which are used to yield the one-step-ahead forecast $\tilde{y}_{t+1|t} = Z_{t+1}\tilde{\alpha}_{t+1|t}$, along with its MSE matrix $F_{t+1} = Z_{t+1}P_{t+1|t}Z_{t+1}' + G_{t+1}G_{t+1}'$.

For multi-step prediction, taking the expectation of both sides of the measurement equation (5.8) conditional on Y_t, gives $\tilde{y}_{t+l|t} = Z_{t+l}\tilde{\alpha}_{t+l|t}$; moreover, $\mathsf{MSE}(\tilde{y}_{t+l|t})$ $= F_{t+l|t} = Z_{t+l}P_{t+l|t}Z_{t+l}' + G_{t+l}G_{t+l}'$, where the l-step-ahead forecast of the state vector, $\tilde{\alpha}_{t+l|t} = \mathsf{E}(\alpha_{t+l}|Y_t)$, and its MSE, $P_{t+l|t} = \mathsf{E}[(\alpha_{t+l} - \tilde{\alpha}_{t+l|t})(\alpha_{t+l} - \tilde{\alpha}_{t+l|t})' | Y_t]$, are built up recursively by the chain rule:

$$\tilde{\alpha}_{t+l|t} = T_{t+l-1}\tilde{\alpha}_{t+l-1|t}, \quad P_{t+l|t} = T_{t+l-1}P_{t+l-1|t}T_{t+l-1}' + H_{t+l-1}H_{t+l-1}'.$$

These expressions are initialized by $\tilde{\alpha}_{t+1|t}$ and $P_{t+1|t}$ delivered by the KF at time t. Two things should be noticed: first, multi-step-ahead prediction errors are correlated and, second, the MSE matrices do not take into account the uncertainty arising from estimation of the parameters in θ. When regression and diffuse initial effects are present, $\tilde{y}_{t+l|t} = Z_{t+l}\tilde{\alpha}_{t+l|t} + X_{t+l}\hat{\beta}$ and $\tilde{\alpha}_{t+l|t} = T_{t+l-1}\tilde{\alpha}_{t+l-1|t} + W_{t+l-1}\hat{\beta}$ where $\hat{\beta} = \mathsf{E}(\beta|Y_t) = S_t^{-1}s_t$ and the initialization for $\tilde{\alpha}_{t+l|t}$ and $P_{t+l|t}$ is provided by the second row of (5.19). In such cases the MSE matrices will reflect the uncertainty associated with the regression and the initial diffuse effects, the same holding when β is incorporated into the state vector.

Writing $\tilde{y}_{t+l|t} = Z_{t+l}T_{t+l,t+1}\tilde{\alpha}_{t+1|t}$, where $T_{j,s} = T_{j-1}T_{j-2}\ldots T_s$ for $j > s$ and $T_{j,s} = I$ for $j = s$, the forecasts can be expressed as a weighted linear combination of past and current innovations:

$$\tilde{y}_{t+l|t} = Z_{t+l}T_{t+l,t+1}\sum_{j=0}^{t-1}[T_{t+1,t+1-j}K_{t-j}v_{t-j}].$$

Also, writing $\tilde{\alpha}_{t+1|t} = L_t\tilde{\alpha}_{t|t-1} + K_t y_t$, where $L_t = T_t - K_t Z_t$, repeated substitution allows the forecast function to be written as a weighted average of past and current observations:

$$\tilde{y}_{t+l|t} = Z_{t+l}T_{t+l,t+1}\sum_{j=0}^{t-1}[L_{t+1,t+1-j}K_{t-j}y_{t-j}],$$

where we have set $L_{j,s} = L_{j-1}L_{j-2}\ldots L_s$ for $j > s$ and $L_{j,s} = I$ for $j = s$. Once new information, y_{t+1} becomes available the forecast of y_{t+l} can be updated by the formula $\tilde{y}_{t+l|t+1} = \tilde{y}_{t+l|t} + Z_{t+l}T_{t+l,t+2}K_{t+1}v_{t+1}$, which stresses that the forecast revision depends on the innovation at time $t + 1$.

Example 5.10.1: The forecast function of the LLM (5.1) is a horizontal straight line, being given by $\tilde{y}_{t+l|t} = \tilde{\mu}_{t+1|t}$, $l = 1, 2, \ldots$, where $\tilde{\mu}_{t+1|t} = \tilde{\mu}_{t|t-1} + K_t v_t$; moreover, $\text{MSE}(\tilde{y}_{t+l|t}) = P_{t+1|t} + (l - 1)\sigma_\eta^2 + \sigma_\varepsilon^2$. When the KF has reached a steady state, $K_t = K = P/(P + \sigma_\varepsilon^2)$ so that the previous forecast is revised by a fraction of the one-step-ahead forecast error. This fraction measures the *persistence* of the innovations and is always between 0 and 1. The constant P can be obtained as the only admissible solution of (5.11): $P = \sigma_\varepsilon^2(q + \sqrt{q^2 + 4q})/2$, where $q = \sigma_\eta^2/\sigma_\varepsilon^2$ is the signal-to-noise ratio. Furthermore, the forecasts are generated as an *exponentially weighted moving average* of the available observations, since $\tilde{y}_{t+l|t} = Ky_t + (1 - K)Ky_{t-1} + (1 - K)^2Ky_{t-2} + \ldots + (1 - K)^jKy_{t-j} + \ldots$. The discounting of past observations varies with q: the larger q is, the greater the weight placed on the most recent observations.

For a time-invariant model with uncorrelated measurement and transition disturbances ($HG' = 0$), it is also useful to write the multi-step forecasts in terms of $\tilde{\alpha}_{t|t}$, as $\tilde{y}_{t+l|t} = ZT^l\tilde{\alpha}_{t|t}$. This formulation can be employed to evaluate the shape of the forecast function: for instance, for the structural model $y_t = \mu_t + \psi_t + \gamma_t + \varepsilon_t$, with μ_t as in (2) and trigonometric seasonality,

$$\tilde{y}_{t+l|t} = \tilde{\mu}_{t|t} + l\tilde{\beta}_{t|t} + \rho^l[\tilde{\psi}_{t|t}\cos(l\lambda_c) + \tilde{\psi}_{t|t}^*\sin(l\lambda_c)]$$

$$+ \sum_{j=1}^{[s/2]}[\tilde{\gamma}_{t|t}\cos(l\lambda_j) + \tilde{\gamma}_{t|t}^*\sin(l\lambda_j)];$$

it should be noted that the trend forecasts are linear in the forecast horizon, l, with intercept and slope that depend on the forecast origin, the cycle, and the seasonal contribution via sine and cosine waves, the former vanishing as $l \to \infty$. Moreover, writing $\tilde{\alpha}_{t|t} = T\tilde{\alpha}_{t-1|t-1} + P_{t|t-1}Z'F_t^{-1}v_t$, we can view forecasting with structural time-series models as an "error learning" process or generalized *exponential smoothing*. The weights attached to the observations by the components can be obtained recursively from $\tilde{\alpha}_{t|t} = (I - P_{t|t-1}Z'F_t^{-1}Z)T\tilde{\alpha}_{t-1|t-1} + P_{t|t-1}Z'F_t^{-1}y_t$.

Example 5.10.2: For the LLTM of example 5.7.1, the forecast function is $\tilde{y}_{t+l|t} = \tilde{\mu}_{t|t} + l\tilde{\beta}_{t|t}$; the steady state recursions for $\tilde{\mu}_{t|t}$ and $\tilde{\beta}_{t|t}$ are equivalent to those of the Holt–Winters' forecasting technique:

$$\tilde{\mu}_{t|t} = \tilde{\mu}_{t-1|t-1} + \tilde{\beta}_{t-1|t-1} + \lambda_0 v_t,$$

$$\tilde{\beta}_{t|t} = \qquad + \tilde{\beta}_{t-1|t-1} + \lambda_0\lambda_1 v_t,$$

with $\lambda_0 = p_{11}/(p_{11} + \sigma_\varepsilon^2)$ and $\lambda_1 = p_{12}/p_{11}$, where $P = \{p_{ij}\}$ satisfies (5.11). The smoothing constants λ_0 and λ_1, both in the range (0, 1), as $\sigma_\eta^2 \geq 0$ implies $0 < p_{12} < p_{11}$, are functionally related to the signal-to-noise ratios $q_\eta = \sigma_\eta^2/\sigma_\varepsilon^2$ and $q_\zeta = \sigma_\zeta^2/\sigma_\varepsilon^2$ (see Harvey, 1989, pp. 175–7). The forecast MSE is a quadratic function of the forecast horizon: $\text{MSE}(\tilde{y}_{t+l|t}) = p_{11} + 2(l-1)p_{12} + (l-1)^2 p_{22} + (l-1)\sigma_\eta^2 + l(l-1)\sigma_\zeta^2/2 + \sigma_\varepsilon^2$. The steady state weights attributed to the observations can be derived from replacing $PZ'F^{-1} = [\lambda_0 \ \lambda_0\lambda_1]'$ in $\tilde{\alpha}_{t|t} = [I - (I - PZ'F^{-1}Z)TL]^{-1}PZ'F^{-1}y_t$. This gives $\tilde{\mu}_{t|t} = \theta(L)^{-1}\lambda_0[1 - (1 - \lambda_1)L]y_t$ and $\tilde{\beta}_{t|t} = \theta(L)^{-1}\lambda_0\lambda_1\Delta y_t$, where $\theta(L) = 1 - [2 - \lambda_0(1 + \lambda_1)]L + (1 - \lambda_0)L^2$. Note that the weights are less than 1 in modulus and sum up to 1 and to 0 respectively for the level and the slope.

In the ARIMA framework the forecast function can be decomposed into components associated with the roots of the autoregressive polynomial (Box et al., 1994, ch. 5). It would appear that for *any* ARIMA model a structural interpretation can be provided (that is, in terms of trends, cycles, and so forth), but this is unwarranted. This point can be illustrated with respect to the ARIMA(1, 1, 1) model $(1 - \rho L)\Delta y_t = (1 + \theta L)\xi_t$, with $\rho, \theta \in (-1, 1)$ and $\xi_t \sim \text{NID}(0, \sigma^2)$: the forecast function can be written $y_{t+l|t} = m_t + \rho^l c_t$, where the updating equations for the components are:

$$m_t = m_{t-1} + [(1 + \theta)/(1 - \rho)]\xi_t, \quad c_t = \rho c_{t-1} - [(\rho + \theta)/(1 - \rho)]\xi_t. \quad (5.22)$$

The sequence $\{m_t, c_t\}$ is also known as the Beveridge and Nelson (1981) decomposition of y_t into a permanent and a transitory component, and the constant $[(1 + \theta)/(1 - \rho)]$ is referred to as persistence, since it represents the scalar multiple of the innovation determining the amount of revision in the long-run forecast of the series.

It is easily shown that the trend is related to the observations via $m_t = [(1 + \theta)/(1 - \rho)](1 - \rho L)(1 + \theta L)^{-1}y_t$, so that the weights attributed to y_{t-j} are geometrically decreasing from time $t - 1$ on and sum up to one. However, they can be greater than 1 if persistence is greater than 1. For instance, when $\theta = 0.8$, $\rho = 0.5$, the weights attributed to y_{t-j}, $j = 0, 1, 2, 3$, are 3.60, −4.68, 3.74, −3.00, respectively. In this situation the trend is, loosely speaking, more volatile than the series itself, since the innovations are not discounted, but their effect is amplified (in the example above by a factor of 3.60), and its time-series plot will have a very uneven appearance. It is questionable whether this can be called a trend.

The structural time-series model with ARIMA(1, 1, 1) reduced form is the trend plus AR(1) model $y_t = \mu_t + \psi_t$, $\mu_{t+1} = \mu_t + \eta_t$, $\psi_{t+1} = \rho\psi_t + \kappa_t$, with independent disturbances $\eta_t \sim \text{NID}(0, \sigma_\eta^2)$ and $\kappa_t \sim \text{NID}(0, \sigma_\kappa^2)$, and is such that persistence is constrained to be less than unity. The stationary representation of the structural model is $(1 - \rho L)\Delta y_t = (1 - \rho L)\eta_{t-1} + \Delta\kappa_{t-1}$, and equating the autocovariances of $(1 - \rho L)\Delta y_t$ at lags 0 and 1 yields $\sigma^2(1 + \theta^2) = (1 + \rho^2)\sigma_\eta^2 + 2\sigma_\kappa^2$ and $\sigma^2\theta = -\rho\sigma_\eta^2 - \sigma_\kappa^2$, which can be solved for σ_η^2 and σ_κ^2 to give $\sigma_\eta^2 = \sigma^2[(1 + \theta)/(1 - \rho)]^2$ and $\sigma_\kappa^2 = -\sigma^2[\rho(1 + \theta)^2/(1 - \rho)^2 + \theta]$. Now, $\sigma_\kappa^2 \geq 0$ requires $\theta \leq -\rho$, and this amounts to constraining persistence to be not greater than one. The state-space representation has $Z = [1 \ 1]$, $G = 0'$, $T = \text{diag}(1, \rho)$, $H = \text{diag}(\sigma_\eta, \sigma_\kappa)$, so that $PZ'F^{-1} = [(1 + \theta)/(1 - \rho), -(\rho + \theta)/(1 - \rho)]'$; therefore, the steady state recursions for the components are exactly as in (5.22), with m_t, c_t replaced by $\tilde{\mu}_{t|t}$, $\tilde{\psi}_{t|t}$, and $\xi_t = v_t$.

5.10.1. Post-sample predictive testing and model evaluation

Diagnostic checking is usually carried out using the standardized innovations $v_t = F_t^{-1/2} v_t$, which play a role in detecting various types of misspecifications, such as serial correlation, heteroskedasticity, nonnormality, and structural change (see Harvey, 1989, sections 5.4 and 8.4.2).

Assessing the goodness of fit of a structural model is closely bound up with forecasting: a basic measure is the prediction error variance (*pev*), defined as the variance of the one-step-ahead prediction errors in the steady state. For a time-invariant SSM, the *pev* is the steady state matrix $F = \lim_{t \to \infty} F_t$, which can be approximated by F_T (*finite pev*), and corresponds to the variance of the ARIMA reduced form disturbances.

The definition of a scale-free measure of goodness of fit, analogous to the coefficient of determination in regression, varies according to the nature of the series under investigation. A comparison is made with a corresponding naive forecasting model: for instance, if the BSM is fitted to a univariate seasonal time series, the sum of squares of the one-step-ahead prediction errors (SSE) is compared to the sum of squares of the first differences of the series around the seasonal means (SSDSM); this is the sum of the prediction errors arising from a random walk with seasonal drift model, and the coefficient of determination is correspondingly defined as $R_s^2 = 1 - \text{SSE}/\text{SSDSM}$.

The availability of post-sample observations, $y_{T+1}, \ldots, y_{T+l}$ (for simplicity we refer to the univariate case), can be exploited for assessing forecasting performance. Two types of prediction errors emerge: the one-step-ahead prediction errors, $v_{T+j}, j = 1, \ldots, l$, and the extrapolative residuals or j-steps-ahead prediction errors $v_{T+j|T} = y_{T+j} - \tilde{y}_{T+j|T}$. Various measures of forecast accuracy can be built upon them, such as the sum of their absolute values and of their squares, in order to compare rival models.

A test of predictive failure aims to compare model performance in the future relative to its past performance. To assess whether the prediction errors in the post-sample period are significantly greater than those within the sample period the following *post-sample predictive failure* statistic is used:

$$\xi(l) = \frac{T-d}{l} \left(\sum_{h=1}^{l} v_{T+h}^2 \right) \left(\sum_{t=d+1}^{T} v_t^2 \right)^{-1},$$

where $v_t = v_t / \sqrt{F_t}$ are the standardized one-step-ahead prediction errors and d the number of nonstationary elements. If the model is correctly specified, $v_t \sim$ NID(0, 1) and the distribution of $\xi(l)$ is $F(l, T-d)$. The cumulative sum (CUSUM) of the standardized prediction errors is useful for detecting if the model is systematically over- or underpredicting.

5.11. NONLINEAR AND NON-GAUSSIAN MODELS

The literature on nonlinear and non-Gaussian structural models has been growing very rapidly during the last decade, paralleling the advances in computational inference using stochastic simulation techniques. This section provides only an incomplete and nontechnical account, placing more emphasis on applications in economics and finance; introductory material can be found in Harvey (1989, sections 3.7, 6.5, and 6.6), Kitagawa and Gersh (1996, ch. 6), and West and Harrison (1997, chs. 12–15).

An important class of nonlinear models arises when the system matrices are functionally related to the information available at time $t − 1$; that is, $Z_t = Z_t(Y_{t-1})$, $G_t = G_t(Y_{t-1})$, $T_t = T_t(Y_{t-1})$, $H_t = H_t(Y_{t-1})$. The resulting SSM is *conditionally Gaussian*, as given Y_{t-1} the system matrices can be regarded as fixed. The KF still delivers the MMSLE of the state vector, but $\tilde{\alpha}_{t|t-1}$ is no longer coincident with $E(\alpha_t | Y_{t-1})$, latter being nonlinear in $y_1, \ldots, y_{t-1}$; similarly, $P_{t|t-1}$ represents only the conditional MSE matrix of $\tilde{\alpha}_{t|t-1}$. The attractive feature is that the likelihood function can be still obtained via the prediction error decomposition. Forecasting is discussed in Harvey (1989, p. 159). A conditionally Gaussian setup is used in Harvey et al. (1992) in order to provide approximate filtering and quasi-maximum likelihood estimation for structural models with ARCH disturbances (STARCH models). Another example is provided by the smooth transition structural models used by Proietti (1999) to model business cycle asymmetries, such as when contractions are steeper, but shorter, than expansions.

The general framework for handling nonlinear and non-Gaussian models is such that the measurement equation is replaced by the observation conditional density

$$f(y_1, \ldots, y_T | \alpha_1, \ldots, \alpha_T; \theta) = \prod_{t=1}^{T} f(y_t | \alpha_t; \theta),$$

which specifies that α_t is sufficient for y_t, and the transition equation is replaced by the Markovian transition density, $f(\alpha_1, \ldots, \alpha_T; \theta) = f(\alpha_0; \theta)\Pi_{t=1}^{T-1} f(\alpha_{t+1} | \alpha_t; \theta)$. A unified treatment of statistical inference via simulation in this framework is provided in Shephard and Pitt (1997) and Durbin and Koopman (1997, 2000). Leaving aside further details, we highlight the following applications:

STRUCTURAL MODELS WITH MARKOV SWITCHING
This class of models, introduced by Harrison and Stevens (1976) as a particular case of the *multi-process* class, postulates that the system matrices vary according to the states of a latent first order Markov chain. It is adopted in Kim (1993), who proposes an approximate filter and smoother, to decompose the U.S. inflation rate into a random walk trend plus stationary AR(1) component with heteroskedastic disturbances, whose variances vary according to two independent two-state (low and high uncertainty) Markov chains. Simulated inference is

considered in Shephard (1994) and the monograph by Kim and Nelson (1999) provides a comprehensive treatment and illustrations.

MULTIPLICATIVE MODELS

Multiplicative models arise in nonlinear seasonal adjustment, when the trend and the seasonal component combine multiplicatively and the irregular variance depends on the underlying trend; see Harvey (1989, p. 174) and Shephard (1994).

DYNAMIC GENERALIZED LINEAR MODELS

This class of models arises for time-series observations originating from the exponential family, such as count data with Poisson and binomial distribution and continuous data with skewed distributions such as the exponential and the gamma distributions. A binomial application concerning advertising awareness is illustrated in West and Harrison (1997, section 14.4), whereas Durbin and Koopman (2000) present a Poisson application with respect to monthly series of van drivers killed in road accidents in the U.K.

OUTLIER MODELS

Outlying observations and structural breaks in the components can be handled as in section 5.8 by the inclusion of appropriate dummy variables on the right-hand side of the measurement and transition equations. This strategy has several drawbacks: for instance, when a dummy is used to model an additive outlier, this amounts to considering the observation as missing, so that a weight of zero is assigned to it in signal extraction and forecasting; on the contrary, the observation may still contain some information, which could be elicited by downweighting it suitably. Moreover, in some empirical applications, a specification compatible with the Gaussian assumption entails a number of occurrences of outliers and structural breaks, which could rather be taken as evidence for departure from Gaussianity. The alternative strategy consists in allowing the disturbances of a structural model to possess a heavy tailed density, such as Students' t-distribution, the general error distribution (Durbin and Koopman, 1997), or a mixture of Gaussian (Harrison and Stevens, 1976).

STOCHASTIC VARIANCE MODELS

This class of models allows the variability of the series to change over time. The basic univariate specification for a time series of stock returns is $y_t = \varepsilon_t \exp(h_t/2)$, $h_{t+1} = \beta + \rho h_t + \eta_t$, where ε_t and η_t are independent Gaussian processes with variances 1 and σ_η^2 respectively. This specification captures the empirical regularities found in financial time series, such as leptokurtosis, volatility clustering, and the fact that returns exhibit little or no serial correlation, whereas their squares show pronounced serial dependence. A comprehensive review of the various approaches to inference for stochastic variance models is provided by Shephard (1996); a freeware package (SVpack) linked to the Ox programming language (Doornik, 1998) is also made available by the same author (http://www.nuff.ox.ac.uk/users/shephard/ox/). A recent addition implementing the approach of Durbin and Koopman (1997) is Sandmann and Koopman (1998).

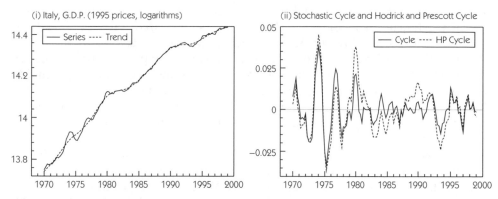

Figure 5.2 Italy, Gross Domestic Product at constant 1995 prices (logarithms), 1970.1–1999.1. (i) Series with trend, $\tilde{\mu}_{t|T}$. (ii) Comparison of $\tilde{\psi}_{t|T}$ from the model ln $y_t = \mu_t + \psi_t$, and the cycle resulting from the Hodrick and Prescott (1997) detrending procedure

5.12. ILLUSTRATIONS

5.12.1. Italian Gross Domestic Product

The first illustration deals with the quarterly series of the Italian Gross Domestic Product at 1995 prices (source: ISTAT, *National Economic Accounts*), shown in panel (i) of figure 5.2. The series displays a clear upward trend, with a changing slope: in effect, average yearly growth declines from about 3.5 percent at the beginning of the sample period to about 1.0 percent at the end. Moreover, there is some graphical evidence for the presence of some cyclic behavior, especially in the period between the two oil crises and from 1993 onwards.

When the local linear trend model (5.2) is fitted to the logarithms of the series using **STAMP 6**, the interactive menu-driven program for fitting and forecasting structural time-series models documented in Koopman et al. (2000), the maximum likelihood estimates are $\hat{\sigma}_\varepsilon^2 = 0$ (the irregular is absent), $\hat{\sigma}_\eta^2 = 183 \times 10^{-7}$, $\hat{\sigma}_\zeta^2 = 347 \times 10^{-7}$. Elaborating results from example 5.10.2 the forecast function implied by the model is ln $\tilde{y}_{t+l|t} = \tilde{\mu}_{t|t} + l\tilde{\beta}_{t|t}$ with $\tilde{\mu}_{t|t} = y_t$ (notice that $\hat{\sigma}_\varepsilon^2 = 0$ implies $\lambda_0 = 1$), so that the trend is coincident with the observations, and $\tilde{\beta}_{t|t} = [1 - (1 - \lambda_1)L]^{-1}\lambda_1\Delta$ ln y_t – the current estimate of the slope is an *exponentially weighted moving average* of current and past growth rates. As far as goodness of fit is concerned, the *pev* is 0.000065 and the coefficient of determination is 0.08. However, the model is misspecified as the Ljung–Box test of residual autocorrelation, $Q(P) = T^*(T^* + 2)\sum_{\tau=1}^{P}(T^* - \tau)r_v^2(\tau)$, where $T^* = T - d$ and $r_v(\tau)$ is the autocorrelation coefficient of v_t at lag τ, is significant at the 5 percent level for all $\tau < 13$.

Diagnostic checking and *a priori* considerations suggest fitting the trend plus cycle model ln $y_t = \mu_t + \psi_t$: the estimated parameters for the trend are $\hat{\sigma}_\eta^2 = 2 \times 10^{-7}$, $\hat{\sigma}_\zeta^2 = 25 \times 10^{-7}$, $\hat{\sigma}_\psi^2 = 1402 \times 10^{-7}$, $\hat{\rho} = 0.92$, $\lambda_c = 0.52$, which implies a period of 12 quarters (3 years). As a result, the trend extracted, $\tilde{\mu}_{t|T}$, has a fairly smooth appearance (see figure 5.2, panel (i)), whereas $\tilde{\psi}_{t|T}$ provides a good representation of the Italian business cycle. The latter is is compared with the deviations from the Hodrick and Prescott trend, which is the trend extracted by the model (5.2) with the following restrictions on the parameters: $\sigma_\eta^2 = 0$ and $\sigma_\zeta^2/\sigma_\varepsilon^2 = 0.000625$. This is clearly a misspecified model and the resulting cycle, although highly coherent with that extracted by the trend plus cycle model, overemphasizes the short-run dynamics, especially during the second decade, which is commonly acknowledged as a period of steady growth with little or no business cycle fluctuations.

The absence of residual autocorrelation ($Q(P)$ is never significant at the 5 percent level) and of departures from the normality assumption, coupled with the better within sample performance ($pev = 0.000052$; the coefficient of determination is 0.27), suggest that the trend plus cycle model is to be preferred.

5.12.2.   BEA Auto Unit Sales

We now provide an example of univariate modeling and forecasting with structural time-series models with respect to the monthly domestic auto unit sales made available by the U.S. *Bureau of Economic Analysis* (BEA) at the URL http://www.bea.doc.gov/bea/pn/ndn0207.exe. The series covers the sample period 1967.1–1998.6, and is an extension of that studied in Findley et al. (1998), to compare a subjective pre-adjustment made by an expert analyst and an objective one, based upon five user-defined regressors and automatic outlier identification. These adjustments are made prior to the seasonal adjustment of the series and aim at removing the effects of short-duration sales incentive programs used by automobile manufacturers, causing "a large increase in the month or two in which they occur, followed by a substantial decrease in the subsequent month or two" (Findley et al., 1998, p. 146).

The series, shown in panel (i) of figure 5.3, along with time-varying level and seasonal components, contains also a relevant calendar component in the form of trading days effects, since the level of sales varies with the day of the week, for example, being higher than average on Monday and Thursday. This effect is modeled including six trading days regressors measuring, respectively, the number of Mondays, Tuesdays, . . . , Saturdays minus the number of Sundays in every month. Actually, the treatment of this component is less trivial than it appears at first sight, due to the reporting habits of the manufacturers; see the comment by Cleveland on the paper by Findley et al. (1998, p. 153).

The initial specification of a structural time-series model for the logarithmic transformation of the series is the following: $\ln y_t = \mu_t + \gamma_t + x_t'\boldsymbol{\beta} + \varepsilon_t$, where μ_t is a random walk, $\mu_{t+1} = \mu_t + \eta_t$, γ_t has the trigonometric specification (5.5), $\varepsilon_t \sim \text{NID}(0, \sigma_\varepsilon^2)$, and x_t contains six trading days regressors and the five user-defined regressors employed by Findley et al. (1998).

This model is estimated using the package STAMP 6.0; diagnostic checking highlights that the standardized innovations are affected by excess kurtosis and significant autocorrelation (as revealed by the Ljung–Box statistic). Moreover, the shape of the autocorrelation function and the estimated spectral density, which

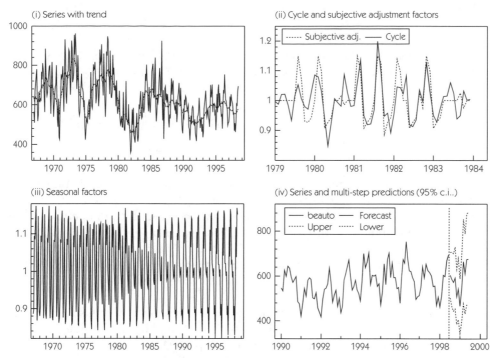

Figure 5.3   BEA Domestic Unit Auto Sales, 1967.1–1999.6. (i) Series with trend, exp $(\tilde{\mu}_{t|T})$. (ii) Comparison of subjective pre-adjustment factors and the cycle extracted, exp $(\tilde{\psi}_{t|T})$, for the period 1979.1–1983.12. (iii) Plot of seasonal factors, exp $(\tilde{\gamma}_{t|T})$. (iv) l-step-ahead forecasts with upper and lower 95% confidence limits

shows a peak around the frequency 0.9 corresponding to a period of 6–7 months, seems to suggest the inclusion of a cyclical component.

When the component ψ_t in (5.3) is added there is a considerable improvement in the fit: the prediction error variance is $pev = 0.006394$ and the coefficient of determination $R_s^2 = 0.44$ (for the previous specification we had $pev = 0.006954$ and $R_s^2 = 0.39$). Furthermore, the Ljung–Box statistic is never significant and excess kurtosis is reduced. The maximum likelihood estimates of the parameters are $\hat{\sigma}_\eta^2 = 13,279 \times 10^{-7}$, $\hat{\sigma}_\omega^2 = 36 \times 10^{-7}$, $\hat{\sigma}_\varepsilon^2 = 4,361 \times 10^{-7}$, $\hat{\sigma}_\kappa^2 = 16,898 \times 10^{-7}$, $\hat{\rho} = 0.6785$, $\hat{\lambda}_c = 0.8964$.

The stochastic cycle, with variance $\hat{\sigma}_\psi^2 = 31,316 \times 10^{-7}$ and period equal to 7 months, captures the quasi-seasonal effect of short-duration sales programs. Panel (ii) of figure 5.3 shows that the smoothed estimates of the cycle are highly coherent with the subjective pre-adjustment factors. Of course, the cycle extracted is no substitute for genuine external information on the timing and extent of sales programmes, but structural modeling appears to capture this feature of the series.

Forecasts up to 12 steps ahead are displayed in panel (iv) in the original scale of the observations: if we denote $z_t = \ln y_t$, and we write $z_{T+l} \mid z_1, \ldots, z_T \sim N(\tilde{z}_{T+l|T}, F_{T+l|t})$, then by properties of the lognormal distribution, the forecast in the original scale is obtained as $\tilde{y}_{T+l|T} = \exp(\tilde{z}_{T+l|T} + F_{T+l|T}/2)$.

For comparison, a regression model with ARIMA errors was fitted to the same series using the **RegARIMA** module included in X-12-ARIMA package with GiveWin interface (see the URL http://www.nuff.ox.ac.uk/use for downloads and information about GiveWin. Documentation and downloads for X-12-ARIMA are available from http://www.census.gov/pub/ts/x12a/final/). The model selected according to various information criteria is ARIMA $(2, 0, 1) \times (0, 1, 1)$:

$$(1 - 1.4007L + 0.4382L^2)\Delta_{12}(\ln y_t - C_t) = (1 - 0.7180L)(1 - 0.7786L^{12})\xi_t,$$

$$\xi_t \sim \text{NID}(0, 0.006623),$$

where C_t represents the regression kernel, including six trading days regressors and five user-defined regressors.

The reduced form of the structural model with a cyclic component has the same autoregressive structure, but the implied representation of the stationary AR(2) polynomial is $(1 - 0.8473L + 0.4604L^2)$, with a pair of complex conjugates roots with modulus 1.4738 and phase 0.8964, whereas the roots of $(1 - 1.4007L + 0.4382L^2)$ are real and equal 1.0614, 2.1500. Moreover, the MA part is additive (with order 14) rather than multiplicative.

The comparison of the prediction error variance of the structural model (0.006394) with that of the ARIMA model (0.006623) highlights that the performance of the former is superior as far as one-step-ahead forecast errors are concerned. Comparison of **MSE** of out-of-sample multi-step forecasts can be based on the following rolling forecast exercise: starting from 1989.12, three alternative models, namely the structural model without (Stsm) and including (StsmC) the cyclic component and the ARIMA$(2, 0, 1) \times (0, 1, 1)$ model, are estimated using the observations through a given forecast origin; l-steps-ahead forecasts, $l = 1, \ldots,$ 12, are computed. The procedure is repeated shifting the forecast origin by one month until the end of the sample period is reached; this yields a total of 102 one-step-ahead forecast errors and 91 12-steps-ahead forecast errors for the three models.

For this computationally demanding task we use the library of state-space function **SsfPack** 2.2 by Koopman et al. (1999), linked to the object-oriented matrix programming language **Ox** 2.1 of Doornik (1998). Moreover, a considerable simplification is obtained considering only one trading days regressor (accounting for the number of weekdays in the month minus (5/2) times the number of Saturdays and Sundays in the month), and dropping the five user-defined regressors.

The main results are summarized in figure 5.4, which displays for the three models the mean of the forecast errors at forecast horizons ranging from 1 to 12 months (panel (i)) and the ratio of the mean square forecast error of the Stsm and the ARIMA models to that of StsmC (panel (ii)). All models present a negative bias at all forecast horizons, which is less pronounced for StsmC. The best forecast performance is provided by StsmC, which clearly outperforms the ARIMA model at horizons from 2–9, and the Stsm specification, particularly at longer horizons.

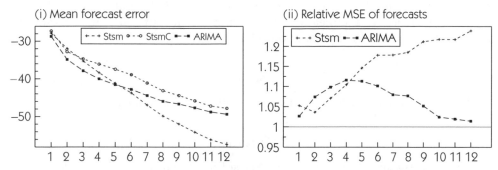

Figure 5.4 BEA Domestic Unit Auto Sales: comparison of forecast accuracy of structural model without a cyclic component (Stsm), including a cyclical component (StsmC) and the ARIMA(2, 0, 1) × (0, 1, 1) model, based on rolling l-step-ahead forecasts ($l = 1, \ldots, 12$) 1989.12–1999.5

Further empirical evidence on the forecasting performance of structural time-series models is reported in Harvey and Todd (1983) and Andrews (1994). The overall conclusion is that their performance is no worse than, and often superior to, that of rival specifications.

Appendix: Proof of the Kalman filter

The preliminary result which is used to determine the optimality of the KF is that for any two random variables x and z, the MMSE of x given z is the conditional expectation $E(x \mid z)$. Assuming that at time t $\tilde{\alpha}_{t \mid t-1}$ and $P_{t \mid t-1}$ are given, taking the expectation of both sides of the measurement equation conditional on Y_{t-1} produces $\tilde{y}_{t \mid t-1} = E(y_t \mid Y_{t-1}) = Z_t \tilde{\alpha}_{t \mid t-1}$. Denoting the one-step-ahead prediction error, $y_t - \tilde{y}_{t \mid t-1}$, by v_t, and substituting from (5.8), gives $v_t = Z_t(\alpha_t - \tilde{\alpha}_{t \mid t-1}) + G_t \varepsilon_t$. Then, $Var(y_t \mid Y_{t-1}) = Z_t P_{t \mid t-1} Z'_t + G_t G'_t = F_t$, since $\alpha_t - \tilde{\alpha}_{t \mid t-1}$ is uncorrelated with ε_t (as a matter of fact, repeated substitution from the transition equation shows that α_t is linear in $\varepsilon_1, \ldots, \varepsilon_{t-1}$).

The updating equations for the state and its covariance matrix are produced as follows: writing $Y_t = \{Y_{t-1}, y_t\}$, by properties of the normal distribution,

$$E(\alpha_{t+1} \mid Y_t) = E(\alpha_{t+1} \mid Y_{t-1}) + Cov(\alpha_{t+1}, y_t \mid Y_{t-1})[Var(y_t \mid Y_{t-1})]^{-1}(y_t - E(y_t \mid Y_{t-1})),$$

$$Var(\alpha_{t+1} \mid Y_t) = Var(\alpha_{t+1} \mid Y_{t-1})$$

$$- Cov(\alpha_{t+1}, y_t \mid Y_{t-1})[Var(y_t \mid Y_{t-1})]^{-1}Cov(y_t, \alpha_{t+1} \mid Y_{t-1})). \qquad (5.23)$$

Now, the expectation and variance of both sides of (5.9) conditional on Y_{t-1} are $E(\alpha_{t+1} \mid Y_{t-1}) = T_t \tilde{\alpha}_{t \mid t-1}$ and $Var(\alpha_{t+1} \mid Y_{t-1}) = T_t P_{t \mid t-1} T_t + H_t H'_t$, respectively; moreover, $Cov(\alpha_{t+1}, y_t \mid Y_{t-1}) = T_t P_{t \mid t-1} Z'_t + H_t G'_t$. Replacing into (5.23) and writing $K_t = (T_t P_{t \mid t-1} Z'_t + H_t G'_t)F_t^{-1}$ yields the last line of (5.10).

The KF performs a Choleski transformation of the observations: if v denotes the stack of the innovations and y that of the observations: then $v = Cy$, where

C is a lower triangular matrix such that $\mathsf{Cov}(y) = C^{-1}FC'^{-1}$ and $F = \text{diag}\,(F_1, \ldots, F_t, \ldots, F_T)$. Hence, v_t is a linear combination of the current and past observations and is orthogonal to the information set Y_{t-1}.

Note

1   This section is more technical and can be omitted on first reading.

References

Anderson, B.D.O. and J.B. Moore (1979). *Optimal Filtering*. Englewood Cliffs, NJ: Prentice-Hall.

Andrews, R.L. (1994). Forecasting performance of structural time series models. *Journal of Business and Economic Statistics*, 12, 129–33.

Ansley, C.F. and R. Kohn (1985). Estimation, filtering and smoothing in state space models with incompletely specified initial conditions. *The Annals of Statistics*, 13, 1286–316.

Ansley, C.F., and R. Kohn (1990). Filtering and smoothing in state space models with partially diffuse initial conditions. *Journal of Time Series Analysis*, 11, 275–93.

Beveridge, S. and C.R. Nelson (1981). A new approach to the decomposition of economic time series into permanent and transitory components with particular attention to the measurement of the "business cycle." *Journal of Monetary Economics*, 7, 151–74.

Box, G.E.P., G.M. Jenkins, and G.C. Reinsel (1994). *Time Series Analysis*, 3rd edn. Englewood Cliffs, NJ: Prentice-Hall.

de Jong, P. (1988). A cross-validation filter for time series models. *Biometrika*, 75, 594–600.

de Jong, P. (1989). Smoothing and interpolation with the state space model. *Journal of the American Statistical Association*, 84, 1085–88.

de Jong, P. (1991). The diffuse Kalman filter. *Annals of Statistics*, 19, 1073–83.

de Jong, P. and J. Penzer (1998). Diagnosing shocks in time series. *Journal of the American Statistical Association*, 93, 796–806.

Doornik, J.A. (1998). *Object-Oriented Matrix Programming Using Ox 2.0*. London: Timberlake Consultants Press.

Durbin, J. and S.J. Koopman (1997). Monte Carlo maximum likelihood estimation for non-Gaussian state space models. *Biometrika*, 84, 669–84.

Durbin, J. and S.J. Koopman (2000). Time series analysis of non-Gaussian observations based on state space models from both classical and Bayesian perspectives. *Journal of the Royal Statistical Society, Series B*, 62, 3–56.

Engle, R.F. and C.W.J. Granger (1987). Co-integration and error correction: representation, estimation and testing. *Econometrica*, 55, 251–76.

Fernandez, F.J. and A.C. Harvey (1990). Seemingly unrelated time series equations and a test for homogeneity. *Journal of Business and Economic Statistics*, 8, 71–81.

Findley, D.F., B.C. Monsell, W.R. Bell, M.C. Otto, and B. Chen (1998). New capabilities and methods of the X-12-ARIMA seasonal adjustment program (with comments). *Journal of Business and Economic Statistics*, 16, 127–77.

Godolphin, E.J. (1976). Discussion on the paper by P.J. Harrison and C.F. Stevens "Bayesian Forecasting." *Journal of the Royal Statistical Society, Series B*, 38, 238–9.

Harrison, P.J. and C.F. Stevens (1976). Bayesian forecasting (with discussion). *Journal of the Royal Statistical Society, Series B*, 38, 205–47.

Harvey, A.C. (1989). *Forecasting, Structural Time Series and the Kalman Filter*. Cambridge: Cambridge University Press.

Harvey, A.C. and S.J. Koopman (1992). Diagnostic checking of unobserved components time series models. *Journal of Business and Economic Statistics*, 10, 377–89.

Harvey, A.C. and S.J. Koopman (1993). Forecasting hourly electricity demand using time-varying splines. *Journal of the American Statistical Association*, 88, 377–89.

Harvey, A.C. and S.J. Koopman (1997). Multivariate structural time series models. In C. Heij, H. Schumaker, B. Hanzon and C. Praagman (eds.), *Systematic Dynamics in Economic and Financial Models*. Chichester: John Wiley.

Harvey, A.C. and S.J. Koopman (2000). Signal extraction and the formulation of unobserved component models. *Econometrics Journal*, 3, 84–107.

Harvey, A.C., E. Ruiz, and E. Sentana (1992). Unobserved component time series models with ARCH disturbances. *Journal of Econometrics*, 52, 129–57.

Harvey, A.C. and P.H.J. Todd (1983). Forecasting economic time series with structural and Box-Jenkins models (with discussion), *Journal of Business and Economic Statistics*, 1, 299–315.

Hodrick, R.J., and E.C. Prescott (1997). Postwar U.S. business cycles: an empirical investigation. *Journal of Money, Credit and Banking*, 29, 1–16.

Hylleberg, S., Ed. (1992). *Modelling Seasonality*. Oxford: Oxford University Press.

Kim, C.J. (1993). Unobserved-component time series models with Markov-switching heteroscedasticity: changes in regime and the link between inflation rates and inflation uncertainty. *Journal of Business and Economic Statistics*, 11, 341–9.

Kim, C.J. and C.R. Nelson (1999). *State-Space Models with Regime Switching*. Cambridge, MA: MIT Press.

Kitagawa, G. and W. Gersch (1996). *Smoothness Priors Analysis of Time Series*. New York: Springer-Verlag.

Koopman, S.J. (1993). Disturbance smoother for state space models. *Biometrika*, 80, 117–26.

Koopman, S.J. (1997). Exact initial Kalman filtering and smoothing for non-stationary time series models. *Journal of the American Statistical Association*, 92, 1630–8.

Koopman, S.J., A.C. Harvey, J.A. Doornik, and N. Shephard (2000). *STAMP 6.0 Structural Time Series Analyser, Modeller and Predictor*. London: Timberlake Consultants Ltd.

Koopman, S.J. and N. Shephard (1992). Exact score for time series models in state form. *Biometrika*, 79, 823–6.

Koopman, S.J., N. Shepard, and J.A. Doornik (1999). Statistical algorithms for models in state space using SsfPack 2.2. *Econometrics Journal*, 2, 113–66.

Marshall, P. (1992). Estimating time-dependent means in dynamic models for cross-sections of time series. *Empirical Economics*, 17, 25–33.

Ord, J.K., A.B. Koehler, and R.D. Snyder (1997). Estimation and prediction for a class of dynamic nonlinear statistical models. *Journal of the American Statistical Association*, 92, 1621–9.

Proietti, T. (1998). Seasonal heteroscedasticity and trends. *Journal of Forecasting*, 17, 1–17.

Proietti, T. (1999). Characterising asymmetries in business cycles using smooth transition structural time series models. *Studies in Nonlinear Dynamics and Econometrics*, 3.3, 141–56.

Proietti, T. (2000). Comparing seasonal components for structural time series models. *International Journal of Forecasting*, 16, 247–60.

Rosenberg, B. (1973). Random coefficient models: the analysis of a cross-section of time series by stochastically convergent parameter regression. *Annals of Economic and Social Measurement*, 2, 399–428.

Sandmann, G. and S.J. Koopman (1998). Estimation of stochastic volatility models via Monte Carlo maximum likelihood. *Journal of Econometrics*, 87, 271–301.

Shephard, N.G. (1994). Partial non-Gaussian state space. *Biometrika*, 81, 115–31.

Shephard, N.G. (1996). Statistical aspects of ARCH and stochastic volatility. In D.R. Cox, D.V. Hinkley, and O.E. Barndorff-Nielsen (eds.), *Time Series Models in Econometrics, Finance and Other Fields*. London: Chapman and Hall.

Shephard, N.G. and A.C. Harvey (1990). On the probability of estimating a deterministic component in the local level model. *Journal of Time Series Analysis*, 11, 339–47.

Shephard, N.G. and M.K. Pitt (1997). Likelihood analysis on non-Gaussian measurement time series. *Biometrika*, 84, 653–67.

Snyder, R.D. (1985). Recursive estimation of dynamic linear models. *Journal of the Royal Statistical Society, Series B*, 47, 272–6.

Tunnicliffe-Wilson, G. (1989). On the use of marginal likelihood in time series model estimation. *Journal of the Royal Statistical Society, Series B*, 51, 15–27.

West, M. and J. Harrison (1997). *Bayesian Forecasting and Dynamic Models*, 2nd edn. New York: Springer-Verlag.

Judgmental Forecasting

Dilek Önkal-Atay, Mary E. Thomson,
and Andrew C. Pollock

6.1.   INTRODUCTION

Human judgment permeates forecasting processes. In economic forecasting, judgment may be used in identifying the endogenous and exogenous variables, building structural equations, correcting for omitted variables, specifying expectations for economic indicators, and adjusting the model predictions in light of new information, official announcements, or "street" talk. Studies with economic forecasters indicate that judgment is given more weight than the modeling techniques in constructing predictions (Batchelor and Dua, 1990). In fact, judgment is "the primary factor that the economist uses in converting mere statistical and theoretical techniques into a usable forecast" (McAuley, 1986, p. 384). As accentuated by Larry Summers (a former Harvard and MIT professor of economics who is currently U.S. Treasury Secretary), "ultimately there's no alternative to judgment – you can never get the answers out of some model" (cf., Fox, 1999, p. 66).

Judgmental forecasting focuses on the incorporation of forecasters' opinions and experience into the prediction process. Hence, it covers an extensive base, ranging from situations where there exists no quantifiable information so that the forecast is based exclusively on judgment, to cases where the econometric or extrapolative methods are heavily consulted, with judgment supporting the model building phase and/or fine-tuning the given predictions. Various surveys have indicated that judgmental forecasting methods enjoy the highest degree of usage by practitioners on a regular basis (Dalrymple, 1987; Mentzer and Cox, 1984; Rothe, 1978; Sparkes and McHugh, 1984; Winklhofer, Diamantopoulos, and Witt, 1996). Forecasters appear to be highly satisfied with judgmental approaches, preferring them over quantitative techniques due to reasons of accuracy and difficulties in obtaining the necessary data for quantitative approaches. Judgmental methods are also stated to add a "common sense element" to the forecast, creating a sense of "ownership" (Sanders and Manrodt, 1994). Firm size does not seem to make a difference, only that larger firms appear to use more sophisticated judgmental techniques (Sanders, 1997b). Even when forecasts are generated quantitatively, judgmental adjustments are regularly performed (Fildes and Hastings, 1994), as they incorporate the forecaster's knowledge of special events and changing conditions, in addition to his/her general knowledge of the prediction environment (Jenks, 1983; Soergel, 1983). Furthermore, forecast users appear to rely more on judgmental methods than on quantitative techniques (Wheelwright and Clarke, 1976).

Given their extensive usage and significant consequences, judgmental forecasts offer challenging research venues across disciplines. This chapter aims to review the relevant work on judgmental forecasting, providing a synopsis of research findings to date, while highlighting issues that demand future scrutiny. Accordingly, the next section details the elicitation formats used in judgmental forecasting studies, followed by discussions of factors affecting accuracy, comparisons of judgmental versus model-based forecasts, issues of judgmental adjustments, and forecast combinations.

6.2. FORECASTING FORMAT

Judgmental forecasts may be expressed via various formats (for example, point forecasts, prediction intervals, or probability forecasts), the choice of which is dictated usually by the user specifications and/or the task environment. Although point forecasting is extensively used, providing only point predictions may convey a misleading message of precision. It could be argued, however, that the uncertainty surrounding the point forecasts may have a direct influence on the decision-making process (Eckel, 1987; Howard, 1988). Prediction intervals and probability forecasts provide alternative formats for revealing this uncertainty. The use of the latter in economics and finance is surveyed by Tay and Wallis in chapter 3 of this volume.

Studies have indicated a distinct preference for interval forecasts over point predictions for the communication of forecasts to users (Baginski, Conrad, and Hassell, 1993; Pownall, Wasley, and Waymire, 1993). Prediction intervals are reportedly influenced by the choice of the presentation scale, as well as the trend, seasonality, and variability in the series (Lawrence and O'Connor, 1993). Furthermore, judgmental prediction intervals are found to reflect overconfidence (that is, for intervals given a confidence coefficient of XX percent, less than XX percent of the intervals actually include the true value; Lichtenstein, Fischhoff, and Phillips, 1982; Russo and Schoemaker, 1992).

Probability forecasting serves as an alternative elicitation format in which the judgments are expressed via subjective probabilities. Probability forecasts reveal detailed information regarding forecaster's uncertainty, acting as a basic communication channel for the transmission of this uncertainty to the users of these predictions, who can, in turn, better interpret the presented forecasts (Murphy and Winkler, 1984). From the forecast provider's point of view, a distinct advantage is that probability forecasting enables the forecaster to more completely express his/her true judgments, thus reducing any tendencies to bias the forecasts (Daan and Murphy, 1982). Probabilistic directional or multiple-interval forecasts are used extensively in economic and financial forecasting, with various measures of accuracy being developed to address diverse aspects of a forecaster's performance like calibration, over/underconfidence, over/underforecasting, and discrimination (Murphy, 1972a,b, 1973; Wilkie and Pollock, 1996; Yates, 1982, 1988). Using these measures to assess probabilistic forecasting performance, previous research has mainly examined predictions of financial variables like stock prices (Muradoglu and Önkal, 1994; Önkal and Muradoglu, 1994, 1995, 1996; Stael von Holstein, 1972; Yates, McDaniel and Brown, 1991) and exchange rates (Wilkie-Thomson, Önkal-Atay and Pollock, 1997), suggesting the importance of factors like contextual information, time-series characteristics, forecaster bias, and expertise for predictive performance. It is to these issues we turn next.

6.3. FACTORS AFFECTING THE ACCURACY OF JUDGMENTAL FORECASTS

Primary benefits of judgmental forecasting entail the incorporation of forecasters' contextual knowledge, including the identification of "special case insights" or "broken leg cues"; that is, unusual pieces of information that cannot be modeled, despite their importance for prediction accuracy (Meehl, 1954). Hence, contextual information promises to be a critical factor influencing the relative performance of judgmental forecasts. If properly incorporated into judgment, such information could signal important changes like upcoming discontinuities in series (Kleinmuntz, 1990). Thus, contextual information could give judgmental forecasts a distinct edge over model-based forecasts since the latter necessarily treats such sporadic influences as merely noise, due to their infrequency (Goodwin and Fildes, 1999).

With most studies on judgmental performance utilizing constructed series with no contextual frames, the effects of such information remains underexplored. Only a few studies have controlled for contextual information, finding higher accuracy for judgmental forecasts constructed with contextual knowledge as opposed to predictions not benefiting from such information (Edmundson, Lawrence, and O'Connor, 1988; Sanders and Ritzman, 1992), and relative to statistical predictions (Edmundson, Lawrence, and O'Connor, 1988; Fildes, 1991). Further work to systematically investigate the sensitivity of judgmental forecasts to variations in factors like the accessibility, timing, and predictive contribution of contextual information would prove valuable for enhancing our understanding of judgmental predictive performance.

Exploring the potential effects of time-series characteristics on the accuracy of judgmental extrapolations constitutes another stream attracting research interest. In attempts to isolate the effects of time-series components on predictive accuracy, previous studies have mainly utilized constructed series, arguing that this practice eliminates the effects of outside cues while enabling control of the pertinent time-series characteristics (O'Connor and Lawrence, 1989). Trend has been the most thoroughly investigated component, with its presence shown to affect the performance of judgmental point and interval forecasts (Lawrence and Makridakis, 1989; O'Connor and Lawrence, 1992; O'Connor, Remus, and Griggs, 1997). Furthermore, past work has found a distinct tendency of participants to dampen both upward and downward trends (Bolger and Harvey, 1993; Eggleton, 1982; Harvey, 1995). Recent evidence showing that forecasting performance could be contingent on the strength of trend (Wilkie-Thomson, 1998) suggests a clear need for detailed studies on the effects of the strength of time-series movements.

Judgmental performance has been reported to deteriorate in constructed series with high seasonality (Adam and Ebert, 1976; Sanders, 1992), and similarly for series with white noise (Adam and Ebert, 1976; Eggleton, 1982; Sanders, 1992; O'Connor, Remus, and Griggs, 1993). However, due to the nested factors in experimental designs, conclusive statements as to the superiority of judgmental versus statistical methods for differential levels of seasonality and noise cannot be made given the results of existing research. Past work on judgmental forecasting for series with discontinuities or temporal disturbances have reported relatively poor performance as compared to statistical techniques (Sanders, 1992; O'Connor, Remus, and Griggs, 1993), and such findings have in part been explained by the absence of contextual information provided to participants. Interestingly, Wilkie-Thomson (1998) found that professionals and academics in currency forecasting outperformed various statistical techniques, sharing the same noncontextual information basis as the models. However, these participants were proficient with chartist forecasting techniques (that is, methods based on the belief that all indicators of change – economic, political, psychological, or otherwise – are reflected in the price series itself and, therefore, a study of price action is all that is needed to forecast future movements). Hence, the absence of contextual information in these circumstances may not carry the same connotations as in previous work, where contextual information may potentially constitute a more critical determinant of performance.

Judgmental forecasts have also been reported to be influenced by the data presentation format, with graphical presentation generally superior to tabular format (Angus-Leppan and Fatseas, 1986; Dickson, DeSanctis, and McBride, 1986), especially for trended series (Harvey and Bolger, 1996). However, forecast horizon (Lawrence, Edmundson, and O'Connor, 1985) and environmental complexity (Remus, 1987) are found to mediate the effects of presentation format, such that the tabular format appears to give better results for constructing long-term forecasts on series with high noise.

Accuracy of judgmental forecasts could also be influenced by biases in judgment (Bolger and Harvey, 1998; Goodwin and Wright, 1994), potentially resulting from the forecasters' use of heuristics or simplifying mental strategies (Tversky and Kahneman, 1974). Heuristics like anchoring and adjustment (that is, giving too much weight to a particular reference point – for example, the last observed value in a time series – and making typically insufficient adjustments to it in arriving at a forecast) may be responsible for the common finding on participants' underestimation of trends (Bolger and Harvey, 1993; Lawrence and Makridakis, 1989), although excessive adjustments from anchors are also reported (Lawrence and O'Connor, 1995).

Judgmental biases argued to be especially relevant to forecasting include: illusory correlations (that is, false beliefs regarding the relatedness of certain variables), hindsight (that is, the feeling that the forecaster knew all along that a particular event would happen anyway), selective perception (discounting information on the basis of its inconsistency with the forecaster's beliefs or expectations), attribution of success and failure (that is, the tendency to attribute good forecasts to one's own skill, while attributing inaccurate forecasts to environmental factors or chance), underestimating uncertainty, optimism, overconfidence, and inconsistency in judgment (Hogarth and Makridakis, 1981). These biases could also be related to the organizational incentive systems (Bromiley, 1987). For instance, forecasters mostly prefer to underforecast, justifying this tendency typically by their motivation to look better if the stated goals are surpassed (Sanders and Manrodt, 1994), or by their choice to be conservative (Peterson, 1991). In a similar motivational vein, Ehrbeck and Waldmann (1996) report that professional forecasters may not merely aim to minimize expected squared forecast errors, but rather, they may "strategically bias" their forecasts. That is, less able forecasters may try to balance their need for accuracy with their concern to appear competent by trying to mimic forecasting patterns typical of recognized experts. Whether real or imaginary, perceived controllability of outcomes could also have a powerful effect on judgmental predictions (Langer, 1982).

Economic forecasting is argued to be particularly vulnerable to belief and expectation biases; that is, there may exist tendencies to construct forecasts that conform to one's beliefs/expectations, while being critical of results that conflict with them (Evans, 1987). Given that in economics, "... rival theories are persistently maintained in the face of all evidence" (p. 43), Evans (1987) points out that "the world inevitably provides excuses for the failures of forecasts" (p. 44), promoting the maintenance of beliefs and expectations.

With debates surrounding the actual forecasting performance of experts, expertise provides another factor that has not received proper research attention in judgmental predictions. A review of studies on the quality of expert judgment reveals contradictory findings that could stem from differences in research methodology, as well as task differences (Bolger and Wright, 1994). The high accuracy of judgmental forecasts provided by financial experts (see Önkal-Atay, 1998, for a review) signals a clear need for detailed studies under realistic conditions; for example, where the forecast may affect the task environment or where the forecaster may have a distinct preference over certain outcomes (Goodwin and Wright, 1993).

6.4. MODEL-BASED VERSUS JUDGMENTAL FORECASTS

Comparisons of judgmental forecasts with model-based or statistical forecasts have appealed to researchers attempting to delineate conditions for their best comparative use. Model-based forecasts enjoy consistency over repetitive settings as well as reliable combination of different information. They may also have immunity from organizational politics as well as from the motivational and cognitive biases, inconsistencies, and limitations that permeate individual judgments. Judgmental forecasts, on the other hand, benefit from human ability to evaluate information that is difficult to quantify, as well as to accommodate changing constraints and dynamic environments.

A number of studies have shown judgment to outperform model-based forecasts (Edmundson, Lawrence, and O'Connor, 1988; Lawrence, Edmundson, and O'Connor, 1985; Murphy and Winkler, 1992; Stewart, Roebber, and Bosart, 1997), especially when few data points are available and when the forecast horizon is extended (Bailey and Gupta, 1999). Other work has supplied evidence favoring statistical models (Armstrong, 1985; Makridakis, 1988; Carbone and Gorr, 1985; Holland, Lorek, and Bathke, 1992). In constructed series with high variability and major discontinuities, participants appeared to overreact to each data point as values were revealed, reading signal into noise, hence performing worse than statistical models (O'Connor, Remus, and Griggs, 1993). Even though predictive performance improved as the accuracy of information on discontinuities improved, individuals were found to overreact to immediate past information, thus not fully utilizing the information provided on the discontinuities (Remus, O'Connor, and Griggs, 1995).

Task characteristics and the differing nature of judgments elicited could account for the discrepancies in findings. Previous work has remained mostly confined to laboratory settings with artificial series constrained to various levels of noise and trend. However, extensive studies with security analysts have repeatedly shown superior accuracy as compared to model-based forecasts (Armstrong, 1983; Branson, Lorek, and Pagach, 1995; Brown, Hagerman, Griffin, and Zmijewski, 1987; Hopwood and McKeown, 1990; O'Brien, 1988), suggesting that real forecasting performance could be different. Regardless, "the evidence is that even if judgmental forecasts perform worse than a statistical model, it is often the former that will be used in any substantive decisions" (Goodwin and Fildes, 1999, p. 50). Practitioners' emphasis on judgmental forecasting is also pronounced in a survey of corporate planners from the 500 largest corporations in the world, where they clearly express the severe limitations of using only statistical techniques for forecasting (Klein and Linneman, 1984). To utilize judgment most effectively in improving forecasting performance for certain tasks, it might be preferable to use judgment in adjusting model-based forecasts, or to combine judgmental predictions with statistical forecasts. The main motivation behind judgmental interventions and combining forecasts involves capturing a richer information base, thus improving accuracy, as discussed in the following section.

6.5. JUDGMENTAL ADJUSTMENTS AND COMBINING FORECASTS

Judgmental adjustments are frequently encountered in business (Sanders and Manrodt, 1994) and economic forecasting (Granger and Newbold, 1986; Young,

1984), and are mostly made informally (Bunn, 1996). The overall value of judgmental interventions to business and econometric forecasts has been well established (Donihue, 1993; Glendinning, 1975; Huss, 1985; Matthews and Diamantopoulos, 1986, 1989; McNees, 1990; Wallis, 1985–1988). Such modifications to statistical or "baseline" forecasts serve the role of incorporating expert knowledge on variables omitted in the models, potentially due to the presumed insignificance of these variables, their judgmental nature, multicollinearity problems, and/or insufficient data (Bunn and Salo, 1996). These modifications can also be automatic, as with the "intercept corrections" discussed extensively in Clements and Hendry (1999).

Results from econometric models are frequently adjusted judgmentally for specification errors and structural changes (Corker, Holly, and Ellis, 1986; McAuley, 1986; Turner, 1990). When no contextual information is provided, the effectiveness of judgmental adjustment may depend on the quality of the statistical forecast (Carbone, Andersen, Corriveau, and Corson, 1983; Willemain, 1991). In particular, judgmental adjustments are argued to not harm the "good" or near-optimal forecasts, while generally improving the "not-so-accurate" predictions (Willemain, 1989). These results appear to be contingent on series characteristics, however. In particular, when regular time series are interrupted by sporadic discontinuities (that is, special events like government announcements, competitor's introduction of a new product, etc.), human judgment is found to be inefficient in using the supplied statistical forecasts. Model-based predictions appear to be modified when, in fact, they are reliable, and yet ignored when they would have provided a good base value for adjustment (Goodwin and Fildes, 1999). As expected, biases may surface again, with forecasters displaying a tendency to favor their own judgmental predictions over other information, suggesting a possible anchoring effect (Lim and O'Connor, 1995). It is also plausible that individuals may feel more "in control" when they use their own judgment (Langer, 1975) to supplement the model-based forecasts. With an insightful perspective, McNees and Perna (1987) contend that a basic advantage of judgmentally overriding the quantitative forecasts is the emergence of a forecast "story" (that is, explanations underlying the forecast and the risks accompanying the forecast); they argue that "most users need to know not only *what* will happen, but why it will happen" (p. 350).

The reverse issue of statistically correcting the judgmental forecasts has received scant research attention (Ashton, 1984; Goodwin, 1997; Moriarty, 1985; Theil, 1971). The role of statistical interventions on judgmental predictions is particularly emphasized in organizational settings where the motivational factors for biasing the forecasts may be quite apparent and where such corrections could also serve as feedback mechanisms (Goodwin, 1996).

In addition to forecast adjustments, the accuracy benefits of combining statistical and judgmental forecasts have been repeatedly demonstrated (Blattberg and Hoch, 1990; Bunn and Wright, 1991; Collopy and Armstrong, 1992; Clemen, 1989; Lawrence, Edmundson, and O'Connor, 1986). See also chapter 12 by Newbold and Harvey in this volume for a review of the literature on the combination of forecasts. Superior accuracy appears to especially hold when there is information asymmetry; that is, when the experts have access to information not captured by the models (Hoch and Schkade, 1996; Yaniv and Hogarth, 1993). Combining could also lead to predictions that are inferior to judgmental forecasts, when statistical model performs poorly (Fildes, 1991). It appears that the contextual information can play an important mediating role in deciding when to combine, given the appraised value of the statistical model generating the forecasts. Supporting this assertion, Sanders and Ritzman (1995) have shown that, especially when the time series exhibits moderate to high variability, heavy emphasis should be given to judgmental forecasts based on contextual knowledge in making combination forecasts.

Mechanical combination is recommended over subjective combination (Goodwin and Wright, 1993; Lee and Yum, 1998; Lim and O'Connor, 1995), with some studies favoring regression-based weights (Guerard and Beidleman, 1987; Lobo, 1991; Newbold, Zumwalt, and Kannan, 1987) while others defend simple averaging of forecasts (Ashton and Ashton, 1985; Blattberg and Hoch, 1990; Bohara, McNown and Batts, 1987; Conroy and Harris, 1987). While the appropriate combination formula appears to depend on a myriad of factors, Armstrong and Collopy (1998) argue that the integration of statistical methods and judgment is effective when there exist structured methods for integration, when judgment brings information not captured by the statistical model, and when judgment is used as an input to statistical techniques (as in selecting variables and defining functional forms).

Combining individual judgmental forecasts provides another gateway for improving predictive accuracy (Ashton, 1986; Ferrell, 1985; Hill, 1982). Group forecasts commonly encountered in practice provide a variety of approaches to combining individual judgments (see Sniezek, 1989, for a review). Judgment accuracy has been found to change in the group process of combining individual assessments into a final group judgment, with group predictions displaying higher accuracy (Ang and O'Connor, 1991) as well as higher confidence (Sniezek and Henry, 1990), accompanied by increased member confidence following group discussion (Sniezek, 1992). Communication between group members can be beneficial as long as they are based on sharing differential information or insights about the possible variability of future outcomes, with measures taken to counteract "groupthink" and similar bias-inducing frames or dominating members (Lock, 1987).

Aside from the "interactive group forecasts" discussed above, statistical models could be used to aggregate individual judgments into "staticized group forecasts" (Hogarth, 1978), with the latter potentially yielding superior predictive performance than both the individual judgments (Einhorn, Hogarth, and Klempner, 1977) and the interactive group forecasts (Sanders, 1997a). Similarly, simple averaging of judgmental forecasts was found to display higher predictive accuracy than the judgmental combination of individual forecasts (Lawrence, Edmundson, and O'Connor, 1986). However, while improving performance aspects like calibration, simple averaging may simultaneously have deteriorating effects on other dimensions like discrimination (Wilkie and Pollock, 1994). Also, judgmental combinations of individual judgmental predictions are found to be no better than the best individual forecast, with judgmental combinations of judgmental and statistical forecasts performing worse than the best individual judgmental prediction (Angus-Leppan and Fatseas, 1986). Fischer and Harvey (1999) assert that these conclusions are only valid if no error histories of individual forecasters are available to the person combining these forecasts. The authors show that when summaries of past errors are available, judgmental combinations perform better than simple averaging of forecasts.

When forecasts are constructed in groups, recognition of member expertise and use of expertise from differential domains may lead to effective utilization of such knowledge for improved group forecasting performance (Littlepage, Robison, and Reddington, 1997). Covering a wide application umbrella extending from forecasts in technology management (Ward, Daview, and Wright, 1999) to predictions in economics (Cicarelli, 1984; Gibson and Miller, 1990), the Delphi technique provides an exemplary group process that aims to benefit from effective judgmental combinations of forecasts. The technique consists of a successive series of forecasting sessions whereby each expert revises his/her predictions in light of other experts' forecasts. Main characteristics include anonymity, iterations of judgment elicitation, group feedback, and statistical aggregation of forecasts in the last session to represent the final forecast (for an extensive review, see Gupta and Clarke, 1996). As a judgmental forecasting technique, Delphi assumes an especially critical role when geographically separated experts with diverse knowledge bases need to interact under conditions of scarce data – an archetypical economic forecasting scenario given the globalization process.

6.6. CONCLUSION

Research reviewed in this chapter attests to the wide use of judgmental forecasts, with their role highlighted under conditions of scarce data or when data sources are dubious and data quality is debatable. Even when operating in information-rich environments, however, judgmental forecasts are typically elicited to enhance the model-based forecasts, given their edge in incorporating expectations on structural changes and/or sporadic influences, as well as assimilating information on contemporaneous factors. Extensive implications of judgmental forecasting performance necessitates detailed analyses targeted at educating the users and providers of forecasts to their benefits as well as shortcomings. Such research should aim to develop modular and credible platforms for methodical incorporation of judgment into forecasting processes. As succinctly stated by Goodwin and Fildes (1999), "the challenge . . . is to develop forecasting support systems that encourage forecasters to recognize those elements of the task which are best delegated to a statistical model and to focus their attention on the elements where their judgment is most valuable" (p. 50).

Evaluation of judgmental forecasting performance poses significant research questions. Previous work has primarily focused on comparative accuracy, delineating forecast errors. Interestingly, surveys of practitioners indicate that accuracy is rated lower than "does the forecast make sense" in the list of important attributes (Huss, 1987), with academics assigning higher ratings of importance to accuracy (Carbone and Armstrong, 1982). Often, forecasts are intertwined with organizational concerns for establishing performance goals and reward systems (Welch, Bretschneider, and Rohrbaugh, 1998). Features of concern mostly center around forecast meaningfulness, intuition, and validation, thus stressing the importance of balancing data with judgment in the forecasting process (Bunn, 1996). In a similar vein, Geistauts and Eschenbach (1987) suggest validity (that is, forecast accuracy), credibility (that is, users' perceptions regarding the reliability of forecasts), and acceptability (that is, decision-maker's evaluation as to the utility and implementability of the forecast) as the prominent criteria for under-standing the implementation of forecasts. Implementation of judgmental fore-casts is argued to be especially difficult since (i) they appear less "scientific" than model-based forecasts, (ii) steps used in arriving at a judgmental forecast are more difficult to describe, (iii) judgmental biases are in effect, and (iv) such forecasts carry a "signature" so that the forecasters' personalities and qualifica-tions may overshadow the evaluation process. Organizational politics, reward systems, and communication processes interact with both the users' relations with forecast providers, and the users' goals and expectations to influence the implementation of a forecast (Geistauts and Eschenbach, 1987).

Regarding accuracy, it may be argued that forecast errors suggest windows of opportunity reflecting dimensions with an improvement potential. To promote learning, such aspects of accuracy may effectively provide mechanisms for indi-vidual feedback (Benson and Önkal, 1992; Önkal and Muradoglu, 1995; Remus, O'Connor, and Griggs, 1996; Sanders, 1997a), as well as group feedback for Delphi-like procedures (Rowe and Wright, 1996).

Feedback becomes particularly critical in rolling forecasts. Forecasts in organ-izational settings are not treated as permanent unchanging statements (Georgoff and Murdick, 1986) but, rather, they are revised to take into account new data, sporadic events like official announcements, and changing user needs. Similarly, economic forecasts are typically updates given periodic information releases or benchmark factors (McAuley, 1986). Rolling forecasts remain a promising topic, involving critical issues like timing decisions, contextual information sensitivity, feedback presentation, and organizational contingencies for effective judgmental adjustments. Relatedly, contextual information in both "hard" and "soft" forms assumes a critical role. It is not merely the continuity, consistency, and accessibil-ity of the information that is crucial for predictive performance, but also the reliability, completeness, and meaningfulness of the information that drives fore-casting accuracy, suggesting promising research agendas.

In revising predictions given new information, Batchelor and Dua (1992) report that economic forecasters assign too much weight to their own previous forecasts (as compared to previous consensus forecasts), interpreted as a tendency to appear variety-seeking instead of consensus-seeking. The authors speculate that this tendency could be due to perceived pressures to provide "worthy" forecasts, where forecasts close to the consensus are thought to be "valueless." They also note that it could be due to users not trusting the forecasters who revise their forecasts substantially, hence producing an anchoring effect on the previously announced forecast. These reports may signal that, especially in rolling forecasts, forecast consistency may be more important than accuracy as a performance criterion for users, given tolerable error bounds (White, 1986). Interestingly, Clements (1995) finds that, although forecasters' revisions may influence accuracy, there appears no evidence of their effects on the rationality of forecasts. In any case, forecast evaluation could be flawed in the absence of detailed knowledge of the forecaster's loss function. That is, unlike the statistical models, forecasters may pursue goals other than minimizing a particular function of the forecast error (Ehrbeck and Waldmann, 1996). Credibility considerations or other motivational pressures may suppress, for instance, the immediate and complete reflection of new information in the revised forecasts. These issues highlight the critical role that the user perspective can play in forecast quality and attest to the importance of provider–user communication. Detailed research into formats that systematically acknowledge and disseminate the uncertainty in forecasts remains crucial.

When the statistical model has not been performing up to expectations or non-time-series information exogenous to the model is expected to affect future outcomes, judgmental adjustments are called for. It has been pointed out that there could be a double-counting bias in making unstructured judgmental interventions to model-based forecasts (Bunn and Salo, 1996). In particular, it is argued that the omission of a variable from a model may not necessarily imply that its effect is not conveyed via other variables (correlated with the omitted variable) already included in the model. Thus, using "model-consistent expectations" for such omitted variables is suggested as a means to explore whether judgmental expectations are different enough to warrant a need for model adjustment (Bunn and Salo, 1996). Adjustments could also be made for behavioral reasons such as to make the predictions appear "plausible," to adhere to certain targets, and to meet the users' expectations (Fildes, 1987). Given that judgmental modifications are often made under implied organizational and political contingencies, systematic work on ecologically valid settings is definitely needed to enable reliable conclusions in this important area.

Combining forecasts is a related topic with disparate findings. Mechanical combinations of judgmental forecasts do not permit any exchange of information among forecasters but avoid behavioral problems that could stem from group dynamics. In settings where group forecasts are deemed desirable, it is recommended that multiple forecasts are elicited from each forecaster, and whenever possible, multiple experts with diverse information backgrounds are used to minimize biases. Hogarth (1978) concludes that predictions from six to 20 forecasters should be combined, with the number increasing as the divergence between forecasters increases; with Ashton's (1986) study providing full support. Naturally, combining becomes redundant when one forecast encompasses all the relevant information in the other forecasts – there has to be unique information to justify the inclusion of each in the aggregated forecast.

Structured research on group techniques like Delphi are needed to resolve the disparities in research findings on behavioral combinations of forecasts (Rowe, 1998). It is argued that the content validity of scenarios used in Delphi methods influences the performance of such groups (Parente and Anderson-Parente, 1987). Relatedly, scenario methods suggest a viable approach to enhancing the effectiveness of judgmental forecasting. These methods involve basing predictions on smoothly unfolding narratives that suggest plausible future conditions (van der Heijden, 1994). Conditioning scenarios, depicting various combinations of event outcomes, could be used for decomposition in the assessment of judgmental probability forecasts (Salo and Bunn, 1995). Given its emphasis on the wide range of plausible future outcomes, scenario analysis counterbalances the judgmental tendency to elide uncertainties (Bunn and Salo, 1993), providing a promising research direction for propagating and conveying uncertainties in judgmental forecasting.

In conclusion, the central tenet of judgmental forecasting is enhancing predictive performance via effectively incorporating nonmodel-based information into the forecasting processes. As shown by Clements and Hendry (1998), combination is valuable precisely when different sources are used, while leading to potentially poor results if all the forecasts are based on the same information set. In domains like economic forecasting, where the markets are in flux and where vast inflows of information permeate expectations, requisite flexibility in allowing for judgmental considerations will continue providing research impetus to benefit both the users and providers of forecasts.

References

Adam, E.E. and R.J. Ebert (1976). A comparison of human and statistical forecasting. *AIIE Transactions*, 8, 120–7.

Ang, S. and M. O'Connor (1991). The effect of group interaction processes on performance in time series extrapolation. *International Journal of Forecasting*, 2, 141–9.

Angus-Leppan, P. and V. Fatseas (1986). The forecasting accuracy of trainee accountants using judgmental and statistical techniques. *Accounting and Business Research*, 16, 179–88.

Armstrong, J.S. (1983). Relative accuracy of judgmental and extrapolative methods in forecasting annual earnings. *Journal of Forecasting*, 2, 437–47.

Armstrong, J.S. (1985). *Long Range Forecasting*. New York: Wiley.

Armstrong, J.S. and F. Collopy (1998). Integration of statistical methods and judgment for time series forecasting: principles from empirical research. In G. Wright and P. Goodwin, (eds.), *Forecasting with Judgment*. Chichester: John Wiley, 269–93.

Ashton, A.H. (1984). A field test of the implications of laboratory studies of decision making. *Accounting Review*, 59, 361–89.

Ashton, R.H. (1986). Combining the judgments of experts: How many and which ones?. *Organizational Behavior and Human Decision Processes*, 38, 405–14.

Ashton, A.H. and R.H. Ashton (1985). Aggregating subjective forecasts: Some empirical results. *Management Science*, 31, 1499–508.

Baginski, S.P., E.J. Conrad, and J.M. Hassell (1993). The effects of management forecast precision on equity pricing and on the assessment of earnings uncertainty. *Accounting Review*, 68, 913–27.

Bailey, C.D. and S. Gupta (1999). Judgment in learning-curve forecasting: a laboratory study. *Journal of Forecasting*, 18, 39–57.

Batchelor, R. and P. Dua (1990). Forecaster ideology, forecasting technique, and the accuracy of economic forecasts. *International Journal of Forecasting*, 6, 3–10.

Batchelor, R. and P. Dua (1992). Conservatism and consensus-seeking among economic forecasters. *Journal of Forecasting*, 11, 169–81.

Benson, P.G. and D. Önkal (1992). The effects of feedback and training on the performance of probability forecasters. *International Journal of Forecasting*, 8, 559–73.

Blattberg, R.C. and S.J. Hoch (1990). Database models and managerial intuition: 50 percent model + 50 percent manager. *Management Science*, 36, 887–99.

Bohara, A., R. McNown, and J.T. Batts (1987). A re-evaluation of the combination and adjustment of forecasts. *Applied Economics*, 19, 437–45.

Bolger, F. and N. Harvey (1993). Context-sensitive heuristics in statistical reasoning. *Quarterly Journal of Experimental Psychology*, 46A, 779–811.

Bolger, F. and N. Harvey (1998). Heuristics and biases in judgmental forecasting. In G. Wright and P. Goodwin (eds.), *Forecasting with Judgment*. Chichester: Wiley, 113–37.

Bolger, F. and G. Wright (1994). Assessing the quality of expert judgment: issues and analysis. *Decision Support Systems*, 11, 1–24.

Branson, B.C., K.S. Lorek, and D.P. Pagach (1995). Evidence on the superiority of analysts' quarterly earnings forecasts for small capitalization firms. *Decision Sciences*, 26, 243–63.

Bromiley, P. (1987). Do forecasts produced by organizations reflect anchoring and adjustment? *Journal of Forecasting*, 6, 201–10.

Brown, L.D., R.L. Hagerman, P.A. Griffin, and M.E. Zmijewski (1987). Security analyst superiority relative to univariate time-series models in forecasting quarterly earnings. *Journal of Accounting and Economics*, 9, 61–87.

Bunn, D.W. (1996). Non-traditional methods of forecasting. *European Journal of Operational Research*, 92, 528–36.

Bunn, D.W. and A.A. Salo (1993). Forecasting with scenarios. *European Journal of Operational Research*, 68, 291–303.

Bunn, D.W. and A.A. Salo (1996). Adjustment of forecasts with model consistent expectations. *International Journal of Forecasting*, 12, 163–70.

Bunn, D.W. and G. Wright (1991). Interaction of judgmental and statistical forecasting methods: Issues and analysis. *Management Science*, 37, 501–18.

Carbone, R., A., Andersen, Y., Corriveau and P.P. Corson (1983). Comparing for different time series methods the value of technical expertise, individualized analysis and judgmental adjustment. *Management Science*, 29, 559–66.

Carbone, R. and J.S. Armstrong (1982). Evaluation of extrapolative forecasting methods: Results of a survey of academicians and practitioners. *Journal of Forecasting*, 1, 215–17.

Carbone, R. and W.L. Gorr (1985). Accuracy of judgmental forecasting of time series. *Decision Sciences*, 16, 153–60.

Cicarelli, S. (1984). The future of economics: a Delphi study. *Technological Forecasting and Social Change*, 25, 139–57.

Clemen, R.T. (1989). Combining forecasts: a review and annotated bibliography. *International Journal of Forecasting*, 5, 559–83.

Clements, M.P. (1995). Rationality and the role of judgment in macroeconomic forecasting. *The Economic Journal*, 105, 410–20.

Clements, M.P. and D.F. Hendry (1998). *Forecasting Economic Time Series*. Cambridge: Cambridge University Press.

Clements, M.P. and D.F. Hendry (1999). *Forecasting Non-Stationary Economic Time Series*. Cambridge: MIT Press.

Collopy, F. and J.S. Armstrong (1992). Rule-based forecasting: development and validation of an expert systems approach to combining time series extrapolations. *Management Science*, 38, 1394–414.

Conroy, R. and R. Harris (1987). Consensus forecasts of corporate earnings: Analysts' forecasts and time series methods. *Management Science*, 33, 725–38.

Corker, R.J., S. Holly, and R.G. Ellis (1986). Uncertainty and forecast precision. *International Journal of Forecasting*, 2, 53–70.

Daan, H. and A.H. Murphy (1982). Subjective probability forecasting in the Netherlands: Some operational and experimental results. *Meteorologische Rundschau*, 35, 99–112.

Dalrymple, D.J. (1987). Sales forecasting practices: results from a United States survey. *International Journal of Forecasting*, 3, 379–91.

Dickson, G.W., G. DeSanctis, and D.J. McBride (1986). Understanding the effectiveness of computer graphics for decision support: A cumulative experimental approach. *Communications of the ACM*, 29, 40–7.

Donihue, M.R. (1993). Evaluating the role judgment plays in forecast accuracy. *Journal of Forecasting*, 12, 81–92.

Eckel, N. (1987). The interaction between the relative accuracy of probabilistic vs deterministic predictions and the level of prediction task difficulty. *Decision Sciences*, 18, 206–16.

Edmundson, B., M. Lawrence, and M. O'Connor (1988). The use of non-time series information in sales forecasting: a case study. *Journal of Forecasting*, 7, 201–11.

Eggleton, I.R.C. (1982). Intuitive time-series extrapolation. *Journal of Accounting Research*, 20, 68–102.

Ehrbeck, T. and R. Waldmann (1996). Why are professional forecasters biased? Agency versus behavioral explanations. *Quarterly Journal of Economics*, 111, 21–40.

Einhorn, H.J., R.M. Hogarth, and E. Klempner (1977). Quality of group judgment. *Psychological Bulletin*, 84, 158–72.

Evans, J. St. B.T. (1987). Beliefs and expectations as causes of judgmental bias. In G. Wright and P. Ayton (eds.), *Judgemental Forecasting*. Chichester: John Wiley, 31–47.

Ferrell, R. (1985). Combining individual judgments. In G. Wright (eds.), *Behavioural Decision Making*. New York: Plenum Press, 111–45.

Fildes, R. (1987). Forecasting: the issues. In S. Makridakis and S.C. Wheelwright (eds.), *The Handbook of Forecasting*, 2nd edn., New York: John Wiley, 150–70.

Fildes, R. (1991). Efficient use of information in the formation of subjective industry forecasts. *Journal of Forecasting*, 10, 597–617.

Fildes, R. and R. Hastings (1994). The organization and improvement of market forecasting. *Journal of the Operational Research Society*, 45, 1–16.

Fischer, I. and N. Harvey (1999). Combining forecasts: What information do judges need to outperform the simple average? *International Journal of Forecasting*, 15, 227–46.

Fox, J. (1999). What in the world happened to economics? *Fortune*, March 15, 60–6.

Geistauts, G.A. and T.G. Eschenbach (1987). Bridging the gap between forecasting and action. In G. Wright and P. Ayton (eds.), *Judgemental Forecasting*. Chichester: John Wiley, 177–95.

Georgoff, D.M. and R.G. Murdick (1986). Manager's guide to forecasting. *Harvard Business Review*, 64, 110–20.

Gibson, L. and M. Miller (1990). A Delphi model for planning "preemptive" regional economic diversification. *Economic Development Review*, 8, 34–41.

Glendinning, R. (1975). Economic forecasting. *Management Accounting*, 11, 409–11.

Goodwin, P. (1996). Statistical correction of judgmental point forecasts and decisions. *Omega: International Journal of Management Science*, 24, 551–9.

Goodwin, P. (1997). Adjusting judgmental extrapolations using Theil's method and discounted weighted regression. *Journal of Forecasting*, 16, 37–46.

Goodwin, P. and R. Fildes (1999). Judgmental forecasts of time series affected by special events: Does providing a statistical forecast improve accuracy?. *Journal of Behavioral Decision Making*, 12, 37–53.

Goodwin, P. and G. Wright (1993). Improving judgmental time series forecasting: a review of the guidance provided by research. *International Journal of Forecasting*, 9, 147–61.

Goodwin, P. and G. Wright (1994). Heuristics, biases and improvement strategies in judgmental time series forecasting. *Omega: International Journal of Management Science*, 22, 553–68.

Granger, C.W.J. and P. Newbold (1986). *Forecasting Economic Time Series*, 2nd edn. San Diego: Academic Press.

Guerard, J.B. and C.R. Beidleman (1987). Composite earnings forecasting efficiency. *Interfaces*, 17, 103–13.

Gupta, U.G. and R.E. Clarke (1996). Theory and applications of the Delphi technique: a bibliography (1975–1994). *Technological Forecasting and Social Change*, 53, 185–211.

Harvey, N. (1995). Why are judgments less consistent in less predictable task situations? *Organizational Behavior and Human Decision Processes*, 63, 247–63.

Harvey, N. and F. Bolger (1996). Graphs versus tables: effects of data presentation format on judgmental forecasting. *International Journal of Forecasting*, 12, 119–37.

Hill, G.W. (1982). Group versus individual performance: Are $N+1$ heads better than one? *Psychological Bulletin*, 91, 517–39.

Hoch, S.J. and D.A. Schkade (1996). A psychological approach to decision support systems. *Management Science*, 42, 51–64.

Hogarth, R.M. (1978). A note on aggregating opinions. *Organizational Behavior and Human Performance*, 21, 40–6.

Hogarth, R.M. and S. Makridakis (1981). Forecasting and planning: an evaluation. *Management Science*, 27, 115–38.

Holland, R.G., K.S. Lorek, and A.W. Bathke Jr. (1992). A comparative analysis of extrapolative and judgmental forecasts. *Advances in Accounting*, 10, 279–303.

Hopwood, W.S. and J.C. McKeown (1990). Evidence on surrogates for earnings expectations within a capital market context. *Journal of Accounting, Auditing and Finance*, 5, 339–68.

Howard, R.A. (1988). Decision analysis: practice and promise. *Management Science*, 34, 679–89.

Huss, W.R. (1985). Comparative analysis of company forecasts and advanced time series techniques using annual electric utility energy sales data. *International Journal of Forecasting*, 1, 217–39.

Huss, W.R. (1987). Forecasting in the electric utility industry. In S. Makridakis and S.C. Wheelwright (eds.), *The Handbook of Forecasting*, 2nd edn. New York: John Wiley, 87–117.

Jenks, J.M. (1983). Non-computer forecasts to use right now. *Business Marketing*, 68, 82–4.

Klein, H.E. and R.E. Linneman (1984). Environmental assessment: an international study of corporate practice. *Journal of Business Strategy*, 5, 66–84.

Kleinmuntz, B. (1990). Why we still use our heads instead of formulas: towards an integrative approach. *Psychological Bulletin*, 107, 296–310.

Langer, E.J. (1975). The illusion of control. *Journal of Personality and Social Psychology*, 32, 311–28.

Langer, E.J. (1982). *The Psychology of Control*. Beverly Hills: Sage.

Lawrence, M.J., R.J. Edmundson, and M. O'Connor (1985). An examination of the accuracy of judgmental extrapolation of time series. *International Journal of Forecasting*, 1, 25–35.

Lawrence, M.J., R.J. Edmundson, and M. O'Connor (1986). The accuracy of combining judgmental and statistical forecasts. *Management Science*, 32, 1521–32.

Lawrence, M.J. and S. Makridakis (1989). Factors affecting judgmental forecasts and confidence intervals. *Organizational Behavior and Human Decision Processes*, 42, 172–87.

Lawrence, M.J. and M. O'Connor (1993). Scale, variability, and the calibration of judgmental prediction intervals. *Organizational Behavior and Human Decision Processes*, 56, 441–58.

Lawrence, M.J. and M. O'Connor (1995). The anchoring and adjustment heuristic in time series forecasting. *Journal of Forecasting*, 14, 443–51.

Lee, J.K. and C.S. Yum (1998). Judgmental adjustment in time series forecasting using neural networks. *Decision Support Systems*, 2, 135–54.

Lichtenstein, S., B. Fischhoff, and L.D. Phillips (1982). Calibration of probabilities: The state of the art to 1980. In D. Kahneman and A. Tversky (eds.), *Judgment Under Uncertainty: Heuristics and Biases*. New York: Cambridge University Press, 306–34.

Lim, J.S. and M. O'Connor (1995). Judgmental adjustment of initial forecasts: its effectiveness and biases. *Journal of Behavioral Decision Making*, 8, 149–68.

Littlepage, G., W. Robison, and K. Reddington (1997). Effects of task experience and group experience on group performance, member ability, and recognition of expertise. *Organizational Behavior and Human Performance*, 69, 133–47.

Lobo, G.J. (1991). Alternative methods of combining security analysts' and statistical forecasts of annual corporate earnings. *International Journal of Forecasting*, 7, 57–63.

Lock, A. (1987). Integrating group judgments in subjective forecasts. In G. Wright and P. Ayton (eds.), *Judgemental Forecasting*. Chichester: John Wiley, 109–27.

Makridakis, S. (1988). Metaforecasting. *International Journal of Forecasting*, 4, 467–91.

Matthews, B.P. and A. Diamantopoulos (1986). Managerial intervention in forecasting: an empirical investigation of forecast manipulation. *International Journal of Research in Marketing*, 3, 3–10.

Matthews, B.P. and A. Diamantopoulos (1989). Judgmental revision of sales forecasts: a longitudinal extension. *Journal of Forecasting*, 8, 129–40.

McAuley, J.J. (1986). *Economic Forecasting for Business*. Englewood Cliffs: Prentice-Hall.

McNees, S.K. (1990). The role of judgment in macroeconomic forecasting accuracy. *International Journal of Forecasting*, 6, 287–99.

McNees, S.K. and N.S. Perna (1987). Forecasting macroeconomic variables: an eclectic approach. In S. Makridakis and S.C. Wheelwright (eds.), *The Handbook of Forecasting*, 2nd edn. New York: John Wiley, 349–72.

Meehl, P.E. (1954). *Clinical versus Statistical Prediction: A Theoretical Analysis and a Review of the Evidence*. Minneapolis: University of Minnesota Press.

Mentzer, J.T. and Cox, J.E. (1984). Familiarity, application, and performance of sales forecasting techniques. *Journal of Forecasting*, 3, 27–36.

Moriarty, M.M. (1985). Design features of forecasting systems involving management judgments. *Journal of Marketing Research*, 22, 353–64.

Muradoglu, G. and D. Önkal (1994). An exploratory analysis of the portfolio managers' probabilistic forecasts of stock prices. *Journal of Forecasting*, 13, 565–78.

Murphy, A.H. (1972a). Scalar and vector partitions of the probability score: Part I. Two-state situation. *Journal of Applied Meteorology*, 11, 273–82.

Murphy, A.H. (1972b). Scalar and vector partitions of the probability score: Part II. N-state situation. *Journal of Applied Meteorology*, 11, 1183–92.

Murphy, A.H. (1973). A new vector partition of the probability score. *Journal of Applied Meteorology*, 12, 595–600.

Murphy, A.H. and R.L. Winkler (1984). Probability forecasting in meteorology. *Journal of the American Statistical Association*, 79, 489–500.

Murphy, A.H. and R.L. Winkler (1992). Diagnostic verification of probability forecasts. *International Journal of Forecasting*, 7, 435–55.

Newbold, P., J.K. Zumwalt, and S. Kannan (1987). Combining forecasts to improve earnings per share prediction. *International Journal of Forecasting*, 3, 229–38.

O'Brien, P. (1988). Analysts' forecasts as earnings expectations. *Journal of Accounting and Economics*, 10, 53–83.

O'Connor, M. and M. Lawrence (1989). An examination of the accuracy of judgmental confidence intervals in time series forecasting. *Journal of Forecasting*, 8, 141–55.

O'Connor, M. and M. Lawrence (1992). Time series characteristics and the widths of judgmental confidence intervals. *International Journal of Forecasting*, 7, 413–20.

O'Connor, M., W. Remus, and K. Griggs (1993). Judgemental forecasting in times of change. *International Journal of Forecasting*, 9, 163–72.

O'Connor, M., W. Remus, and K. Griggs (1997). Going up – going down: How good are people at forecasting trends and changes in trends? *Journal of Forecasting*, 16, 165–76.

Önkal, D. and G. Muradoglu (1994). Evaluating probabilistic forecasts of stock prices in a developing stock market. *European Journal of Operational Research*, 74, 350–8.

Önkal, D. and G. Muradoglu (1995). Effects of feedback on probabilistic forecasts of stock prices. *International Journal of Forecasting*, 11, 307–19.

Önkal, D. and G. Muradoglu (1996). Effects of task format on probabilistic forecasting of stock prices. *International Journal of Forecasting*, 12, 9–24.

Önkal-Atay, D. (1998). Financial forecasting with judgment. In G. Wright and P. Goodwin (eds.), *Forecasting with Judgment*. Chichester: John Wiley, 139–67.

Parenté, F.J. and J.K. Anderson-Parenté (1987). Delphi inquiry systems. In G. Wright and P. Ayton (eds.), *Judgemental Forecasting*. Chichester: John Wiley, 129–56.

Peterson, R.T. (1991). The role of experts' judgment in sales forecasting. *The Journal of Business Forecasting*, 9, 16–21.

Pownall, G., C. Wasley, and G. Waymire (1993). The stock price effects of alternative types of management earnings forecasts. *The Accounting Review*, 68, 896–912.

Remus, W. (1987). A study of graphical and tabular displays and their interaction with environmental complexity. *Management Science*, 33, 1200–4.

Remus, W., M. O'Connor, and K. Griggs (1995). Does reliable information improve the accuracy of judgmental forecasts?. *International Journal of Forecasting*, 11, 285–93.

Remus, W., M. O'Connor, and K. Griggs (1996). Does feedback improve the accuracy of recurrent judgmental forecasts? *Organizational Behavior and Human Decision Processes*, 66, 22–30.

Rothe, J.T. (1978). Effectiveness of sales forecasting methods. *Industrial Marketing Management*, April, 114–8.

Rowe, G. (1998). The use of structured groups to improve judgmental forecasting. In G. Wright and P. Goodwin (eds.), *Forecasting with Judgment*. Chichester: John Wiley, 201–35.

Rowe, G. and G. Wright (1996). The impact of task characteristics on the performance of structured group forecasting techniques. *International Journal of Forecasting*, 12, 73–89.

Russo, J.E. and P.J.H. Schoemaker (1992). Managing overconfidence. *Sloan Management Review*, 33, 7–17.

Salo, A.A. and D.W. Bunn (1995). Decomposition in the assessment of judgmental probability forecasts. *Technological Forecasting and Social Change*, 49, 13–25.

Sanders, N.R. (1992). Accuracy of judgmental forecasts: a comparison. *Omega: International Journal of Management Science*, 20, 353–64.

Sanders, N.R. (1997a). The impact of task properties feedback on time series judgmental forecasting tasks. *Omega: International Journal of Management Science*, 25, 135–44.

Sanders, N.R. (1997b). The status of forecasting in manufacturing firms. *Production and Inventory Management Journal*, 38, 32–5.

Sanders, N.R. and K.B. Manrodt (1994). Forecasting practices in U.S. corporations: Survey results. *Interfaces*, 24, 92–100.

Sanders, N.R. and L.P. Ritzman (1992). The need for contextual and technical knowledge in judgmental forecasting. *Journal of Behavioral Decision Making*, 5, 39–52.

Sanders, N.R. and L.P. Ritzman (1995). Bringing judgment into combination forecasts. *Journal of Operations Management*, 13, 311–21.

Sniezek, J.A. (1989). An examination of group process in judgmental forecasting. *International Journal of Forecasting*, 5, 171–8.

Sniezek, J.A. (1992). Groups under uncertainty: an examination of confidence in group decision making. *Organizational Behavior and Human Decision Processes*, 52, 124–55.

Sniezek, J.A. and R.A. Henry (1990). Revision, weighting, and commitment in consensus group judgment. *Organizational Behavior and Human Decision Processes*, 45, 66–84.

Soergel, R.F. (1983). Probing the past for the future. *Sales and Marketing Management*, 130, 39–43.

Sparkes, J.R. and A.K. McHugh (1984). Awareness and use of forecasting techniques in British industry. *Journal of Forecasting*, 3, 37–42.

Stael von Holstein, C.-A.S. (1972). Probabilistic forecasting: an experiment related to the stock market. *Organizational Behavior and Human Performance*, 8, 139–58.

Stewart, T.R., P.J. Roebber, and L.F. Bosart (1997). The importance of the task in analyzing expert judgment. *Organizational Behavior and Human Decision Processes*, 69, 205–19.

Theil, H. (1971). *Applied Economic Forecasting*. Amsterdam: North-Holland.

Turner, D.S. (1990). The role of judgment in macroeconomic forecasting. *Journal of Forecasting*, 9, 315–45.

Tversky, A. and D. Kahneman (1974). Judgment under uncertainty: heuristics and biases. *Science*, 185, 1124–31.

van der Heijden, K. (1994). Probabilistic planning and scenario planning. In P. Ayton and G. Wright (eds.), *Subjective Probability*. Chichester: John Wiley, 549–72.

Wallis, K.F. (1985–1988). *Models of the U.K. Economy: Reviews 1–4*. Oxford: Oxford University Press.

Ward, P., B.J. Davies, and H. Wright (1999). The diffusion of interactive technology at the customer interface. *International Journal of Technology Management*, 17, 84–108.

Welch, E., S. Bretschneider, and J. Rohrbaugh (1998). Accuracy of judgmental extrapolation of time series data: Characteristics, causes, and remediation strategies for forecasting. *International Journal of Forecasting*, 14, 95–110.

Wheelwright, S.C. and D.G. Clarke (1976). Corporate forecasting: promise and reality. *Harvard Business Review*, 54, 40–8.

White, H.R. (1986). *Sales Forecasting: Timesaving and Profit-making Strategies That Work*. London: Scott, Foresman and Company.

Willemain, T.R. (1989). Graphical adjustment of statistical forecasts. *International Journal of Forecasting*, 5, 179–85.

Willemain, T.R. (1991). The effect of graphical adjustment on forecast accuracy. *International Journal of Forecasting*, 7, 151–4.

Wilkie, M.E. and A.C. Pollock (1994). Currency forecasting: an investigation into probability judgment accuracy. In L. Peccati and M. Virén (eds.), *Financial Modeling*. Heidelberg: Physica-Verlag, 354–64.

Wilkie, M.E. and A.C. Pollock (1996). An application of probability judgment accuracy measures to currency forecasting. *International Journal of Forecasting*, 12, 25–40.

Wilkie-Thomson, M.E. (1998). An examination of judgment in currency forecasting. Unpublished Ph.D. Thesis. Glasgow, Glasgow Caledonian University.

Wilkie-Thomson, M.E., D. Önkal-Atay, and A.C. Pollock (1997). Currency forecasting: An investigation of extrapolative judgment. *International Journal of Forecasting*, 13, 509–26.

Winklhofer, H., A. Diamantopoulos, and S.F. Witt (1996). Forecasting practice: a review of the empirical literature and an agenda for future research. *International Journal of Forecasting*, 12, 193–221.

Yaniv, I. and R.M. Hogarth (1993). Judgmental versus statistical prediction: information asymmetry and combination rules. *Psychological Science*, 4, 58–62.

Yates, J.F. (1982). External correspondence: decompositions of the mean probability score. *Organizational Behavior and Human Performance*, 30, 132–56.

Yates, J.F. (1988). Analyzing the accuracy of probability judgments for multiple events: an extension of the covariance decomposition. *Organizational Behavior and Human Decision Processes*, 41, 281–99.

Yates, J.F., L.S. McDaniel, and E.S. Brown (1991). Probabilistic forecasts of stock prices and earnings: the hazards of nascent expertise. *Organizational Behavior and Human Decision Processes*, 49, 60–79.

Young, R.M. (1984). Forecasting with an econometric model: the issue of judgmental adjustment. *Journal of Forecasting*, 1, 189–204.

CHAPTER SEVEN

Forecasting for Policy

Adrian R. Pagan and John Robertson

7.1. INTRODUCTION

Any complete account of "forecasting for policy" could be formidably long. There are an enormous number of economic policy issues that require a forecast. For example, the effects of changes in taxes and tariffs upon output and employment, the impact of legislation relating to retirement incomes upon savings behavior, questions relating to variations in regional growth rates and even the setting of greenhouse emission targets.[1] This diversity is naturally associated with a corresponding diversity in what is forecast, the interval of time between which successive forecasts must be made, the nature of the association between those making forecasts and the policy-makers, and the forecasting methods that are deemed to be most suitable. Contemplating such a list, it is clear that we need to narrow the focus considerably in order to make the topic manageable. Perhaps the one thing about which there may be agreement is that forecasts, whether explicit or implicit, are at the heart of policy (Budd, 1999), while the methods for making a forecast often engender much less agreement.

Given both our own experiences, interests, and expertise, and the fact that it is probably macroeconomic forecasts that feature most prominently in public discussion, it is natural that we concentrate upon that strand. Even with such a constraint, there is still too much variety, as macroeconomic policy resides in at least two institutions – finance ministries (treasury departments) and central banks. This institutional division sometimes results in independent decisions being taken with respect to the fiscal and monetary instruments in attempts to influence the macroeconomy. Whenever this happens, it will be necessary for each to take account of the actions of the other when forming a forecast. Such considerations suggest that the framework used for forecasting will most likely be institution dependent. Nevertheless, there could be considerable overlap and we believe that this is probably true today, if not in the past.

It is also necessary that we identify the individuals who are making forecasts. It has to be the case that policy-makers possess some strategy for forming a view about the future when making their decisions but it is unlikely that one can discover this with any accuracy. Reading some of the published statements of the attitudes of policy-makers such as Blinder (1999), the transcripts of meetings such as the Federal Open Market Committee (FOMC) – see Edison and Marquez (1998) – and reflections by advisers such as Stevens (1999) on how policy-makers react to forecasts suggests that there is no real consensus that we can draw upon about who ultimately makes the forecasts that underlie policy decisions. In some cases, such as in the U.S., a staff forecast is presented to the policy-makers simply as a baseline for discussion by the policy-makers, and these forecasts do not represent the forecasts of the individual policy-makers (see Reifschneider, Stockton, and Wilcox, 1997). In other cases, such as at the Bank of England, the forecast is the result of a process of interaction between the bank staff and the policy-makers (George, 1997). We propose to concentrate upon the forecasting process of policy advisers rather than that of policy-makers. How influential the former is upon the latter is largely unknown. We don't feel that it is zero but a reading of some of the FOMC discussion (Edison and Marquez, 1998), shows that the responses by policy-makers to the projections of policy advisers can vary a great deal with the individual involved.

It is also important to remark that a good deal of what we discuss below is concerned with some of the mechanics of forecasting. However, in practice a considerable amount of a policy analyst's time is occupied in ascertaining whether there are quirks in the data and how a piece of evidence should be counted in any forecast. There are many reasons why data can be hard to interpret. Examples include changes in the method of data collection; the impact of natural events such as hurricanes and snowstorms; feasts such as Christmas occurring on a weekend; and the presence of extra pay-periods in a quarter. All of these can make a difference to any assessment of the current position of the economy and its likely evolution. Moreover, even when it is impossible to isolate reasons for any perceived aberrant behavior, the analyst may well feel that "something is wrong" and that later data revisions are likely to shed a different light on the series under consideration.[2] A deep knowledge of the nature of these particular statistics as well as a grasp of the lessons of economic history is incredibly important to being a successful forecaster for policy-makers. Such difficulties with the data inevitably impact upon forecasting, regardless of which method is finally adopted.

We therefore propose to focus upon forecasting for monetary policy, limiting ourselves to occasional comments about how this might differ if it was fiscal policy that was being considered. Sometimes the differences are too extreme for us to do this in any satisfactory way. These situations arise when fiscal policy is more concerned with resource allocation than stabilization issues; the most appropriate framework then tends to be one of dynamic general equilibrium. For example, the Dutch Central Planning Bureau places a heavy emphasis upon such models in setting policy. In the next section we set out what we perceive to be common elements in the forecasting processes of central banks around the world. Section 7.3 then looks at some case studies, summarizing the forecasting process in five central banks – the U.S., the U.K., Australia, New Zealand and Canada. These tend to be the best documented and our conversations with representatives of other central banks would suggest that their forecast procedures have one or other of the approaches represented in the chosen quintet. In some instances all of the styles were experimented with by each institution until the method that was judged to be most suitable for its own circumstances was settled upon. Chapter 16 in this volume, by Eitrheim, Husebø, and Nymoen, discusses the experiences of the Norges Bank in forecasting with its macroeconomic model. Section 7.4 concludes.

7.2. The Basis of Forecasts

Those faced with the task of forecasting in a policy environment need to make decisions about a number of issues. We canvass eight of these in the following subsections through a series of questions. Although segmented, they are not really independent and often the answers provided to one of the questions posed will depend upon the solutions proposed to another.

7.2.1.   What needs to be forecast?

There are always a minimal number of variables that policy-makers wish to see forecasts about. For monetary policy decisions, inflation and output growth are the obvious candidates, but aggregate demand, future wage developments, and the global outlook may be others. Even so, this list is rarely exhaustive, simply because the construction of a forecast for (say) inflation may require a forecast of other variables such as productivity. Whether these intermediate forecasts even make their way to policy-makers is more problematic, although often they are implicitly provided when discussing the environment surrounding a forecast. A second reason for why a relatively large number of variables may need to be forecast is that, in order to motivate the forecasts that are being presented, an adviser needs to tell a story about them. For example, a forecast of aggregate demand may need to be separated into consumption and investment components, since the current economic environment may suggest that these are likely to evolve in different directions. As Dawes (1999) observes, it is easier to convince the recipient of the forecast of its validity if it can be given a plausible interpretation, and some degree of disaggregation may aid this process. Policy-makers would need to weigh up the plausibility of the aggregate forecasts by considering their own beliefs about the constituent parts. Policy-makers may also occasionally ask for information about a variable on which forecast information is not routinely available, particularly when there has been some institutional change. For example, in some countries the impact of privatization and demutualization upon consumption has been an important topic during the 1990s. Disaggregation does have problems associated with it, however. It will often be the case that some components are difficult to predict compared to either the aggregate or other components. An example would be forecasting the output of the manufacturing sector, where data is relatively accessible, versus forecasting the quantitatively more important service sector. Also, the degree of disaggregation cannot be too extreme, as it can easily become very hard to present a consistent story about the whole picture.

7.2.2. What is the forecast horizon and interval?

One can distinguish a few separate issues under this title. First, how long the forecast period should be will depend upon the impact of policy instruments. If these are swift, as is often the case with a temporary tax change, the forecast horizon can be relatively short. Generally, though, there are enough lags in the system coming from inertia in the responses of households and firms as to mean that forecasts will be prepared using a one- to two-year horizon. In the case of monetary policy the relevant period is generally set at between six to eight quarters, although sometimes longer-term forecasts are made. Fiscal authorities are increasingly looking at horizons of at least three years. Second, it is necessary to decide on how often a forecast is to be made. To use some jargon, how often does a "forecasting round" occur and what is to be done in the inter-forecast period, a period that is sometimes referred to as the "monitoring quarters"? There are a number of institutional constraints that decide the answer to this question, including how often policy-makers meet to consider a change in policy, how often (if at all) the institutions are required to produce a public forecast, and the frequency of publication of the national accounts.[3]

7.2.3. Should one develop a model?

At one level, the question here is simply semantic. One U.S. policy-maker, Laurence Meyer (1999), argues strongly for the utility of models in the policy process. Mostly what is at issue is the type of model. Thus, the question we are posing here has to be one concerning whether a forecast might be produced without any economic model, even a very informal one. For the likely readership of this chapter, the question may sound somewhat odd, but there are two reasons for raising it. First, if the forecast period is relatively short, there are often accurate surveys available on the plans of economic agents over its length. For example, one generally gets data available on whether agents are expecting their prices to rise over the next six months and by how much, as well as a record of what happened in the previous quarter. Balance statistics representing the difference between the proportion of respondents expecting output to rise or fall are also often used to shed information on output growth; for example, see Bank of England (1999, pp. 11–12). All these pieces of information can be used to produce a forecast, although relating the pieces of information will generally require some statistical model. Second, even if the forecast horizon is relatively long, a large number of forecasts relating to any country for a one- to two-year period now emanate from many sources for example *The Economist*, Consensus Economics, the IMF, the OECD, newsletters from banks and domestic funds managers. All this information might be collated and used; one motivation for doing so is that one thereby acquires information from a wide variety of "models," something that policy-makers often find attractive. The main disadvantage of a strict reliance on pooled information is often the lack of a story that can be associated with the forecasts. This is an obvious impediment to their use by policy-makers, but also for policy advisers, as the latter generally need to address policy meetings and so must have formed some view on the rationale for a particular forecast outcome. Finally, another point in favor of having a model relates to the issue of "transparency." Even if a model and its forecasts are only one element in the thinking behind a policy action, examination of its structure can be very useful in educating and informing markets about the reasoning behind changes in policy instruments. Perhaps in order to focus on key issues and to avoid being distracted by excessive detail, most central banks appear to have adopted relatively small-scale macroeconometric models as the main vehicles for their medium-term forecasting exercises.

7.2.4.   What type of forecasting system is desirable?

Often forecasting is performed in different sections of a policy-making institution, each with responsibilities for specific parts of the forecast horizon. In particular, it is very common to have two sections. One section concentrates upon modeling of the whole system with a "core" model, adopting an horizon that is longer than six months, while the other focuses upon the initial six months. This latter group generally employs either an "indicator" or "spreadsheet" model, but also uses a good deal of judgment in forming the short-term forecast. The knowledge of sector specialists is relied upon quite heavily in this regard. Models may be involved but they are mostly statistical in nature, although economic ideas may guide and inform the choices. It is rare for much economic structure to be formally imposed at this level, and the methods do not lend themselves to producing a consistent statement about the evolution of the complete system. Whilst it is certainly possible to preserve national account identities by sufficient iteration between the different sector specialists, having a large number of different "local" opinions can sometimes lead to seemingly inconsistent behavioral relations. For example, if a Phillips curve connects wage and price inflation and unemployment, each person producing forecasts for their own series may have a different view of this relation in their own minds (or none at all). In the case of a specific series such as the consumer price index (CPI) a great deal of disaggregation may be undertaken in order to enable "sector specialists" to incorporate their knowledge about events such as tax changes, modifications of statistical procedures for compiling the data, etc.

Perhaps the most important issue to be resolved when faced with such a separation in responsibility is how to make the forecasts of the two groups cohere over the total forecast horizon. In many instances the two strands coexist rather uneasily and with little interaction. In that case it is generally those receiving the forecasts who must resolve any conflicts. Recently, some central banks have tried to fully integrate the two groups within a comprehensive forecasting system. The leader in this endeavor has been the Bank of Canada in their Quarterly Projection System (QPS), and their techniques have been transplanted to at least one other site, the Reserve Bank of New Zealand through its Forecasting and Policy System (FPS). There is a strong case for having a seamless approach to forecasting and the appropriate way of doing this is likely to receive quite a lot of attention in the years ahead.

7.2.5.   What type of model should be constructed?

A decision also has to be made about which type(s) of model(s) are to be used. As mentioned earlier, it is unlikely that there will be a single model. A consistent theme that emerges from reading policy documents is that policy-makers would prefer to see forecasts from a range of approaches rather than a single forecast. A member of the Bank of England Monetary Policy Committee, Vickers (1999, p. 11) sums this up in the following words:

> Models get two cheers. The pluralist approach to modeling gets three. That is why the Bank, like many other organisations, has a suite of models, rather than being wedded to a single model. In the context of the forecasting process there has to be a core model in order to ensure overall consistency, but how it used is informed by a variety of other models.

Thus, for example, although a detailed model may give a relatively precise forecast of inflation, a simpler and more stylized model may be of greater use for understanding the relation between the instruments of policy and targets such as output growth and inflation.[4] In part this reflects the fact that models are used in the policy process for other purposes, such as simulating the effects of alternative policy rules or changes in the way inflation expectations are formed. These types of simulations may be difficult to implement in the primary forecasting model. Even if it is feasible there is often a desire to provide consistency checks on the simulations using smaller theoretically-based models. Moreover, it is doubtful if policy-makers place great emphasis upon the point forecasts presented to them, and frequently see the forecasting process simply as an aid to bolstering their understanding of the available options. Duguay and Longworth (1998, p. 368) note that the Governor and Deputy Governor of the Bank of Canada expressed the opinion in an internal survey conducted in 1988 that:

> They regarded the staff projection as a basis for policy discussion . . . but what mattered most for policy discussion was the macroeconomic picture and the analysis of the major issues facing the economy. . . . As well they wanted the presentation to highlight the more contentious assumptions and the major risks.

The Bank of England details five types of models used in supporting decisions taken by their Monetary Policy Committee and we will use their categories to make some brief comments on the nature of models used in forecasting in a policy environment.

The "core" model

Most policy-setting institutions have a "core" model that summarizes the main relationships within the macroeconomy and is the reference point for forecasting and policy evaluation in the medium term. These models usually contain about 30 or so stochastic equations and determine another 100–150 variables through identities. The modeling philosophy often involves the selection of a set of long-run relations such as a constant labor share, a production function, a constant long-run real exchange rate, and interest rate arbitrage. To this is sometimes added uncovered interest rate parity at the short end of the term structure. A variety of mechanisms are invoked to relate the short run and the long run, with departures from the long-run equilibrium values being an important factor in ensuring long-run convergence. Of course this philosophy is now a very standard one in macroeconomic modeling, finding its most precise expression in equilibrium correction models.[5] Even though there is a shared vision in most of these models, there are also significant differences, particularly in regard to the relative roles played by forward- and backward-looking expectations in determining expenditures. Thus, for example, some models would have investment being determined by the gap between expected future returns and the current cost of capital while others would replace expected future returns by current returns. The Bank of England's core model seems to be of the latter variety, whereas the QPM model of the Bank of Canada takes the former approach.

The way that empirical evidence is used in constructing the models can also vary substantially. The Bank of Norway's RIMINI model uses standard econometric estimation methods with a heavy emphasis upon cointegration tools, whereas Coletti et al. (1996, p. 3) say about the Bank of Canada's QPM model that

> ... the model is calibrated to reflect the empirical evidence, rather than directly estimated.

In practice this means "QPM's short-run properties have been configured to reflect a number of key assessments as to how the economy functions and how monetary policy works." A similar situation exists for the Reserve Bank of New Zealand's FPS model with the parameters and even the structure being chosen to produce outcomes that are regarded as being plausible for the New Zealand economy. That is, the dynamics of this model reflect quite a bit of judgment from specialists within the Bank. One argument in favor of the latter strategy is if it is felt that there have been large structural changes to the economy so that the correlation amongst historical data series may not be very informative about the influence of current policy changes. The possibility of such shifts can also make it difficult to specify reliable numerical values for long-run equilibrium ratios; for example, the debt to GDP ratio. Both the Canadian and New Zealand core models have steady state solutions for such a ratio. However, these are unlikely to represent what agents perceive the short-run equilibrium values to be at any point in time, since those individuals must learn about the long-run equilibrium in the face of many changes; for example, the liberalization of financial markets. Exactly what to use as historical short-run equilibria, and how to "smooth paste" these into the steady state values, is a contentious issue. Often, it seems to involve the use of trends extracted with a Hodrick–Prescott filter from the historical data on the ratios. In other instances, as in the core U.S. model, the equilibrium trajectory is forecast from auxiliary vector autoregression models. Such constructed values are then forced to decay to the steady state at some prescribed rate.

Core models are) often not the best way to produce accurate forecasts at a fairly short-term horizon. But it is hard to see what the alternative is when the forecast horizon lengthens and one wishes to look at the sensitivity of outcomes to a policy change. Thus the importance of a core model will depend a good deal on the relative mix of scenario analysis and forecasts in the making of policy decisions. Some of the features that well-designed core models can have may also be of assistance when formulating policy. One of these is a steady-state solution that can be consulted to view the long-run consequences of a policy action. Another, once forecasts of their exogenous variables are fed in, is the generation of "medium-term equilibrium" paths; that is, where the core model predicts that the economy is heading in the medium term.

VECTOR AUTOREGRESSIONS

In some situations, a vector autoregression (VAR) is used to model the complete economy, but more often they are adopted to explore specific questions such as the role of monetary aggregates in predicting inflation and output growth. Their record in forecasting output growth in countries such as the U.S. and Australia during the Asian crisis tends to have been quite good, possibly because of the fact that an event like the Asian shock was absent from the sample used for estimation, so that the models continued to predict strong economic growth. Consequently, the fact that they are rarely used as a core model has to be explained by something other than the magnitude of forecasting errors. Part of the explanation lies in the difficulty of using them for policy analysis, since they treat policy as partly unexpected (exogenous) events and partly as determined by the past history of the variables appearing in a VAR. It is true that a policy shock may be identified through a VAR with some loose economic reasoning, but such shocks are rarely easy to relate to actual policy events (see Rudebusch, 1998). Moreover, in practice VARs ascribe most of the variation in policy instruments to systematic behavior; for example, Dungey and Pagan (1999) find that 85 percent of the variation in the monetary policy instrument in Australia was allocated to that source. So a user of VAR forecasts has to accept that the policy instrument will vary continuously over the forecast horizon, something that is not easy to explain to policy-makers who are considering whether to change a policy instrument that they feel will be sustained over the forecast horizon.[6] Such reservations mean that VARs tend to be used simply as forecasting devices and not for policy analysis. In the former role, the emphasis can be placed upon their statistical characteristics, and this perhaps accounts for why the most popular versions have been Bayesian VARs. The latter involve prior stochastic restrictions upon the coefficients that might be regarded as plausible given the nature of many economic times series – see Robertson and Tallman (1999) for a review of the different type of restrictions that have been used. Even in that role they have the disadvantage that it is hard to isolate the story that underlies any predictions made with them – see Meyer's (1999) comment in this vein. Fundamentally, the case for a VAR in prediction is based on the first category in Whittle's (1963, p. 2) pithy summary: "Prediction can be based upon recognition of a regularity as well as upon explanation of a regularity."

Small forward-looking models

These models embroider what has sometimes been referred to as the "central bank model" (see Clarida et al., 1999; McCallum, 1999). They contain an IS curve with forward-looking expectations and past dynamics, a Phillips curve with both forward- and backward-looking expectations, an aggregate supply constraint, and some mechanism for setting policy. If money supply is the instrument then a money demand function needs to be appended to the system, but in most cases the system is closed with a simple interest rate rule. These models differ from the "Core" models in terms of the degree of aggregation. However, they also often tend to place greater emphasis upon forward-looking behavior in the IS curve and the wage–price sector than do the larger scale models. It is probably true that they are rarely used for forecasting *per se*, but the distinction between forecasting and simulations of policy actions is a fine one. The Batini–Haldane model discussed in Bank of England (1999) is a good example of an open-economy version of this framework, which augments the fundamental elements above with an uncovered interest parity condition. Because of the relatively small size of these types of model, it is relatively easy to experiment with alternative assumptions and parameter settings. Hence they can provide a useful cross-check on the policy simulations from the core model. However, the high degree of aggregation and the tendency to have a simplified dynamic structure means that they may not be very useful for either short-term forecasting or for explaining sources of business cycle variation.

Single equation regression models

Examples of these would be Phillips curve models and relations summarizing the connection between the exchange rate and the terms of trade (or commodity prices) in open economies. The main advantage of such models is their simplicity and that they can be readily used to calculate forecasts conditional on a range of alternative paths for the explanatory variables. In some cases the conditional forecasts might be used as cross-checks on the forecasts from the core model, and sometimes the purpose is to give policy-makers some feel for longer-term movements in the economy. For example, there is an extensive literature on equilibrium exchange rates, and studying movements in predictions of these can be informative.

Dynamic optimizing models

Often, it is necessary to form a view about the likely economic consequences of a particular structural change or an atypical shock. One general problem with using regression-based models for this task is that their coefficients may be functions of underlying preferences and technology, as well as government policy, and it is usually difficult to predict the effect that a change in these parameters would have for the estimated coefficients. Largely because of their stronger structural basis, dynamic optimizing models tend to be the mainstay of the academic literature. They rarely produce forecasts directly but can be an ingredient in a forecast and are sometimes important in producing an understanding of forecasts. This class of model ranges from dynamic stochastic general equilibrium (DSGE) models (King and Wolman, 1996) and asset pricing models to more deterministic versions such as McKibbin and Wilcoxen's (1998) G-cubed model.

Dynamic optimizing models are often used to study issues that are hard to address satisfactorily with the first and third types of model, particularly welfare issues and those that relate to structural changes and events that are unusual in historical perspective. An example of the latter would be the Asian crisis, where simulations from a model such as G-Cubed can be very informative about global developments and can assist in thinking about the global environment; for example, see the experiments in McKibbin and Martin (1998). As McKibbin (2000, p. 50) says: "Indeed it is in providing consistent scenarios and highlighting general equilibrium issues for input into a broader forecasting exercise, rather than as pure number generators, where the newer generation of global economic models have been most valuable in recent years."

As such, it is clear that these models are much more closely related to scenario analysis than to traditional forecasting.

Representatives from the classes of models outlined above are found to a greater or lesser extent in most central bank policy and research departments, and we will illustrate this point when summarizing the forecasting process in a range of central banks in the next section. Consequently, an important point to be derived from our discussion is that it is rare for a decision to be taken to build a single model, although it is not unknown. In some respects this is a break with the prevailing philosophy of the 1960s and 1970s, where the objective seems to have been to devise a single model that was capable of answering many questions. This change in emphasis has come about in part because of the large increase in computing capabilities, making it relatively easy today to develop and maintain a suite of models. However, it is also appears that there is a growing consensus that a single model is unlikely to be a reliable and useful tool in all circumstances.

7.2.6. Conditional or unconditional forecasts?

The type of forecast to be performed is often described as being conditional or unconditional, and the distinction relates to the assumption made about how nonmodeled variables and the policy instrument are to be set over the forecasting horizon. Specifically, if the latter is treated as exogenous and either held constant or shifted in a permanent manner, then the resulting forecast is often termed a conditional one. If, however, the policy instrument path is set in response to objectives such as inflation and output growth, then the forecast is said to be unconditional, even though this ignores any conditioning upon the nonmodeled variables. Generally, forecasts going to policy-makers are conditional, but there is an emerging debate about whether one should ignore the fact that historically the policy instrument may not have been held constant in the face of variations in inflation and output and other factors. The issue here is the extent to which the policy instrument is set according to a reaction function when forming the forecasts. As Blinder (1997, p. 9) observes in describing rules for monetary policy, one might want to substitute a fully-specified path for a future policy instrument rather than just assume a constant path, and be prepared to continually re-appraise that path as new information becomes available.

A related problem is the treatment of variables such as asset prices for which the forecasting record is very poor. It is very difficult to forecast quarter to quarter movements in such variables, although it may be easier to pick up longer-term movements. The dilemma is often resolved by conditioning forecasts upon such variables, perhaps using values which are thought to be representative of longer-run values. Some analysis of the sensitivity of the forecasts to this assumption is then often provided to policy-makers so that they can incorporate this uncertainty into their assessment of the forecast. In passing one might note that, to some extent, the choice between conditional and unconditional forecasts reflects the fact that the forecasting is being done for policy-makers. It is clear that a private-sector forecaster would want an unconditional forecast.

7.2.7. Initial conditions?

Because current values for many variables are not available at the time of the forecast, some decision has to be made about how to handle this "initial conditions" problem. Generally there will be many partial measures available, mostly of the indicator variety, and these may be assembled to produce some estimates of quantities such as GDP. It is very common to see these being identified with the short-run forecasts made using indicator or judgmental methods.

7.2.8. Adjusting for a lack of fit?

Linear, time-invariant core models may not produce a close fit to historical data, even if some allowance has been made for short-run dynamic behavior in their specification. Clearly, this failure to fit the past history has some bearing upon their ability to forecast the future. Various adjustments involving "add factors" and "intercept corrections" may be used to try to make an adjustment to the forecasts. As described in Clements and Hendry (1998), intercept corrections can be divided into two broad categories: (1) discretionary adjustments representing the influence of anticipated future events that are not explicitly part of the model, and (2) projecting into the future past forecast errors to get the model "back on track." It is the latter type that we discuss here; the first is captured by our "judgment" category. Typically, these automatic corrections involve finding a sequence of residuals that would enable the model to reproduce the recent past history and any short-term (usually one or two quarters) forecasts made with indicator methods. If a time-series model is fit to these residuals, then the add factors will generally be forecasts of future values for the residuals (with the residuals from the indicator-based forecast being the initial conditions). If the residuals follow a stable stationary process, then the influence of the initial conditions will decay to zero and so the forecasts in the medium term will be just those from the core model. Some judgment may also be applied to set this rate of decay.

7.2.9. Summary

The discussion above suggests that, at a broad level of abstraction, the basic mechanism of the forecasting process in a policy environment might be summarized as comprising of four elements:

1 A series of models or methods that are used to produce short-run (1–2 quarter ahead) forecasts.
2 A relatively small core model that produces forecasts of major aggregates of interest over a 1–3 year horizon.
3 A method for disaggregating the aggregated forecasts from the core model so as to utilize the insights of sector specialists.
4 A collection of auxiliary models that are designed to provide information about policy actions (such as policy simulations), or yield information relating to forecasts which are hard to analyze with the core model (such as the effects of unusual events).

These elements are part of most of the forecasting systems we study although the emphasis given to each differs across institutions. Moreover, the way each component is implemented varies a great deal; for example, the degree to which the core model is closely linked to data, versus how much theoretical structure is imposed. Additional theoretical structure might reduce the model's forecast accuracy but will generally aid its economic interpretability.

Finally, the role of judgment in forecasting is one important aspect of the forecasting process that will not be discussed very systematically in what follows, basically because it is hard to get precise information on how it is used. One thing that is clear, however, is that policy institutions rarely, if ever, rely solely on mechanical model-based forecasts. If the science of forecasting is the model, then the art of forecasting is the judgment that is applied by the individuals involved.

7.3. SOME CASE STUDIES

7.3.1. The U.S. Federal Reserve

THE PROCESS

Monetary policy in the United States is set by the Federal Open Market Committee (FOMC) and consists of 12 voting members: seven members of the Board of Governors of the Federal Reserve System, and the presidents of five of the 12 Reserve Banks ("regional Feds").[7] The staff of the Board of Governors prepares forecasts of U.S. and international economic activity prior to each of the eight

FOMC meetings held each year. Independently, the staff of each of the regional Feds may also produce forecasts as part of their briefing of their Bank's president prior to an FOMC meeting. The various Board and regional Fed forecasts are not made publicly available until several years after an FOMC meeting. However, a summary of the outlook of the policy-makers is contained in the forecasts of GDP, inflation and unemployment documented in the "Humphrey–Hawkins" testimony on monetary policy submitted to the Congress twice each year. We will focus here on the forecasting system implemented at the Board of Governors.

Information available to the FOMC policy-makers comes from a number of sources. First, each Federal Reserve Bank gathers anecdotal information on current economic conditions in its District through reports from Bank and Branch directors and interviews with key business contacts, economists, market experts, and other sources. The so-called Beige Book summarizes this information. In addition the Board receives information directly from various advisory councils who can provide an assessment of recent economic developments. Second, staff at the Board of Governors produce several documents for FOMC meetings. One document is entitled "Current Economic and Financial Conditions" and is commonly referred to as the Green Book because of its green cover. The Green Book lays out the staff's assessment of recent developments in the domestic macroeconomy, together with an analysis of the financial and international developments. The Green Book also presents quarterly point forecasts for key aggregates in the domestic economy such as the broad components of GDP, unemployment, and prices and wages. The forecast horizon in the Green Book is up to nine quarters ahead, although it is sometimes as short as six quarters. Another document, the Blue Book, contains model simulations to examine alternative strategies for policy over a longer period, often up to five years. These simulations are presented formally at least twice each year.

Published accounts of the forecasting system suggest that, despite its role in the overall policy-making process, a core macroeconometric model is not the tool used for producing the Green Book forecasts (Reifschneider, Stockton, and Wilcox, 1997). In fact, the forecasts are primarily judgmental in nature, relying heavily on the expertise of sector specialists and senior advisers. The process of generating a Green Book forecast begins with a forecast coordinator who provides the conditioning assumptions and initial forecasts for several key aggregates such as inflation and output.[8] Staff experts on various sectors of the economy then quantify the impact on the aggregate baseline forecast as well as data that has become available since the last FOMC meeting on their sector-specific forecasts. Each sector specialist would potentially use a range of econometric models relevant to their sector for guidance in preparing their forecasts. The sector forecasts are then blended by the coordinator into revised aggregate forecasts, which are returned to the sector specialists, who may again adjust their sector forecasts in view of the new aggregate baseline. After some iteration, the "consensus" forecast is reported in the Green Book.

High-frequency time-series data (monthly, weekly) are used to tune the short-range forecasts by providing better estimates of initial conditions. For example, a newly available monthly labor market or retail sales report might impact upon the assessment of current quarter GDP growth. Several statistical models are used to filter the high-frequency data. The near-term forecast is considered important because the dynamics of spending and production are linked to the nature of short-term changes. For example, an increase in final sales might be expected to have different medium-term effects on production if it is being borne by foreign rather than domestic producers. Anecdotal evidence also plays a potentially important role in identifying trends that may not yet have shown up in official statistics.

THE CORE MODEL

The Board maintains a core domestic model, the FRB/U.S. model. This model contains about 40 stochastic behavioral equations – see Brayton and Tinsley (1996) for an overview. There is no money supply and demand relationship, with short-term interest rates determined by policy rules that can be toggled on or off. The FRB/U.S. model is the successor to the larger MPS model that was used until the early 1990s, and is distinguished from its predecessor mainly by its explicit separation of the macro-dynamics of the nonfinancial sector into adjustment cost and expectations-formation components. In particular, most nonfinancial-sector variables are assumed to move gradually to eliminate past disequilibria (deviations of actual from desired levels), and also respond to the path that the equilibrium is expected to follow in the future. This "target-seeking" feature is also common to models used at the Bank of Canada and the Reserve Bank of New Zealand. The financial sector of FRB/U.S. is based on various instantaneous arbitrage equilibria. For example, long-term interest rates are determined via the expected path of short rates plus a time-varying term premium, while the real value of the stock market is determined via the discounted expected future flow of dividend payments.

The core model is used as input to the Green Book forecasting system, primarily as a check on the plausibility of the forecasts, and for identifying the sources of any discrepency. Also, if a major change in underlying assumptions occurs between meetings, then the FRB/U.S. model may be used to provide a new benchmark baseline. In practice the core model is add factored in order to replicate the final Green Book forecasts over the forecast horizon. This adjusted version of the core model is then used for various exercises, such as generating intervals around the Green Book forecasts based on stochastic simulations, and occasionally for producing forecasts at horizons beyond two years. The core model also appears to play an important role in simulation experiments, such as predicting the effects of alternative policy paths and/or alternative assumptions about exogenous variables. The simulation results are typically presented in the Blue Book at FOMC meetings.

7.3.2.   The Bank of Canada

THE PROCESS

Monetary policy in Canada is set within the Bank of Canada with no outside members involved in decisions to raise or lower interest rates. As described by

Duguay and Poloz (1996), the Bank of Canada's staff formally prepares forecasts for senior Bank management at least four times a year. These are of two types. A semi-annual long-term forecast (after the release of the second and fourth quarter national accounts) with up to a seven-year horizon; and two quarterly medium-term updates (after the release of the first and third quarter National accounts) that have a two-year horizon. A core model, called the Quarterly Projection Model (QPM) (see Poloz, Rose and Tetlow, 1994, for an overview), provides the framework for each forecasting round. Embedded within the core model is a steady-state model upon which experiments can be performed to assess the long-term implications of a shock or a policy action. Although dynamic adjustment is allowed for in the model, it was not designed to replicate the very short-run dynamics that might be found from the data. Consequently, it was decided that "very short-run forecasts (for the first couple of quarters) would be done entirely outside the core model – by staff judgment" (Coletti et al., 1996, p. 14).

The Bank staff begins each major forecasting round by analyzing the United States and Mexican economies, which are taken as exogenous to the QPM. An assessment is then made of the domestic current quarter situation, compared to what was previously forecast. The potential sources of forecast errors are examined in order to try to distinguish between temporary special factors, such as weather events, and more fundamental changes.

Next, the QPM is simulated to produce paths for the core macroeconomic variables, including policy variables, that are consistent with the Bank's inflation targets. Satellite models are used to translate this projection into implications for more disaggregated variables. The use of satellite models arose since it was believed that it would be hard to maintain the rigorous theoretical structure in QPM if the core model was made too disaggregated. Not a great deal of information seems to be available about these models. At this stage, some judgment is applied in order to reconcile differences between the results of the sector-specific forecasts and the aggregate forecasts. As a consequence, several iterations of the process are often required before there is convergence to a consensus outlook. Finally, sensitivity analysis is performed with the QPM in order to get a feel for the likely implications of alternative conditioning assumptions, such as changes in world oil prices or the rate of real growth in the economies of key trading partners, as well as changes in key model parameters.

In the inter-forecast period, sector specialists monitor new data relative to their current forecasts and make a judgment as to whether the new data are consistent with the existing aggregate forecasts. The signals from each sector are then evaluated and some revision to the overall short-term forecasts may be made. As well, the likely implications for the next baseline forecasts will be discussed with senior management.

THE CORE MODEL

Prior to the mid-1990s, a large-scale quarterly econometric model called RDXF had been used as an organizing framework for incorporating the judgment of sector specialists into the four formal forecast exercises (see Robertson and McDougall, 1980). Since about 1994, a more aggregated model that places greater emphasis on theoretical consistency, particularly in stock-flow relations, has replaced the large-scale model (see Coletti et al., 1996). The QPM model contains a mixture of rational and adaptive expectations, a steady-state equilibrium, overlapping contracts, and full stock-flow accounting. Monetary policy is accounted for by a policy reaction function based on forward-looking inflation control targets with a six to seven quarter horizon. As with the FRB/U.S. model, the QPM emphasizes the separation of dynamic terms into two separate components; one of which effectively describes how agents learn about the new equilibrium while the other reflects dynamic adjustments toward the equilibrium positions due to lags, etc. Compared to a standard equilibrium-correction framework, much of what would have represented pure disequilibrium effects would now appear as equilibrium dynamics. Numerical values of parameters in the QPM model are set to produce "reasonable" responses rather than being estimated directly from time-series data. As a consequence, not a great deal of attention is paid to the model's short-term fit to data.

AUXILIARY MODELS

In addition to its role in providing a framework for the preparation of economic forecasts, the QPM has been used as a policy analysis tool. The basic technique of analysis is stochastic simulation. However, as Coletti et al. (1996, p. 5) observe: "For pure policy research, for example, QPM is perhaps too complicated and takes too long to solve . . . in part because of the extra structure that is necessary to make the model useful for economic projections."

This has led to the development of a newer model, the Canadian Policy Analysis Model (CPAM) – see Black and Rose (1997). All in all, CPAM is a smaller version of QPM and has been configured to simulate much faster than that model so that large-scale stochastic simulations for policy analysis become feasible. It has many features in common with QPM, containing the same basic economic theory and exhibiting similar dynamic properties.[9] The CPAM is also the template used for the core model of the forecasting system employed at the Reserve Bank of New Zealand.

7.3.3. The Reserve Bank of New Zealand

THE PROCESS

A few years ago, the accepted wisdom seemed to be that models used for forecasting should be divorced from models used for policy – see, for example, Wren-Lewis (1995). The usual argument was that forecasting models are unreliable for policy analysis because they tend to have inconsistent or "old fashioned" theoretical foundations. It may be true that this dichotomy is still present, but today there is a serious attempt to integrate the various models into a single framework. One of the institutions which is most advanced in this task is the Reserve Bank of New Zealand (RBNZ). As its name implies, the Forecasting and Policy System (FPS) is an integrated approach to forecasting and policy evaluation. The system was clearly inspired by the builders of the Canadian quarterly projection system and was actually built under contract by some of the members of that group. Moreover, as the introduction to the CPAM model in Black and Rose (1997) notes, that model was built using many of the principles underlying FPS. Not only do the forecasting systems of the RBNZ and the Bank of Canada have a common origin, but many of the other arrangements relating to monetary policy are the same. For example, the Governor sets policy after advice from an internal monetary policy committee. The forecasts published in the Monetary Policy Statement are actually issued under his name. Given all this one might think of treating the Bank of Canada and the RBNZ as a single unit in discussion. However, there are some advantages to a partial separation simply because the FPS system is so well documented, with much of the documentation readily accessible via the RBNZ website (http://www.rbnz.govt.nz/). In many ways, a study of forecasting at the RBNZ can be very informative about gaps in the documentation of the Bank of Canada system, so we have opted to produce a separate treatment.

Forecasts are published each quarter for a wide range of variables, not just output and inflation. In particular, a forecast is given for the 90-day bill rate. Since this is quite closely related to the instrument of policy (since the change in operating procedures in March 1999), the cash rate, the RBNZ is effectively providing a statement about the anticipated future course of policy. It seems to be unique among central banks in doing this on a regular basis. Provision of such a future path complies with Alan Blinders' recommendation mentioned earlier, and is fully compatible with the core model in the sense that the path of future rates is chosen to achieve the target inflation rate. However, as Drew and Frith (1998, p. 317) observe: "It is during the process of producing a projection that the tools of the FPS and the 'human element' come together. . . . During the projection process, judgment is applied to the projected path for the economy until a plausible macroeconomic picture emerges. . . . it is people who produce the projections, rather than models."

Because of the close connection with the Bank of Canada the differences in the forecasting process are relatively minor. Forecasts of variables thought to be exogenous to the economy are taken from a number of outside sources. The forecasting round begins with an unmodified forecast. Indicator models are used to produce forecasts for the monitoring quarters and these become the starting points in producing forecasts from the core model for the longer horizons. Modifications are then made through add factors in each of the equations of the model until a central scenario emerges, and this then forms the basis of the published forecasts.

THE CORE AND RELATED MODELS

In terms of our division of the forecasting process into four elements, the FPS explicitly deals with three of them:

1 Indicator models to handle short-run (up to two quarters) predictions.
2 A core model that is used to produce medium-term (1–2 year) forecasts and to perform policy analysis.
3 Satellite models that disaggregate the forecasts from the core model.

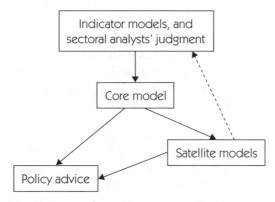

Figure 7.1 Basic structure of the FPS model

The basic structure of the FPS can be summarized in figure 7.1, which is based on figure 1 in Breece and Cassino (1998).[10]

The indicator models used within the bank are not publically documented but are designed to capture the short-term time-series characteristics of detailed macroeconomic data and to utilize the sectoral analyst's judgment. For example, tonnes of cement produced has been found to have a close relationship to commercial construction – Drew and Frith (1998, p. 318).

The core model contains the key features that were present in the Bank of Canada CPAM model. That is, the presence of a well-defined steady state, explicit stock-flow accounting and budget constraints, endogenous monetary policy with an inflation target as the nominal anchor, and the separation of dynamic adjustments in nonfinancial sectors into "expectational" and "intrinsic" components. On the supply side, there is a system of relative prices and an underlying inflation process that is driven primarily by the output gap, wages and indirect taxes, foreign prices and exchange rates, and inflation expectations.

Three satellite models disaggregate the simulated values from the aggregate projections made with the forecasting system. Initially there were plans for a number of these, but the demand for extra ones has turned out to be nonexistent (St Clair and McDermott, 2000). The method used for disaggregation is to first prescribe an equilibrium share, based on some idea about where particular components are headed. The dynamics around the equilibrium path for variables in the satellite models are then derived from estimated "autoregressive" functions. The adjustment rate is not constant, but is modified according to variables such as relative prices and disequilibrium in stocks and flows. In practice, the equilibrium paths are derived using a Hodrick–Prescott filter that converges to a fixed steady-state share – see Breece and Cassino (1998) for a complete discussion. The main advantage of this process is that it allows the dynamics of the core model to be kept relatively simple and the satellite models are quite transparent and amenable to modification by sector specialists. As McKibbin (2000) observes, this is important when using forward-looking models. Otherwise, the order of dynamics in the system becomes very high, thereby creating difficulties for numerical algorithms.

AUXILIARY MODELS

A smaller forward-looking demand-side model has been developed by Hargreaves (1999), and denoted as the SDS–FPS model. Designed to produce simulations more cheaply than the larger FPS core model, it is nonetheless calibrated to replicate the dynamic properties of the core model for key aggregates. The heart of the SDS–FPS model is a forward-looking IS curve, a Phillips curve, an exchange rate equation, and a monetary policy reaction function. It also contains additional equations to determine the relative prices of consumption goods, inflation and exchange rate expectations, interest rates, and the prices of exports and imports. A VAR model was constructed in Drew and Hunt (1998a) and this is mainly used to produce shocks that could be fed into the FPS and SDS–FPS models for stochastic simulation purposes.

7.3.4. The Bank of England

THE PROCESS

In the United Kingdom monetary policy is set by a Monetary Policy Committee (MPC) composed of three Bank of England representatives and six non-Bank members. Forecasts of inflation and output have been presented quarterly in the Inflation Report since February 1993. These forecasts are meant to be a summary of the views of the members of the MPC and, as such, are intended to explain any policy actions. The current forecasting process at the Bank of England and the resulting inflation and output "fan charts," represent an explicit attempt to map the uncertainty that the policy-maker has about alternative economic assumptions onto a distribution of future outcomes via a combination of models and judgment. Figure 7.2 (from Vickers, 1999) provides a schematic summary of the forecasting process, and how it relates to policy decisions.

As described in Britton, Fisher, and Whitley (1998), and by Vickers (1999), a series of meetings take place between the MPC and the Bank of England's forecasting staff, beginning about one month before the Inflation Report is published. At the first meeting current issues, key assumptions and an initial assessment

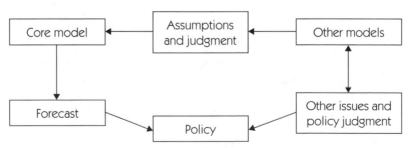

Figure 7.2 The Bank of England forecasting process.

of the relative likelihood of various future paths for the economic variables are discussed.[11] Following these discussions, the forecasting staff prepares central (most likely) forecast paths together with forecast distributions constructed to reflect as accurately as possible the MPC's assessment of relative risks (skewness) and the overall uncertainty (variability). These forecast distributions might be revised following subsequent meetings between the MPC and Bank staff. If the MPC judges that the distribution is inconsistent with its assessment of the issues then the staff will be asked to make changes. For example, the type of assumptions, their probability, or perhaps the core model itself might be changed. Notably, two sets of forecasts are published in the Inflation Report. The first is based on the assumption of unchanged U.K. short-term interest rates during the forecast period, while the second allows interest rates to follow the MPC's assessment of market expectations.

THE CORE MODEL

As presaged earlier, the Bank of England maintains a suite of models and has made descriptions of the various models publicly available (see Bank of England, 1999). However, exactly what relative weights are ultimately given to these models in the committee's published forecast is unknown. Speeches made by the members of the MPC have not shed a great deal of light upon this. The core model, termed MM in Bank of England (1999), involves about 20 behavioral relations and 130 variables in total. In some respects, the MM model can be categorized as having been constructed from a "bottom-up" (equation by equation) perspective rather than the "top-down" philosophy that is a feature of the Bank of Canada's QPM. Also, unlike some other central bank models, the parameters of the MM are estimated econometrically from time-series data.

The underlying structure of the MM involves: (1) the specification of an equilibrium position in real variables which is independent of the price level and displays a vertical long-run Phillips curve; (2) a nominal variable equilibrium determined via an inflation target and a feedback rule for short-term nominal interest rates; and (3) a sluggish adjustment to shocks due to both real and nominal rigidities. The explicitly forward-looking aspects of the MM are limited to the foreign exchange market, and the dynamics of nonfinancial sectors are generally determined by conventional equilibrium-correction mechanisms. Thus, for example, a forward-looking Phillips curve cannot be derived analytically from the wage–price system within MM. The MM is used to simulate the effects of various exogenous shocks such as a shift in the inflation target or a temporary change in short-term interest rates. Presumably these types of experiments are conducted as part of the preparations for the forecast in which alternative risks are assessed.

AUXILIARY MODELS

The Bank also maintains some small forward-looking models, of which the leading example is that due to Batini and Haldane (1999). This model is a less detailed but more theoretically consistent version of MM, and its estimated parameters are chosen to satisfy numerous theoretically motivated constraints.

The smaller size makes it more tractable and the results are often easier to inter-pret in economic terms. Also, because there are fewer equations and parameters it is easier to experiment with alternative behavioral assumptions, such as the degree of forward-looking behavior in agents' decision-making. Against this, the higher level of aggregation means that the smaller model is not necessarily as accurate or reliable a forecasting tool as the larger-scale version, particularly at short horizons.

Bank of England staff have also used various single-equation Phillips curve models to investigate the relationship between inflation and summary measures of disequilbrium in the real economy, and to simulate the implications for inflation of alternative unemployment rate paths. Along with VAR models, these are used as a cross-check on the inflation forecasts produced by the core model.

Finally, the MPC also makes use of business and consumer survey data obtained from private organizations and Bank of England regional agencies. Because of their timeliness, and their focus on forward-looking behavior, they are viewed as being particularly important from a forecasting perspective. That is, these surveys represent one form of nonmodel information used in constructing the Inflation Report projections.

7.3.5. The Reserve Bank of Australia

THE PROCESS

Monetary policy in Australia is set by the Reserve Bank of Australia (RBA) Board. This Board consists of nine members, seven of whom are external to the Bank. No regular set of published forecasts is provided but they can sometimes be gleaned, at least on a qualitative dimension, from studying the Semi-Annual Statement on Monetary Policy, the quarterly reports on The Economy and Financial Markets and speeches of RBA officials.[12] One peculiarity of monetary policy in Australia is that the Secretary of the Treasury sits on the Board. Perhaps this is responsible for another unusual arrangement in the form of a Joint Forecasting Group, which involves both the Treasury and the RBA forecasters along with representatives of other Commonwealth Government Departments with input into economic policy formation. Although there is no requirement that a single forecast should be adopted by all members of this group, it would be surprising if the differences in forecasts are very large. The presence of the Joint Forecasting Group means that concentrating upon the forecasting activities at the RBA in isolation may be a little misleading regarding the overall forecasting system.

The RBA constructs forecasts using several of the approaches described earlier and these are presented to internal staff meetings in the lead-up to each Board meeting. A small core macroeconometric model is used to produce a set of no-policy change forecasts, adjusted in light of special anticipated events using intercept corrections. For example, inflation forecasts for the year 2000 have to recognize the impact of the pending introduction of a Goods and Services Tax. The model-based forecasts are then compared to those from the groups respons-ible for producing separate forecasts of real and nominal variables. These groups use a variety of spreadsheet or indicator models, as well as incorporating their own judgment and survey data. For example, survey data on expected future capital expenditure by the private sector in Australia have proved to be quite accurate predictors of investment. There is often conflict between the projections of the "spreadsheet" and "core modeling" groups and this is resolved by the former deciding whether to adjust their forecasts in light of the those produced by the latter. The forecasts of both the modeling and "spreadsheet" groups are then passed up to senior management who impose another round of judgment in reaching a final forecast. Sometimes these adjustments are quite large owing to a feeling that there is too much inertia in the forecasts that come out of the indicator framework. After all these modifications, a final set of forecasts is sent to the Board for use in its deliberations.

The process just described is similar for both short- and long-term forecasts. Unlike some other institutions, the model doesn't become more influential as the forecast horizon lengthens, although long-term forecasts do tend to revert toward trend values that are found in historical data. Such long-run convergence is very common among forecasters. A striking example was recently afforded when the 1999 benchmark revisions to U.S. real GDP data raised the average historical growth rate by 50 basis points. Almost immediately, most forecasters raised their long-term forecasts of U.S. growth by exactly this amount.

Overall, although both indicator models and a core model are used in the RBA for forecasting purposes, there is extensive modification of their output through the judgment of higher-level bank officials, albeit in a way that is hard to systematize. Certainly, there is nothing like either the Bank of Canada or Reserve Bank of New Zealand approach to the task. Simulations are sometimes run with the core model to compute the optimal policy path consistent with that model and this is taken as a useful check on policy actions that are either proposed or have been taken. With that exception, it seems rare for the RBA to formally study different policy scenarios, and that may be an important part of the explanation for why the core model has a much smaller role in the policy process compared to the situation in other central banks.

THE CORE AND RELATED MODELS

There are core models in both the RBA and the Treasury. The current RBA model is described in Beechey et al. (2000) and the Treasury's has the acronym TRYM (see www.treasury.gov.au for documentation of this model). The RBA model is relatively small, with five stochastic equations and about 19 exogenous variables. It does not feature forward-looking behavior. Perhaps the best way to describe it would be as a slimmed down version of the MM model used at the Bank of England, even though it was not developed in the same manner. The TRYM model is much closer to the type of core model used at the Reserve Bank of New Zealand, having a relatively strong theoretical base, although forward-looking expectations are mainly confined to financial markets. To some extent there would be a limited need for these public institutions to develop core models for evaluating different scenarios (and even for making forecasts), since Australia has had models like those in Canada commercially available for quite a long period. This is primarily due to the work of Chris Murphy of ECONOTECH – see Powell and

Murphy (1995) for a good description of this class of model, variants of which are used at the New Zealand Treasury and the Monetary Authority of Singapore. These models have a strong theoretical core, forward-looking behavior and the parameters are generally estimated from data, although in equations such as the Phillips curve the parameter values are sometimes calibrated to produce "economically sensible responses" rather than to obtain a tight fit to historical data. Both the RBA and Treasury subscribe to the current version of Murphy's model. Another model that is commercially available and which can be used for analyzing the impact of international developments upon the Australian economy is the model developed by the McKibbin Software Group, denoted as MSG2.

A variety of indicator models are used. In many instances these are equilibrium-correction equations. An example would involve the forecasting of the volume of imports using an equilibrium-correction model that links imports to gross national expenditure and relative prices. However, because there are always some lumpy items in Australian imports, dummy variables might need to be added over the estimation period, with add factors used to account for similar events in the forecast period.

7.4. CONCLUSIONS

We have tried to summarize some of the basic issues that arise when forecasting is being conducted in the context of a macroeconomic policy decision, specifically monetary policy, and have described some of the responses that have been made to these issues at several central banks. One thing that becomes apparent from the chapter is the diversity of approaches that are currently taken. Some institutions favor an approach that is structured explicitly within a model framework that encapsulates their consensus "world view." Of the institutions we study, the Reserve Bank of New Zealand and the Bank of Canada appear to be representative of this approach. Others, of which the Reserve Bank of Australia is an example, place much greater emphasis upon the judgments of sector experts and the experience of policy advisors. In some ways, the distinction is between those favoring relatively formal methods of forecasting and those who find the use of expert systems appealing. Of course, the distinction is not a sharp one. For example, while the Board of Governors of the U.S. Federal Reserve primarily uses an expert-based system for producing baseline forecasts, they rely on a detailed core macroeconometric model for policy simulation analysis as well as a cross-check on the economic plausibility of the baseline forecasts. At the Bank of England, a core model is used to produce forecasts, but the policy-makers assign subjective weights to various alternative assumptions in producing a forecast distribution. Ultimately, no institution relies entirely on formal models to produce forecasts, but inevitably they must use an economic model of some sort to provide the story that accompanies the forecast numbers.

Exactly why some institutions adopt a particular approach while others don't is not known to us. To some extent, it may reflect the personalities of the policy-makers and their senior advisors; that is, the recipients of the forecasts. If these individuals are convinced of the merits of experience and judgment and are cautious about the utility of models, then it is highly likely that the first methodology will prevail. This is probably most telling when the track record of a model-based forecast has been poor. For example, in the U.S., models based solely on historical relationships generally failed to anticipate the sustained combination of low rates of inflation and unemployment over the latter part of the 1990s. Cost cannot be ruled out as a factor as well. Having many sector specialists can be quite expensive and also raises the likelihood of coordination problems. Having a single system that all the forecasting staff subscribes to, as in the Forecasting and Policy System at the Reserve Bank of New Zealand, can be a very cost-effective method of producing forecasts and policy analysis in a small central bank. Further investigation into the sources of diversity in approach across institutions seems warranted.

One striking feature of our investigation, at least based on published accounts, is that many institutions seem to be quite happy with the general structure of their current forecasting system. St. Clair and McDermott (2000) express this opinion explicitly about the forecasting system at the Reserve Bank of New Zealand. Nevertheless, there is also continued interest in experimenting with new forecasting techniques such as Bayesian VARs. In this regard, academic researchers could profitably devote some time to the issues that arise when a variety of models are used to produce forecasts within an institution, a preference that has been expressed by many policy-makers.

Acknowledgments

Thanks are due to John McDermott, Warwick McKibbin, and Ellis Tallman for valuable comments on earlier drafts. Chris Aylmer, Anthony Dickman, Lynne Cockerell, Malcom Edey, David Gruen, and Glenn Stevens have also been very helpful in discussing their experiences with the forecasting process. However, the views expressed here are those of the authors and do not necessarily reflect the opinions of the Reserve Bank of Australia, the Federal Reserve Bank of Atlanta, or the Federal Reserve System.

Notes

1   We will use the words "forecasting" and "projection" interchangeably in this chapter, simply because much of the literature does so.
2   As Reserve Bank of New Zealand Governor Brash (1998) notes, the first estimate of GDP growth in the March quarter of 1996 provided by Statistics New Zealand was 1.5 percent, while a year later it had been revised to 4.2 percent. As he comments, "The policy implications of these two numbers are radically different".
3   The increasing availability of survey and other high-frequency data that sheds light on the development of the national aggregates has probably meant that this latter issue has become less of a constraint over time.
4   In commenting on an early forecasting model used in the Bank of Canada, RDXF, Duguay and Longworth (1998, p. 369) observe that "considerable top-down judgment was imposed so that the output from the projection process resembled what one would get from a reduced form aggregate demand equation and a Phillips curve."

5 Equilibrium correction equations relate current changes to past deviations from equilibrium and lagged changes. However, some models describe the out of equilibrium behavior of nonfinancial variables either in terms of so-called polynomial adjustment cost (Brayton et al., 1997) or target-seeking behavior (Coletti et al., 1996). The resulting equations differ from standard error correction equations by also including discounted expected future equilibrium levels. This forward-looking aspect is a key feature of the core models of the Board of Governors of the U.S. Federal Reserve, the Bank of Canada, and the Reserve Bank of New Zealand.

6 Of course, there is nothing to preclude one from doing forecasts by constructing shocks which keep the monetary policy instrument on some given path (Leeper and Zha, 1999). However, to be consistent with the notion of rational expectations, the required shock sequence could not be not too persistent or large.

7 The President of the Federal Reserve Bank of New York is a permanent member of the FOMC; the other presidential members rotate on an annual basis.

8 The key conditioning assumptions, such as the path for the federal funds rate, fiscal policy, as well as stock and energy prices are described in the text of the Green Book. However, the wording is generally nonspecific about the exact values and timings involved.

9 However, the inflation dynamics in CPAM are based on a staggered real wage contracts model, rather than a generalized adjustment cost mechanism that is a feature of the QPM and the FRB/U.S. models.

10 It seems reasonable to suppose that a similar schematic summarizes the forecasting system at the Bank of Canada based on the QPM.

11 As an example, the MPC might decide that, following a previously unexpected increase in income, the most likely outcome for expenditure is a 2.5 percent increase during the first year, but that the balance of risks lies in the upward direction, in that a greater change than 2.5 percent is more likely than one that is less.

12 There are many statements by bank officials about how policy is governed by forecasts, so it is surprising there has been little expressed demand for a description of the forecasting process.

References

Bank of England (1999). *Economic Models at the Bank of England*. Bank of England.

Batini, N. and A.G. Haldane (1999). Forward-looking rules for monetary policy. In J.B. Taylor (ed.), *Monetary Policy Rules*. Chicago: University of Chicago Press for NBER.

Beechey, M., N. Bharucha, A. Cagliarini, D. Gruen, and C. Thompson (2000). A small model of the Australian macroeconomy. Reserve Bank of Australia Discussion Paper.

Black, R., V. Cassino, A. Drew, E. Hansen, B. Hunt, D. Rose, and A. Scott (1997). The forecasting and policy system: the core model. Reserve Bank of New Zealand Research Paper No. 43.

Black, R. and D. Rose (1997). Canadian policy analysis model: CAPM. Working paper 97-16, Bank of Canada.

Blinder, A.S. (1997). What central bankers could learn from academics – and vice versa. *Journal of Economic Perspectives*, 11, 3–19.

Brash, D. (1998). Reserve bank forecasting: Should we feel guilty? *RBNZ Bulletin*, December Quarter, 61(4), 328.

Brayton, F., A. Levin, R. Tryon, and J. Williams (1997). The evolution of macro models at the Federal Reserve Board. *Carnegie-Rochester Conference Series on Public Policy*, 47, 43–81.

Brayton, F. and P. Tinsley (1996). A guide to FRB/U.S.: a macroeconometric model of the United States. Discussion Paper 96-42. Board of Governors of the Federal Reserve System.

Breece, J. and V. Cassino (1998). The forecasting and policy system: demand-side satellite models. Reserve Bank of New Zealand Discussion Paper G98/3.

Britton, E., P. Fisher, and J. Whitley (1998). The inflation report projections: understanding the fan chart. *Bank of England Quarterly Review*, February, 30–37.

Budd, A. (1999). Economic models, with and without forecasts (Caircross Lecture, available at www.bankofengland.co.uk).

Clarida, R., J. Gali, and M. Gertler (1999). The science of monetary policy: a new Keynesian perspective. *Journal of Economic Literature*, 37, 1661–707.

Clements, M.P. and D.F. Hendry (1998). *Forecasting Economic Time Series*. Cambridge: Cambridge University Press.

Coletti, D., B. Hunt, D. Rose, and R. Tetlow (1996). The dynamic model: QPM. Reserve Bank of Canada Technical Report No. 75.

Dawes, R. (1999). A message from pyschologists to economists: mere predictability doesn't matter like it should (without a good story appended to it). *Journal of Economic Behavior and Organization*, 39, 29–40.

Drew, A. and M. Frith (1998). Forecasting at the Reserve Bank of New Zealand. *Reserve Bank of New Zealand Bulletin*, 61, 317–27.

Drew, A. and B. Hunt (1998a). The forecasting and policy system: stochastic simulations of the core model. Reserve Bank of New Zealand Discussion Paper G98/6.

Drew, A. and B. Hunt (1998b). The forecasting and policy system: preparing economic projections. Reserve Bank of New Zealand Discussion Paper G98/7.

Duguay, P. and D. Longworth (1998). Macroeconomic models and policymaking at the Bank of Canada. *Economic Modeling*, 15, 357–75.

Duguay, P. and S. Poloz (1994). The role of economic projections in Canadian monetary policy formulation. *Canadian Public Policy*, 20 (June), 189–99.

Dungey, M. and A.R. Pagan (1999). A structural VAR model of the Australian economy. *Economic Record*.

Edison, H. and J. Marquez (1998). U.S. monetary policy and econometric modeling: tales from the FOMC Transcripts, 1984–1991. *Economic Modeling*, 15, 411–28.

George, E. (1997). Evolution of the monetary framework, Loughborough University Banking Lecture. Reprinted in *Bank of England Quarterly Review*, February, 98–103.

Hargreaves, D. (1999). SDS-FPS: a small demand-side version of the Forecasting and Policy System Core Model. Reserve Bank of New Zealand Discussion Paper G99/10.

King, R.G. and A.L. Wolman (1996). Inflation targeting in a St Louis model of the 21st century. Federal Reserve Bank of St Louis Review, 78, 83–107.

Leeper, E.M. and T. Zha (1999). Modest policy interventions. Working Paper 99-22, Federal Reserve Bank of Atlanta.

McCallum, B. (1999). Recent developments in the analysis of monetary policy rules. *Federal Reserve Bank of St Louis Review*, 81(6), 3–11.

McKibbin, W.J. (2000). Forecasting the world economy. In P. Abelson and R. Joyeux, *Economic Forecasting*. St Leonards: Allen and Unwin.

McKibbin, W.J. and W. Martin (1998). The East Asian crisis: investigating causes and policy responses. Brookings Discussion Paper In International Economics, #142. Washington, D.C.: The Brookings Institution.

McKibbin, W.J. and P. Wilcoxen (1998). The theoretical and empirical structure of the G-Cubed model. *Economic Modeling*, 16(1), 123–48.

Mayes, D. and W. Razzak (1998). Transparency and accountability: empirical models and policy making at the RBNZ. *Economic Modelling*, 15, 377–94.

Meyer, L.H. (1999). Start with a paradigm, end with a story: the value of model-based forecasting and policy analysis (speech before the Stern Graduate School of Business, New York University, available at www.federalreserve.gov).

Poloz, S., D. Rose, and R. Tetlow (1994). The Bank of Canada's new quarterly projection model (QPM): an introduction. *Bank of Canada Review*, Autumn, 23–38.

Powell, A. and C. Murphy (1995). *Inside A Modern Macroeconometric Model: A Guide to the Murphy Model*. Springer-Verlag.

Reifschneider, D.L., D.J. Stockton, and D.W. Wilcox (1997). Econometric models and the monetary policy process. *Carnegie-Rochester Conference Series on Public Policy*, 47, 1–37.

Robertson, H. and M. McDougall (1980). The structure and dynamics of RDXF. Technical Report no. 26, Bank of Canada.

Robertson, J.C. and E.W. Tallman (1999). Vector autoregressions: forecasting and reality. *Federal Reserve Bank of Atlanta Economic Review*, First quarter.

Rudebusch, G. (1998). Do measures of monetary policy in a VAR make sense? *International Economic Review*, 39, 907–31.

St. Clair, R. and J. McDermott (2000). The Reserve Bank of New Zealand's model and its role in forecasting and policy: a review. Paper prepared for the Seminar on Macroeconometric Modelling and Public Policy.

Stevens, G. (1999). Economic forecasting and its role in making monetary policy. *Reserve Bank of Australia Bulletin*, September, 1–9.

Whittle, P. (1963). *Prediction and Regulation by Linear Least-Square Methods*. Princeton: Van Nostrand.

Wren-Lewis, S. (1993). Macroeconometric models and economic theory: another failed partnership? ICMM Discussion Paper 9, University of Strathclyde

Vickers, J. (1999). Economic models and monetary policy (speech to the National Institute of Economic and Social Research, available at www.bankofengland.co.uk).

CHAPTER EIGHT

Forecasting Cointegrated VARMA Processes

Helmut Lütkepohl

8.1.   MOTIVATION AND CHAPTER OUTLINE

In forecasting time-series variables, the information in past values of the series is used to extract potential future developments. In other words, a forecast is a function of past values of a time-series variable. If only linear functions are considered, this leads to autoregressive (AR) models where a variable at time t, y_t say, depends on lagged values plus the forecast error, $y_t = v + \alpha_1 y_{t-1} + \ldots + \alpha_p y_{t-p} + u_t$. Here u_t represents the forecast error, α_i $(i = 1, \ldots, p)$ are autoregressive parameters and v is an intercept term. Similarly, if more than one variable is involved, say $y_{1t}, \ldots, y_{Kt}$, each component is viewed as a linear function of lags of all the variables plus an error term in order to use information from all the past variables. Using vector and matrix notation, this leads to vector autoregressive (VAR) models of the form $y_t = v + A_1 y_{t-1} + \ldots + A_p y_{t-p} + u_t$, where $y_t = (y_{1t}, \ldots, y_{Kt})'$, the A_i $(i = 1, \ldots, p)$ are $(K \times K)$ coefficient matrices, v is a $(K \times 1)$ intercept term and u_t is a K-dimensional error term.

In small samples, the precision of forecasts based on these models will be affected by the precision of the parameter estimators. Since an adequate description of the data generation process (DGP) of a multiple time series may require a fairly large VAR order and hence a large number of parameters, the estimation precision in such models may be low. Consequently, forecasts based on VAR processes may suffer from the uncertainty in the parameter estimators. In such a situation it may be worth considering a larger model class with processes which may be able to represent the DGP of interest in a more parsimonious way. Vector autoregressive moving-average (VARMA) models constitute such a class. In this chapter, the analysis of models from that class will be discussed.

One of the problems in dealing with VARMA models is that generally their parameterization is not unique. For inference purposes it is necessary to focus on a unique representation of a DGP. In the following a variant of the *echelon form* of a VARMA process will be considered. It has the advantage of providing a relatively parsimonious parameterization in general and, following Poskitt (1992), we use the acronym ARMA$_E$ for the echelon form. In the next section, this representation of a VARMA process will be described formally. Generally, the variables are allowed to be integrated of order one ($I(1)$) and they may be cointegrated. Therefore it will be convenient to supplement the echelon form with an error correction or equilibrium correction (EC) term. Thereby it is possible to separate the long-run cointegration relations from the short-term dynamics. This results in an EC-ARMA$_E$ form which turns out to be a convenient framework for modeling and forecasting cointegrated variables. The model and some of its pertinent properties will be discussed in section 8.2.

In using these models for forecasting, a specific candidate from the general model class has to be chosen, its parameters have to be estimated, and then point forecasts may be computed and, if desired, forecast intervals may be established. In this procedure, we have to pass through the usual model specification, estimation, and model-checking cycles before the forecasts are determined. The necessary steps and procedures will be considered in this chapter. In section 8.3, estimation procedures will be discussed under the assumption that a well specified model is available. The ARMA$_E$ form of a VARMA process is characterized by a set of integer parameters called Kronecker indices. A procedure for consistently estimating these quantities and also the cointegrating rank from a given multiple time series will be discussed in section 8.4. Moreover, some comments on model-checking will be given in that section. Thereby a complete strategy for analyzing EC-ARMA$_E$ models is provided. Once a well specified model is available it can be used for forecasting, which is considered in section 8.5. Conclusions follow in section 8.6.

This chapter draws heavily on material from Lütkepohl and Claessen (1997) who introduced the error correction echelon form of a VARMA process, Poskitt and Lütkepohl (1995) who presented consistent estimation procedures for the Kronecker indices, and Bartel and Lütkepohl (1998) who explored the small sample properties of some such procedures. To simplify the exposition, some important ideas and concepts will be discussed in the framework of VAR models first, which are treated as special VARMA models.

8.2. THE VARMA FRAMEWORK

8.2.1. Characteristics of variables

The characteristics of the variables involved determine to some extent which model is a suitable representation of the DGP. For instance, the trending properties of the variables and their seasonal fluctuations are of importance in setting up a suitable model. In the following a variable is called *integrated of order d* $(I(d))$ if stochastic trends or unit roots can be removed by differencing the variable d times. A variable without a stochastic trend or unit root is sometimes called $I(0)$. In the present chapter it is assumed that all variables are at most $I(1)$ if not otherwise stated. In other words, for any time-series variable y_{kt} it is assumed that $\Delta y_{kt} \equiv y_{kt} - y_{k,t-1}$ has no stochastic trend. Note, however, that in general Δy_{kt} may still have deterministic terms such as a polynomial trend and seasonal components. For convenience it is assumed in the following that there are no deterministic terms. In other words, polynomial trends, seasonal dummy variables or nonzero mean terms are not considered. It is straightforward to include a nonzero mean or regard the variables as being mean-adjusted, and for most procedures discussed in the following other deterministic terms can be accommodated in a straightforward manner.

A set of $I(1)$ variables is called *cointegrated* if a linear combination exists which is $I(0)$ (Engle and Granger, 1987). Generally, it is convenient to consider systems with both $I(1)$ and $I(0)$ variables. In this case the concept of cointegration is extended by calling any linear combination which is $I(0)$ a cointegration relation. Clearly, this terminology is not in the spirit of the original definition because it leads to a linear combination of $I(0)$ variables being called a cointegration relation. For our purposes, a distinction between genuine cointegration and more general forms is not necessary, however.

8.2.2. VAR and EC models

As mentioned in the introduction, for a system of K time-series variables $y_t = (y_{1t}, \ldots, y_{Kt})'$ a VAR model is a useful forecasting tool. The basic VAR model is of the form

$$y_t = A_1 y_{t-1} + \ldots + A_p y_{t-p} + u_t, \tag{8.1}$$

where $u_t = (u_{1t}, \ldots, u_{Kt})'$ is an unobservable zero-mean, independent, white-noise process with time-invariant positive-definite covariance matrix $E(u_t u_t') = \Sigma_u$, the A_i $(i = 1, \ldots, p)$ are $(K \times K)$ coefficient matrices. This model is often briefly referred to as a VAR(p) process because the number of lags is p.

The process is said to be *stable* if

$$\det (I_K - A_1 z - \ldots - A_p z^p) \neq 0 \quad \text{for} \quad |z| \leq 1. \tag{8.2}$$

Here I_K denotes the $(K \times K)$ identity matrix. Assuming that a stable process has been initiated in the infinite past, it generates *stationary* time series which have time-invariant means, variances, and covariance structure. If the determinantal polynomial in (8.2) has unit roots (that is, roots for $z = 1$), then some or all of the variables are $I(1)$ and they may also be cointegrated. Thus, the present model accommodates variables with stochastic trends. On the other hand, it is not the most suitable setup for analyzing cointegration relations because these relations do not appear explicitly in (8.1). They are more easily analyzed within a model obtained by rewriting (8.1) as

$$\Delta y_t = \Pi y_{t-1} + \Gamma_1 \Delta y_{t-1} + \ldots + \Gamma_{p-1} \Delta y_{t-p+1} + u_t, \qquad (8.3)$$

where $\Pi = -(I_K - A_1 - \ldots - A_p)$ and $\Gamma_i = -(A_{i+1} + \ldots + A_p)$ for $i = 1, \ldots, p - 1$. This reparameterization of the process is obtained from (8.1) by subtracting y_{t-1} from both sides and rearranging terms. The model form (8.3) is the so-called *vector error correction* or *equilibrium correction model* (VECM). Because Δy_t does not contain stochastic trends by our assumption that all variables can be at most $I(1)$, the term Πy_{t-1} is the only one which may include $I(1)$ variables. Hence, Πy_{t-1} must also be $I(0)$. Thus, it contains the cointegrating relations. These relations represent long-run or equilibrium relations and the model is written in a form which shows how the variables respond to deviations from the long-run relations. In other words, it can be seen how equilibrium errors are corrected, which explains the name of the model. The Γ_j ($j = 1, \ldots, p - 1$) in (8.3) are often referred to as the short-term or short-run parameters.

To distinguish the VECM from the VAR model the latter is sometimes called the levels version. Of course, it is also possible to determine the A_j levels parameter matrices from the coefficients of the VECM as $A_1 = \Gamma_1 + \Pi + I_K$, $A_i = \Gamma_i - \Gamma_{i-1}$ for $i = 2, \ldots, p - 1$, and $A_p = -\Gamma_{p-1}$. Thus, the two forms (8.1) and (8.3) are equivalent representations of a stochastic process. Which one of the two representations is used for a specific analysis is mainly a question of convenience with respect to model specification, estimation, or analysis.

If the VAR(p) process has unit roots – that is, det $(I_K - A_1 z - \ldots - A_p z^p) = 0$ for $z = 1$ – the matrix Π is singular. Suppose it has rank r; that is, rk(Π) $= r$. It is well-known that in this case, Π can be represented as a product $\Pi = \alpha \beta'$, where α and β are ($K \times r$) matrices with rank r. Premultiplying $\Pi y_{t-1} = \alpha \beta' y_{t-1}$ by $(\alpha' \alpha)^{-1} \alpha'$ shows that $\beta' y_{t-1}$ is $I(0)$ because premultiplying an $I(0)$ vector by some constant matrix results again in an $I(0)$ process. Hence, $\beta' y_{t-1}$ contains the cointegrating relations and it is obvious that there are $r = $ rk(Π) linearly independent such relations among the components of y_t. The matrices α and β are not unique, however, so that there are many possible β matrices which contain the cointegrating relations or linear transformations of them. Consequently, those relations with economic content, for instance as economic equilibrium relations, cannot be extracted purely from the observed time series. In other words, nonsample information is required to identify the economically interesting relations uniquely.

Special cases included in (8.3) are $I(0)$ processes for which $r = K$ and systems that have a stable, stationary VAR representation in first differences. In the latter case, $r = 0$ and the term Πy_{t-1} disappears in (8.3). These boundary cases do not represent cointegrated systems in the usual sense. There are also other cases which are not in line with the original idea of the concept of cointegration even if the cointegrating rank is strictly between zero and K. An obvious example is obtained if all variables but one are $I(0)$. In that case the cointegrating rank is $K - 1$ although the only $I(1)$ variable is not cointegrated with the other variables. For our purposes, it is no problem to include those cases here.

So far, I have not been precise about the range of the index t. If the process is $I(0)$, then assuming that the range consists of all integers is convenient. In that case, in each period t, the process is already in operation for an infinite time and, hence, the moments and distributions have stabilized and are therefore time invariant. On the other hand, if there are $I(1)$ variables, it is usually more convenient from a theoretical point of view to assume that the process has been initialized in some period, say in $t = 0$ or $t = 1$, and has only a finite past, because otherwise the variables may have infinite variances. Since $I(1)$ variables are generally allowed for in the following, it will be assumed that the process under consideration has been initiated at some finite time if not otherwise stated. All variables indexed by integers smaller than the initial period may be assumed to be zero if not otherwise specified. For instance, if the process y_t is initialized at $t = 1$, the variables y_0, y_{-1}, etc. which may appear in a VAR model are assumed to be zero. Again this is just a convenient simplification for expository purposes. More general assumptions are possible for the theoretical results of the following sections to hold.

8.2.3. VARMA models

As mentioned in the introduction, the VAR class of processes sometimes has the disadvantage that a quite large order p is necessary for a proper representation of the DGP. In fact, in some cases theoretical considerations lead to infinite order VAR processes (see also the section on linear transformations). Therefore we consider the following more general process class which includes infinite order VAR processes as well.

GENERAL FORM

It is assumed that the DGP of the K-dimensional multiple time series $y_1, \ldots, y_T$ is from the VARMA class:

$$A_0 y_t = A_1 y_{t-1} + \ldots + A_p y_{t-p} + M_0 u_t + M_1 u_{t-1} + \ldots + M_p u_{t-p}, \quad t = 1, 2, \ldots, \qquad (8.4)$$

or

$$A(L) y_t = M(L) u_t, \quad t = 1, 2, \ldots, \qquad (8.5)$$

where u_t is again a white-noise process with zero mean and nonsingular, time-invariant covariance matrix $E(u_t u_t') = \Sigma_u$. As mentioned previously, the initial values are assumed to be zero for convenience; that is, $u_t = y_t = 0$ for $t \leq 0$. Moreover, $A(L) = A_0 - A_1 L - \ldots - A_p L^p$ and $M(L) = M_0 + M_1 L + \ldots + M_p L^p$ are matrix polynomials in the lag or backshift operator L, which is defined as usual by $L y_t = y_{t-1}$. The zero-order matrices A_0 and M_0 are assumed to be nonsingular. Later on, it will be argued that $A_0 = M_0$ may be assumed without loss of generality. Some of the A_i and M_j coefficient matrices may be zero, so that the AR or MA order may actually be less than p. The matrix polynomials are assumed to satisfy

$$\det A(z) \neq 0, \ |z| \leq 1, z \neq 1, \quad \text{and} \quad \det M(z) \neq 0, \ |z| \leq 1. \qquad (8.6)$$

The second part of this condition is the usual *invertibility condition* for the MA operator which is imposed to ensure the existence of a pure (possibly infinite order) VAR representation of the type discussed below. As in the pure VAR case, the possibility that the operator $A(z)$ can have zeros for $z = 1$ implies that the components of y_t may be integrated and perhaps cointegrated variables.

Clearly, without further restrictions on the operators $A(L)$ and $M(L)$ the representation (8.4)/(8.5) is not unique. This phenomenon is easily seen by writing (8.5) in AR form:

$$y_t = \sum_{i=1}^{t-1} \Xi_i y_{t-i} + u_t, \tag{8.7}$$

where $A_0 = M_0$ is assumed and $\Xi(z) = I_K - \sum_{i=1}^{\infty} \Xi_i z^i = M(z)^{-1}A(z)$. Every pair of operators $A(z)$, $M(z)$ which leads to the same transfer function $\Xi(z)$ defines an equivalent VARMA representation for y_t. For instance, premultiplying by some nonsingular matrix results in an equivalent representation. In fact, premultiplying by some operator $D(L) = D_0 + D_1L + \ldots + D_qL^q$ satisfying det $D_0 \neq 0$ and det $D(z) \neq 0$ for $|z| \leq 1$, results in an equivalent VARMA representation of the process. In other words, cancellation of factors of $A(L)$ and $M(L)$ is possible. Therefore it is usually assumed that there are no redundancies. This condition is imposed by assuming that the operator $[A(z) : M(z)]$ is left-coprime, meaning that only unimodular operators $D(z)$ can be factored from $[A(z) : M(z)]$. In other words, $[A(z) : M(z)]$ is left-coprime if the existence of $(K \times K)$ matrix polynomials $D(z)$, $\bar{A}(z)$, $\bar{M}(z)$ such that $[A(z) : M(z)] = D(z)[\bar{A}(z) : \bar{M}(z)]$ implies that $D(z)$ is unimodular.

Recall that a matrix polynomial $D(z)$ is unimodular if det $D(z)$ is a constant which does not depend on z. For example,

$$D(z) = D_0 \quad \text{or} \quad D(z) = \begin{bmatrix} 1 & \delta z \\ 0 & 1 \end{bmatrix}$$

are unimodular matrix polynomials. (See Lütkepohl (1996) for definitions and properties of matrix polynomials.) Obviously, requiring that $[A(z) : M(z)]$ is left-coprime therefore does not solve the nonuniqueness problem completely because the possibility of premultiplying by some nonsingular matrix, for example, is still not excluded. Even if this possibility is excluded by assuming $A_0 = M_0 = I_K$, the nonuniqueness problem is not solved because there are unimodular operators $D(z) = I_K + D_1z + \ldots + D_qz^q$ with zero-order matrix I_K (see the foregoing example). Premultiplying by such an operator still leaves $[A(z) : M(z)]$ left-coprime. Clearly, more restrictions are needed for uniqueness. One possible set of restrictions is given by the echelon form, which is discussed next.

THE ECHELON FORM

In order to obtain a unique representation, we denote the kl-th elements of $A(z)$ and $M(z)$ by $\alpha_{kl}(z)$ and $m_{kl}(z)$, respectively, and impose the following constraints. First of all, let $[A(z) : M(z)]$ be left-coprime. Moreover,

$$m_{kk}(L) = 1 + \sum_{i=1}^{p_k} m_{kk,i} L^i, \quad \text{for } k = 1, \ldots, K, \tag{8.8a}$$

$$m_{kl}(L) = \sum_{i=p_k-p_{kl}+1}^{p_k} m_{kl,i} L^i, \quad \text{for } k \neq l, \tag{8.8b}$$

and

$$\alpha_{kl}(L) = \alpha_{kl,0} - \sum_{i=1}^{p_k} \alpha_{kl,i} L^i, \quad \text{with} \quad \alpha_{kl,0} = m_{kl,0} \quad \text{for } k, l = 1, \ldots, K. \tag{8.8c}$$

Here

$$p_{kl} = \begin{cases} \min(p_k + 1, p_l) & \text{for } k > l, \\ \min(p_k, p_l) & \text{for } k < l, \end{cases} \quad k, l = 1, \ldots, K.$$

The process is said to be in echelon form or, briefly, ARMA_E form if $A(L)$ and $M(L)$ satisfy these restrictions. The row degrees p_k in this representation are the *Kronecker indices* (see Hannan and Deistler, 1988; and Lütkepohl, 1991). In (8.4)/(8.5), $p = \max(p_1, \ldots, p_K)$; that is, p is the maximum row degree or Kronecker index. $\text{ARMA}_E(p_1, \ldots, p_K)$ denotes an echelon form with Kronecker indices $p_1, \ldots, p_K$. The sum of the Kronecker indices $p_1 + \ldots + p_K$ is said to be the *McMillan degree*.

As an example consider a three-dimensional process with Kronecker indices $(p_1, p_2, p_3) = (1, 2, 1)$. In this case,

$$[p_{kl}] = \begin{bmatrix} \bullet & 1 & 1 \\ 1 & \bullet & 1 \\ 1 & 2 & \bullet \end{bmatrix}.$$

Hence, an $\text{ARMA}_E(1, 2, 1)$ has the following form:

$$\begin{bmatrix} 1 & 0 & 0 \\ 0 & 1 & 0 \\ 0 & \alpha_{32,0} & 1 \end{bmatrix} y_t = \begin{bmatrix} \alpha_{11,1} & \alpha_{12,1} & \alpha_{13,1} \\ \alpha_{21,1} & \alpha_{22,1} & \alpha_{23,1} \\ \alpha_{31,1} & \alpha_{32,1} & \alpha_{33,1} \end{bmatrix} y_{t-1} + \begin{bmatrix} 0 & 0 & 0 \\ \alpha_{21,2} & \alpha_{22,2} & \alpha_{23,2} \\ 0 & 0 & 0 \end{bmatrix} y_{t-2}$$

$$+ \begin{bmatrix} 1 & 0 & 0 \\ 0 & 1 & 0 \\ 0 & \alpha_{32,0} & 1 \end{bmatrix} u_t + \begin{bmatrix} m_{11,1} & m_{12,1} & m_{13,1} \\ 0 & m_{22,1} & 0 \\ m_{31,1} & m_{32,1} & m_{33,1} \end{bmatrix} u_{t-1}$$

$$+ \begin{bmatrix} 0 & 0 & 0 \\ m_{21,2} & m_{22,2} & m_{23,2} \\ 0 & 0 & 0 \end{bmatrix} u_{t-2}. \tag{8.9}$$

Note that in the formulation of the echelon form in (8.8) the autoregressive operator is unrestricted except for the constraints imposed by the maximum row degrees or Kronecker indices and the zero order matrix $(A_0 = M_0)$, whereas additional zero restrictions are placed on the moving average coefficient matrices attached to low lags of the u_t. For example, in (8.9), there are two zero restrictions on M_1. This representation of the echelon form was proposed by Lütkepohl and Claessen (1997) for processes with integrated and cointegrated variables. It differs from the $ARMA_E$ form usually found in the literature on stationary processes where the restrictions on low order lags are imposed on the AR coefficient matrices (for example, Hannan and Deistler, 1988; Lütkepohl, 1991). The advantage of (8.8) in the present context is that it can be combined easily with the EC form, as will be seen shortly.

It may be worth noting that an $ARMA_E$ form may have more zero coefficients than those specified in (8.8). Further zero restrictions may lead to models where the AR and MA orders are not identical. Such constraints are not excluded in an echelon form. However, the echelon from does not need them to ensure uniqueness of the representation of the operator $\Xi(L)$. Note also that the echelon form does not exclude processes. In other words, every VARMA process can be written in echelon form.

THE EC ECHELON FORM

An EC form may be obtained from (8.4) by subtracting $A_0 y_{t-1}$ on both sides and rearranging terms as for the VECM representation of a VAR in section 8.2:

$$A_0 \Delta y_t = \Pi y_{t-1} + \Gamma_1 \Delta y_{t-1} + \ldots + \Gamma_{p-1} \Delta y_{t-p+1} + M_0 u_t + M_1 u_{t-1} + \ldots + M_p u_{t-p}, \qquad (8.10)$$

where $\Pi = -(A_0 - A_1 - \ldots - A_p)$ and $\Gamma_i = -(A_{i+1} + \ldots + A_p)$ $(i = 1, \ldots, p-1)$ as before. Again Πy_{t-1} is the EC term and $r = \text{rk}(\Pi)$ is the cointegrating rank of the system, which specifies the number of linearly independent cointegration relations.

If the operators $A(L)$ and $M(L)$ satisfy the echelon form restrictions, it is easily seen that the Γ_i satisfy similar identifying constraints as the A_i. More precisely, Γ_i obeys the same zero restrictions as A_{i+1} for $i = 1, \ldots, p-1$, because a zero restriction on an element $\alpha_{kl,i}$ of A_i implies that the corresponding element $\alpha_{kl,j}$ of A_j is also zero for $j > i$. For the same reason, the zero restrictions on Π are the same as those on $A_0 - A_1$. This means in particular that there are no echelon form zero restrictions on Π if all Kronecker indices $p_k \geq 1$ $(k = 1, \ldots, K)$ because in that case the echelon form does not impose zero restrictions on A_1. On the other hand, if there are zero Kronecker indices this has implications for the integration and cointegration structure of the variables. A specific analysis of the relations between the variables is called for in that case. Denoting by ϱ the number of Kronecker indices which are zero, it can be shown that

$$\text{rk}(\Pi) \geq \varrho. \qquad (8.11)$$

This result has to be taken into account in the procedure for specifying the cointegrating rank of a VARMA system, discussed in section 8.6.

If the model (8.10) satisfies the echelon form restrictions it is denoted as EC-ARMA$_E$ in the following. As an example consider again the system (8.9). Its EC-ARMA$_E$ form is

$$
\begin{bmatrix} 1 & 0 & 0 \\ 0 & 1 & 0 \\ 0 & \alpha_{32,0} & 1 \end{bmatrix} \Delta y_t = \begin{bmatrix} \pi_{11} & \pi_{12} & \pi_{13} \\ \pi_{21} & \pi_{22} & \pi_{23} \\ \pi_{31} & \pi_{32} & \pi_{33} \end{bmatrix} y_{t-1} + \begin{bmatrix} 0 & 0 & 0 \\ \gamma_{21,1} & \gamma_{22,1} & \gamma_{23,1} \\ 0 & 0 & 0 \end{bmatrix} \Delta y_{t-1}
$$

$$
+ \begin{bmatrix} 1 & 0 & 0 \\ 0 & 1 & 0 \\ 0 & \alpha_{32,0} & 1 \end{bmatrix} u_t + \begin{bmatrix} m_{11,1} & m_{12,1} & m_{13,1} \\ 0 & m_{22,1} & 0 \\ m_{31,1} & m_{32,1} & m_{33,1} \end{bmatrix} u_{t-1}
$$

$$
+ \begin{bmatrix} 0 & 0 & 0 \\ m_{21,2} & m_{22,2} & m_{23,2} \\ 0 & 0 & 0 \end{bmatrix} u_{t-2}.
$$

As a further example, consider the three-dimensional ARMA$_E$(0, 0, 1) system

$$
y_t = \begin{bmatrix} 0 & 0 & 0 \\ 0 & 0 & 0 \\ \alpha_{31,1} & \alpha_{32,1} & \alpha_{33,1} \end{bmatrix} y_{t-1} + u_t + \begin{bmatrix} 0 & 0 & 0 \\ 0 & 0 & 0 \\ m_{31,1} & m_{32,1} & m_{33,1} \end{bmatrix} u_{t-1}. \tag{8.12}
$$

Because two of the Kronecker indices are zero, the cointegrating rank of this system must be at least 2. The EC-ARMA$_E$ form is easily seen to be

$$
\Delta y_t = \begin{bmatrix} 1 & 0 & 0 \\ 0 & 1 & 0 \\ \pi_{31} & \pi_{32} & \pi_{33} \end{bmatrix} y_{t-1} + u_t + \begin{bmatrix} 0 & 0 & 0 \\ 0 & 0 & 0 \\ m_{31,1} & m_{32,1} & m_{33,1} \end{bmatrix} u_{t-1}.
$$

Obviously, the rank of

$$
\Pi = \begin{bmatrix} 1 & 0 & 0 \\ 0 & 1 & 0 \\ \pi_{31} & \pi_{32} & \pi_{33} \end{bmatrix}
$$

is at least 2.

Specifying an EC-ARMA$_E$ model requires that the cointegrating rank r is determined, the Kronecker indices $p_1, \ldots, p_K$ are specified and possibly further overidentifying zero restrictions are placed on the coefficient matrices Γ_i and M_j. Before we discuss strategies for this task, some useful properties of linearly transformed VARMA processes are considered in the next section.

LINEAR TRANSFORMATIONS

In many cases, systems of linearly transformed variables are of interest. For example, the gross national product of a country is the sum of the gross products of the different regions, or the money stock variable M1 consists of currency plus sight deposits. Moreover, temporal aggregation is often just a linear transformation. For instance, the quarterly value of a variable may be the sum or the average of the monthly values or it may just be the value of the last month of a quarter. Furthermore, seasonal adjustment procedures are sometimes linear transformations, such as finite moving averages of the unadjusted variables. In other words, quite often a system of variables z_t is of interest which is obtained as a linear transformation of the original system y_t, say $z_t = Fy_t$, where F is a suitable transformation matrix. Notice that this notation also covers temporal aggregation if the process y_t is defined in an appropriate way (see, for example, Lütkepohl, 1987; 1991, ch. 6). Also any marginal process of y_t can be written in the form Fy_t by a suitable choice of F.

An important result regarding linear transformations of VARMA processes is that they are again VARMA processes. More precisely, if y_t has a VARMA representation, the same is true for z_t. Hence, the VARMA class of processes is closed with respect to linear transformations (see Lütkepohl, 1984a, 1987). In general, the autoregressive and moving-average orders, or Kronecker indices, associated with z_t will be different from those of y_t, however. Furthermore, if y_t is a finite-order VAR(p) process, z_t will in general not have a finite-order VAR representation but will be of a mixed VARMA type. In particular, if the individual component series of a VAR process y_t are considered, they will usually not have a finite-order AR representation. Therefore, for internal consistency in the modeling process it is sometimes useful to consider the more general VARMA class of processes rather than pure VAR models. In practice, pure VAR processes are often used because they are usually more easily dealt with in terms of inference than mixed VARMA processes as we will see in the following sections. More discussion of the structure of linearly transformed VARMA processes may be found in Lütkepohl (1987).

8.3. ESTIMATION

Although model specification precedes estimation, I discuss the latter first because estimates are needed in the specification procedures considered later.

8.3.1. Maximum likelihood estimation

If the distribution of u_t is Gaussian, the log-likelihood function of the model (8.4) for a given multiple time series $y_1, \ldots, y_T$ is

$$l(\theta) = \sum_{t=1}^{T} l_t(\theta), \tag{8.13}$$

where θ represents the vector of all parameters to be estimated and

$$l_t(\theta) = -\frac{K}{2} \log 2\pi - \frac{1}{2} \log \det \Sigma_u - \frac{1}{2} u_t' \Sigma_u^{-1} u_t$$

with

$$u_t = M_0^{-1}(A_0 y_t - A_1 y_{t-1} - \ldots - A_p y_{t-p} - M_1 u_{t-1} - \ldots - M_q u_{t-p}).$$

In general, maximization of $l(\theta)$ is a nonlinear optimization problem, which is complicated by the fact that inequality constraints have to be observed to ensure invertibility of the MA operator. Iterative optimization algorithms have to be used for the maximization. Suitable start-up values may be obtained from one of the algorithms considered in the following.

If the DGP is stable and invertible and the parameters are identified, the ML estimator $\hat{\theta}$ has standard limiting properties; that is, $\hat{\theta}$ is consistent and

$$\sqrt{T}(\hat{\theta} - \theta) \xrightarrow{d} N(0, \Sigma_{\hat{\theta}}),$$

where $\xrightarrow{d}$ signifies convergence in distribution and $\Sigma_{\hat{\theta}}$ is the inverse asymptotic information matrix. On the other hand, if the variables are cointegrated, the estimators of the long-run and short-run parameters have different convergence rates. In special cases, simple estimation algorithms exist. Some of them will be considered in the following.

8.3.2. VAR models

Because estimation of some special-case models is computationally particularly easy, these cases will be considered in more detail in the following. We begin with the levels VAR representation (8.1) under the condition that no parameter restrictions are imposed. Then estimation of the unrestricted VECM (8.3) is treated and VECMs with parameter restrictions are discussed.

Given a sample of size T, $y_1, \ldots, y_T$, and p presample values, $y_{-p+1}, \ldots, y_0$, it is well-known that the K equations of the VAR model (8.1) may be estimated separately by least squares (LS) without losing efficiency relative to generalized LS (GLS). That is, $a = \text{vec}[A_1 : \ldots : A_p]$ may be estimated by a regression based on

$$y_t = (Y_{t-1}^{t-p'} \otimes I_K)a + u_t, \tag{8.14}$$

where $Y_{t-1}^{t-p'} = (y_{t-1}', \ldots, y_{t-p}')$. Under standard assumptions, the resulting estimator $\hat{a}$ is consistent and asymptotically normally distributed (see, for example, Lütkepohl, 1991),

$$\sqrt{T}(\hat{a} - a) \xrightarrow{d} N(0, \Sigma_{\hat{a}})$$

or, written in an alternative way,

$$\hat{a} \overset{a}{\sim} N(a, \Sigma_{\hat{a}}/T).$$ (8.15)

Here vec denotes the column stacking operator which stacks the columns of a matrix in a column vector. The covariance matrix of the asymptotic distribution is

$$\Sigma_{\hat{a}} = \text{plim}\left(T^{-1}\sum_{t=1}^{T} Y_{t-1}^{t-p} Y_{t-1}^{t-p\prime}\right)^{-1} \otimes \Sigma_u.$$ (8.16)

Although these results also hold for cointegrated systems it is important to note that in this case the covariance matrix $\Sigma_{\hat{a}}$ is singular, whereas it is nonsingular in the usual $I(0)$ case (see Park and Phillips, 1988, 1989; Sims, Stock, and Watson, 1990; Lütkepohl, 1991, ch. 11). In fact, some estimated coefficients or linear combinations of coefficients converge with a faster rate than $T^{1/2}$ if there are integrated or cointegrated variables. Therefore, in this case the usual t-, χ^2-, and F-tests used for inference regarding the VAR parameters may not be valid, as shown, for example, by Toda and Phillips (1993).

If the cointegrating rank of y_t is known and one wishes to impose the corresponding restrictions, it is convenient to work with the VECM (8.3). Following Johansen (1995), we denote the residuals from a regression of Δy_t and y_{t-1} on ΔY_{t-1}^{t-p+1} by R_{0t} and R_{1t}, respectively, and define

$$S_{ij} = T^{-1}\sum_{t=1}^{T} R_{it}R'_{jt}, \quad i, j = 0, 1.$$

The parameter estimators under the restriction $\text{rk}(\Pi) = r$ are then obtained by solving the generalized eigenvalue problem

$$\det(\lambda S_{11} - S_{10}S_{00}^{-1}S_{01}) = 0.$$ (8.17)

Let the ordered eigenvalues be $\lambda_1 \geq \ldots \geq \lambda_K$ with corresponding eigenvectors $V = [v_1, \ldots, v_K]$ satisfying $\lambda_i S_{11} v_i = S_{10}S_{00}^{-1}S_{01}v_i$ ($i = 1, \ldots, K$) and normalized such that $V'S_{11}V = I_K$. Then β and α may be estimated as

$$\hat{\beta} = [v_1, \ldots, v_r] \quad \text{and} \quad \hat{\alpha} = S_{01}\hat{\beta}(\hat{\beta}'S_{11}\hat{\beta})^{-1},$$ (8.18)

respectively, that is, $\hat{\alpha}$ may be viewed as the LS estimator from the model

$$R_{0t} = \alpha\hat{\beta}'R_{1t} + \tilde{u}_t.$$

An estimator of Π is $\hat{\Pi} = \hat{\alpha}\hat{\beta}'$ and, using $\Delta y_t - \hat{\Pi}y_{t-1} = \Gamma\Delta Y_{t-1}^{t-p+1} + \tilde{u}_t$, $\Gamma = [\Gamma_1 : \ldots : \Gamma_{p-1}]$ may be estimated as

$$\hat{\Gamma} = [\hat{\Gamma}_1 : \cdots : \hat{\Gamma}_{p-1}] = \left(\sum_{t=1}^{T} (\Delta y_t - \hat{\Pi} y_{t-1}) \Delta Y_{t-1}^{t-p+1\prime} \right) \left(\sum_{t=1}^{T} \Delta Y_{t-1}^{t-p+1} \Delta Y_{t-1}^{t-p+1\prime} \right)^{-1}.$$

Under Gaussian assumptions, these estimators are ML estimators conditional on the presample values (Johansen, 1995).

In this approach, the parameter estimator $\hat{\beta}$ is made unique by normalizing the eigenvectors from the eigenvalue problem (8.17) and $\hat{\alpha}$ is adjusted accordingly. However, these are not econometric identification restrictions. Without such restrictions, only the product $\alpha\beta' = \Pi$ can be estimated consistently. For consistent estimation of the matrices α and β, identifying restrictions have to be imposed. For example, in a specific model it may be reasonable to assume that the first part of β is an identity matrix, so that $\beta' = [I_r : \beta_1']$, where β_1 is a $((K - r) \times r)$ matrix. For $r = 1$, this restriction amounts to normalizing the coefficient of the first variable. This identifying restriction has attracted some attention in the cointegration literature. If uniqueness restrictions are imposed it can be shown that $T(\hat{\beta} - \beta)$ and $\sqrt{T}(\hat{\alpha} - \alpha)$ converge in distribution (Johansen, 1995). In other words, the estimator of β converges with the fast rate T. It is therefore sometimes called *superconsistent*, whereas the estimator of α converges with the usual rate $\sqrt{T}$.

The estimators of Γ and Π are consistent and asymptotically normal under general assumptions and converge at the usual $\sqrt{T}$ rate, $\sqrt{T}\text{vec}(\hat{\Gamma} - \Gamma) \xrightarrow{d} N(0, \Sigma_{\hat{\Gamma}})$ and $\sqrt{T}\text{vec}(\hat{\Pi} - \Pi) \xrightarrow{d} N(0, \Sigma_{\hat{\Pi}})$. The asymptotic distribution of $\hat{\Gamma}$ is nonsingular and, hence, standard inference may be used for Γ. In contrast, the $(K^2 \times K^2)$ covariance matrix $\Sigma_{\hat{\Pi}}$ has rank Kr. It is singular if $r < K$. This result is obtained because Π involves the cointegrating relations which are estimated superconsistently.

Interestingly, if an estimator of the levels parameters A is computed via the estimates of Π and Γ and thereby satisfies the cointegration restriction, that estimator has the same asymptotic distribution as in (8.15) where no restrictions have been imposed in estimating A. Important results on estimating models with integrated variables are due to Phillips and his co-workers (for example, Phillips and Durlauf, 1986; Phillips, 1987, 1991).

In practice, it is often desirable to place restrictions on the parameters to reduce the dimensionality of the parameter space. For instance, it is quite common that different lags of the differenced variables appear in the individual equations. In other words, there may be zero restrictions on the short-run parameters Γ. Moreover, some of the cointegrating relations may be confined to specific equations by imposing zero constraints on the loading matrix α. Efficient estimation of a model with parameter restrictions is more complicated than in the unrestricted case because LS is no longer identical to GLS and ML in general. A possible estimation procedure estimates β in a first stage, ignoring the restrictions on the short-run parameters. Let the estimator be $\hat{\beta}$. Because the estimators of the cointegrating parameters converge at a faster rate than the estimators of the short-run parameters, the former may be treated as fixed in a second stage of the estimation procedure. In other words, a systems estimation procedure may be applied to

$$\Delta y_t = (y'_{t-1}\hat{\beta} \otimes I_K)\text{vec}(\alpha) + (\Delta Y_{t-1}^{t-p+1'} \otimes I_K)\text{vec}(\Gamma) + \tilde{u}_t. \tag{8.19}$$

If only exclusion restrictions are imposed on the parameter vectors $\text{vec}(\alpha)$ and $\text{vec}(\Gamma)$ in this form, standard GLS or similar methods may be applied. They result in estimators of the short-run parameters with the usual asymptotic properties. Feasible GLS estimation of more general VARMA models is discussed next.

8.3.3. Feasible GLS estimation of VARMA models

For given Kronecker indices, an ARMA_E model can be estimated even if the cointegrating rank is unknown. The Kronecker indices are assumed to be known in the following. Strategies for specifying them will be described in section 8.4.

Let $a = S_a\text{vec}(A_1 : \ldots : A_p)$, $\lambda = S_\lambda\text{vec}(A_0 - I_K)$, and $m = S_m\text{vec}(M_1 : \ldots : M_p)$ denote the freely-varying elements in the coefficient matrices. The selection matrices S_a, S_λ, and S_m are defined such that they have a one in the column corresponding to the unrestricted coefficient being chosen. Then $\theta = (a' : \lambda' : m')'$ contains the freely-varying coefficients of $[A(z) : M(z)]$ not restricted to be zero or one, and we can rewrite the system (8.4) in the following compact regression model form:

$$y_t = R'_t\theta + u_t, \tag{8.20}$$

where

$$R_t = \begin{bmatrix} S_a[Y_{t-1}^{t-p} \otimes I_K] \\ S_\lambda[(u_t - y_t) \otimes I_K] \\ S_m[U_{t-1}^{t-p} \otimes I_K] \end{bmatrix},$$

and $U_{t-1}^{t-p} = (u'_{t-1}, \ldots, u'_{t-p})'$. As an example consider the two-dimensional $\text{ARMA}_E(2, 1)$ model

$$\begin{bmatrix} 1 & 0 \\ \alpha_{21,0} & 1 \end{bmatrix} y_t = \begin{bmatrix} \alpha_{11,1} & \alpha_{12,1} \\ \alpha_{21,1} & \alpha_{22,1} \end{bmatrix} y_{t-1} + \begin{bmatrix} \alpha_{11,2} & \alpha_{12,2} \\ 0 & 0 \end{bmatrix} y_{t-2}$$

$$+ \begin{bmatrix} 1 & 0 \\ \alpha_{21,0} & 1 \end{bmatrix} u_t + \begin{bmatrix} m_{11,1} & 0 \\ m_{21,1} & m_{22,1} \end{bmatrix} u_{t-1}$$

$$+ \begin{bmatrix} m_{11,2} & m_{12,2} \\ 0 & 0 \end{bmatrix} u_{t-2}.$$

Here,

$$\theta' = [a' : \lambda' : m']$$

$$= [\alpha_{11,1}, \alpha_{21,1}, \alpha_{12,1}, \alpha_{22,1}, \alpha_{11,2}, \alpha_{12,2} : \alpha_{21,0} : m_{11,1}, m_{21,1}, m_{22,1}, m_{11,2}, m_{12,2}]$$

and

$$R_t' = \begin{bmatrix} y_{1,t-1} & 0 & y_{2,t-1} & 0 & y_{1,t-2} & y_{2,t-2} & 0 \\ 0 & y_{1,t-1} & 0 & y_{2,t-1} & 0 & 0 & (u_{1,t} - y_{1,t}) \end{bmatrix}$$

$$\left. \begin{array}{ccccc} u_{1,t-1} & 0 & 0 & u_{1,t-2} & u_{2,t-2} \\ 0 & u_{1,t-1} & u_{2,t-1} & 0 & 0 \end{array} \right].$$

Clearly, since R_t involves unknown residuals, estimating the parameters θ directly by regression from (8.20) is not feasible. Therefore, in a first step, an unrestricted long VAR model of order h_T, say, is fitted by LS as in (8.14). Denoting the residuals by $\hat{u}_t$, we let $\hat{R}_t$ be defined as R_t except that the residuals $\hat{u}_t$ are substituted for the unknown u_t's. Moreover, let $\hat{\Sigma}_u = T^{-1} \sum_{t=1}^T \hat{u}_t \hat{u}_t'$ be the corresponding estimator of the white-noise covariance matrix Σ_u. Then a feasible GLS estimator of θ is given by

$$\hat{\theta} = \left(\sum_{t=1}^T \hat{R}_t \hat{\Sigma}_u^{-1} \hat{R}_t' \right)^{-1} \sum_{t=1}^T \hat{R}_t \hat{\Sigma}_u^{-1} y_t. \tag{8.21}$$

Here the choice of h_T should be such that significant residual autocorrelation is largely eliminated in the empirical model. Poskitt and Lütkepohl (1995) argue that the estimator $\hat{\theta}$ is strongly consistent under suitable conditions for y_t and h_T.

If the cointegrating rank is known, or has been determined by some procedure, and one wishes to take it into account in the estimation procedure, it is preferable to estimate the EC-ARMA$_E$ form (8.10). This may be done by first estimating θ in the ARMA$_E$ form as in (8.21). The estimator $\hat{\theta}$ implies, of course, estimators $\hat{A}_i$ of the A_i. It is natural to consider estimating the EC specification in (8.10) via its relation to the A_i. Let $\hat{\Pi} = -(\hat{A}_0 - \hat{A}_1 - \ldots - \hat{A}_p)$ and $\hat{\Gamma}_i = -(\hat{A}_{i+1} + \ldots + \hat{A}_p)$ ($i = 1, \ldots, p - 1$). These estimators are also strongly consistent, of course, if the $\hat{A}_j$ have this property. Provided that identifying restrictions for α and β are available, we may then obtain estimators for these parameters via their relation to $\Pi = \alpha\beta'$. For instance, if β' has the form $\beta' = [I_r : \beta_1']$, we get estimators

$$\hat{\alpha} = \hat{\Pi}_1 \quad \text{and} \quad \hat{\beta}_1' = (\hat{\alpha}'[\hat{\Psi}\hat{\Sigma}_u\hat{\Psi}']^{-1}\hat{\alpha})^{-1}(\hat{\alpha}'[\hat{\Psi}\hat{\Sigma}_u\hat{\Psi}']^{-1}\hat{\Pi}_2), \tag{8.22}$$

where $[\hat{\Pi}_1 : \hat{\Pi}_2]$ denotes a partition of $\hat{\Pi}$ into submatrices of dimension $(K \times r)$ and $(K \times (K - r))$, respectively, and $\hat{\Psi} = \hat{A}_0 + \hat{M}_1 + \ldots + \hat{M}_p$. Again these estimators are strongly consistent under usual assumptions. Alternatively, if no specific identifying restrictions for β are available, we may estimate this matrix as in the Johansen procedure in (8.18) on the basis of a long VAR(h_T). In the next step this estimator may be fixed and substituted in (8.10). The remaining parameters of the EC-ARMA$_E$ form may then be estimated by a feasible GLS procedure similar to the one described in the foregoing.

These estimators may be used as starting values for a Gaussian maximum likelihood or pseudo maximum likelihood procedure. Using a scoring algorithm, for example, will result in asymptotically fully-efficient estimators after one iteration. In the scoring iterations, the estimator $\hat{\beta}$ may be fixed or iterated together with the other parameters because this estimator has a higher rate of convergence than the estimators of the autoregressive and moving-average parameters if identifying restrictions are available for β. In this case, the other parameter estimators have an asymptotic normal distribution which is the same as if β were known. This, of course, is analogous to the pure VAR case considered in section 8.3.2; see also Phillips (1991), Yap and Reinsel (1995), or Lütkepohl and Claessen (1997).

As mentioned earlier, before a model can be estimated, the Kronecker indices and possibly the cointegrating rank have to be specified. How to do that is discussed in the next section.

8.4. Model Specification

8.4.1. Specification of the Kronecker Indices

For stationary processes, a number of proposals have been made for specifying the Kronecker indices of an ARMA$_E$ model. For example, Hannan and Kavalieris (1984), Poskitt (1992), and Nsiri and Roy (1992) are important contributions where practical specification and analysis tools for stationary processes are introduced. In Lütkepohl and Poskitt (1996), several specification strategies are surveyed and extensions to integrated and cointegrated processes are considered by Lütkepohl and Claessen (1997), Claessen (1995), and Poskitt and Lütkepohl (1995). The strategies for specifying the Kronecker indices of cointegrated ARMA$_E$ processes presented in this section are proposed in the latter paper, where they are also shown to result in consistent estimators of the Kronecker indices under suitable conditions. In a simulation study, Bartel and Lütkepohl (1998) found that they work reasonably well in small samples at least for the processes explored in the Monte Carlo study.

The specification procedures may be partitioned in two stages. The first stage is the same in the procedures considered here. It consists of fitting a long VAR of order h_T, say, by least squares in order to obtain estimates of the unobservable innovations u_t as in the estimation procedure of the previous section. In a second stage the residuals are then substituted for the unknown lagged u_t in the individual equations of an ARMA$_E$ form which may be estimated by linear LS procedures. Based on the equations estimated in this way, a choice of the Kronecker indices is made using model selection criteria. Poskitt and Lütkepohl (1995), Guo, Huang, and Hannan (1990), and Huang and Guo (1990) show that the estimation residuals $\hat{u}_t$ are "good" estimates of the true residuals if the VAR order h_T approaches infinity at a suitable rate as T goes to infinity.

The methods differ in the way they choose the Kronecker indices in the next step. An obvious idea is to search over all models associated with Kronecker indices which are smaller than some prespecified upper bound p_{max}, $\{(p_1, \ldots, p_K) \mid 0 \le p_k \le p_{max}, k = 1, \ldots, K\}$, and choose the set of Kronecker indices which optimizes some model selection criterion. Unfortunately, this procedure is extremely computer-intensive for systems of moderate or large dimension. Therefore, procedures have been proposed which are computationally more efficient. One possibility is to use linear regressions to estimate the individual equations separately for different lag lengths. A choice of the optimal lag length is then based on some prespecified model selection criterion which includes the residual variance as a measure of goodness of fit. For example, a criterion of the general form

$$\Lambda_{k,T}(n) = \log \hat{\sigma}^2_{k,T}(n) + C_T n / T, \quad n = 0, 1, \ldots, P_T,$$

may be used, where C_T is a suitable function of the sample size T and $T\hat{\sigma}^2_{k,T}(n)$ is the residual sum of squares from a regression of y_{kt} on $(\hat{u}_{jt} - y_{jt})$ ($j = 1, \ldots, K$, $j \ne k$) and y_{t-s} and $\hat{u}_{t-s}$ ($s = 1, \ldots, n$). Here the maximum lag length P_T may depend on the sample size.

Because each equation is treated separately, restrictions from the echelon structure are not explicitly taken into account in this procedure. Instead, for each equation it is implicitly assumed that the current index under consideration is the smallest and thus no restrictions are imported from other equations. Still, the kth equation will be misspecified whenever the lag order is less than the true Kronecker index, because in that case lagged values required for a correct specification are omitted. On the other hand, if the lag order is greater than the true Kronecker index, the kth equation will be correctly specified but may include redundant parameters and variables. Therefore, for an appropriate choice of C_T, the criterion function $\Lambda_{k,T}(n)$ will possess a global minimum asymptotically when n is equal to the true Kronecker index. For practical purposes, possible choices of C_T are $C_T = h_T \log T$ or $C_T = h_T^2$. More details on the procedure may be found in the aforementioned articles.

Poskitt and Lütkepohl (1995) also propose a modification of this procedure where coefficient restrictions derived from those equations in the system which have smaller Kronecker indices are taken into account. In that modification, after specifying the Kronecker indices with the previous procedure, the smallest Kronecker index is fixed and the procedure is repeated for the remaining equations. In this second application of the procedure, the restrictions implied by the smallest Kronecker index found in the first round are taken into account when the second smallest index is determined. We proceed in this way by fixing the smallest Kronecker index found in each successive round until all the Kronecker indices have been specified. The variables are ordered in such a way that the Kronecker indices of the final system are ordered from largest to smallest. That is, the variable whose equation is associated with the smallest Kronecker index is placed last in the list of variables. The one with the second smallest Kronecker index is assigned the next to the last place, and so on.

Poskitt and Lütkepohl (1995) argue that for a suitable choice of C_T the procedure results in consistent estimators of the Kronecker indices. In this version of the specification procedure, the coefficient restrictions derived from the echelon form are directly incorporated into the identification stage. The idea is that this may result in a superior performance of the selection procedure. Bartel and Lütkepohl (1998) found in their Monte Carlo study that this is indeed the case. On the other hand, the computational burden is increased substantially relative to a procedure which treats all equations independently. Therefore the procedure may be problematic for high-dimensional systems.

It should be understood that the Kronecker indices found in such a procedure for a given time series of finite length can only be expected to be a reasonable starting point for a more refined analysis of the system under consideration. Based on the specified Kronecker indices, a more efficient procedure for estimating the parameters may be applied, as discussed in the previous section and the model may be modified subsequently. Before we consider possibilities for model-checking, we will discuss procedures for specifying the cointegrating rank.

8.4.2. Specification of the cointegrating rank

For pure VAR processes, Johansen (1995) provides LR tests for specifying the cointegrating rank. Under Gaussian assumptions, ML estimation of unrestricted VECMs with a specific cointegrating rank r was found to be relatively easy in section 8.3.2. Therefore the LR statistic for a pair of hypotheses $H_0 : r = r_0$ versus $H_1 : r > r_0$ is easily determined by evaluating the maxima of the likelihood functions for $r = r_0$ and for $r = K$. In fact, it can be shown that the LR statistic has the form

$$LR(r_0) = -T \sum_{j=r_0+1}^{K} \log (1 - \lambda_j), \qquad (8.23)$$

where the λ_j are the eigenvalues from (8.17). The asymptotic distribution of the LR statistic is nonstandard but has been tabulated in Johansen (1995, ch. 15), for example. It depends on the deterministic terms in the DGP such as intercept and trend terms. Hence, in this case it makes a difference which deterministic terms are included.

Saikkonen and Luukkonen (1997) show that Johansen's LR tests can be justified even if a finite-order VAR process is fitted although the true underlying process has an infinite-order VAR structure, provided that the VAR order goes to infinity with the sample size. Consequently, these tests may be applied at the beginning of the specification procedure even if the true DGP is a mixed VARMA process. Lütkepohl and Saikkonen (1999) discuss the choice of the VAR order in this case. Alternatively, Yap and Reinsel (1995) have extended the likelihood ratio principle to VARMA processes and develop tests for the cointegrating rank under the assumption that the lag orders of $A(z)$ and $M(z)$ are known. Thus, these tests may be applied once the Kronecker indices have been identified. Whatever approach is adopted, for our purposes a modification is useful. It is known from

(8.11) that the cointegrating rank $r \geq \varrho$, the number of zero Kronecker indices. Hence, only null hypotheses should be considered where r is greater than or equal to ϱ so that the sequence of null hypotheses $H_0 : r = \varrho$, $H_0 : r = \varrho + 1, \ldots,$ $H_0 : r = K - 1$, is tested. The estimator of r is chosen as the smallest value for which H_0 cannot be rejected.

8.4.3. Model checking

Once a model has been specified and estimated by some efficient procedure, some checks for model adequacy are in order and possible further model reductions or modifications may be called for. For instance, insignificant parameter estimates may be restricted to zero. Here it is convenient that the t-ratios of the short-run and loading parameters have their usual asymptotic standard normal distributions under the null hypothesis due to the limiting normal distribution of the ML estimators. In this way, overidentifying restrictions may be imposed.

A number of model-checking tools are based on the residuals of the final model. Some of them are applied to the residuals of individual equations and others are based on the full residual vectors. Examples of specification checking tools are visual inspection of the plots of the residuals and their autocorrelations. In addition, autocorrelations of squared residuals may be considered to check for possible autoregressive conditional heteroskedasticity (ARCH). Although it may be quite insightful to inspect the autocorrelations visually, formal statistical tests for remaining residual autocorrelation should also be applied. Such tests are often based on LM (Lagrange Multiplier) or Portmanteau statistics. Moreover, normality tests of the Lomnicki–Jarque–Bera type may be applied to the residuals (see, for example, Lütkepohl, 1991; Doornik and Hendry, 1997).

There are also procedures for checking a model for potential structural shifts during the sample period. For example, prediction tests as discussed in Lütkepohl (1991) may be performed or recursive residuals (Doornik and Hendry, 1997) may be inspected. In addition, out-of-sample forecasts are sometimes used for model-checking when new data become available. For a more detailed discussion of model-checking, see Hendry (1995) or Doornik and Hendry (1997). If model defects are detected at the checking stage, efforts have to be made to find a better representation of the DGP by adding other variables or lags to the model, by modifying the sampling period, considering nonlinear terms, etc.

8.5. FORECASTING

In discussing forecasts based on VARMA processes, it is again instructive to begin with pure VAR models. An extension to mixed VARMA processes will then be relatively simple. I will first consider forecasts based on known processes and then discuss the consequences of using models with estimated rather than known parameters. Finally, in subsection 8.5.4, forecasting linearly transformed processes will be considered. In this section it is assumed that a VAR or VARMA process is the true DGP also during the forecasting period, so that structural breaks or other model complications are excluded *a priori*. This assumption is made for convenience in order to simplify the exposition, although it may not be very realistic when the models are applied for solving actual forecasting problems. Model extensions are possible to take care of nonlinearities or other complications.

8.5.1. VAR processes

The VAR form (2.1) is particularly easy to use in forecasting the variables y_t. The optimal, minimum mean squared error (MSE) one-step forecast in period T is the conditional expectation

$$y_{T+1|T} \equiv E(y_{T+1}|y_T, y_{T-1}, \dots) = A_1 y_T + \dots + A_p y_{T+1-p}, \tag{8.24}$$

where the latter equality holds if u_t is independent white noise; that is, u_t and u_s are independent random vectors for $s \neq t$. In that case, $E(u_{T+1}|y_T, y_{T-1}, \dots) = 0$. Forecasts for longer horizons $h > 1$ may be obtained recursively as

$$y_{T+h|T} = A_1 y_{T+h-1|T} + \dots + A_p y_{T+h-p|T}, \tag{8.25}$$

where $y_{T+j|T} = y_{T+j}$ for $j \leq 0$. The corresponding forecast errors are $y_{T+1} - y_{T+1|T} = u_{T+1}$, $y_{T+2} - y_{T+2|T} = u_{T+2} + A_1 u_{T+1}$, and, more generally,

$$y_{T+h} - y_{T+h|T} = u_{T+h} + \Phi_1 u_{T+h-1} + \dots + \Phi_{h-1} u_{T+1}, \tag{8.26}$$

where it is easy to see by successive substitution that the weight matrices in the latter equation may be obtained as

$$\Phi_s = \sum_{j=1}^{s} \Phi_{s-j} A_j, \quad s = 1, 2, \dots, \tag{8.27}$$

with $\Phi_0 = I_K$ and $A_j = 0$ for $j > p$ (see Lütkepohl, 1991, section 11.3). Obviously, the forecasts are unbiased; that is, the forecast errors have expectation 0.

As mentioned earlier, these are the minimum MSE forecasts. The MSE matrix of an h-step forecast is

$$\Sigma_y(h) \equiv E\{[y_{T+h} - y_{T+h|T}][y_{T+h} - y_{T+h|T}]'\} = \sum_{j=0}^{h-1} \Phi_j \Sigma_u \Phi_j'. \tag{8.28}$$

For any other h-step forecast with MSE matrix $\Sigma_y^*(h)$, say, the difference $\Sigma_y^*(h) - \Sigma_y(h)$ is a positive-semidefinite matrix. This result relies on the assumption that u_t is independent white-noise. If u_t is just uncorrelated white-noise so that u_t and u_s are uncorrelated for $s \neq t$ and not necessarily independent, the forecasts computed by the recursions in (8.25) are just best linear forecasts (see Lütkepohl (1991, section 2.2.2) for an illustrative example).

It may be worth pointing out that the forecast MSEs for integrated processes are generally unbounded as the horizon h goes to infinity. Thus the forecast uncertainty increases without bounds for forecasts of the distant future. This contrasts with the case of stationary $I(0)$ variables for which the forecast MSEs are bounded by the unconditional covariance of y_t. Because cointegration relations are $I(0)$, this means, in particular, that forecasts of cointegration relations have bounded MSEs even for horizons approaching infinity. For a more detailed discussion of forecasting cointegrated processes, see Clements and Hendry (1995).

Of course, this result is also reflected in the corresponding forecast intervals. Assuming that the process y_t is Gaussian and, hence, $u_t \sim$ iid $N(0, \Sigma_u)$, the forecast errors are also multivariate normal. This result may be used to set up forecast intervals of the form

$$[y_{k,T+h|T} - c_{1-\gamma/2}\sigma_k(h), \ y_{k,T+h|T} + c_{1-\gamma/2}\sigma_k(h)], \tag{8.29}$$

where $c_{1-\gamma/2}$ is the $(1 - \frac{\gamma}{2})100$ percentage point of the standard normal distribution, $y_{k,T+h|T}$ denotes the kth component of $y_{T+h|T}$ and $\sigma_k(h)$ denotes the square root of the kth diagonal element of $\Sigma_y(h)$; that is, $\sigma_k(h)$ is the standard deviation of the h-step forecast error for the kth component of y_t. I will now turn to forecasts based on VARMA processes, still assuming that the parameters are known.

8.5.2. VARMA processes

Forecasts of the variables of the VARMA process (8.4)/(8.5) are obtained easily from the pure VAR form (8.7). Assuming again independent white noise, an optimal one-step forecast at forecast origin T is

$$y_{T+1|T} = \sum_{i=1}^{T} \Xi_i y_{T+1-i}. \tag{8.30}$$

More generally, optimal h-step forecasts may be computed recursively for $h = 1$, $2, \ldots,$ as

$$y_{T+t|T} = \sum_{i=1}^{T+h-1} \Xi_i y_{T+t-i|T}. \tag{8.31}$$

Because for given $y_1, \ldots, y_T$ the $u_1, \ldots, u_T$ may be computed from (8.7), the one-step forecast may be obtained alternatively as

$$y_{T+1|T} = A_0^{-1}(A_1 y_T + \ldots + A_p y_{T+1-p}) + A_0^{-1}(M_1 u_T + \ldots + M_p u_{T+1-p}),$$

where $M_0 = A_0$ is assumed as in the echelon form. Again more generally, the h-step forecasts may be determined as

$$y_{T+h|T} = A_0^{-1}(A_1 y_{T+h-1|T} + \ldots + A_p y_{T+h-p|T}) + A_0^{-1} \sum_{i=h}^{p} M_i u_{T+h-i}, \qquad (8.32)$$

where, as usual, the sum vanishes if $h > p$.

Both ways of computing h-step forecasts from VARMA models are relatively computer-intensive, especially for long time series. Moreover, they rely on our initial value assumption which states that $y_t = 0$ for $t \leq 0$. If such an assumption is not made, the true error terms cannot be computed and also (8.30) and (8.31) are only approximations. In that case, precise formulas based on $y_1, \ldots, y_T$ may be obtained via the so-called *Multivariate Innovations Algorithm* of Brockwell and Davis (1987, §11.4).

Under our assumptions, the properties of the forecast errors are easily derived by expressing the process (8.5) as

$$y_t = u_t + \sum_{i=1}^{t-1} \Phi_i u_{t-i}, \qquad (8.33)$$

where

$$\Phi(z) = I_K + \sum_{i=1}^{\infty} \Phi_i z^i = A(z)^{-1} M(z). \qquad (8.34)$$

Note that, in general, if there are unit roots, for $A(z)^{-1}$ to exist, z must be strictly within the complex unit circle. Nevertheless, we can, of course, get the coefficient matrices Φ_i from (8.34). In terms of the representation (8.33) the optimal h-step forecast may be expressed as

$$y_{T+h|T} = \sum_{i=h}^{T+h-1} \Phi_i u_{T+h-i}. \qquad (8.35)$$

Hence, the forecast errors are seen to be

$$y_{T+h} - y_{T+h|T} = u_{T+h} + \Phi_1 u_{T+h-1} + \ldots + \Phi_{h-1} u_{T+1}, \qquad (8.36)$$

just as in the pure VAR case in (8.26). Thus, the MSE or forecast error covariance matrix is also obtained in the same way as in that section; that is, $\Sigma_y(h)$ has precisely the form given in (8.28). Moreover, forecast intervals, etc. may be derived from these results in the familiar way under Gaussian assumptions.

8.5.3.   Forecasting using estimated processes

In practice, processes with estimated parameters are usually used for forecasting. To investigate the implications for the forecast precision, we denote the h-step forecast based on estimated parameters by $\hat{y}_{T+h|T}$; that is,

$$\hat{y}_{T+h\mid T} = \hat{A}_0^{-1}(\hat{A}_1\hat{y}_{T+h-1\mid T} + \ldots + \hat{A}_p\hat{y}_{T+h-p\mid T}) + \hat{A}_0^{-1}\sum_{i=h}^{p}\hat{M}_i\hat{u}_{T+h-i}, \quad h = 1, 2, \ldots, \qquad (8.37)$$

where, of course, $\hat{y}_{T+j\mid T} = y_{T+j}$ for $j \le 0$ and the $\hat{u}_{T+h-i}$ are estimation residuals. The corresponding forecast error is

$$y_{T+h} - \hat{y}_{T+h\mid T} = [y_{T+h} - y_{T+h\mid T}] + [y_{T+h\mid T} - \hat{y}_{T+h\mid T}]$$

$$= \sum_{j=1}^{h-1}\Phi_j u_{T+h-j} + [y_{T+h\mid T} - \hat{y}_{T+h\mid T}].$$

If T marks the end of the sample period used for estimation and is at the same time the forecast origin, then the first term on the right-hand side of the foregoing expression consists of future residuals only, whereas the second term involves present and past variables only. Hence, assuming that u_t is independent white noise, the two terms are independent. Moreover, under standard assumptions, the difference $y_{T+h\mid T} - \hat{y}_{T+h\mid T}$ is small in probability as T gets large. Consequently, the forecast error covariance matrix is

$$\Sigma_{\hat{y}}(h) = E\{[y_{T+h} - \hat{y}_{T+h\mid T}][y_{T+h} - \hat{y}_{T+h\mid T}]'\}$$

$$= \Sigma_y(h) + o(1).$$

Here $o(1)$ denotes a term which approaches zero as the sample size tends to infinity. Thus, for large samples the estimation uncertainty may be ignored in evaluating the forecast precision and setting up forecast intervals. On the other hand, in small samples the forecast precision will depend on the quality of the parameter estimators. Hence, if precise forecasts are desired, good parameter estimators are needed. A more precise form of the difference between $\Sigma_{\hat{y}}(h)$ and $\Sigma_y(h)$ may be found, for example, in Lütkepohl (1991) and a more complete discussion of forecasting estimated cointegrated processes with further references is given in Clements and Hendry (1995).

8.5.4. Forecasting linearly transformed and aggregated processes

As mentioned in section 8.2.3, linearly transformed VARMA processes are again VARMA processes. Hence, if y_t has a VARMA representation, the same is true for $z_t = Fy_t$, where F is some fixed $(M \times K)$ transformation matrix. The VAR and MA orders can change considerably, however. Nevertheless, it can be shown that if forecasts of z_t are desired, it is generally preferable to forecast the untransformed process y_t first and then transform the forecasts rather than forecast z_t directly. More precisely, it can be shown that $Fy_{T+h\mid T}$ is generally a better forecast of z_{T+h} than $z_{T+h\mid T}$ in the sense that $\Sigma_z(h) - F\Sigma_y(h)F'$ is positive-semidefinite (see Lütkepohl, 1984a, 1987). Here $F\Sigma_y(h)F'$ is the MSE matrix associated with $Fy_{T+h\mid T}$, of course.

This result implies that if forecasts of an aggregate are of interest, then it is generally useful to consider disaggregated series, forecast them in a multivariate model and aggregate the forecasts. Because temporal aggregation can also be viewed as a linear transformation of a process observed at a higher frequency, this result also means that if forecasts of quarterly variables, say, are of interest forecasting monthly values and aggregating the monthly forecasts to obtain a quarterly forecast is preferable to forecasting the quarterly process directly (see also Lütkepohl (1984b, 1986a,b) for examples).

To illustrate these issues consider the following example from Lütkepohl (1991). Suppose y_t is a bivariate VAR(1) process,

$$\begin{bmatrix} 1 - 0.5L & 0.66L \\ 0.5L & 1 + 0.3L \end{bmatrix} \begin{bmatrix} y_{1t} \\ y_{2t} \end{bmatrix} = \begin{bmatrix} u_{1t} \\ u_{2t} \end{bmatrix} \quad \text{with} \quad \Sigma_u = I_2. \tag{8.38}$$

Furthermore, suppose that we are interested in the aggregate $z_t = y_{1t} + y_{2t}$. It can be shown that z_t has the representation

$$(1 - 0.2L - 0.48L^2)z_t = (1 - 0.504L)v_t \quad \text{with} \quad \sigma_v^2 = 2.70.$$

Obviously, the one-step forecast error variance of $z_{T+1|T}$ is $\Sigma_z(1) = \sigma_v^2 = 2.70$, whereas $\Sigma_y(1) = \Sigma_u = I_2$ and, hence, for $F = [1, 1]$, $F\Sigma_y(1)F' = 2$.

Unfortunately, in general, aggregated forecasts are not necessarily better than forecasting the aggregate directly if the true process is unknown and the parameters have to be estimated, for example. More details and examples illustrating this case may be found in Lütkepohl (1984b, 1986a) and other references given there. Notice also that forecasting the disaggregate series individually using univariate time-series methods and then aggregating them may result in a forecast which is inferior to a direct forecast of the aggregate.

8.6. CONCLUSIONS AND EXTENSIONS

In this chapter, the use of VARMA processes for forecasting systems of variables has been considered. In this procedure, the usual steps of model specification, estimation, and diagnostic checking have to be done first. Once a well-specified and efficiently estimated model has been established, it can be used for forecasting in a straightforward manner. Procedures are presented that may be used in the different steps of the analysis. It is assumed that all variables are at most $I(1)$, so that stochastic trends can be removed by differencing once. Possible cointegration between the variables is accommodated by including an EC term which makes it particularly easy to analyze the cointegration relations. Moreover, it is argued that the echelon form offers a framework for a unique parameterization of the VARMA structure which may be combined conveniently with the EC form.

It should be noted, however, that other possibilities exist for unique parameterizations of VARMA models. For instance, the scalar component models of

Tiao and Tsay (1989) and Tsay (1989) have received some attention in the literature. Moreover, early attempts of econometric VARMA modeling have focused on so-called final equations forms (Zellner and Palm, 1974; Wallis, 1977). These approaches may be useful occasionally, but have not found widespread use in applications.

Throughout, I have focused on models with time-invariant coefficients and without deterministic terms. Adding mean terms, seasonal dummy variables, or polynomial trends is a straightforward extension for most of the models and procedures presented in the foregoing. Some adjustments are necessary in some of the procedures, however. In particular, deterministic terms lead to changes in the asymptotic distributions of the cointegration tests. More generally, there may be additional unmodeled or exogenous variables. In that case, the VARMAX class of models considered by Hannan and Deistler (1988), for example, may offer an appropriate framework.

Another limitation of the previous analysis is the exclusion of variables with higher-order integration. In practice, some variables such as price indices may be modeled more appropriately as $I(2)$ variables. If variables of higher-order integration are present, the analysis and modeling of the cointegration relations becomes more difficult. Except for that problem, forecasts can be set up as discussed in section 8.5 on the basis of the levels version if that is available. A proper analysis of the cointegration properties may be very important for longer-term forecasts, however.

Acknowledgments

I thank the Deutsche Forschungsgemeinschaft, SFB 373, and the European Commission under the Training and Mobility of Researchers Programme (contract No. ERBFMRXCT980213) for financial support. Moreover, I am grateful to the editors for helpful comments.

References

Bartel, H. and H. Lütkepohl (1998). Estimating the Kronecker indices of cointegrated echelon form VARMA models. *Econometrics Journal*, 1 C76–C99.

Brockwell, P.J. and R.A. Davis (1987). *Time Series: Theory and Methods*. New York: Springer-Verlag.

Claessen, H. (1995). *Spezifikation und Schätzung von VARMA-Prozessen unter besonderer Berücksichtigung der Echelon-Form*. Bergisch Gladbach: Verlag Josef Eul.

Clements, M.P. and D.F. Hendry (1995). Forecasting in cointegrated systems. *Journal of Applied Econometrics*, 10, 127–46.

Doornik, J.A. and D.F. Hendry (1997). *Modeling Dynamic Systems Using PcFiml 9.0 for Windows*, London: International Thomson Business Press.

Engle, R.F. and C.W.J. Granger (1987). Co-integration and error correction: representation, estimation and testing. *Econometrica*, 55, 251–76.

Guo, L., D.W. Huang, and E.J. Hannan (1990). On ARX(∞) approximation. *Journal of Multivariate Analysis*, 32, 17–47.

Hannan, E.J. and M. Deistler (1988). *The Statistical Theory of Linear Systems*. New York: John Wiley.

Hannan, E.J. and L. Kavalieris (1984). Multivariate time series models. *Advances in Applied Probability*, 16, 492–561.

Hendry, D.F. (1995). *Dynamic Econometrics*. Oxford: Oxford University Press.

Huang, D. and L. Guo (1990). Estimation of nonstationary ARMAX models based on the Hannan–Rissanen method. *Annals of Statistics*, 18, 1729–56.

Johansen, S. (1995). *Likelihood Based Inference in Cointegrated Vector Autoregressive Models*. Oxford: Oxford University Press.

Lütkepohl, H. (1984a). Linear transformations of vector ARMA processes. *Journal of Econometrics*, 26, 283–293.

Lütkepohl, H. (1984b). Forecasting contemporaneously aggregated vector ARMA processes. *Journal of Business and Economic Statistics*, 2, 201–14.

Lütkepohl, H. (1986a). Forecasting vector ARMA processes with systematically missing observations. *Journal of Business and Economic Statistics*, 4, 375–90.

Lütkepohl, H. (1986b). Forecasting temporally aggregated vector ARMA processes. *Journal of Forecasting*, 5, 85–95.

Lütkepohl, H. (1987). *Forecasting Aggregated Vector ARMA Processes*. Berlin: Springer-Verlag.

Lütkepohl, H. (1991). *Introduction to Multiple Time Series Analysis*. Berlin: Springer-Verlag.

Lütkepohl, H. (1996). *Handbook of Matrices*. Chichester: John Wiley.

Lütkepohl, H. and H. Claessen (1997). Analysis of cointegrated VARMA processes. *Journal of Econometrics*, 80, 223–39.

Lütkepohl, H. and D.S. Poskitt (1996). Specification of echelon form VARMA models. *Journal of Business and Economic Statistics*, 14, 69–79.

Lütkepohl, H. and P. Saikkonen (1999). Order selection in testing for the cointegrating rank of a VAR process. In R.F. Engle and H. White (eds.), *Cointegration, Causality, and Forecasting. A Festschrift in Honour of Clive W.J. Granger*. Oxford: Oxford University Press, 168–99.

Nsiri, S. and R. Roy (1992). On the identification of ARMA echelon–form models. *Canadian Journal of Statistics*, 20, 369–86.

Park, J.Y. and P.C.B. Phillips (1988). Statistical inference in regressions with integrated processes: Part 1. *Econometric Theory*, 4, 468–97.

Park, J.Y. and P.C.B. Phillips (1989). Statistical inference in regressions with integrated processes: Part 2. *Econometric Theory*, 5, 95–131.

Phillips, P.C.B. (1987). Time series regression with a unit root. *Econometrica*, 55, 277–301.

Phillips, P.C.B. (1991). Optimal inference in cointegrated systems. *Econometrica*, 59, 283–306.

Phillips, P.C.B. and S.N. Durlauf (1986). Multiple time series regression with integrated processes. *Review of Economic Studies*, 53, 473–95.

Poskitt, D.S. (1992). Identification of echelon canonical forms for vector linear processes using least squares. *Annals of Statistics*, 20, 195–215.

Poskitt, D.S. and H. Lütkepohl (1995). Consistent specification of cointegrated autoregressive moving-average systems. Discussion Paper 54 1995, SFB 373, Humboldt–Universität zu Berlin.

Saikkonen, P. and R. Luukkonen (1997). Testing cointegration in infinite order vector autoregressive processes. *Journal of Econometrics*, 81, 93–126.

Sims, C.A., J.H. Stock, and M.W. Watson (1990). Inference in linear time series models with some unit roots. *Econometrica*, 58, 113–44.

Tiao, G.C. and R.S. Tsay (1989). Model specification in multivariate time series (with discussion). *Journal of the Royal Statistical Society*, B51, 157–213.

Toda, H.Y. and P.C.B. Phillips (1993). Vector autoregressions and causality. *Econometrica*, 61, 1367–93.

Tsay, R.S. (1989). Parsimonious parameterization of vector autoregressive moving average models. *Journal of Business and Economic Statistics*, 7, 327–41.

Wallis, K.F. (1977). Multiple time series analysis and the final form of econometric models. *Econometrica*, 45, 1481–97.

Yap, S.F. and G.C. Reinsel (1995). Estimation and testing for unit roots in a partially non-stationary vector autoregressive moving average model. *Journal of the American Statistical Association*, 90, 253–67.

Zellner, A. and F. Palm (1974). Time series analysis and simultaneous equation econometric models. *Journal of Econometrics*, 2, 17–54.

CHAPTER NINE

Multi-Step Forecasting

R.J. Bhansali

9.1. INTRODUCTION

An established approach for prediction of an observed time series centers on building a statistical model to characterize its salient features, including the structure of dependence between the successive observations; the unknown future values are then predicted dynamically by repeatedly iterating the model and by replacing (plugging in) the unknown future values by their own forecasts. This standard approach is known to be optimal in a linear least squares sense if the postulated model coincides with the data generating process, but the optimality property does not hold when the two differ and now it is possible to improve on the standard approach, especially for multi-step prediction. As the former assumption is usually untenable for an observed time series, there has been much development recently in a direct method in which either a new model is selected and/or the parameters of a postulated model are reestimated separately for each step of prediction. An aim of this chapter is to provide an introduction and an overview of some of these developments, especially for multi-step prediction of economic time series.

9.2. A MOTIVATING EXAMPLE

Suppose that the observed time series actually follows an autoregressive model of order 1, an AR(1) model:

$$x_t = ax_{t-1} + \varepsilon_t, \quad |a| < 1, \tag{9.1}$$

where $\{\varepsilon_t\}$ is a sequence of uncorrelated random variables, each with mean 0 and variance σ^2 and a is a known constant. Suppose also that for some integer n and an $h \geq 1$, the linear least-squares forecast, $\tilde{x}_n(h)$, say, of x_{n+h} is desired when x_{n-j}, $j \geq 0$, are treated as known. By a standard argument, see Whittle (1963),

$$\tilde{x}_n(h) = a^h x_n, \ h \geq 1. \tag{9.2}$$

Suppose next that $\{x_t\}$ is erroneously assumed to follow the AR(1) model, (1), but the data generating process does not actually follow this model. The one-step linear least squares forecast, $\tilde{x}_n(1)$, may still be written as

$$\tilde{x}_n(1) = ax_n, \tag{9.3}$$

where $a = R(1)/R(0)$ and $R(u) = E(x_t x_{t+u})$ $(t, u = 0, \pm 1, \dots)$ denotes the covariance function of $\{x_t\}$. For $h > 1$, however, the direct multi-step linear least squares forecasts are given by

$$\tilde{x}_{nD}(h) = r(h)x_n, \tag{9.4}$$

where $r(u) = R(u)/R(0)$ $(u = 1, 2, \dots)$ denotes the correlation function of $\{x_t\}$. By contrast, the plug-in forecasts, obtained by erroneously treating (9.1) as the correct model, are given by

$$\tilde{x}_{nP}(h) = \{r(1)\}^h x_n. \tag{9.5}$$

It follows therefore that if $\{x_t\}$ actually follows an AR(1) model, or if $h = 1$ and the true generating process is not AR(1), $r(h) = r(1)^h$ and (9.4) and (9.5) coincide. However, (9.4) may be preferred to (9.5) in a linear least squares sense for multi-step prediction when the assumed model is misspecified. Thus, if $V_D(h)$ and $V_P(h)$ denote the h-step mean squared errors of prediction of the direct and plug-in methods respectively, then, for each $h \geq 1$,

$$V_D(h) = R(0)\{1 - r(h)^2\},$$
$$V_P(h) = R(0)\{1 - 2r(1)^h r(h) + r(1)^{2h}\},$$
$$[V_P(h) - V_D(h)]/R(0) = \{r(h) - r(1)^h\}^2,$$

and the difference between the mean squared errors of prediction of the plug-in and direct methods increases as the magnitude of the difference between $r(h)$ and $r(1)^h$ increases.

9.3. GENERALIZATIONS AND EXTENSIONS

The advantages in adopting the direct method for multi-step prediction with misspecified models extend to a variety of different situations. To gain an appreciation of the current state of the art, we distinguish between the following scenarios:

(a) The actual stochastic structure generating an observed time series is postulated to belong to a model class admitting an infinite number of parameters, and a finite-order model of this class is fitted, but the selected order is specified to be a function of T, the series length, and allowed to approach infinity simultaneously but sufficiently slowly with T.

(b) The actual stochastic structure is explicitly recognized as being unknown and perhaps highly complex, but, for ease of implementation, a simple and possibly underparameterized procedure, exponential smoothing, for example, is adopted for multi-step prediction.

The two modeling approaches described above may be contrasted with a standard approach in which, after appropriate diagnostic testing, a finite parameter model, such as an autoregressive moving average, ARMA, model is fitted to an observed time series and all further statistical inferences about the data, including multi-step prediction of the unknown future values, are based on the premise that the chosen model is suitable and it coincides with the process actually generating the data. In this sense, (a) and (b) above describe two situations in which model misspecification could arise and for which multi-step prediction by the direct method may be considered.

The modeling approach outlined in (a) is known as "nonparametric" and for its implementation the class of autoregressive models is usually chosen, though alternative model classes, for example, the Exponential model of Bloomfield (1973), may also be envisaged; Moulines and Soulier (1999) have recently employed the latter class for modeling the short-memory component of a long-range dependent time series. For applying the direct method within the context of a nonparametric approach, a new model is selected and fitted for each step of prediction by a model selection criterion. By contrast, the modeling approach described in situation (b) only involves reestimation of the parameters of the fitted model separately for each step of prediction, and the actual model being fitted is treated as fixed.

Next, we consider these two approaches in greater detail.

9.4. Direct Method for Autoregressive Models

Suppose that the observed time series, $x_1, \ldots, x_T$, is a part realization of a stationary process admitting an autoregressive representation:

$$\sum_{j=0}^{\infty} a(j)x_{t-j} = \varepsilon_t, \, a(0) = 1, \tag{9.6}$$

where $\{\varepsilon_t\}$ is a sequence of independent random variables, each with mean 0, variance σ^2, and finite fourth moment, and the $a(j)$ are absolutely summable real coefficients such that

$$\sum_{j=0}^{\infty} a(j)z^j \neq 0, |z| \leq 1. \tag{9.7}$$

In an important paper, Shibata (1980) suggested that a new autoregressive model be selected and fitted for each step of prediction, h, by an ordinary linear least squares, OLS, regression procedure in which x_{t+h} is regressed on $x_t, x_{t-1}, \dots, x_{t-k+1}$ and the value of k, the autoregressive order, is selected anew for each h by an order selection criterion. Let $\hat{\Phi}_{Dh}(k) = [\hat{\varphi}_{Dhk}(1), \dots, \hat{\varphi}_{Dhk}(k)]'$ denote the estimated regression coefficients and $\hat{V}_{Dh}(k)$ the residual error variance in this regression. We have

$$\hat{\Phi}_{Dh}(k) = -\hat{\Gamma}_h(k)^{-1}\hat{r}_h(k), \tag{9.8}$$

$$\hat{V}_{Dh}(k) = \hat{d}_h(0) + \hat{r}_h(k)'\hat{\Phi}_{Dh}(k), \tag{9.9}$$

where $\hat{\Gamma}_h(k) = [C_{hT}(u, v)]$ $(u, v = 1, \dots, k)$, $\hat{r}_h(k) = [C_{hT}(-h + 1, 1), \dots, C_{hT}(-h + 1, k)]'$, $\hat{d}_h(0) = C_{hT}(-h + 1, -h + 1)$, the subscript D stands for the direct method and, with K denoting a known upper bound for the autoregressive order and $N = T - h - K + 1$,

$$C_{hT}(u, v) = N^{-1}\sum_{t=K}^{T-h} x_{t-u+1}x_{t-v+1}. \tag{9.10}$$

For $h = 1$, we put $\hat{a}(k) = \hat{\Phi}_{Dh}(k)$, where $\hat{a}(k)$ now defines an OLS estimator of the autoregressive coefficients.

Shibata (1980) suggested the following order selection criterion, with $\alpha = 2$, for determining separately the value of k to be used for each h:

$$\text{Sh}_\alpha(k) = \hat{V}_{Dh}(k)(N + \alpha k) \quad (k = 0, 1, \dots, K) \tag{9.11}$$

and the order is selected by minimizing this criterion. It is clear, however, that the value of α in (9.11) need not be restricted to 2 and other values for α could be considered. Moreover, as in Bhansali (1996), the use of alternative order selection criteria is also possible and one may let $\alpha = \alpha(T)$, a function of T, such that $\alpha(T) \to \infty$ as $T \to \infty$.

By contrast, the corresponding plug-in estimator, $\hat{\Phi}_{Ph}(k) = [\hat{\varphi}_{Phk}(1), \dots, \varphi_{Phk}(1)]'$ (see Yamamoto, 1976), is given by, with $e_1(k) = [1, 0, \dots, 0]'$,

$$\hat{\Phi}_{Ph}(k) = -e_1'(k)\hat{\Omega}(k)^h. \tag{9.12}$$

Here, $\hat{\Omega}(k)$ is the companion-form matrix for $\hat{a}(k)$, that is,

$$\hat{\Omega}(k) = \left[\begin{array}{c} -\hat{a}(k)' \\ \hline I_{k-1} \vdots O_{k-1} \end{array}\right], \tag{9.13}$$

in which I_{k-1} denotes an identity matrix of dimension $k - 1$ and 0_{k-1} denotes a vector of zeroes, also of dimension $k - 1$, and the value of k, the autoregressive order, may be selected, see Bhansali (1993), by the Akaike information criterion, or the Shibata criterion, (9.11), with $h = 1$, amongst others.

For one-step prediction, $h = 1$, the plug-in and direct estimators coincide and correspond to OLS estimators of the autoregressive coefficients of order k. For $h > 1$, however, these two methods differ; to appreciate the difference, suppose that $k = 1$, but $\{x_t\}$ actually follows an autoregressive model of order greater than 1. Now, for each $h > 1$, $\hat{\Phi}_{Dh}(k)$ provides an estimator of $r(h)$, the h-step linear least squares prediction constant of order 1 discussed in section 9.1; but $\hat{\Phi}_{Ph}(k)$, by contrast, provides an estimator of $r(1)^h$, the corresponding h-step plug-in prediction constant. This difference extends to higher-order models as well. Thus (see Bhansali, 1999a), under the hypothesis that $\{x_t\}$ does not degenerate to a finite-order autoregressive process, the $\hat{\varphi}_{Dh}(j)$, for each $h \geq 1$, provide OLS estimators of the h-step linear least squares prediction constants of order k, but, by contrast, the $\hat{\varphi}_{Ph}(j)$ only estimate the corresponding plug-in prediction constants.

Bhansali (1996) has investigated the relative advantages of the direct and plug-in methods for multi-step prediction within the class of autoregressive processes which do not degenerate to a finite autoregression. An asymptotic lower bound for the h-step mean squared error of prediction of the direct method is developed for each $h \geq 1$, by assuming that the prediction constants are estimated by solving equation (9.8) above, but $k = \hat{k}_h$, say, is a random variable whose value is selected anew for each h by an order selection criterion. The order selected by the $Sh_\alpha(k)$ criterion, (9.11), among others, is shown to be asymptotically efficient for each fixed $\alpha > 1$ in the sense that the bound is attained in the limit if $\tilde{k}_h$ is selected by this criterion. A lower bound for the h-step mean squared error of prediction of the plug-in method, but with the initial order treated as a random variable and determined by a selection criterion, is also derived. A two-fold advantage for the direct method is indicated by these results: first, the asymptotic lower bound on its mean squared error of prediction is smaller than that for the plug-in method; second, while the latter bound is not attainable even asymptotically, the former is asymptotically attainable.

If, on the other hand, $\{x_t\}$ follows an autoregressive process of finite order, m say, then for all $k \geq m$, the direct estimator, $\hat{\Phi}_{Dh}(k)$, of the h-step prediction constants is asymptotically inefficient relative to the plug-in estimator, $\hat{\Phi}_{Ph}(k)$; Bhansali (1997) gives explicit asymptotic expressions for evaluating the loss in parameter estimation and predictive efficiency in this situation. A motivation for adopting an h-step order selection criterion is given in a least squares framework by Bhansali (1999b); see also Hurvich and Tsai (1997). For additional references, the review by Bhansali (1999a) may be consulted.

9.5. MULTI-STEP PARAMETER ESTIMATION METHODS

A standard method for forecasting a possibly nonstationary time series is Exponentially Weighted Moving Average, according to which, for all $h \geq 1$, the forecast of x_{n+h}, based on a knowledge of $\{x_{n-j}, j \leq 0\}$ is given by, for a $\beta \in (0, 1)$,

$$\hat{x}_n(h) = (1 - \beta) \sum_{j=1}^{\infty} \beta^j x_{n+1-j}. \tag{9.14}$$

Although this procedure is known to be optimal in a linear least squares sense only for the class of ARIMA(0, 1, 1) models (see Box and Jenkins, 1970), it is convenient to use and in practice it is routinely applied even when an ARIMA(0, 1, 1) model may not be appropriate for the data, and, as in section 9.2, the direct method of parameter estimation is appropriate for this scheme.

Tiao and Xu (1993) investigate this last possibility. In their approach, β is estimated separately for each h by a least squares procedure; see also Cox (1961) for related work.

Haywood and Tunnicliffe-Wilson (1997) extend the work of Tiao and Xu to the structural models of Harvey (1993), and more widely to models in which the spectral density function is postulated to follow a linear model in terms of "spectral components." These authors characterize in the frequency domain the manner in which the direct method improves the fit of their model to the periodogram of the data.

Care is required, however, in generalizing the work of Tiao and Xu to other forecasting schemes, since two different procedures are possible: (a) direct estimation of the h-step prediction constants separately for each h; or (b) reestimation of the parameters of the assumed model for each h by treating it as if it specifies the actual data generating process. While these two procedures coincide for the exponentially weighted moving average forecasting scheme, this need not be so for other models. As an example, consider the ARMA(1, 1) model

$$x_t - \delta x_{t-1} = \varepsilon_t - \beta \varepsilon_{t-1}, \ |\delta| < 1, |\beta| < 1, \tag{9.15}$$

where $\delta \neq \beta$, and $\{\varepsilon_t\}$ is as in (6) above. On replacing t by $n + 2$ and substituting for x_{n+1} in terms of x_n, ε_{n+1}, and ε_n, we get

$$x_{n+2} = \delta^2 x_n - \delta \beta \varepsilon_n + z_{n+2}, \tag{9.16}$$

where

$$z_{n+2} = \varepsilon_{n+2} + (\delta - \beta)\varepsilon_{n+1}, \tag{9.17}$$

denotes the two-step prediction error in predicting x_{n+2} from the infinite past $\{x_{n-j}, j \leq 0\}$ by the linear least squares method. Also, the autoregressive representation for $\{x_t\}$ implies that

$$\varepsilon_n = x_n + (\beta - \delta) \sum_{j=1}^{\infty} \beta^{j-1} x_{n-j}. \tag{9.18}$$

Hence, it follows that for two-step prediction, $h = 2$, we may express x_{n+2} as follows:

$$x_{n+2} = \hat{x}_n(2) + z_{n+2}, \tag{9.19}$$

where, with B denoting the backward shift operator, $B^j x_t = x_{t-j}$, and $\tau = (\beta - \delta)\delta$,

$$\hat{x}_n(2) = -\tau(1 - \beta B)^{-1} x_n, \tag{9.20}$$

defines the linear least squares predictor of x_{n+2} from the infinite past, $\{x_{n-j}, j \le 0\}$.

For an observed time series of length T, the two-step method described in (a) yields the direct estimate, $\hat{\Theta}(2) = [\hat{\tau}, \hat{\beta}]'$, of $\Theta(2) = [\tau, \beta]'$, by minimizing the sum of squares of z_{t+2}, the two-step prediction errors; that is,

$$\hat{\Theta}(2) = \operatorname{argmin}_{(\tau,\beta)} \sum_{t=1}^{T} \{x_{t+2} - \tau(1 - \beta B)^{-1} x_t\}^2. \tag{9.21}$$

By contrast, according to method (b), the parameters, δ and β, of the model (9.15) are reestimated by minimizing the same sum of squares as on the right of (9.20), but with respect to δ and β; that is, if $\hat{\Theta}_2(1) = [\hat{\delta}_2, \hat{\beta}_2]'$ denote the resulting estimates,

$$\hat{\Theta}_2(1) = \operatorname{argmin}_{(\delta,\beta)} \sum_{t=1}^{T} \{x_{t+2} - \delta(\beta - \delta)(1 - \beta B)^{-1} x_t\}^2. \tag{9.22}$$

However, see Stoica and Soderstrom (1984), whereas $\hat{\Theta}(2)$ obtained as in (9.21) is unique, $\hat{\Theta}_2(1)$ need not be so; see also Dahlhaus and Wefelmeyer (1996) on this point. A second difficulty with the method (b) is that unless the assumed ARMA(1, 1) model coincides with the actual data generating process, the pseudo-true parameter value, $\Theta_2^0(1) = [\delta_2^0, \beta_2^0]'$, say, corresponding to $\hat{\Theta}_2(1)$ may not coincide with that corresponding to the estimator for one-step prediction. To illustrate this point further, consider the AR(1) model, (9.1), which is also the model M_1^* of Clements and Hendry (1996). For fitting this model to an observed time series with $h = 2$, when the actual data generating process may not necessarily be of the form specified in (9.1), the method (a) described above is to find an estimate, $\hat{\mu}$, say of the two-step pseudo-true prediction constant, $\mu^0 = r(2)$, by

$$\hat{\mu} = \operatorname{argmin}_{\mu} \sum_{t=2}^{T} \{x_t - \mu x_{t-2}\}^2. \tag{9.23}$$

By contrast, Clements and Hendry find the two-step estimate, $\hat{a}_2$, say, by

$$\hat{a}_2 = \operatorname{argmin}_a \sum_{t=2}^{T} \{x_t - (a^2) x_{t-2}\}^2. \tag{9.24}$$

As discussed earlier, the resulting estimate $\hat{a}_2$ need not be unique, a point also noted by Clements and Hendry (1996, p. 667). Moreover, as is readily seen from (9.4), the pseudo-true parameter value, a_2^0, say, corresponding to $\hat{a}_2$ is $a_2^0 = \sqrt{r(2)}$ and if the actual data generating process is not AR(1), a_2^0 need not equal $r(1)$, the pseudo-true parameter value corresponding to the least squares estimate of a^0 obtained for one-step prediction by (9.8), and this may cause confusion.

Clements and Hendry (1996) also examine the efficacy of a multi-step parameter estimation method by a Monte Carlo study in which a nonseasonal Holt model such that its second differences follow an MA(2) model is simulated and fit autoregressive models with and without a constant "drift" term to either the original undifferenced data or to observations obtained by taking first differences. While these authors do identify certain conditions which, from the point of view of multi-step prediction, favor the particular estimation procedure they use, it should be recognized that this procedure corresponds to adopting the method (b) rather than the method (a) discussed above.

Stoica and Nehorai (1989), by contrast, fail to discern an improvement when applying a particular "multi-step" estimation method, with the possible exception occurring when an underparametrized model is fitted. These authors consider estimation of the parameters of an ARMA model by minimizing a weighted sum of the mean squared prediction errors up to J steps ahead, $J > 1$, and study possible merits of this approach. However, estimation of the coefficients of the original ARMA model is considered and in this sense their approach corresponds to adopting the method (b) rather than the method (a) above. A common conclusion emerging from these studies is that for the direct method of parameter estimation to yield a discernible improvement in multi-step forecasts, the model misspecification is a necessary condition, in the sense that the actual process generating the data is much more complex than the model actually used for generating the multi-step forecasts, and this conclusion accords with the general guidance given in section 9.3 as regards when it would be appropriate to use the direct method of parameter estimation.

For an application of a multi-step estimation method for time-series regresion models, see Weiss (1991) and the references therein; see also Greco et al. (1984), among others, for the use of direct method in Control Engineering applications. Farmer and Sidorowich (1987) discuss advantages of using a multi-step estimation method for prediction of chaotic time series.

9.6. DIRECT METHOD FOR ARMA MODELS

A number of authors (see Hannan, 1987; Newbold et al., 1993, and the references therein) have suggested that an ARMA model fitted to an observed time series should not be viewed as the true generating process, but as a parsimonious approximation to it, and even as a "whitening" filter which uses only the family of rational transfer functions for producing as output a serially uncorrelated process.

As this point of view accords with some of the reasons for considering the direct method, it is apposite to investigate the question of selecting and fitting a new ARMA model for each step of prediction. Below we indicate how a procedure for doing so may be developed, our suggestion being based on the Hannan and Rissanen (1982) three-stage procedure for ARMA model selection but using an improvement to their procedure due to Bhansali (1991).

For illustrating the underlying idea, suppose that $\{x_t\}$ follows an ARMA(1, 1) model defined by equation (9.15). On multiplying both sides of this equation by x_{t-1} and ε_{t-1} and taking expectations, we get the equations

$$R(1) = \delta R(0) - \beta c(0),$$

$$c(1) = (\delta - \beta)c(0), \tag{9.25}$$

where $c(u) = E(x_{t+u}\varepsilon_t)$ ($t, u = 0, \pm 1, \ldots$), and provided that $\{x_t\}$ does not degenerate into a white-noise process, they may be solved for δ and β in terms of the $R(u)$ and $c(u)$.

As discussed by Bhansali (1991), estimates of ARMA parameters obtained at stage II of the Hannan and Rissanen (1982) procedure may be interpreted as being solutions of equations (9.25), and of similar equations when $p > 1$, or $q > 1$, but with the $R(u)$ and $c(u)$ replaced by their estimators, where an estimator of the latter is based on an initial autoregression fitted to the data at stage I by a method similar to that discussed in section 9.3 for $h = 1$. This interpretation increases the computational economy of the original procedure because a recursive algorithm of Franke (1985) may be employed for solving these equations and also because the estimates of $R(u)$ and $c(u)$ may be computed once and for all and do not need to be recomputed as p and q are varied.

A new ARMA model may be selected for each step of prediction by extending the above procedure to $h > 1$. Suppose that $h = 2$. On letting $t = t + 1$ and substituting for x_t in terms of x_{t-1}, ε_t, and ε_{t-1}, we may, as in (16), rewrite equation (9.15) as

$$x_{t+1} - \delta^2 x_{t-1} = \delta\beta\varepsilon_{t-1} + z_{t+1}, \tag{9.26}$$

where $z_{t+1} = (\delta - \beta)\varepsilon_t + \varepsilon_{t+1}$ is the two-step prediction error when predicting x_{t+1} from $\{x_{t-j}, j \leq 1\}$. Hence, on multiplying both sides of (9.26) by x_{t-1} and ε_{t-1} and taking expectations, we get the equations, with $d = \delta^2$ and $g = \delta\beta$,

$$R(2) = dR(0) - gc(0),$$

$$c(2) = (d - g)c(0), \tag{9.27}$$

and since these equations are of the same form as equations (9.25) they may also be solved for d and g, provided that $\{x_t\}$ does not degenerate to a white-noise process.

In general, suppose that $\{x_t\}$ is an ARMA(p, q) process:

$$x_t = \sum_{j=1}^{p} \delta_{pq}(j)x_{t-j} - \sum_{j=1}^{q} \beta_{pq}(j)\varepsilon_{t-j} + \varepsilon_t, \tag{9.28}$$

where $p \geq 0$, $q \geq 0$, are some integers, $\{\varepsilon_t\}$ is as in (9.6), the $\delta_{pq}(j)$ and $\beta_{pq}(j)$ are real coefficients such that

$$1 - \sum_{j=1}^{p} \delta_{pq}(j)z^j \neq 0, 1 - \sum_{j=1}^{q} \beta_{pq}(j)z^j \neq 0, |z| \leq 1, \tag{9.29}$$

and these two polynomials do not have a common zero. On letting $t = t + h - 1$, where $h \geq 1$, and on substituting repeatedly for $x_{t+h-j-1}, j = 1, \ldots, h - 1$, in terms of x_{t-u} and $\varepsilon_{t-v}, u = 1, \ldots, p; v = 1, \ldots, q$, we may write (9.28) as

$$x_{t+h-1} = \sum_{j=1}^{p} d_{hpq}(j) x_{t-j} - \sum_{j=1}^{q} g_{hpq}(j) \varepsilon_{t+h-j-1} + z_{t+h}, \tag{9.30}$$

where the $d_{hpq}(j)$ and $g_{hpq}(j)$ are some functions of the $\delta_{pq}(j)$ and $\beta_{pq}(j)$ and denote the coefficients in a linear least-squares predictor of x_{t+h-1} based on $\{x_{t-u}, \varepsilon_{t-v}; u = 1, \ldots, p, v = 1, \ldots, q\}$ and z_{t+h-1} is the h-step prediction error which coincides also with the error, denoted later in section 9.7 by $z_t(h)$, in predicting x_{t+h-1} from $\{x_{t-j}, j \leq 1\}$ by the linear least squares method. Hence, on multiplying both sides of (9.30) by x_{t-u} and $\varepsilon_{t-u}, u = 1, \ldots, p; v = 1, \ldots, q$, equations (9.27) generalize to each $h \geq 1$ and all $p \geq 1, q \geq 1$ as follows:

$$R(h - 1 + u) = \sum_{j=1}^{p} d_{hpq}(j) R(u - j) - \sum_{j=1}^{q} g_{hpq}(j) c(j - u) \quad (u = 1, \ldots, p),$$

$$c(h - 1 + v) = \sum_{j=1}^{p} d_{hpq}(j) c(v - j) - \sigma^2 g_{hpq}(v) \quad (v = 1, \ldots, q), \tag{9.31}$$

where $c(0) = \sigma^2$ and $c(j) = 0, j < 0$.

On replacing the $R(u)$ and $c(v)$ by their estimators and provided that $\{x_t\}$ does not degenerate to an ARMA$(p - 1, q - 1)$ process, equations (9.31) may be solved recursively in order by the algorithm of Franke (1985), but extended to $h > 1$, and estimators of the $d_{hpq}(j)$ and $g_{hpq}(j)$ obtained separately for each h.

To complete the procedure, a relevant order selection criterion, analogous to (9.11), needs to be developed and properties of the order selected studied.

9.7. CHECKING MODEL ADEQUACY FOR MULTI-STEP PREDICTION

For the class of processes admitting an autoregressive representation, (9.6), we have, for all t and each $h \geq 1$,

$$x_{t+h} = \bar{x}_t(h) + z_t(h), \tag{9.32}$$

where (see Bhansali, 1996) $\bar{x}_t(h)$ is the linear least squares predictor in predicting x_{t+h} from the infinite past $\{x_{t+1}, j \leq 1\}$,

$$z_t(h) = \sum_{j=0}^{h-1} b(j) \varepsilon_{t+h-j} \tag{9.33}$$

is the h-step prediction error, and the $b(j)$ are the coefficients in the moving average representation of $\{x_t\}$; that is, $b(j)$ is the coefficient of z^j in the power series expansion of $[\sum a(j) z^j]^{-1}$.

Many of the existing diagnostic techniques (for example, Harvey, 1993, p. 76), for checking the adequacy of a time-series model focus on testing whether the residuals obtained after fitting the model are serially uncorrelated. However, as explained in section 9.1 (see also Whittle, 1963), a model may appear suitable for one-step prediction and yet its performance for multi-step prediction may be far from satisfactory. Hence, especially within the context of the direct approach, it is pertinent to examine the question of whether a given h-step predictor, $h > 1$, is suitable for an observed time series.

The representation (9.32) shows that the h-step prediction error, $z_t(h)$, follows a moving-average process of order $h - 1$, an MA($h - 1$) process. Hence, for a fixed $h \geq 1$, a time-series model may be said to be suitable for h-step prediction if its h-step residuals (approximately) follow an MA($h - 1$) model. By contrast, the existing methods only test whether the residuals follow an MA(0) model, and their suitability for checking the model adequacy for h-step prediction, $h > 1$ is unclear. Below, we discuss how diagnostic tools for testing this hypothesis may be developed:

Bhansali (1983a,b) has considered the question of moving-average order selection for an observed time series, and the techniques discussed there may be applied to the h-step residuals, $\hat{z}_t(h)$, say, of a model fitted for h-step prediction, provided that proper allowance for the effect of parameter estimation has been made. We distinguish between graphical, hypothesis-testing, and order-selection procedures:

A simple graphical procedure would be to plot the estimated correlations of $\hat{z}_t(h)$, where $\hat{z}_t(h) = x_{t+h} - \hat{x}_t(h)$, and where $\hat{x}_t(h)$ is the estimated h-step predictor of x_{t+h} for each $t \geq 1$ and a fixed h; if, for example, the direct method for autoregressive models is used for h-step prediction, $\hat{z}_t(h) = x_{t+h} + \hat{\phi}_{Dhk}(1)x_t + \ldots + \hat{\phi}_{Dhk}(k)x_{t-k+1}$. If the fitted model is adequate for h-step prediction then, as in Box and Jenkins (1970), the estimated correlations of $\hat{z}_t(h)$ may be expected to have a "cut-off" at lag $h - 1$, but, if the converse holds, then the estimated correlations may be expected to be significantly different from 0 at higher lags. A main difficulty with this procedure, although it has an intuitive appeal, is that a theoretical yardstick is usually needed against which departures from the expected behavior may be judged, but, even for an observed time series, care is required in interpreting the sample correlogram at higher lags, whose appearance may be obscured because the sample correlations are themselves mutually correlated. An alternative graphical procedure is to inspect a plot of the estimated inverse partial correlation function of $\hat{z}_t(h)$. For an observed MA(q) process, the inverse partial correlation function, $\pi i(s)$, say, behaves like the partial correlation function, $\pi(s)$ say, of an AR(q) process; moreover, for all $s > q$, the autoregressive estimates, $\hat{\pi}i(s)$, say, of the $\pi i(s)$ are asymptotically independent and normally distributed, each with mean 0 and approximate variance T^{-1}, see Bhansali (1983a) for a proof of these results.

The hypothesis-testing procedures are also considered by Bhansali (1983a), who has suggested a test of the hypothesis that an observed time series follows an MA(q_0) model against the alternative that the order is $q_0 + q_1$, where q_0 and q_1 are pre-specified, and this test is especially suitable in the present context because by (9.32) $z_t(h)$ follows an MA model of pre-specified order, $h - 1$. A difficulty, however, is that $z_t(h)$ is not observed and only its estimate $\hat{z}_t(h)$ is available, and effects of working with the latter instead of the former on the distribution of the relevant test statistic may not even be asymptotically negligible (see Harvey, 1993, p. 76) for further discussion of this problem. It is relevant to note also that the order-selection procedures are inappropriate in the present context, since, see Bhansali (1983a,b), they are based on the assumption that the order of the moving average process has not been pre-specified; however, this order is prescribed to be $h - 1$ for the problem at hand.

9.8.   SIMULATION RESULTS

For the class of linear autoregressive-moving average models, a comparison of the predictive efficiency of the direct and plug-in methods of fitting autoregressions has been carried out by Bhansali (1997) in whose simulation study a nonlinear model is also considered. Moreover, the behavior of these two methods with actual time series has been investigated by Bhansali (1992).

Economic time series generally tend to be nonstationary and possess trend and seasonal components; furthermore, the value of T, the series length, also tends to be invariably small for economic time series, and there is no certainty that their innovations process is necessarily Gaussian. Taking these features into account, a stretch of 111 observations from the following model was simulated:

$$\text{Model 1: } y_t = m_t + x_t, \tag{9.34}$$

where $\{x_t\}$ is an autoregressive process of order 9:

$$x_t + 0.363x_{t-1} + 0.235x_{t-2} + 0.21x_{t-3} + 0.339x_{t-9} = \varepsilon_t, \tag{9.35}$$

but with $\{\varepsilon_t\}$ simulated as a sequence of independent exponentially distributed random variables, each with mean 10.0, and m_t denotes a deterministic seasonal component defined as follows:

$$m_t = \sum_{s=1}^{12} \delta_{st} D' e_s(12), \tag{9.36}$$

in which $D = [343.3, 466.7, 1{,}606.5, 1{,}272.2, 1{,}070.9, 1{,}002.7, 972.2, 1{,}011.0, 1{,}142.8, 1{,}230.0, 1{,}006.3, 1{,}530.3]'$, and $e_s(12) = [0, \dots, 0, 1, 0, \dots, 0]'$ denote two 12×1 vectors, $e_s(12)$ has 1 in the sth position and 0's everywhere else and $\delta_{st} = 1$, if $(t - s)/12$ is an integer including 0, and $\delta_{st} = 0$, otherwise.

The precise form of the seasonal pattern and the generated autoregressive process defined by equations (9.34)–(9.36) above was suggested by analysis of an actual time series. However, for examining the importance of seasonality when constructing multi-step forecasts by the direct and plug-in methods, the magnitude of m_t was varied as shown in the following models, but without altering $\{x_t\}$, which is still defined by (9.35):

$$\text{Model 2: } y_t = (0.1)m_t + x_t;$$

$$\text{Model 3: } y_t = (0.01)m_t + x_t;$$

$$\text{Model 4: } y_t = x_t.$$

For each model, a comparison of the forecasts provided by the direct and plug-in methods up to 12 steps ahead was carried out by applying these two methods to the first 99 observations of the seasonally-adjusted series, $\tilde{x}_t$, where $\tilde{x}_t$ was obtained as follows:

$$\tilde{x}_{j+12k} = y_{j+12k} - \hat{m}_j, \quad j = 1, \ldots, 12; \, k = 0, 1, \ldots, n - 1, \tag{9.37}$$

$$\hat{m}_j = n^{-1} \sum_{i=0}^{n-1} y_{j+12i}, \tag{9.38}$$

and $n = 10$, if $1 \le j \le 3$, and $n = 9$, $4 \le j \le 12$; the last 12 observations were used for a comparison of the forecasts with the actual values. The number of simulations, J, say, equalled 200.

At each simulation, the plug-in and direct forecasts were computed by applying the methodology described in section 9.4; the value of K, the maximum autoregressive order fitted, was set equal to 14 and that of α to 3.0.

As a measure of forecast accuracy, we computed the individual h-step average mean squared errors of prediction, AMSE(h), $h = 1, \ldots, 12$, and the overall average mean squared error of prediction, OAMSE, as follows:

$$\text{AMSE}(h) = J^{-1} \sum_{j=1}^{J} \{\hat{x}_j(h) - \tilde{x}_j\}^2, \quad h = 1, \ldots, 12, \tag{9.39}$$

$$\text{OAMSE} = \sum_{h=1}^{12} \text{AMSE}(h), \tag{9.40}$$

where $J = 200$ is the total number of simulations, $\hat{x}_j(h)$ denotes the h-step forecast given by the direct or plug-in method at the jth simulation, while $\tilde{x}_j(h)$ denotes the corresponding h-step value of the seasonally-adjusted series, $\tilde{x}_t$, that is to be forecast and which were obtained as in (9.37) above.

The ratios of the average h-step mean squared errors of prediction, AMSE(h), of the plug-in and direct methods for $h = 1, \ldots, 12$ and each of models 1–4 are shown in table 9.1, together with the ratio of the overall average mean squared error of prediction, OAMSE, and the frequency with which the criterion (9.11) selected a model of order 0.

It may be gleaned that for models 1–3, the plug-in method has a slightly smaller overall average mean squared error of prediction than the direct method, though the converse holds for model 4, where the direct method has a slightly smaller overall average mean squared error of prediction than the plug-in method.

Table 9.1 The ratios* of the average h-step mean squared errors of prediction for the plug-in and direct methods and the frequency[†] of selecting a 0th order model

Lead time (h)	Model 1		Model 2		Model 3		Model 4	
	AMSE(h) ratio	Order 0 freq.	AMSE(h) ratio	Order 0 freq.	AMSE(h) ratio	Order 0 freq.	AMSE(h) ratio	Order 0 freq.
1	1.000	89.5	1.000	88.5	1.000	87.5	1.000	81.5
2	1.002	86.5	1.002	87.0	1.000	86.5	1.003	80.0
3	1.013	91.5	1.013	91.5	1.011	88.5	1.011	81.0
4	1.013	90.5	0.997	91.0	0.989	89.5	1.010	79.0
5	0.986	94.0	1.003	94.0	1.000	89.5	0.990	79.0
6	0.975	90.0	0.965	90.0	0.971	82.5	0.953	75.0
7	0.973	90.5	0.967	89.5	0.984	83.5	0.976	69.5
8	0.988	88.0	1.003	89.0	0.954	74.0	1.004	58.5
9	1.001	86.0	0.998	85.5	1.010	64.5	1.060	45.0
10	0.975	85.5	0.974	85.5	0.978	95.5	0.986	85.0
11	0.982	84.0	0.980	84.5	0.988	83.0	0.992	82.0
12	0.983	86.0	0.983	86.0	0.981	84.5	0.980	82.5
Overall	0.990	88.5	0.989	88.5	0.990	83.3	1.001	74.8

* The ratio shown is AMSE(h) Plug-in Method/AMSE(h) Direct Method.
[†] The frequencies are shown as percentages over 200 simulations

The difference between their respective mean squared errors of prediction is, however, quite small and well within sampling fluctuations so as not to reject the hypothesis of a lack of superiority of one method over the other for multi-step prediction with models 1–4.

The behavior of the ratios of AMSE(h) for the individual values of h is consistent with the overall behavior described above and does not provide evidence for preferring one method to the other for multi-step prediction with the models considered here.

The simulation results, thus, do not quite accord with the asymptotic theoretical results described in section 9.4, though they do agree with the empirical findings of Clements and Hendry (1996) in a slightly different setting.

An explanation is probably three-fold and could center, first, around the nature of the simulated autoregressive model, (9.35); second, the value of T being relatively small; and, third, that the seasonal adjustment procedure defined by (9.37)–(9.38) may mask or even swamp the underlying serial dependence structure of the simulated process, especially for models 1 and 2. Thus, the coefficients of the simulated autoregression are all less than 0.5 in absolute value and, as may be seen from table 9.1, the Sh_α criterion, (9.11), selected a model of order 0 with a very high frequency, especially with models 1–2, where this frequency does not fall below 84 percent for any value of h. Although this frequency is slightly smaller with model 4 and to a lesser extent with model 3, it is still relatively high and, except for $h = 7, 8, 9$, it does not fall below 75 percent for other values of h. As a consequence, the theoretical advantage of the direct method for multi-step prediction is not apparent in the simulations described here.

References

Bhansali, R.J. (1983a). The inverse partial correlation function of a time series and its applications. *Journal of Multivariate Analysis*, 13, 310–27.

Bhansali, R.J. (1983b). Estimation of the order of a moving average model from auto-regressive and window estimates of the inverse correlation function. *Journal of Time Series Analysis*, 4, 137–62.

Bhansali, R.J. (1991). Consistent recursive estimation of the order of an autoregressive moving average process. *International Statistical Review*, 59, 81–96.

Bhansali, R.J. (1993). Order selection for linear time series models: a review. In T. Subba Rao (ed.), *Developments in Time Series Analysis*. London: Chapman and Hall, 50–66.

Bhansali, R.J. (1996). Asymptotically efficient autoregressive model selection for multi-step prediction. *Annals of the Institute of Statistical Mathematics*, 48, 577–602.

Bhansali, R.J. (1997). Direct autoregressive predictors for multi-step prediction: order selection and performance relative to the plug in predictors. *Statistica Sinica*, 7, 425–49.

Bhansali, R.J. (1999a). Parameter estimation and model selection for multi-step prediction of a time series: a review. In S. Ghosh (ed.), *Asymptotics, Nonparametrics and Time Series*. New York: Marcel Dekker, 201–25.

Bhansali, R.J. (1999b). Autoregressive model selection for multi-step prediction. *Journal of Statistical Planning and Inference*, 78, 295–305.

Bloomfield, P. (1973). An exponential model for the spectrum of a scalar time series, *Biometrika*, 60, 217–26.

Box, G.E.P. and G.M. Jenkins (1970). *Time Series Analysis: Forecasting and Control*. New York: Holden Day.

Clements, M.P. and D.F. Hendry (1996). Multi-Step estimation for forecasting. *Oxford Bulletin of Economics and Statistics*, 58, 657–84.

Cox, D.R. (1961). Prediction by exponentially weighted moving averages and related methods. *Journal of the Royal Statistical Society*, B23, 414–22.

Dahlhaus, R. and Wefelmeyer, W. (1996). Asymptotically optimal estimation in misspecified time series models. *Annals of Statistics*, 24, 952–74.

Farmer, J.D. and J. Sidorowich (1987). Predicting chaotic time series. *Physics Review Letters*, 59, 845–48.

Franke, J. (1985). A Levinson–Durbin recursion for autoregressive-moving average process. *Biometrika*, 72, 573–81.

Greco, C., G., Menga, E. Mosca, and G. Zappa (1984). Performance improvement of self-tuning controllers by multi-step horizons: the musmar approach. *Automatica*, 20, 681–99.

Hannan, E.J. (1987). Rational transfer function approximation. *Statistical Science*, 2, 135–61.

Hannan, E.J. and J. Rissanen (1982). Recursive estimation of mixed autoregressive-moving average order. *Biometrika*, 69, 81–94. Correction (1983), 70, 303.

Harvey, A.C. (1993). *Time Series Models*, 2nd edn. New York: Harvester.

Haywood, J. and G. Tunnicliffe Wilson (1997). Fitting time series models by minimizing multi-step-ahead errors: a freqency domain approach. *Journal of the Royal Statistical Society*, 59, 237–54.

Hurvich, C.M. and C.-L. Tsai (1994). Selection of a multi-step linear predictor for short time series. *Statistica Sinica*, 7, 395–406.

Moulines, E. and P. Soulier (1999). Broad band log-periodogram regression of time series with long range dependence. *Annals of Statistics*, 27, 1415–39.

Newbold, P., C. Agiakloglou and J. Miller (1993). Long-term inference based on short-term forecasting models. In T. Subba Rao (ed.), *Developments in Time Series Analysis*. London: Chapman and Hall, 9–25.

Shibata, R. (1980). Asymptotically efficient selection of the order of the model for estimating the parameters of a linear process. *Annals of Statistics*, 8, 147–64.

Stoica, P. and A. Nehorai (1989). On multi-step prediction error methods for time series models. *Journal of Forecasting*, 8, 357–68.

Stoica, P. and T. Soderstrom (1984). Uniqueness of estimated k-step prediction models of ARMA processes. *Systems and Control Letters*, 4, 325–31.

Tiao, G.C. and D. Xu (1993). Robustness of MLE for multi-step predictions: the exponential smoothing case. *Biometrika*, 80, 623–41.

Weiss, A.A. (1991). Multi-step estimation and forecasting in dynamic models. *Journal of Econometrics*, 48, 135–49.

Whittle, P. (1963). *Prediction and Regulation by Linear Least Squares Methods*. London: English University Press.

Yamamoto, T. (1976). Asymptotic mean square prediction error for an autoregressive model with estimated coefficients. *Applied Statistics*, 25, 123–7.

CHAPTER TEN

The Rationality and Efficiency of Individuals' Forecasts

Herman O. Stekler

10.1. INTRODUCTION

Most forecast evaluations examine the rationality and efficiency of economic predictions made by individuals. There are two justifications for this procedure. First, the study may be concerned with testing the Rational Expectations Hypothesis, developed by Muth (1961), who argued that expectations about an economic variable were rational if they were formed in the same way as the theory explained the actual values of that variable. Because Muth had indicated (p. 316) that expectations were "informed predictions of future events," economists realized that forecast evaluations could be used to test the Rational Expectations Hypothesis.[1]

The second reason why an evaluation might be concerned about the rationality and efficiency of forecasts concerns the accuracy of the predictions themselves and whether they could have been improved. Suppose that *ex post* rationality studies show that the forecasts were biased or had not taken into account information available to the forecaster at the time the predictions were made. Then, in principle, the accuracy of the *ex ante* predictions could have been improved if this information had been taken into account (although this might not have been possible in real time if the forecaster had not had an appropriate model for incorporating this information into the prediction). This chapter will focus on the second issue.

For the forecasts to be rational, they must be unbiased and efficient, with efficiency meaning that the errors must be uncorrelated with information known by the forecaster at the time that the predictions were prepared. Over the years there have been many different operational definitions of the terms rationality and efficiency. It is, therefore, necessary to define these terms as they are currently used. The statistical procedures that are used to test for bias and efficiency will be presented below.

10.2.   RATIONALITY: WEAK AND STRONG (EFFICIENCY)

The two main concepts of rationality used in the current literature are weak and strong rationality. Weak rationality means that the forecasts are conditionally unbiased, so that forecasters do not make systematic errors. Strong rationality has also been called efficiency. The forecasts are efficient if they are unbiased *and* if the forecast errors are not correlated with any other information known at the time the forecast is prepared. If there is a correlation, the forecaster has not efficiently utilized those data.[2]

Since a myriad of series are available whenever a forecast is prepared, as a practical matter it is impossible to definitively test whether an individual has efficiently utilized *all* available information. One researcher using a particular set of data series might find that strong rationality is not rejected, while another study, using a different set of series does reject this hypothesis. A different approach is to test for efficiency using only information that the forecaster certainly has, that is the individual's own past forecasts and forecast errors. Efficiency in this sense requires that one-period-ahead forecast errors not be serially correlated and that these errors be uncorrelated with past forecast values or errors. If these conditions are met, the forecasts are said to exhibit weak form informational efficiency. If the forecasts are both unbiased and exhibit this type of efficiency, the forecasts have also been called weakly rational (for example, Bonham and Dacy, 1991).[3]

10.3.   TYPES OF FORECASTS

These concepts of rationality have been applied to two different categories of forecasts. Most studies have examined the rationality of "rolling event" forecasts. These are forecasts of the value of a variable at different instants of time but made with a fixed lead; that is, the forecast of the value of GDP in 1999I, 1999II, etc. always made one quarter in advance of the quarter for which the prediction is made. "By rolling event we mean that the forecast length *h* is fixed as we move through the available sample of forecasts and outcomes" (Clements, 1995, p. 411). There could be other samples of forecasts made for the same periods but which have leads of two, three, or four quarters. In testing for rationality each of these samples would usually be analyzed separately.

The second category of forecasts consists of "fixed event" predictions. In this case the evaluations analyze the properties of forecasts made of the same event but with different leads. This analysis is possible if there are multiple forecasts for the value of GDP say in 1999I. It is then possible to examine the *revisions* in the forecasts made for *a particular* quarter as the horizon decreased. Although virtually every forecast evaluation of the absolute or relative accuracy of multi-period forecasts examines the tradeoff between prediction lead and the size of the errors

– that is, rolling event projections – there have been fewer studies that have tested the rationality of such fixed event predictions. In analyzing fixed event forecasts made for 1999I, for example, the multiple GDP predictions that are made for that quarter but which have different lead times are evaluated separately from the multiple forecasts made for 1999II, etc. However, as discussed below, Batchelor and Dua (1991) and Davies and Lahiri (1995, 1998) have developed econometric methodologies in which fixed event forecasts made for different target quarters can be analyzed simultaneously. Using these procedures, it is possible to test the rationality of forecasts where the data set consists of multiple predictions for multiple target dates.

10.4. STATISTICAL TESTS

The statistical tests for rationality and efficiency are different for the two categories of forecast sets.

10.4.1. Rolling event forecasts

REGRESSION TESTS

The customary procedure for testing whether rolling event forecasts are unbiased is to use the regression

$$A_t = \alpha + \beta F_t + \varepsilon_t, \tag{10.1}$$

where A_t is the actual value (outcome) and F_t is the prediction. The forecasts would be considered unbiased if the joint hypothesis that $\alpha = 0$ and $\beta = 1$ is not rejected. This joint null on α and β is a sufficient but not a necessary condition for unbiasedness. Holden and Peel (1990, pp. 126–7) presented the necessary and sufficient condition; that is, $\alpha = (1 - \beta)E(F_t)$.

The regression approach can also be used to test for both weak and strong efficiency. Variables that presumably were known by the forecaster when the prediction was made would be included in the equation

$$A_t = \alpha + \beta F_t + C'X_{t-1} + \varepsilon_t. \tag{10.2}$$

The null hypothesis would be that all the coefficients in the C vector were zero; that is, that the information contained in the X variables provided no explanatory power and that all available information had been used efficiently. If the null were not rejected, then the forecasts would exhibit strong efficiency. If only past values of the relevant variable were included in (10.2) and the null hypothesis was not rejected, the forecasts would have displayed weak form informational efficiency. Weak form efficiency also requires that there be no serial correlation in the one-period-ahead prediction errors.[4]

Earlier studies sometimes used a somewhat different regression procedure. Using Muth's insight that expectations were rational if they were formed in the same way as the theory explained the actual values of that variable, Turnovsky (1970) suggested that an autoregressive approach be used to test the rationality of price expectations.[5] He, however, actually tested whether $\alpha = 0$ and $\beta = 1$ as in equation (10.1).

Both Pesando (1975) and Mullineaux (1978), however, used variants of the autoregressive approach to test for efficiency. In particular, they tested whether the outcomes and the forecasts were generated by the same model:

$$A_t = \beta_1 A_{t-1} + \beta_2 A_{t-2} + \ldots\ldots\ldots\ldots + \beta_n A_{t-n} + u_{1t}, \tag{10.3a}$$

$$F_t = b_1 A_{t-1} + b_2 A_{t-2} + \ldots\ldots\ldots\ldots + b_n A_{t-n} + u_{2t}, \tag{10.3b}$$

where A_t and F_t are the actual rates of inflation and the inflation forecast, respectively. Pesando assumed that the β_i and b_i coefficients were equal and used a Chow test in testing the significance of this null. Mullineaux argued that this approach was inappropriate. Mullineaux pointed out that this Chow test requires that the error variances of the realized inflation and the predicted inflation equations be identical. This is not likely to be met in practice, because the variance of a set of forecasts is usually smaller than the variance of the set of outcomes. Mullineaux then suggested an alternative test based on (10.3c).

Subtracting (10.3b) from (10.3a) yields (10.3c), which can be used to test for efficiency because it shows the relationship between the forecast error and past values of the variable:

$$A_t - F_t = (\beta_1 - b_1)A_{t-1} + (\beta_2 - b_2)A_{t-2} + \ldots + (\beta_n - b_n)A_{t-n} + (u_{1t} - u_{2t}). \tag{10.3c}$$

Efficiency requires that all the coefficients in (10.3c) be zero because all of the past values of the inflation rate were known at the time the forecast was prepared. It should be noted that equation (10.3c) is essentially the same as equation (10.2), with the past values of the inflation rate representing the variables in the X vector of equation (10.2).

Variance-bound tests

Muth had demonstrated that when the forecast was optimal, the variance of the predictions would be less than the variance of the series being predicted. This led to the development of variance-bound tests in which the variances of the actual data and the variances of the forecasts are compared. The forecasts would be judged rational if $\text{Var}(A_t) > \text{Var}(F_t)$, but this test may not be valid under some conditions. (See Jeong and Maddala (1991) for a survey of some of the earlier criticism.) In any event, these tests have been primarily applied to financial forecasts and have not been used in testing for the rationality of GDP or inflation predictions.[6]

Cointegration

When the forecast series, F_t, and the series of actuals, A_t, are nonstationary with unit roots, the traditional regression methods that are used to test for bias can yield erroneous results. The result is that the approach embodied in equation (10.1) can lead to falsely rejecting rationality.[7] In this case cointegration techniques would be appropriate for testing whether the forecasts are biased.

The A_t and F_t should be cointegrated; the cointegrating factor should be 1; and the error series, $A_t - F_t$, should not have a unit root. This is a necessary, but not sufficient, condition for unbiasedness. Additional conditions are that $E(A_t - F_t) = 0$, and the error series, $e_t = (A_t - F_t)$, for one-period-ahead forecasts should be serially uncorrelated (Jeong and Maddala, 1991).

SOME PROBLEMS WITH THE STATISTICAL TECHNIQUES

Although these statistical techniques continue to be used, questions have been raised about their validity. First, the predictions could be measured with error. If this occurred, the regression coefficients would be biased downward and rationality might be rejected too often. There are several reasons why the forecasts could be mismeasured: the respondents might not provide their true beliefs; there might be sampling errors; and the questions might be ambiguous[8] (Maddala, 1991; Jeong and Maddala, 1991).

Another criticism is that using the mean prediction of a group of respondents rather than the individual predictions yields an aggregation bias (Figlewski and Wachtel, 1981). It has been noted that the small sample properties of the regression approach cause rationality to be rejected too frequently (Mankiw and Shapiro, 1986). Other criticisms are that the assumptions of the regression approach may not be met in practice.

It is for this reason that nonparametric techniques have been suggested as an alternative approach for testing the unbiasedness and efficiency of forecasts[9] (Campbell and DuFour, 1991, 1995). These statistics focus on the median (rather than the mean) of the forecast errors.[10] The suggested tests can be used to determine whether (1) the forecasts are unbiased, (2) there is an absence of serial correlation among the errors, and (3) the errors are independent from past information. In each case, a sign test and a Wilcoxon signed rank test are used in the evaluations.

The test for unbiasedness is presented here. Median unbiasedness means that the median forecast error should be zero. The sign test statistic is calculated by counting the number of observations where the error, $e_t > 0$, $t = 1, 2, \ldots, T$. Let $z_i = 1$ if $e_t > 0$ and 0 otherwise. Then under the null that the errors are independently distributed, their sum, $u = \Sigma z_i$, which is the sign statistic, will be distributed as a binomial variable $(T, 0.5)$,[11] based on T observations and a probability that the event will occur 50 percent of the time. This null hypothesis is that the forecast errors are independent and have a zero median. The sign test does not indicate whether the distribution of the errors is symmetric. The Wilcoxon signed-ranks test can be used to test whether the forecast errors are symmetric about a zero median. In order to use this test the errors are ranked by their absolute size. Then the sum of the ranks of the errors that originally were positive is obtained; similarly for the errors that were negative. For large samples, the test statistic

$$T^* = \{T - n(n + 1)/4\}/\{n(n + 1)(2n + 1)/24\}^{-(1/2)}$$

has approximately the standard normal distribution. Variants of the sign and Wilcoxon statistics can also be used to test for the absence of serial correlation among the errors and to determine whether the forecast errors are independent of past information.

10.4.2.   Fixed event predictions

Although most rationality studies have analyzed rolling event forecasts, a number have examined fixed event forecasts and have developed the techniques for testing their efficiency (Nordhaus, 1987; Clements, 1995, 1997; Davies and Lahiri, 1995, 1998). Weak efficiency is tested by examining the revisions in the forecasts made of the same event but with different lead times. The two conditions for weak efficiency are that (1) the forecast error made with a h-period lead is independent of all forecast revisions made with a lead longer than h periods, and (2) the revision made with a lead of h periods is independent of all earlier revisions. Thus the series of forecast revisions should be white noise and the fixed event predictions should follow a random walk. These conditions imply that the next revision is unforecastable. If these conditions are not met, the forecaster has not efficiently used all the available information.

10.5.   EMPIRICAL RESULTS – WEAK FORM INFORMATIONAL EFFICIENCY

There have been many studies of the rationality of forecasts of different economic variables. Only a subset of the results of these studies are reported in this chapter. We limit ourselves to reporting findings about the rationality of GDP (GNP) and inflation predictions. First, these are important variables that virtually every macroeconomic forecaster would be interested in. Second, while financial forecasts of interest rates and exchange rates have also been tested for rationality, these tests involve a joint hypothesis: the forecasts are rational and the relevant market is efficient. We avoid this complication by focusing exclusively on the GDP and inflation predictions.[12] Most of the published studies examined the rationality and efficiency of U.S. and U.K. predictions, and these are the results that are presented here. In this section we report on the bias tests and those weak form informational efficiency tests that involve the forecasters' own past forecasts and past errors. The results with respect to the efficiency of the predictions when other variables are introduced into the information set are presented in section 10.5.4 below.

10.5.1.   U.S. inflation studies

The studies that examined the rationality of U.S. inflation forecasts have used a variety of different sources. The first studies were based on the Livingston Surveys, forecasts by economists that Livingston had been collecting since 1947. Later studies examined the forecasts contained in the consumer surveys conducted by the Michigan Survey Research Center, the predictions in the ASA/

NBER surveys (now called the Survey of Professional Forecasters), the Blue Chip Economic Indicators, or the Money Market Surveys (MMS). The Blue Chip Economic Indicators is a consensus forecasting service run by Bob Eggert. Once a month this service conducts a telephone survey to obtain the forecasts of prominent economists in major U.S. business and financial institutions. The MMS is a weekly survey of 60 U.S. securities dealers that collects their predictions of changes in economic variables to be announced in the near future. (The survey of the CPI predictions is conducted two weeks prior to the publication of this number). Finally, the forecasts of econometric models and forecasting services have also been analyzed.

LIVINGSTON SURVEYS

Since 1970, 11 published papers have used this data set to investigate the rationality of price forecasts. The empirical results derived from these studies have varied. In some cases the expectations were judged to be rational, only for this conclusion to be contradicted by other parts of the same study, or to flip-flop in the next study.

Turnovsky (1970) was the first to test the Livingston data for rationality. The results were conflicting. The null that the 1954–64 forecasts were rational was rejected for all of the data. For the years 1962–69, however, the hypothesis that the expectations are unbiased was not rejected for the six-month predictions but was rejected for the 12-month forecasts.[13]

Subsequent analyses of the Livingston forecasts used statistical methodologies that differed somewhat. Pesando (1975) uses two autoregressions based on current and past price changes. The forecasts would be rational if they incorporate all of the information contained in the previously observed rates of inflation. Thus the first-period forecasts would be efficient if this condition were met. Multi-period forecasts would be consistent (and thus rational) if they were generated by the same process; that is, Wold's chain principle of forecasting. Despite a slight difference in methodologies, Pesando's results for the years 1962–69 agree with Turnovsky's (both studies do not reject rationality for six months, but do for 12 months).

Carlson's (1977) analysis of the Livingston data showed how data problems could affect the conclusions regarding rationality. He argues that the data used in the previous studies do not reflect the actual conditions existing at the time that the economists were preparing their predictions. For example, the previous studies assumed that the December levels of the CPI were known at the time that the economists made their predictions of the level of this variable for June and December of the following year. In actuality when the forecasts were made, only the October figures were known. Thus, economists were in fact making predictions 8 and 14 months into the future instead of 6 and 12 months as had previously been assumed. Therefore these forecasts had to be compared with the actual changes that occurred over 8 and 14 month periods rather than over a half year or year. Using the adjusted data, the shorter-term forecasts are no longer rational. Thus, rationality is rejected for the CPI forecasts, but rationality is not rejected for the forecasts of the Wholesale Price Index (WPI) made by the same group of economists. Carlson suggests that it is extremely unlikely that the forecasts are rational in one case and irrational in the other.

Mullineaux (1978) then demonstrated how methodological problems can affect the results. As explained above, he argued that the previous methodology used by Pesando and Carlson was inappropriate. Using the new procedure (equation (10.3c)), Mullineaux runs tests for two time periods, 1959–69 and 1962–69, using two sets of data, Pesando's and Carlson's. The null of rationality was not rejected in most cases.

Although there are seven other studies that examine the rationality of the Livingston forecasts and their results sometimes conflict, we only discuss those where a significant new procedure is used. Figlewski and Wachtel (1981), using a pooled cross-section time-series approach, rejected the null of unbiasedness because the errors were autocorrelated.

Brown and Maital (1981) used the Hansen–Hodrick estimation procedure for the multi-period estimates and indicated that the unbiasedness null was not rejected, but Schroeter and Smith (1986) question that result. Moreover, Brown and Maital were the first to test the Livingston data for strong form informational efficiency. (Their findings will be presented in section (10.5.4 below.) The latest study using these data is by Batchelor and Dua (1989) who find that the Livingston data are rational for most periods.[14]

The evidence that is presented here documents that there are conflicting findings within and across the 11 studies that have examined the Livingston data. The results depend crucially on the data that are used and the appropriateness of the econometric methodology that is employed.[15] In section 10.5.3 we will discuss one possible technique for reconciling conflicting results.

MICHIGAN SURVEY

The Michigan Survey Research Center collects information from consumers about their expectations of inflation. A number of economists have examined these data.[16] Only Smyth (1992) rejected the rationality null.

ASA/NBER SURVEYS

Although there have been only a limited number of studies that have examined the rationality of the forecasts in the ASA/NBER surveys, the results have been controversial. Zarnowitz (1985) used OLS to test the forecasts of 78 individuals. He separately analyzed the predictions that were made with leads of one to four quarters. He concluded that the null that the *current* quarter inflation predictions were unbiased could not be rejected for most forecasters. However, this null was rejected for a majority of the forecasters' longer-lead inflation predictions.

Keane and Runkle (1990) used the same data source over a longer time period and a different methodology, but only analyzed the one-period-ahead projections.[17] The individual forecasts were combined into a panel and a GMM estimator was used to take into account the possibility that the prediction errors were correlated across forecasters because of the aggregate shocks that affected all forecasters. They also assumed that forecasters were trying to predict the outcomes as measured by the first published numbers rather than later revised figures. They, therefore, used the first published numbers as their measure of the actual changes that occurred. The results indicate that the forecasts were unbiased. While the errors were serially correlated, they did not explain future prices; consequently the rationality condition is not violated.

It should be noted that the substance of Zarnowitz's results was not over-turned. While he had reported that most individuals' one-period ahead forecasts were rational, the later study merely showed that a larger percentage of those predictions were unbiased. Keane and Runkle explained that this increase in the percentage of individuals whose forecasts were rational occurred because they used unrevised data as their measure of the outcomes whereas Zarnowitz had used the "final" data.

Davies and Lahiri (1998) also used panel data and a GMM framework but developed a more general model of the process that generated the forecast errors in these surveys. They combined the rolling and fixed event aspects of these forecasts by considering that N individuals made forecasts for T multiple target quarters at H multiple horizons. Using their terminology an individual's forecast error is

$$A_t - F_{ith} = \Phi_i + \lambda_{th} + E_{ih}, \tag{10.4}$$

where F_{ith} is the forecast of the inflation rate for year t, made by individual i with a lead of h periods; Φ_i is the individual's average bias; λ_{th} represents the sum of aggregate shocks between period $t - h$ and t; and E_{ih} is the forecaster's "idiosyncratic" error. The test for bias is that $\Phi_i = 0$. For both the one-period-ahead and for forecasts at all horizons combined, Davies and Lahiri found that only 12 of 45 individuals had made biased predictions. These results are similar to those of Zarnowitz and Keane and Runkle but are not directly comparable, because neither the time periods nor the individuals whose records were examined were identical across these studies. These results demonstrate that most, but not all, professional forecasters who must meet the test of the market were able to generate unbiased predictions.

BLUE CHIP FORECASTS

As noted above, the Blue Chip Economic Indicators is a forecasting service that obtains the predictions of business and financial economists and then issues a consensus projection. In the first half of each year, the monthly forecasts are the annual average rate of inflation for the current year. In the latter half of the current year, the forecast is for the inflation rate expected in the subsequent year. Thus there are 12 forecasts of the inflation rate for each target year, made over horizons of seven to 18 months. These forecasts are for fixed events and their rationality must be judged using techniques appropriate to that type of forecast.

Batchelor and Dua (1991) and Davies and Lahiri (1995) have analyzed these forecasts. Batchelor and Dua concluded that the consensus inflation forecasts failed most tests, but that most individuals produced unbiased predictions – only five of 19 forecasters failed to pass the test that the errors were orthogonal to their current forecast. Moreover, when they revised their predictions, most individuals efficiently used the information contained in their own past forecasts. This result was contradicted by Davies and Lahiri (1995), who used a methodology that differed from that of Batchelor and Dua as did their sample size.[18] Davies and Lahiri used the same framework that was employed in their study of the ASA/NBER forecasts and concluded that 27 of 35 forecasters showed a significant bias. It is interesting to note that the individuals who are included in the Blue Chip panel are also professional forecasters, but, unlike the ASA/NBER participants, these people did not make unbiased predictions.

CONCLUSIONS – U.S. INFLATION STUDIES

After reviewing these studies, it is apparent that there is no definitive answer about the weak form informational efficiency of these U.S. inflation forecasts. The results differ depending on which database is used, when the study was conducted, and which methodology is employed.

10.5.2. U.S. GNP forecasts

There are many fewer studies of the weak form of informational efficiency of the U.S. GNP/GDP predictions. Mincer and Zarnowitz (1969) were the first to analyze the rationality of those predictions. They concluded that two of the three forecasters that were in their sample made unbiased predictions. McNees (1978) examined the forecasts of three econometric services at different horizons and obtained mixed results. Brown and Maital (1981) did not reject weak form informational efficiency in the mean GNP forecasts obtained from the Livingston Surveys. Zarnowitz (1985) examined the individual forecasts of economists participating in the ASA/NBER surveys and found that the null of weak form informational efficiency was not rejected in most cases. Similarly, this null was not rejected for four of six econometric models (Joutz, 1988).

None of these databases have been used a second time. The only database that has been used in more than one study involved the fixed event Blue Chip Forecasts. Batchelor and Dua (1991) tested the individual forecasts for bias and efficiency with respect to own past errors. They did not reject these nulls for any of the forecasts. However, Davies and Lahiri (1995) used the data as a panel, applied the methodology described above, and found that half of the forecasters made biased forecasts. We conclude that while a larger percentage of U.S. GNP forecasts displayed weak form informational efficiency than did the inflation predictions, even these forecasts yielded conflicting results.

10.5.3. Reconciling conflicting rationality findings

We have discovered that many of our results about rationality are in conflict with each other. Sometimes the conflicts arose when a new statistical technique was applied to the original data set. At other times, the results obtained from one survey would differ from those obtained from another data set. Moreover, the availability of additional data points might have affected the results.

This problem of conflicting results is important, because these conflicts make it difficult to reach a conclusion about the rationality of the forecasts. When there are conflicting economic results, our profession often reviews these empirical literatures in survey articles. In such reviews, the surveys typically discuss the inferences that might plausibly be drawn from that literature. Analogous problems involving conflicting empirical results also exist in disciplines other than economics, and a nonsurvey statistical approach is sometimes used to reconcile the conflicts. This approach, called meta-analysis, has been employed in the psychology and the biostatistics literatures, for example. What a meta-analysis adds to a survey article is a formal statistical analysis of what inferences are warranted from the body of existing studies.[19]

Goldfarb and Stekler (1999) used this technique to try to reconcile the conflicting results obtained from studies (published between 1969 and 1998) that examined the weak form informational efficiency of forecasts of U.S. GNP/GDP and inflation. They analyzed the results at three different horizons: one quarter, two quarters, and four quarters. Because these studies were not independent, it was necessary to develop the methodology for combining those results, but each horizon was treated separately.[20] They showed that the results of the meta-analysis differed depending on which meta null is used. If the null is that "all forecasters are rational": (1) this hypothesis would have been rejected for the price forecasts at all horizons and for two of the three sets of GNP predictions, and (2) the same conclusions were obtained whenever the meta-analysis was conducted during the period 1985–98; that is, every meta-analysis yielded the same finding.

However, the results obtained from using a less stringent meta null, "80 percent of forecasters are rational," are different. The results showed that since 1985 the rationality hypothesis was not rejected for any of the real GNP forecasts or for the current quarter price forecasts. However, since 1985 the null that the price forecasts are rational is consistently rejected for two of the horizons. Again we are forced to conclude that, even with the use of this statistical technique, the results concerning the weak form informational efficiency of U.S. inflation and real growth forecasts are ambiguous.

10.5.4. Strong form informational efficiency

The studies that rejected unbiasedness and weak form informational efficiency merely demonstrated that individuals made systematic errors. They did not identify information that could have been used to improve the accuracy of the forecasts. The test for strong rationality can identify relevant information that economists failed to use in preparing their forecasts. This hypothesis has been tested using variables that are of importance to the economy and that, theoretically, should have been considered in preparing the forecast. These include policy variables, such as changes in the money supply and government outlays, and variables that characterize the state of the economy, such as changes in prices, industrial production, wages, unemployment, etc.

Using the Livingston data, Brown and Maital (1981) found that information had not been used efficiently in predicting inflation.[21] This was true for both the

CPI and WPI predictions at both the six and 12 month horizons. Prior changes in wholesale prices explained the errors in the CPI, and the effect of prior changes in the money supply was not fully recognized. On the other hand, Keane and Runkle (1990) found that the ASA/NBER inflation forecasts were efficient with respect to prior monetary movements.

Batchelor and Dua (1989, 1991) tested the Livingston, Michigan, and Blue Chip forecasts for strong form rationality. A large set of policy and economic state variables were used in performing this test. They concluded that the errors of the mean Livingston and Michigan inflation forecasts were not orthogonal to the information in this data set, thus rejecting strong form rationality. When the *individual* Blue Chip predictions were tested, they found similar evidence for both the real GNP and inflation forecasts. For example, 8 of 19 individuals did not use the policy information efficiently in making inflation forecasts and 11 of the 19 did not do so when making real GNP forecasts.[22] More disturbingly, 17 of the 19 did not incorporate all of the information contained in their *own* forecasts of *other* variables when they prepared the inflation estimates.

The most comprehensive analysis of (semi)strong rationality was undertaken by Joutz (1988). He examined 49 information variables in studying whether the GNP and inflation predictions of six econometric forecasting services were efficient. He found that forecasters could have benefitted from the information contained in housing starts, M1 growth, and the degree of slackness in capacity utilization and in the labor market.

There is no definitive explanation for the failure of U.S. forecasters to take account of such important information. Several possible explanations will be presented in section 10.7 below.

10.6. U.K. EMPIRICAL RESULTS

There have been far fewer studies of the rationality of the U.K. forecasts. Batchelor and Dua (1987) found that the individual inflation forecasts in the Gallup Poll's 1982–85 surveys were biased and inefficient. Bakhshi and Yates (1998) also used the Gallup data and likewise found that the predictions for 1984–96 were biased. Holden and Thompson (1997) examined the growth and inflation predictions of four U.K. econometric models and obtained mixed results. Some models made biased forecasts for some variables at some horizons, but there was no consistent pattern.

Britton and Pain (1992) undertook a more comprehensive analysis of the quarterly forecasts of the National Institute of Economic and Social Research. Using the initial values of the published figures as their measure of the actual outcomes, they concluded that for the entire period, 1968IV–1991I, efficiency was not rejected for either the growth or the consumer price inflation forecasts. This hypothesis was, however, rejected in several subperiods for both variables. The number of rejections depended on which set of actual data was used; with the latest available data, this hypothesis was rejected less frequently.

Clements (1995) examined the fixed event forecasts of the Oxford Economic Forecasting macromodel of the U.K. economy. He questioned whether the judgmental adjustments to that model were rational or were excessively smooth. He found no evidence that any of the revisions were excessively smooth. Clements (1997) then analyzed the forecasts of the National Institute of Economic and Social research and found that the revisions displayed negative autocorrelation rather than being white noise. Nevertheless, he argued that this result was not necessarily inconsistent with rationality.

Even with the limited number of studies that examined the rationality of U.K. forecasts, the results are in conflict.

10.7. WHY ARE SOME FORECASTS NOT RATIONAL?

Our survey demonstrates that some individuals' forecasts of some variables did not violate the rationality null. The next question is why other predictions are biased or inefficient. Zellner (1985) advanced the hypothesis that forecasts might be biased and not rational if forecasters had an asymmetric loss function and issued predictions so as to minimize this function.[23] However, the studies referenced here have provided evidence that forecasters made rational forecasts for some variables but not for others. For Zellner's hypothesis to apply, it would be necessary to explain why individuals had asymmetric loss functions only for some variables.

An alternative hypothesis was suggested by Fildes and Fitzgerald (1983), who expressed the view that forecasters did not completely understand the dynamic process that they were trying to predict. This view is consistent with the findings of the Batchelor and Dua (1991) analysis of the Blue Chip predictions in which they found that most forecasters did not incorporate the information contained in their own predictions of *other* variables when they prepared their estimates of the inflation rate. This same view is stated more forcefully in the Batchelor and Dua (1987) study of the U.K. Gallup Poll survey of inflation expectations: "It is then likely that consumers hold an incorrect model of inflation" (p. 825) and "the inefficiency is mainly the result of consumers failing to utilize at all the information in a broad range of relevant published economic indicators . . ." (p. 826). Finally, Britton and Pain (1992, p. 16) show that the "[efficiency] null is only accepted for [a few] variables. . . . A similar finding is reported in Brown and Maital (1981), suggesting that the interrelationships between the variables of interest may not be fully appreciated by forecasters."

10.8. RELATED TOPICS AND UNRESOLVED ISSUES

There are a number of topics in the forecast evaluation literature that are related to the rationality tests. These include combining forecasts and encompassing tests. Important references to the combining literature are Bates and Granger (1969) and Clemen (1989), while encompassing is analyzed by Chong and Hendry (1986) and Harvey et al. (1998). For specific discussion of the relationship of these concepts with rationality, see Holden and Peel (1989) and Holden and Thompson (1997).

It is not surprising that encompassing and efficiency tests are related. The former test asks whether the second of two models adds anything to the explanatory power of the first model (see chapter 12 by Newbold and Harvey). This is similar to the efficiency test which determines whether there is any information in the forecasts of the second model that was not considered when the predictions of the first model were issued.[24] Whether forecasts should be combined is a similar problem because one would only combine if the forecasts contained different information.

Forecast evaluations have also shown that forecasters make systematic errors, failing to predict turning points, underestimating the inflation rate when it is rising and overestimating it when it is falling, etc. (For a survey of these findings, see Fildes and Stekler, 1999.) Despite these qualitative findings, the customary tests frequently do not reject the rationality null. These results seem inconsistent and must still be resolved. One possibility might be that other tests are required to supplement the traditional methods.

On the other hand, there might be some systematic errors that should not be considered evidence of irrationality. This would involve a situation where "agents . . . use all available information efficiently and in this sense are rational" (Lewis, 1989, p. 621) but these errors occur because there is a fundamental change in the structure of a market or the economy that is only recognized over time. In this case "forecast errors may be systematically incorrect while the market rationally learns the true process that generates fundamentals" (Lewis, p. 622). Forecast evaluations and rationality tests would be required to determine whether or not the regime change could have been predicted on the basis of existing information. If it could have been forecast, then the systematic error would be evidence that all information had not been optimally utilized.[25] If the change in fundamentals were truly unpredictable in advance, subsequent analyses would have to investigate the framework in which learning about this structural change occurred.

A final possibility is that the forecasts are economically rational in the sense that individuals either measure the marginal costs and benefits of expanding their information sets or place different values on the costs associated with different types of errors. "In practice, however, since these costs and benefits are difficult to observe, it is hard to say what the information set . . . ought to be" (Maddala, 1991, p. 325; also see Clements, 1997). Zellner (1986) indicated that biased forecasts may be optimal from the forecaster's perspective if costs are taken into account.

10.9. CONCLUSIONS

Although there have been many evaluations of U.S. and U.K. forecasts, there is no definitive conclusion about their rationality and efficiency. The results are in conflict, with some forecasts displaying these characteristics in some periods and not in others, and/or some forecasters able to generate unbiased and efficient forecasts while others were unable to do so. Even using a sophisticated technique for reconciling conflicting results, we could not obtain a definitive conclusion. We were also unable to determine why information was not always used effectively. This leads to the obvious plea that more research be done on this topic.

Notes

1 Some observers have noted that some individuals responding to surveys or preparing forecasts may not have as strong incentives as others to prepare accurate forecasts displaying rational expectations. Therefore, using these forecasts might not yield a valid test of the rationality hypothesis (Sheffrin, 1983). Zarnowitz (1985) and Keane and Runkle (1990) argue that the respondents to the ASA/NBER surveys provide forecasts that meet the market test, and these individuals have the appropriate incentives to make accurate predictions.

2 This requirement has also been called the orthogonality condition; that is, the error should be orthogonal, or unrelated, to the information that had been available.

3 Other studies have used additional definitions of rationality: sufficient rationality, and strict rationality. Also the term conditional efficiency has been used (see Bonham and Dacy, 1991, p. 248). Since the literature primarily uses the terms weak and strong rationality and weak and strong informational efficiency, these are the concepts that will be examined in this chapter.

4 If the data are overlapping, the error term of the equation would have a moving-average structure that is dependent upon the number of periods in the forecast horizon. Because an optimal k-period-ahead forecast has a MA $(k-1)$ process, efficiency requires that the MA process be no longer than $k-1$ periods.

5 "Consequently a test for rationality . . . is obtained by regressing the actual changes on the same variables generating the expectations and by comparing the magnitude of the corresponding coefficients" (Turnovsky, 1970, p. 1445). Also, see Modigliani and Shiller (1973) and Mishkin (1981).

6 There have been several studies that examined this relationship between the standard deviations of the predicted and actual changes. These analyses were not, however, concerned with the rationality of the forecasts. See Stekler (1975) and Smyth and Ash (1985).

7 If the series of actual values is a random walk, the OLS estimates of the coefficients in equation (10.1) are biased downwards.

8 These error-in-variables problems can be solved if two or more sets of forecasts that measure the same variable are used together. Although the data are available, this approach has not been employed in studies of the rationality of GDP or inflation predictions.

9 This approach was used to analyze government budget forecasts (Campbell and Ghysels, 1995).

10 If the distribution of errors is symmetric and has a finite mean, median and mean unbiasedness are equivalent.

11 For larger sized samples, the normal approximation to the binomial may be used. However, a continuity correction factor must be used in this case.

12 Maddala (1991) surveys some of the studies that examined the rationality of the interest rate and exchange rate predictions. Lovell (1986) has a survey of some earlier rationality studies.

13 Turnovsky did not use an F-test, but separately examined the two coefficients in the equation: $A_t = a_0 + a_1 F_t$.

14 Other studies of the Livingston data were by Pearce (1979), Hafer and Resler (1982), and Bryan and Gavin (1987).

15 Thomas (1999) reaches a similar conclusion. Moreover, the results can differ if the median rather than the mean forecast is examined.

16 Such studies include Fackler and Stanhouse (1977), Noble and Fields (1982), Gramlich (1983), Bryan and Gavin (1987), Batchelor and Dua (1989), Rich (1989, 1993), Baghestani (1992, 1992a), and Smyth (1992).

17 Keane and Runkle criticize the fact that survey means and pooled data were used. While Zarnowitz did report these results, he focused on the performance of individuals' predictions for various forecasting leads.

18 Davies and Lahiri had an incomplete panel. Missing data were replaced by zeroes and the estimation process was adjusted for these missing observations.

19 A very useful general reference on the meta-analysis literature focusing largely on psychology and educational evaluation is Cooper and Hedges, *Handbook of Research Synthesis* (1994). See also Lipsey and Wilson (1993).

20 They conducted the meta-analysis as though it would have been done in each year from 1969 to 1999, based on the studies that would have been available at the end of each of those years. However, prior to 1985 there were an insufficient number of observations to have been able to draw any statistically warranted inferences about the rationality of either the real growth rate or inflation forecasts.

21 The variables that Brown and Maital used for this test were ones that the respondents were, in fact, trying to predict. Thus they were obviously aware of their prior values at the time that the predictions were made.

22 Unfortunately, Batchelor and Dua do not identify the specific variables that contained this information.

23 Clements (1997) explored this issue further and noted that the rejection of weak efficiency implied either irrationality or optimally biased forecasts.

24 This assumes that the predictions of the second model were available at the time the forecasts of the first model were issued.

25 It should be noted that the analyses of U.S. forecasts that used the panel approach and the GMM estimating technique implicitly assumed that the shocks that were common to all forecasters were unpredictable. Some such as the two oil shocks would clearly fall into this category. Regime changes that led to cycles would, however, not be in this category; forecasters should be expected to predict them.

References

Baghestani, H. (1992). On the formation of expected inflation under various conditions: some survey evidence. *Journal of Business*, 65, 281–93.

Baghestani, H. (1992a). Survey evidence on the Muthian rationality of the inflation forecasts of U.S. consumers. *Oxford Bulletin of Economics and Statistics*, 54, 173–86.

Bakhshi, H. and A. Yates (1998). Are U.K. inflation expectations rational? Bank of England, mimeo.

Batchelor, R.A. and P. Dua (1987). The accuracy and rationality of U.K. inflation expectations: some quantitative results. *Applied Economics*, 19, 819–28.

Batchelor, R.A. and P. Dua (1989). Household versus economist forecasts of inflation: a reassessment. *Journal of Money, Credit and Banking*, 21, 252–57.

Batchelor, R.A. and P. Dua (1991). Blue chip rationality tests. *Journal of Money, Credit, and Banking*, 23, 692–705.

Bates, J.M. and C.W.J. Granger (1969). The combination of forecasts. *Operations Research Quarterly*, 20, 451–68.

Bonham, C.S. and D.C. Dacy (1991). In search of a strictly rational forecast. *Review of Economics and Statistics*, 73, 245–53.

Britton, A. and N. Pain (1992). *Economic Forecasting in Britain*, Report Series Number 4. London: National Institute of Economic and Social Research.

Brown, B.W. and S. Maital (1981). What do economists know? An empirical study of experts' expectations. *Econometrica*, 49, 491–504.

Bryan, M.F. and W.T. Gavin (1986). Models of inflation expectations formation; a comparison of household and economist forecasts. *Journal of Money, Credit, and Banking*, 18, 539–44.

Campbell, B. and J.-M. Dufour (1991). Over-rejection in rational expectations models: a non-parametric approach to the Mankiw–Shapiro problem. *Economics Letters*, 35, 285–90.

Campbell, B. and J.-M. Dufour (1995). Exact nonparametric orthogonality and random walk tests. *Review of Economics and Statistics*, 77, 1–16.

Campbell, B. and E. Ghysels (1995). Federal budget projections: a nonparametric assessment of bias and efficiency. *Review of Economics and Statistics*, 77, 17–31.

Carlson, J.A. (1977). A study of price forecasts. *Annals of Economic and Social Measurement*, 6, 27–56.

Chong, Y.Y. and D.F. Hendry (1986). Econometric evaluation of linear macroeconomic models. *Review of Economic Studies*, 53, 671–90.

Clemen, R.T. (1989). Combining forecasts: a review and annotated bibliography. *International Journal of Forecasting*, 5, 559–83.

Clements, M.P. (1995). Rationality and the role of judgment in macroeconomic forecasting. *Economic Journal*, 105, 410–20.

Clements, M.P. (1997). Evaluating the rationality of fixed event forecasts. *Journal of Forecasting*, 16, 225–39.

Cooper, H. and L. Hedges (eds.) (1994). *The Handbook of Research Synthesis*. New York: Russell Sage Foundation.

Davies, A. and K. Lahiri (1995). A new framework for analyzing three-dimensional panel data. *Journal of Econometrics*, 68, 205–27.

Davies, A. and K. Lahiri (1998). Reexamining the rational expectations hypothesis using panel data on multiperiod forecasts. In C. Hsiao, K. Lahiri, M.H. Pesaran, and L.F. Lee (eds.), *Analysis of Panels and Limited Dependent Variable Models*. Cambridge and New York: Cambridge University Press.

Fackler, J. and B. Stanhouse (1977). Rationality of the Michigan price expectations data. *Journal of Money Credit and Banking*, 9, 662–6.

Fildes, R. and M.D. Fitzgerald (1983). The use of information in balance of payments forecasting. *Economica*, 50, 249–58.

Fildes, R. and H.O. Stekler (1999). The state of macroeconomic forecasting. Mimeo.

Figlewski, S. and P. Wachtel (1981). The formation of inflationary expectations. *Review of Economics and Statistics*, 63, 1–10.

Goldfarb, R. and H.O. Stekler (1999). Testing for rationality: would meta-analysis help? Mimeo.

Gramlich, E.M. (1983). Models of inflation expectations formation. *Journal of Money, Credit and Banking*, 15, 155–73.

Hafer, R.W. and D.H. Resler (1982). On the rationality of inflation forecasts: a new look at the Livingston data. *Southern Economic Journal*, 48, 1049–56.

Hansen, L.-P. and R.J. Hodrick (1980). Foreign exchange rates as optimal predictors of future spot prices: an econometric analysis. *Journal of Political Economy*, 88, 829–53.

Harvey, D., S. Leybourne, and P. Newbold (1998). Tests for forecast encompassing. *Journal of Business and Economic Statistics*, 16, 254–9.

Holden, K. and D.A. Peel (1989). Unbiasedness, efficiency and the combination of economic forecasts. *Journal of Forecasting*, 8, 175–88.

Holden, K. and D.A. Peel (1990). On testing for unbiasedness and efficiency of forecasts. *The Manchester School*, 58, 120–7.

Holden, K. and D.A. Peel, and J. Thompson (1997). Combining forecasts, encompassing and the properties of U.K. macroeconomic forecasts. *Applied Economics*, 29, 1447–58.

Jeong, J. and G.S. Maddala (1991). Measurement errors and tests for rationality. *Journal of Business and Economic Statistics*, 9, 431–9.

Joutz, F.L. (1988). Informational efficiency tests of quarterly macroeconometric GNP forecasts from 1976 to 1985. *Managerial and Decision Economics*, 9, 311–30.

Keane, M.P. and D.E. Runkle (1990). Testing the rationality of price forecasts: new evidence from panel data. *American Economic Review*, 80, 714–35.

Lewis, K.K. (1989). Changing beliefs and systematic rational forecast errors with evidence from foreign exchange. *American Economic Review*, 79, 621–36.

Lovell, M.C. (1986). Tests of the rational expectations hypothesis. *American Economic Review*, 76, 110–24.

Maddala, G.S. (1991). Survey data on expectations: what have we learnt? In Marc Nerlove (ed.), *Issues in Contemporary Economics vol. 2: Macroeconomics and Econometrics*. New York: NYU Press, 319–44.

Mankiw, N.G. and M.D. Shapiro (1986). Do we reject too often? Small sample properties of rational expectations models. *Economics Letters*, 20, 139–45.

McNees, S.K. (1978). The rationality of economic forecasts. *American Economic Review Papers and Proceedings*, 68, 301–5.

Mincer, J. and V. Zarnowitz (1969). The evaluation of economic forecasts. In Jacob Mincer (ed.), *Economic Forecasts and Expectations*. New York: National Bureau of Economic Research, 3–46.

Mishkin, F.S. (1981). Are market forecasts rational? *American Economic Review*, 71, 295–305.

Modigliani, F. and R.J. Shiller (1973). Inflation, rational expectations and the term structure of interest rates. *Economica*, 40, 12–43.

Mullineaux, D.J. (1978). On testing for rationality: another look at the Livingston price expectations data. *Journal of Political Economy*, 86, 329–36.

Muth, J.F. (1961). Rational expectations and the theory of price movements. *Econometrica*, 29, 315–35.

Noble, N.R. and T.W. Fields (1982). Testing the rationality of inflation expectations derived from survey data: a structure-based approach. *Southern Economic Journal*, 49, 361–73.

Nordhaus, W.D. (1987). Forecasting efficiency: concepts and applications. *Review of Economics and Statistics*, 69, 667–74.

Pearce, D.K. (1979). Comparing survey and rational measures of expected inflation. *Journal of Money, Credit, and Banking*, 11, 447–56.

Pesando, J.E. (1975). A note on the rationality of the Livingston price expectations. *Journal of Political Economy*, 83, 849–58.

Rich, R.W. (1989). Testing the rationality of inflation forecasts from survey data: another look at the SRC expected price change data. *Review of Economics and Statistics*, 71, 682–86.

Schroeter, J.R. and S.L. Smith (1986). A reexamination of the rationality of the Livingston price expectations. *Journal of Money, Credit and Banking*, 18, 239–46.

Sheffrin, S. (1983). *Rational Expectations*. Cambridge: Cambridge University Press.

Smyth, D. (1992). Measurement errors in survey forecasts of expected inflation and the rationality of inflation expectations. *Journal of Macroeconomics*, 14, 439–48.

Smyth, D. and J.C.K. Ash (1985). The underestimation of forecasts and the variability of predictions and outcomes. *Economics Letters*, 19, 141–43.

Swidler, S. and D. Ketcher (1990). Economic forecasts, rationality, and the processing of new information over time. *Journal of Money, Credit, and Banking*, 22, 65–76.

Stekler, H.O. (1975). Why do forecasters underestimate? *Economic Inquiry*, 13, 445–9.

Thomas, L.B. (1999). Survey measures of expected U.S. inflation. *Journal of Economic Perspectives*, 13, 125–44.

Turnovsky, S.J. (1970). Empirical evidence on the formation of price expectations. *Journal of the American Statistical Association*, 65, 1441–54.

Zarnowitz, V. (1985). Rational expectations and macroeconomic forecasts. *Journal of Business and Economic Statistics*, 3, 293–311.

Zellner, A. (1986). Biased predictors, rationality and the evaluation of forecasts. *Economics Letters*, 21, 45–8.

CHAPTER ELEVEN

Decision-Based Methods for Forecast Evaluation

M. Hashem Pesaran and Spyros Skouras

11.1. INTRODUCTION

This chapter provides an overview of techniques for evaluation of forecasts when the primary purpose of forecasting is to make better decisions. The traditional literature on forecast evaluation focuses on purely statistical measures of forecast accuracy without making specific reference to the way the forecasts are used. See, for example, Box and Jenkins (1970), Granger and Newbold (1977, 1986), and Clements and Hendry (1998, 1999). The approach reviewed here assumes the forecast user's decision environment is known, and addresses the issue of forecast evaluation as an integral part of the decision-making process. Both approaches are clearly useful, as they address the same problem in different contexts. The statistical approach focuses on general measures of forecast accuracy intended to be relevant in a variety of circumstances, while the decision-based approach provides techniques with which to evaluate the economic value of forecasts to a particular decision-maker or a group of decision-makers. Theil (1960, sections 8.4 and 8.5) provides an early discussion of the usefulness of the decision approach to forecast evaluation. Other important early contributions include Nelson (1972) and White (1966), who are amongst the first to consider the problem of forecast evaluation from the perspective of decision theory and dynamic programming. Nelson, in particular, articulates the concept of the "value of a (probability) forecast" to an individual decision-maker as the expected value of his/her payoff using the probability forecasts relative to the payoff expected if unconditional probability estimates are used. This "economic" approach to forecast evaluation and its various extensions have been applied extensively in the literature on meteorological forecasting. See, for example, Murphy (1977, 1985), Katz, Brown, and Murphy (1987), and the recent edited volume by Katz and Murphy (1997) for more recent references.

Similar ideas have emerged in empirical finance since early attempts by Cowles (1933) to determine whether financial analysts' forecasts were of any value to investors. However, until recently, little effort had been made to nest this problem in a general decision-based approach to forecast evaluation. This has been somewhat rectified during the last decade as the observation that financial series are predictable has led to an attempt to understand the economic significance of this finding. See, for example, Breen, Glosten, and Jagannathan (1989), Leitch and Tanner (1991), McCulloch and Rossi (1990), West, Edison, and Cho (1993), Pesaran and Timmermann (1994, 1995), Satchell and Timmermann (1995), and Skouras (1998). For the time being, work in this area has emerged primarily in empirical finance even though it is natural to expect the application of the decision-based approach in other settings, including for example macroeconomic forecasting. For further references, see also Granger and Pesaran (2000a,b).

The chapter is organized as follows. Section 11.2 discusses the issue of forecast evaluation from the respective perspectives of the producers and the users of the forecasts, and whether the forecasts are intended for general or specific use. Section 11.3 develops a decision-based framework to forecast evaluation and illustrates its application in the context of simple examples covering the standard quadratic cost function as well as an application to finance with a negative exponential utility function and a two-action two-state decision problem employed extensively in evaluation of weather forecasts. Section 11.4 provides an overview of recent developments in forecast evaluation within a decision-based framework to forecast evaluation, and shows how a decision-based approach can provide a unifying theme for these developments, including providing an economic rationale for the use of generalized cost-of-error functions, statistics for market-timing skills in finance, and the evaluation of interval and probability forecasting. Section 11.5 considers the problem of forecast comparisons and develops a measure based on the mean of realized loss-differentials that arise in a particular decision from the use of one forecast distribution (density) function as compared to another. The problem of forecast comparisons from the perspective of a forecast producer is also discussed briefly. Section 11.6 discusses the statistical problem of testing the "equivalence" of two forecast distributions in the context of a particular decision. The relationship between this test and forecast encompassing tests is also discussed. Section 11.7 concludes with a discussion of some likely future developments.

11.2. PRODUCERS AND USERS OF FORECASTS

As in any evaluation process, the purpose of forecast evaluation is paramount. Forecasts could be subject to evaluation for a number of different purposes and from a variety of perspectives. For example, it is important to distinguish between whether the evaluation is to be carried out from the perspective of the producers or the consumers of the forecasts, and whether the forecasts are intended for general use or for use by a particular individual (or a group of individuals) for a specific purpose. Forecast evaluation also plays a central role in the process of model selection and model evaluation. One prominent example in the model selection literature is the Predictive Least Squares principle advocated by Rissanen (1987).

Evaluation of forecasting skills of a forecast producer may best be carried out using any one of the purely statistical measures, such as root mean squared forecast errors, errors in forecasting turning points, or general probability measures based on probability integral transforms. There now exists a distinguished literature that deals with such purely statistical measures of forecast evaluation. See, for example, Stock and Watson (1993), Diebold and Mariano (1995), Diebold and Lopez (1996), West (1996), and Clements and Hendry (1998, 1999), and the chapters by Mariano; Eitrheim, Husebø, and Nymoen; McCracken and West; and Tay and Wallis in this volume.

In contrast, for a user (or a group of users) forecast evaluation requires a decision-based approach. Purely statistical measures, by their very nature, need not be directly relevant to a particular user's utility function and budget constraints. From a user's perspective, forecast accuracy is best judged by its expected economic value, the characterization of which requires a full specification of the user's decision environment. Evaluation of forecasts within a decision framework has been considered in the meteorology literature and a simple two-action two-state version of the decision problem is routinely applied in the evaluation of weather forecasts for use by various clients, such as Florida orange growers wishing to protect their crops against frost damage, or U.K. county councils in their decisions as to whether to grit the roads to avoid icy road conditions. See for example, Murphy and Winkler (1987), Ehrendorfer and Murphy (1988), and Katz and Murphy (1990). In contrast, the forecasting literature in economics has focussed almost exclusively on statistical measures. In finance, where the objective of forecasting is relatively uncontroversial (making profits without taking excessive risks), the importance of economic measures of forecast accuracy has been widely acknowledged, but most applications in finance fall short of a fully integrated decision-based approach to forecast evaluation. See, for example, McCulloch and Rossi (1990), Leitch and Tanner (1991), West, Edison, and Cho (1993), Pesaran and Timmermann (1995, 2000), and Granger and Pesaran (2000b).

There seem to be four main reasons for the limited use of the decision-based approach to forecast evaluation in economics. First, the focus of forecast evaluation has been on the models/producers of the forecasts rather than their use in decision-making. Second, the decision-based approach is highly information intensive and requires full articulation of the decision environment, which is often absent from the formulation of the forecasting models considered in economics. Third, until recently, there has been little evidence that such an approach would lead to different evaluations of forecasts in practice than a purely statistical approach. Fourth, the application of the approach is likely to involve technical difficulties.

In subsequent sections we will discuss a number of important economic situations in which forecasting and decision-making are naturally integrated and the decision environment can be readily characterized. That this is worthwhile is suggested by a substantial literature pointing to the idea that the evaluation of realistic economic forecasts is sensitive to the use to which they will be put (see, for example, Zellner, 1973; Leitch and Tanner, 1991, 1995; Gerlow and Irwin, 1991; Boothe, 1983, 1987).

11.3. A DECISION-BASED FORECAST EVALUATION FRAMEWORK

As Whittle (1979, p. 177) notes "Prediction is not an end in itself, but only a means of optimizing current actions against the prospect of an uncertain future." To make better decisions we need better forecasts, and to evaluate forecasts we need to know how and by whom forecasts are used. As argued above, from a user's perspective, the criteria for forecast evaluation must depend on her decision environment.

Consider a one-shot decision problem faced by a single individual with a globally convex cost function, $C(y_t, x_{t+1})$, where x_{t+1} is a state variable of relevance to the decision with the conditional probability distribution function

$$F_t(x) = \Pr(x_{t+1} < x \mid \Omega_t), \tag{11.1}$$

and y_t is the decision variable to be chosen by the decision-maker. Ω_t is the information set containing at least observations on current and past values of x_t. To simplify the analysis, we assume that the choice of y_t does not affect $F_t(x)$, although clearly changes in $F_t(x)$ will influence the decisions. In general, the cost and the probability distribution functions, $C(y_t, x_{t+1})$ and $F_t(x)$, also depend on a number of parameters characterizing the degree of risk aversion of the decision-maker and her (subjective) specification of the future uncertainty characterized by the curvature of the conditional distribution function of x_{t+1}.

Suppose now that at time t, a forecaster provides the decision-maker with the predictive distribution $\hat{F}_t$, being an estimate of $F_t(x)$, and we are interested in computing the value of this forecast to the decision-maker. Under the traditional approach, the forecasts $\hat{F}_t$ are evaluated using statistical criteria which may not be directly relevant to the decision-maker under consideration. The appropriate criterion for forecast evaluation in the present context is implicit in the decision problem and simplifies to a familiar statistical criterion only under restrictive assumptions on the decision environment.

Under the decision-based approach, we first need to solve for the decision variable y_t based on the predictive distribution function $\hat{F}_t$. We shall assume that this is carried out by means of standard decision-based procedures, namely expected utility/cost optimization using Bayes rule with respect to $\hat{F}_t$. Hence, for the optimal value of y_t, which we denote by y_t^*, we have

$$y_t^* = \operatorname*{argmin}_{y_t} \{E_{\hat{F}}[C(y_t, x_{t+1}) \mid \Omega_t]\}, \tag{11.2}$$

where $E_F[C(y_t, x_{t+1}) | \Omega_t]$ is the conditional expectations operator with respect to the predictive distribution function, $\hat{F}_t$. The decision-making problem under parameter and model uncertainty will not be addressed in this chapter. Here we focus on the formulation of the forecast evaluation problem when a single decision-maker is faced with a given probability forecast function.

A "population average" criterion function for the evaluation of the probability distribution function, $\hat{F}_t$, is given by

$$\Psi_C(F_t, \hat{F}_t) = E_F[C(y_t^*, x_{t+1}) | \Omega_t], \tag{11.3}$$

where the conditional expectations are taken with respect to $F_t(x)$, the "true" probability distribution function of x_{t+1} conditional on Ω_t. The above function can also be viewed as the average cost of making forecast errors when large samples of forecasts and realizations are available, for the same specifications of cost and predictive distribution function.[1]

To simplify notation, we drop the subscript F when the expectations are taken with respect to the true distribution functions. We now turn to some decision problems of particular interest, to study the dependence of (11.3) on the cost function $C(y_t, x_{t+1})$.

11.3.1. Quadratic cost functions and the MSFE criteria

In general, the decision based forecast evaluation criterion given by (11.3) depends on the parameters of the underlying cost (utility) function as well as on the difference between $F_t(x)$ and its estimate $\hat{F}_t$. The only exception, as far as we know, arises when the utility (cost) function is quadratic and the constraints (if any) are linear; the so called LQ decision problem. To see this, consider the following quadratic specification for the cost function:

$$C(y_t, x_{t+1}) = ay_t^2 + 2by_t x_{t+1} + cx_{t+1}^2, \tag{11.4}$$

where $a > 0$ and $ca - b^2 > 0$, thus ensuring that $C(y_t, x_{t+1})$ is globally convex in y_t and x_{t+1}. Based on the forecasts, $\hat{F}_t$, the unique optimal decision rule for this problem is given by

$$y_t^* = \left(\frac{-b}{a} \right) E_{\hat{F}}(x_{t+1} | \Omega_t)$$

$$= \left(\frac{-b}{a} \right) \hat{x}_{t,1},$$

where $\hat{x}_{t,1}$ is the one-step forecast of x formed at time t based on the estimate, $\hat{F}_t$. Substituting this result in the utility function, after some simple algebra we have

$$C(y_t^*(\hat{x}_{t,1}), x_{t+1}) = \left(c - \frac{b^2}{a}\right)x_{t+1}^2 + \frac{b^2}{a}(x_{t+1} - \hat{x}_{t,1})^2.$$

Therefore,

$$\Psi_C(F_t, \hat{F}_t) = \left(c - \frac{b^2}{a}\right)E(x_{t+1}^2 \mid \Omega_t) + \frac{b^2}{a}E[(x_{t+1} - \hat{x}_{t,1})^2 \mid \Omega_t].$$

In this case, the evaluation criterion implicit in the decision problem is proportional to the familiar statistical measure $E[(x_{t+1} - \hat{x}_{t,1})^2 \mid \Omega_t]$, namely the Mean Squared Forecast Error (MSFE) criterion, which does not depend on the parameters of the underlying cost function.

This is a special result, and does not carry over to the multivariate context even within the rather restrictive LQ setup.[2] To see this, consider the following multivariate version of (11.4):

$$C(\mathbf{y}_t, \mathbf{x}_{t+1}) = \mathbf{y}_t'\mathbf{A}\mathbf{y}_t + 2\mathbf{y}_t'\mathbf{B}\mathbf{x}_{t+1} + \mathbf{x}_{t+1}'\mathbf{C}\mathbf{x}_{t+1}, \tag{11.5}$$

where $\mathbf{y}_t$ is an $m \times 1$ vector of decision variables, $\mathbf{x}_{t+1}$ is a $k \times 1$ vector of state variables, and $\mathbf{A}$, $\mathbf{B}$, and $\mathbf{C}$ are $m \times m$, $m \times k$ and $k \times k$ coefficient matrices. To ensure that $C(\mathbf{y}_t, \mathbf{x}_{t+1})$ is globally convex in its arguments we also assume that the $(m + k) \times (m + k)$ matrix

$$\begin{pmatrix} \mathbf{A} & \mathbf{B} \\ \mathbf{B}' & \mathbf{C} \end{pmatrix}$$

is positive-definite and symmetric. As before due to the quadratic nature of the cost function the optimal decision depends only on the first conditional moment of the assumed conditional probability distribution function of the state variables and is given by

$$\mathbf{y}_t^* = -\mathbf{A}^{-1}\mathbf{B}\hat{\mathbf{x}}_{t,1}, \tag{11.6}$$

where $\hat{\mathbf{x}}_{t,1}$ is the point forecast of $\mathbf{x}_{t+1}$ formed at time t, with respect to the conditional probability distribution function, $\hat{F}_t$. Substituting this result in (11.5) and taking conditional expectations with respect to the $F_t(\mathbf{x})$, the true conditional probability distribution function of $\mathbf{x}_{t+1}$, we have:

$$\Psi_C(F_t, \hat{F}_t) = E(\mathbf{x}_{t+1}'(\mathbf{C} - \mathbf{H})\mathbf{x}_{t+1} \mid \Omega_t) + E[(\mathbf{x}_{t+1} - \hat{\mathbf{x}}_{t,1})'\mathbf{H}(\mathbf{x}_{t+1} - \hat{\mathbf{x}}_{t,1}) \mid \Omega_t],$$

where $\mathbf{H} = \mathbf{B}'\mathbf{A}^{-1}\mathbf{B}$. Therefore, the implied forecast evaluation criterion is given by

$$E[(\mathbf{x}_{t+1} - \hat{\mathbf{x}}_{t,1})'\mathbf{H}(\mathbf{x}_{t+1} - \hat{\mathbf{x}}_{t,1}) \mid \Omega_t],$$

which, through $\mathbf{H}$, depends on the parameters of the underlying cost function. Only in the univariate LQ case can the implied evaluation criterion be cast in terms of a purely statistical criterion function.

The dependence of the evaluation criterion in the multivariate case on the parameters of the cost (or utility) function of the underlying decision model has direct bearing on the noninvariance critique of MSFEs to scale-preserving linear transformations discussed by Clements and Hendry (1993). In multivariate (or multistep) forecasting problems, the choice of the evaluation criterion is not as clear cut as in the univariate case even if we confine our attention to MSFE-type criteria. One possible procedure, commonly adopted, is to use $E[(\mathbf{x}_{t+1} - \hat{\mathbf{x}}_{t,1})'(\mathbf{x}_{t+1} - \hat{\mathbf{x}}_{t,1}) \,|\, \boldsymbol{\Omega}_t]$, or equivalently the trace of the MSFE matrix $E[(\mathbf{x}_{t+1} - \hat{\mathbf{x}}_{t,1})(\mathbf{x}_{t+1} - \hat{\mathbf{x}}_{t,1})' \,|\, \boldsymbol{\Omega}_t]$. Alternatively, the determinant of the MSFE matrix has also been suggested. In the context of the LQ decision problem, both of these purely statistical criteria are inappropriate, as they also are in general in the statistical approach. The trace MSFE criterion is justified only when $\mathbf{H}$ is proportional to an identity matrix of order $m + k$.

11.3.2. Negative exponential utility: A finance application

The link between purely statistical and decision-based forecast evaluation criteria becomes even more tenuous for nonquadratic cost or utility functions. One important example is the negative exponential utility function often used in finance for the determination of optimal portfolio weights in asset allocation problems. Consider a risk-averse speculator with a negative exponential utility function who wishes to decide on his long ($y_t > 0$), and short positions ($y_t < 0$), in a given security.[3] To simplify the exposition we abstract from transaction costs. At the end of the period (the start of period $t + 1$) the speculator's net worth will be given by

$$W_{t+1} = y_t \rho_{t+1},$$

where ρ_{t+1} is the rate of return on the security. The speculator chooses y_t in order to maximize the expected value of the negative exponential utility function

$$U(y_t, \rho_{t+1}) = -\exp(-\lambda y_t \rho_{t+1}), \quad \lambda > 0, \tag{11.7}$$

with respect to the publicly available information, Ω_t.

Suppose now that the speculator is told that conditional on Ω_t, excess returns are forecastable assuming that[4]

$$\rho_{t+1} \,|\, \Omega_t \sim N(\hat{\rho}_{t,1}, \hat{\sigma}_{t,1}^2) \tag{11.8}$$

What is the economic value of this forecast to the speculator?

Under (11.8), we have[5]

$$E_f[U(y_t, \rho_{t+1}) \,|\, \Omega_t] = -\exp\left(-\lambda y_t \hat{\rho}_{t,1} + \frac{1}{2}\lambda^2 y_t^2 \hat{\sigma}_{t,1}^2\right),$$

and

$$\frac{\partial E_f[U(y_t, \rho_{t+1})|\Omega_t]}{\partial y_t} = -(-\lambda\hat{\rho}_{t,1} + \lambda^2 y_t \hat{\sigma}_{t,1}^2) \exp\left(-\lambda y_t \hat{\rho}_{t,1} + \frac{1}{2}\lambda^2 y_t^2 \hat{\sigma}_{t,1}^2\right).$$

Setting this derivative equal to zero, we now have the following familiar result for the speculator's optimal decision:

$$y_t^* = \frac{\hat{\rho}_{t,1}}{\lambda\hat{\sigma}_{t,1}^2}. \tag{11.9}$$

Hence

$$U(y_t^*, \rho_{t+1}) = -\exp\left(-\frac{\rho_{t+1}\hat{\rho}_{t,1}}{\hat{\sigma}_{t,1}^2}\right), \tag{11.10}$$

and the expected economic value of the forecasts in (11.8) is given by

$$\Psi_U(F_t, \hat{F}_t) = E_F\left[-\exp\left(-\frac{\rho_{t+1}\hat{\rho}_{t,1}}{\hat{\sigma}_{t,1}^2}\right)\bigg|\Omega_t\right], \tag{11.11}$$

where expectations are taken with respect to the true distribution of returns, $F_t(\rho)$.[6] This result has three notable features. The decision-based forecast evaluation measure does not depend on the risk-aversion coefficient, λ. It has little bearing to the familiar purely statistical forecast evaluation criteria such as the MSFEs of the mean return, given by $E_F[(\rho_{t+1} - \hat{\rho}_{t,1})^2|\Omega_t]$. Finally, even under Gaussian assumptions (often violated in practice) the evaluation criterion involves return predictions, $\hat{\rho}_{t,1}$, as well as volatility predictions, $\hat{\sigma}_{t,1}^2$.

It is also interesting to note that under the assumption that (11.8) is based on a correctly specified model, we have

$$\Psi_U(F_t, F_t) = -\exp\left[-\frac{1}{2}\left(\frac{\rho_{t,1}}{\sigma_{t,1}}\right)^2\right],$$

where $\rho_{t,1}/\sigma_{t,1}$ is a single-period Sharpe ratio routinely used in the finance literature for the economic evaluation of risky portfolios.

11.3.3.   Two-state, two-action decision problems[7]

The examples considered so far assume that the state variables (x_t and ρ_t) vary continuously. It is also interesting to illustrate the decision-based approach when

Table 11.1 Payoff matrix for a two-state, two-action decision problem

		States (s_{t+1})	
		Bad $(s_{t+1} = 1)$	Good $(s_{t+1} = 0)$
Decisions (y_t)	Yes $(y_t = 1)$	$U_{by}(t)$	$U_{gy}(t)$
	No $(y_t = 0)$	$U_{bn}(t)$	$U_{gn}(t)$

the state and the decision variables can only take a finite number of values. A simple, but important, example is the two-state, two-action decision problem considered in some detail in the weather forecasting literature. Similar problems also arise in finance and economics; for example, whether to switch between bonds and stocks, and whether to raise interest rates. An empirical finance application is provided in Granger and Pesaran (2000b).

Consider a decision problem where there are two states, called "Bad" and "Good" for convenience, and two possible actions, "Yes" and "No." The states are denoted by s_{t+1} taking the value of unity if the Bad state materializes and 0 otherwise. The payoff matrix associated with this decision problem is given in table 11.1.

In table 11.1, $U_{by}(t)$ represents the decision-maker's utility if the Bad state occurs after the Yes decision is taken, $U_{bn}(t)$ the utility in the Bad state when no action is taken, and so on.

Suppose now that at the beginning of period t the decision-maker is supplied with a forecast probability of the Bad event occurring in period $t + 1$, and denote this forecast probability by $\hat{\pi}_{t,1}$, being an estimate of

$$\pi_{t,1} = Pr(s_{t+1} = 1 \mid \Omega_t).$$

As before, we assume that actions do not alter $\pi_{t,1}$, namely

$$Pr(s_{t+1} = 1 \mid \Omega_t, y_t) = Pr(s_{t+1} = 1 \mid \Omega_t),$$

and

$$Pr(s_{t+1} = 0 \mid \Omega_t, y_t) = Pr(s_{t+1} = 0 \mid \Omega_t) = 1 - \pi_{t,1}.$$

Thus, action will be taken if

$$\hat{\pi}_{t,1} > \frac{c_t}{1 + c_t} = q_t.$$

where[8]

$$c_t = \frac{U_{gn}(t) - U_{gy}(t)}{U_{by}(t) - U_{bn}(t)} > 0, \quad \text{for all } t.$$

Hence, in this example the decision variable takes a particularly simple form

$$y_t^* = I(\hat{\pi}_{t,1} - q_t),$$

where $I(\cdot)$, is the indicator function defined by $I(\mathfrak{A}) = 1$ if $\mathfrak{A} > 0$, and $I(\mathfrak{A}) = 0$, otherwise.

Using the above solution, the time $(t + 1)$ realized value of the economic decision based on the probability forecast, $\hat{\pi}_{t,1}$, is given by

$$U(y_t^*, s_{t+1}) = a_{t+1} + b_t(s_{t+1} - q_t)I(\hat{\pi}_{t,1} - q_t), \tag{11.12}$$

where

$$a_{t+1} = s_{t+1}U_{bn}(t) + (1 - s_{t+1})U_{gn}(t), \tag{11.13}$$

and

$$b_t = U_{by}(t) - U_{bn}(t) + U_{gn}(t) - U_{gy}(t) > 0. \tag{11.14}$$

Only the second term of (11.12) depends on the probability forecast estimate, $\hat{\pi}_{t,1}$, and the appropriate loss function for the evaluation of the probability forecasts in the case of this decision problem is given by

$$b_t(s_{t+1} - q_t)I(\hat{\pi}_{t,1} - q_t). \tag{11.15}$$

Finally, the expected economic value of using the probability forecast $\hat{\pi}_{t,1}$ is given by

$$\Psi_U(\pi_{t,1}, \hat{\pi}_{t,1}) = E[U(y_t^*, s_{t+1}) | \Omega_t] = E(a_{t+1} | \Omega_t) + b_t(\pi_{t,1} - q_t)I(\hat{\pi}_{t,1} - q_t). \tag{11.16}$$

Notice that the relevant second term of this expression can be negative for some values of $\pi_{t,1}$, $\hat{\pi}_{t,1}$, and q_t, unless $\hat{\pi}_{t,1} = \pi_{t,1}$; namely, if $\hat{\pi}_{t,1}$ is estimated using the correct conditional model of s_{t+1}.

Once again the appropriate forecast evaluation criteria, given by (11.15), differs markedly from the usual MSFE.

11.4.   Recent Developments in Forecast Evaluation: An Overview

Apart from clarifying the rationale behind the use of MSFEs in forecast evaluation, the decision-based approach also provides a unifying theme for other recent developments in the area of forecast evaluation, namely the use of generalized cost-of-error functions, the analysis of market-timing skills in finance, and the evaluation of interval and probability forecasts (event and density forecasts). We provide an overview of these recent developments from the perspective of the decision-based framework set out in the previous section.

11.4.1. Generalized cost-of-error functions

The generalized cost-of-error function has been proposed as a possible way of dealing with asymmetries in the costs of over- and under-predicting.[9] In many instances, the costs associated with making positive and negative forecast errors are not the same. For example, arriving late for a transatlantic flight is more costly than arriving early! A central banker concerned with controlling the inflation rate to lie within a given target range is likely to aim for the lower rather than the upper end of the range since under-shooting the set target rate is likely to be less costly (in terms of her job security) than over-shooting it.

In terms of forecasting returns, for example, the generalized cost-of-error function can be written as $\varphi(\rho_{t+1} - \hat{\rho}_{t,1})$, where $\varphi(\cdot)$ is a convex function having a global minimum at the origin. In particular, $\varphi(0) = 0$ and $\varphi(e) > 0$ for all $e \neq 0$. The use of $\varphi(e)$ in many instances is an improvement over the quadratic specification, e^2. However, from a decision-based viewpoint the generalized error cost function is still arbitrary and need not coincide with the cost function implied by the decision problem. As we saw above, the optimal cost function for return predictions in the case of the investment decision of a speculator with a negative exponential utility function is given by $\left(-\exp\left(-\dfrac{\rho_{t+1}\hat{\rho}_{t,1}}{\hat{\sigma}_{t,1}^2}\right)\right)$, which involves volatility forecasts and in general cannot be approximated by a function in the forecast errors $\rho_{t+1} - \hat{\rho}_{t,1}$.[10]

In practice, the choice of $\varphi(e)$ is likely to be arbitrary, and may prove more difficult to justify than the specification of the cost/utility functions that underlie the decision problem. An important example of $\varphi(e)$ is the LINEX function due to Varian (1975):

$$\varphi(e) = 2(\exp(\alpha e) - \alpha e - 1)/\alpha^2.$$

This specification tends to the quadratic form, e^2, as $\alpha \to 0$. When $\alpha > 0$ it is more costly to underpredict, while the reverse is true when $\alpha < 0$. Once again an informed choice of α requires a full and detailed knowledge of the decision problem that motivates the forecasting process in the first instance. Nobay and Peel (1998) use the LINEX function to provide an analysis of monetary policy under asymmetric central bank preferences with respect to the departures of the inflation rate from its target value.

11.4.2. Directional forecast evaluation criteria

Another important example of a nonquadratic forecast error cost function is the Kuipers score used in evaluation of weather forecasts and the market-timing test statistics originally due to Henriksson and Merton (1981) in finance. These are directional type evaluation criteria and, as pointed out earlier, can be justified in the context of the two-state, two-action decision problem discussed above. In

Table 11.2   Contingency matrix of forecasts and realizations

| | | Actual outcomes (s_{t+1}) | |
		Up $(s_{t+1} = 1)$	Down $(s_{t+1} = 0)$
Forecasts	Up $(\hat{s}_{t,1} = 1)$	Hits (N_{uu})	False alarms (N_{ud})
	Down $(\hat{s}_{t,1} = 0)$	Misses (N_{du})	Correct rejections (N_{dd})

their simplest form they apply to bivalued qualitative forecasts (up, down) and are best cast in the form of a contingency table in realizations and forecasts. See table 11.2.

The Kuipers score (KS) mentioned earlier is defined by[11]

$$KS = H - F, \tag{11.17}$$

where H is the proportion of Ups that were correctly forecast to occur, and F is the proportion of Downs that were incorrectly forecast. These two proportions, known as the "hit rate" and the "false alarm rate" respectively, in terms of the cell frequencies of the above contingency table, can be readily computed as

$$H = \frac{N_{uu}}{N_{uu} + N_{du}}, F = \frac{N_{ud}}{N_{ud} + N_{dd}}. \tag{11.18}$$

The total number of forecasts is clearly given by $N = N_{uu} + N_{ud} + N_{du} + N_{dd}$.

Henriksson and Merton's (HM) market-timing statistic is based on the conditional probabilities of making correct forecasts. Denoting as before the (excess) return on a given security by ρ_{t+1} and its forecast by $\hat{\rho}_{t,1}$, Merton (1981) postulates the following conditional probabilities of taking correct actions:

$$p_1(t) = \Pr(\hat{\rho}_{t,1} \geq 0 \,|\, \rho_{t+1} \geq 0),$$

$$p_2(t) = \Pr(\hat{\rho}_{t,1} < 0 \,|\, \rho_{t+1} < 0).$$

Assuming that $p_1(t)$ and $p_2(t)$ do not depend on the size of the excess returns $|\rho_{t+1}|$, he shows that $p_1(t) + p_2(t)$ is a sufficient statistic for the evaluation of the forecasting ability. Together with Henriksson, he then develops a nonparametric statistic for testing the hypothesis

$$H_0 : p_1(t) + p_2(t) = 1,$$

or equivalently

$$H_0 : p_1(t) = 1 - p_2(t),$$

that a market-timing forecast ($\hat{\rho}_{t,1} \geq 0$ or $\hat{\rho}_{t,1} < 0$) has no economic value against the alternative

$$H_1 : p_1(t) + p_2(t) > 1$$

that it has positive economic value.[12] As HM point out, their test is essentially a test of the independence between the forecasts and whether the excess return on the market portfolio is positive. In terms of the notation in the above contingency table, the sample estimate of the HM statistic, $p_1(t) - (1 - p_2(t))$, is *exactly* equal to the Kuipers score given by (11.17). The hit rate, H, is the sample estimate of $p_1(t)$ and the false alarm rate, F, is the sample estimate of $1 - p_2(t)$.

An alternative formulation of the HM test and its extension has been advanced in Pesaran and Timmermann (1992), where the market-timing test is based on

$$PT = \frac{\hat{P} - \hat{P}_*}{\{\hat{V}(\hat{P}) - \hat{V}(\hat{P}_*)\}^{1/2}} \overset{a}{\sim} N(0, 1), \tag{11.19}$$

where $\hat{P}$ is the proportion of Ups that are correctly predicted, $\hat{P}_*$ is the estimate of the probability of correctly predicting the events assuming predictions and realizations are independently distributed, and $\hat{V}(\hat{P})$ and $\hat{V}(\hat{P}_*)$ are consistent estimates of the variances of $\hat{P}$ and $\hat{P}_*$, respectively.

Granger and Pesaran (2000b) have established the following relationship between the KS and the PT statistic:

$$PT = \frac{\sqrt{N}KS}{\left[\dfrac{\hat{\pi}_f(1 - \hat{\pi}_f)}{\hat{\pi}_a(1 - \hat{\pi}_a)}\right]^{1/2}}, \tag{11.20}$$

where $\hat{\pi}_a = \dfrac{N_{uu} + N_{du}}{N}$, is the estimate of the probability that the realizations are

Up, and $\hat{\pi}_f = \dfrac{N_{uu} + N_{ud}}{N}$ is the estimate of the probability that outcomes are forecast to be Up. The above results also establish the asymptotic equivalence of the HM and PT statistics.

As HM note, under certain conditions, their test has a direct bearing on the economic value of the forecasts. The exact conditions depend on the underlying decision problem. For example, in the context of the two-action, two-state decision problem of section 11.3.3, the link between the realized loss function, the decision problem given by (11.15), and the market-timing criterion function, namely $\hat{p}_1(t) - (1 - \hat{p}_2(t)) = H - F$, depends on b_t and q_t, the parameters of the decision problem. As shown in Granger and Pesaran (2000b), in the special case where $q_t = q$ and $b_t = b$ for all t, the sample counterpart of (11.16) can be written as[13]

$$\hat{\Psi}_U(\pi_{t,1}, \hat{\pi}_{t,1}) = b\hat{\pi}_a(1 - \hat{\pi}_a)(H - F), \tag{11.21}$$

where an Up forecast is defined by $\hat{s}_{t,1} = I(\hat{\pi}_{t,1} - q)$. In the HM set-up, q is set equal to $1/2$, which is justified given their assumption that $p_1(t)$ and $p_2(t)$ do not depend on the size of the excess returns. But, in general, where the probability forecasts, $\hat{\pi}_{t,1}$, are likely to be used by different individuals making decisions having different cost–benefit ratios the use of a homogeneous probability threshold of 1/2 may not be justified.

11.4.3. Evaluation of probability event and density forecasts

As shown above, point forecasts are sufficient for decision-making in the case of LQ problems (see section 11.3.1). However, in the general case where the decision environment involves nonquadratic cost functions and/or nonlinear constraints, probability forecasts are needed, or even the entire predictive joint probability distribution function of the state variables.

For expositional purposes, it is useful to make a distinction between probability event forecasting and probability distribution or density forecasting. To clarify this distinction consider the decision problem of section 11.3, and suppose that the true conditional probability distribution function of the state variable x_{t+1} is stable and denote its conditional density by $f(x_{t+1} | \Omega_t)$, and its one-step-ahead estimate formed at time t by $\hat{f}_t(x_{t+1} | \Omega_t)$. The probability event forecast refers to the probability of a particular event, say the probability that the event $\mathfrak{A}_{t+1} = \{b \leq x_{t+1} \leq a\}$ occurs, while density forecasting is concerned with $\hat{f}_t(x_{t+1} | \Omega_t)$ for all feasible values of x_{t+1}, or equivalently with its probability distribution function, $\hat{F}_t(x) = \int_{-\infty}^{x} \hat{f}_t(u | \Omega_t) du$, for all feasible values of x. The former is a special case of the latter and we have

$$\hat{\Pr}(\mathfrak{A}_{t+1} | \Omega_t) = \hat{F}_t(a) - \hat{F}_t(b).$$

The probability event forecasts focus on single or joint events of general interest. Events such as inflation falling within a pre-announced target range, a rise in the Fed interest rate, a stock market crash, or the joint event that output growth will be positive over two successive quarters and that the inflation rate does not exceed 3 percent per annum, are all events of general interest.[14] But for a particular decision, the whole of the forecast probability distribution function, $\hat{F}_t(x)$, could be needed. From a decision-based viewpoint probability forecasts are therefore more appropriate than categorical forecasts.[15]

Another important distinction is between probability event forecasting and event forecasting. An event forecast is often in the form of an indicator function and states whether an event is forecast to occur. For example, in the case of $\mathfrak{A}_{t+1} = \{b \leq x_{t+1} \leq a\}$, the event forecast will simply be:

$$\hat{I}(\mathfrak{A}_{t+1} | \Omega_t) = 1, \text{ if } \mathfrak{A}_{t+1} \text{ is predicted to occur,}$$

$$\hat{I}(\mathfrak{A}_{t+1} | \Omega_t) = 0, \text{ otherwise.}$$

It is always possible to compute event forecasts from probability event forecasts, but not vice versa. This could be done with respect to a probability threshold, p, often taken to be 1/2 in practice. In the case of the above example we have

$$\hat{I}(\mathfrak{A}_{t+1} \mid \Omega_t) = I(\hat{F}_t(a) - \hat{F}_t(b) - p).$$

In general, probability event forecasts are likely to be more useful than event forecasts.

Probability event and density forecasts are used extensively in financial risk management, turning point predictions, and inflation forecasting. For example, J.P. Morgan presents "Event Risk Indicators" in its analysis of foreign exchange markets.[16] The Bank of England publishes a range of outcomes for its inflation and output growth forecasts, discussed, for example, in Britton, Fisher, and Whitley (1998), and Wallis (1999). The use of probability forecasting in a sequential Bayesian context has also been advocated by Dawid (1984). Probability forecasts based on macroeconometric models have been reported for the U.S. economy by Fair (1980, 1993) and Stock and Watson (1993), and for the U.K. by Blake (1996), Poulizac et al. (1996), and Garratt, Lee, Pesaran, and Shin (2000).

These recent developments are gradually shifting the focus of the forecast evaluation literature from the analysis of point (and interval) forecasts to the evaluation of probability forecasts. Purely statistical techniques for the evaluation of density forecasts have been advanced by Dawid (1984) and elaborated upon more recently by Diebold, Gunther, and Tay (1998) in the case of univariate predictive densities, and by Diebold, Hahn, and Tay (1999) and Clements and Smith (2000) for the evaluation of multivariate density forecasts. These techniques are based on the idea of the probability integral transform that originates in the work of Rosenblatt (1952). Suppose that we have the N consecutive pairs $\{x_{t+1}, \hat{f}_t(x_{t+1} \mid \Omega_t), t = T, T + 1, \ldots, T + N - 1\}$ of the realizations and density forecasts. As shown by Diebold, Gunther, and Tay (1998), under the null hypothesis that $\hat{f}_t(x_{t+1} \mid \Omega_t)$ and $f(x_{t+1} \mid \Omega_t)$ coincide and assuming a nonzero Jacobian and continuous partial derivatives, the N sequence of probability integral transforms

$$z_{t+1} = \int_{-\infty}^{x_{t+1}} \hat{f}_t(u \mid \Omega_t) du, \quad t = T, T + 1, \ldots, T + N - 1, \qquad (11.22)$$

is $i.i.d.$ Uniform $(0,1)$. The statistical adequacy of the predictive distributions, $\hat{F}_t$, can then be assessed by testing whether $\{z_{t+1}, t = T, T + 1, \ldots, T + N - 1\}$ forms an $i.i.d.$ $U(0, 1)$ sequence. This test can be carried out using a number of familiar statistical procedures.[17] But it is worth noting that the application of this test requires fairly large N. Also the $i.i.d.$ uniform property is a necessary but not a sufficient condition for the optimality of the underlying predictive distribution. For example, expanding the information set Ω_t will lead to a different predictive distribution but $\hat{f}_t$ continues to satisfy the $i.i.d.$ uniform property.[18]

11.5. DECISION-BASED FORECAST COMPARISONS

The statistical approaches to forecast evaluation and comparison reviewed briefly in the previous section are *intended* to be universal, in the sense that they do not depend on the decision environment of a particular decision-maker. However, for a forecast to be universally applicable, it must coincide with the true distribution function.[19] For example, in the context of the density forecast evaluation problem, $\hat{f}(x_{t+1} \mid \Omega_t)$ is universally applicable if it coincides with $f(x_{t+1} \mid \Omega_t)$. In such a case the forecasts are optimal and all individuals should use $\hat{f}(x_{t+1} \mid \Omega_t)$ regardless of their decision environment. But this is unlikely to be the case in practice, and there will be discrepancies between $f(x_{t+1} \mid \Omega_t)$ and $\hat{f}(x_{t+1} \mid \Omega_t)$ that could be more serious for some ranges of the state variable, x, and for some decisions as compared with other ranges or decisions. For example, in risk management the extreme values of x (portfolio returns) are of interest, while in macroeconomic management values of x (inflation or output growth) in the middle of the distribution may be of concern. In general, the forecast density function $\hat{f}(x_{t+1} \mid \Omega_t)$ can at best provide an approximation to the true density and from a decision perspective its evaluation is best carried out following the approach advanced in section 11.3. Such an evaluation can be made from an individual or a group perspective. In what follows, initially we shall focus on an individual decision-maker who wishes to evaluate the forecast distribution function, $\hat{F}_t$, over the period $t = T, T + 1, \ldots, T + N - 1$. For this purpose the sample counterpart of (11.3), namely

$$\Psi_N(\hat{F}_t) = \frac{1}{N} \sum_{t=T}^{T+N-1} C(y_t^*(\hat{F}_t), x_{t+1}), \tag{11.23}$$

may be used, where the dependence of the decision variable, y_t^*, on the choice of the probability forecast distribution, $\hat{F}_t$, is made explicit here.[20] The average Ψ_N provides an estimate of the realized cost to the decision-maker of using $\hat{F}_t$ over the period $t = T, T + 1, \ldots, T + N - 1$. Clearly, the decision-maker will be interested in forecasts that minimize Ψ_N. An absolute standard for forecast evaluation could then be defined by

$$\bar{\Delta}_N(\hat{F}_t, F_t) = \Psi_N(\hat{F}_t) - \Psi_N(F_t) \geq 0,$$

with the equality holding when $\hat{F}_t = F_t$.

In general, when one does not expect $\hat{F}_t$ to coincide with F_t, a sensible approach to forecast evaluation is to resort to forecast comparisons rather than seek absolute standards of forecast accuracy. For example, suppose in addition to $\hat{F}_t$ the alternative predictive distribution function $\tilde{F}_t$, is also available. A baseline alternative could be the unconditional probability distribution function of the state variable, or some other simple conditional model. Then the average economic loss arising from using the predictive distribution $\hat{F}_t$ as compared to $\tilde{F}_t$ is given by

$$L_N(\hat{F}_t, \tilde{F}_t) = \frac{1}{N} \sum_{t=T}^{T+N-1} [C(\mathbf{y}_t^*(\hat{\mathbf{F}}_t), \mathbf{x}_{t+1}) - C(\mathbf{y}_t^*(\tilde{\mathbf{F}}_t), \mathbf{x}_{t+1})], \tag{11.24}$$

which can also be written as the simple average of the loss-differential series,

$$d_{t+1} = C(\mathbf{y}_t^*(\hat{\mathbf{F}}_t), \mathbf{x}_{t+1}) - C(\mathbf{y}_t^*(\tilde{\mathbf{F}}_t), \mathbf{x}_{t+1}), \quad t = T, T + 1, \ldots, T + N - 1,$$

considered in Diebold and Mariano (1995) in the special case where $C(y_t^*(\hat{F}_t), x_{t+1})$ $= \varphi(x_{t+1} - \hat{x}_{t,1})$, $C(y_t^*(\tilde{F}_t), x_{t+1}) = \varphi(x_{t+1} - \tilde{x}_{t,1})$, and $\varphi(\cdot)$ is a generalized cost-of-error function as discussed in section 11.4.1. But in a decision-based framework it is $C(y_t^*, x_{t+1})$ which determines the appropriate cost-of-error function and, as can be seen below, is *equally* applicable to the evaluation of point and probability forecasts.

In the case of the illustrative examples of section 11.3 we have the following expressions for the loss-differential series. For the multivariate quadratic decision model we have[21]

$$d_{t+1} = (\mathbf{x}_{t+1} - \hat{\mathbf{x}}_{t,1})'\mathbf{H}((\mathbf{x}_{t+1} - \hat{\mathbf{x}}_{t,1}) - (\mathbf{x}_{t+1} - \tilde{\mathbf{x}}_{t,1})'\mathbf{H}(\mathbf{x}_{t+1} - \tilde{\mathbf{x}}_{t,1}), \tag{11.25}$$

for the finance example in section 11.3.2, using (11.10) the loss-differential becomes

$$d_{t+1} = \exp\left(-\frac{\rho_{t+1}\,\hat{\rho}_{t,1}}{\hat{\sigma}_{t,1}^2}\right) - \exp\left(-\frac{\rho_{t+1}\,\tilde{\rho}_{t,1}}{\tilde{\sigma}_{t,1}^2}\right), \tag{11.26}$$

and finally for the two-action two-state problem using (11.15) we have

$$d_{t+1} = b_t[(s_{t+1} - q_t)I(\tilde{\pi}_{t,1} - q_t) - (s_{t+1} - q_t)I(\hat{\pi}_{t,1} - q_t)]. \tag{11.27}$$

According to the above decision-based measures the predictive distribution function $\hat{F}_t$ is preferable to $\tilde{F}_t$ if $L_N(\hat{F}_t, \tilde{F}_t) = (1/N)\sum_{t=T}^{T+N-1} d_{t+1} = \bar{d}_N < 0$, otherwise the probability distribution function $\tilde{F}_t$ would be preferable to $\hat{F}_t$.

The criterion function (11.27) is related to the forecasting skill measures (often referred to as scoring rules) used for the evaluation of probability event forecasts in meteorology. A leading example, the quadratic or Brier score (Brier, 1950), is defined by[22]

$$B_N = \frac{1}{N}\sum_{t=T}^{T+N-1}(s_{t+1} - \hat{\pi}_{t,1})^2. \tag{11.28}$$

The analogy with MSFE is clear and there are various extensions along the lines of generalized cost-of-error functions. Pearl (1978) discusses how some of the scoring rules advanced in the literature may be justified on the basis of decision-based considerations. As with the conventional MSFE for point forecasts, the Brier score is identically zero only in the case of perfect deterministic forecasts and has a maximum value of unity in the case of forecasts that are consistently wrong. An interesting decomposition of the Brier score into measures of "reliability," "resolution," and "uncertainty" has been derived by Murphy (1973). In the context of the two-state, two-action decision problem, however, the Brier score need not be appropriate. As was noted earlier, in the special case where $b_t = b$, the decision-based evaluation criterion (11.27), is related to the Kuipers score, (11.21), also used extensively in the meteorology literature.

So far, we have focused on the economic value of forecasts to a given user. But it is also often of interest to evaluate skills of a forecast producer who produces forecasts for general use. To formalize the issues involved, consider m different potential individual users of the same sequence of forecast distributions, $\{\hat{F}_t, t = T, T + 1, \ldots, T + N - 1\}$. In terms of the notations of section 11.3, denote the cost function of individual i by $C_i(\mathbf{y}_{it}, \mathbf{x}_{t+1})$, where $\mathbf{y}_{it}$ is the vector of decision variables of the ith individual. Also assume that all individuals use the same information set Ω_t, and the same forecast distribution, $\hat{F}_t$, to resolve the uncertainty surrounding the future values of $\mathbf{x}_{t+1}$. As before, we have

$$\mathbf{y}_{it}^* = \underset{\mathbf{y}_{it}}{\text{argmin}} \ \{E_{\hat{F}}[C_i(\mathbf{y}_{it}, \mathbf{x}_{t+1}) \,|\, \Omega_t]\},$$

with the implied realized mean cost function

$$\Psi_{iN}(\hat{F}_t) = \frac{1}{N} \sum_{t=T}^{T+N-1} C_i(\mathbf{y}_{it}^*(\hat{F}_t), \mathbf{x}_{t+1}).$$

Aggregation of these cost functions across the individuals requires formulation of a suitable social welfare function.[23] For the linear specification

$$C(\mathbf{y}_{it}, \mathbf{x}_{t+1}) = \sum_{i=1}^{m} w_i C_i(\mathbf{y}_{it}, \mathbf{x}_{t+1}),$$

where the weights $w_i \geq 0$, and $\sum_{i=1}^{m} w_i = 1$, the "social" value (cost) of the forecasts, $\{\hat{F}_t, t = T, T + 1, \ldots, T + N - 1\}$, is given by

$$\Psi_{mN}(\hat{F}_t) = \frac{1}{N} \sum_{t=T}^{T+N-1} \sum_{i=1}^{m} w_i C_i(\mathbf{y}_{it}^*(\hat{F}_t), \mathbf{x}_{t+1}).$$

As a simple example, consider the two-action, two-state problem of section 11.3.3 and suppose that we are interested in a comparison of forecast probabilities $\hat{\pi}_{t,1}$ and $\hat{\pi}_{t,1}$ with respect to a group of decision-makers composed of m individuals with the same decision problem but with different payoff ratios, q_{it}, $i = 1, 2, \ldots, m$. Assuming a linear social welfare function with individual i having weight w_i, we would then say that $\hat{\pi}_{t,1}$ is preferable to $\tilde{\pi}_{t,1}$ from the viewpoint of the group if

$$\frac{1}{N} \sum_{t=N}^{T+N-1} \sum_{i=1}^{m} w_i(s_{t+1} - q_{it}) I(\hat{\pi}_{t,1} - q_{it}) > \frac{1}{N} \sum_{t=N}^{T+N-1} \sum_{i=1}^{m} w_i(s_{t+1} - q_{it}) I(\tilde{\pi}_{t,1} - q_{it}),$$

where it is assumed that $b_{it} = b_t$, for all t. In this example, it may be reasonable to carry out the aggregation assuming simple cross-sectional distributions for the weights and the payoff ratios q_{it}. For further details, see Granger and Pesaran (2000b).

11.6. TESTING THE EQUIVALENCE OF FORECAST VALUES

Our discussion of forecast evaluation so far assumes a given sequence of point or density forecasts and does not address the issue of whether the economic value (cost) of one forecast relative to another is statistically significant. The problem of statistical significance of the mean loss-differential, $L_N(\hat{F}_t, \tilde{F}_t)$ defined by (11.24), arises at two levels. (i) Abstracting from the process of how the forecasts are constructed, it may be asked whether the mean loss-differential is statistically significant (alternatively, how large N should be before we can be reasonably confident that one forecast distribution is preferable to another). (ii) If we know how the forecasts were constructed, we should incorporate this knowledge in our statistical tests, for example by accounting for the effect of parameter uncertainty when forecasts originate from an estimated parametric model.

Both of these problems have been considered in the literature. In the case of point forecasts the issue of the statistical efficiency of one set of forecasts relative to another was originally discussed by Granger and Newbold (1973). Consider two sets of one-step-ahead scalar point forecasts, $\hat{x}_{t,1}$ and $\tilde{x}_{t,1}$ over the period $t = T$, $T + 1, \ldots, T + N - 1$. The null hypothesis that $\hat{x}_{t,1}$ is "conditionally efficient" relative to $\tilde{x}_{t,1}$ in Granger and Newbold terminology, or that $\hat{x}_{t,1}$ "encompasses" $\tilde{x}_{t,1}$ in Chong and Hendry's (1986) terminology, is given by $\theta = 0$ in the combined forecasts

$$x_{t,1}(\theta) - \hat{x}_{t,1} = \theta(\tilde{x}_{t,1} - \hat{x}_{t,1}).$$

Alternatively, this null hypothesis can be written as

$$E(\hat{d}_{t+1}) = 0,$$

where

$$\hat{d}_{t+1} = (x_{t+1} - \hat{x}_{t,1})(\tilde{x}_{t,1} - \hat{x}_{t,1}),$$

$$= \hat{e}_{t,1}(\hat{e}_{t,1} - \tilde{e}_{t,1}), \tag{11.29}$$

and $\hat{e}_{t,1} = x_{t+1} - \hat{x}_{t,1}$, and $\tilde{e}_{t,1} = x_{t+1} - \tilde{x}_{t,1}$ are the forecast errors. Similarly, the null hypothesis that $\tilde{x}_{t,1}$ "encompasses" $\hat{x}_{t,1}$ can be written as

$$E(\tilde{d}_{t+1}) = 0,$$

where

$$\tilde{d}_{t+1} = \tilde{e}_{t,1}(\tilde{e}_{t,1} - \hat{e}_{t,1}). \tag{11.30}$$

The above encompassing tests can be rationalized in the context of the decision-based framework if the underlying cost function is quadratic, containing a single state variable. In this case the appropriate loss-differential criterion is given by

$$d_{t+1} = (x_{t+1} - \hat{x}_{t,1})^2 - (x_{t+1} - \tilde{x}_{t,1})^2,$$

which reduces to

$$d_{t+1} = \hat{d}_{t+1} + \tilde{d}_{t+1},$$

where $\hat{d}_{t+1}$ and $\tilde{d}_{t+1}$ are defined by (11.29) and (11.30), respectively. Therefore, in the decision-based framework the appropriate null hypothesis is $E(d_{t+1}) = 0$, namely that the population mean loss-differential is zero. In the case of point forecasts the two forecast encompassing tests of $E(\hat{d}_{t+1}) = 0$ and $E(\tilde{d}_{t+1}) = 0$ clearly imply the forecast equivalence hypothesis $E(d_{t+1}) = 0$, but not vice versa.

The null hypothesis $E(d_{t+1}) = 0$ is applicable more generally, with d_{t+1} appropriately defined in terms of the decision environment of the forecast user(s). In general, we have

$$d_{t+1} = C(\mathbf{y}_t^* (\hat{\mathbf{F}}_t), \mathbf{x}_{t+1}) - C(\mathbf{y}_t^* (\tilde{\mathbf{F}}_t), \mathbf{x}_{t+1}),$$

and for the various examples considered in section 11.5, d_{t+1} is given by (11.25), (11.26), and (11.27).

Testing the null hypothesis that $E(d_{t+1}) = 0$ can be carried out using the recently developed statistical techniques by Diebold and Mariano (1995) and its various modifications by Harvey, Leybourne, and Newbold (1998, 1999). (See chapters 12 and 13 by Newbold and Harvey, and Mariano, in this volume.) The basic problem is to derive the asymptotic distribution of the mean loss-differential criterion, $L_N(\hat{F}_t, \tilde{F}_t) = \frac{1}{N}\sum_{t=T}^{T+N-1}d_{t+1} = \bar{d}_N$. Under certain regularity conditions on the underlying cost function and the distribution of the state variables, it is possible to show that under $E(d_{t+1}) = 0$, the statistic $\sqrt{N}\bar{d}_N$ is asymptotically normally distributed with a zero mean and a finite variance given by $2\pi g_d(0)$, where $g_d(0)$ is the spectral density at zero frequency of d_{t+1}. The exact conditions under which this result holds for nonquadratic decision problems need to be established on a case-by-case basis.

The above forecast comparison analysis assumes two given sets of forecasts and is silent on the different degrees of uncertainty that may be associated with the estimates used in forming the forecasts. This problem is addressed by West (1996) (see also chapter 14, by McCracken and West, in this volume) who considers the case where forecasts are computed from regression models estimated recursively over the period $t = 1, 2, \ldots, T, T + 1, \ldots, T + N - 1$ and the forecasts are evaluated over the period, $t = T, T + 1, \ldots, T + N - 1$. He also confines his analysis to the situations where d_{t+1} is a smooth function of forecasts and forecast errors, and there exists a sufficiently long series of predictions and realizations, such that $N \to \infty$ and $T \to \infty$ as the total available sample $T + N - 1 \to \infty$. In the special case where $N/T \to 0$, the effect of parameter uncertainty on the forecast equivalence test tends to zero and the Diebold–Mariano and West statistics become asymptotically (as $N \to \infty$) identical.

11.7. CONCLUDING REMARKS

The decision-based approach to forecast evaluation provides a unifying framework for the analysis of point as well as density forecasts. It should also help establish a closer link between economic and financial analysis and forecasting. However, despite these attractive features a widespread application of the decision-based approach in economics is likely to take decades rather than years before becoming a reality.

First, the approach requires a complete specification of the decision environment of individual agents and a cross-sectional aggregation rule if the aim is to evaluate the forecasts from the viewpoint of the producer rather than an individual user (client). Most forecasting exercises are carried out without much attention being paid to the uses of the forecasts, and consequently do not readily lend themselves to decision-based evaluation. Much closer links between forecast producers and forecast users are needed. As documented in this chapter, important steps in this direction are being taken in empirical finance, but a great deal more still needs to be done.

Second, even when a full specification of the underlying decision model is available, technical details need to be worked out. The examples considered above all possessed closed-form solutions and were easy to implement. But this is an exception. In practice, the solutions of most decision problems require numerical techniques which add further complications to the derivation of realized loss-differential series used in the decision-based approach to forecast evaluation.

Third, for the analysis of discrete-decision variables, as illustrated in the two-action, two-state problem, further developments of the existing statistical theory are needed. For example, the work of West (1996) considers criteria that are smooth functions of the predictions and prediction errors and are not readily adaptable to the case where the loss-differential criterion is not a smooth function of the forecasts.

Fourth, the decision-based approach poses new methodological and technical problems for specification search and the analysis of model uncertainty.

Finally, all these difficulties will be greatly compounded in the case of decision problems where the action of an agent (such as a central banker) affects the forecast process that is being evaluated. Similarly, further difficulties arise when agents' decisions interact with others and the strategic aspect of the behavior needs to be taken into account both at decision-making level and at the stage of forecast evaluation.

These are some of the challenges that lie ahead for the development of this literature. It is hoped that these challenges are taken up so as to bring forecasting closer to decision-making.

Acknowledgments

We are grateful to Clive Granger for helpful discussions on many of the topics discussed in this chapter. We would also like to acknowledge helpful comments and suggestions by Michael Binder, Frank Diebold, and the editors on an earlier version of this chapter.

Notes

1 Skouras (2000) proposes (3) as a decision-based measure of the value of information in $\hat{F}_t$ about F_t. He shows that it is a discrepancy that generalises to the Kullback–Leibler Information Discrepancy and refers to it as a "Value of Information Discrepancy."
2 The multivariate LQ decision problem has been used extensively in the inflation targeting literature to model the tradeoff between inflation and output in the conduct of monetary policy. See, for example, Barro and Gordon (1983), Rogoff (1985), Green (1996), Svensson (1997), and Beetsma and Jensen (1998).
3 West, Edison, and Cho (1993) consider a utility-based procedure for comparisons of exchange rate volatility models. Skouras (1998) discusses asset allocation decisions and forecasts of a "risk neutral" investor.
4 We assume that y_t is small relative to the size of the market and the choice of y_t does not influence the returns distribution.
5 In general, where the conditional distribution of returns are not normally distributed we have

$$E_{\hat{F}}[U(y_t, \rho_{t+1}) \mid \Omega_t] = -M_{\hat{F}}(-\lambda y_t),$$

where $M_{\hat{F}}(\theta)$ is the moment generating function of the assumed conditional distribution of returns. In this more general case the optimal solution is y_t^* that solves

$$\frac{\partial M_{\hat{F}}(-\lambda y_t)}{\partial y_t} = 0.$$

6 Notice that under (11.8) we have

$$\hat{F}_t(\rho) = \int_{-\infty}^{\rho} (2\pi\hat{\sigma}_{t,1}^2)^{-1/2} \exp\left[\frac{-(u - \hat{\rho}_{t,1})^2}{2\hat{\sigma}_{t,1}^2}\right] du.$$

7 The exposition in this subsection is based on Granger and Pesaran (2000b), where a more detailed account can be found.
8 Notice that since in the present example taking an action in the bad state is beneficial and taking an action in the good state is costly, so $U_{by}(t) > U_{bn}(t)$, and $U_{gn}(t) > U_{gy}(t)$.
9 Generalized cost-of-error functions have been discussed, for example, by Granger (1969, 1999), Christoffersen and Diebold (1996, 1997), Weiss (1996), and Granger and Pesaran (2000b), and in a Bayesian context by Varian (1975) and Zellner (1986).
10 Christoffersen and Diebold (1997) consider general error cost functions when the underlying forecast error distribution is conditionally heteroskedastic.
11 For more details, see Murphy and Dann (1985) and Wilks (1995, ch. 7).
12 The alternative that $H_1 : p_1(t) + p_2(t) < 1$ corresponds to the case of negative economic value.

13 Notice that the estimate of the term $E(a_{t+1} \mid \Omega_t)$ which does not vary with the forecasts has been dropped for notational convenience.

14 See Schnader and Stekler (1990) and Cicarelli (1983) for evaluation of turning point forecasts and Wilks (1995, ch. 7) for a discussion of how meteorological event forecasts are evaluated.

15 The present discussion assumes the absence of prohibitive costs associated with the provision, communication, and processing of the additional information contained in probability forecasts. Such issues are discussed by Nelson and Winter (1964).

16 See, for example, Duffie and Pan (1997), Berkowitz (1999), and in particular Lopez (1999), who discusses the evaluation of value-at-risk forecasts.

17 For further details, see Diebold, Gunther, and Tay (1998).

18 We are grateful to Clive Granger for pointing this out to us.

19 See, for example, Granger and Pesaran (2000a).

20 Under certain regularity conditions on the distribution of the state variable and the underlying cost function, $C(\cdot, \cdot)$ it is reasonable to expect that (by appealing to a suitable law of large numbers)

$$\plim_{N \to \infty} [\Psi_N(\hat{F}_t)] = \lim_{N \to \infty} \left[\frac{1}{N} \sum_{t=T}^{T+N-1} \Psi_C(F_t, \hat{F}_t) \right],$$

namely that $\Psi_N(\hat{F}_t)$ is an asymptotically consistent estimate of $E_F[\Psi_C(F_t, \hat{F}_t)]$. Establishing this result for a general cost function may involve strict conditions on Ψ_C, F_t and $\hat{F}_t$ that rule out some interesting decision problems (for example, the Risk Neutral Forecasting problem of Skouras, 1998) More generally, these results are only approximately valid in finite samples and (for now) sufficient experience with these approximations is not available in the literature.

21 For a fixed choice of **H**, specified independently of the parameters of the underlying cost function $C(y_t, x_{t+1})$, the loss differential series d_t is not invariant under nonsingular linear transformations of the state variables, x_{t+1}, a point emphasized by Clements and Hendry (1993) and alluded to above. But d_{t+1} is invariant to the nonsingular linear transformations of the state variables once it is recognized that such linear transformations will also alter the weighting matrix **H**, in line with the transformation of the state variables, thus leaving the loss differential series, d_{t+1} unaltered.

22 See, for example, Wilks (1995, ch. 7) and Katz and Murphy (1997, ch. 2). As Wilks (1995, p. 260) points out, the ordinal measure proposed by Brier (1950) was in fact twice the measure commonly used.

23 This requirement is similar to using social welfare functions for interpersonal utility/cost comparisons in welfare economics.

References

Barro, R. and D. Gordon (1983). A positive theory of monetary policy in a natural rate model. *Journal of Political Economy*, 91, 589–610.

Beetsma, R. and H. Jensen (1998). Inflation targets and contracts with uncertain central bank preferences. *Journal of Money, Credit and Banking*, 30, 384–403.

Berkowitz, J. (1999). Evaluating the forecast of risk models. Federal Reserve Bank Finance and Economic Discussion Paper Series No. 1999-11.

Blake, A.P. (1996). Forecast error bounds by stochastic simulation. *National Institute Economic Review*, May, 72–79.

Boothe, P.M. (1983). Speculative profit opportunities in the Canadian foreign exchange market, 1974–78. *Canadian Journal of Economics*, 16, 603–11.

Boothe, P. (1987). Comparing exchange rate forecasting models: accuracy versus profitability. *International Journal of Forecasting*, 65–79.

Box, G.E.P. and G.M. Jenkins (1970). *Time Series Analysis, Forecasting and Control*. San Francisco: Holden–Day.

Breen, W., L.R. Glosten, and R. Jagannathan (1989). Economic significance of predictable variations in stock index returns. *Journal of Finance*, 44, 1177–89.

Brier, G.W. (1950). Verification of forecasts expressed in terms of probabilities. *Monthly Weather Review*, 78, 1–3.

Britton, E., P. Fisher, and J. Whitley (1998). The inflation report projections: understanding the fan chart. *Bank of England Quarterly Bulletin*, 33, 30–7.

Christofferson, P.F. and F.X. Diebold (1996). Further results on forecasting and model selection under asymmetric loss. *Journal of Applied Econometrics*, 11, 561–71.

Christofferson, P.F. and F.X. Diebold (1997). Optimal prediction under asymmetric loss. *Econometric Theory*, 13, 808–17.

Chong, Y.Y. and D.F. Hendry (1986). Econometric evaluation of linear macroeconometric models. *Review of Economic Studies*, 53, 671–90.

Cicarelli, J. (1983). A new method for evaluating the accuracy of economic forecasts. *Journal of Macroeconomics*, 4, 469–75.

Clements, M.P. and D.F. Hendry (1993). On the limitations of comparing mean square forecast errors. *Journal of Forecasting*, 12, 617–37.

Clements, M.P. and D.F. Hendry (1998). *Forecasting Economic Time Series*. Cambridge: Cambridge University Press.

Clements, M.P. and D.F. Hendry (1999). *Forecasting Non-Stationary Economic Time Series*. Cambridge, MA: MIT Press.

Clements, M.P. and J. Smith (2000). Evaluating the forecast densities of linear and nonlinear models: applications to output growth and unemployment. *Journal of Forecasting*, 19, 255–76.

Cowles, A. (1933). Can stock market forecasters forecast? *Econometrica*, 1, 309–24.

Dawid, A.P. (1984). Present position and potential developments: some personal views – statistical theory, the prequential approach. *Journal of the Royal Statistical Society Series A*, 147, 278–92.

Diebold, F.X., T.A. Gunther, and A.S. Tay (1998). Evaluating density forecasts, with applications to financial risk management. *International Economic Review*, 39, 863–84.

Diebold, F.X., J. Hahn, and A.S. Tay (1999). Multivariate density forecast evaluation and calibration in financial risk management: high-frequency returns on foreign exchange. *Review of Economics and Statistics*, 81, 661–73.

Diebold, F.X. and J.A. Lopez (1996). Forecast evaluation and combination. In G.S. Maddala and C.R. Rao (eds.), *Handbook of Statistics*, Amsterdam: North Holland.

Diebold, F.X. and R.S. Mariano (1995). Comparing predictive accuracy. *Journal of Business and Economic Statistics*, 13, 253–65.

Duffie, D. and J. Pan (1997). An overview of value at risk. *Journal of Derivatives*, 4, 7–49.

Ehrendorfer, M. and A.H. Murphy (1988). Comparative evaluation of weather forecasting systems sufficiency, quality and accuracy. *Monthly Weather Review*, 116, 1757–70.

Fair, R.C. (1980). Estimating the expected predictive accuracy of econometric models. *International Economic Review*, 21, 355–78.

Fair, R.C. (1993). Estimating event probabilities from macroeconometric models using stochastic simulations. In J.H. Stock and M.W. Watson (eds.), *Business Cycles, Indicators, and Forecasting*. National Bureau of Economic Research, Studies in Business Cycles Volume 28, University of Chicago Press.

Garratt, A., K. Lee, M.H. Pesaran, and Y. Shin (2000). Forecast uncertainties in macro-econometric modeling. DAE Working Paper 0004, University of Cambridge.

Gerlow, M.E. and S.H. Irwin (1991). The performance of exchange rate forecasting models: an economic evaluation. *Applied Economics*, 23, 133–42.

Granger, C.W.J. (1969). Prediction with a generalized cost-of-error function. *Operational Research Quarterly*, 20, 199–207.

Granger, C.W.J. (1999). *Empirical Modelling in Economics: Specification and Evaluation*. Cambridge: Cambridge University Press.

Granger, C.W.J. and P. Newbold (1973). Some comments on the evaluation of economic forecasts. *Applied Economics*, 5, 35–47.

Granger, C.W.J. and P. Newbold (1977, 2nd edn. 1986). *Forecasting Economic Time Series*. San Diego: Academic Press.

Granger, C.W.J. and M.H. Pesaran (2000a). A decision-based approach to forecast evaluation. In W.S. Chan, W.K. Li, and H. Tong (eds.), *Statistics and Finance: An Interface*. London: Imperial College Press.

Granger, C.W.J. and M.H. Pesaran (2000b). Economic and statistical measures of forecast accuracy. *Journal of Forecasting*, 19, 537–60.

Green, J.H. (1996). Inflation targeting: theory and implications. *IMF Staff Papers*, 43, 779–95.

Harvey, D.I., S.J. Leybourne, and P. Newbold (1998). Tests for forecast encompassing. *Journal of Business and Economic Statistics*, 16, 254–9.

Harvey, D.I., S.J. Leybourne, and P. Newbold (1999). Forecast evaluation tests in the presence of ARCH. *Journal of Forecasting*, 18, 435–45.

Henriksson, R.D. and R.C. Merton (1981). On market-timing and investment performance. II. Statistical procedures for evaluating forecasting skills. *Journal of Business*, 54, 513–33.

Katz, R.W., B.G. Brown, and A.H. Murphy (1987). Decision-analytic assessment of the economic value of weather forecasts: the fallowing/planting problem. *Journal of Forecasting*, 6, 77–89.

Katz, R.W. and A.H. Murphy (1990). Quality/value relationships for imperfect weather forecasts in a prototype multistage decision-making model. *Journal of Forecasting*, 9, 75–86.

Katz, R.W. and A.H. Murphy (eds.) (1997). *Economic Value of Weather and Climate Forecasts*. Cambridge: Cambridge University Press.

Leitch, G. and J.E. Tanner (1991). Economic forecast evaluation: profits versus the conventional error measures. *American Economic Review*, 81, 580–90.

Leitch, G. and J.E. Tanner (1995). Professional economic forecasts: are they worth their costs?. *Journal of Forecasting*, 14, 143–57.

Lopez, J.A. (1999). Methods for evaluating value-at-risk estimates. *Federal Reserve Bank of San Francisco Economic Review*, 3–17.

McCulloch, R. and P.E. Rossi (1990). Posterior, predictive and utility based approaches to testing the arbitrage pricing theory. *Journal of Financial Economics*, 28, 7–38.

Merton R.C. (1981). On market-timing and investment performance: an equilibrium theory of market forecasts. *Journal of Business*, 54, 363–406.

Murphy, A.H. (1973). A new vector partition of the probability score. *Journal of Applied Meteorology*, 12, 595–600.

Murphy, A.H. (1977). The value of climatological, categorical and probabilistic forecasts in the cost-loss ratio situation. *Monthly Weather Review*, 105, 803–16.

Murphy, A.H. (1985). Decision making and the value of forecasts in a generalized model of the cost-loss ratio situation. *Monthly Weather Review*, 113, 362–69.

Murphy, A.H. and H. Dann (1985). Forecast evaluation. In A.H. Murphy and R.W. Katz (eds.), *Probability, Statistics, and Decision Making in the Atmospheric Sciences*. Boulder: Westview. 379–437.

Murphy, A.H. and R.L. Winkler (1987). A general framework for forecast verification. *Monthly Weather Review*, 115, 1330–38.

Nelson, C.R. (1972). The Prediction Performance of the FRB-MIT-PENN Model of the U.S. Economy. *American Economic Review*, 62, 902–48.

Nelson, R.R. and S.G. Winter (1964). A case study in the economics of information and coordination: The weather forecasting system. *Quarterly Journal of Economics*, 78, 420–41.

Nobay, R.A. and D.A. Peel (1998). Optimal monetary policy in a model of asymmetric central bank preferences. Mimeo, London School of Economics.

Pearl, J. (1978). An economic basis for evaluating certain methods of probabilistic forecasts. *An International Journal of Man-Machine Studies*, 10, 175–83.

Pesaran, M.H. and A.G. Timmermann (1992). A simple nonparametric test of predictive performance. *Journal of Business and Economic Statistics*, 10, 461–65.

Pesaran, M.H. and A.G. Timmermann (1994). Forecasting stock returns. An examination of stock market trading in the presence of transaction costs. *Journal of Forecasting*, 13, 330–65.

Pesaran, M.H. and A.G. Timmermann (1995). Predictability of stock returns: robustness and economic significance. *Journal of Finance*, 50, 1201–28.

Pesaran, M.H. and A.G. Timmermann (2000). Recursive modeling approach to predicting U.K. stock returns. *The Economic Journal*, 110, 159–91.

Poulizac, D., M. Weale, and G. Young (1996). The performance of national institute economic forecasts. *National Institute Economic Review*, 55–62.

Rissanen, J. (1987). Stochastic Complexity and the MDL Principle. *Econometric Reviews*, 6, 85–102.

Rogoff, K. (1985). The optimal degree of commitment to a monetary target. *Quarterly Journal of Economics*, 100, 1169–90.

Rosenblatt, M. (1952). Remarks on a multivariate transformation. *Annals of Mathematical Statistics*, 23, 470–2.

Satchell, S. and A.G. Timmermann (1995). An assessment of the economic value of nonlinear foreign exchange rate forecasts. *Journal of Forecasting*, 14, 477–97.

Schnader, M.H. and H.O. Stekler (1990). Evaluating predictions of change. *Journal of Business*, 63, 99–107.

Skouras, S. (1998). Risk neutral forecasting. EUI Working Papers, Eco No. 98/40, European University Institute.

Skouras, S. (2000). Decisionmetrics: a decision-based approach to econometric modeling. Mimeo, Cambridge: University of Cambridge.

Stock, J.H. and M.W. Watson (1993). A procedure for predicting recessions with leading indicators: econometric issues and recent experience. In J.H. Stock and M.W. Watson (eds.), *Business Cycles, Indicators and Forecasting*, National Bureau of Economic Research, Studies in Business Cycles Volume 28, Chicago: University of Chicago Press, 95–153.

Svensson, L.E.O. (1997). Optimal inflation targets, conservative central banks, and linear inflation contracts. *American Economic Review*, 87, 98–114.

Theil, H. (1960). *Economic Forecasts and Policy*, 2nd edn. Amsterdam: North-Holland.

Varian, H.R. (1975). A Bayesian approach to real estate assessment. In S.E. Fienberg and A. Zellner (eds.), *Studies in Bayesian Econometrics and Statistics in Honor of Leonard J. Savage*. Amsterdam: North-Holland.

Wallis, K.F. (1999). Asymmetric density forecasts of inflation and the Bank of England's fan chart. *National Institute Economic Review*, 106–12.

Weiss, A.A. (1996). Estimating time series models using the relevant cost function. *Journal of Applied Econometrics*, 11, 539–60.

West, K.D. (1996). Asymptotic inference about predictive ability. *Econometrica*, 64, 1067–84.

West, K.D., H.J. Edison, and D. Cho (1993). A utility-based comparison of some models of exchange rate volatility. *Journal of International Economics*, 35, 23–45.

White, D.J. (1966). Forecasts and decisionmaking. *Journal of Mathematical Analysis and Applications*, 14, 163–73.

Whittle, P. (1979). Why predict? Prediction as an adjunct to action. In D. Anderson (ed.), *Forecasting*. Amsterdam: North Holland.

Wilks, D.S. (1995). *Statistical Methods in the Atmospheric Sciences: An Introduction*. London: Academic Press.

Zellner, A. (1973). The quality of quantitative economic policymaking when targets and costs of change are misspecified. In W. Sellakaerts (ed.), *Selected Readings in Econometrics and Economic Theory: Essays in Honour of Jan Tinbergen*, London: Macmillan.

Zellner, A. (1986). Bayesian estimation and prediction using asymmetric loss functions. *Journal of the American Statistical Association*, 81, 446–51.

CHAPTER TWELVE

Forecast Combination and Encompassing

Paul Newbold and David I. Harvey

12.1. INTRODUCTION

It is very often the case that two or more forecasts, of the same quantity from different sources or different methodological approaches, are available. On occasions these forecasts may be created by the same analyst, either to compare alternative methodologies and models or to provide benchmarks against which the merits of an *a priori* preferred forecast can be assessed. One possibility in these circumstances is to opt for one of the alternatives, chosen on subjective or objective grounds. However, this strategy discounts the possibility that the discarded forecasts could embody useful information about the future not contained in the preferred forecast. Both intuition and experience suggest that such a strategy will frequently be sub-optimal.

The concept and methodology of forecast combination were introduced by Bates and Granger (1969) in a seminal paper that has become a citation classic. Surveys and discussions of some subsequent developments and applications by Clemen (1989), Granger (1989), and Diebold and Lopez (1996) testify to the widespread interest that has developed in the topic. Bates and Granger urged that, when alternative forecasts are available, the analyst should consider creating a *combined* forecast, possibly as a weighted average of the individual constituent forecasts. When a record is available of past performance, the weights to be attached to each individual forecast in the combination can be chosen objectively, so that most weight is given to the approach that has performed best in the recent past.

Four factors account for the extensive and continued interest in forecast combination. First, the concept is intuitively appealing. Second, although some technically elaborate methodologies have subsequently been proposed, the approaches suggested by Bates and Granger, and those still most frequently used, to determine a specific combination are very simple to understand and implement. Third, and most important, there is a wealth of evidence from empirical studies that combination works well in practical applications. Indeed, it is often found that the combined forecast outperforms *all* individual forecasts. Finally, combination leads naturally to the concept of forecast *encompassing* as a very valuable tool in the evaluation of forecasts.

The intuitive appeal of forecast combination is analogous to that of investment in a portfolio of securities in preference to a single stock: risk is diversified. Economic forecasts are developed through a broad range of methodological approaches, and often embody some subjective judgmental component. When, as in macroeconomic forecasting, several agencies exhaust substantial effort in generating predictions, the option of discarding all but one may seem unattractive. Rather, it may pay to investigate the possibility that several competing forecasts embody useful information absent in the others, and that such information can be profitably impounded through amalgamation of the individual forecasts.

The combination methods proposed by Bates and Granger require very simple calculations to determine appropriate weights, and moreover many studies have found that such straightforward methods generate high-quality forecasts. One would expect combination to be most effective when composites are formed from forecasts generated by widely divergent methodologies. For example, Montgomery et al. (1998) combine unemployment rate forecasts from nonlinear time-series models with median forecasts from a survey of professional economic forecasters. However, gains have also been reported from the combination of forecasts from apparently quite similar sources. For example, Newbold and Granger (1974) and Winkler and Makridakis (1983) demonstrated benefits from combining alternative forecasts obtained through different univariate time-series methods. Many studies analysing practical applications of combination are briefly summarized in Clemen (1989).

In reviewing methods proposed for the evaluation of forecasts, and in particular the concept of *forecast efficiency*, Granger and Newbold (1973) argued that the assessment in isolation of a set of forecasts was of limited value. Rather, it is potentially more informative to compare one's forecast performance with that of a competitor. Ideally, not only should the competing forecasts be outperformed, they should contain no useful information about the future not embodied in one's preferred forecasts. In terms of our previous discussion, the competing forecasts should optimally receive zero weight in combination with the preferred forecasts, a notion that had previously been applied by Nelson (1972). If this is the case, the preferred forecasts are said to be *conditionally efficient* with respect to their competitors. Subsequently, Chong and Hendry (1986) described this as the preferred forecasts *encompassing* their competitors, employing the terminology of Mizon (1984) and Mizon and Richard (1986) for a concept originally designed to assess fitted models in-sample. Further discussion of the encompassing principle as it applies to forecast evaluation is provided by Lu and Mizon (1991) and Clements and Hendry (1993).

It is useful to have available formal tests of the null hypothesis that one set of forecasts encompasses its competitors. Rejection at low significance levels of this null hypothesis would of course suggest that forecast combination is likely to prove rewarding. However, such an outcome might also stimulate an analyst to seek directions in which a forecasting model can be improved. For example, if forecasts from some simple time series model are not encompassed, it may prove rewarding to more carefully assess the dynamic specification of the preferred model. The most direct approaches to forecast combination are based on linear regression analysis, which generates formal hypothesis tests in a straightforward way. This approach to testing for encompassing has been applied, for example, by Cooper and Nelson (1975), Fair and Shiller (1989, 1990), Fisher and Wallis (1990), Ericsson and Marquez (1993), and Holden and Thompson (1997). However, as we shall see in the third section of this chapter, the standard regression-based approach strongly depends for its validity on the assumption that the forecast errors are normally distributed. When, as seems prudent, the analyst is unwilling to make this assumption, alternative tests, offering robustness to nonnormality, are available.

12.2. Forecast Combination

In introducing forecast combination, we shall for ease of exposition, concentrate in the main on the combination of a pair of forecasts. Extension to the case of combining several forecasts is generally technically straightforward, and some details are given in Newbold and Granger (1974) and Granger and Newbold (1986).

Let f_{1t} and f_{2t} be two forecasts, made h time periods earlier, of the quantity y_t. Assume for now, as will often be reasonable, that these forecasts are unbiased in the sense that their errors

$$e_{it} = y_t - f_{it}; \quad i = 1, 2$$

each have mean zero. Denote by σ_i^2 ($i = 1, 2$) the forecast error variances, and by ρ the correlation between the forecast errors. Bates and Granger (1969) then propose consideration of the composite forecast

$$f_{ct} = (1 - \lambda)f_{1t} + \lambda f_{2t} \tag{12.1}$$

which, for $0 \le \lambda \le 1$, is a weighted average of the two individual forecasts. The error of the combined forecast is then

$$\varepsilon_t = y_t - f_{ct} = (1 - \lambda)e_{1t} + \lambda e_{2t} \tag{12.2}$$

which has mean zero, and variance

$$E(\varepsilon_t^2) = (1 - \lambda)^2\sigma_1^2 + \lambda^2\sigma_2^2 + 2\lambda(1 - \lambda)\rho\sigma_1\sigma_2$$

This is minimized by setting the weight λ equal to

$$\lambda_{opt} = \frac{\sigma_1^2 - \rho\sigma_1\sigma_2}{\sigma_1^2 + \sigma_2^2 - 2\rho\sigma_1\sigma_2}, \tag{12.3}$$

giving the optimal weighting in a composite predictor when the cost of forecast error function is proportional to squared error.

In practice $(\sigma_1^2, \sigma_2^2, \rho)$ will be unknown, but, provided that a record of forecast performance has been observed, these parameters can be estimated. Suppose that a record of T consecutive sets of forecasts, together with the corresponding outcomes, is available, giving the forecast errors (e_{1t}, e_{2t}), $t = 1, \ldots, T$. Then the natural sample estimator of (12.3) is

$$\hat{\lambda}_{opt} = \frac{\sum_{t=1}^{T} e_{1t}^2 - \sum_{t=1}^{T} e_{1t} e_{2t}}{\sum_{t=1}^{T} e_{1t}^2 + \sum_{t=1}^{T} e_{2t}^2 - 2\sum_{t=1}^{T} e_{1t} e_{2t}}. \tag{12.4}$$

This estimator has a straightforward interpretation in a regression context. Writing ε_t for the error of the combined forecast, it follows from (12.1) or (12.2) that

$$e_{1t} = \lambda(e_{1t} - e_{2t}) + \varepsilon_t. \tag{12.5}$$

Viewing (12.5) as a regression equation with error term ε_t, corresponding to

$$y_t = (1 - \lambda)f_{1t} + \lambda f_{2t} + \varepsilon_t, \tag{12.6}$$

(12.4) is simply the ordinary least squares estimator of λ.

Granger and Ramanathan (1984) have argued that it may often be desirable to generalize (12.6) to

$$y_t = \alpha + \beta_1 f_{1t} + \beta_2 f_{2t} + \varepsilon_t \tag{12.7}$$

estimating $(\alpha, \beta_1, \beta_2)$ by least squares. Of course, (12.6) is simply (12.7) with the constraints $(\alpha = 0, \beta_1 + \beta_2 = 1)$. Given only a limited amount of data, there are obviously gains from imposing these constraints when it is reasonable to believe they are approximately true. On the other hand, the more general form (12.7) allows for the possibility of biased forecasts. One difficulty with (12.7) is that frequently economic time series are generated by *integrated processes*. To circumvent inferential difficulties from least squares regressions involving such processes, it seems most appropriate for (y_t, f_{1t}, f_{2t}) in (12.7) to represent actual and predicted *changes* of the variable of interest. Diebold (1988) argues that, in situations where the more general form (12.7) is appropriate, serial correlation in the error terms ε_t is likely. In consequence, Coulson and Robins (1993) propose adding a lagged dependent variable to the right-hand-side of (12.7) when y_t is stationary, but working with actual and predicted changes when y_t is integrated.

As in any applied statistical work, the degree of sophistication of the methodology that can sensibly be applied depends to a considerable extent on the amount of available sample data – that is, in our notation, on the number T of observations available on (y_t, f_{1t}, f_{2t}). In many applications, for example in forecasting low-frequency macroeconomic data, this will not be large. In those circumstances, it is obviously sensible to base estimation of combining weights on relatively simple approaches. However, in some circumstances, particularly the prediction of high-frequency financial data, quite long series should be available, so that a more sophisticated approach might be reasonable. Of course, it is worth asking whether one should use a very long series of observations when such a possibility is open. Intuitively, one might suspect some form of nonstationarity, believing that the relative performances of individual forecasters, or forecasting models, might change over time. This could occur because the process predicted evolves over time, from one whose dominant features are best captured by one approach to one most easily predicted by an alternative method. It is also possible that individual forecasters evolve over time, for example through learning from past errors and modifying forecasting models accordingly. Bates and Granger (1969) anticipated such concerns, suggesting that combination weights be most strongly influenced by *recent* past performance. For example, even when more data are available, the summations in (12.4) might be calculated from just the few most recent observations. Alternatively, the regressions (12.5) or (12.7) could be estimated by *discounted* least squares. These strategies are probably about the best that can be done unless the analyst has available a very large data set, in which case more sophisticated econometric analyses of the possibility of time-varying regressions and structural change could be applied. Procedures of this sort have been proposed in the context of forecast combination by Diebold and Pauly (1987), LeSage and Magura (1992), and Deutsch et al. (1994).

In theory, the formula (12.3) need not produce a value between zero and one for the optimal combining weight. However, if the assumptions on which it is based are correct, it is difficult to treat such a result as more than a theoretical curiosity. Otherwise it would be necessary to believe that one forecaster was of perverse value – worse, for example, than a coin in assessing whether to increase or decrease the superior forecast. Such a forecaster would be unlikely to stay in business long – unless the value of his perversity was detected! Discounting this possibility, it can still often occur as a result of sampling error that the estimator (12.4) will not satisfy $0 \leq \hat{\lambda}_{opt} \leq 1$. Given the apparent absurdity of such an estimate, many, including Granger and Newbold (1986), recommend its replacement with the nearest boundary value. The situation can become more acute in the case of combining three or more forecasts. First, the greater the number of forecasts in the putative combination, the more likely are least squares estimates of the weights to be attached to some of them to be negative. Newbold et al. (1987) encountered this problem, treating it through an *ad hoc* backward elimination algorithm. Gunter (1992) and Gunter and Aksu (1997) have explored a more rigorously proper, though computationally far more demanding, approach through nonnegativity restricted least squares.

When data are plentiful, it is not necessary to restrict attention to combined forecasts that are *linear* functions of the constituent forecasts. For example, Donaldson and Kamstra (1996) discuss the use of neural networks, while Fiordaliso (1998) explores the selection of nonlinear combinations through fuzzy systems. A further possibility, considered by West (1996), is that the analyst may be interested in the combination of forecasts of several related, or similar, time series at several different horizons, constituent forecasts in each case having been produced by the same forecaster or the same methodology. It seems sub-optimal in such a case to view the choice of each individual set of combination weights as a separate problem. Rather, there could well be gains from a joint analysis of these problems. Although the approaches considered by West are quite *ad hoc*, further analysis of this issue could well prove rewarding.

In spite of the intricacy of some of the methodology just discussed, in fact the combination methods that have most often been used in practical applications are far more straightforward. For example, Bates and Granger (1969) suggested that weights attached to individual forecasts might be taken as inversely proportional to mean squared forecast error in the recent past. Thus, in place of (12.4) one would use

$$\hat{\lambda}_{inv} = \frac{\sum_{t=1}^{T} e_{1t}^2}{\sum_{t=1}^{T} e_{1t}^2 + \sum_{t=1}^{T} e_{2t}^2},$$

(12.8)

neglecting entirely the sample covariance term in (12.4). Again, if it is suspected that relative forecast performance might evolve over time, the summations in (12.8) might incorporate only the few most recent forecast errors, rather than all available observations.

Of course, the formula (12.8) will, in contrast to (12.4), always produce weights between zero and one. By the same token, it will always assign some weight to any individual forecaster, however poor the recent performance. This point may be especially troublesome when (12.8) is generalized to combining a moderately large number of forecasts, some of which are from forecasters with a poor track record, and who in the event have nothing of value to contribute. There may then be some benefit in eliminating some forecasts before attempting this approach. This could, for example, be achieved through an initial backward-elimination stepwise regression, dropping those forecasts whose estimated weights differ insignificantly from zero.

Beginning with Newbold and Granger (1974), several published large-scale empirical studies, many of which are discussed by Clemen (1989), have found in the aggregate better mean squared error performance when combination weights were based on (12.8) rather than (12.4). This finding, for which we know of no completely convincing theoretical explanation, is somewhat perplexing, as (12.4) is the more obviously defensible choice. Moreover, for purposes of statistical inference, as in the tests for encompassing to be discussed in the next section, it is certainly convenient to base analysis on that estimator. One possibility is that the published studies have generally based the choice of combination weights on a relatively small number of observations – as we have suggested might often be desirable – so that there is considerable sampling variability in (12.4) viewed as an estimator of the theoretically optimal weight (12.3).

In fact, an even simpler approach to forecast combination has often proved remarkably successful. Makridakis et al. (1982), Makridakis and Winkler (1983), and several subsequent studies discussed in Clemen (1989) have reported that simple averaging of alternative single series time-series forecasts often does at least as well as methods where weights are chosen on the basis of past performance. It is difficult to see quite how one should react to such results. The implication is surely not that one should always simply average forecasts, whatever is known about particular forecasters' methodologies and recent track records. However, these considerations do prompt the thought that the selection of combining weights might be viewed within a Bayesian framework, and a number of authors, beginning with Bunn (1975), have taken this view. Subsequently, Clemen and Winkler (1986) and Diebold and Pauly (1990) have advocated an approach, via Bayes' theorem, through which the usual least squares estimators of the regressions (12.5) or (12.7) are shrunk toward some prior mean, in effect mitigating the effect of sampling variability. As is not infrequently the case, the difficulty lies in the choice of prior. Although shrinkage toward the equal weights case has been advocated, it is not difficult to think of situations where this is far from representing the analysts' true prior belief. For example, having spent a great deal of effort developing a forecasting model, we might be tempted to try combining our own forecasts with those of some competitors. However, we might be quite reluctant to thrust modesty aside to the extent of belief in an equal weights-centered prior. A considerably fuller discussion of Bayesian issues in the combination of both forecasts and models is provided by Min and Zellner (1993).

12.3. Forecast Encompassing

We now turn to the issue of forecast encompassing, concentrating on the case where a pair of competing forecasts is available. Extension to the case of more than two forecasts is discussed in Harvey and Newbold (2000). It should be emphasized that the tests of this section are of *forecast* encompassing. They make no allowance for sampling error in the estimation of competing forecast-generating models, and in general do not constitute valid tests for *model* encompassing when the model fitting period is not very large compared with the forecast period (see, for example, the discussion in West, 1996, and chapter 14 by McCracken and West in this volume). It is further assumed that the data-generating model remains stable over the forecast period, and our tests make no allowance for the possibility of structural change in this period, an issue whose relevance is extensively discussed by Clements and Hendry (1999).

The methodology of forecast combination can be exploited to test the null hypothesis that one forecast encompasses another – that is, given that the first forecast is available, the second provides no further useful incremental information for prediction. If combination is to be based on a weighted average, a natural test of the null hypothesis that forecast 1 encompasses forecast 2 is a test of $\lambda - 0$ in the regression (12.5). In addition to this possibility, Chong and Hendry (1986) also suggested a test of the hypothesis $\alpha = 0$ in the regression

$$e_{1t} = \alpha f_{2t} + \varepsilon_t. \tag{12.9}$$

The rationale is that, optimally, the error e_{1t} to be made by forecaster 1 should be uncorrelated with all information available when the forecast is made, while correlation of that error with forecast 2 implies that information in the latter is of some value in anticipating the former. Nevertheless, application of a test based on the regression (12.9) can lead to difficulties, particularly when, as is often the case, the series of interest, and consequently any reasonable predictor series, is integrated. Besides noting that an encompassing test statistic based on the estimation of (12.9) is not invariant to nonsingular linear transformations of a data set and can have lower power than one based on (12.5), Ericsson (1992, 1993) stresses the problem when the series of interest is integrated. Not only would any reasonable predictor series, such as f_{2t}, also be integrated, but any reasonable predictor would generate stationary forecast errors e_{1t}. The regression (12.9) is then "unbalanced" in the sense that, unless $\alpha = 0$, the left- and right-hand sides have different orders of integration, and the usual test statistics will have nonstandard limiting distributions. Indeed, Phillips (1995) has proved that in these circumstances the spurious regression phenomenon is generated, in that as the sample size tends to infinity the t-ratio test on $\alpha = 0$ always leads to a rejection of a true null hypothesis.

In addition to encompassing tests based on (12.5), several studies have based tests on the Granger–Ramanathan regression (12.7), though again, as noted by for example Fair and Shiller (1989) and Diebold and Lopez (1996), if the time series to be predicted is integrated the variables in the regression should be actual and predicted changes. There does not, however, seem to be unanimity on precisely what null hypothesis is to be tested. While Fair and Shiller test $\beta_2 - 0$, Diebold and Lopez test $(\alpha, \beta_1, \beta_2) = (0, 1, 0)$. An intermediate possibility that appears to be preferred by Andrews et al. (1996) would be to impose the restriction $\beta_1 + \beta_2 = 1$, but allow α to be unrestricted, so permitting bias in the forecasts. If the Fair–Shiller null hypothesis is correct, then (12.7) reduces to

$$y_t = \alpha + \beta_1 f_{1t} + \varepsilon_t. \tag{12.10}$$

Since the forecast f_{2t} does not enter into (12.10), one could say that forecast 1 encompasses forecast 2 in the sense that there exists a predictor that is a linear function, $\alpha + \beta_1 f_{1t}$, of f_{1t} that cannot be improved in a squared error sense through combination with forecast 2. Diebold and Lopez further require $(\alpha, \beta_1) = (0, 1)$. This is precisely the condition required on (12.10) for forecast 1 to be deemed "efficient" according to a definition of Mincer and Zarnowitz (1969). Thus, the hypothesis tested by Diebold and Lopez is that forecast 1 is at the same time both Mincer-Zarnowitz efficient and conditionally efficient with respect to forecast 2, in the sense of Granger and Newbold (1973). The Fair–Shiller null hypothesis does not require Mincer–Zarnowitz efficiency, and indeed it is theoretically possible that forecast 1 could encompass forecast 2 according to this definition, yet have larger expected squared error.

Turning now to concentrate on the case of combination as a simple weighted average, tests for forecast encompassing can be based on the fitting of the regression (12.5), as noted above, given a series of T observations. The null hypothesis that forecast 1 encompasses forecast 2 corresponds to $\lambda = 0$, and the natural alternative is that forecast 2 should receive *positive* weight in the optimal combination; that is, $\lambda > 0$. The "obvious" approach is to estimate (12.5) by ordinary least squares, the test statistic being the usual OLS-based t-ratio associated with the least squares estimate $\hat{\lambda}$ of λ.

There are two difficulties with this "obvious" approach. First, although the errors of optimal one-step forecasts are nonautocorrelated, those of optimal h-steps forecasts follow a moving average process of order $h - 1$. Thus, for prediction beyond one step ahead it would be inappropriate to assume that the error terms in (12.5) are white noise. Second, as pointed out by Harvey et al. (1998), it would be unsurprising to find in (12.5) a form of conditional heteroskedasticity in which $Var\,(\varepsilon_t \,|\, e_{1t} - e_{2t})$ is a function of $(e_{1t} - e_{2t})$. This might be induced, for example, by nonnormality in (e_{1t}, e_{2t}). The assumption that forecast errors are normally distributed is unappealing. Experience suggests that, on occasions, very large absolute forecast errors will occur so that a heavier-tailed distribution, such as Student's t, might be more plausible. Indeed, in some current work in progress studying predictions of U.S. macroeconomic variables reported in the "Survey of Professional Forecasters," we have found strong evidence that the forecast error series are leptokurtic, to the extent that if these series were generated by Student's t distributions, the appropriate degrees of freedom would be in the range 5–10. Harvey et al. considered the case where (e_{1t}, e_{2t}) is an independent sequence, as might be appropriate for one-step forecasting, but their distribution is bivariate Student's t. In that case, the usual test will reject a true null hypothesis of forecast encompassing far too often. For example, for five degrees of freedom, it can be shown that, as the sample size becomes large, a nominal 5 percent-level test will produce a rejection rate of 17.1 percent for a true null hypothesis.

These difficulties can be overcome through the use of autocorrelation- and heteroskedasticity-consistent methods, in the spirit of those of Newey and West (1987) and Andrews (1991). Let $\hat{\lambda}$ be the least squares estimator of λ from the regression (12.5). Then, under certain regularity conditions,

$$D^{-1/2}T^{1/2}(\hat{\lambda} - \lambda) \xrightarrow{d} N(0, 1),$$

where

$$D = M^{-2}Q; \; M = E[(e_{1t} - e_{2t})^2],$$

$$Q = \lim_{T \to \infty} Var\left[T^{-1/2}\sum_{t=1}^{T}(e_{1t} - e_{2t})\varepsilon_t\right]. \tag{12.11}$$

Given consistent estimators $\hat{M}$, $\hat{Q}$, and therefore $\hat{D}$, a test statistic of the form

$$R = \hat{D}^{-1/2}T^{1/2}\hat{\lambda} \tag{12.12}$$

will then have a limiting standard normal distribution under the null hypothesis $\lambda = 0$. A natural estimator of M is

$$\hat{M} = T^{-1} \sum_{t=1}^{T} (e_{1t} - e_{2t})^2$$

Now (12.11) is $2\pi f(0)$, where $f(0)$ is the spectral density at zero frequency of $(e_{1t} - e_{2t})\varepsilon_t$. For forecasting h steps ahead, it may be reasonable to assume the sequence of forecast errors is $(h-1)$-dependent. In that case, a sensible estimator of Q is

$$\hat{Q}_1 = T^{-1} \sum_{\tau=-(h-1)}^{h-1} \sum_{t=|\tau|+1}^{T} (e_{1t} - e_{2t})\hat{\varepsilon}_t (e_{1,t-|\tau|} - e_{2,t-|\tau|})\hat{\varepsilon}_{t-|\tau|}, \qquad (12.13)$$

where $\hat{\varepsilon}_t$ are the residuals from the least squares estimation of (12.5). Then, corresponding to (12.12), the test statistic is

$$R_1 = T^{-1/2}\hat{Q}_1^{-1/2} \sum_{t=1}^{T} (e_{1t} - e_{2t})^2 \hat{\lambda}. \qquad (12.14)$$

It is easily shown that the statistic (12.14) has a limiting standard normal distribution, though Student's t critical values are preferable in small samples. However, Harvey et al. (1998) reported simulation evidence suggesting that tests based on this result could be quite seriously oversized in small samples. This occurs because $\hat{Q}_1$ of (12.13) converges only very slowly to Q of (12.11), even in the simplest case of one-step forecasting. An alternative estimator of Q that is consistent under the null hypothesis, but not under the alternative, follows immediately from setting $\lambda = 0$ in (12.5), thus obtaining

$$\hat{Q}_2 = T^{-1} \sum_{\tau=-(h-1)}^{h-1} \sum_{t=|\tau|+1}^{T} (e_{1t} - e_{2t})e_{1t}(e_{1,t-|\tau|} - e_{2,t-|\tau|})e_{1,t-|\tau|}$$

and a test statistic R_2 of identical form to R_1 of (12.14), but with $\hat{Q}_2$ in place of $\hat{Q}_1$. A third possibility follows from noting that the statistic R_2 can be written as

$$R_2 = T \left[\sum_{\tau=-(h-1)}^{h-1} \sum_{t=|\tau|+1}^{T} d_t d_{t-|\tau|} \right]^{-1/2} \bar{d}, \qquad (12.15)$$

where

$$d_t = (e_{1t} - e_{2t})e_{1t} \qquad (12.16)$$

and $\bar{d}$ is the sample mean of the d_t sequence. Viewed in this way, the problem is seen as one of testing the null hypothesis $E(d_t) = 0$, though it is unorthodox to estimate the variance of $\bar{d}$ consistently only under the null hypothesis. In fact, an orthodox approach along these lines to a related problem – testing the equality of prediction mean squared errors, so that $d_t = e_{1t}^2 - e_{2t}^2$ – has been proposed by Diebold and Mariano (1995). Then, applied to our problem, with d_t given by (12.16), the Diebold–Mariano test statistic is

$$DM = T \left[\sum_{\tau=-(h-1)}^{h-1} \sum_{t=|\tau|+1}^{T} (d_t - \bar{d})(d_{t-|\tau|} - \bar{d}) \right]^{-1/2} \bar{d}. \qquad (12.17)$$

A further modification of (12.17) and the associated test is desirable in small samples. Harvey et al. (1997) investigated the Diebold–Mariano test of equality of prediction mean squared errors, recommending the use of the modified test statistic

$$MDM = T^{-1/2}[T + 1 - 2h + T^{-1}h(h - 1)]^{1/2}DM. \qquad (12.18)$$

They further recommend comparison of this statistic with critical values from Student's t distribution with $(T - 1)$ degrees of freedom rather than from the standard normal distribution. Notice that in the case of one-step forecasts, so that $h = 1$ and independence over time of the sequence (e_{1t}, e_{2t}) is assumed, this test based on (12.18) is then precisely the standard test of the null hypothesis $E(d_t) = 0$, based on the sample mean. Of course, tests of this form are well known to be robust to nonnormality, arguing their value in the present situation.

The test statistics R_1, R_2, DM, and MDM all have limiting standard normal distributions under the null hypothesis of forecast encompassing. However, simulation results reported by Harvey et al. (1998), covering error processes generated by both the bivariate normal and bivariate t distributions, suggested that in small samples the test based on MDM has empirical size somewhat closer to the nominal size than any of the alternatives. Unfortunately, obtaining this advantage is not costless. For small sample sizes, the statistic R_1 and particularly the usual OLS-based regression statistic can have markedly higher size-adjusted powers than MDM. Thus, the protection in terms of size reliability in the presence of nonnormality afforded by MDM has to be balanced against the loss in power when in fact the true generating process is approximately normal. However, as the sample size increases, this ambiguity dissipates, as the size-adjusted power of MDM quickly approaches that of its competitors. Harvey et al. (1998) note a further possibility, directly applicable only to one-step forecasting. The null hypothesis of zero correlation between $(e_{1t} - e_{2t})$ and e_{1t} can be tested through Spearman's rank correlation coefficient. This test has somewhat higher power than MDM in small samples.

The recommendation to adopt the MDM test in the form just discussed has to be tempered by a further possibility. Forecast errors might well exhibit autoregressive conditional heteroskedasticity (ARCH). In its simplest form this could occur in one-step forecasting when the error series is nonautocorrelated but the sequence of squared errors is autocorrelated. Such an outcome would not be surprising in practice, since it is easy to believe for example that a variable that is difficult to forecast accurately this quarter will also prove to be relatively difficult to forecast next quarter. In terms of our previous analysis, the presence of ARCH effects invalidates the assumption of $(h - 1)$-dependence in sequences (e_{1t}, e_{2t}) of h-steps forecast errors. This issue has been investigated by Harvey et al. (1999), who found for the type of ARCH effects most likely to occur in practice, that, even asymptotically, the encompassing tests discussed thus far will generate spurious rejections of the null hypothesis. These authors proposed a simple modification that should considerably alleviate this problem. When the presence of ARCH is suspected, simply pretend one is forecasting a few steps further ahead than is in fact the case, replacing h by $(h + [0.5T^{1/3}])$, where [.] denotes integer part, in (12.14), (12.15), and (12.18).

We have noted that forecast encompassing tests are often based on the Granger–Ramanathan regression (12.7). Of course, the problems of autocorrelated errors and forecast error nonnormality will cause difficulties here too. Some of the tests just described can be adapted in an obvious way to deal with this regression. For example, suppose as in Fair and Shiller (1989) the null hypothesis to be tested is $\beta_2 = 0$. Now, write the regression (12.7) as

$$y_t = x_t'\beta + \varepsilon_t; \quad t = 1, \ldots, T,$$

where

$$x_t' = (1, f_{1t}, f_{2t}); \beta' = (\alpha, \beta_1, \beta_2).$$

In matrix form this is

$$y = X\beta + \varepsilon.$$

Then, as for example in theorem 5.16 of White (1984, p. 119), if $\hat{\beta}$ is the least squares estimator of β,

$$D^{-1/2}T^{1/2}(\hat{\beta} - \beta) \xrightarrow{d} N(0, I),$$

where

$$D = M^{-1}QM^{-1}, \quad M = E(x_t x_t'),$$
$$Q = \lim_{T\to\infty} Var\, [T^{-1/2}X'\varepsilon].$$

Then, to test the null hypothesis $\beta_2 = 0$, a test statistic of the form

$$R = \hat{d}_{33}^{-1/2}T^{1/2}\hat{\beta}_2, \tag{12.19}$$

where $\hat{d}_{33}$ is the (3, 3) element of $\hat{D}$, a consistent estimator of D, has a limiting standard normal distribution under the null hypothesis. The matrix M is consistently estimated by

$$\hat{M} = T^{-1}X'X$$

while, corresponding to (12.13), with $\hat{\varepsilon}_t$ denoting the residuals from least squares estimation of (12.7), the matrix Q can be consistently estimated by

$$\hat{Q}_1 = T^{-1}\left[\sum_{t=1}^{T} x_t x_t' \hat{\varepsilon}_t^2 + \sum_{\tau=1}^{h-1}\sum_{t=\tau+1}^{T} x_{t-\tau}\hat{\varepsilon}_{t-\tau}x_t'\hat{\varepsilon}_t + \sum_{\tau=1}^{h-1}\sum_{t=\tau+1}^{T} x_t \hat{\varepsilon}_t x_{t-\tau}'\hat{\varepsilon}_{t-\tau}\right]. \quad (12.20)$$

Substitution of these estimates into (12.19) then generates a test statistic R_1 analogous to (12.14). A statistic analogous to R_2 of (12.15) would be obtained by estimating the matrix Q under the null hypothesis by $\hat{Q}_2$ in the same form as (12.20), but now with $\hat{\varepsilon}_t$ denoting residuals from the least squares estimation of (12.7) when $\beta_2 = 0$ is imposed.

12.4. Summary

In a world of increasingly complex technical methodology, much of it, one suspects, destined never to be used outside of academic econometrics, the combination of forecasts is a beautiful rarity – a simple idea, easily implemented, that works well and therefore *is* used in practice. Although some sophisticated elaborations will undoubtedly prove of value on occasions, the basic simple methodology has often proved to perform remarkably well, as witnessed by many published applications. Possibly some of this apparent success stems from a form of publication bias, it being easier to publish positive rather than negative results. However, several published analyses have contained the results of "forecasting competitions," involving large numbers of time series, that would have appeared in print whatever the outcome. The reason for the success of this simple idea is also not difficult to see. The amalgamation, in-sample, of complex models can be very difficult and potentially a violation of the principle of parsimony, leading to disappointing post-sample forecast performance. By contrast, combination permits the amalgamation of forecasts from a range of sources, including efficiently parameterized models.

A natural application of forecast combination is in testing the hypothesis of forecast encompassing – that is, the conditional efficiency of one forecast with respect to others. It is perhaps a pity that simple methods cannot necessarily be recommended here also. Some consolation might be derived from the fact that the elaborations outlined in the previous section are motivated by a well-appreciated property of real world forecasts: it is implausible to assume that their errors are normally distributed. In that sense, the recommended methods are pragmatic, following from experience of reality rather than an apparently convenient academic assumption. Doubtless further elaborations and extensions of these test procedures remain to be developed, but it seems clear that robust tests will be the paradigm within which such developments take place.

References

Andrews, D.W.K. (1991). Heteroskedasticity and autocorrelation consistent covariance matrix estimation. *Econometrica*, 59, 542–47.

Andrews, M.J., A.P.L. Minford, and J. Riley (1996). On comparing macroeconomic models using forecast encompassing tests. *Oxford Bulletin of Economics and Statistics*, 58, 279–305.

Bates, J.M. and C.W.J. Granger (1969). The combination of forecasts. *Operational Research Quarterly*, 20, 451–68.

Bunn, D.W. (1975). A Bayesian approach to the linear combination of forecasts. *Operational Research Quarterly*, 26, 325–29.

Chong, Y.Y. and D.F. Hendry (1986). Econometric evaluation of linear macro-economic models. *Review of Economic Studies*, 53, 671–90.

Clemen, R.T. (1989). Combining forecasts: a review and annotated bibliography. *International Journal of Forecasting*, 5, 559–83.

Clemen, R.T. and R.L. Winkler (1986). Combining economic forecasts. *Journal of Business and Economic Statistics*, 4, 39–46.

Clements, M.P. and D.F. Hendry (1993). On the limitations of comparing mean square forecast errors. *Journal of Forecasting*, 12, 617–37.

Clements, M.P. and D.F. Hendry (1999). *Forecasting Non-stationary Economic Time Series*. Cambridge, MA: M.I.T. Press.

Cooper, J.P. and C.R. Nelson (1975). The *ex ante* prediction performance of the St. Louis and FRB–MIT–PENN econometric models and some results on composite predictors. *Journal of Money, Credit and Banking*, 7, 1–32.

Coulson, N.E. and R.P. Robins (1993). Forecast combination in a dynamic setting. *Journal of Forecasting*, 12, 63–7.

Deutsch, M., C.W.J. Granger, and T. Teräsvirta (1994). The combination of forecasts using changing weights. *International Journal of Forecasting*, 10, 47–57.

Diebold, F.X. (1988). Serial correlation and the combination of forecasts. *Journal of Business and Economic Statistics*, 6, 105–11.

Diebold, F.X. and J.A. Lopez (1996). Forecast evaluation and combination. In G.S. Maddala and C.R. Rao (eds.), *Handbook of Statistics*, Vol. 14. Amsterdam: North Holland, 241–68.

Diebold, F.X. and R.S. Mariano (1995). Comparing predictive accuracy. *Journal of Business and Economic Statistics*, 13, 253–63.

Diebold, F.X. and P. Pauly (1987). Structural change and the combination of forecasts. *Journal of Forecasting*, 6, 21–40.

Diebold, F.X. and P. Pauly (1990). The use of prior information in forecast combination. *International Journal of Forecasting*, 6, 503–8.

Donaldson, R.G. and M. Kamstra (1996). Forecast combining with neural networks. *Journal of Forecasting*, 15, 49–61.

Ericsson, N.R. (1992). Parameter constancy, mean square forecast errors, and measuring forecast performance: an exposition, extensions, and illustration. *Journal of Policy Modeling*, 14, 465–95.

Ericsson, N.R. (1993). On the limitations of comparing mean square forecast errors: clarifications and extensions. *Journal of Forecasting*, 12, 644–51.

Ericsson, N.R. and J. Marquez (1993). Encompassing the forecasts of U.S. trade balance models. *Review of Economics and Statistics*, 75, 19–31.

Fair, R.C. and R.J. Shiller (1989). The informational content of *ex ante* forecasts. *Review of Economics and Statistics*, 71, 325–31.

Fair, R.C. and R.J. Shiller (1990). Comparing information in forecasts from econometric models. *American Economic Review*, 80, 375–89.

Fiordaliso, A. (1998). A nonlinear forecasts combination method based on Takagi-Sugeno fuzzy systems. *International Journal of Forecasting*, 14, 367–79.

Fisher, P.G. and K.F. Wallis (1990). The historical tracking performance of U.K. macro-econometric models 1978–85. *Economic Modelling*, 7, 179–97.

Granger, C.W.J. (1989). Combining forecasts – twenty years later. *Journal of Forecasting*, 8, 167–73.

Granger, C.W.J. and P. Newbold (1973). Some comments on the evaluation of economic forecasts. *Applied Economics*, 5, 35–47.

Granger, C.W.J. and P. Newbold (1986). *Forecasting Economic Time Series*, 2nd edn. London: Academic Press.

Granger, C.W.J. and R. Ramanathan (1984). Improved methods of combining forecasts. *Journal of Forecasting*, 3, 197–204.

Gunter, S.I. (1992). Nonnegativity restricted least squares combinations. *International Journal of Forecasting*, 8, 45–59.

Gunter, S.I. and C. Aksu (1997). The usefulness of heuristic N(E)RLS algorithms for combining forecasts. *Journal of Forecasting*, 16, 439–63.

Harvey, D.I., S.J. Leybourne and P. Newbold (1997). Testing the equality of prediction mean squared errors. *International Journal of Forecasting*, 13, 281–91.

Harvey, D.I., S.J. Leybourne and P. Newbold (1998). Tests for forecast encompassing. *Journal of Business and Economic Statistics*, 16, 254–59.

Harvey, D.I., S.J. Leybourne, and P. Newbold (1999). Forecast evaluation tests in the presence of ARCH. *Journal of Forecasting*, 18, 435–45.

Harvey, D.I. and P. Newbold (2000). Tests for multiple forecast encompassing. *Journal of Applied Econometrics*, 15, 471–82.

Holden, K. and J. Thompson (1997). Combining forecasts, encompassing and the properties of U.K. macroeconomic forecasts. *Applied Economics*, 29, 1447–58.

LeSage, J.P. and M. Magura (1992). A mixture-model approach to combining forecasts. *Journal of Business and Economic Statistics*, 10, 445–52.

Lu, M. and G.E. Mizon (1991). Forecast encompassing and model evaluation. In P. Hackl and A.H. Westlund (eds.), *Economic Structural Change Analysis and Forecasting*. Berlin: Springer-Verlag, 123–38.

Makridakis, S., A. Andersen, R. Carbone, R. Fildes, M. Hibon, R. Lewandowski, J. Newton, E. Parzen, and R. Winkler (1982). The accuracy of extrapolation (time series) methods: results of a forecasting competition. *Journal of Forecasting*, 1, 111–53.

Makridakis, S. and R.L. Winkler (1983). Averages of forecasts: some empirical results. *Management Science*, 29, 987–96.

Min, C. and A. Zellner (1993). Bayesian and non-Bayesian methods for combining models and forecasts with applications to forecasting international growth rates. *Journal of Econometrics*, 56, 89–118.

Mincer, J. and V. Zarnowitz (1969). The evaluation of economic forecasts. In J. Mincer (ed.), *Economic Forecasts and Expectations*. New York: National Bureau of Economic Research, 3–46.

Mizon, G.E. (1984). The encompassing approach in econometrics. In D.F. Hendry and K.F. Wallis (eds.), *Econometrics and Quantitative Economics*. Oxford: Basil Blackwell, 135–72.

Mizon, G.E. and J.-F. Richard (1986). The encompassing principle and its application to testing non-nested hypotheses. *Econometrica*, 54, 657–78.

Montgomery, A.L., V. Zarnowitz, R.S. Tsay, and G.C. Tiao (1998). Forecasting the U.S. unemployment rate. *Journal of the American Statistical Association*, 93, 478–93.

Nelson, C.R. (1972). The prediction performance of the FRB-MIT-PENN model of the U.S. economy. *American Economic Review*, 62, 902–17.

Newbold, P. and C.W.J. Granger (1974). Experience with forecasting univariate time series and the combination of forecasts. *Journal of the Royal Statistical Society, Series A*, 137, 131–46.

Newbold, P., J.K. Zumwalt, and S. Kannan (1987). Combining forecasts to improve earnings per share prediction: an examination of electric utilities. *International Journal of Forecasting*, 3, 229–38.

Newey, W.K. and K.D. West (1987). A simple positive semi-definite heteroskedasticity and autocorrelation consistent covariance matrix. *Econometrica*, 55, 703–8.

Phillips, P.C.B. (1995). Spurious regression in forecast-encompassing tests. *Econometric Theory*, 11, 1188–90.

West, C.T. (1996). System-based weights versus series-specific weights in the combination of forecasts. *Journal of Forecasting*, 15, 369–83.

West, K.D. (1996). Asymptotic inference about predictive ability. *Econometrica*, 64, 1067–84.

White, H. (1984). *Asymptotic Theory for Econometricians*. London: Academic Press.

Winkler, R.L. and S. Makridakis (1983). The combination of forecasts. *Journal of the Royal Statistical Society, Series A*, 146, 150–57.

Testing Forecast Accuracy

Roberto S. Mariano

13.1.   Introduction

The predictive ability of an estimated model is critical not only to the quality of model forecasts but also to the adequacy of the model for policy analysis. Despite the obvious desirability of formal testing procedures, earlier efforts at assessing the forecast accuracy of an estimated model revolved around the calculation of summary forecast error statistics – for example, see Klein (1991), Clements and Hendry (1993), Wallis (1995), Newbold, Harvey, and Leybourne (1999), and Stock and Watson (1999). Resort to such an informal approach may be ascribed mainly to the complexities involved in dealing with sampling uncertainties and correlations that are present in forecast errors.

Efforts toward the construction of appropriate statistical tests of forecast accuracy started with loss functions that are quadratic in forecast errors. Furthermore, forecast errors are assumed to be Gaussian and serially uncorrelated. More recent activity has led to tests under more relaxed conditions – where loss functions may be nonquadratic and asymmetric and forecast errors need not be Gaussian. These tests generally are based on large-sample asymptotic analysis – with some limited experimental studies of their size and power properties in small samples.

This chapter reviews such significance tests. The review is necessarily outpaced by on-going research; it is necessarily limited as well – focusing on statistical tests of the accuracy of forecasts and tests comparing accuracy of competing forecasts.

13.2.   Significance Tests of Forecast Accuracy

Tests of forecast accuracy can be either model-based or model-free. The first type assumes that the econometric model is parametric, estimated from a given data sample, and both the data and model are available for testing forecast accuracy. Tests of this genre have been developed for large macroeconometric models based on deterministic and stochastic simulations of the estimated model – see Mariano and Brown (1983), Chong and Hendry (1986), Pagan (1989), Mariano and Brown (1991), and Wallis (1995).

For model-free tests, on the other hand, we assume that the information set at the disposal of the investigator consists only of a set of forecasts and actual values of the predictand. We also consider the case where we have two or more sets of forecasts from competing models, together with actual values, and wish to determine the relative accuracies of the forecasts.

Most of the tests we discuss here are model-free. These tests are intimately related to the encompassing tests that have been developed in the econometric literature (for example, Clements and Hendry, 1998) and are covered by Newbold and Harvey in chapter 12 of this volume. Two important topics – asymptotic inference for predictive ability and reality checks for data snooping – are also discussed. The latter is treated at length by McCracken and West in chapter 14 of this volume.

Our order of presentation of model-free tests of forecast accuracy follows the historical development of the literature – starting with tests developed under squared-error loss and zero-mean, serially uncorrelated forecast errors and proceeding to more recent tests that are asymptotically valid under more general conditions, allowing loss functions other than the quadratic, and covering situations when forecast errors are non-Gaussian, nonzero-mean, serially correlated, and contemporaneously correlated.

13.2.1. The Morgan–Granger–Newbold (MGN) test

For our discussion, assume that the available information consists of the following:

- actual values $\{y_t : t = 1, 2, 3, \ldots, T\}$
- two forecasts: $\{\hat{y}_{t1} : t = 1, 2, 3, \ldots, T\}$ and $\{\hat{y}_{t2} : t = 1, 2, 3, \ldots, T\}$

Define the forecast errors as

$$e_{it} = \hat{y}_{it} - y_t, \quad \text{for } i = 1, 2.$$

The loss associated with forecast i is assumed to be a function of the actual and forecast values only through the forecast error, e_{it}, and is denoted by

$$g(y_t, \hat{y}_{it}) = g(\hat{y}_{it} - y_t) = g(e_{it}).$$

Typically, $g(e_{it})$ is the square (squared-error loss) or the absolute value (absolute error loss) of e_{it}. Other measures that introduce alternative functional dependence or asymmetry in the loss function or express loss in terms of economic costs are discussed in, for example, Clements and Hendry (1993), Pesaran and Timmermann (1994), Christoffersen and Diebold (1996), Granger and Pesaran (1999), and Stock and Watson (1999). See also chapter 11 by Pesaran and Skouras in this volume.

We denote the loss differential between the two forecasts by

$$d_t = g(e_{1t}) - g(e_{2t})$$

and say that the two forecasts have equal accuracy if and only if the loss differential has zero expectation for all t.

So, we would like to test the null hypothesis

$$H_0 : E(d_t) = 0 \text{ for all } t$$

versus the alternative hypothesis

$$H_1 : E(d_t) = \mu \neq 0.$$

For our first test, consider the following assumptions:

A1. Loss is quadratic.
A2. The forecast errors are (a) zero mean, (b) Gaussian, (c) serially uncorrelated, or (d) contemporaneously uncorrelated.

Maintaining assumptions A1 and A2(a)–A2(c), Granger and Newbold (1986) develop a test for equal forecast accuracy based on the following orthogonalization (see Morgan, 1939–40):

$$x_t = e_{1t} + e_{2t},$$
$$z_t = e_{1t} - e_{2t}.$$

In this case, the null hypothesis of zero mean loss differential is equivalent to equality of the two forecast error variances or, equivalently, zero covariance between x_t and z_t, since it follows directly from the definition of x_t and z_t that

$$\operatorname{cov}(x_t, z_t) = E(e_{1t}^2 - e_{2t}^2).$$

Hence the test statistic is

$$\mathrm{MGN} = r/[(1 - r^2)/(T - 1)]^{1/2},$$

where

$$r = x'z/[(x'x)(z'z)]^{1/2}$$

and x and z are the $T \times 1$ vectors with tth elements x_t and z_t, respectively. Under the null hypothesis of a zero covariance between x_t and z_t, MGN has a t-distribution with $T - 1$ degrees of freedom.

Note that this test is based on the maintained assumption that forecast errors are white noise – hence, the test is applicable only to one-step predictions. Also, the test is valid as a test of equality of forecast accuracy only under squared error loss.

13.2.2.   Variations of the MGN test

Harvey, Leybourne, and Newbold (HLN, 1997) set up the MGN test in a regression framework,

$$x_t = \beta z_t + \varepsilon_t,$$

and note that the MGN test statistic is exactly the same as that for testing the null hypothesis that $\beta = 0$ in the above regression. Specifically,

$$\text{MGN} = b/(s^2/z'z)^{1/2},$$

where

$$b = x'z/z'z,$$

$$s^2 = (x - bz)'(x - bz)/(T - 1).$$

Thus, the test would work – and in fact, be uniformly most powerful unbiased – in the ideal situation where assumptions A1 and A2(a)–A2(c) all hold.

When the forecast errors come from a heavy-tailed distribution, however, HLN argue that the estimate of the variance of b, which appears in the denominator of MGN, is biased, and recommend the following modification of MGN:

$$\text{MGN}^* = b/[(\textstyle\sum z_t^2 \hat{\varepsilon}_t^2)/(\textstyle\sum z_t^2)^2]^{1/2},$$

where $\hat{\varepsilon}_t$ is the calculated OLS residual at time t. In this modification, a White-correction for heteroskedasticity is utilized to estimate the variance of b. Thus, in fact, the modification is a correction for heteroskedasticity, not fat tails, in the distribution of the forecast errors. HLN further suggest comparing MGN* with critical values of the t-distribution with $T - 1$ degrees of freedom.

The simulation study in HLN verifies that the original MGN test has empirical sizes that are equal to nominal sizes when forecast errors are drawn from a Gaussian distribution. However, when the forecast error generating process is t_6 (t-distribution with six degrees of freedom), the MGN test becomes seriously oversized – with the deficiency getting worse as sample size increases.

For the modified MGN test, the simulation results are mixed. As theory suggests, the modified test registered the correct size when the sample size was large. However, oversizing shows up when samples are small, both when the forecast error distribution is Gaussian or t_6. In fact, in the latter case (with small samples), the modified test performed worse than the original MGN test.

These simulation results led HLN to consider yet another variation of the MGN test – a nonparametric approach using Spearman's rank test for correlation between x and z. Strictly speaking, just like the MGN and MGN* tests, this variation would be valid for testing one-period forecasts in situations where forecast errors are white noise.

The real drawback of these variations of the MGN test is the limitation of their applicability to one-step predictions and to squared error loss. Also, there are inherent difficulties in extending the procedure to multi-period forecast horizons.

13.2.3. The Meese–Rogoff (MR) test

Meese and Rogoff (1988) developed a test of equal forecast accuracy when the forecast errors are serially and contemporaneously correlated (relaxing assumptions A2(c) and A2(d), but maintaining assumptions A1, A2(a), and A2(b)). They assume squared error loss and base their test directly on the sample covariance between x_t and z_t.

Given the maintained assumptions, the following result holds under the hypothesis of equal forecast accuracy:

$$T^{1/2}\hat{\gamma}_{xz}(0) \to N(0, \Omega) \text{ in distribution,}$$

where

$$\hat{\gamma}_{xz}(0) = x'z/T,$$

$$\Omega = \sum_{k=-\infty}^{\infty} [\gamma_{xx}(k)\gamma_{zz}(k) + \gamma_{xz}(k)\gamma_{zx}(k)],$$

$$\gamma_{xz}(k) = \text{cov}(x_t, z_{t-k}), \ \gamma_{zx}(k) = \text{cov}(z_t, x_{t-k}),$$

$$\gamma_{xx}(k) = \text{cov}(x_t, x_{t-k}), \quad \text{and} \quad \gamma_{zz}(k) = \text{cov}(z_t, z_{t-k}).$$

The own- and cross-autocovariances can be estimated consistently by their sample counterparts, and a consistent estimate of Ω is

$$\hat{\Omega} = \sum_{k=-m(T)}^{m(T)} (1 - |k|/T)[\hat{\gamma}_{xx}(k)\hat{\gamma}_{zz}(k) + \hat{\gamma}_{xz}(k)\hat{\gamma}_{zx}(k)].$$

The truncation lag $m(T)$ increases with sample size T but at a slower rate. The statistic for the Meese–Rogoff test is then

$$\text{MR} = \hat{\gamma}_{xz}(0)/(\hat{\Omega}/T)^{1/2}.$$

13.2.4. The Diebold–Mariano (DM) test

Diebold and Mariano (DM, 1995) consider model-free tests of forecast accuracy that are directly applicable to nonquadratic loss functions, multi-period forecasts, and forecast errors that are non-Gaussian, nonzero-mean, serially correlated, and contemporaneously correlated. The basis of the test is the sample mean of the observed loss differential series $\{d_t : t = 1, 2, 3, \ldots, T\}$, when assumptions A1 and A2(a)–(d) need not hold. Assuming covariance stationarity and other regularity conditions on the process $\{d_t\}$, DM use the standard result that

$$T^{1/2}(\bar{d} - \mu) \rightarrow N(0, 2\pi f_d(0)), \text{ in distribution,}$$

where $f_d(\bullet)$ is the spectral density of $\{d_t\}$ and $\bar{d}$ is the sample mean differential:

$$f_d(\lambda) = (1/2\pi) \sum_{k=-\infty}^{\infty} \gamma_d(k) \exp(-ik\lambda), \quad -\pi \leq \lambda \leq \pi,$$

$$\bar{d} = \sum_{t=1}^{T} [g(e_{1t}) - g(e_{2t})]/T,$$

and $\gamma_d(k)$ is the autocovariance of d_t at displacement k:

$$\gamma_d(k) = E[(d_t - \mu)(d_{t-k} - \mu)].$$

The Diebold–Mariano test statistic is

$$DM = \bar{d}/[2\pi \hat{f}_d(0)/T]^{1/2},$$

where $\hat{f}_d(0)$ is a consistent estimate of $f_d(0)$. The null hypothesis that $E(d_t) = 0$ for all t is rejected in favor of the alternative hypothesis that $E(d_t) \neq 0$ when DM, in absolute value, exceeds the critical value of a standard unit Gaussian distribution.

Consistent estimators of $f_d(0)$ can be of the form

$$\hat{f}_d(0) = (1/2\pi) \sum_{k=-m(T)}^{m(t)} w(k/m(T)) \hat{\gamma}_d(k),$$

where

$$\hat{\gamma}_d(k) = (1/T) \sum_{t=|k|+1}^{T} (d_t - \bar{d})(d_{t-|k|} - \bar{d}).$$

$m(T)$, the bandwidth or lag truncation, increases with T but at a slower rate, and $w(\bullet)$ is the weighting scheme or kernel (see, for example, Andrews (1991) for econometric applications). One weighting scheme, called the truncated rectangular kernel and used in Diebold and Mariano (1995), is the indicator function that takes the value of unity when the argument has an absolute value less than one:

$$w(x) = I(|x| < 1).$$

The Monte Carlo analysis in DM provides some insight into the finite-sample behavior of the DM test statistic, relative to MGN and MR. The experimental design covers a variety of contemporaneous and serial correlation in the forecast errors. In addition to Gaussian distributions for forecast errors, the t-distribution with six degrees of freedom was also used to represent fat tails in the distribution of forecast errors. For comparison purposes, only quadratic loss is considered in the analysis.

In the case of Gaussian forecast errors, the main results are as follows.

MGN is robust to contemporaneous correlation and it remains correctly sized as long as there is no serial correlation in the forecast errors. With serial correlation present, the empirical size of MGN exceeds nominal size.

MR is unaffected by contemporaneous and serial correlation in large samples, as expected. In the presence of serial correlation, it tends to be oversized in small samples. Asymptotic behavior sets in rather quickly; the test shows approximately the correct size for sample sizes exceeding 64.

The behavior of DM is similar to that of MR: robust to contemporaneous and serial correlation in large samples and oversized in small samples. Empirical size converges to nominal size a bit more slowly than for MR.

When forecast errors are non-Gaussian, MGN and MR are drastically mis-sized in large as well as small samples. DM, on the other hand, maintains approximately correct size for all but very small sample sizes.

13.2.5.   Small-sample modifications to the Diebold–Mariano test

Harvey, Leybourne, and Newbold (HLN, 1997) propose a small-sample modification of the Diebold–Mariano test. The modification revolves around an approximately unbiased estimate of the variance of the mean loss differential when forecast accuracy is measured in terms of mean squared prediction error and h-step-ahead forecast errors are assumed to have zero autocorrelations at order h and beyond.

Since optimal h-step-ahead predictions are likely to have forecast errors that are MA(h − 1) – a moving average process of order h − 1, HLN assume that for h-step-ahead forecasts, the loss differential d_t has autocovariance

$$\gamma(k) = 0, \quad \text{for } k \geq h.$$

In this case, for $0 \leq k \leq h$,

$$\hat{\gamma}(k) = (1/T) \sum_{t=k+1}^{T} (d_t - \bar{d})(d_{t-k} - \bar{d}).$$

The exact variance of the mean loss differential is

$$V(\bar{d}) = (1/T)[\gamma_0 + (2/T) \sum_{k=1}^{h-1} (T - k)\gamma_k].$$

The original DM test would estimate this variance by

$$\hat{V}(\bar{d}) = (1/T)[\hat{\gamma}*(0) + (2/T)\sum_{k=1}^{h-1}(T-k)\hat{\gamma}*(k)],$$

$$\hat{\gamma}*(k) = T\hat{\gamma}(k)/(T-k).$$

With d based on squared prediction error, HLN obtain the following approximation to the expected value of $\hat{V}(\bar{d})$:

$$E(\hat{V}(\bar{d})) \sim V(\bar{d})[T + 1 - 2h + h(h-1)/T]/T,$$

and therefore suggest modifying the DM test statistic to

$$DM* = DM/[[T + 1 - 2h + h(h-1)/T]/T]^{1/2}.$$

Further, HLN suggest comparing $DM*$ with critical values from the t-distribution with $(T-1)$ degrees of freedom, instead of the standard unit normal distribution.

HLN perform a Monte Carlo experiment of these tests. Their simulation study allows for forecast horizons up to 10 periods and uses expected squared prediction error as the criterion of forecast quality. Their main findings are as follows:

1   The tendency of the original DM test to be oversized becomes more severe as the forecast horizon grows, especially in smaller samples. Table 1 in HLN illustrates this problem for samples as small as 16 observations when dealing with one-step-ahead forecasts and for samples with up to 128 observations for four-step-ahead forecasts.
2   In all cases, the modified test performs considerably better, although it also tends to be oversized, but not as much. Thus, the finite-sample modification suggested by HLN for the DM test provides an important (although not complete) size correction.
3   These findings also apply when forecast errors are contemporaneously correlated, serially correlated, or generated by heavy-tailed distribution (in the study, the t-distribution with six degrees of freedom was used).
4   HLN also provide simulation results on power comparisons – restricting the scope to one-step predictions and quadratic loss and two forecast error distributions – Gaussian and t_6. Under Gaussian error distributions, the original MGN test is considerably more powerful than the modified DM test when the sample is small (up to $T = 32$). For larger sample sizes, the original MGN and modified DM tests show just about equal power while the modified MGN rank test is somewhat inferior. Under a t_6 error distribution, the rank test is more powerful than the modified DM test for all sample sizes and all levels of contemporaneous correlation between forecast errors.

13.2.6.   Nonparametric tests

We summarize three nonparametric tests that have been proposed in the literature. The first is the standard sign test which is based on the assumption that the loss differential series is independent and identically distributed, and tests the null hypothesis that the median of the loss-differential distribution is equal to zero. Under this null hypothesis, the number, N, of positive loss-differentials in a sample of size T has a binomial distribution with the number of trials equal to T and success probability equal to $1/2$. The test statistic in this case is

$$\text{SIGN} = (N - 0.5T)/(0.5T^{1/2}),$$

which is asymptotically $N(0, 1)$ as sample size increases.

Wilcoxon's signed rank test also has been used. This test considers the sum of the ranks of the absolute values of positive forecast loss differentials (d_t):

$$\text{SR} = \sum I(d_t > 0) \text{ rank } (|d_t|),$$

where $I(d_t > 0)$ is the indicator function, taking the value one when $d_t > 0$.

For loss-differentials that are independent, identically distributed with a symmetric distribution around zero, the exact critical values of SR are tabulated in standard texts on nonparametric methods. Under the null hypothesis, it is also known that, as T goes to infinity,

$$[SR - T(T + 1)/4]/[T(T + 1)2T + 1)/24]^{1/2} \to N(0, 1), \text{ in distribution.}$$

Pesaran and Timmermann (1992) focus on the sign of the predictand y_t, and a nonparametric test is developed based on the number of correct predicted signs in the forecast series of size T. The maintained assumptions are that the distributions of the predictand and predictor are continuous, independent, and invariant over time.

Let

p = sample proportion of times that the sign of y_t is correctly predicted,

$\pi_1 = \text{Pr}(y_t > 0)$,

$\pi_2 = \text{Pr}(\hat{y}_t > 0)$,

p_1 = sample proportion of times that actual y is positive,

p_2 = sample proportion of times that forecast y is positive.

Under the null hypothesis that $\hat{y}_t$ and y_t are independently distributed of each other (so that the forecast values have no ability to predict the sign of y_t), then the number of correct sign predictions in the sample has a binomial distribution with T trials and success probability equal to

$$\pi_* = \pi_1\pi_2 + (1 - \pi_1)(1 - \pi_2).$$

If π_1 and π_2 are known (for example, if the distributions are symmetric around zero), the test statistic is simply

$$\text{PTK} = (p - \pi_*)/[\pi_*(1 - \pi_*)/T]^{1/2}.$$

When π_1 and π_2 are not known, they can be estimated by the sample proportions p_1 and p_2, so that π_* can be estimated by

$$p_* = p_1p_2 + (1 - p_1)(1 - p_2).$$

The test statistic in this case, which Pesaran and Timmermann show to converge in distribution to $N(0, 1)$ under the null hypothesis, is

$$\text{PTNK} = (p - p_*)[\widehat{\text{var}}\,(p) - \widehat{\text{var}}\,(p_*)]^{1/2},$$

where

$$\widehat{\text{var}}\,(p) = p_*(1 - p_*)/T,$$

$$\widehat{\text{var}}\,(p_*) = (2p_1 - 1)^2 p_2(1 - p_2)/T + (2p_2 - 1)^2 p_1(1 - p_1)/T + 4p_1p_2(1 - p_1)(1 - p_2)/T^2.$$

Pesaran and Timmermann generalize this test to situations where there are two or more meaningful categories for the actual and forecast values of the predictand. They also remark that, in the case of two categories, the square of PTNK is asymptotically equal to the chi-squared statistic in the standard goodness-of-fit test using the 2×2 contingency table categorizing actual and forecast values by sign. The authors apply their methodology to analyze reported price changes in the Industrial Trends Survey of the Confederation of British Industries (CBI) and demand data from business surveys of the French manufacturing industry conducted by the Institut de la Statistique et des Etudes Economiques (INSEE).

13.2.7. West's asymptotic inference on predictive ability

While the Diebold–Mariano test applies to forecasts from models whose parameters have been estimated, forecast uncertainty due to parameter estimation is not taken into account explicitly. West (1996) provides the formal asymptotic theory for inference about moments of smooth functions of out-of-sample predictions and prediction errors – thus establishing a framework for testing predictive ability of models. See chapter 14 in this volume by McCracken and West for a review. The machinery allows for nonnested and nonlinear models and dependence of predictions on estimated regression parameters. The analysis is carried out in environments where there is a long time series of predictions that have been made from a sequence of base periods. Furthermore, if predictions are based on regression estimates, it is also assumed that these regression estimates come from a long time series. In West and McCracken (1998), the framework is utilized to develop regression-based tests of hypotheses about out-of-sample prediction errors, when predictions depend on estimated parameters. The hypotheses tested include (1) zero-mean prediction error and (2) zero correlation between a prediction error and a vector of predictors.

13.2.8.   White's Reality Check p-value

When using a data set repeatedly for purposes of inference – say, for evaluating the predictive ability of a large number of alternative models – there is a possibility of getting apparently satisfactory results simply by chance. Such data-snooping bias has been recognized, especially in empirical finance. White (2000) builds on Diebold and Mariano (1995) and West (1996) and develops what he calls his Reality Check Bootstrap methodology for purposes of testing "whether a given model has predictive superiority over a benchmark model after accounting for the effects of data-snooping."

We proceed with a broad outline of the method and refer the reader to White (2000) and Sullivan, Timmermann, and White (1999) for technical details. If f_j measures performance (not loss) of the jth forecasting model relative to the benchmark, the methodology tests the null hypothesis that the maximum of $E(f_j)$, over all models under study, is less than or equal to zero. Correction for data-snooping is achieved by extending the maximization of $E(f_j)$ over all relevant forecasting models. Rejection of the null hypothesis supports the proposition that the best model has superior performance relative to the benchmark.

Suppose there are L models under study and T sample observations on the performance measures f_{jt} ($j = 1, 2, 3, \ldots, L$; $t = 1, 2, 3, \ldots, T$). White's test statistic is

$$\max_j T^{1/2}\bar{f}_j,$$

where

$$\bar{f}' = \Sigma f_t'/T = (\bar{f}_1, \bar{f}_2, \bar{f}_3, \ldots, \bar{f}_L), \text{ and } f_t' = (f_{1t}, f_{2t}, f_{3t}, \ldots, f_{Lt}).$$

Under appropriate assumptions – for example, in West (1996) and White (2000) – for some positive definite Ω,

$$T^{1/2}(\bar{f} - E(f_t)) \to N(0, \Omega).$$

White (2000) shows further that his test statistic converges in distribution to the maximum element of a random vector with distribution $N(0, \Omega)$. The distribution of this maximum is not known for the general case. Thus, White uses resampling techniques to determine asymptotic p-values of his test.

White points out that a Monte Carlo p-value can be obtained. One first computes a consistent estimate $\hat{\Omega}$ through block resampling or block subsampling. The next step requires repeated draws from $N(0, \hat{\Omega})$, followed by calculation of the *p*-value from the pseudo-sampling distribution of the maximum component of the $N(0, \hat{\Omega})$ draws.

For his analysis, White suggests using a bootstrap reality check *p*-value. The approach resamples from the empirical distribution of f_t using the "stationary bootstrap" procedure of Politis and Romano (PR, 1994). Earlier development in the bootstrap literature has led to the moving blocks method (Kuensch, 1989; Liu and Singh, 1992) for resampling from a stationary dependent process. This technique constructs a resample from blocks of observations with fixed length and random starting indices. PR modify this technique by introducing randomness in the length of the moving blocks. The lengths are assumed to follow a geometric distribution with mean value that increases with sample size. PR call their method "stationary bootstrap" because of the fact that their resampled time series is stationary (conditional on the original data). PR also show that their method produces valid bootstrap approximations for means of α-mixing processes. The procedure also avoids certain biases associated with fixed lengths in the moving blocks bootstrap.

Corradi, Swanson, and Olivetti (1999) study the extension of the results in Diebold and Mariano (1995), West (1996), and White (2000) to the case of cointegrated variables. In dealing with predictive tests of an econometric model, Kitamura (1999) studies the use of nonparametric bootstrap smoothing as a device for explicitly incorporating parameter estimation uncertainty in a forward validation of the estimated model.

13.3. APPLICATIONS

There is a myriad of empirical papers dealing with forecast evaluation. Here, we briefly review four recent ones that apply the testing methodologies that we have discussed.

In studying the predictability of nominal exchange rates, Mark (1995) estimates regressions of multi-period changes in the log exchange rate on the deviation of the log exchange rate from its "fundamental value." For operational purposes, the fundamental value is defined as a linear combination of log relative money stocks and log relative income. Four currencies are analyzed: the Canadian dollar, the German deutschemark, the Swiss franc, and the Japanese yen. The Diebold–Mariano test is used to compare the predictive ability of the estimated regressions with a driftless random walk and leads to the general conclusion that out-of-sample point forecasts of the regressions based on fundamentals outperform forecasts from the random walk model at longer horizons. "While short-horizon changes (in log exchange rate) tend to be dominated by noise, this noise is apparently averaged out over time, thus revealing systematic exchange-rate movements (over longer horizons) that are determined by economic fundamentals. These findings are noteworthy because it has long been thought that log exchange rates are unpredictable."

Kaufman and Stern (1999) analyze the effects of model specification, data aggregation, and data quality on the predictive ability of an equilibrium-correction time-series model for global temperature as explained by radiative forcing of greenhouse gases, anthropogenic sulfur emissions and solar irradiance. An important variable in the model is what the authors call the "global temperature reconstruction," which appears in both the cointegration relationship and the short-run dynamics of the model. Alternative estimated versions of the model (and hence, also temperature forecasts) result from alternative measures of this variable. Two measures were used in their paper – one based on a diffusion energy balance model (EBM) and the other on an atmosphere ocean general circulation model (GCM) of the climate. Utilizing absolute prediction error loss, the authors implement the Diebold–Mariano test and find that the predictive accuracy of the EBM construction is statistically superior to that of GCM.

Swanson and White (SW, 1997a,b) study the usefulness of a variety of flexible-specification, fixed-specification, linear, and nonlinear econometric models in predicting future values of nine macroeconomic variables. These variables are the civilian unemployment rate, Aaa corporate bond yield, industrial production index, nominal gross national product, real gross national product, corporate profits after taxes, personal consumption expenditures, change in business inventories, and net exports of goods and services. Using a variety of out-of-sample forecast-based model selection criteria and tests (including Granger–Newbold, Diebold–Mariano, the Wilcoxon signed rank test, and a contingency test based on forecast direction accuracy or confusion rate), the authors find in SW (1997a) that "multivariate adaptive linear vector autoregression models often outperform adaptive and nonadaptive univariate models, nonadaptive multivariate models, adaptive nonlinear models, and professionally available survey predictions." In SW (1997b), the authors point out that flexible artificial neural networks (ANN) appear to offer a viable alternative to fixed specification linear models (such as random walk, random walk with drift, and unrestricted vector autoregressive models), especially for forecast horizons greater than one period ahead. However, there is mixed evidence on the performance of the flexible ANN models used in the study – perhaps pointing to the need for extending the analysis to include more elaborate ANN models. The study also tends to support the notion that alternative cost functions (for example, those based on market timing and profitability instead of prediction error) can lead to conflicting ranking of the forecasting ability of the models.

Sullivan, Timmermann, and White (STW, 1999) apply the Reality Check bootstrap methodology of White (2000) for significance testing of the predictive superiority of technical trading rules in the stockmarket after accounting for data-snooping over the universe from which the trading rules were drawn. Revisiting Brock, Lakonishok, and LeBaron (BLL, 1992), STW expands the universe from the 26 trading rules considered by BLL to almost 8,000 trading rules. These were drawn from previous academic studies and the literature on technical analysis, and were in use in a substantial part of the sample period. Two performance measures relative to a benchmark were used: market returns and a Sharpe ratio relative to a risk-free rate. STW report the following major findings.

Over the sample period covered by BLL (1897–1986), the best technical trading rule generates superior performance even after accounting for data-snooping.

However, the best technical trading rule does not deliver superior performance when used to trade in the subsequent ten-year post-sample period. When applied to Standard and Poor's 500 futures contracts, the analysis taking into account data-snooping provides no evidence of superior performance of the best trading rule.

13.4. CONCLUSION

This chapter has reviewed the development of significance tests of forecast accuracy. Developments in the decade of the 1990s have yielded model-free testing procedures that are applicable in a wide variety of cases – where performance measures are nonquadratic and asymmetric, where forecast errors are serially correlated and contemporaneously correlated (when multivariate in nature), and where underlying distributions need not be Gaussian.

So now, there are no more excuses for settling for simply descriptive statistics when assessing the predictive ability of forecasting procedures. There are statistical tests of significance that can be used. And, as our selective examples illustrate, they have been used effectively in substantive empirical applications in economics, business and other disciplines. But there remains a wide research frontier in this area, as more complications are taken into account in the testing environment for forecast accuracy – for example, parameter estimation in West's tests of predictive ability, nonstandard test statistics in White's treatment of data-snooping, and nonstationarity.

References

Andrews, D.W.K. (1991). Heteroskedasticity and autocorrelation consistent covariance matrix estimators. *Econometrica*, 59, 817–58.

Brock, W., J. Lakonishok, and B. LeBaron (1992). Simple technical trading rules and the stochastic properties of stock returns. *Journal of Finance*, 47, 1731–64.

Chong, Y. and D. Hendry (1986). Econometric evaluation of linear macro-economic models. *Review of Economic Studies*, 53, 671–90.

Christoffersen, P.F. and F.X. Diebold (1996). Further results on forecasting and model selection under asymmetric loss. *Journal of Applied Econometrics*, 11, 561–71.

Clements, M.P. and D.F. Hendry (1993). On the limitations of comparing mean square forecast errors (with discussion). *Journal of Forecasting*, 12, 617–76.

Clements, M.P. and D.F. Hendry (1998). *Forecasting Economic Time Series*. Cambridge: Cambridge University Press.

Corradi, V., N. Swanson, and C. Olivetti (1999). Predictive ability with cointegrated variables. Working paper, Department of Economics, Texas A&M University.

Diebold, F.X. and R.S. Mariano (1995). Comparing predictive accuracy. *Journal of Business and Economic Statistics*, 13, 253–63.

Engle, R.F. and H. White (1999). *Cointegration, Causality, and Forecasting*. Oxford: Oxford University Press.

Granger, C.W.J. and M.H. Pesaran (1999). Economic and statistical measures of forecast accuracy. DAE Working Paper # 9910. Cambridge: University of Cambridge.

Harvey, D., S. Leybourne, and P. Newbold (1997). Testing the equality of prediction mean squared errors. *International Journal of Forecasting*, 13, 281–91.

Kaufman, R.K. and D.I. Stern (1999). The effect of specification, aggregation, and data quality on climate model temperature simulations. Working paper, Center for Energy and Environmental Studies, Boston University.

Kitamura, Y. (1999). Predictive inference and the bootstrap. Discussion paper, Department of Economics, University of Wisconsin.

Klein, L.R. (ed.) (1991). *Comparative Performance of U.S. Econometric Models*. Oxford: Oxford University Press.

Kuensch, H.R. (1989). The jackknife and bootstrap for general stationary observations. *Annals of Statistics*, 17, 1217–41.

Liu, R.Y. and K. Singh (1992). Moving blocks jackknife and bootstrap capture weak dependence. In R. Lepage and L. Billiard (eds.), *Exploring the Limits of Bootstrap*. Chichester: John Wiley, 225–48.

Mariano, R.S. and B.W. Brown (1983). Prediction-based tests for misspecification in nonlinear simultaneous systems. In S. Karlin, T. Amemiya, and L. Goodman (eds.), *Studies in Econometrics, Time series, and Multivariate Statistics*. London: Academic Press, 131–51.

Mariano, R.S. and B.W. Brown (1991). Stochastic simulation tests of nonlinear econometric models. In Klein (1991), 250–9.

Mark, N.C. (1995). Exchange rates and fundamentals: evidence on long-horizon predictability. *American Economic Review*, 85, 201–18.

Morgan, W.A. (1939–40). A test for significance of the difference between the two variances in a sample from a normal bivariate population. *Biometrika*, 31, 13–19.

Newbold, P., D.I. Harvey, and S.J. Leybourne (1999). Ranking competing multi-step forecasts. In Engle and White, 91–101.

Pagan, A. (1989). On the role of simulation in the statistical evaluation of econometric models. *Journal of Econometrics*, 40, 125–40.

Pesaran, M.H. and A. Timmermann (1992). A simple nonparametric test of predictive performance. *Journal of Business and Economic Statistics*, 10, 461–5.

Pesaran, M.H. and A. Timmermann (1994). Forecasting stock returns: an examination of stock market trading in the presence of transaction costs. *Journal of Forecasting*, 13, 330–65.

Pesaran, M.H. and M.R. Wickens (eds.) (1995). *Handbook of Applied Econometrics, Vol. I: Macroeconomics*. Oxford: Blackwell.

Politis, D. and J. Romano (1994). The stationary bootstrap. *Journal of the American Statistical Association*, 89, 1303–13.

Stock, J.H. and M.W. Watson (1999). A comparison of linear and nonlinear univariate models for forecasting macroeconomic time series. In Engle and White, 1–44.

Sullivan, R., A. Timmermann, and H. White (1999). Data-snooping, technical trading rule performance, and the bootstrap. *Journal of Finance*, 54, 1647–91.

Swanson, N. and H. White (1997). Forecasting economic time series using flexible versus fixed specification and linear versus nonlinear econometric models. *International Journal of Forecasting*, 13, 439–61.

Swanson, N. and H. White (1997). A model selection approach to real-time macroeconomic forecasting using linear models and artificial neural networks. *The Review of Economics and Statistics*, 79, 540–50.

Wallis, K.F. (1995). Large-scale macroeconometric modeling. In Pesaran and Wickens (1995), 312–55.

West, K.D. (1996). Asymptotic inference about predictive ability. *Econometrica*, 64, 1067–84.

West, K.D. and M.W. McCracken (1998). Regression-based tests of predictive ability. *International Economic Review*, 39, 817–40.

White, H. (2000). A reality check for data snooping. *Econometrica*, 68, 1097–1126.

CHAPTER FOURTEEN

Inference About Predictive Ability

Michael W. McCracken and Kenneth D. West

14.1. INTRODUCTION

Traditionally, statistical evaluation of an econometric model focuses on "in-sample" analysis of the residuals from a fitted model. This methodology has powerful theoretical and practical justification. However, it is not always particularly natural or effective. A number of studies (see references below) find that models that seem to fit well by conventional in-sample criteria do poorly at out-of-sample prediction. This has led observers such as Klein (1992) to argue that the "ability to make useful ex-ante forecasts is the *real* test of a model."

In this chapter we provide a brief review of how out-of-sample methods can be used to construct tests that evaluate a time-series model's ability to predict. Although we touch on a wide range of issues, we focus on the role that parameter estimation plays in constructing asymptotically valid tests of predictive ability. We explain why forecasts and forecast errors that depend upon estimated parameters do not necessarily have the statistical properties of their population counterparts: asymptotic inference sometimes requires explicitly accounting for uncertainty about the population values of such parameters. Although this is well known when using fitted values and residuals (for example, Durbin, 1970; Pagan and Hall, 1983), it is commonly ignored when using out-of-sample methods.

We survey a literature that evaluates forecasts and forecast errors generated over an "out-of-sample" period. The forecasts may be truly *ex ante*, generated before the data on the predictand are available. More commonly, the investigator sets the out-of-sample period aside, specifically to allow model evaluation. Dawid (1984), who refers to it as the "prequential" approach to testing, has paid considerable attention to this method.

Because the sample is split into in-sample and out-of-sample portions, this method of evaluating a model is somewhat different from that commonly taught in econometric textbooks, in both minor and major ways. An example of a technical difference is that in many applications parameters are updated as more data becomes available throughout the out-of-sample period; if so, each new forecast is constructed using a potentially different estimate of the population level parameter vector. More generally, since forecasts of (say) y_{t+1} may lie off of the time t empirical support, we expect the predictions to be less prone to biases induced by parameter estimation and, more generally, to overfitting and pre-test biases.

The remainder of the chapter proceeds as follows. Section 14.2 provides a review of the literature in which out-of-sample methods have been used to test for predictive ability. Section 14.3 consists of four subsections. The first is an analytic example illustrating why error in estimation of regression parameters used to make forecasts affects the asymptotic distribution of test statistics. The second and third subsections present general discussions of the asymptotic effects of such error, and of how to feasibly account for such error in construction of test statistics. The final subsection reviews Monte Carlo evidence on the importance of such accounting. Section 14.4 concludes and provides directions for future research.

One bit of terminology: because we need to refer frequently to error induced by estimation of regression parameters used to make forecasts, we denote such error as "parameter estimation error" or "parameter uncertainty." Similarly, "parameter estimation" is used as shorthand for "estimation of regression parameters used to make forecasts," an abuse of terminology in that the out-of-sample object of interest (say, mean squared forecast error) is also a parameter that is estimated.

14.2. Literature Review

While use of out-of-sample forecasts for model evaluation is less common than use of in-sample evidence, forecast evaluation has a long and distinguished history in economics. Early references include Christ (1956) and Goldberger (1959), each of which evaluates the predictive ability of the Klein–Goldberger model of the U.S. economy. Here we review more recent papers, citing both methodological contributions and recent representative applied papers.

There are many measures of forecast quality, but most tests that are used in practice can be grouped into one of five categories: *equal forecast accuracy* between two (or more) predictive models, forecast *encompassing*, forecast *efficiency*, zero forecast *bias*, and *sign predictability*. We discuss each in turn while referencing relevant methodological and applied work. Throughout, we assume that the forecasting model is parametric and, for expositional ease, that the (scalar) predictand is y_{t+1}. The parameter estimate $\hat{\beta}_t$ is a function of observables known at time t. Let the forecast be based upon a function $\hat{y}_{t+1}(\beta)$ such that the time $t = R, \ldots, T - 1$ forecast of y_{t+1} is $\hat{y}_{t+1} \equiv \hat{y}_{t+1}(\hat{\beta}_t)$. If we let P denote the number of one-step-ahead forecast errors $\hat{u}_{t+1} = y_{t+1} - \hat{y}_{t+1}$, then

$$R + P = T + 1. \tag{14.1}$$

When two forecasting models exist, an additional index $i = 1, 2$ will be used to distinguish between the parameter estimates, forecasts, and forecast errors from each of the two models.

A very general test of predictive ability is one that tests for *equal forecast accuracy* across two or more models. To construct a test of this type one needs to select a measure of accuracy. McCulloch and Rossi (1990), Leitch and Tanner (1991), and West, Edison and Cho (1993) compare predictive ability using economic measures of accuracy. It is more common to use statistical measures. In particular, the most common comparison is whether two predictive models have the same mean squared error (MSE).

Granger and Newbold (1977) propose a test for equal MSE that is similar to a test suggested by Morgan (1939). They note that if the sequence of forecast errors form a random sample from a bivariate normal population then the sample correlation coefficient, associated with $(\hat{u}_{1,t+1} + \hat{u}_{2,t+1})$ and $(\hat{u}_{1,t+1} - \hat{u}_{2,t+1})$, can be used to construct a test for equal MSE. This test has been applied by a number of authors, including Granger and Deutsch (1992), who compare the predictive ability of models of the unemployment rate. Ashley, Granger, and Schmalensee (1980), Ashley (1981), Alpert and Guerard (1988), and Bradshaw and Orden (1990) use the statistic to test for causality between two nested models.

Extensions include Brandt and Bessler (1983), who explicitly adjust for the fact that forecast errors may be biased away from zero. A test used by Meese and Rogoff (1988) and Diebold and Rudebusch (1991) allows for serial correlation in the forecast errors. Park (1990), Tegene and Kuchler (1994), and Granger and Swanson (1997) apply a variant of this statistic based upon Fisher's z-test.

A more general test for equal forecast accuracy is that suggested by Diebold and Mariano (1995). They base their test for equal MSE upon the loss differential, $d_{t+1} = \hat{u}_{1,t+1}^2 - \hat{u}_{2,t+1}^2$. Let $\gamma_j = Ed_{t+1}d_{t+1-j}$ and let $\hat{S}_{dd}$ denote a consistent estimate of $S_{dd} = \gamma_0 + 2\sum_{j=1}^{\infty}\gamma_j$, the long-run covariance associated with the covariance stationary sequence d_{t+1}. The authors argue that the statistic $P^{-1/2}\sum_{t=R}^{R+P-1}d_{t+1}/\hat{S}_{dd}^{1/2}$ converges in distribution to a standard normal variable and hence normal tables can be used to test the null of equal forecast accuracy.

This statistic has been frequently used in recent years. Engel (1994), Chinn and Meese (1995), and Blomberg and Hess (1997) test whether regime-shifting models, error correction models, and models of political behavior, respectively, outperform the random walk in the prediction of exchange rates. Mark (1995) and Kilian (1999) use a bootstrapped version of this statistic to compare the predictive ability of long-horizon models of exchange rates to the random walk. Bram and Ludvigson (1998) use a modified version of this test, suggested by Harvey, Leybourne, and Newbold (1997), to determine a causal relationship between consumer confidence and household expenditure.

An advantage of the technique proposed by Diebold and Mariano (1995) is that it can be extended to other measures of loss (say) $L(.)$. To do so we need only define $d_{t+1} = L(\hat{u}_{1,t+1}) - L(\hat{u}_{2,t+1})$ and proceed to construct the test as we did when the loss was quadratic. Based upon this observation, Chen and Swanson (1996) use squared forecast error, absolute forecast error, and absolute percentage forecast error as loss functions to evaluate several parametric and semiparametric forecasting models of U.S. inflation. Swanson and White (1997a,b) use the same three loss functions to evaluate how well parametric and neural net models predict several macroeconomic variables.

The test of forecast *encompassing* is related to the literature on the combination of forecasts introduced by Bates and Granger (1969) (see Diebold, 1989). The idea of forecast combination is that if two (or more) forecasting models are available, then taking a weighted combination of the available forecasts may generate a better forecast. Granger and Ramanathan (1984) suggest doing this using regression-based methods. Suppose that $\hat{y}_{1,t+1}$ and $\hat{y}_{2,t+1}$ are competing forecasts for y_{t+1} and that we already have an observed series of these *ex ante* forecasts. They construct future forecasts using the weights α_0, α_1, and α_2 estimated by the OLS regression

$$y_{t+1} = \alpha_0 + \alpha_1 \hat{y}_{1,t+1} + \alpha_2 \hat{y}_{2,t+1} + \text{error term.} \qquad (14.2)$$

Based upon this regression, Chong and Hendry (1986) observe that under the null that forecasts from model 1 encompass the forecasts from models 2, α_1 and α_2 should be 1 and 0 respectively. If this is the case, then a test for forecast encompassing can be constructed using the t-statistic associated with α_2 in the OLS estimated regression

$$\hat{u}_{1,t+1} = \alpha_0 + \alpha_2 \hat{y}_{2,t+1} + \text{error term.} \qquad (14.3)$$

Under the null that the model 1 forecast encompasses model 2, they argue that the t-statistic should be asymptotically standard normal and hence normal tables can be used to conduct a test of encompassing.

Tests related to that in (14.3) include one suggested by Fair and Shiller (1989, 1990). They construct a regression-based test that is closer to (14.2) than (14.3). Their test for "information content" in m-step-ahead forecasts does not impose the null that one particular model forecast encompasses the other and hence can be considered more general than that in (14.3). Ericsson (1992) constructs a regression-based test that is designed to allow for forecasts generated by models with cointegrating relationships. He notes that if the population level forecast errors are I(0) but the population level forecasts are I(1), then equation (14.3) is "unbalanced." To rectify this possibility he suggests using the t-statistic associated with $(\hat{y}_{2,t+1} - \hat{y}_{1,t+1})$ when it and a constant are regressed on $\hat{u}_{1,t+1}$.

These tests of encompassing have been implemented by a number of authors. Day and Lewis (1992) determine the information content in volatility forecasts. Ericsson and Marquez (1993) test whether certain models of the U.S. trade balance forecast encompass other models. They also argue that by estimating the equation using GLS they can account for the "asymptotically negligible" autocorrelation in the forecast errors due to parameter uncertainty. Oliner, Rudebusch, and Sichel (1995) determine whether "new" models of business investment forecast encompass "old" models. Lo and MacKinlay (1997) test for forecast encompassing in models of asset returns from the stock and bond markets. Amano and van Norden (1995) test whether or not error correction models forecast encompass the random walk model. Andrews, Minford, and Riley (1996) conduct a series of tests of encompassing that includes (14.3). Fair (1999) compares the information content in structural models of exchange rates with the random walk model. Stock and Watson (1999a,b) test for information content in forecasts of inflation and several other macroeconomic variables.

Mincer and Zarnowitz (1969) introduce the test of forecast *efficiency*. The test for forecast efficiency is based upon the observation that if the forecast is constructed using all available information, then the optimal forecast (in the sense of minimum mean square error) and the forecast error should be uncorrelated. If this is the case, then a test of efficiency may be constructed using the t-statistic associated with the estimate of α_1 in the OLS estimated regression

$$\hat{u}_{t+1} = \alpha_0 + \alpha_1 \hat{y}_{t+1} + \text{error term.} \tag{14.4}$$

Authors who have used this test of efficiency include the following. McNees (1978) estimates (14.4) by both OLS and GLS to allow for multi-step forecasts and then applies the method to predictions of the unemployment rate, real GNP, and the GNP deflator. Berger and Krane (1985) evaluate the efficiency of forecasts of real GNP made by D.R.I. and Chase Econometrics. Pagan and Schwert (1990), Day and Lewis (1992), and West and Cho (1995) evaluate the efficiency of volatility forecasts. Stock and Watson (1993) construct a comparable test for the efficiency of forecasts of the probability of recessions. Hatanaka (1974) and Keane and Runkle (1989) have suggested extensions to this type of test.

The test for zero forecast *bias* is sometimes referred to as a test for *zero-mean prediction error*. Mincer and Zarnowitz (1969) introduce this test in the context of tests of efficiency. For example, note that in (14.4) we have included an intercept term in the regression. They note that if the forecasts are unbiased then the intercept term should be zero. Ericsson and Marquez (1993) also give this argument in the context of regression-based tests of encompassing like that in (14.3). Because of this, tests for zero bias are commonly reported along with (and tested jointly with) tests of efficiency and encompassing. Day and Lewis (1992) report the t-statistics associated with the intercept term in both regression-based tests of efficiency as in (14.4) and regression-based tests of encompassing as in (14.3). Berger and Krane (1985) use an F-test to construct a joint test for both efficiency and zero bias. Ericsson and Marquez (1993) do the same but for encompassing and zero bias. It is also possible to take a more direct approach when testing for zero bias. Stock and Watson (1993) and Oliner, Rudebusch, and Sichel (1995) construct a test for zero bias by regressing the forecast error on a constant. They then use the t-statistic associated with the intercept term to test for zero bias.

Perhaps the most well known test of *sign predictability* was developed in a series of papers by Merton (1981) and Henriksson and Merton (1981). These authors are interested in evaluating whether decisions based upon $\hat{y}_{t+1}$ are useful in the absence of knowing the actual value of y_{t+1}. The context that the authors had in mind was one where decisions had to be made to either buy or sell an asset.

For example, let y_{t+1} denote the return on an asset and let $\hat{y}_{t+1}$ denote the forecasted return. If the sign of $\hat{y}_{t+1}$, denoted sgn $(\hat{y}_{t+1})$, is positive then the decision is made to buy shares of the asset. If sgn $(\hat{y}_{t+1})$ is negative then the decision is made to sell shares of the asset. Notice that the actual value of the forecast is not important *per se*, just the sign of the forecast.

In this decision-based forecasting literature, we are interested in whether the sign of $\hat{y}_{t+1}$ is useful as a predictor of the sign of y_{t+1}. If it is not useful then sgn $(\hat{y}_{t+1})$ is independent of sgn (y_{t+1}). To test this null hypothesis, Henriksson and Merton (1981) suggest a test using the t-statistic associated with α_1 in the following OLS estimated regression:

$$1(\hat{y}_{t+1} \geq 0) = \alpha_0 + \alpha_1 1(y_{t+1} \geq 0) + \text{error term}, \tag{14.5}$$

where the function $1(.)$ takes the value one if the argument is true and zero otherwise.

Applications of this test of sign predictability include Breen, Glosten, and Jagannathan (1989), who are concerned with the sign predictability of indices of stock returns. Park (1990) tests for sign predictability of changes in the price of U.S. cattle. Tegene and Kuchler (1994) evaluate the sign predictive ability of changes in farmland prices in the U.S. Midwest. Kuan and Liu (1995), Chen and Swanson (1996), and Swanson and White (1995, 1997a,b) evaluate the sign predictive ability of both parametric and neural net models.

Other sign tests include one suggested by Cumby and Modest (1986), who argue that their test of sign predictability is more powerful than that in (14.5). Pesaran and Timmermann (1992) suggest a test, similar to that in (14.5), that they use in Pesaran and Timmermann (1995). More recently, Pesaran and Timmermann (1994) extend the Henriksson and Merton (1981) test to situations where there are more than two choices available. This is potentially useful since, for example, when making investment decisions one usually has the choice to not only buy or sell an asset but also to hold and not act in the relevant market. Chinn and Meese (1995) use a test of sign predictability that is based upon the binomial distribution.

It is interesting to note that this literature on sign prediction runs parallel to the literature on probability forecasting that is particularly important in meteorology. For example, suppose that a decision is made to take an action based upon the probability forecast, $\hat{p}_{t+1}$, of rain. A farmer has to make a decision as to whether to spread fertilizer onto his fields. If it rains, then the fertilizer may wash away and not have time to penetrate the soil. In this case, the farmer makes the decision to spread the fertilizer only if the probability forecast of rain is (say) less than 20 percent. In this case, the farmer is interested in the sign of $\hat{y}_{t+1} \equiv \hat{p}_{t+1} - 20\%$. The obvious difficulty with evaluating these types of forecasts is that we do not have the luxury of observing the actual probability p_{t+1} unless $p_{t+1} = 1.00$ or $p_{t+1} = 0$. See Brier (1950), as well as the review by Murphy and Daan (1985), for a discussion on the evaluation of probability forecasts in meteorology. See Granger and Pesaran (2000) and Lopez (2001) for discussions relevant to economists.

One common feature of all of the *applied* papers cited above is that the predictions are made using estimated regression models. This is in sharp contrast to all

of the *methodological* papers cited above. None of these explicitly consider possible effects from use of an estimated regression model to construct forecasts.
That is, their arguments make use of conditions that are not obviously applicable
when such models are used.

This difference, between the applied papers and the methodological papers,
raises a question. Do the results of the methodological papers remain valid when
regression models are estimated rather than known? West (1996) and McCracken
(2000) use first-order asymptotics to address this question, assuming parametric
regression models and stationary data. Their results delineate conditions under
which the results of these papers remain valid, and, more generally, present the
appropriate limiting results when forecasts rely on estimated regression parameters. A discussion of these and other theoretical results, along with some
related Monte Carlo evidence, is provided in the next section.

14.3. THEORETICAL AND MONTE CARLO EVIDENCE

This section contains four subsections. The first illustrates how parameter estima-
tion error can affect the asymptotic distribution of out-of-sample test statistics.
The second section presents general asymptotic results, focusing on the results in
West (1996) and McCracken (2000). The third section describes how to feasibly
account for parameter estimation error. The final section summarizes some Monte
Carlo results.

14.3.1. How parameter estimation affects inference: An example

Before presenting the theoretical results, we provide a simple illustrative example
of how parameter estimation error can affect the limiting distribution of out-of-
sample test statistics. Suppose that the forecasting model is a simple univariate
linear regression estimated by OLS. If we let y_t denote the scalar predictand and
x_{t-1} denote the scalar covariate, then we have the regression model

$$y_t = \beta_0^* + x_{t-1}\beta_1^* + u_t = X_{t-1}'\beta^* + u_t, \tag{14.6}$$

where $X_{t-1} = (1, x_{t-1})'$ and $\beta^* = (\beta_0^*, \beta_1^*)'$. For the sake of presentation let u_t be an
i.i.d. zero mean conditionally homoskedastic disturbance term with uncondi-
tional variance σ^2 and let X_{t-1} be covariance stationary. Suppose that the one-
step-ahead predictions are made in the obvious way using $\hat{y}_{t+1} = X_t'\hat{\beta}_t$. Write the
one-step-ahead forecast error as $\hat{u}_{t+1} = y_{t+1} - \hat{y}_{t+1}$. For ease of presentation, assume
that the parameter estimate $\hat{\beta}_t$ is estimated once by OLS using information available
through $s = 1, \ldots, R$. Hence for any $t \geq R$, $\hat{\beta}_t = (R^{-1}\sum_{s=1}^{R}X_{s-1}X_{s-1}')^{-1}(R^{-1}\sum_{s=1}^{R}X_{s-1}y_s)$.

Consider the test for zero-mean prediction error conducted by, for example,
Oliner, Rudebusch, and Sichel (1995). The test for zero-mean prediction error
can be constructed using the t-statistic associated with α from the regression
$\hat{u}_{t+1} = \alpha +$ error term. The t-statistic has the form

$$P^{-1/2}\sum_{t=R}^{R+P-1}\hat{u}_{t+1}/[(P-1)^{-1}\sum_{t=R}^{R+P-1}(\hat{u}_{t+1}-\bar{u})^2]^{1/2}, \tag{14.7}$$

where $\bar{u}$ is the sample average of the forecast errors $\hat{u}_{t+1}$.

To show that a statistic of this type is limiting standard normal usually requires three steps. The first is to show that the numerator of the t-statistic is asymptotically normal with a limiting variance Ω. The second is to show that the denominator converges in probability to $\Omega^{1/2}$. The final step is simply to apply Slutsky's Theorem and conclude that the t-statistic is asymptotically standard normal.

Consider the numerator. By definition,

$$P^{-1/2}\sum_{t=R}^{R+P-1}\hat{u}_{t+1} \tag{14.8}$$

$$= P^{-1/2}\sum_{t=R}^{R+P-1}u_{t+1} + (-P^{-1}\sum_{t=R}^{R+P-1}X_t')(R^{-1}\sum_{s=1}^{R}X_{s-1}X_{s-1}')^{-1}((P/R)^{1/2}R^{-1/2}\sum_{s=1}^{R}X_{s-1}u_s).$$

If we assume, as in Hoffman and Pagan (1989), that

$$P,R \to \infty, \; P/R \to \pi < \infty, \tag{14.9}$$

then it is straightforward to show that, under general conditions,

$$P^{-1/2}\sum_{t=R}^{R+P-1}\hat{u}_{t+1} = (1 -(EX_t')(EX_tX_t')^{-1})\begin{pmatrix} P^{-1/2}\sum_{t=R}^{R+P-1}u_{t+1} \\ \pi^{1/2}R^{-1/2}\sum_{s=1}^{R}X_{s-1}u_s \end{pmatrix} + o_p(1). \tag{14.10}$$

Since the disturbance terms are i.i.d., zero mean, and conditionally homoskedastic, we know that the two components of the column vector in (14.10) are independent and hence

$$\begin{pmatrix} P^{-1/2}\sum_{t=R}^{R+P-1}u_{t+1} \\ \pi^{1/2}R^{-1/2}\sum_{s=1}^{R}X_{s-1}u_s \end{pmatrix} \to_d N\left(0_{3\times1}, \begin{pmatrix} \sigma^2 & 0 \\ 0 & \pi\sigma^2(EX_tX_t') \end{pmatrix}_{3\times3}\right). \tag{14.11}$$

We then know that $P^{-1/2}\sum_{t=R}^{R+P-1}\hat{u}_{t+1} \to_d N(0, \Omega)$, where

$$\Omega = \sigma^2 + \pi\sigma^2(EX_t')(EX_tX_t')^{-1}(EX_t). \tag{14.12}$$

The right-hand side of (14.12) should seem familiar. It is directly comparable to the variance of a one-step-ahead prediction error (Goldberger, 1991, p. 175). It differs because it is the variance of a scaled sample average of one-step-ahead predictions rather than just a single one-step-ahead prediction error.

Now consider the denominator in (14.7). To show that $(P-1)^{-1}\sum_{t=R}^{R+P-1}(\hat{u}_{t+1}-\bar{u})^2 = (P-1)^{-1}\sum_{t=R}^{R+P-1}\hat{u}_{t+1}^2 - P(\bar{u})^2/(P-1)$ converges in probability to σ^2, first notice that equations (14.8)–(14.12) imply that $P(\bar{u})^2/(P-1)$ converges in probability to zero.

We then need only show that $(P-1)^{-1}\sum_{t=R}^{R+P-1}\hat{u}_{t+1}^2$ converges in probability to σ^2. By definition,

$$(P-1)^{-1}\sum_{t=R}^{R+P-1}\hat{u}_{t+1}^2 = (P-1)^{-1}\sum_{t=R}^{R+P-1}u_{t+1}^2 - 2((P-1)^{-1}\sum_{t=R}^{R+P-1}u_{t+1}X_t')(\hat{\beta}_R - \beta^*)$$
$$+ (\hat{\beta}_R - \beta^*)'((P-1)^{-1}\sum_{t=R}^{R+P-1}X_tX_t')(\hat{\beta}_R - \beta^*). \qquad (14.13)$$

Since the first right-hand side term in (14.13) converges in probability to σ^2, the result will follow if the last two right-hand side terms converge in probability to zero. This is evident, since $(P-1)^{-1}\sum_{t=R}^{R+P-1}u_{t+1}X_t' \to_p 0$, $(P-1)^{-1}\sum_{t=R}^{R+P-1}X_tX_t' \to_p EX_tX_t'$, and $\hat{\beta}_R - \beta^* \to_p 0$.

By Slutsky's Theorem we can now conclude that the t-statistic in (14.7) converges in distribution to a normal variable with limiting variance V,

$$V = 1 + \pi(EX_t')(EX_tX_t')^{-1}(EX_t). \qquad (14.14)$$

This limiting distribution is in direct contrast to that when the parameters are known. If the parameters are known, then the t-statistic is asymptotically normal but with a limiting variance $V = 1$. Since parameters are generally not known, and since $\pi(EX_t')(EX_tX_t')^{-1}(EX_t)$ is positive semidefinite, (14.14) will be greater than or equal to 1. When (14.14) is greater than 1, any test that uses standard normal tables, without accounting for the extra term induced by parameter estimation, will reject the null of zero-mean prediction error too often and may lead to a less powerful test of the null.

14.3.2. How parameter estimation affects inference: A general result

The argument of the preceding section can be expanded to include parametric functions other than that used to construct the test of zero-mean prediction error. Suppose that we are interested in testing the (scalar) null that for some parametric function $f_{t+1}(\beta)$, $Ef_{t+1}(\beta^*) = \theta$. Here, β^* is the unknown vector of parameters needed to make a forecast. For one-step-ahead forecasts, examples of $f(.)$ include (in each case, $\theta = 0$):

Test	$f_{t+1}(\beta)$	(14.15)
Equal mean square error	$(y_{t+1} - X_{1,t}'\beta_1)^2 - (y_{t+1} - X_{2,t}'\beta_2)^2$	
Equal mean absolute error	$\lvert y_{t+1} - X_{1,t}'\beta_1\rvert - \lvert y_{t+1} - X_{2,t}'\beta_2\rvert$	
Forecast encompassing in (14.3)	$(y_{t+1} - X_{1,t}'\beta_1)X_{2,t}'\beta_2$	
Forecast efficiency in (14.4)	$(y_{t+1} - X_t'\beta)X_t'\beta$	
Zero-mean prediction error	$y_{t+1} - X_t'\beta$	
Sign predictability in (14.5)	$[1(X_t'\beta \geq 0) - E1(X_t'\beta \geq 0)][1(y_{t+1} \geq 0) - E1(y_{t+1} \geq 0)]$	

In (14.15), we have assumed that when two forecasting models are needed, they both are linear with covariate vector $X_{i,t}$ and parameter vector β_i^* for models $i = 1, 2$ respectively. We then define $\beta^* = (\beta_1^{*\prime}, \beta_2^{*\prime})'$.

West's (1996) results cover those functions in (14.15) associated with the tests of equal mean square error, encompassing, efficiency, and zero-mean prediction error. More generally, his results cover tests that use any twice continuously differentiable function $f(.)$. McCracken (2000) extends West's results to situations where the moment function $Ef(.)$ is continuously differentiable but where the function $f(.)$ need not be differentiable. This extension allows for the remaining tests in (14.15), those for equal mean absolute error and sign predictability. The key to both of their results is an asymptotic expansion like that in (14.10) that has two distinct components: a first component that involves the population level forecasts and forecast errors and a second that is due to the fact that parameters are not known and must be estimated.

Again suppose that we are interested in the (scalar) null $Ef_{t+1}(\beta^*) = \theta$. To test this null we first construct a scaled sample average of the form $P^{-1/2}\sum_{t=R}^{R+P-1}(f_{t+1}(\hat{\beta}_t) - \theta)$. Furthermore, let the sequence of parameter estimates be constructed using one of the three schemes that figure prominently in the forecasting literature: the *recursive*, *rolling*, or *fixed* schemes. These schemes are defined as follows, with the formulas applicable for OLS estimation given in (14.16) below.

The *recursive* scheme is used in, for example, Pagan and Schwert (1990). In this scheme, the parameter estimates are updated as more data becomes available. Hence for any time $t = R, \dots, T - 1$ the parameter estimates use all relevant information from time $s = 1, \dots, t$.

The *rolling* scheme is used in, for example, Swanson (1998). Here, the parameter estimates are updated as more data becomes available, but always using only the most recent (say) R observations. This scheme is sometimes used when there are concerns about changepoints and biases from the use of older observations.

Finally, the *fixed* scheme is used in, for example, Ashley, Granger, and Schmalensee (1980). Here the parameter estimate is estimated only once, using data from (say) 1 to R and hence is not updated as forecasting moves forward in time from $t = R, \dots, T - 1$. This scheme may seem inefficient, but is frequently used in the neural net literature where computational concerns are a serious issue. This scheme was used for presentation purposes in the zero-mean prediction error example of (14.7).

To see how each of these parameter estimation schemes differ consider the simple linear regression in (14.6). If the parameter estimate(s) is constructed using OLS, then:

Scheme	Estimator	(14.16)
Recursive	$\hat{\beta}_t = (t^{-1}\sum_{s=1}^{t}X_{s-1}X_{s-1}')^{-1}(t^{-1}\sum_{s=1}^{t}X_{s-1}y_s),$	(a)
Rolling	$\hat{\beta}_t = (R^{-1}\sum_{s=t-R+1}^{t}X_{s-1}X_{s-1}')^{-1}(R^{-1}\sum_{s=t-R+1}^{t}X_{s-1}y_s),$	(b)
Fixed	$\hat{\beta}_t = (R^{-1}\sum_{s=1}^{R}X_{s-1}X_{s-1}')^{-1}(R^{-1}\sum_{s=1}^{R}X_{s-1}y_s).$	(c)

Notice that each has essentially the same form but that they vary because different observations are being used.

To present our asymptotic results, suppose that we are considering a univariate least squares model. Asymptotic results extend directly when considering multivariate models, or two or more nonnested models, say to compare their forecast accuracy. They extend directly when the estimation method is maximum likelihood (ML) or generalized method of moments (GMM), as indicated in parenthetical comments in the exposition below. Finally, they extend to multi-step rather than one-step-ahead forecasts. Essential technical conditions for these extensions include stationarity (no unit roots), existence of moments of sufficient order, and, if two or more models are being compared, that the models be nonnested. See the cited papers for exact details.

In our least squares example, define $h_s = X_{s-1}u_s$ and let $H(t)$ equal $(t^{-1}\sum_{s=1}^{t}h_s)$, $(R^{-1}\sum_{s=t-R+1}^{t}h_s)$, and $(R^{-1}\sum_{s=1}^{R}h_s)$ respectively for the recursive, rolling, and fixed schemes. Let $B = (EX_tX'_t)^{-1}$. (In general, h_s is the score if the estimation method is ML and is the set of orthogonality conditions used to estimate β^* if the estimation method is GMM; B is the inverse of the expectation of the Hessian (ML) or the asymptotic linear combination of orthogonality conditions (GMM).) Define

$$F = \partial Ef_{t+1}(\beta^*)/\partial\beta. \tag{14.17}$$

For the test of zero-mean prediction error, for example, this is $-EX'_t$ (see (14.10)). Then

$$P^{-1/2}\sum_{t=R}^{R+P-1}(f_{t+1}(\hat{\beta}_t) - \theta) = P^{-1/2}\sum_{t=R}^{R+P-1}(f_{t+1}(\beta^*) - \theta) + FBP^{-1/2}\sum_{t=R}^{R+P-1}H(t) + o_p(1). \tag{14.18}$$

The first component involves the population level forecasts and forecast errors. The second arises because parameters are not known and must be estimated.

Define S as the long-run covariance of $(f_{t+1}(\beta^*) - \theta, h'_t)'$ with diagonal elements S_{ff} and S_{hh} and off-diagonal element S_{fh}. That is,

$$S = \begin{pmatrix} S_{ff} & S_{fh} \\ S'_{fh} & S_{hh} \end{pmatrix}. \tag{14.19}$$

Under mild conditions, $P^{-1/2}\sum_{t=R}^{R+P-1}(f_{t+1}(\hat{\beta}_t) - \theta)$ converges in distribution to a normal variable with limiting covariance matrix Ω, defined by

$$\Omega = S_{ff} + \lambda_{fh}(FBS'_{fh} + S_{fh}B'F') + \lambda_{hh}FBS_{hh}B'F', \tag{14.20}$$

where

Scheme	λ_{fh}	λ_{hh}	(14.21)
Recursive	$1 - \pi^{-1} \ln (1 + \pi)$	$2[1 - \pi^{-1} \ln (1 + \pi)]$	
Rolling, $\pi \leq 1$	$\pi/2$	$\pi - \pi^2/3$	
Rolling, $1 < \pi < \infty$	$1 - (2\pi)^{-1}$	$1 - (3\pi)^{-1}$	
Fixed	0	π	

The formulae in (14.20) and (14.21) illustrate the statement made in the introduction that parameter estimation can affect the limiting variance of out-of-sample test statistics. In (14.20), the first component, S_{ff}, is precisely the limiting variance accounted for by authors such as Diebold and Mariano (1995). The remaining components arise from estimation of β^*.

The intuition for the form of the variance can be seen in (14.18). There are two sources of uncertainty. The first is the uncertainty that would exist even if population level parameters were known. This is represented by the term $P^{-1/2} \sum_{t=R}^{R+P-1} (f_{t+1}(\beta^*) - \theta)$. Authors such as Mincer and Zarnowitz (1969), Granger and Newbold (1977), Diebold and Mariano (1995), and Harvey, Leybourne, and Newbold (1997, 1998, 1999) have accounted for this uncertainty when deriving their out-of-sample tests of predictive ability.

The second type of uncertainty arises because parameters are not known and must be estimated. This is represented by the term $FBP^{-1/2} \sum_{t=R}^{R+P-1} H(t)$ in (14.18). This is the source of uncertainty not explicitly considered by the previously mentioned authors. It generates a variance term, $\lambda_{hh} FBS_{hh} B'F'$, and a covariance term, $\lambda_{fh}(FBS'_{fh} + S_{fh} B'F')$. Randles (1982) derives the in-sample equivalent of the expansion in (14.18) and the limiting variance in (14.20). He also discusses the importance of accounting for parameter estimation uncertainty when in-sample tests are constructed. As well, Hoffman and Pagan (1989) provide a similar result for out-of-sample inference when the fixed scheme is used.

We close this subsection by discussing several papers that derive additional asymptotic results. The first paper is White (2000), which develops a bootstrap test of predictive ability that accounts for potential effects due to parameter estimation. The bootstrap, which is also suggested by Ashley (1998), potentially brings asymptotic refinements. It is also a computationally convenient method to compare predictive ability across a potentially large number of models. Perhaps most importantly, White's bootstrap algorithm explicitly accounts for the potential existence of data snooping effects of the kind discussed by Lo and MacKinlay (1990).

Corradi, Swanson, and Olivetti (2001) extends some of the results of West (1996) and White (2000) to unit-root environments. One result concerns tests of equal forecast accuracy between two nonnested parametric regression models that contain cointegrating relationships. Based upon an expansion akin to that in (14.18) they show that when MSE is the measure of accuracy, parameter uncertainty is asymptotically irrelevant and hence the standard tests for equal forecast accuracy will be asymptotically standard normal. When other measures of accuracy are used, they show that parameter uncertainty can have an effect. That effect causes the standard tests to have nonstandard limiting distributions that are not well approximated by the standard normal distribution. They also extend the results in White (2000) by validating the use of White's bootstrap method in environments where forecasts are generated using estimated regression models with cointegrating relationships.

McCracken (1999) and Clark and McCracken (2001) derive results for tests of equal forecast accuracy and encompassing when the two models are nested rather than nonnested. They show that these tests are not asymptotically normal but instead have nonstandard limiting distributions. This occurs since, when models are nested and the parameters are known in advance, the forecast errors associated with the two models are identical. In particular, the difference in (say) the loss differential d_{t+1} must be zero by definition. This set of results is potentially useful, since tests of causality by Ashley, Granger, and Schmalensee (1980), tests of long-horizon predictive ability by Mark (1995), and tests of market efficiency by Pesaran and Timmermann (1995) each involve the comparison of two nested rather than nonnested models.

Finally, Kitamura (1999) proposes bootstrap methods that can be used to improve the accuracy of point estimates of moments of functions of out-of-sample forecasts and forecast errors. In particular, he shows that the bootstrap can be used to smooth over the added variability in these point estimates induced by parameter estimation. His results are general enough to be applied to functions $f(.)$ that are either differentiable or nondifferentiable, and hence can be applied to measures of forecast accuracy like MSE and sign predictability.

14.3.3. Accounting for parameter uncertainty

We return now to the result in (14.20). We remarked in section 14.2 that the applied papers we cited do not explicitly account for error in estimation of parameters used to make forecasts. Even so, the analysis just presented can be used to show that, in some cases, the extra terms introduced by such error vanish, at least asymptotically. One important contribution of the preceding analysis is that it delineates an exact set of conditions under which there is no need to account for such error, thereby providing conditions under which the inference in those papers is asymptotically valid.

One such condition is that the out-of-sample size, P, is small relative to the in-sample size, R. This is transparent if we return to the limiting variance in (14.20). Each of the terms due to the existence of parameter estimation error depends upon the value π through λ_{fh} and λ_{hh}. In either case, if $\pi = 0$ then parameter estimation uncertainty is asymptotically irrelevant, since both $\lambda_{fh} = 0$ and $\lambda_{hh} = 0$ (the result for the recursive scheme follows, since $1 - \pi^{-1} \ln (1 + \pi) \to 0$ as $\pi \to 0$). When this is the case $\Omega = S_{ff}$ and hence parameter uncertainty can be safely ignored. As noted by Chong and Hendry (1986), the intuition behind this result is that when R is large relative to P, uncertainty about β^* is small relative to uncertainty that would be present even if β^* were known. Examples where this condition may be useful include Fair (1980, $P/R = 0.156$), Pagan and Schwert (1990, $P/R = 0.132$ and 0.4), and Kuan and Liu (1995, $P/R = 0.042$, 0.087 and 0.137).

It is important to point out that it will not always, or perhaps even usually, be the case that P/R (the obvious sample analog to π) is small enough for parameter estimation error to be irrelevant for inference. There are many applications in which P/R is numerically large. Examples include Mark (1995), for which P/R ranges from 0.69 to 1.11, and Pesaran and Timmermann (1995), for which P/R ranges from 0.38 to 5.55. In any case, inspection of the asymptotic variance formula (14.20) shows that the value of π alone does not determine the effects of parameter estimation error; the parameters of the data generating process, and the estimator used, are also relevant. The Monte Carlo simulations summarized in section 14.3.4 show that serious biases result when parameter estimation error is ignored, for data generating processes, and choice of P and R, that are calibrated to actual economic data.

A second set of circumstances is also immediate from (14.20). When $F = 0$, the second and third terms disappear and hence $\Omega = S_{ff}$. Perhaps the most useful application of this result is to the test of equal MSE. When the test of interest is one of equal MSE between two linear parametric models, $F = (-2Eu_{1,t+1}X'_{1,t}, 2Eu_{2,t+1}X'_{2,t})$. Note that both components of F are essentially the moment conditions used to identify the parameters when they are estimated by OLS. Since these are both equal to zero we know that when OLS provides consistent estimates of the parameters it must be the case that F is a vector of zeroes. When this is the relevant environment, the Granger and Newbold (1977) and Diebold and Mariano (1995) tests of equal MSE can be applied without adjustment and still obtain a statistic that is asymptotically standard normal.

A third set of circumstances is not quite so obvious. We see in (14.21) that when the recursive scheme is used, $\lambda_{hh} = 2\lambda_{fh}$ and hence $\Omega = S_{ff} + \lambda_{fh}(FBS'_{fh} + S_{fh}B'F' + 2FBS_{hh}B'F')$. This is potentially useful since it is possible that

$$FBS'_{fh} + S_{fh}B'F' + 2FBS_{hh}B'F' = 0, \tag{14.22}$$

regardless of whether F or π equals zero.

A particularly intriguing example of this occurs when one is testing for first-order serial correlation, disturbances are i.i.d., and a lagged dependent variable is used as a predictor in a linear regression model. From Durbin (1970) we know that when constructing an in-sample test for serial correlation this is potentially a problem. When the test is constructed out-of-sample, *and* the recursive scheme is used, this problem does not occur. The reason for this is that for this scalar test, it can be shown that $-FBS'_{fh} = FBS_{hh}B'F'$. This implies that (14.22) is satisfied and hence parameter estimation error is asymptotically irrelevant. For a discussion and other examples of this type of cancellation, see West (1996) and West and McCracken (1998).

Note that for the rolling and fixed schemes, parameter estimation error is asymptotically relevant for this test (because for these schemes, $\lambda_{hh} \neq 2\lambda_{fh}$). When this is the case, one must specifically account for parameter estimation error. There are a number of ways to do so. The obvious method is simply to use (14.23) below when constructing tests, using the obvious sample analogues. That is, if $\hat{F}$, $\hat{B}$, $\hat{S}_{fh}$, $\hat{S}_{hh}$, $\hat{\lambda}_{fh}$, and $\hat{\lambda}_{hh}$ are consistent estimates of their population level counterparts (see below), construct test statistics of the form

$$\hat{\Omega}^{-1/2}P^{-1/2}\sum_{t=R}^{R+P-1}(f_{t+1}(\hat{B}_t) - \theta), \text{ where} \tag{14.23}$$

$$\hat{\Omega} = \hat{S}_{ff} + \hat{\lambda}_{fh}(\hat{F}\hat{B}\hat{S}'_{fh} + \hat{S}_{fh}\hat{B}'\hat{F}') + \hat{\lambda}_{hh}(\hat{F}\hat{B}\hat{S}_{hh}\hat{B}'\hat{F}').$$

In this way, the test statistic is limiting standard normal, and standard normal tables can be used to construct an asymptotically valid test of the null.

To compute the terms in (14.23), begin with the scalars λ_{fh} and λ_{hh}. Since these are both continuous functions of $\pi = \lim P/R$, they can be computed by substituting P/R for π. Since the term B varies with the methodology used to estimate the parameters (that is, OLS, maximum likelihood, GMM, etc.) so will its estimator. When OLS is used to estimate the parameters, as in the zero-mean prediction error example of (14.7), $B = (EX_tX'_t)^{-1}$. Here, a consistent estimate of B could take the form $\hat{B} = (P^{-1}\sum_{t=R}^{R+P-1}X_tX'_t)^{-1}$. Similarly, since the term F varies with the function of interest, $f(.)$, so will its estimator. In the zero-mean prediction error example of (14.7), $F = -EX'_t$. A consistent estimate of F could take the form $\hat{F} = -P^{-1}\sum_{t=R}^{R+P-1}X'_t$.

The remaining terms, S_{ff}, S_{fh}, and S_{hh}, require a bit more knowledge of the data that is being used. At times, consistent estimates are quite simple. For example, under the conditions assumed for the linear model in (14.6) and the test of zero-mean prediction error in (14.7), $S_{ff} = \sigma^2$, $S_{fh} = -\sigma^2 EX'_t$, and $S_{hh} = \sigma^2 EX_tX'_t$. Consistent estimates of S_{ff}, S_{fh}, and S_{hh} include $\hat{S}^0_{ff} = P^{-1}\sum_{t=R}^{R+P-1}\hat{u}^2_{t+1}$, $\hat{S}^0_{fh} = -(P^{-1}\sum_{t=R}^{R+P-1}\hat{u}^2_{t+1})$ $(P^{-1}\sum_{t=R}^{R+P-1}X'_t)$, and $\hat{S}^0_{hh} = (P^{-1}\sum_{t=R}^{R+P-1}\hat{u}^2_{t+1})(P^{-1}\sum_{t=R}^{R+P-1}X_tX'_t)$. These estimates, however, are based upon knowledge that the disturbances are i.i.d. and conditionally homoskedastic. If the disturbances are i.i.d. but conditionally heteroskedastic, then $\hat{S}^0_{ff}$ remains consistent for S_{ff} but $\hat{S}^0_{fh}$ and $\hat{S}^0_{hh}$ are no longer consistent for S_{fh} and S_{hh}. In this case, consistent estimators include $\hat{S}^1_{fh} = -P^{-1}\sum_{t=R}^{R+P-1}\hat{u}^2_{t+1}X'_t$ and $\hat{S}^1_{hh} = P^{-1}\sum_{t=R}^{R+P-1}\hat{u}^2_{t+1}X_tX'_t$. More generally, if the disturbances are serially correlated and conditionally heteroskedastic, then standard nonparametric kernel estimators, such as the Bartlett or quadratic spectral, can be used to consistently estimate the long-run covariances S_{ff}, S_{fh}, and S_{hh}. See West and McCracken (1998) and McCracken (2000) for further discussion on estimating these quantities.

Such calculations may be quite involved. Fortunately, in some cases, the formula for Ω simplifies. For example, in the test for zero-mean prediction error above, it can be shown that not only does $-FBS'_{fh} = FBS_{hh}B'F'$, but also $-FBS'_{fh} = FBS_{hh}B'F' = S_{ff}$. Using (14.20) we see that Ω can be rewritten as λS_{ff}, where λ is defined as $1 - 2\lambda_{fh} + \lambda_{hh}$. When this is the case, one need only estimate S_{ff} and λ to form a consistent estimate of Ω. This technique can be particularly useful when the test of interest is for either efficiency or zero-mean prediction error. See West and McCracken (1998) for further examples.

As well, judiciously designed regression-based tests, which introduce seemingly irrelevant variables, can cause the usual least squares standard errors to be the appropriate ones. West and McCracken (1998) demonstrate this, building on related results for in-sample tests in Pagan and Hall (1983) and Davidson and MacKinnon (1984). Leading examples of tests that can be constructed using augmented regression-based tests include those for serial correlation in the forecast errors and forecast encompassing. For an illustration, consider the encompassing test and assume that the putatively encompassing model is linear with vector of predictors $X_{1,t}$. An adjustment for parameter uncertainty can be made using the augmented regression

$$\hat{u}_{1,t+1} = \alpha_0 + \tilde{\alpha}_2 \hat{y}_{2,t+1} + \alpha_3' X_{1,t} + \text{error term}. \tag{14.24}$$

(Compare to the usual regression in (14.3).) Under mild conditions, the least squares standard errors associated with the estimate of $\tilde{\alpha}_2$ can be appropriate even when those associated with the estimate of α_2 are not. See West and McCracken (1998) for a discussion on how to choose the augmenting variables.

14.3.4. Monte Carlo evidence

Here we briefly summarize some Monte Carlo evidence on the adequacy of the asymptotic approximations referenced above. In choosing the Monte Carlo studies, we restrict attention to ones that evaluate the finite sample size and size adjusted power properties of tests that use estimated regression models. Thus we do not discuss simulations of out-of-sample tests that do not involve the estimation of parameters, such as those in Diebold and Mariano (1995), Harvey, Leybourne, and Newbold (1997, 1998, 1999), and Clark (1999).

Unfortunately, the number of Monte Carlo studies that evaluate predictive ability using estimated regression models is extremely limited. We cite West (1996, 2001a,b), West and McCracken (1998), McCracken (2000), Corradi, Swanson, and Olivetti (2001), and Clark and McCracken (2001). All of these studies consider one-step-ahead forecast errors and use linear DGPs. Although Corradi, Swanson, and Olivetti (2001) allow the disturbances to be autoregressive, the remaining authors restrict attention to i.i.d. disturbances (usually normal). No doubt equally good finite sample behavior would require larger sample sizes for multi-step forecasts and conditionally heteroskedastic disturbances.

The basic results from these papers are as follows. First, test statistics relying on the asymptotic approximation in (14.18) can work quite well even in sample sizes as small as eight. For example, one set of experiments in West (1996) considers certain tests in which parameter estimation error is asymptotically irrelevant (that is, tests in which $\lambda_{fh}(FBS'_{fh} + S_{fh}B'F') + \lambda_{hh}FBS_{hh}B'F' = 0$ in (14.20)). Of 30 nominal 0.05 tests computed from sample splits in which R ranges from 25 to 100 and P from 25 to 175, all but one had an actual size between 0.03 and 0.08 (the remaining actual size was 0.10). Results in the other papers cited in the previous paragraph are generally comparable. There are, however, occasional exceptions. A dramatic one is the regression-based test of encompassing in (14.24), when the rolling scheme is used. West and McCracken (1998) find that sample sizes greater than a thousand are required for test statistics to be reasonably accurately sized. (Peculiarly, the same regression-based test works well with small sample sizes when the recursive or fixed schemes are used, for reasons that are not clear to us.)

Second, when the approximation calls for adjusting for parameter estimation error (that is, when $\lambda_{fh}(FBS'_{fh} + S_{fh}B'F') + \lambda_{hh}FBS_{hh}B'F' \neq 0$ in (14.20)), test statistics adjusting for parameter estimation error perform better than those that do not, sometimes dramatically so. West (2001a,b) conducts simulations in which parameter estimation affects the limiting distribution of tests of encompassing. In both papers the simulated tests are conducted with and without adjustment ("Without adjustment" means use only S_{ff} [the first term in (14.20)].). Consider, for example, the simulations in West (2001a). P and R ranged from 8 to 512. For nominal 0.05 tests, sizes of adjusted test statistics ranged from 0.04 to 0.10; the range for unadjusted test statistics was 0.04 to 0.25. (In this particular experiment, it can be shown that failure to adjust will asymptotically result in a size greater than 0.05. In other setups, it is possible that failure to adjust will result in asymptotic sizes less than 0.05.) Consistent with the asymptotic theory and with the intuition of Chong and Hendry (1986), the smaller P/R is, the better is the performance of the unadjusted test statistic. For example, for the unadjusted test statistic, with $P = 32$, nominal 0.05 tests behaved as follows: when $R = 16$ (that is, $P/R = 2$), actual size = 0.208; when $R = 256$ (that is, $P/R = 0.125$), actual size = 0.055. (The comparable figures for the test statistic that adjusts for parameter estimation error are 0.065 for $R = 16$ and 0.050 for $R = 256$.)

Third, when the approximation calls for adjusting for parameter estimation error, size adjusted power typically is better for adjusted than for unadjusted test statistics. Both Clark and McCracken (2001) and McCracken (2000) conduct simulations in which parameter estimation affects the limiting distribution. In both papers, the asymptotically valid version of the test has greater size-adjusted power than the asymptotically invalid version. Consider, for example, one of the setups in McCracken (2000), in which $R = 432$ and $P = 87$ (that is, $P/R = 0.20$), the recursive scheme is used, and the nominal size of the test is 0.01. As the deviation from the null decreases across four experiments, the adjusted tests have size-adjusted powers of 1.000, 0.988, 0.748, and 0.118, while the unadjusted tests have size-adjusted powers of 0.999, 0.948, 0.383, and 0.054 respectively.

In addition, for size-adjusted tests, power is increasing in P/R. This tendency occurs in each of the simulations conducted by Corradi, Swanson, and Olivetti (2001), Clark and McCracken (2001), and McCracken (2000). For example, in the first of two simulations conducted by Corradi, Swanson, and Olivetti (2001) they construct tests for equal MSE estimating parameters associated with both stationary regressors and those with a unit root. They find that nominal 0.05 tests have size-adjusted powers that range across 0.170, 0.261, 0.466, 0.632, 0.764, and 0.847 when $R = 50$ and $P = 25, 50, 100, 150, 200, 250$ (that is, $P/R = 0.50, 1, 2, 3, 4, 5$) respectively.

14.4. CONCLUSION

We hope that we have made four contributions in this chapter. The first is simply to introduce the methodology of out-of-sample hypothesis testing. We think this is important. The applied papers cited in section 14.2 convince us that out-of-sample methods provide an insight into econometric models that is not easily obtained with standard in-sample methods.

The second contribution is to emphasize that economic forecasts and forecast errors usually are generated using estimated regression models. Because of this feature, test statistics constructed using forecasts and forecast errors often have statistical properties that differ from those of statistics constructed when the population level forecasts and forecast errors are known. For those tests that are asymptotically normal, we show that the limiting variance may depend on uncertainty about the parameters used to make forecasts.

Our third contribution is to outline how to feasibly account for the uncertainty introduced when estimated regression parameters are used to construct forecasts. We describe circumstances under which such estimation error washes out asymptotically and thus can be ignored in large samples. For other circumstances, we outline how adjustments can be made.

The fourth, and perhaps most important, contribution that our chapter can make is to promote future use of and research on out-of-sample tests of predictive ability. There are more than a few unanswered questions regarding out-of-sample tests of predictive ability. Perhaps the most obvious is how to choose the sample split parameter π (defined in (14.9)). The Monte Carlo results in section 14.3.4 seem to indicate that this can play a significant role in determining both the size and power properties of the test. Further Monte Carlo results and perhaps even local asymptotics may shed light on the optimal choice of π. Steckel and Vanhonacker (1993) provide some suggestions, but conclude that in finite samples a split where $P/R \approx 1$ is not "too" suboptimal.

Other lines of research include extending the work of Corradi, Swanson, and Olivetti (2001) in ways that allow for a broader range of tests than just for equal forecast accuracy between two nonnested models. Examples include tests of efficiency, encompassing, serial correlation in the forecast errors and zero-mean prediction error when cointegrating relationships exist within the estimated regression model(s). Moreover, since tests of causality often involve regression models that include cointegrating relationships (Stock and Watson, 1988) it would be useful to extend their work along the lines of that by McCracken (1999) and Clark and McCracken (2001). In that way, tests of equal forecast accuracy and encompassing between two nested models can be constructed when cointegrating relationships exist.

Another line of work involves tests of predictive ability when nonparametric methods are used to estimate regression functions. Swanson and White (1997a, b), Chung and Zhou (1996), and Jaditz and Sayers (1998) each construct tests of predictive ability based upon forecasts and forecast errors estimated using series-based, kernel-based, and local-linear nonparametric methods respectively. Since each of these methods use regression estimators that have slower rates of convergence than parametric estimates it seems likely that they, too, would affect the distributions of out-of-sample tests of predictive ability.

Other potential questions include determining the importance of parameter uncertainty in the evaluation of probability or interval forecasts. There is also the question of whether out-of-sample methods should be used at all. Fair and Shiller (1990) suggest that this methodology provides a protection against data-mining and overfitting. It would be useful to determine whether their heuristic arguments in favor of out-of-sample methods can be validated analytically. Another question is whether standard information criteria can be used as a consistent testing methodology in an out-of-sample environment. In particular, information criteria are sometimes used to choose among multiple nested and nonnested models based upon out-of-sample forecast errors. Although Swanson (1998) argues in its favor, there is no theoretical evidence to support its use.

Acknowledgments

West thanks the Graduate School of the University of Wisconsin and the National Science Foundation for financial support.

References

Alpert, A.T. and J.B. Guerard (1988). Employment, unemployment and the minimum wage: A causality model. *Applied Economics*, 20, 1453–64.

Amano, R.A. and S. van Norden (1995). Terms of trade and real exchange rates: the Canadian evidence. *Journal of International Money and Finance*, 14, 83–104.

Andrews, M.J., A.P.L. Minford, and J. Riley (1996). On comparing macroeconomic models using forecast encompassing tests. *Oxford Bulletin of Economics and Statistics*, 58, 279–305.

Ashley, R. (1981). Inflation and the distribution of price changes across markets: a causal analysis. *Economic Inquiry*, 19, 650–60.

Ashley, R. (1998). A new technique for postsample model selection and validation. *Journal of Economic Dynamics and Control*, 22, 647–65.

Ashley, R., C.W.J. Granger, and R. Schmalensee (1980). Advertising and aggregate consumption: an analysis of causality. *Econometrica*, 48, 1149–67.

Bates, J.M. and C.W.J. Granger (1969). The combination of forecasts. *Operational Research Quarterly*, 20, 451–68.

Berger, A. and S. Krane (1985). The informational efficiency of econometric model forecasts. *Review of Economics and Statistics*, 67, 128–34.

Blomberg, S.B. and G.D. Hess (1997). Politics and exchange rate forecasts. *Journal of International Economics*, 43, 189–205.

Bradshaw, G.W. and D. Orden (1990). Granger causality from the exchange rate to agricultural prices and export sales. *Western Journal of Agricultural Economics*, 15, 100–10.

Bram, J. and S. Ludvigson (1998). Does consumer confidence forecast household expenditure? A sentiment horse race. *Federal Reserve Bank of New York Economic Policy Review*, 4, 59–78.

Brandt, J.A. and D. Bessler (1983). Price forecasting and evaluation: an application in agriculture. *Journal of Forecasting*, 2, 237–48.

Breen, W., L.R. Glosten, and R. Jagannathan (1989). Economic significance of predictable variations in stock index returns. *Journal of Finance*, 44, 1177–89.

Brier, G.W. (1950). Verification of forecasts expressed in terms of probability. *Monthly Weather Review*, 75, 1–3.

Chen, X. and N.R. Swanson (1996). Semiparametric ARX neural network models with an application to forecasting inflation. Manuscript, London School of Economics and Purdue University.

Chinn, M.D. and R.A. Meese (1995). Banking on currency forecasts: How predictable is change in money? *Journal of International Economics*, 38, 161–78.

Chong, Y.Y. and D.F. Hendry (1986). Econometric evaluation of linear macro-economic models. *Review of Economic Studies*, 53, 671–90.

Christ, C. (1956). Aggregate econometric models. *American Economic Review*, 66, 385–408.

Chung, Y.P. and Z.G. Zhou (1996). The predictability of stock returns – a nonparametric approach. *Econometric Review*, 15, 299–330.

Clark, T.E. (1999). Finite-sample properties of tests for equal forecast accuracy. *Journal of Forecasting*, 18, 489–504.

Clark, T.E. and M.W. McCracken (2001). Tests of equal forecast accuracy and encompassing for nested models. *Journal of Econometrics*, 105, 85–110.

Corradi, V., N.R. Swanson and C. Olivetti (2001). Predictive ability with cointegrated variables. *Journal of Econometrics*, 105, 315–58.

Cumby, R.E. and D.M. Modest (1986). Testing for market timing ability: A framework for forecast evaluation. *Journal of Financial Economics*, 19, 169–89.

Davidson, R. and J.G. MacKinnon (1984). Model specification tests based on artificial linear regressions. *International Economic Review*, 25, 241–62.

Dawid, A.P. (1984). Present position and potential developments: some personal views. Statistical theory. The prequential approach. *Journal of the Royal Statistical Society, Series A*, 147, 278–92.

Day, T.E. and C.M. Lewis (1992). Stock market volatility and the information content of stock index options. *Journal of Econometrics*, 52, 267–87.

Diebold, F.X. (1989). Forecast combination and encompassing: reconciling two divergent literatures. *International Journal of Forecasting*, 5, 589–92.

Diebold, F.X. and R.S. Mariano (1995). Comparing predictive accuracy. *Journal of Business and Economic Statistics*, 13, 253–63.

Diebold, F.X. and G.D. Rudebusch (1991). Forecasting output with the composite leading index: a real time analysis. *Journal of the American Statistical Association*, 86, 603–10.

Durbin, J. (1970). Testing for serial correlation in least squares regression when some of the regressors are lagged dependent variables. *Econometrica*, 38, 410–21.

Engel, C. (1994). Can the Markov switching model forecast exchange rates? *Journal of International Economics*, 36, 151–65.

Ericsson, N.R. (1992). Parameter constancy, mean square forecast errors, and measuring forecast performance: an exposition, extensions, and illustration. *Journal of Policy Modeling*, 14, 465–95.

Ericsson, N.R. and J. Marquez (1993). Encompassing the forecasts of U.S. trade balance models. *Review of Economics and Statistics*, 75, 19–31.

Fair, R.C. (1980). Estimating the predictive accuracy of econometric models. *International Economic Review*, 21, 355–78.

Fair, R.C. (1999). Evaluating the information content and money making ability of forecasts from exchange rate equations. Manuscript, Yale University.

Fair, R.C. and R. Shiller (1989). The informational content of *ex ante* forecasts. *Review of Economics and Statistics*, 71, 325–31.

Fair, R.C. and R. Shiller (1990). Comparing information in forecasts from econometric models. *American Economic Review*, 80, 375–89.

Goldberger, A.S. (1959). *Impact Multipliers and Dynamic Properties of the Klein–Goldberger Model*. Amsterdam: North-Holland.

Goldberger, A.S. (1991). *A Course in Econometrics*. Cambridge: Harvard University Press.

Granger, C.W.J. and M. Deutsch (1992). Comments on the evaluation of policy models. *Journal of Policy Modeling*, 14, 497–516.

Granger, C.W.J. and P. Newbold (1977). *Forecasting Economic Time Series*. London: Academic Press.

Granger, C.W.J. and M.H. Pesaran (2000). A decision theoretic approach to forecast evaluation. In W.S. Chan, W.K. Lin, and H. Tong (eds.), *Statistics and Finance: An Interface*. London: Imperial College Press, 261–78.

Granger, C.W.J. and R. Ramanathan (1984). Improved methods of combining forecasts. *Journal of Forecasting*, 3, 197–204.

Granger, C.W.J. and N.R. Swanson (1997). An introduction to stochastic unit-root processes. *Journal of Econometrics*, 80, 35–62.

Harvey, D.I., S.J. Leybourne, and P. Newbold (1997). Testing the equality of prediction mean squared errors. *International Journal of Forecasting*, 13, 281–91.

Harvey, D.I., S.J. Leybourne, and P. Newbold (1998). Tests for forecast encompassing. *Journal of Business and Economic Statistics*, 16, 254–59.

Harvey, D.I., S.J. Leybourne, and P. Newbold (1999). Forecast evaluation tests in the presence of ARCH. *Journal of Forecasting*, 18, 435–45.

Hatanaka, M. (1974). A simple suggestion to improve the Mincer–Zarnowitz criterion for the evaluation of forecasts. *Annals of Economic and Social Measurement*, 3, 521–4.

Henriksson, R.D. and R.C. Merton (1981). On market timing and investment performance II: Statistical procedures for evaluating forecasting skills. *Journal of Business*, 54, 513–33.

Hoffman, D. and A. Pagan (1989). Practitioners corner: post-sample prediction tests for generalized method of moments estimators. *Oxford Bulletin of Economics and Statistics*, 51, 333–43.

Jaditz, T. and C.L. Sayers (1998). Out-of-sample forecast performance as a test for nonlinearity in time series. *Journal of Business and Economic Statistics*, 16, 110–17.

Keane, M.P. and D.E. Runkle (1989). Are economic forecasts rational? *Federal Reserve Bank of Minneapolis Quarterly Review*, 13.

Kilian, L. (1999). Exchange rates and monetary fundamentals: What do we learn from long-horizon regressions?. *Journal of Applied Econometrics*, 14, 491–510.

Kitamura, Y. (1999). Predictive inference and the bootstrap. Manuscript, University of Wisconsin.

Klein, L.R. (1992). The test of a model is its ability to predict. Manuscript, University of Pennsylvania.

Kuan, C. and T. Liu (1995). Forecasting exchange rates using feedforward and recurrent neural networks. *Journal of Applied Econometrics*, 10, 347–64.

Leitch, G. and J.E. Tanner (1991). Economic forecast evaluation: profits versus the conventional error measures. *American Economic Review*, 81, 580–90.

Lo, A.W. and A.C. MacKinlay (1990). Data snooping biases in tests of financial asset pricing models. *Review of Financial Studies*, 3, 431–67.

Lo, A.W. and A.C. MacKinlay (1997). Maximizing predictability in the stock and bond markets. *Macroeconomic Dynamics*, 1, 118–58.

Lopez, J.A. (2001). Evaluating the predictive accuracy of volatility models. *Journal of Forecasting*, 20, 87–109.

Mark, N.C. (1995). Exchange rates and fundamentals: Evidence on long-horizon predictability. *American Economic Review*, 85, 201–18.

McCracken, M.W. (1999). Asymptotics for out-of-sample tests of causality. Manuscript, University of Missouri-Columbia.

McCracken, M.W. (2000). Robust out-of-sample inference. *Journal of Econometrics*, 99, 195–223.

McCulloch, R. and P.E. Rossi (1990). Posterior, predictive, and utility-based approaches to testing the arbitrage pricing theory. *Journal of Financial Economics*, 28, 7–38.

McNees, S.K. (1978). The rationality of economic forecasts. *American Economic Review; Papers and Proceedings of the Ninetieth Annual Meeting of the American Economic Association*, 68, 301–5.

Meese, R.A. and K. Rogoff (1988). Was it real? The exchange rate-interest differential relation over the modern floating-rate period. *Journal of Finance*, 43, 933–48.

Merton, R.C. (1981). On market timing and investment performance. I. An equilibrium theory of value for market forecasts. *Journal of Business*, 54, 363–406.

Mincer, J. and V. Zarnowitz (1969). The evaluation of economic forecasts. In J. Mincer (ed.), *Economic Forecasts and Expectations*. New York: National Bureau of Economic Research, 3–46.

Morgan, W.A. (1939). A test for significance of the difference between two variances in a sample from a normal bivariate population. *Biometrika*, 31, 13–19.

Murphy, A.H. and H. Daan (1985). Forecast evaluation. In A.H. Murphy and R.W. Katz (eds.), *Probability, Statistics and Decision Making in the Atmospheric Sciences*. Boulder: Westview Press, 379–437.

Oliner, S., G. Rudebusch, and D. Sichel (1995). New and old models of business investment: A comparison of forecasting performance. *Journal of Money, Credit and Banking*, 27, 806–26.

Pagan, A.R. and A.D. Hall (1983). Diagnostic tests as residual analysis. *Econometric Review*, 2, 159–218.

Pagan, A.R. and G.W. Schwert (1990). Alternative models for conditional stock volatility. *Journal of Econometrics*, 45, 267–90.

Park, T. (1990). Forecast evaluation for multivariate time-series models: the U.S. cattle market. *Western Journal of Agricultural Economics*, 15, 133–43.

Pesaran, M.H. and A. Timmermann (1992). A simple nonparametric test of predictive performance. *Journal of Business and Economic Statistics*, 10, 561–5.

Pesaran, M.H. and A. Timmermann (1994). A generalization of the nonparametric Henriksson–Merton test of market timing. *Economics Letters*, 4, 1–7.

Pesaran, M.H. and A. Timmermann (1995). Predictability of stock returns: robustness and economic significance. *Journal of Finance*, 50, 1201–28.

Randles, R. (1982). On the asymptotic normality of statistics with estimated parameters. *Annals of Statistics*, 10, 462–474.

Steckel, J. and W. Vanhonacker (1993). Cross-validating regression models in market research. *Marketing Science*, 12, 415–27.

Stock, J.H. and M.W. Watson (1988). Interpreting the evidence on money-income causality. *Journal of Econometrics*, 40, 161–82.

Stock, J.H. and M.W. Watson (1993). A procedure for predicting recessions with leading indicators: Econometric issues and recent experience. In J.H. Stock and Mark W. Watson (eds.), *Business Cycles, Indicators and Forecasting*. Chicago: University of Chicago Press, 95–153.

Stock, J.H. and M.W. Watson (1999a). Forecasting inflation. *Journal of Monetary Economics*, 44, 293–335.

Stock, J.H. and M.W. Watson (1999b). Diffusion indices. *NBER Working Paper* #6702.

Swanson, N.R. (1998). Money and output viewed through a rolling window. *Journal of Monetary Economics*, 41, 455–73.

Swanson, N.R. and H. White (1995). A model-selection approach to assessing the information in the term structure using linear models and artificial neural networks. *Journal of Business and Economic Statistics*, 13, 265–75.

Swanson, N.R. and H. White (1997a). A model-selection approach to real-time macroeconomic forecasting using linear models and artificial neural networks. *Review of Economics and Statistics*, 79, 265–75.

Swanson, N.R. and H. White (1997b). Forecasting economic time series using flexible versus fixed specification and linear versus nonlinear econometric models. *International Journal of Forecasting*, 13, 439–61.

Tegene, A. and F. Kuchler (1994). Evaluating forecasting models of farmland prices. *International Journal of Forecasting*, 10, 65–80.

West, K.D. (1996). Asymptotic inference about predictive ability. *Econometrica*, 64, 1067–84.

West, K.D. (2001a). Tests for forecast encompassing when forecasts depend on estimated regression parameters. *Journal of Business and Economic Statistics*, 19, 29–33.

West, K.D. (2001b). Encompassing tests when no model is encompassing. *Journal of Econometrics*, 105, 287–308.

West, K.D. and D. Cho (1995). The predictive ability of several models of exchange rate volatility. *Journal of Econometrics*, 69, 367–91.

West, K.D., H.J. Edison, and D. Cho (1993). A utility-based comparison of some models of exchange rate volatility. *Journal of International Economics*, 35, 23–45.

West, K.D. and M.W. McCracken (1998). Regression-based tests of predictive ability. *International Economic Review*, 39, 817–40.

White, H. (2000). A reality check for data snooping. *Econometrica*, 68, 1097–126.

Forecasting Competitions: Their Role in Improving Forecasting Practice and Research

Robert Fildes and Keith Ord

15.1.   INTRODUCTION

Many organizations are confronted with the problem of forecasting a multiplicity of time series. This arises as a natural part of their regular budgeting, planning, and operational activities. Governmental organizations such as health authorities also face a similar set of problems. The dimensionality of the data set may be large, with hundreds if not thousands of series to be considered, updated perhaps weekly with forecasts required weekly. Cost-effective procedures are needed for generating such forecasts and this raises the issue of how to select a suitable approach. The purpose of this chapter is to review the progress that has been made in developing empirical comparisons of competing methods, and to evaluate the strengths and weaknesses of this research.

Typically, the problem is simplified by structuring the problem hierarchically as shown in figure 15.1. Economic and marketing factors such as price, advertising, and income are often used to predict demand at more aggregated levels of the hierarchy, but the lower levels are usually forecast using only the time-series history on the individual item (Fildes and Beard, 1992). Because of the

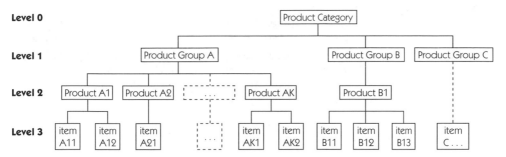

Figure 15.1 Product hierarchy. The diagram shows a typical three-level hierarchy where different product groups contribute to overall sales. Within each group, a number of different products are sold. Product sales, in turn, are composed of sales of different packs (or sales in different regions or to different warehouses). Forecasts are needed at all levels

dimensionality of the problem, the primary approach is to use the extrapolative forecasting procedures automatically. Exponential smoothing or one of its variants, first proposed by Brown in 1955 (see R.G. Brown, 1963) as a convenient solution for this class of problem, is still the method most widely used (Dalrymple, 1987; Sanders and Mandrodt, 1994).

In contrast to the problem area we have just described, time-series statisticians have concentrated on developing methods for analyzing a single time series. The growth of computer processing power over the last 40 years has led to the development of a wide variety of methods. Perhaps the most influential have been the class of ARIMA models proposed by Box and Jenkins (1976). At the time of their development these methods required considerable expertise in model selection (or identification, in the Box–Jenkins terminology). Moreover, the ability to use the data to select a model from a broad class was believed to ensure their superior performance. If there was any justification in continuing to use exponential smoothing, Box and Jenkins argued, it lay in its computational simplicity and ease of use. But at what cost? If the deterioration in accuracy from using simple models was very high, the more complex class of models proposed by Box and Jenkins should clearly be adopted.

These developments raised a number of general issues. How should a practising forecaster choose between different forecasting approaches when they need to be applied to multiple time series over many months, if not years? Is the analysis of individual time series worthwhile when the objective is to improve aggregate performance? The attempt to answer these important practical questions, concerned as they are with comparative forecasting accuracy, has seen the growth of a new research area, known as *forecasting competitions*, a term that is defined in detail in section 15.2.

This chapter is in four parts. We first consider the characteristics of forecasting competitions and the types of problem the research attempts to illuminate. The next section is concerned with the objectives of the various competitions and how they have developed from the earliest studies in the area. Forecasting competitions are controversial and various researchers have criticized their foundations, and the third section considers these objections. By analyzing the major studies, we then highlight the conclusions that can be drawn from the research. The chapter concludes by considering the challenges posed by including multivariate problems and directions for future research.

15.2. The Characteristics of Forecasting Competitions

Here we lay out the core elements defining a forecasting competition together with notes that expand on the problems they pose. The forecasting task may be defined more broadly than the construction given below; for example, we may wish to forecast the timing of future technological progress when no objective data are available. Such tasks are excluded from further analysis in this chapter, although the broad framework of competitive evaluation remains applicable.

A *forecasting competition* has the following six features:

1   A collection of time series to be forecast

Series may be collected in an *ad hoc* fashion or may be selected to represent a given problem area, for example the set of all monthly time series on GNP included in the United Nations Statistical Year Book, published in 1999, starting in 1970 and ending in 1997.

An organization facing the problem of choosing a forecasting approach to support their manufacturing operations will typically have a well-defined database of time series. For example, in an analysis of a company's telecoms data, Fildes et al. (1998) were able to define precisely a homogenous set of time series with which to work.

2   A set of forecasting tasks

The forecasting task may affect the value of a particular forecasting method. A method may perform well in one context but not in another.

For example, it may be a requirement that no human intervention is permitted. Thus, if model selection is reliant on human identification, the modeling process is handicapped in any competition that excludes human intervention; nor is it useful for any problem area which requires automatic modeling. Additional aspects when specifying the forecasting task include the lead time of the forecast, and whether or not the model is re-identified or re-calibrated as additional data points are added.

3   A collection of forecasting procedures

Procedures should be carefully defined and include the information set available when producing the forecasts.

For example, the information set could just be the past data or it could be enhanced by potential explanatory variables. It could also include information provided through human intervention. Where a formal forecasting method is employed there should be no ambiguity about how it is operationalized; for example, the set of trans-

forms considered prior to model building and how the "optimal" transform is to be selected.

4   Calibration/estimation procedures

This characteristic includes defining the data used and the algorithms and software employed.

Research has shown that both the choice of algorithm and the choice of software can be influential in the forecasting results (Newbold, Agiakloglou, and Miller, 1994). For example, in an ARIMA model, the parameters may be estimated by full maximum likelihood, nonlinear least squares or conditional maximum likelihood. The choice affects the results, particularly near the boundaries of the parameter space. In addition, in some software, the algorithms have been inaccurately programmed. For a recent discussion of these issues, see McCullough (1998, 1999a,b) and McCullough and Wilson (1999). Even when the programs are correct, mathematical considerations such as convergence criteria, search procedures, and numerical accuracy may affect results. The same issues apply with exponential smoothing algorithms where initialization and search procedures need to be specified.

In many forecasting methods, key parameters are user selected and their post hoc *manipulation can confuse the results. Neural net forecasting techniques (Zhang et al., 1998) provide a particularly subtle example of this. The data set available for calibrating the model is usually split into two parts (the training set and the validation set). The exact specification of the model (including the number of hidden nodes and hidden layers) may be defined by iterating between the two data sets. The validation set cannot then be used to measure forecasting performance reliably, as the model has effectively been selected* ex post *to perform optimally on the validation data.*

5   An experimental design

The design should include all those factors considered relevant to forecasting performance. The experiment may then be analyzed using analysis of variance and similar techniques.

The various competitions have progressively extended our understanding of those factors that affect comparative performance. Examples include the nature of the system in which the data are generated, the frequency of recording the data, statistical characteristics of seasonality and trend, the noise level in the data, and the number of data points. In addition, decisions as to whether to transform the data prior to modeling may also be examined.

6   Measures of forecast performance

A key feature of forecasting competitions is the separation of the data into two distinct parts, one of which we refer to as the hold-out sample or test set, which must not be used at all during the calibration/estimation process, but only to evaluate performance after fitting is complete. Defining a suitable error measure based on the hold-out sample is discussed in the next section.

No standard terminology has been established and the forecasting literature has often termed these data the validation sample, but we avoid that usage to eliminate confusion with the validation set as used in neural networks.

15.2.1. Forecast performance measures

Most practical problems in forecasting method selection require the repeated production of forecasts based on the selected method. To simulate this when making forecasting comparisons, the time origin of the forecast may be progressively shifted through the hold-out sample to provide a set of rolling forecasts from which to calculate various out-of-sample measures of forecasting performance. The general procedure is as follows:

1   $t + T$ known data points are split initially into t periods for estimation and T periods left over for testing.
2   1 to T step-ahead forecasts are generated for times $t + 1, \ldots, T$ and compared to the observed values.
3   The estimation period is then incremented by one and a new set of 1 to $T - 1$ step-ahead forecasts generated for times $t + 2, \ldots, T$.

This process is repeated, adding one observation to the estimation sample each time until the end of the series is reached. Thus, we generate a set of T one-step-ahead forecast errors, $T - 1$ two-step-ahead errors, etc., down to one T-step-ahead error. For any given lead time these forecast errors can be regarded as a sample from an unknown probability distribution. Based on the hold-out sample, we now let Y_t denote the observation recorded in period t and $e_t(l)$ the error made in forecasting Y_{t+l} at time t; that is, the l-step-ahead forecast error at time t. The characteristics of that probability distribution must be estimated from the errors computed using the hold-out sample as just described.

For a given lead time l and n errors $e_{t+i}(l)$ denoting the l-step-ahead error for the forecast at time $t + i$, standard summary statistics include:

$$\text{Average error} = \frac{1}{n} \sum_{i=1}^{n} e_{t+i-1}(l), \tag{15.1}$$

$$\text{MAE} = \frac{1}{n} \sum_{i=1}^{n} |e_{t+i-1}(l)| \quad \text{(Mean Absolute Error)}, \tag{15.2}$$

$$\text{MAPE} = \frac{1}{n} \sum_{i=1}^{n} \frac{|e_{t+i-1}(l)|}{Y_{t+i+l-1}} \quad \text{(Mean Absolute Percentage Error)}, \tag{15.3}$$

$$\text{RMSE} = \sqrt{\frac{1}{n} \sum_{i=1}^{n} e_{t+i-1}^2(l)} \quad \text{(Root Mean Square Error)}. \tag{15.4}$$

In addition, there are various relative error measures that compare one forecasting method with another. These include the percent better, which counts the relative frequency with which one method outperforms another, and the relative median, defined below. Their advantages are argued by Armstrong and Collopy (1992) and Fildes (1992) but in essence boil down to their robustness in small sample sizes (often the hold-out sample is small) and in the presence of outliers (the sample will often contain extreme outlying observations).

$$\text{MdRAE} = Median_i \left(\left| \frac{e_{1,t+i}(l)}{e_{2,t+i}(l)} \right| \right) \quad \text{(Median Relative Absolute Error),} \quad (15.5)$$

where $e_{j,t}(l)$ is the l-step ahead error made at time t when using method j.

Note that MAPE has the advantage of scale-invariance but should only be used when the series is nonnegative and possesses a natural origin. Most business and economic series are of this type, although some are not, such as company profits. When the set of series relate to common phenomena (for example, stock levels), we may use more specific measures such as probability of stockout or operating costs.

In chapter 13 of this volume, Mariano discusses the question of testing whether there is a significant difference in performance evaluation between various error statistics.

In forecasting competitions, the problem of choosing an appropriate error statistic is compounded by the need to analyze multiple series, as table 15.1 shows, where N data series are compared. Here, e_{jl} is the error for series j at lead time l.

Here SSE (and SAPE) are summary measures based on squared errors (absolute percentage errors) where, as before, they summarize the errors made for a particular series (and for a given lead time). TSE (and TAPE) summarize the errors made across series (for a particular time period). This latter has been the approach adopted in most of the forecasting competition comparisons.

Table 15.1 The error structure and error measures used in forecasting competitions

Time	Series				Summary measures by time period	
	1	2	. .	N	Squared error	Absolute % Error
$t + 1$	–	–		–	–	–
..						
$t + l$	e_{1l}	e_{2l}		e_{Nl}	TSE.$_l$	TAPE.$_l$
..						
..						
$t + T$	e_{1T}	e_{2T}	. .	e_{NT}	TSE.$_T$	TAPE.$_T$
					Overall summary measures	
Summary	SSE$_1$.	SSE$_2$.		SSE$_N$.	SSE..	SAPE..
measures by	SAPE$_1$.	SAPE$_2$.		SAPE$_N$.	TSE..	TAPE..
series						

If the errors are summarized across series, scale-dependent measures such as the MSE (summed over series, designated by $TSE_{.l}$ in table 15.1 above) cannot usually be used. The only exception to this is where the sum is itself a meaningful proxy for the cost of forecast error for the set of time series as a whole. The geometric mean of the MSE (GMMSE) is a valid measure for comparisons across series, since scale changes leave the ratio of GMMSE for two methods unchanged. In the forecasting competitions we discuss here, typically the mean or median of the APE across series (that is, $TAPE_{.l}$) has been used.

To summarize, the errors in a forecasting competition are measured both across series and over time periods, and this raises questions about how comparisons should be made. Clements and Hendry (1993) have proposed a measure which is invariant to linear transformations of the data and that also takes into account the effects of errors, which are correlated across series. (Standard measures ignore such intercorrelation.) Even with such extensions, no single measure is adequate for summarizing the various error distributions shown in table 15.1, so researchers presenting their results should include a number of alternatives that represent the costs of forecast error in the problem under analysis.

15.2.2. The use of forecasting competitions

In our introductory remarks we argued that for many organizations the problem of choosing a forecasting procedure arises naturally from within their organizational activities; in particular, manufacturing and operations. Forecasting competitions directly tackle this problem. The research is built on two fundamental premises:

- that no single class of stochastic model can successfully characterize the data generating process of the time series encountered in business and economics (never mind those from other areas in the social and natural sciences)
- because of identification and estimation errors compounded by structural change, different methods have unexpected performance characteristics that cannot be deduced from their theoretical properties where the data generation process is assumed known.

Thus, competitions are an attempt to establish regularities in comparative performance that are likely to depend on the characteristics of the set of time series being forecast *and* the problem area under study. If the results of the various competitions are convincing, they therefore have the potential to guide researchers in extending established techniques or developing new ones.

When a competition uses a well-specified set of series, such as a (sub)set of a company's sales records, it is reasonable to draw inferences for the whole set and, more tentatively, for future operations. On the other hand, many competitions have used more of a convenience sample, collecting series from diverse sources and related to many different phenomena. We believe that such competitions still provide useful insights into the performance of different methods, with respect to such issues as dealing with outliers, level changes, seasonal patterns, and so on. However, it will not usually be possible to make *formal* inferences about the utility of methods for particular forecasting tasks.

Fildes and Lusk (1984) explored this issue of how competition results should be used by contrasting the results of one of the major competitions, the M-Competition (Makridakis et al., 1982), with a survey of forecasters' beliefs as to the strengths and weaknesses of various established methods. These methods included ARIMA modeling, exponential smoothing, adaptive (time-varying para-meter) smoothing, and trend curve analysis. They concluded that there was a discrepancy between the empirical results of that particular competition and the forecasters' beliefs as to accuracy. Fildes and Makridakis (1995) looked at the same problem in a different fashion through a detailed citation study of statistical journals. They asked the question whether the results of the various competitions had influenced time-series researchers in their choice of stochastic framework adopted in their research. Their answer was a resounding "No." The unexpected results of the forecasting competitions have been ignored by most time-series researchers in their choice of a model structure. The recent volume by Clements and Hendry (1998) is a notable exception to this general observation; in the preface, the authors state that their motivation was "to take up the implicit chal-lenge of developing a theory of economic forecasting with practical implications" (p. xvii).

15.3. THE OBJECTIVES OF FORECASTING COMPETITIONS

Comparative reviews of the forecasting accuracy of alternative forecasting methods established themselves early as an adjunct to the theoretical developments of economic and statistical models. In early studies, Ferber (1956) and Schupack (1962) showed concern that "correctly specified," well-fitted models often under-performed when tested outside the sample data. Prior to 1970, empirical work was limited by computer resources. The accuracy of different methods tended to focus on a single method and a very restricted selection of time series (see Chatfield and Prothero, 1974, for an example of ARIMA modeling). However, by around 1970 studies started to include a wide range of comparisons that covered several methods and used larger numbers of real data series in order to determine the accuracy of such methods.

15.3.1. A brief history of forecasting accuracy studies

The earliest work was carried out by Reid (1969, 1972) as part of his doctoral research, and this was built on by Newbold and Granger (1974) in a funded research project. Newbold and Granger used 106 time series and concentrated on the accuracy of three univariate forecasting methods: the Holt–Winters vari-ant of exponential smoothing with trend and multiplicative seasonal, stepwise autoregressions on first differences of the data with automatic selection of lag length, and the Box–Jenkins methodology applied to ARIMA modeling. They also considered, in depth, various forms of combining forecasts from these three methods. The objectives they set were:

- to assess the loss from using automatic methods compared to manual procedures (the ARIMA models were identified manually while the other two approaches were automatic)
- to assess the relative performance of some univariate forecasting methods on real data.

Newbold and Granger found that the forecasts from ARIMA models were best about 60 percent of the time and that the mean absolute error of these forecasts was about 80 percent of that of the forecasts derived from their exponential smoothing procedures.

With the exception of some studies comparing univariate time-series models to econometric models (for a critical review, see Armstrong, 1978), no further ambitious accuracy comparisons were undertaken until Makridakis and Hibon (1979). The Makridakis and Hibon study was based on 111 series; they considered some 13 core methods[1] in total, including a number of variations of exponential smoothing, adaptive smoothing, and naive benchmarks based on the random walk. Their aim was "to reconcile conflicting evidence [they had perceived] on accuracy."

Commentators on the paper made a number of substantive suggestions (see below) on how the design of comparative studies could be improved. In particular, a consensus view of the commentators was that an explanation for observed differences should be sought in the characteristics of the time series. These reactions led Makridakis to continue this line of research and this resulted in the so-called M-Competition (Makridakis et al., 1982).

In the M-Competition, the number of series considered was increased to 1,001 and the number of core methods was increased to 14 (three new approaches were added and two were dropped). In addition, more accuracy measures were considered and the series were segmented into various subdivisions, in search of an explanation as to the circumstances in which one method outperformed the remainder. There was an increased emphasis on establishing the conditions under which one method outperforms alternatives in order to help forecasting users make a rational choice between methods.

Armstrong and Lusk (1983) provided a commentary that identified weaknesses, clarified results, and suggested paths for further research. Newbold (1983) even hoped that it was "the forecasting competition to end all forecasting competitions," a hope that was soon frustrated.

The authors of the M-Competition drew conclusions that raised as many questions as they answered. Further research has been carried out with the intent of extending the original findings, clarifying some aspects of the methodology (Armstrong and Collopy, 1992; Fildes, 1992), extending the range of univariate methods (Gardner and McKenzie, 1985; Andrews, 1994), including multivariate comparisons (Kling and Bessler, 1985), and, following Newbold (1983), examining comparative performance under conditions more closely matching those experienced by practising forecasters (the M2-Competition; Makridakis et al., 1993).

Of the early studies, that by Meese and Geweke (1984) went furthest in terms of examining the conditions under which one method outperforms its alternatives. They considered "(a) data transformations (logging, detrending, differencing, etc.), (b) data periodicity, (c) the forecast horizon, (d) the metric used to evaluate forecasts, (e) the loss functions used in parameter estimation, and (f) seasonal adjustment procedures." An additional objective was to examine the relationship between fit versus forecast performance. Meese and Geweke found that differencing is among the less effective procedures for trend removal and that the in-sample identification of transformations did not produce any noticeable improvements in forecast performance out-of-sample. However, they also found that careful modeling does produce improved forecast performance.

These early studies attracted considerable academic attention, both within the field of forecasting and in core related areas such as time-series analysis. Nevertheless, apart from the Meese and Geweke study, methodological research in this forecasting competitions paradigm remained the preserve of the forecasting community. A recent study by Fildes et al. (1998) with a commentary by Armstrong et al. (1998) attempted to clarify various issues arising from the discussion of the M-Competition, at the same time adding an additional method (Robust trend) to the range of univariate methods compared. In contrast to the earlier studies discussed above, where the sets of time series were heterogeneous (even in Meese and Geweke, who analyzed a disparate macroeconomic set of data), the set analyzed by Fildes et al. (1998) was all drawn from the same company, the same geographic area, the same level of aggregation in the product hierarchy, and the same start and end periods. This permitted the researchers to draw conclusions about the potential gains to be made when considering similar series, as well as to demonstrate certain methodological points arising from series' commonalities. The key question at issue was how the results of the earlier competitions carried over to this new and totally different data set. Fildes et al. confirmed earlier findings that simple methods appear to perform as well as more complex procedures, although the relative performance depended upon the accuracy measure used. They also found that updating the parameter estimates at successive forecasting origins improves the forecasts.

While the methodology of forecasting competitions has developed only slowly from the major studies of the 1980s, there have been a number of extensions in different applications areas including demographics (Smith, 1997), short-term electricity demand (Engle et al., 1988; Ramanathan et al., 1997), and accounting earnings (Brown, 1996).

The M3 Competition (Makridakis and Hibon, 2000) is the most recent study and is based upon 3,003 series covering primarily yearly, quarterly, and monthly series representing industrial, financial, demographic, and micro- and macroeconomic variables. In addition to the basic core methods, several new methods have been evaluated, notably rules-based[2] forecasting and artificial neural networks. In addition, five commercial software companies participated in the competition. The method and results are described in a series of papers in the *International Journal of Forecasting* (2000), **16**(4), and a commentary is scheduled to appear in the same journal (2002, **17**(4)).

15.4. Objections to Forecasting Competitions

Of the four early competitions considered, the three that included some commentary have provoked objections ranging from the competence of the researchers, to detailed statistical comments. We will limit our remarks to those that have been concerned with the broader issues discussed in the preceding sections, arguing that these objections are not sufficiently serious, either individually or collectively, to invalidate the conclusions drawn from those empirical studies.

15.4.1. Lack of clear objectives

In the various discussions of forecasting accuracy studies, a number of commentators have questioned the value of such comparisons: Priestley, commenting first in Newbold and Granger (1974) and then more explicitly on Makridakis and Hibon (1979), states "we should resist the temptation to read too much into the results of the analyses" concluding that they tell us little about "the relative merits of different types of forecasting methods." Newbold (1983), in a partial recantation of his earlier work, doubts the value of such "horse races" and goes on to note that the results that are reported are necessarily *aggregate*, so that "the forecaster, faced with a specific problem learns little about how such a problem might be attacked."

In commenting on the Newbold and Granger study, Reid (1974) highlighted the problem that without a well-specified population, selection of the time series to analyze cannot be based on sampling theory, but must, instead, be done so that the series are as representative as possible of the problem the researchers choose to address. Durbin (1979) and Newbold (1983) took up this same criticism of the subsequent Makridakis studies, with Newbold stating that no inference on relative forecasting performance was possible.

In order to understand the effects of a nonrandom choice of time series, we need to distinguish two types of competition. Some competitions, as in Fildes (1992) are able to focus upon a well-defined (sub)set of series (for example, sales figures for different product lines for a single company) so that we may examine a random sample or even an entire population of series of interest. In those cases, inference is clearly possible, albeit restricted to the original set of series (company products). In other cases, no well-defined population of series exists and direct inference is not feasible.

This criticism is valid, but the emphasis is misplaced. Many (if not all) field experiments suffer from the same limitation of using a nonrandom sample experimental base. It is overcome by the experimenter increasing the sample size and the diversity of the set (of selected time series) and by ensuring that the nonrandom components in the experiment are of little importance to the possible outcome. As Johnstone (1989) argues, the statistical testing of hypotheses is not dependent on randomness in the sample, only lack of systematic bias. Inexplicable findings should lead to a revised definition of the population under study and a revised view of the results expected. Reid's plea for a stratified selection of series has been responded to in most of the studies in that relative accuracy has been examined in subsets of the data: seasonal/nonseasonal, micro/macro, etc. In addition, quantitative measures such as the number and position of outliers, level of randomness, trend/cycle component relative to noise, etc., have been hypothesized as important factors influencing the results in some systematic way, and their impact has been considered in the some of the recent studies; for example, Fildes et al. (1998).

15.4.2. The use of automatic methods of forecasting

Jenkins (1974, 1982) and many other commentators have concerned themselves with the appropriateness of automatic methods, as contrasted with *personalized* selection whereby the choice is made by the researcher. But as we (and earlier commentators such as Bramson, 1974) have made clear, automatic methods are not an indulgence but a necessity when dealing with the large inventory/production systems that many organizations have implemented. Meese and Geweke (1984) make a similar argument for automatic forecasting of macro time series. In addition, there is no evidence on the benefits of personalized model building (excluding domain knowledge) compared to automatic procedures. Various authors, for example, Libert (1983), Texter and Ord (1989), and Makridakis et al. (1993), all found no substantive improvements from personalized model building. Perhaps even more telling, Beveridge and Oickle (1994) compare automatic procedures with those personalized identifications published in the literature and find certain of the standard automatic identifications better. In fact, experimental evidence has repeatedly demonstrated the dangers of "expert" adjustments to automatic forecasting methods (Goodwin and Fildes, 1998). At the very least, an effective automatic benchmark provides monitoring information to assess the value of subjective adjustments based on expert knowledge.

15.4.3. Aggregation over time series and various horizons of error statistics

Jenkins (1982) argued against aggregating error statistics over time series, pointing out that the errors for different series usually derive from a series-specific distribution. However, relative error measures can be used or the errors may be standardized before aggregation. In addition, Jenkins (1982) claimed that error statistics should not be aggregated over various forecasting horizons, as all relevant information is contained in the one-step-ahead residuals. Such a claim is only valid if the model is correctly identified or when the estimated model is equally appropriate for the out-of-sample data – rarely the case with real-life time series. In fact, Newbold and Granger (1974), Makridakis et al. (1982), and Meese and Geweke (1984) all calculate error statistics for various fixed lead times.

Table 15.2 The characteristics of five accuracy studies

Experimental characteristics	Research studies				
	Newbold/Granger	*Makridakis/Hibon*	*Meese/Geweke*	*Makridakis et al.*	*Fildes et al.*
Methods	Three methods + combining (ARIMA, exponential smoothing, and autoregression)	13 methods + seasonal variants (ARIMA, exponential smoothing)	Autoregressive models – various model selection criteria, for example AIC, BIC	14 methods + seasonal variants + combining (ARIMA, Bayesian, Exponential Smoothing)	Robust trend + exponential smoothing + ARIMA + ARARMA
Estimation	Least squares	Least squares	Least squares, MAD	Least squares	Least squares
Data	106 series: 80 monthly, 20 quarterly; mixture of micro and macro, some seasonal; data trended	111 series; 80% monthly, 12% quarterly, 8% annual: 1/3 macro, 2/3 seasonal. Data did not consistently trend	150 series, all macro, 50 quarterly, 100 monthly, 1/3 seasonally adjusted. 40% financial, 60% real, 1/3 non-U.S.	1001 series + sub-sample of 111: 302 micro data, 236 industry, 319, macro and 144 demographic, with 181 annual, 203 quarterly and 617 monthly	Telecoms data set of 261 non-seasonal monthly series + M-Competition data.
Lead times	1–8	1–6, 9, 12	1, 6, 12	1–18	1–18
Loss functions	Distribution of relative average squared errors (Lead 1), % better for all leads, different time origins	Fit statistics: MAPE, Theil's U; % better	% better measured by Relative MSE, MAPE and relative error calculated across time: no fit or forecast statistics given	MSE, MAPE, Median APE, % better, average rankings	MAPE; MdAPE, Relative AE, % better; 5 time origins
Transforms	None	Log and square root in ARIMA models	Logs to maximize likelihood; various prefilters of data	Log transforms for ARIMA models, none for other methods	None

15.4.4. The use of a single time origin to construct the forecasts

In the two early Makridakis studies (see table 15.2), the error statistics calculated are a summary of a cross-section of forecast errors for different lead times. Newbold and Granger, Meese and Geweke, and Fildes et al. aggregated (fixed lead time) errors across time for each series and then published summary statistics across all series. Although it is possible that the forecast periods and their accuracy are not independent (for example, if they all refer to a period of an economic boom) the problem is minimal when the series are selected in such a way as to end in different time periods and only one set of forecasts is calculated for each series; (this was the case in the Newbold and Granger, Makridakis and Hibon, and the M-Competition studies). Where the set of time series are on the same time scale as in Fildes et al., multiple time origins have been shown to be both useful and necessary (Fildes, 1992) so this design consideration should be kept in mind.

15.4.5. Failure to match estimation methods to error statistics

A number of commentators, (for example, Priestley, 1974, 1979; Zellner, 1986) have criticized the studies for estimating the parameters in a model using least squares, adopting the conditional mean as the point forecast and, subsequently, evaluating forecast accuracy using other measures than mean squared error; for example, MAPE. Whilst such a procedure might significantly affect the results, other researchers have explored this issue and found little if any improvement. In particular, even when optimal estimators with better theoretical performance characteristics are used with a matching out-of-sample evaluation criterion, no difference in performance is detectable (Meese and Geweke, 1984; Makridakis and Hibon, 1991; see also Fildes and Makridakis, 1988). Thus, the choice of accuracy measure is important when comparing methods, but it is relatively unimportant in the estimation phase. That is, although estimation and prediction issues may be combined into an overall loss function framework, little is lost by first using an efficient estimation procedure and then generating predictions from the fitted model.

A related question is the use of dynamic, or multi-step, estimation, where the model is fitted using data lagged l periods if forecasts are required l steps ahead. For a detailed discussion, see chapter 9 by Bhansali in this volume.

15.4.6. The methodological adequacy of forecasting competition research

Table 15.2 summarizes five of the major forecasting competitions. Although all the objections described above carry some weight, at least for some of the studies, the care and objectivity with which the studies have been carried out and the openness of the process by which replication has been encouraged seem to us to counterbalance the criticisms. After reviewing this evidence, Fildes and Makridakis (1995) argued that the intense scrutiny of the results, particularly of the M-Competition, is such as "we can conclude with reasonable confidence that the results of the accuracy competitions . . . have withstood the requirements for objectivity and replicability." They go on "In summary, different researchers, using different methods and different data sets have reached some broadly compatible conclusions" and these conclusions we discuss in the next section.

15.5.   Conclusions from Forecasting Competitions

The results of the various competitions we have described do not readily lead to a simple numerical summary of relative performance. We here describe the qualitative findings as reported by the authors (and any qualifications due to subsequent commentators).

15.5.1.   General versus specific model specification

The early practical forecasting models, such as exponential smoothing, were easy to apply (in a pre-computerized world) because the user was offered little choice. The model structure was preset and the smoothing parameter(s) were fixed *a priori*. In contrast, the ARIMA class of models as developed by Box and Jenkins requires the user to first filter the data to achieve stationarity, specify the autoregressive structure, and estimate the parameters from the data. Exponential smoothing (at least in its additive forms) is a special case of the ARIMA class. In turn, the ARIMA class is a special case (with fixed parameters) of a more general state-space formulation: see chapters 4 and 5 by Pedregal and Young, and Proietti, in this volume. It might be thought that such generality would lead to improved forecasting accuracy. As the argument goes, if the data generation process, the "true model," is of the simpler, specific model class, assuming the more general model and simplifying (usually through statistical testing) will, in theory, lead to similar accuracy as the alternative strategy of starting with the specific "true" model. However, where the data generation process (DGP) is from the more general class, starting with the simple model necessarily leads to a specification error and potentially large losses in relative accuracy.

The broad thrust of the findings in the forecasting competitions has belied this theoretical analysis. The following summary may serve to explain these results. When the series is *short*, model selection may produce poor results. In addition, even with the DGP known, a simpler misspecified model may forecast better due to poor parameter estimates (Gilbert, 1995). When the series is subject to *structural change*, simple methods are often more robust in that they respond to changes more rapidly (the random walk being an obvious example). Conversely, moderate-to-long series with a relatively stable structure will benefit from systematic model development. For example, working with longer macroeconomic series, Newbold and Granger (1974) found some improvement in forecasting accuracy when comparing ARIMA models to an automatic Holt–Winters version of exponential smoothing. Also, Meese and Geweke (1984) concluded that long-memory autoregressions with an estimated pre-filter[3] compare favorably to those where the filter is predetermined. However, Fildes (1983), Huss (1985), Schnaars (1986), Geurts and Kelly (1986), Watson et al. (1987), Koehler and Murphree (1988), and Fildes et al. (1998) all found simpler methods to be at least as effective.

15.5.2. Data-based transformations

Prior to any modeling, the data may be transformed in a variety of ways such as adjusting for seasonality, scaling or, in the ARIMA modeling tradition, differencing. Meese and Geweke (1984) paid particular attention to this issue, showing convincingly that of the three prefilters they considered, linear detrending, an estimated prefilter, and differencing, the linear or estimated filters worked best. This adds support to Pierce's (1977) observation of the inappropriateness of automatically using differencing as is recommended in the Box–Jenkins methodology[4]. In support of this observation, in both the M-Competition and Fildes et al. (1998), Parzen's long-memory method (ARARMA) performed well, a method based on an estimated pre-filter. In a direct analysis of this issue, Makridakis and Hibon (1997) compared differencing versus linear detrending using the 1,001 series in the M-Competition and found that linear detrending improved longer term forecast accuracy, the difference in performance for monthly data being substantial. In the M3 Competition (Makridakis and Hibon, 2000) the ARARMA method does somewhat better than most of the ARIMA-based methods, but the results are less clear-cut. This outcome appears to reflect improvements in the ARMA modeling system that was employed as well as the sheer number of ARIMA-based schemes considered. We continue to believe that the long-memory method has better long-term potential than differencing.

Some forecasting methods simultaneously incorporate a seasonal component into the modeling procedure; for example, Holt–Winters or ARIMA. An alternative is to seasonally adjust the data prior to modeling. While the latter course of action is theoretically less efficient, some of the models that include seasonality may well be overly constraining, neglecting either deterministic or stochastic seasonality. The choice of seasonal specification has been explored in a number of "competitions." Osborn et al. (1999) clarified and extended Clements and Hendry's (1997) study through an analysis of 24 quarterly time series. They concluded that seasonal unit-root tests were not helpful in determining whether to include a seasonal difference in the model. A limited study by Garcia-Ferrer et al. (1997) found evidence of changing seasonality (which would explain Osborn's et al.'s finding) and this was best modeled through a time-varying parameter specification. This contradictory evidence suggests there are further comparisons to be made to understand how best to model seasonality. In chapters 18 and 19 in this volume, Osborn discusses forecasting with seasonal unit-root models, and Franses and Paap consider periodic models of seasonality.

In a comment on the first Makridakis study, Durbin (1979) noted that the results of the study (and later the M-Competition) suggested that deseasonalizing the data and using nonseasonal methods, then re-seasonalizing, led to improved performance when compared to methods such as Winters that explicitly model seasonality. Makridakis and Hibon (1997) further analyzed the 1,001 data series of the M-Competition and confirmed the weakness of the integrated seasonal models as identified through the Box–Jenkins methodology (as well as an automatic variant). The differences were, however, small.

Seasonal effects may be additive or multiplicative. When multiplicative, a logarithmic transformation may suffice to restore the additivity property, but many series appear to have a multiplicative seasonal plus additive error structure. Indeed, the heuristic scheme underlying the Census X-11 method of seasonal adjustment has this form. The multiplicative Holt–Winters scheme is designed to accommodate such structures, but tended to be ignored in the time-series literature, as it lacked an underlying statistical model. Ord et al. (1997) have now provided such a structure, which should enable the development of suitable diagnostics to choose between additive and multiplicative models. However, Franses (1996), among others, has suggested that seasonality is neither additive nor multiplicative, but is inextricably bound up with the trend and cyclical components of the series. Clearly, this is an area where forecasting issues are far from resolved and further comparisons are needed.

15.5.3. Nonlinear models

The core competitions we have described have not paid much attention to modeling any nonlinear characteristics in the data. The results that have appeared mostly consider transformations. Thus, Meese and Geweke (1984) examined the benefits of using a log transform where it was recommended by an in-sample (maximum likelihood) based analysis. In their study, 48 percent of series apparently needed to be transformed but when out-of-sample comparisons were made with the untransformed model, no material improvement in forecast performance was observed. That is, the information from the in-sample analysis regarding transformations was close to worthless. Both Makridakis and Hibon (1979) and the M-Competition found no benefits to using transforms, although Makridakis and Hibon (1997) in their extended analysis of ARIMA models (using M-Competition data) found some minor advantages.

More generally, the development of nonlinear models has been a major area of activity in time-series analysis in recent years, as is evident from chapters 20 and 21 by Tsay, and Lundbergh and Teräsvirta, in this volume.

Insofar as a nonlinear model encompasses a linear alternative, the previous summary of evidence in favor of simplicity suggests there are conflicting factors that in particular circumstances may or may not lead to nonlinear models performing relatively well. In fact, theoretical arguments suggest that some aspects of the economy would be better modeled nonlinearly. However, in an extensive survey of nonlinear models, de Gooijer and Kumar (1992) found little evidence that nonlinear models consistently outperform linear alternatives. Clements and Smith (1999) examined the performance of a number of self-exciting threshold autoregressive (SETAR) models for forecasting certain macroeconomic variables and found that these nonlinear models were advantageous in some states of nature, but not in others.

Artificial neural networks (ANN) represent a particular class of nonlinear models that has attracted attention; see the recent review by Zhang et al. (1998). Protagonists for neural network methods obviously view the nonlinear effects as potentially important and consider the costs of misspecification to be low. Hill et al. (1996) show that, for some of the M-Competition data, neural nets outperform the best of the alternative methods, while Liao (1999) drew the same conclusion from analyzing the telecoms data of Fildes et al. (1998). When the models are known to be linear, Zhang (2000) provides evidence that using ANN instead of the linear (ARIMA) DGP has little adverse impact on forecast quality.

Balkin and Ord (2000) evaluated the performance of neural networks for the 3,003 series of the M3 Competition. Overall, no particular benefit appears to accrue to using neural nets for these series, and they conclude that ANN methods are likely to show material gains in forecasting only when a time series is sufficiently long *and* sufficiently stable for the nonlinear structure to be reliably identified and modeled.

In summary, the issue of whether to use a nonlinear method is moot. However, the evidence seems to suggest that the form of the nonlinearity cannot be identified by in-sample tests. It is perhaps the case that some ANN methods are sufficiently robust as to overcome the downside costs of adopting such a general formulation.

15.5.4. The benefits of combining forecasting methods

One of the few "laws of forecasting" is that forecast accuracy can be improved by combining a number of (preferably distinct) forecasting methods. The competitions themselves broadly confirm this law also. Clemen (1989) provides a detailed review and bibliography on this issue, which extends far beyond the scope of the evidence from forecasting competitions; Armstrong (2001) provides an updated review of this area. Whilst the benefits are best realized when the methods that are combined differ substantially (ideally, they are negatively correlated), in the competitions all the core forecasting methods used in the combinations are univariate and often quite similar in their statistical structure. For example, Newbold and Granger provided a detailed study of combining, justifying it in the case where the models under consideration are similar by a Bayesian argument focusing on the uncertainty in identification of an ARIMA model. In their study, Box–Jenkins was most often ranked as best and was reasonably regarded as the method to beat. But a combination of Box–Jenkins and Holt–Winters outperformed it.

However, the combination of methods does not generally outperform the best possible method – its strength lies in its consistently strong performance, which therefore avoids the problem of choosing between methods; see, for example, Makridakis et al. (1993).

Combining may outperform selection, as the following argument illustrates. Consider two forecasts, *F* and *G*, with respective forecast mean square errors

(FMSE) equal to V and W respectively, and expected cross-product (covariance when the forecasts are unbiased) equal to C. Without loss of generality, we take $V < W$. Given a sufficiently long series we will always select F, with FMSE equal to V.

Now consider the linear combination:

$$F^* = aF + (1 - a)G,$$

with FMSE equal to $a^2V + (1 - a)^2W + 2a(1 - a)C$. This FMSE is minimized when we choose $a = (W - C)/(V + W - 2C)$, $0 < a < 1$. The minimum value of the FMSE is

$$FMSE = V - (1 - a)^2(V + W - 2C),$$

which is always less than V unless $V = C$. This condition is exactly the requirement for F to be fully efficient relative to G (Stuart, Ord, and Arnold, 1998, pp. 22–4). In practice such a condition will rarely be satisfied and combining forecasts leads to improved accuracy.

More generally, a combined forecasting is calculated from: $F^* = d + \sum_{i=1}^{p} b_i \hat{Y}_i$ where

$\hat{Y}_i$ is the forecast from the ith method. A question susceptible to both theoretical and empirical "competition style" research is the choice of weighting schemes and the choice and number of methods to include. Summarizing these various studies, Clemen (1989) concluded that the "equal weights" benchmark is hard to beat. In summary, combining forecasts will often work quite well, particularly when the true DGP is unknown. For a much more detailed discussion on combining and the related notion of encompassing, see chapter 12 by Newbold and Harvey in this volume.

15.5.5. Forecasting accuracy and prediction intervals

A point forecast is usually chosen as a conditional expected value and is associated with an interval that expresses the corresponding uncertainty. Empirical studies (Makridakis et al., 1987; Makridakis and Winkler, 1989) have found that actual forecasts fall outside the theoretically constructed prediction intervals more often than postulated by the theory, whatever model is used to describe the data, Bayesian, recursive methods partially excepted (see Chatfield's (1993) survey of this topic). For example, in Makridakis et al. (1987) it was shown that 17 percent of the forecasts fell outside the 95 percent prediction interval for lead 1, rising to 26 percent for lead 6. A further problem is that increases in sample size do not lead to improved calibration of the prediction intervals (Makridakis and Hibon, 1979; Makridakis et al., 1982; Lusk and Neves, 1984). This leaves open the question of how best to calculate confidence intervals and whether bootstrapping methods or the simpler approach of using the empirically observed error distribution as developed in section 15.2.1 are adequate (Chatfield, 1993). The latter is only useful when there is an ample supply of data. In chapter 2 of this volume, Ericsson considers forecast uncertainty, and in chapter 3 Tay and Wallis discuss density forecasts.

Without an adequate theory to provide prediction intervals for different lead times, the empirical measures used to compare point forecasts have had to suffice. The results of the various competitions have left no doubt that the choice of measure is important in deciding which method is to be preferred. For example, some methods seem less likely to produce extreme errors, despite their average performance being mediocre. Equally, some methods perform better at longer lead times. Thus the researcher needs to use a wide variety of measures (including such standards as MAPE, if only to ensure comparability with earlier studies).

15.5.6. Model selection

A pervasive theme underlying all forecasting competition research is how best to select an appropriate method. Even in Newbold and Granger's framework, it was apparent from their experiments that model identification errors, compounded by estimation errors, often led to inadequate performance of the more general ARIMA class of models. While the Box–Jenkins methodology of model building inevitably led to improved fit, there were no such implications for forecasting performance. In fact, various researchers have used the results from the competitions to analyze the relationship between within sample fit and out-of-sample accuracy and found low correlations, particularly at longer lead times (Koehler, 1985; Makridakis, 1986; Makridakis and Winkler, 1989; Pant and Starbuck, 1990). These results led to attempts to promote statistical measures of fit that more effectively linked with forecast performance. Such methods include Akaike's Information Criterion (AIC) and Schwartz's Bayesian Information Criterion (BIC), but success has been mixed, with conflicting evidence on which should be preferred, the more parsimonious BIC (Beveridge and Oickle, 1994) or AIC (Meese and Geweke, 1984).

By the time of publication of the M-Competition and the associated discussion (Armstrong and Lusk, 1983), forecasters came to view the evidence on relative performance as favoring exponential smoothing and its variants as a highly competitive benchmark, relative to other classes of method. Sophisticated modeling of trend, rather than simple differencing, appears to pay off, whether in the class of autoregressive model (Meese and Geweke, 1984; Meade and Smith, 1985) or in the class of exponential smoothing models (Tashman and Kruk, 1996). These conclusions, firm though they are, have had little impact on the models proposed by most statisticians when analyzing time series (Fildes and Makridakis, 1995).

The gain from selecting a "best method," as measured by the percentage of forecasts that are better than those from an exponential smoothing benchmark, is modest; only around 55 percent show as better, even though there are many data series which are not well described by the models that underpin exponential smoothing (see, for example, the HP data set in the M2 Competition, 1987). This evidence suggested the need to develop methods that build on the particular characteristics of the time series in order to select a model class or a method.

Fildes (1989) showed the potential benefits that could be achieved if it proved possible to match the appropriate method to each of a set of time series. Makridakis (1990) proposed an empirically based approach he called "sliding simulation," which attempted to capitalize on the past success of a method in forecasting a series in selecting a method to forecast ahead for the same series. However, in the M2 Competition it met with little success. A similar approach, associated with the name Focus Forecasting, has had commercial success but no impartial validation, failing to beat exponential smoothing and its extensions (Gardner and Anderson, 1997).

A second approach to model selection aims to use the characteristics of each time series, observed up to time t, to choose a method (from some wide class of alternatives) to forecast ahead. At a fundamental level, this principle has been implicit in all time-series modeling, whether based on automatic algorithms or expert judgment, where summary statistics and graphs, in-sample statistics such as model fit (however measured), and diagnostics were initially regarded as indicative of forecasting performance and informative as to which model to adopt; subsequently these were extended to include out-of-sample statistics. Grambsch and Stahel (1990) illustrate how the detailed analysis of a set of time series can then be successfully applied to other similar series. Shah (1997) achieved some success at formalizing method selection based on combining the statistical characteristics of the data through discriminant analysis. His analysis included such measures as series length, the coefficient of variation, and the first few autocorrelations for both the original and detrended series. Armstrong and Collopy (1993) extended the set of characteristics under consideration to include *a priori* information on the "causal forces" that, they argued, were likely to affect the future trends in the series; that is, whether it is a "growth" series such as population. The logic behind including "causal forces" is straightforward; the social, economic, or market forces which determine a time series, whilst unknown, are expected to remain fixed. Therefore, data-based statistical estimates and *a priori* estimates should on average be compatible and better forecasts could be obtained by rules which reconciled any conflicts. This proved successful when evaluated using a subset of the M-Competition data.

A further consequence of accepting the idea of causal forces is that the careful analysis of the full data history in order to choose a forecasting method, based on data characteristics and forecasting performance on the hold-out data, should lead to equally strong performance when applied in real time. Fildes et al. (1998) examined this issue, using the robust trend method developed by Grambsch and Stahel, for some telecoms data. They compared the robust-trend method to a wide range of methods taken from earlier competitions both on the telecoms data series and the M-Competition data set. The results convincingly demonstrate the principle that methods developed and proven for a homogenous set of data can outperform those that previous research had identified as the best performers. Robust trend substantially outperformed the exponential smoothing class and ARARMA. Also, damped trend smoothing was consistently outperformed by Holt's linear trend (a result in conflict with previous evidence). A different perspective on these results is that prior knowledge of the structure of a homogeneous set of series is much stronger than that for a heterogeneous collection. In consequence, model selection need not be purely data-driven.

15.5.7. An evaluation

This latest research has taken us full-circle; forecasting methods can and should be designed to suit the data series under analysis. The *a priori* selection of a particular model class, without regard to the data generating process,[5] may possibly lead to substantial additional error.

This conclusion is perhaps best understood through an example. The papers on short-term electricity demand forecasting, by Ramanathan et al. (1997) and by Engle et al. (1998), present analyses based upon series that are relatively long and whose patterns are reasonably stable over time. Thus, the researchers were able to identify meaningful and quite complex models, and to obtain efficient parameter estimates. The contextual knowledge that these authors were able to employ to develop their models provides an edge to the model-builder that is not easily captured by automatic methods (although a rules-based system could probably do so, given enough development). Thus quality of information is critical in the selection of a suitable model.

It is worth noting that Box and Jenkins recommend that at least 30 observations should be available for the identification of a regular series, and perhaps 50 for seasonal models. By contrast, many of the series used in forecasting competitions are shorter than this and are often prone to structural change. The nature of many forecasting competitions is often such that a large number of diverse series must be forecast, thereby making the use of contextual knowledge very difficult. Nevertheless, results from the M3 Competition suggest that, even with weak information, rules-based methods can do rather well at longer lead times.

In conclusion, we must recognize that purely data-driven model selection methods need a substantial amount of data to be effective, and that the application of such techniques to very short series may be counterproductive.

15.6. MULTIVARIATE INFORMATION SETS

So far, we have concerned ourselves only with univariate time-series methods in forecasting competitions. In principle, many of the same issues apply when the information available to produce the forecast is multivariate; in particular, whether there is a class of model and associated estimation procedures that has desirable (or undesirable) performance characteristics. However, one of the primary justifications of the design of forecasting competitions, the requirement to include automatic procedures in order to be cost-effective, does not hold in multivariate extensions. In general, multivariate forecasting problems are complex and demand expert modeling attention, not least to select the information set to be included. This effectively means fewer data series (sometimes only one) can be considered. No studies have been identified that have tackled a wide variety of different problems. Allen and Fildes (2001) summarize the empirical evidence derived from a large number of studies and discuss all aspects of econometric model-building relevant to forecasting. While many of the principles they propose are based on limited empirical evidence backed up by theoretical analysis or simulation studies, certain themes we have already discussed in the univariate context have also been studied in much the same way in the multivariate context. These include:

1 The appropriate specification for VAR models. Issues include:
   (a) determining suitable lag length,
   (b) whether to model in levels or differences,
   (c) the effects of cointegrating vectors (that is, the conditions under which a particular VAR specification outperforms another), and
   (d) the benefits from adopting constrained model specifications such as those in an equilibrium correction model.
2 The estimation method that should be adopted (least squares is usually adequate).
3 The accuracy of multivariate models compared to univariate alternatives:
   (a) *Ex post* versus *ex ante* comparisons;
   (b) When forecasting short term versus long term;
   (c) Nonlinear models versus linear models.

Table 15.3 (table 6 in their original), is reproduced here and summarizes their evidence on accuracy. Allen and Fildes conclude, from a mound of disparate research evidence, that the lag lengths should be reduced for each variable in each equation in a VAR, and make several recommendations on how VARs should be specified.

Despite the wealth of empirical evidence presented by Allen and Fildes (2001) the studies have been summarized qualitatively. They are not based on a common methodology; no summary statistics can be calculated, nor are the conditions of the (often implicit) experiment made clear. Finally, the empirical results are not reproducible. Thus, we must conclude that although the questions posed when multivariate information is available are amenable, in principle, to the methodology of forecasting competitions, the majority of studies provide limited information for generalization.

We examine here the objectives of those few studies that have tried to overcome the problems of multivariate forecasting competitions. The area of macro-economic forecasting has seen the most research activity. Fildes and Stekler (1999) survey these studies and find, with Allen and Fildes, that the multivariate macro-forecasts are more accurate than univariate forecasts. Within these comparisons, certain authors have examined various methodological issues. For example, Artis and Zhang (1990) studied the specification of VAR models, and Zellner and his co-workers (Garcia-Ferrer et al., 1987; Zellner and Hong, 1989) took the output growth series from eight countries and asked whether a small number of explanatory variables could enhance simple autoregressive univariate forecasts, and whether advanced time-series models could be used successfully to improve

Table 15.3   Econometric versus univariate forecasts
[Recorded as (better, no difference, worse) according to the specified accuracy criterion, by *series*, with number of studies in parentheses. Most forecasts are one step ahead and RMSE is the usual accuracy criterion.][6]

	Classical single equation	*VAR*	*Structural sector model*	*All econometric*
Pre-1985				
Against				
Naive	18,2,11 (15)		49,6,15 (8)	67,8,26 (23)
ARIMA	53,4,35 (37)	4,0,4 (2)	65,4,64 (15)	122,8,103 (54)
All univariate	71,6,46 (52)	4,0,4 (2)	114,10,79 (23)	189,16,129 (77)
Better as percent of total	*58%*	*50%*	*56%*	*57%*
1985 on				
Against				
Naive	27,4,25 (15)	18,2,5 (6)		45,6,30 (21)
ARIMA	27,8,28 (22)	170,8,39 (37)	77,6,46 (9)	274,22,113 (68)
All univariate	54,12,53 (37)	188,10,44 (43)	77,6,46 (9)	319,28,143 (89)
Better as percent of total	*45%*	*78%*	*59%*	*65%*

accuracy. This work led to certain empirical conclusions in the spirit of "competition research." They must be regarded as more tentative than those derived from the univariate competitions, as they are based on a much more limited set of time series. However, the addition of explanatory variables improved accuracy (confirming the survey evidence in table 15.3 above), the use of concurrent cross-section time series also improved accuracy, as did the use of combining and of time-varying parameters (Garcia-Ferrer et al., 1989).

15.6.1. Stability of relationships

A small study by Geriner and Ord (1991) suggested that bivariate time-series models may be more sensitive to misspecification in either the variables or the lag structure, or more sensitive to structural changes than univariate schemes. Stock and Watson (1996) have examined bivariate forecasting relationships compared to univariate models whilst facing the same methodological issues as the competitions we have studied earlier. They considered 76 U.S. monthly macro time series. Their aim was to examine the stability in the bivariate relationships as "instability in one of these bivariate [constant parameter] VARs implies instability in the higher dimensional VAR, so evidence of instability in the bivariate systems can be extrapolated to implied instability in the larger system." They find such instability common. The implications for forecasting, explored only in one-step-ahead forecasts, was that time-varying parameter methods might well produce improved forecasting and overcome the instability problems.

The question of whether such instability was the result of time-varying behavior or nonlinearity has been picked up by Swanson and White (1997), who used nine U.S. macroeconomic data series in a VAR model. Their interest was whether a nonlinear method (neural network) would outperform a linear method and whether a flexible specification that allowed variables to enter or drop from each equation improved on a fixed specification. Parameters were permitted to evolve in all the models. The results offer some support for all the models they considered, depending on the error measure used. However, for short-term one-quarter ahead forecasting, a fixed specification proved best (compared to a flexible specification) while for four-quarters ahead the opposite conclusion held. Similarly, a linear model won overall in the short term, while the nonlinear (flexible specification) model proved the modest winner for four-quarters ahead.

From this limited evidence of multivariate forecasting competitions, a pattern can be vaguely discerned – of varying parameters, changing economic structure, and hard-to-identify nonlinearities. These tentative conclusions are in accord with the meta-analyses of Allen and Fildes (2001) and Fildes and Stekler (1999). But here, with our focus on the methodology of forecasting competitions, we must not make too much of them. The studies illustrate the complexities of carrying out multivariate forecasting competitions – there are many factors to be taken into account in designing the experiment, perhaps most crucially the information set that is selected for inclusion in the model-building. The nature of that multivariate data set will itself determine the conclusions the researchers can draw, and they run the risk that the research design predetermines the conclusions.

15.7. CONCLUSIONS

Forecasting competitions research has developed over a 30-year period. Such competitions effectively answer a problem common to many organizations of how to select a forecasting approach to support operations. There is evidence that the research has affected forecasting practice, not least through its influence on commercial forecasting packages. Its substantive (rather than methodological) conclusions are controversial and counterintuitive. Fildes et al. (1998) summarize the four major conclusions of earlier competitions as follows:

1 Statistically sophisticated or complex methods [discussed above under the headings of general versus specific model specification and nonlinearity] do not typically produce more accurate forecasts than simpler ones.
2 The ranking of the performance of the various methods varies according to the accuracy measure being used.
3 The accuracy of the combination of various methods outperforms, on average, the individual methods being combined, and does well in comparison with other methods.

4   The performance of the various methods depends on the length of the fore-
    casting horizon.

The additional research of Fildes (1992) and Fildes et al. (1998) has supple-
mented these findings:

5   The characteristics of the set of time series under analysis is an important
    factor in determining relative performance between methods. If the time series
    has a homogeneous structure, that information should be exploited. That is,
    contextual knowledge should be utilized wherever possible.
6   A method specifically designed for the characteristics observed in specific
    data sets (such as the telecoms data) may perform substantially better than the
    methods selected as best in a broad-ranging competition using heterogeneous
    series.
7   Sampling variability of performance measures renders comparisons based
    on a single time-series origin unreliable; comparisons should be based on
    multiple origins.
8   The broad conclusions (listed above) of the M-Competition hold for time
    series drawn from a wide variety of economic and national contexts.

The controversies surrounding these findings are discussed in Fildes and
Makridakis (1995). In essence, they arise from the limited relationship between
in-sample fit and out-of-sample performance and the tendency of more general,
complex methods and the process of model construction itself to produce less
parsimonious models. That is, as we have argued elsewhere in this chapter,
simple methods may be more robust when data are limited or series are subject
to (unpredictable) structural changes (cf., Chen, 1997). The second, more straightforward, issue is the use of differencing to render the data stationary. The research results we report here make it clear that the automatic adoption of this
approach is inappropriate. Unfortunately, it is so embedded in the paradigm of
ARIMA modeling that few time-series researchers have heeded this conclusion
in their theoretical work. At least in part, this tendency reflects an over-reliance
on data-driven methods and a lack of consideration of contextual information.

Despite the success of the univariate competitions in influencing both practice
and, to a lesser extent, research in time-series modeling and forecasting, many
issues remain to be explored in greater depth. The most important research issue
is the need to define the experimental conditions in order to help model selection. As yet, the substantive help competitions offer is limited, although certain
methods appear to dominate others on average (see, for example, the discussion
on ARARMA versus ARIMA in section 15.5.2). What is needed is a more detailed
prescriptive approach based on the characteristics of the time series, developing
the issues discussed in section 15.5.6 on model selection.

Forecasting competitions applied to multivariate problems are in their infancy.
They pose deeper problems, in addition to the question of defining the experimental conditions. That they are needed is not in doubt, at least in our minds. The
difficulty in establishing principles to support effective econometric forecasting
(Allen and Fildes, 2001) demonstrates the deficiencies of relying on current

approaches that combine econometric theory with *ad hoc* case studies. There is a wide range of questions requiring answers based on firmer empirical evidence than is at present available. Building on Stock and Watson's (1996) analysis of instability and Swanson and White's (1997) study linking instability to nonlinearity would be a good place to start.

The importance of the results of forecasting competitions can all too easily be lost in the detail. How many organizations follow the guidelines suggested by these competitions? How many software packages encourage their users to develop effective forecasting methods? There is an important educational effort required here.

Further, the economic benefits to improved organizational forecasting are considerable and yet, as noted in the surveys by Dalrymple (1987) and Sanders and Mandrodt (1994), resource-intensive subjective methods still tend to dominate industrial practice: see also chapter 6 by Önkal-Atay, Thomson, and Pollock, in this volume. Such methods clearly can capture contextual inputs but, as noted by O'Connor et al. (1993, 1997), forecasting judgments are often flawed and may be inferior to even simple quantitative methods (cf., Webby and O'Connor, 1996).

Notes

1 We have counted each method that has both a seasonal and nonseasonal variant as a single method and excluded combined methods.

2 Rule-based forecasting is a type of expert system that is used in time-series extrapolations. Rules are based on forecasting expertise and domain knowledge to combine extrapolative forecasts.

3 The pre-filters used are autoregressive of the form $(1 - \sum \phi_i B^i)$, where B is the back-shift operator, and this effectively transforms Y_t into $Z_t = Y_t - \sum \phi_i Y_{t-i}$. The first difference is the simplest example. In an estimated pre-filter, the parameters $\{\phi_i\}$ are estimated.

4 Franses and Kleibergen (1996), using the Nelson–Plosser annual macro data, found differencing more satisfactory than incorporating a linear trend.

5 Liao's (1999) work with neural nets that successfully outperform robust trend is an apparent contradiction to this finding. However, the input needed to make ANN effective relies on the exploratory statistical analysis of Grambsch and Stahel (1990).

6 The detailed sources for these comparisons are given in Allen and Fildes (2001).

References

Allen, P.G. and R. Fildes (2001). Econometric forecasting. In J.S. Armstrong (ed.), *Principles of Forecasting: A Handbook for Researchers and Practitioners*. Norwell, MA.: Kluwer.

Andrews, R.L. (1994). Forecasting performance of structural time series models. *Journal of Business and Economic Statistics*, 12, 129–33.

Armstrong, J.S. (1978). Forecasting with econometric methods: Folklore versus fact with discussion. *Journal of Business*, 51, 549–600.

Armstrong, J.S. (2001). Combining forecasts. In J.S. Armstrong (ed.), *Principles of Forecasting: A Handbook for Researchers and Practitioners*. Norwell, MA.: Kluwer.

Armstrong, J.S. and F. Collopy (1992). Error measures for generalizing about forecasting methods: empirical comparisons with discussion. *International Journal of Forecasting*, 8, 69–80.

Armstrong, J.S. and F. Collopy (1993). Causal forces: structuring knowledge for time series extrapolation. *Journal of Forecasting*, 12, 103–15.

Armstrong, J.S., A. Koehler et al. (1998). Commentaries on "Generalizing about univariate forecasting methods: further empirical evidence". *International Journal of Forecasting*, 14, 359–66.

Armstrong, J.S. and E.J. Lusk (eds.) (1983). "Commentary on the Makridakis time series competition (M-Competition)." *Journal of Forecasting*, 2, 259–311.

Artis, M.J. and W. Zhang (1990). BVAR forecasts of the G-7. *International Journal of Forecasting*, 6, 349–62.

Balkin, S. and J.K. Ord (2000). A statistical implementation of neural network analysis. *International Journal of Forecasting*, 16, 509–15.

Beveridge, S. and C. Oickle (1994). A comparison of Box–Jenkins and objective methods for determining the order of a non-seasonal ARMA model. *Journal of Forecasting*, 13, 419–34.

Box, G.E.P. and G.M. Jenkins (1976). *Time Series Analysis, Forecasting and Control*, 2nd edn. San Francisco: Holden-Day.

Bramson, M.J. (1974). Comment on Newbold, P. and Granger, C.W.J., Experience with forecasting univariate time series and the combination of forecasts. *Journal of the Royal Statistical Society* (A), 137, 157.

Brown, L.D. (ed.) I/B/E/S Research Bibliography (1996). *The Annotated Bibliography of Earnings Expectation Research*. New York: I/B/E/S International Inc.

Brown, R.G. (1963). *Smoothing, Forecasting and Prediction*. Englewood Cliffs, N.J.: Prentice-Hall.

Chatfield, C. (1993). Calculating interval forecasts. *Journal of Business and Economic Statistics*, 11, 121–35.

Chatfield, C. and D.L. Prothero (1973). Box–Jenkins seasonal forecasting: problems in a case study with discussion. *Journal of the Royal Statistical Society*, (A), 136, 295–336.

Chen, C. (1997). Robustness properties of some forecasting methods for seasonal time series: a Monte Carlo study. *International Journal of Forecasting*, 13, 269–80.

Clemen, R.T. (1989). Combining forecasts: a review and annotated bibliography with discussion. *International Journal of Forecasting*, 5, 559–608.

Clements, M.P. and D.F. Hendry (1993). On the limitations of comparing mean squared forecast errors with discussion. *Journal of Forecasting*, 12, 617–76.

Clements, M.P. and D.F. Hendry (1997). An empirical study of seasonal unit roots in forecasting. *International Journal of Forecasting*, 13, 341–55.

Clements, M.P. and D.F. Hendry (1998). *Forecasting Economic Time Series*. Cambridge: Cambridge University Press.

Clements, M.P. and J. Smith (1999). A Monte Carlo study of the forecasting performance of empirical SETAR models. *Journal of Applied Econometrics*, 14, 123–41.

Dalrymple, D.J. (1987). Sales forecasting practices: results from a United States survey. *International Journal of Forecasting*, 3, 379–91.

De Gooijer, J.G. and K. Kumar (1992). Some recent developments in nonlinear time series modeling, testing and forecasting. *International Journal of Forecasting*, 8, 135–56.

Durbin, J. (1979). Comment on: Makridakis, S. and Hibon, M., "Accuracy of forecasting: an empirical investigation." *Journal of the Royal Statistical Society* (A), 142, 133–4.

Engle, R.F., S.J., Brown, and G. Stern (1988). A comparison of adaptive structural forecasting methods for electricity sales. *Journal of Forecasting*, 7, 149–72.

Ferber, R. (1956). Are correlations any guide to predictive value. *Applied Statistics*, 5, 113–22.

Fildes, R. (1983). An evaluation of Bayesian forecasting. *Journal of Forecasting*, 2, 137–50.

Fildes, R. (1989). Evaluation of aggregate and individual forecast method selection rules. *Management Science*, 39, 1056–65.

Fildes, R. (1992). The evaluation of extrapolative forecasting methods with discussion. *International Journal of Forecasting*, 8, 81–111.

Fildes, R. and C. Beard (1992). Forecasting systems for production and inventory control. *International Journal of Operations and Production Management*, 12, 4–27.

Fildes, R., M. Hibon, S. Makridakis, and N. Meade (1998). Generalising about univariate forecasting methods: further empirical evidence with discussion. *International Journal of Forecasting*, 14, 339–58.

Fildes, R. and E.J. Lusk (1984). The choice of a forecasting model. *Omega*, 12, 427–35.

Fildes, R. and S. Makridakis (1988). Loss functions and forecasting. *International Journal of Forecasting*, 4, 545–50.

Fildes, R. and S. Makridakis (1995). The impact of empirical accuracy studies on time series analysis and forecasting. *International Statistical Review*, 63, 289–308.

Fildes, R. and H.O. Stekler (1999). The state of macroeconomic forecasting. Lancaster, U.K.: Lancaster University Working Paper EC3/99, forthcoming in *Journal of Macroeconomics*.

Franses, P.H. and F. Kleibergen (1996). Unit roots in the Nelson–Plosser data: Do they matter for forecasting? *International Journal of Forecasting*, 12, 283–8.

Franses, P.H. (1996). *Periodicity and Stochastic Trends in Economic Time Series*. Oxford: Oxford University Press.

Garcia-Ferrer, A., J. Del Hoyo, and A.S. Martin-Arroyo (1997). Univariate forecasting comparisons: the case of the Spanish automobile industry. *Journal of Forecasting*, 16, 1–17.

Garcia-Ferrer, A., R.A., Highfield F. Palm, and A. Zellner (1987). Macroeconomic forecasting using pooled international data. *Journal of Business and Economic Statistics*, 5, 53–67.

Gardner, E.S. and E.A. Anderson (1997). Focus Forecasting reconsidered. *International Journal of Forecasting*, 13, 501–8.

Gardner, E.S. Jr. and E. McKenzie (1985). Forecasting trends in time series. *Management Science*, 31, 1237–46.

Geriner, P.A. and Ord J.K. (1991). Automatic forecasting using explanatory variables: a comparative study. *International Journal of Forecasting*, 7, 127–40.

Geurts, M.D. and J.P. Kelly (1986). Forecasting retail sales using alternative models. *International Journal of Forecasting*, 2, 261–72.

Gilbert, P.D. (1995). Combining VAR estimation and state space model reduction for simple good predictions. *Journal of Forecasting*, 14, 229–50.

Goodwin, P. and R. Fildes (1999). Judgmental forecasts of time series affected by special events: Does providing a statistical forecast improve accuracy? *Journal of Behavioural Decision Making*, 12, 37–53.

Grambsch, P. and W.A. Stahel (1990). Forecasting demand for special services. *International Journal of Forecasting*, 6, 53–64.

Hill, T., M. O'Connor, and W. Remus (1996). Neural network models for time series forecasting. *Management Science*, 42, 1082–92.

Huss, W.R. (1985). Comparative analysis of company forecasts and advanced time series techniques using annual electric utility energy sales data. *International Journal of Forecasting*, 1, 217–39.

Jenkins, G.M. (1974). Comments on Newbold, P. and Granger, C.W.J., "Experience with forecasting univariate time series and the combination of forecasts." *Journal of the Royal Statistical Society* (A), 137, 148–50.

Jenkins, G.M. (1982). Some practical aspects of forecasting in organizations. *Journal of Forecasting*, 1, 3–21.

Johnstone, D.J. (1989). On the necessity of random sampling. *British Journal of the Philosophy of Science*, 40, 443–83.

Kling, J.L. and D.A. Bessler (1985). A comparison of multivariate forecasting procedures for economic time series. *International Journal of Forecasting*, 1, 5–24.

Koehler, A.B. (1985). Simple vs. complex extrapolation models. *International Journal of Forecasting*, 1, 63–8.

Koehler, A.B. and E.S. Murphree (1988). A comparison of results from state space forecasting with forecasts from the Makridakis Competition. *International Journal of Forecasting*, 4, 45–55.

Liao, K.P. (1999). Feedforward neural network forecasting, model building and evaluation: theory and application in business forecasting. Ph.D. Thesis. Lancaster, U.K.: University of Lancaster.

Libert, G. (1983). The M-Competition with a fully automatic Box–Jenkins procedure. *Journal of Forecasting*, 2, 325–8.

Lusk, E.J. and J.S. Neves, J.S. (1984). A comparative ARIMA analysis of the 111 series of the Makridakis competition. *Journal of Forecasting*, 3, 329–32.

Makridakis, S. (1983). Empirical evidence versus personal experience: commentary on the Makridakis time series competition. *Journal of Forecasting*, J.S. Armstrong and E.J. Lusk (eds.), 295–309.

Makridakis, S. (1990). Sliding simulation – a new approach to statistical forecasting. *Management Science*, 36, 505–12.

Makridakis, S., A. Andersen, R. Carbone, R. Fildes, M. Hibon, R. Lewandowski, J. Newton, E. Parzen, and R. Winkler (1982). The accuracy of extrapolation (time series) methods; results of a forecasting competition. *Journal of Forecasting*, 1, 111–53.

Makridakis, S., C. Chatfield, M. Hibon, M. Lawrence, T. Mills, J.K. Ord, and L. Simmons (1993). The M-2 Competition: a real-life judgmentally based forecasting study with discussion. *International Journal of Forecasting*, 9, 5–29.

Makridakis, S. and M. Hibon (1979). Accuracy of forecasting: an empirical investigation with discussion. *Journal of the Royal Statistical Society* (A), 142, 97–145.

Makridakis, S. and M. Hibon (1991). Exponential smoothing – the effect of initial values and loss functions on post-sample forecasting. *International Journal of Forecasting*, 7, 317–30.

Makridakis, S. and M. Hibon (1997). ARMA models and the Box–Jenkins methodology. *Journal of Forecasting*, 16, 147–63.

Makridakis, S. and M. Hibon (2000). The M3 Competition. *International Journal of Forecasting*, 16, 451–76.

Makridakis, S., M. Hibon, E. Lusk, and M. Belhadjali (1987). Confidence intervals: an empirical investigation of the series in the M-competition. *International Journal of Forecasting*, 3, 489–508.

Makridakis, S. and R.L. Winkler (1989). Sampling distributions of post-sample forecasting errors. *Applied Statistics*, 38, 331–42.

McCullough, B.D. (1998). Assessing the reliability of statistical software: Part I. *American Statistician*, 52, 358–66.

McCullough, B.D. (1999a). Assessing the reliability of statistical software: Part II. *American Statistician*, 53, 149–59.

McCullough, B.D. (1999b). The reliability of econometric software: Eviews, LIMDEP, SHAZAM and TSP. *Journal of Applied Econometrics*, 14, 191–202.

McCullough, B.D. and B. Wilson (1999). On the accuracy of statistical procedures in Microsoft Excel 97. *Computational Statistics and Data Analysis*, 31, 27–37.

Meade, N. and I.M.D. Smith (1985). ARARMA vs. ARIMA – a study of the benefits of a new approach to forecasting. *Omega*, 6, 519–34.

Meese, R. and J. Geweke (1984). A comparison of autoregressive univariate forecasting procedures for macroeconomic time series. *Journal of Business and Economic Statistics*, 2, 191–200.

Newbold, P. (1983). The competition to end all competitions: commentary on the Makridakis time series competition. *Journal of Forecasting*, J.S. Armstong and E.J. Lusk (eds.), 276–79.

Newbold, P., C. Agiakloglou, and J. Miller (1994). Adventures with ARIMA software. *International Journal of Forecasting*, 10, 573–81.

Newbold, P. and C.W.J. Granger (1974). Experience with forecasting univariate time-series and the combination of forecasts with discussion. *Journal of the Royal Statistical Society* (A), 137, 131–65.

Ord, J.K., A.B. Koehler, and R.D. Snyder (1997). Estimation and prediction for a class of dynamic nonlinear statistical models. *Journal of the American Statistical Association*, 92, 1621–9.

Osborn, D.R., S. Heravi, and C.R. Birchenhall (1999). Seasonal unit roots and forecasts of two-digit European industrial production. *International Journal of Forecasting*, 15, 27–47.

O'Connor, M., W. Remus, and K. Griggs (1993). Judgemental forecasting in times of change. *International Journal of Forecasting*, 9, 163–72.

Pant, P.N. and W. Starbuck (1990). Innocents in the forecast: forecasting and research methods. *Journal of Management*, 16, 433–60.

Pierce, D.A. (1977). Relationships – and the lack thereof – between economic time series, with special reference to money and interest rates. *Journal of the American Statistical Association*, 72, 11–26.

Priestley, M.B. (1974). Comment on Newbold, P. and Granger, C.W.J., "Experience with forecasting univariate time series and the combination of forecasts." *Journal of the Royal Statistical Society* (A), 137, 152–3.

Priestley, M.B. (1979). Comment on Makridakis, S. and Hibon, M., "Accuracy of forecasting: an empirical investigation with discussion." *Journal of the Royal Statistical Society* (A), 142, 127–8.

Ramanathan, R., R. Engle, C.W.J. Granger, F. Vahid-Araghi, and C. Brace (1997). Short-run forecasts of electricity loads and peaks. *International Journal of Forecasting*, 13, 161–74.

Reid, D.J. (1969). A comparative study of time series prediction techniques on economic data. Ph.D Thesis, Nottingham: University of Nottingham.

Reid, D.J. (1972). A comparison of forecasting techniques on economic time series. In M.J. Bramson, I.G. Helps, and J.A.C.C. Watson-Gandy (eds.), *Forecasting in Action*. Birmingham, U.K.: Operational Research Society.

Reid, D.J. (1974). Comments on Newbold, P. and Granger, C.W.J. "Experience with forecasting univariate time series and the combination of forecasts." *Journal of the Royal Statistical Society* (A), 137, 146–8.

Sanders, N.R. and K.B. Mandrodt (1994). Forecasting practices in United-States corporations – survey results. *Interfaces*, 24: (2), 92–100.

Schnaars, S.P. (1986). A comparison of extrapolation models on yearly sales forecasts. *International Journal of Forecasting*, 2, 71–85.

Schupack, M.P. (1962). The predictive accuracy of empirical demand analysis. *Economic Journal*, 72, 550–75.

Shah, C. (1997). Model selection in univariate time series forecasting using discriminant analysis. *International Journal of Forecasting*, 13, 489–500.

Smith, S.K. (1997). Further thoughts on simplicity and complexity in population projection models. *International Journal of Forecasting*, 13, 557–65.

Stock, J.H. and M.W. Watson (1996). Evidence on structural instability in macroeconomic time series relations. *Journal of Business and Economic Statistics*, 14, 11–30.

Stuart, A., J.K. Ord, and S.F. Arnold (1999). *Kendall's Advanced Theory of Statistics*, Vol. 2A. 6th edn. London: Arnold.

Swanson, N.R. and H. White (1997). Forecasting economic time series using flexible versus fixed specification and linear versus nonlinear econometric models. *International Journal of Forecasting*, 13, 439–61.

Tashman, L.J. and J.M. Kruk (1996). The use of protocols to select exponential smoothing procedures: a reconsideration of forecasting competitions. *International Journal of Forecasting*, 12, 235–53.

Texter, P.A. and J.K. Ord (1989). Forecasting using automatic identification procedures: A comparative analysis. *International Journal of Forecasting*, 5, 209–15.

Watson, M.W., L.M. Pastuszek, and E. Cody (1987). Forecasting commercial electricity sales. *Journal of Forecasting*, 6, 117–36.

Webby, R. and M. O'Connor (1996). Judgemental and statistical time series forecasting: a review of the literature. *International Journal of Forecasting*, 12, 91–118.

Zellner, A. (1986). A tale of forecasting 1001 series: the Bayesian knight strikes again. *International Journal of Forecasting*, 2, 491–4.

Zellner, A. and C. Hong (1989). Forecasting international growth rates using Bayesian Shrinkage and other procedures. *Journal of Econometrics*, 40, 183–202.

Zhang, G.P., B.E. Patuwo, and M.Y. Hu (1998). Forecasting with artificial neural networks. The state of the art. *International Journal of Forecasting*, 14, 35–62.

Zhang, G.P. (2001). An investigation of neural networks for linear time-series forecasting. *Computers and Operational Research*, 28, 1183–1202.

CHAPTER SIXTEEN

Empirical Comparison of Inflation Models' Forecast Accuracy

Øyvind Eitrheim, Tore Anders Husebø, and Ragnar Nymoen

16.1. INTRODUCTION

Producers and consumers of empirical models take a shared interest in comparison of model forecasts. As pointed out by Granger (1990), consumers of models care about out-of-sample model properties and consequently put weight on comparisons of model forecasts. Since producers of models in turn wish to influence the beliefs of model consumers, comparison of model forecasts provides an important interface between producers and consumers of empirical models.

A comparison of forecasts from empirical models can be based on "raw" model forecasts (for example, provided by the producers) or on the published forecasts that include the effects of judgmental corrections (intercept corrections). In this chapter, the aim is to focus on the mapping from model specification to forecast properties, so we consider the raw model forecast, without the intervening corrections made by forecasters. Another issue is that any comparison will inevitably consider only a subset of macroeconomic variables, and the choice of variables will influence the outcome of the comparison. This problem extends to whether it is levels variables that are forecasted or their growth rates, since the ranking of forecast accuracy may depend on which linear transformation one uses: see Clements and Hendry (1993) and Clements and Hendry (1998, ch. 3).

In the following, these issues are pushed somewhat in the background by focusing on inflation forecasting. The vector of variables that enters the comparison is the "typical" list of variables that are forecasted in central banks' economic bulletins and outlooks. The typical list includes a limited number of *annual growth rates*: inflation (in Norway, this is CPI inflation), wage growth, import price growth, GDP growth, growth in consumer expenditure, housing price growth (asset inflation), but also at least one levels variable, namely the rate of unemployment.

In the 1990s, inflation targeting has emerged as a candidate intermediate target for monetary policy. An explicit inflation target for monetary policy means a quantified inflation target, for example 2 percent per year, and a tolerance interval around it of (for example) ±1 percentage point, and that the central bank is given full control of monetary instruments. New Zealand and Canada are the pioneering countries. Sweden moved to inflation targeting in 1993, and since 1997 an inflation target has represented the nominal anchor of the U.K. economy.

As emphasized in Svensson (1997b), an explicit inflation target implies that the central bank's conditional forecasts 1–2 years ahead become the intermediate target of monetary policy. If the inflation forecast is sufficiently close to the target, the policy instruments (a short-term interest rate) is left unaltered. If the forecasted rate of inflation is higher (lower) than the target, monetary instruments are changed until the revised forecast is close to the inflation target. In such instances the properties of the forecasting model (the dynamic multipliers) can have a large influence on how much the interest rate is changed.

It is seen that with the conditional inflation forecasts as the operational target of monetary policy, there is an unusually strong linkage between forecasting and policy analysis. Decisions are more explicitly forward-looking than in other instances of macroeconomic policy making, where the assessment of the current economic situation plays a prominent role. That said, inflation forecasts are also important elements in policy discussions for exchange rate "regimes" other than explicit inflation targeting. Thus, Svensson (1997a) notes that inflation forecasts prepared by Norges Bank are "more explicit and detailed than Sveriges Riksbank's forecast," even though Norway has no formal inflation target.[1]

In this chapter we compare forecasts that are made for policy purposes. Section 16.2 gives the economic background and discusses the relationship between model specification and inflation forecasting and section 16.3 provides an empirical investigation example of how the models perform econometrically and in forecasting inflation. In section 16.4 we outline four different forecasting models for the Norwegian economy. First, we present two large scale macroeconometric models which contain monetary policy channels (transmission mechanisms) linking monetary policy instruments like short-run money market interest rates and exchange rates to other economic variables (for example, those listed above), through causal mechanisms which allow for monetary policy analysis. Second, we also look at two simple noncausal forecasting models in differences. Section 16.5 discuss the forecasting properties of the four models using stochastic simulation.

16.2. MODEL SPECIFICATION AND INFLATION FORECASTING

One of the inflation models with the longest track record is the Phillips curve. It was integrated into macroeconometric models in the 1970s. In the mid-1980s, however, the Phillips curve approach has been challenged by a model consisting of a negative relationship between the level of the real wage and the rate of unemployment, dubbed the wage curve by Blanchflower and Oswald (1994), together with firms' price-setting schedules.[2] The wage curve is consistent with a wide range of economic theories (see Blanchard and Katz, 1997), but its original impact among European economists was due the explicit treatment of union behavior and imperfectly competitive product markets: see Layard and Nickell (1986), Rowlatt (1987), and Hoel and Nymoen (1988). Because the modern theory of wage- and price-setting recognizes the importance of imperfect competition on both product and labor markets, we refer to this class of models as the Imperfect Competition Model – ICM hereafter.

In equation (16.1) pc_t denotes the log of the consumer price index in period t. Δ is the first difference operator, so Δpc_t is CPI inflation:

$$\Delta pc_t = \gamma_1(u_{t-1} - u^n) + \gamma_2'(L)\Delta z_t - \sum_{i=1}^{n} \alpha_i EC_{i,t-1} + \varepsilon_t \qquad (16.1)$$

The first term on the right-hand side is the (log of) the rate of unemployment (u_{t-1}) minus its (unconditional) mean u^n, hence $E[u_{t-1} - u^n] = 0$. It represents "excess demand" in the labor market and how wage increases are transmitted on to CPI inflation. Empirical equations often include a product market output-gap variable alongside the unemployment term. However, this variable is not needed in order to discriminate between theories, and is omitted from (16.1).

The term z_t is a vector of variables that enter in differenced form and $\gamma_2'(L)$ is the corresponding coefficient vector of lag polynomials. Typical elements in this part of the model are the lagged rate of inflation; that is, Δpc_{t-1}, the rate of change in import prices and changes in indirect tax-rates.

The case where the remaining coefficients in the equation are zero, that is $\alpha_1 = \ldots = \alpha_n = 0$, corresponds to the Phillips curve model. The Phillips curve is an important model in current macroeconomics, for example in the theory of monetary policy as laid out in Clarida and Gertler (1999), and it dominates the theoretical literature on inflation targeting (see Svensson, 2000). The Bank of England (1999) includes Phillips curve models in their suite of models for monetary policy. Mervyn King, the Deputy Governor of the Bank of England puts it quite explicitly: "the concept of a natural rate of unemployment, and the existence of a vertical long-run Phillips curve, are crucial to the framework of monetary policy."[3]

The empirical literature shows that the Phillips curve holds its ground when tested on U.S. data – see Fuhrer (1995), Gordon (1997), Gali and Gertler (1999), and Blanchard and Katz (1999). Studies from Europe usually conclude differently: the preferred models tend to imply a negative relationship between the real wage level and the rate of unemployment: see, for example, Drèze and Bean (1990, table 1.4), OECD (1997, table 1.A.1), Wallis (1993), and Rødseth and Nymoen (1999). These findings are consistent with the seminal paper of Sargan (1964), and the later theoretical developments leading to the ICM class of wage- and price-setting equations.

The negative relationship between the real wage level and the rate of unemployment, which is also referred to in the literature as the *wage-curve* (see Blanchflower and Oswald, 1994), can be incorporated in (16.1) in the following way: Let w_t denote the log of the nominal wage rate in period t, so $w_t - pc_t$ is the real-wage, then the equilibrium correction term $EC_{1,t}$ can be specified as

$$EC_{1,t} = w_t - pc_t + \beta_{11}u_t - \mu_1, \quad \text{with } \alpha_1 \geq 0 \text{ and } \beta_{11} \geq 0. \tag{16.2}$$

Thus, the future rate of inflation is influenced by a situation "today" in which the real wage is high/low relative to the "equilibrium" real wage $\beta_{11}u_t + \mu_1$. The parameter μ_1 denotes the (long-run) mean of the relationship; that is, $E[EC_{1,t}] = 0$. Disequilibria in firms' price-setting have similar implications, and the inflation equation therefore contains a second term $EC_{2,t}$ that relates the price level in period t to the equilibrium price level. Hence, in a simple specification,

$$EC_{2,t} = (pc_t - w_t) - \beta_{12}(pi_t - pc_t) + \mu_2 \quad \text{with } \alpha_2 \geq 0 \text{ and } \beta_{12} \geq 0, \tag{16.3}$$

where pi_t is the log of the import price index.

It is seen that both the Phillips curve and ICM theories focus on the labor and product markets. Although in theory disequilibria in other markets, such as the money market and the market for foreign exchange, might have predictive power for inflation, we only consider the case of $n = 2$ in equation (16.1). Thus, the Phillips curve equation takes the simple form

$$\Delta pc_t = \gamma_1(u_{t-1} - u^n) + \gamma_2'(L)\Delta \mathbf{z}_t + \varepsilon_{\text{phil},t}, \tag{16.4}$$

while an inflation equation consistent with the ICM is given by

$$\Delta pc_t = \gamma_2'(L)\Delta \mathbf{z}_t + \alpha_1 EC_{1,t-1} + \alpha_2 EC_{2,t-1} + \varepsilon_{\text{ICM},t}. \tag{16.5}$$

In (16.5) the unemployment term $(u_{t-1} - u^n)$ is omitted because, according to theory, unemployment creates inflation via wage-setting. Thus, if the wage-curve implicit in (16.2) is correctly modeled, there is no additional predictive power arising from the inclusion of $(u_{t-1} - u^n)$ in the equation: see Kolsrud and Nymoen (1998) for a discussion.

The two models take different views on the causal mechanisms in the inflation process, and as a result, they can lead to conflicting policy recommendations. Consider, for example, a situation where both models forecast a rise in inflation; say, because of a sudden rise in domestic spending. Based on the Phillips curve, one might recommend a rise in the Bank's interest rate, since otherwise it would take several periods before unemployment rises enough to curb inflation. Moreover, since any departure of unemployment from its natural rate is temporary, one might as well provoke a temporary rise in u_t, "today," in order to cut off inflation pressure directly. The ICM model suggests mechanisms other than unemployment which can stabilize inflation. For example, in an open economy, a rise in inflation leads to a fall in profits, and wage claims will be reduced as a result even at the going rate of unemployment. According to the ICM it is also possible that a rise in the interest rate has lasting effects on the rate of unemployment; that is, the natural rate may not be invariant to policy changes (see Kolsrud and Nymoen, 1998; Bårdsen and Nymoen, 2000). Thus, the recommendation could be a more moderate rise in the interest rate.

However, equations (16.4) and (16.5) have in common that they include causal information about the effects of other variables on inflation. In this respect they stand apart from univariate time-series models which only include causal information in the form of lagged values of inflation itself. A simple example is given by

$$\Delta pc_t = \gamma_0 + \gamma_{3p}\Delta pc_{t-1} + \varepsilon_{AR,t}, \tag{16.6}$$

which is a first-order autoregressive model of inflation. Finally, we consider forecasting models of the *random-walk* type; that is,

$$\Delta\Delta pc_t = \varepsilon_{dAR,t}. \tag{16.7}$$

We use the acronym *dAR* for the disturbance in (16.7), since an interpretation of (16.7) is that it is an autoregression in differences, obtained by setting $\gamma_{3p} = 1$ in (16.6) (and $\gamma_0 = 0$).

A common thread in many published evaluations of forecasts is the use of time-series models as a benchmark for comparison with forecasts derived from large-scale econometric systems of equations: see Granger and Newbold (1986, ch. 9.4) for a survey. The finding that the benchmark models often outperformed the econometric models represents an important puzzle that has not been fully resolved until recently, by the work of Michael Clements and David Hendry. In short, the solution lies in the insight that, for example, the *random walk* model is not the "naive" forecasting tool that it appears at first sight. Instead, its forecasts are relatively robust to some types of structural change that occurs frequently in practice, and that are damaging to forecasts derived from econometric models.

Equations (16.4)–(16.7) are special cases of the general equation (16.1). Assume now that the disturbances in that equation are innovations relative to the avaiable information. A strategy of choosing a forecasting model for period $T + 1$ is to test the validity of the restrictions of the different models on the sample ($t = 1, 2, \ldots T$). Only models which are valid reductions of (16.1) will have disturbances that are innovations relative to the information set. For models which are correctly specified, the conditional expectation of the variable (inflation) in period $T + 1$, based on the model, will yield the predictor with the minimum mean squared forecast error (MMSFE): see, for example, Clements and Hendry (1998, ch. 2.7). This suggests that congruent models will generate accurate forecasts.

However, this result implicitly assumes that the process that we forecast is stable over the forecast horizon. But experience tells us that parameters frequently change. Suppose, for example, that a "regime shift" occurs in period $T + 1$. The congruent model then no longer reflects the true process in the forecast period, and thus we cannot use the above theorem to show that its conditional mean is the MMSFE forecast. Conversely, simple univariate models like (16.6) and (16.7) are unlikely to be congruent representations. Despite this, they offer some degree of protection against damage caused by nonstationarities.

Clements and Hendry (1998, 1999) have developed the theory of forecasting economic time series to account for instability and nonstationarity in the processes. One important result is that there is no way of knowing *a priori* which model will have the best forecast properties – an econometric model that includes relevant causal information, or a simple random walk model like (16.7): see, for example, Clements and Hendry (1998, ch. 2.9). In our case, the econometric ICM may be the encompassing model, but if the parameters of the inflation process alter in the forecast period, its forecasts may still compare unfavourably with the forecasts of simple time-series models.

As an example, suppose that the parameter μ_1 of the wage-curve changes in period $T + 1$; that is, there is a shock to wage-setting. The ICM-forecast $E[\Delta pc_{T+2} | \mathcal{I}_{T+1}]$ then becomes biased. Moreover, in the case that μ_1 changes within sample (in period T, say), and that change is undetected by the forecaster, the ICM model will produce a biased forecast for period $T + 1$, while the random-walk forecast from (16.7) may be unbiased. Thus the better model in terms of causal information actually loses in a comparison to the random walk on this measure of forecast accuracy. Moreover, it is also possible that the Phillips curve model outperforms the ICM. The reason is that the Phillips curve shares the one-step forecast properties of the random walk in this case, since it omits the $EC_{1,t-1}$ term that is affected by the structural break.

So far we have only considered one-step forecasts, but it is clear that the same issues arise for dynamic multi-step forecasts. For example, in the Phillips curve and in the ICM model, u_{T+1} has to be forecasted in order to calculate $E[\Delta pc_{T+2} | \mathcal{I}_T]$. Hence a larger econometric model is needed for forecasting, and if a structural break occurs in those parts of the economy that determine u_{T+1}, the inflation forecast is damaged. Conversely, simple univariate forecasting tools are by construction insulated from structural changes elsewhere in the system. Also in that sense they produce robust forecasts.

Systems of equations that are developed with econometric methods are referred to as equilibrium-correcting models, EqCMs. The generalization of the simple autoregressive inflation models in (16.6) and (16.7) are systems of equations that only use differences of the data, without equilibrium correction terms; that is, VARs in differences (DVs: Clements and Hendry, 1999, ch. 5) and double-differences (DDVs). The Phillips curve and the ICM are examples of EqCMs. At first sight it may seem that this tag only applies to the ICM, since the terms $EC_{1,t-1}$ and $EC_{2,t-1}$ are omitted from the Phillips curve. However, the Phillips curve conveys the alternative view that inflation is stabilized by $u_t - u^n \to 0$ in steady-state. Thus the equilibrating term is the rate of unemployment itself, rather than $EC_{1,t-1}$ and $EC_{2,t-1}$.

In the following, these issues are investigated by comparison of the forecasts of the different model specifications: ICM, Phillips curve, univariate autoregression in differences, and double differencing forecasting rules. In the next section, small-scale models of inflation are evaluated econometrically prior to forecast comparison. In section 16.4 we investigate different versions of the macroeconomic models used by Norges Bank (the Central Bank of Norway).

16.3. TWO INFLATION MODELS

In this section[4] we compare forecasts of the two contending quarterly inflation models over the period 1995.1–1998.4. The estimation sample is 1968.1–1994.4. The sample-split coincides with an important change in the Norwegian economy: the move from a high-inflation regime to a new regime with low and stable inflation. The means of the annual CPI growth rate of are 6.7 percent (estimation sample) and 2.1 percent (forecast period). The corresponding standard deviations are 3 percent and 0.6 percent. Thus the experiment is relevant for elucidating how well the different models forecast the new regime, conditional on the old regime.

A VAR for the five endogenous variables Δw_t, Δpc_t, Δp_t, Δy_t, and Δu_t was estimated with data 1968.1–1994.4 ($N = 108$). The definitions of the variables are:

- w_t = log of nominal wage cost per man hour in Norwegian manufacturing.
- y_t = log of manufacturing value-added (fixed prices) per man hour.
- p_t = log of the manufacturing value-added deflator.
- u_t = log of the rate of unemployment.
- pc_t = log of the consumer price index.

The equilibrium-correction mechanisms in equations (16.8) and (16.9) were taken as known, thus.

$$w_t = p_t + y_t - 0.08u_t + EC_{1,t}, \tag{16.8}$$

$$pc_t = 0.6(w - y)_t + 0.4pi_t + \tau_{3,t} + EC_{2,t}. \tag{16.9}$$

pi_t is log of the import price index of manufactures, and $\tau_{3,t}$ is an indirect tax-rate. These two equations are the empirical counterparts to (16.2) and (16.3). The estimates are taken from Bjørnstad and Nymoen (1999), and are also consistent with the findings for annual data in Johansen (1995). Equation (16.9) is from Bårdsen, Fisher, and Nymoen (1998).[5]

The unrestricted system is large (43 coefficients in each equation), due to fourth-order dynamics and the inclusion of 18 nonmodeled variables, for example, current and lagged import price growth (Δpi_t), the change in normal working hours in manufacturing (Δh_t), a variable that captures the coverage of labor markets programmes ($prog_t$), and changes in the payroll and indirect tax-rates ($\Delta \tau_{1,t}$ and $\Delta \tau_{3,t}$). The deterministic terms include intercepts, three centered seasonal dummies, incomes policy dummies for 1979 and 1988, and a VAT dummy for 1970q1. Finally, dummies that capture both deterministic shifts in the mean of the rate of unemployment as well as a changing seasonal pattern (see Akram, 1999).

The upper part of table 16.1 shows residual properties of the estimated VAR. The residual standard errors of wage growth ($\hat{\sigma}_{\Delta w}$) and inflation ($\hat{\sigma}_{\Delta pc}$) are similar

Table 16.1 Diagnostics for the ICM system and model

Diagnostic tests for the VAR

$$\hat{\sigma}_{\Delta w} = 0.0113$$

$$\hat{\sigma}_{\Delta pc} = 0.0054$$

$$\hat{\sigma}_{\Delta p} = 0.0299$$

$$\hat{\sigma}_{\Delta y} = 0.0277$$

$$\hat{\sigma}_{\Delta u} = 0.084$$

$$vAR\ 1 - 5F(125, 182) = 1.94[0.53]$$

$$vNormality\ \chi^2(10) = 20.00[0.03]$$

Diagnostic tests for the ICM

$$Overidentification\ \chi^2(152) = 175.3[0.10]$$

$$vAR\ 1 - 5F(125, 334) = 0.99[0.52]$$

$$vNormality\ \chi^2(10) = 18.0[0.06]$$

Notes: Sample period: 1968.1–1994.4. The VAR is estimated by OLS. The model is estimated by FIML. *p*-values in brackets.

to what we expect from earlier studies (cf., Nymoen, 1989a; Bårdsen, Jansen, and Nymoen, 1999). The estimated standard errors for product price growth and productivity are both close to 3 percent, and they are clearly going to induce a lump of uncertainty in inflation forecasts based on this system. For the rate of unemployment, $\hat{\sigma}_{\Delta u} = 0.084$ corresponds to a residual standard error of 0.18 percentage points (using that the sample mean of the rate of unemployment is 2.2 percent). There is no evidence of vector residual autocorrelation, as shown by the joint test of absence of fifth-order autocorrelation. However, the vector normality test is significant at the 5 percent level. In the lower part of table 16.1, *Overidentification* $\chi^2(152)$ shows that the overidentifying restrictions implied by the ICM model, are jointly data acceptable. That the ICM encompasses the VAR is also confirmed by the (vector) test statistics for absence of residual autocorrelation and nonnormality.

Next, table 16.2 focuses on the FIML estimates for the wage and price equations of the ICM. The equation for manufacturing wages resembles earlier models of this variable (see Nymoen, 1989a,b). Structural break-dummies are present in the form of WD_t, which captures the effects of wage-freeze periods and the highly centralized settlements in 1988 and 1989, and a dummy for the devaluation of the Norwegian currency in May 1986. The price equation includes the devaluation dummy, and a dummy for the introduction of VAT ($i70q1$), price freeze ($i79q1$),

Table 16.2   The wage and price equations of the estimated ICM

The wage equation

$$\widehat{\Delta w_t} = 0.341 + 0.512\Delta_3 pc_{t-1} - 0.199\Delta_3 w_{t-1} + 0.06\Delta_3 pi_{t-1} + 0.074\Delta_4 y_{t-1}$$
$$\phantom{\widehat{\Delta w_t} =}{\scriptstyle(0.007)}{\scriptstyle(0.04)}\phantom{\Delta_3 pc_{t-1} - }{\scriptstyle(0.04)}\phantom{\Delta_3 w_{t-1} + }{\scriptstyle(--)}{\scriptstyle(0.03)}$$

$$+ 0.494\Delta\tau_{1,t-2} - 0.023\Delta u_t - 1\Delta h_t - 0.045 WD_t$$
$${\scriptstyle(0.143)}\phantom{\Delta\tau_{1,t-2} - }{\scriptstyle(0.004)}{\scriptstyle(--)}{\scriptstyle(0.005)}$$

$$+ 0.023 i86q3_t - 0.078[(w - p - y)_{t-4} + 0.08 u_{t-1}]$$
$${\scriptstyle(0.011)}{\scriptstyle(0.0193)}$$

$$\hat{\sigma}_{\Delta w} = 0.0124$$

The price equation

$$\widehat{\Delta pc_t} = -0.065 + 0.079\Delta w_t + 0.167\Delta_3 pc_{t-1} - 0.041\Delta^2 y_{t-1}$$
$$\phantom{\widehat{\Delta pc_t} = }{\scriptstyle(0.015)}{\scriptstyle(0.003)}{\scriptstyle(0.025)}\phantom{\Delta_3 pc_{t-1} - }{\scriptstyle(0.009)}$$

$$- 0.031[p_{t-1} - 0.6(w_{t-1} - y_{t-2}) - 0.4 pi_{t-1} - \tau_{3,t-1}]$$
$${\scriptstyle(0.007)}$$

$$+ 0.037(\Delta pi_{t-1} + \Delta pi_{t-4}) - 0.007\Delta u_{t-2} - 0.005\Delta u_{t-5}$$
$${\scriptstyle(0.011)}\phantom{(\Delta pi_{t-1} + \Delta pi_{t-4}) - }{\scriptstyle(0.0022)}\phantom{\Delta u_{t-2} - }{\scriptstyle(0.0024)}$$

$$+ 0.114\Delta\tau_{3,t-2} + 0.039 i70q1_t - 0.028 i79q1_t + 0.067 i86q3_t$$
$${\scriptstyle(0.034)}\phantom{\Delta\tau_{3,t-2} + }{\scriptstyle(0.005)}{\scriptstyle(0.005)}{\scriptstyle(0.005)}$$

$$+ 0.022 S_{1,t} + 0.013 S_{2,t} + 0.008 S_{3,t}$$
$${\scriptstyle(0.002)}\phantom{S_{1,t} + }{\scriptstyle(0.002)}\phantom{S_{2,t} + }{\scriptstyle(0.0021)}$$

$$\hat{\sigma}_{\Delta pc} = 0.0049$$

Notes: Sample period: 1968.1–1994.4. Estimation by FIML, jointly with equations for Δp_t; Δy_t and Δu_t. Standard errors are in parentheses below the estimates.

and seasonal dummies ($S_{i,t}$ ($i = 1, 2, 3$)). When we replace Δw_t by the right hand side of the wage equation, we obtain the empirical counterpart to equation (16.1) in section 16.2. The two equilibrium-correction terms in particular are significant, and imposition of the Phillips curve restrictions on the model produces a highly significant test statistic.

Next, consider a "Phillips curve VAR"; that is, we start from a VAR that omits the equilibrium-correction terms while retaining u_{t-1} as an unrestricted variable. Table 16.3 gives the diagnostics for the system and the model, and table 16.4 shows the estimated Phillips curve wage equation together with the Δpc_t equation.

The Phillips curve wage equation has a residual standard error a little lower than its ICM counterpart. The equation implies a natural rate of unemployment (u^n in (4)) of 1.5 percent, which may seem low, but the average rate of unemployment over the sample period is only 2.2 percent.

We first compare the forecasts of the models for the 16-quarter period from 1995.1 to 1998.4. The forecasts are dynamic and are conditional on the actual

Table 16.3 Diagnostics for the system and the Phillips curve model

Diagnostic tests for the Phillips curve VAR

$$\hat{\sigma}_{\Delta w} = 0.0188$$

$$\hat{\sigma}_{\Delta pc} = 0.0533$$

$$\hat{\sigma}_{\Delta p} = 0.0302$$

$$\hat{\sigma}_{\Delta y} = 0.0276$$

$$\hat{\sigma}_{\Delta u} = 0.0836$$

$$vAR\ 1 - 5F(125, 191) = 0.977[0.55]$$

$$vNormality\ \chi^2(10) = 21.84[0.02]$$

Diagnostic tests for the Phillips curve model

$$Overidentification\ \chi^2(139) = 159.1[0.11]$$

$$vAR\ 1 - 5F(125, 329) = 0.977[0.55]$$

$$vNormality\ \chi^2(10) = 18.19[0.05]$$

Notes: See table 16.1.

Table 16.4 The wage and inflation equations of the estimated Phillips curve

The wage Phillips curve

$$\widehat{\Delta w_t} = \underset{(0.0019)}{0.0094} + \underset{(0.07)}{0.503\Delta_2 pc_{t-1}} - \underset{(0.06)}{0.195\Delta w_{t-1}} + \underset{(--)}{0.06\Delta_3 pi_{t-1}} + \underset{(0.14)}{0.395\Delta\tau_{1,t-2}}$$

$$- \underset{(0.006)}{0.013\Delta u_t} - \underset{(0.0016)}{0.0067 u_{t-1}} - \underset{(--)}{1\,\Delta h_t} - \underset{(0.006)}{0.046 WD_t} + \underset{(0.011)}{0.027 i86q3_t}$$

$$- \underset{(0.003)}{0.005 S_{1,t}} - \underset{(0.004)}{0.001 S_{2,t}} - \underset{(0.004)}{0.001 S_{3,t}}$$

$$\hat{\sigma}_{\Delta w} = 0.0122$$

The price equation

$$\widehat{\Delta pc_t} = \underset{(0.016)}{-0.065} + \underset{(0.037)}{0.108\Delta w_{t-1}} + \underset{(0.025)}{0.216\Delta_3 pc_{t-1}} + \underset{(0.013)}{0.039\,(\Delta pi_{t-1} + \Delta pi_{t-4})}$$

$$- \underset{(0.0095)}{0.029\Delta^2 y_{t-1}} - \underset{(0.0025)}{0.007\Delta u_{t-2}} + \underset{(0.0342)}{0.129\Delta\tau_{3,t-2}}$$

$$+ \underset{(0.0056)}{0.038\,i70q1_t} - \underset{(0.0055)}{0.025\,i79q1_t} + \underset{(0.0055)}{0.013\,i86q3_t}$$

$$- \underset{(0.0024)}{0.021 S_{1,t}} - \underset{(0.0027)}{0.012 S_{2,t}} - \underset{(0.0022)}{0.010 S_{3,t}}$$

$$\hat{\sigma}_{\Delta pc} = 0.0055$$

Notes: See table 16.2.

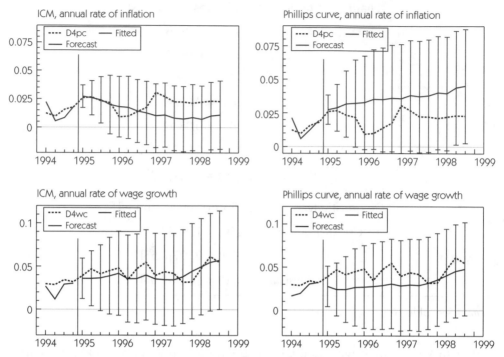

Figure 16.1 Sixteen quarters dynamic forecasts for the ICM
and the Phillips curve

values of the nonmodeled variables: import prices, the payroll and indirect tax-rate, and labor market policy stance.

In figure 16.1 the two graphs in the first row are for the annual rate of inflation, $\Delta_4 pc_t$, the ICM on the left and the Phillips curve on the right. The two bottom graphs compare the annual wage growth forecasts, $\Delta_4 wc_t$, of the two rival models. Each graph in figure 16.1 also contains the 95 percent prediction intervals in the form of ±2 standard errors, as a direct measure of the uncertainty of the forecasts. The inflation forecasts differ both in terms of bias and uncertainty. The Phillips curve systematically over-predicts the rate of inflation, and the Phillips curve prediction intervals appear to overstate the degree of uncertainty in inflation forecasting: see Sgherri and Wallis (1999) for a similar finding on U.K. inflation forecast uncertainty.

We next consider the following sequences of forecasts: first, a sequence up to 16 steps ahead for 1995.1 to 1998.4 based on information up to 1994.4, then a sequence up to 12 periods ahead for 1996.1 to 1998.4 conditional on information up to and including 1995.4, then a sequence up to eight periods, and then up to four periods.

Figure 16.2 shows the forecasts for $\Delta_4 pc_t$ over all four horizons. Both 12-period forecasts over-predict significantly in 1996.1. In that quarter there was a reduction

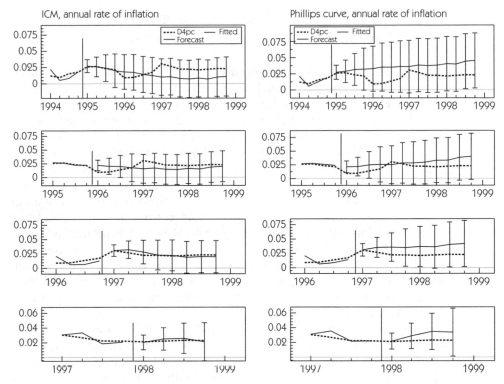

Figure 16.2 Sixteen, twelve, eight, and four quarters dynamic inflation forecasts for the ICM and the Phillips curve

in the excises on cars (which explains around 40 percent of the over-prediction), so this is an example of a nonconstancy in the process in the forecast period. Interestingly, the eight-quarter horizon shows that both models are "back on track" in 1997.1; that is, when the excise reduction is in the conditioning information set. However, the Phillips curve continues to over-predict, also for the eight- and four-quarter horizons. In fact, it is also evident from the graphs that on a comparison of biases, the Phillips curve model would be beaten by a no-change rule; that is, a double difference "model" $\Delta\Delta_4 pc_t = 0$.

In sum, although both the ICM and the Phillips curve appear to be congruent models within sample, their forecast properties are indeed significantly different from a user's point of view. In this one-off "test," the Phillips curve is poor on forecasting the mean of inflation in the new low-inflation regime, and it over-states the uncertainty in inflation forecasting. Causal information does not necessarily lead to successful forecasts; that is, the finding that the Phillips curve loses to a random-walk model of inflation over the latter part of the sample. In the next two sections the empirical analysis of these issues are carried one step further when we compare forecasts derived from large-scale systems of the Norwegian economy, using stochastic simulation techniques.

16.4. Large-Scale Macroeconomic Models of the Norwegian Economy

RIMINI[6] is the Norges Bank macroeconometric model, which is routinely used for practical forecasting and policy analysis. RIMINI is a large-scale model which links together several important submodels of the Norwegian economy. One of the submodels is an ICM-type wage/price submodel of the labor market, similar to the model discussed in section 16.3: hence we adopt the same labels and denote this as an EqCM submodel. Other key submodels in RIMINI (for example, for household and corporate sector behavior, and for housing and credit markets, etc.) are also represented as equilibrium correcting dynamic equations, and in the following we will label RIMINI as an EqCM-type model. Section 16.2 pointed out that the Phillips curve model, which is easily obtained from the ICM model as a special case, could logically be labeled as an EqCM model, although with the exception of the level of unemployment all variables enter in differences only, thus also pointing in the direction of a dVAR model. The issues raised in section 16.3 on modeling considerations, emphasizing model selection criteria and their consequences, easily generalizes to a broader and more realistic modeling framework in the RIMINI-model.

In this section we will first outline the EqCM-type RIMINI-model, and then briefly describe how we have constructed a contending dVAR-type model in differences. Typically we have remodeled the econometric equations, replacing EqCM-type models with models in differences only (Eitrheim, Husebø, and Nymoen, 1999), and notwithstanding the somewhat ambiguous labeling of the Phillips curve, the ICM submodel of the labor market has been replaced by a Phillips curve model in the dVAR system counterpart to RIMINI, along the same lines as in section 16.3. Finally, in light of the forecasting comparison in Clements and Hendry (1999), we have also developed noncausal forecasting models in first-order and second order differences, which will be denoted as dAR and dARr respectively in the following.

Clements and Hendry (1999) brought out that, even for very simple systems, when comparing models with and without causal information, it is in general difficult to predict which version of the model will have the smallest forecast error. In our case EqCM and dVAR, on the one hand, and dAR and dARr on the other, represent models with and without causal information.

In section 16.5 we generate multi-period forecasts from the econometric model RIMINI used by Norges Bank, and compare these to the forecasts from models based on differenced data, focusing on both forecast error biases and uncertainty using stochastic simulation. The latter extends the analysis in Eitrheim, Husebø, and Nymoen (1999), and we have also extended the maximum forecasting horizon from 12 to 28 quarters. As a background for the simulations, the rest of this section describes the main features of the incumbent EqCM and how we have designed the three rival forecasting systems.

16.4.1.   The incumbent EqCM model – eRIM

The typical forecast horizon when RIMINI is used as a forecasting tool in the preparation of Norges Bank's forecasts for the Norwegian economy is four to eight quarters in the Bank's Inflation report, but forecasts for up to five years ahead are also published regularly as part of the assessment of the medium-term outlook for the Norwegian economy. Simulations of the RIMINI model can also provide estimates of the quantitative effects on inflation, economic growth, and unemployment of changes in monetary policy instruments, and the RIMINI model is frequently used to analyze monetary policy issues. A requirement for policy analysis is that the model contains the necessary links between monetary policy instruments, such as interest rates and the exchange rate, and the variables of interest. In addition, we have to rely on invariance properties and that the monetary policy instruments work through channels which satisfy the requirements for super exogeneity (Engle, Hendry, and Richard, 1983).

The 205 equations of RIMINI (version 2.9) fall into three categories:

- 26 estimated stochastic equations, representing economic behavior.
- 146 definitional equations; for example, national accounting identities, composition of the workforce, etc.
- 33 estimated "technical" equations; for example, price indices with different base years and equations that serve special reporting purposes (with no feedback to the rest of the model).

It is the specification of 26 stochastic equations representing economic behavior that distinguishes the models. Together, they contain putative quantitative knowledge about behavior relating to aggregate outcome: for example, consumption, savings and household wealth; labour demand and unemployment; wage and price interactions (inflation); capital formation; and foreign trade. The oil and shipping sectors are treated exogenously in the model, as are agriculture, forestry, and fisheries. The rest of the private nonfinancial sector is divided between the manufacturing and construction sectors (producers of traded goods) and services and retail trade (producers of nontraded goods).

Seasonally unadjusted data are used for the estimation of the equations. To a large extent, macroeconomic interdependencies are contained in the dynamics of the model. For example, prices and wages Granger-cause output, trade, and employment, and similarly the level of real activity feeds back on to wage–price inflation. The model is an open system. Examples of important nonmodeled variables are the level of economic activity by trading partners, as well as inflation and wage costs in those countries. Indicators of economic policy (the level of government expenditure, the short-term interest rate, and the exchange rate) are also nonmodeled, and forecasts are therefore conditional on a particular scenario for these variables. The **EqCM** model RIMINI will be labeled **eRIM** in the following.

To provide some insights in the type of causal information which is reflected in the behavioral relationships in **eRIM** (and **dVARc** below), consider the link

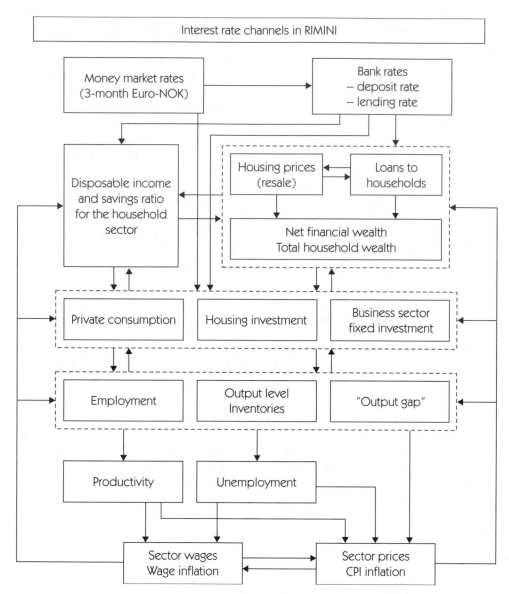

Figure 16.3   Interest rate channels in RIMINI. Effects on CPI inflation
assuming constant exchange rates

between interest rates and other economic variables in figure 16.3. The main links
between short-term interest rates and aggregated variables like output, employment, and CPI inflation in RIMINI, are often denoted as the "interest rate channel"
of monetary policy.

The main mechanisms of the interest rate channel in RIMINI are as follows. A
partial rise in the short-term money market interest rate (typically 3-month NOK

rates), assuming fixed exchange rates, leads to an increase in banks' borrowing and lending interest rates with a lag. Aggregate demand is influenced by the interest rate shift through several mechanisms, such as a negative effect on housing prices which (for a given stock of housing capital) causes real household wealth to decline and suppresses total consumer expenditure. Likewise, there are negative direct and indirect effects on real investments in sectors producing traded and nontraded goods and on housing investments. The housing and credit markets in RIMINI are interrelated through the housing price and household loans equations, which reflects the fact that housing capital is collateralized against household loans (mainly in private and state-owned banks) and that the ownership rate among Norwegian households exceeds 80 percent. CPI inflation is reduced after a lag, mainly as a result of the effects of changes in aggregate demand on aggregate output and employment (productivity), but also as a result of changes in unit labor costs.

16.4.2. A full-scale dVAR model – dRIMc

Because all the stochastic equations in RIMINI are in equilibrium-correction form, a simple dVAR version of the model can be obtained by omitting the equilibrium-correcting terms from the equation and re-specifying all the affected equations in terms of differences alone. In our earlier paper, however, we found that this left us with seriously misspecified equations due to the autocorrelation in the omitted equilibrium-correction terms. This model was denoted dRIM in Eitrheim, Husebø, and Nymoen (1999), and we have discarded this model in the present analysis.

The previous paper also showed that a more interesting rival was a re-modeled version of dRIM (a similar procedure was applied in section 16.3). In order to make the residuals of the dVAR equations empirically white-noise, additional terms in differences often had to be added to remove autocorrelation from the model residuals. The corrected dVAR version of RIMINI is denoted dRIMc, and, bearing in mind the potential bias in the estimation of the drift term in small samples, we have made simulations with a version of dRIMc where we systematically excluded the constant term from typical no-drift variables like unemployment rates and interest rates: see Eitrheim, Husebø, and Nymoen (1999) for discussion.

Hence, the two complete system forecasting models, eRIM and the no-drift version of dRIMc, both broadly satisfy the same set of single-equation model design criteria and have residuals which are close to white-noise, zero-mean innovations.

16.4.3. Difference and double difference models – dAR and dARr

Both models considered so far are "system of equations" forecasting models. For comparison, we have also prepared univariate model forecasts for each variable, in line with equations (16.6) and (16.7) in section 16.2 (see also Clements and

Hendry, 1999, ch. 5) but allowing for higher-order dynamics and seasonality. The first set is dubbed dAR, and is based on unrestricted estimation of AR(4) models, including a constant term and three seasonal dummies. Finally, we generate forecasts from $\Delta_4 \Delta \ln X_t = 0$, for each variable X_t in the set of endogenous variables. This set of forecasts is called dARr, where the r is a reminder that the forecasts are based on completely restricted AR(4) processes. The univariate dARr "models" are specified without drift terms; hence their forecasts are protected against trend-misrepresentation.

16.5. Forecast Comparisons of the Large-Scale Models

Table 16.5 summarizes the four models of the previous section in terms of the incumbent "baseline" EqCM model and the three "rival" dVAR type models.

All models that enter this exercise were estimated on a sample ending in 1991.4. The period 1992.1–1998.4 is used for forecast comparisons.

In this section we use graphs to allow direct inspection of the bias and uncertainty of Monte Carlo simulated prediction intervals. The set of variables that we consider is the rate of inflation, $\Delta_4 cpi$, and some of the key factors affecting it: the annual growth in import prices, $\Delta_4 pbi$, (imported inflation), the annual growth in wage costs per hour, $\Delta_4 wcf$, (cost-push), the level of unemployment, $UTOT$, (labor market pressure), and annual nonoil GDP growth, $\Delta_4 yf$ (product market pressure).

We evaluate four dynamic forecasts, distinguished by the start period: the first forecast is for the whole 28-quarter horizon, so the first period being forecasted is 1992.1. The second simulation starts in 1995.1 (16-quarters horizon), the third in 1997.1 (8-quarters horizon) and the fourth in 1998.1 (4-quarters horizon). Furthermore, all forecast are conditional on the actual values of the models' exogenous variables and the initial conditions, which of course change accordingly when we initialize the forecasts in different start periods.

Table 16.5   The models used in the forecasts

Model	Name	Description
Baseline	eRIM	26 behavioral equations, equilibrium-correcting equations 33 + 146 technical and definitional equations
1. Rival	dRIMc	26 behavioral equations, remodeled without levels information, restricting drift terms to zero 33 + 146 Technical and definitional equations
2. Rival	dAR	71 equations modeled as 4.order unrestricted AR models
3. Rival	dARr	71 equations modeled as restricted 4.order AR models, restricting drift terms to zero

Figures 16.4–16.8 show the results from stochastic simulations of each of the four models at the different forecasting horizons. For each of the reported variables we have plotted the mean of 500 replications (using antithetic drawings) against the observed historical values. The uncertainty of the model forecasts at different horizons is illustrated by putting a 95 percent prediction interval around the mean. Some important theoretical properties about the second-order moments of EqCM-type and differenced models are discussed in Clements and Hendry (1999, ch. 5).

We first consider the results for annual inflation, $\Delta_4 cpi$, in figure 16.4. The eRIM model seems to do better than its dVAR rivals in the first half of the 28-quarter forecasting horizon, both in terms of a smaller forecast error bias, and less forecast uncertainty. We note, however, that as we approach the end of the horizon eRIM starts to overpredict CPI inflation from 1996 and onwards. As we move the starting point of the simulations forward, the simple univariate dARr model outperforms all the other forecasting models in terms of the forecast error bias: compare figure 16.4(d). Similar results were reported in Eitrheim, Husebø, and Nymoen (1999) for the 1992.1–1994.4 period. They illustrate the inherent ability of the differencing models to intercept-correct for structural changes occurring after the estimation period (which ends in 1991.4 for all simulations), as well as they insulate against shocks occurring in other parts of a larger system.

While eRIM only overpredicts CPI inflation from 1996 and onwards, the rival system forecast from dRIMc consistently over-predicts CPI inflation over the entire forecasting horizon. This is also in line with the results from the Phillips curve model in section 16.3. From figure 16.4 we see that the extra unit-root assumption built into models in differences give rise to wider prediction intervals as we increase the forecast horizon, and in particular we see that this is the case for dARr models where there is a clear trend. In contrast to the models eRIM and dRIMc, however, which are designed such that the residuals are close to being zero-mean innovations, to the extent the two univariate "models," and in particular dARr, have autocorrelated residuals. Thus their prediction intervals may be overstated, Clements and Hendry (1999, ch. 5).

Turning to the tendency to over-predict inflation, note that for eRIM and dRIMc, this can be tracked down to two channels: first, through the growth in import prices (figure 16.5); and, second, through wage growth (figure 16.6)[7]. Import price growth is over-predicted by both eRIM and dRIMc in 1997–1998, as shown in figures 16.5(c) and 16.5(d), and wage growth forecasts seems to largely follow the same pattern as CPI inflation forecasts in eRIM and dRIMc respectively. Again, the noncausal models dominate on the shortest forecast horizon: compare figure 16.6(d). The forecasts for wage and price inflation in eRIM is consistent with the forecast of the total rate of unemployment in figure 16.7, which is under-predicted in the latter part of the simulation period.

Whereas the eRIM model underpredicts the rate of total unemployment from 1996 and onwards, this is not the case for the dRIMc model. The rate of unemployment seems to be more or less uncoupled from the wage–price formation process in dRIMc, overpredicting unemployment from 1996 and onwards in the 28-quarter forecast and being close to spot on the actual values when simulation starts in 1997.1. This is due to an insulation property in the dRIMc model, namely

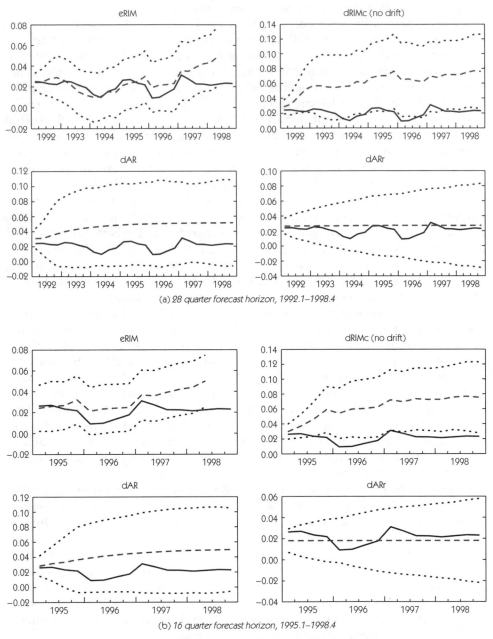

(a) *28 quarter forecast horizon, 1992.1–1998.4*

(b) *16 quarter forecast horizon, 1995.1–1998.4*

Figure 16.4 Forecast comparisons over different horizons based on stochastic simulation. Annual consumer price inflation $\Delta_4 cpi$

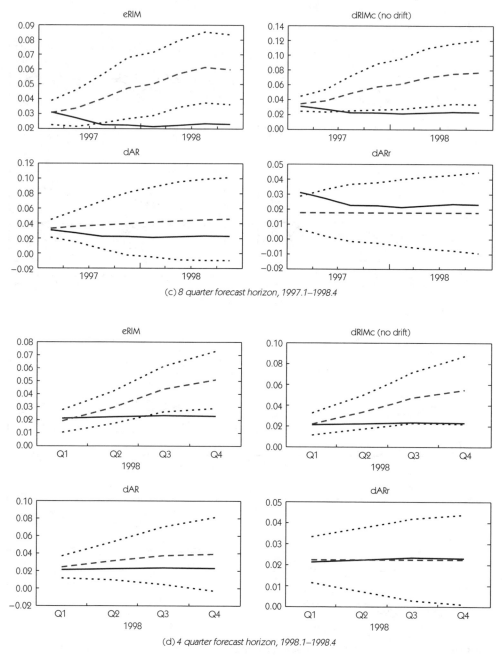

(c) *8 quarter forecast horizon, 1997.1–1998.4*

(d) *4 quarter forecast horizon, 1998.1–1998.4*

Figure 16.4 *(cont'd)*

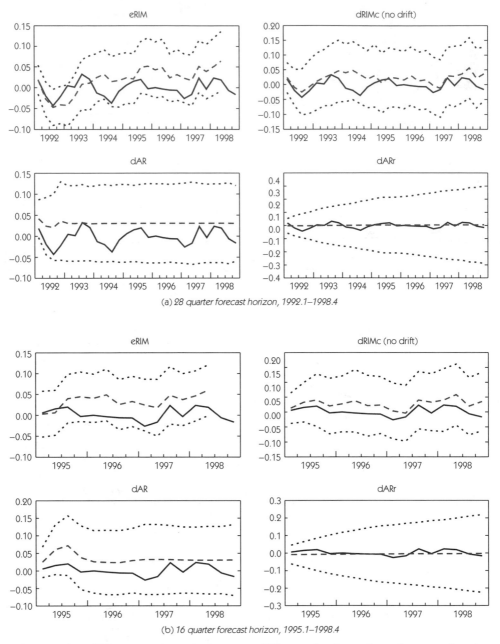

(a) *28 quarter forecast horizon, 1992.1–1998.4*

(b) *16 quarter forecast horizon, 1995.1–1998.4*

Figure 16.5   Forecast comparisons over different horizons based on stochastic simulation. Annual import price growth $\Delta_4 pbi$

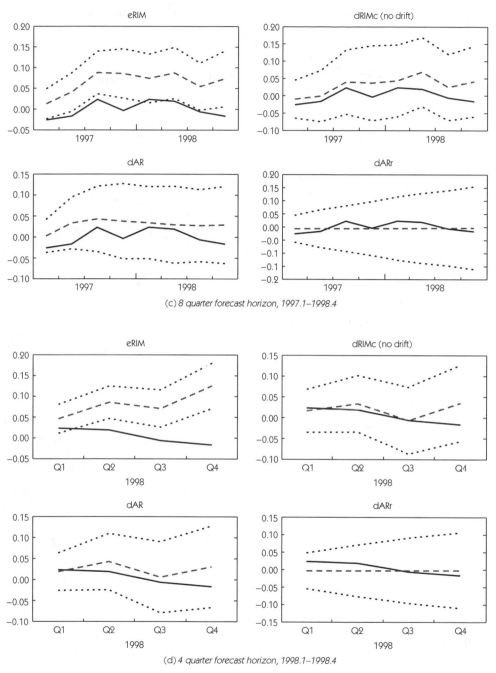

(c) *8 quarter forecast horizon, 1997.1–1998.4*

(d) *4 quarter forecast horizon, 1998.1–1998.4*

Figure 16.5 (*cont'd*)

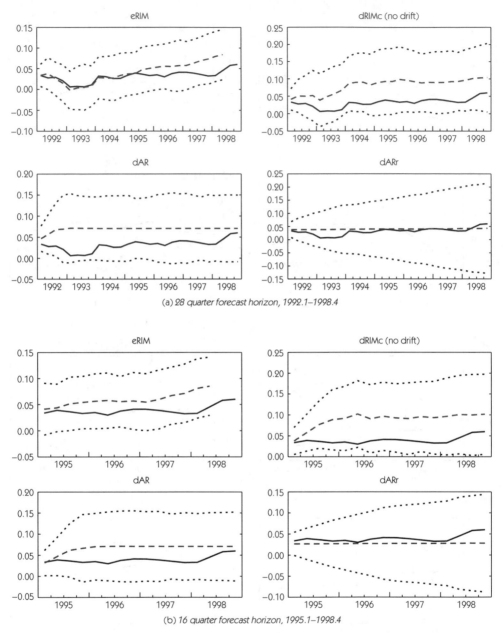

(a) 28 quarter forecast horizon, 1992.1–1998.4

(b) 16 quarter forecast horizon, 1995.1–1998.4

Figure 16.6 Forecast comparisons over different horizons based on stochastic simulation. Annual growth in wage costs per hour $\Delta_4 wcf$

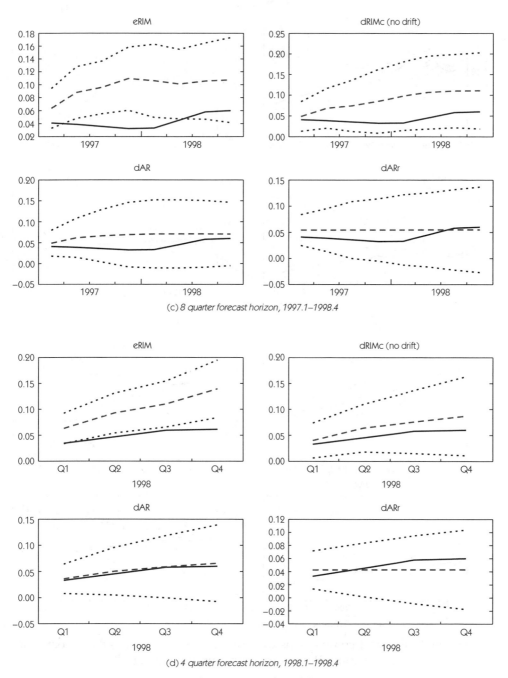

(c) *8 quarter forecast horizon, 1997.1–1998.4*

(d) *4 quarter forecast horizon, 1998.1–1998.4*

Figure 16.6   (*cont'd*)

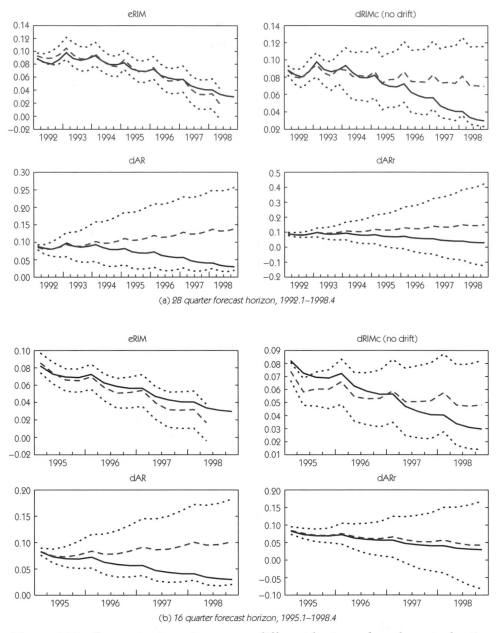

(a) *28 quarter forecast horizon, 1992.1–1998.4*

(b) *16 quarter forecast horizon, 1995.1–1998.4*

Figure 16.7   Forecast comparisons over different horizons based on stochastic simulation. Rate of total unemployment *UTOT*

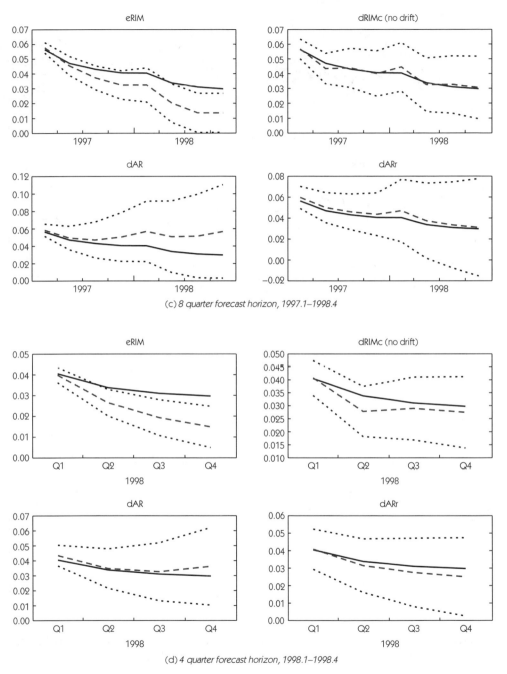

(c) *8 quarter forecast horizon, 1997.1–1998.4*

(d) *4 quarter forecast horizon, 1998.1–1998.4*

Figure 16.7 *(cont'd)*

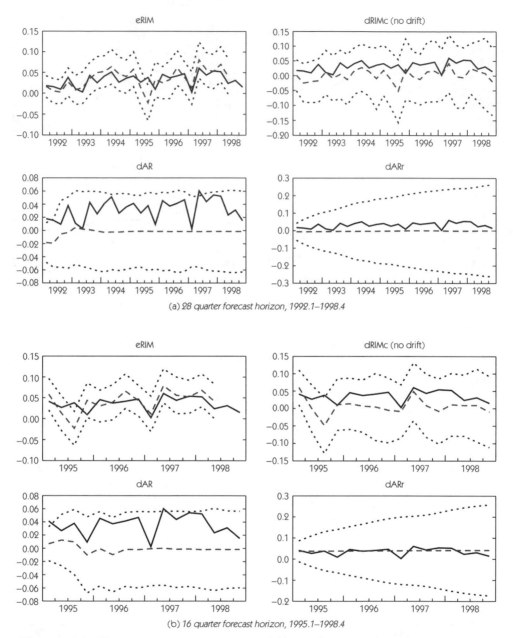

(a) 28 quarter forecast horizon, 1992.1–1998.4

(b) 16 quarter forecast horizon, 1995.1–1998.4

Figure 16.8 Forecast comparisons over different horizons based on stochastic simulation. Annual growth in mainland GDP $\Delta_4 yf$

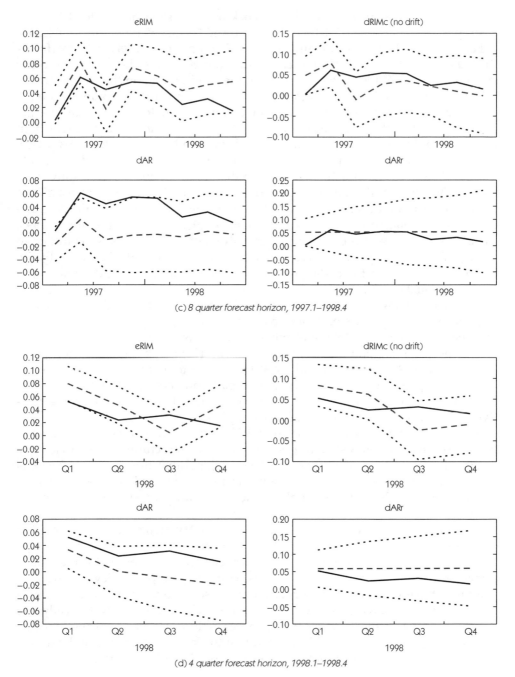

(c) 8 quarter forecast horizon, 1997.1–1998.4

(d) 4 quarter forecast horizon, 1998.1–1998.4

Figure 16.8   *(cont'd)*

that forecast errors in the price/wage block of the system do not feed into the unemployment block (see Eitrheim, Husebø, and Nymoen (1999) for discussion).

For the annual growth in mainland GDP (see figure 16.8), eRIM outperforms the other models on the 28-quarter forecast horizon. Like the eRIM, the other system forecast, dRIMc, also benefits from the conditioning on the true values of the exogenous variables, although the dRIMc shows a tendency to under-predict output growth compared with eRIM. The two univariate forecasts under-predict output growth really badly at the 28-quarter horizon, due to the fact that both forecasts tend to extrapolate the low growth rates in Norway in the early 1990s. As we move to the 16-quarter forecast starting in 1995.1, the restricted univariate model dARr does much better on average than both the unrestricted univariate model dAR which still badly under-predicts, and the dVAR system forecast dRIMc which also shows the same tendency to under-predict output growth. With the exception of a single-year instance of under-predicting output growth in 1995, the eRIM continues to predict output growth relatively well. As we continue to the eight- and four-quarter forecasts starting in 1997.1 and 1998.1, respectively, the two open system forecasts continue to benefit from their conditioning on a larger information set.

The main findings conveyed by the graphs can be summarized in the following four points. First, the simulations confirm earlier results presented in Eitrheim, Husebø, and Nymoen (1999) that while eRIM tends to improve the forecast on longer horizons (extending earlier result from 12 to a 28 periods), noncausal "models" like dAR and in particular dARr still seem to frequently outperform the forecast properties of their system counterparts on shorter horizons, thus corroborating the theoretical results in Clements and Hendry (1999) on the relative robustness of the two types of models.

Second, we have shown evidence that dVAR-type models offer some degree of protection against forecast failure stemming from structural breaks that have occurred prior to the forecast period. This suggests that if a structural break is suspected to have occurred, or is known from nonmodeled sources, the dVAR model may provide information about the magnitude of the required intercept correction.

Third, another form of robustness in dAR and dARr stems from the insulation of, for example, the inflation forecasts from errors in other variables like the growth rate in import prices. In other words, forecasts from models with less causal information are more robust than models with, for example, policy channels.

Fourth, the estimated second-order moments seem to be in line with the forecasting theory in Clements and Hendry (1999, ch. 5) and show typically the differences between the forecast error variances in the causal and noncausal models respectively, although it should be noted that the latter may overstate the uncertainty, since the model residuals may be autocorrelated in practice.

16.6. Discussion

The fact that the underlying inflation process is unknown, and that competing models exist, makes it attractive for forecasters to draw on several models. This is reflected by operational inflation forecasting, where a multitude of models are currently in use. Models range from large macroeconometric models to simpler Phillips curve models, and from data-based VARs to full blown theoretical optimizing models. Given that all models are necessarily partial in nature, it is easy to acknowledge the wisdom of a pragmatic and pluralist use of economic models, of which the Bank of England's suite of model approach is one example.

However, the pluralist view has a cost in terms of lost transparency. When many models are used to forecast inflation, it may become difficult for the central bank to communicate its forecasts to the general public, the markets, and the political authorities. Thus section 16.2 showed that it may be difficult to draw the correct policy implications from a combined forecast of two models that have different theoretical content, and that the combined forecast can be less accurate than the forecast of the model with best econometric properties. Hence, model pluralism can be carried too far. An alternative is represented by the encompassing principle and progressive research strategies. In practice, this entails a strategy where one tests competing models as thoroughly as practically feasible, and keeps only the encompassing model in the suite of models. Our example in section 16.2 focused on competing models of the supply side, the ICM and the Phillips curve. But several other issues in the modeling of inflation can in principle be tackled along the same lines; for example, the role of rational expectations, and forward-looking optimizing behavior (see, for example, Hendry, 1995, ch. 14).

A more specific argument for pluralism stems from the insight that an EqCM is incapable of correcting forecasts sufficiently for the impact of parameter changes that occur prior to the start of the forecast period. In contrast, a univariate dVAR forecast moves back on track once it is conditional on the period when the parameter change took place. Section 16.5 provided several empirical examples. This supports the view that an EqCM and simple dVARs could constitute a suite of models for forecasting, where the role of the dVAR is primarily to help intercept correct the policy model.

Acknowledgments

The views expressed in this paper are solely the responsibility of the authors and should not be interpreted as reflecting those of Norges Bank. We would like to thank the editors for advice and suggestions. Please address correspondence to Ragnar Nymoen.

Notes

1 Norway changed its monetary policy regime to that of inflation targeting from March, 29, 2001.
2 Wallis (1993) gives an excellent exposition, emphasizing the impact on macroeconometric modeling and policy analysis.
3 King (1998, p. 12).
4 All results in this section were obtained using GiveWin 1.20 and PcFIML 9.20: see Doornik and Hendry (1996a) and Doornik and Hendry (1996b).
5 However, this relationship was obtained for *total economy* wages and productivity, and therefore cointegration may be weaker for our manufacturing wage cost data.

6   RIMINI was originally an acronym for a model for the Real economy and Income accounts – a MINI-version. The model version used in this paper has 205 endogenous variables, although a large fraction of these are accounting identities or technical relationships creating links between variables: see Eitrheim and Nymoen (1991) for a brief documentation of a predecessor of the model.

7   Note that the forecasts in section 16.3 were conditional on actual import prices.

References

Akram, Q.F. (1999). Multiple unemployment equilibria – do transitory shocks have permanent effects? Working paper 1999/6, Oslo: Norges Bank.

Bank of England (1999). *Economic Models at the Bank of England*. Bank of England.

Bårdsen, G., P.G. Fisher, and R. Nymoen (1998). Business cycles: Real facts or fallacies? In S. Strøm (ed.), *Econometrics and Economic Theory in the 20th Century: The Ragnar Frisch Centennial Symposium*, Number 32 in Econometric Society Monograph Series. Cambridge: Cambridge University Press, chapter 16, 499–527.

Bårdsen, G., E.S. Jansen, and R. Nymoen (1999). Econometric inflation targeting. Working paper 1999/5, Oslo: Norges Bank.

Bårdsen, G., and R. Nymoen (2000). Testing steady-state implications of the Nairu. Working paper 2000/3, Oslo: Norges Bank.

Bjørnstad, R. and R. Nymoen (1999). Wages and profitability: Norwegian manufacturing 1967q1–1998q2. Working paper 1999/7, Oslo: Norges Bank.

Blanchard, O.J. and L. Katz (1997). What do we know and do not know about the natural rate of unemployment. *Journal of Economic Perspectives*, 11, 51–72.

Blanchard, O.J. and L. Katz (1999). Wage dynamics: reconciling theory and evidence. NBER Working Paper Series 6924, National Bureau of Economic Research.

Blanchflower, D.G. and A.J. Oswald (1994). *The Wage Curve*. Cambridge, MA: The MIT Press.

Clarida, Richard, J.G. and M. Gertler (1999). The science of monetary policy: a new Keynesian perspective. *Journal of Economic Literature*, 37(4), 1661–707.

Clements, M.P. and D.F. Hendry (1993). On the limitations of comparing mean squared forecasts errors. *Journal of Forecasting*, 12, 669–76 (with discussion).

Clements, M.P. and D.F. Hendry (1998). *Forecasting Economic Time Series*. Cambridge: Cambridge University Press.

Clements, M.P. and D.F. Hendry (1999). *Forecasting Non-stationary Economic Time Series*. Cambridge, MA: The MIT Press.

Doornik, J.A. and D.F. Hendry (1996a). *GiveWin. An Interface to Empirical Modeling*. London: International Thomson Publishing.

Doornik, J.A. and D.F. Hendry (1996b). *Modeling Dynamic Systems Using PcFiml 9.0 for Windows*. London: International Thomson Publishing.

Drèze, J. and C.R. Bean (1990). Europe's unemployment problem; Introduction and synthesis. In J. Drèze and C.R. Bean (eds.), *Europe's Unemployment Problem*. Cambridge: MIT Press, chapter 1.

Eitrheim, Ø., T.A. Husebø and R. Nymoen (1999). Error-correction versus differencing in macroeconometric forecasting. *Economic Modeling*, 16, 515–44.

Eitrheim, Ø. and R. Nymoen (1991). Real wages in a multisectoral model of the Norwegian economy. *Economic Modeling*, 8(1), 63–82.

Engle, R.F., D.F. Hendry, and J.-F. Richard (1983). Exogeneity. *Econometrica*, 51, 277–304.

Fuhrer, J.C. (1995). The Phillips curve is alive and well. *New England Economic Review*, 41–56.

Gali, J. and M. Gertler (1999). Inflation dynamics: A structural econometric analysis. *Journal of Monetary Economics*, 44(2), 233–58.

Gordon, R.J. (1997). The time-varying NAIRU and its implications for economic policy. *Journal of Economic Perspectives*, 11(1), 11–32.

Granger, C.W.J. (1990). General introduction: Where are the controversies in econometric methodology? In C.W.J. Granger (ed.), *Modeling Economic Series. Readings in Econometric Methodology*. Oxford: Oxford University Press, 1–23.

Granger, C.W.J. and P. Newbold (1986). *Forecasting Economic Time Series*. San Diego: Academic Press.

Hendry, D.F. (1995). *Dynamic Econometrics*. Oxford: Oxford University Press.

Hoel, M. and R. Nymoen (1988). Wage formation in Norwegian manufacturing. An empirical application of a theoretical bargaining model. *European Economic Review*, 32, 977–97.

Johansen, K. (1995). Norwegian wage curves. *Oxford Bulletin of Economics and Statistics*, 57, 229–47.

King, M. (1998). Mr King explores lessons from the U.K. labour market. *BIS Review* (103).

Kolsrud, D. and R. Nymoen (1998). Unemployment and the open economy wage-price spiral. *Journal of Economic Studies*, 25, 450–467.

Layard, R. and S. Nickell (1986). Unemployment in Britain. *Economica*, 53, 121–66. Special issue.

Nymoen, R. (1989a). Modeling wages in the small open economy: an error-correction model of Norwegian manufacturing wages. *Oxford Bulletin of Economics and Statistics*, 51, 239–58.

Nymoen, R. (1989b). Wages and the length of the working day. An empirical test based on Norwegian quarterly manufacturing data. *Scandinavian Journal of Economics*, 91, 599–612.

OECD (1997). *Employment Outlook*. Number July 1997. OECD.

Rødseth, A. and R. Nymoen (1999). Nordic wage formation and unemployment seven years later. Memorandum 10/99, Department of Economics, University of Oslo.

Rowlatt, P.A. (1987). A model of wage bargaining. *Oxford Bulletin of Economics and Statistics*, 49, 347–72.

Sargan, J.D. (1964). Wages and prices in the United Kingdom: a study of econometric methodology. In P.E. Hart, G. Mills, and J.K. Whitaker (eds.), *Econometric Analysis for National Economic Planning*. London: Butterworth, 25–63.

Sgherri, S. and K.F. Wallis (1999). Inflation targetry and the modeling of wages and prices. Mimo ESRC Macroeconomic Modeling Bureau, University of Warwick.

Svensson, L.E.O. (1997a). Exchange rate target or inflation target for Norway? In A.B. Christiansen and J.F. Qvigstad (eds.), *Choosing a Monetary Policy Target*. Oslo: Scandinavian University Press, chapter 7, 121–38.

Svensson, L.E.O. (1997b). Inflation forecast targeting: Implementing and monitoring inflation targets. *European Economic Review*, 41, 1111–46.

Svensson, L.E.O. (2000). Open economy inflation targeting. *Journal of International Economics*, 50, 155–83.

Wallis, K.F. (1993). On macroeconomic policy and macroeconomic models. *The Economic Record*, 69, 113–30.

CHAPTER SEVENTEEN

The Forecasting Performance of the OECD Composite Leading Indicators for France, Germany, Italy, and the U.K.

Gonzalo Camba-Mendez,[a]
George Kapetanios,[a] *Martin R. Weale,*
and Richard J. Smith

17.1. INTRODUCTION

In their broadest sense, cyclic indicators might be seen as forecasts. They are intended to provide a guide to the future evolution of some variable of interest. For those concerned about the volume of economic activity (rather than the level of prices or the inflation rate) the predicend is usually GDP, industrial pro-

[a] Work carried out while at the National Institute of Economic and Social Research, London. The views expressed in this chapter are those of the authors and do not necessarily reflect the views of the Bank of England or the European Central Bank.

duction, or a composite coincident indicator which is believed to represent the state of the economy. Industrial production is often chosen in preference to GDP because the data are usually available monthly rather than quarterly, while composite indicators are used in an attempt to include, on a monthly basis, the 70 percent or so of economic activity which lies outside the scope of industrial production. It is often suggested that the function of the indicators is not to forecast the level or change of the predicend but some nonlinear transformation of it, such as a cyclical turning point or a recession; in fact, of course, different users may have different needs.

Lahiri and Moore (1991) provide a valuable source of different methods of indicator construction and suggests ways of assessing their performance; in particular, in their book de Leeuw (1991) offers – despite the famous criticism of such indicators as "measurement without theory" by Koopmans (1947) – a number of reasons why one would expect *a priori* it to be possible to construct leading indicators of economic activity in some form or other. He suggests, among other things, that this is possible because:

1   There are lags between production decisions and actual production.
2   Some variables adjust more slowly than others to the same economic stimulus.
3   Some series are influenced by expectations of future changes in economic activity.
4   Some variables, such as monetary and fiscal policy instruments, may drive the whole of the economy.

The existence of leading indicators invites an assessment of their performance. As with the indicators themselves, this can focus either on the capacity of the indicator to predict its predicend (see, for example, Layton, 1991) or to predict cyclic turning points: see a number of papers in Lahiri and Moore (1991) and Artis, Bladen-Hovell, Osborn, Smith, and Zhang (1995).

In this chapter, we look specifically at the OECD's leading indicators. These are constructed from a range of indicator variables using a method close to that suggested by Burns and Mitchell (1946) for the original leading indicator produced by the United States. Economic time series are selected which show clear turning points. A leading indicator is produced from those which show turning points well in advance of the "reference cycle." The OECD assumes that the cycle is represented by industrial production (because this is, as noted above, available monthly, while GDP is available only quarterly). It constructs its indicators by identifying series which have a reasonably stable lead and which anticipate industrial production even away from turning points. Thus the indicator is intended to "cohere" with the cycle as well as to anticipate turning points. Each series is detrended if it appears to have a trend. It is then scaled so that its variation over the cycle corresponds to the cyclical variation of the economy as a whole. Averaging over these series then provides a composite cyclic indicator which can be presented either as it is or, as the OECD do, after the trend has been restored. The exercise is not in any conventional sense econometric. Not only are the usual criteria absent, but there is difficulty in giving too much weight to turning points because there are relatively few of these. With a shortage of degrees of freedom the risk of inclusion of spurious variables is increased.

Emerson and Hendry (1996) presented a critique of the U.K.'s leading indicator system which was first published by the Office for National Statistics (then the Central Statistical Office) in 1975 (see O'Dea, 1975) but which applies equally to the OECD indicators. They made the point that the index was a linear combination of the underlying indicator variables, but that the method of construction ensured that the weights used to combine the indicators were very different from those which would be found if regression methods were used to produce a forecasting system; given the optimality of the weights found from regression methods, it follows that the weighting scheme used to construct the leading indicators must be sub-optimal. The position becomes more complicated when the indicator variables are I(1). If the variable they are supposed to lead is also I(1), then a cointegrating vector has to link them if the structure is to have any coherence at all. In the light of the criticisms made by Emerson and Hendry and others, the Office for National Statistics stopped publishing the U.K. leading (and coincident) indicators in 1996; publication was taken up, however, by a private-sector consultancy, using the same approach. At much the same time, the United States Bureau of Census stopped publishing coincident and leading indicators for the United States; they were taken up by the Conference Board, the United States equivalent of the CBI.

However, the OECD has continued to produce leading indicators for most of its members. In this chapter we present an assessment of the performance of these leading indicators for four major European countries (France, Germany, Italy, and the U.K.). Our assessment focuses on the forecasting properties of the indicators rather than specifically on their capacity to anticipate turning points. We compare the forecasts generated from the indicators with forecasts generated by a number of alternative models. We consider both VAR models constructed from the data used by the OECD in the construction of its indicators and those which include a wider range of financial variables as well as more restricted models; we present a new means of comparing the forecasts from these VARs with those which can be generated from the leading indicators.

The chapter is organized as follows. Section 17.2 describes the forecasting models. Section 17.3 discusses our forecast evaluation strategy. Section 17.4 presents the data for the empirical analysis. Empirical results are presented in section 17.5. Section 17.6 concludes.

17.2. Forecasting Models

We compare the forecasts of a number of different models of the log of industrial output (y_t) in order to assess the performance of the OECD leading indicators for the four countries. These models are as follows.

17.2.1. Model 1: An autoregressive model

This is frequently used as a reference point against which to compare other models. We treat it as such in this chapter:

$$\Delta y_t = \sum_{k=1}^{n} \alpha_k \Delta y_{t-k} + \gamma + \varepsilon_t.$$

17.2.2. Model 2: A naive model

This model is recommended by Clements and Hendry (1999) as it is robust to structural breaks. It is plainly a restricted form of model 1:

$$\Delta y_t = \Delta y_{t-1} + \varepsilon_t$$

or

$$\Delta^2 y_t = \varepsilon_t.$$

17.2.3. Model 3: A bivariate VAR with the log of the OECD leading indicator, z_t

An error-correction term is included to deal with the case, which may arise for some countries and not others, when industrial production and the leading indicator are cointegrated:

$$\Delta y_t = \sum_{k=1}^{n} \alpha_{1k} \Delta y_{t-k} + \sum_{k=1}^{n} \beta_{1k} \Delta z_{t-k} + \delta_1(y_{t-1} - z_{t-1}) + \gamma_1 + \varepsilon_{1t},$$

$$\Delta z_t = \sum_{k=1}^{n} \alpha_{2k} \Delta y_{t-k} + \sum_{k=1}^{n} \beta_{2k} \Delta z_{t-k} + \delta_2(y_{t-1} - z_{t-1}) + \gamma_2 + \varepsilon_{2t}.$$

17.2.4. Model 4: An equation which reflects the fact that the indicator is supposed to have a lead of 6–9 months (interpreted as eight months)

$$\Delta y_t = \sum_{k=1}^{n} \alpha_{1k} \Delta y_{t-k} + \sum_{k=1}^{n} \beta_{1k} \Delta z_{t-k-7} + \delta_1(y_{t-1} - z_{t-8}) + \gamma_1 + \varepsilon_{1t}.$$

This equation allows us to forecast up to eight months ahead (the limit of the horizon we consider) without requiring any means of projecting the indicator variable. If the leading indicator is functioning as intended, one might hope that

$\alpha_{1k} = 0$ for all k and that the lags represented by β_{1k} would be short. Thus this structure incorporates that which would be found if the leading indicator has a clear and direct link to industrial production, with the lead claimed.

17.2.5.   Model 5: A VAR forecasting system constructed using a vector of indicator variables, x_t

We split these into two groups, either of which may be empty. The first group, x_{at}, is I(0) and the second, x_{bt}, is I(1). It is assumed that y_t is I(1). c is the number of cointegrating relations between the I(1) variables:[1]

$$\Delta y_t = \sum_{k=1}^{n} \alpha_{1k} \Delta y_{t-k} + \sum_{k=1}^{n} b_{yak} x_{at-k} + \sum_{k=1}^{n} b_{ybk} \Delta x_{bt-k} + \sum_{k=1}^{c} \Theta_{yk} \begin{bmatrix} y_{t-1} \\ x_{bt-1} \end{bmatrix} + \gamma_y + \varepsilon_{yt},$$

$$x_{at} = \sum_{k=1}^{n} \alpha_{ak} \Delta y_{t-k} + \sum_{k=1}^{n} B_{aak} x_{at-k} + \sum_{k=1}^{n} B_{abk} \Delta x_{bt-k} + \sum_{k=1}^{c} \Theta_{ak} \begin{bmatrix} y_{t-1} \\ x_{bt-1} \end{bmatrix} + \gamma_a + \varepsilon_{at},$$

$$\Delta x_{bt} = \sum_{k=1}^{n} \alpha_{bk} \Delta y_{t-k} + \sum_{k=1}^{n} B_{bak} x_{at-k} + \sum_{k=1}^{n} B_{bbk} \Delta x_{bt-k} + \sum_{k=1}^{c} \Theta_{bk} \begin{bmatrix} y_{t-1} \\ x_{bt-1} \end{bmatrix} + \gamma_b + \varepsilon_{at}.$$

Each of the categories 17.2.1–17.2.4 represents only one model, although, except in the case of model 2 some criterion such as the BIC must be used to determine the lag length. But there is a large number of possibilities under model 5. With up to eight indicator variables for each country there is a risk of over-fitting, particularly if a good part of the sample is to be saved to allow for an assessment of out-of-sample forecast performance. On the other hand, it may be difficult to distinguish between different components of the vector x_t as candidates for inclusion. We resolve this problem by looking at the performance of all possible well-behaved VAR models which include output and a subset of the indicator variables. This allows us to compare the forecasts produced by models 1–4 with the forecasts that could be produced by all acceptable VAR models including between two and six of the variables (with industrial production counted as one variable).

Ideally, we should expect an acceptable VAR model to be a model which passes two specification tests. First, we should be able to reject the hypothesis that the other variables do not Granger-cause industrial output growth. Second, we should be able to accept the hypothesis that the parameters of the model are constant over time. We test for Granger causality using a likelihood ratio test (see Hamilton, 1994) and for parameter constancy using the CUSUM-OLS test of Ploberger and Kramer (1992). Unfortunately, as we note in section 17.5, in a great majority of VAR models considered, the null hypothesis of the Granger causality test cannot be rejected for some countries. We therefore disregard it for the forecasting evaluation of the models.

We finally note that the categories of models we consider are all linear both in variables and parameters. We have not examined the possibility that the use of leading indicators in nonlinear models may provide a useful forecasting tool (but see Osborn, 1999; Anderson and Vahid, 2000).

17.3. MODEL ASSESSMENT

Our assessment is based on forecasting performance. For this purpose, we split our data set into two parts. The first runs to 1990M4, with the starting date in the late 1970s varying slightly from country to country. We use this part of the data purely for estimation purposes. We use the second part, from 1990M5 to 1998M4, both for estimation and assessment of forecast performance. We consider the root mean square forecast error (RMSFE) of the forecast n periods ahead ($n = 1$ to 8); we estimate our models recursively so as always to replicate what a practitioner would have been able to do.[2] In computing the forecast at time $t + n$, only data to time t are used.

17.3.1. Comparison of predictive performance

As it is common in the literature, we use the results from the forecasting performance of the AR(p) model (model 1) as a benchmark and measure the performance of our models relative to this. This means that whenever the relative RMSFE of a particular model is larger than 1, its forecasting performance is worse than that of the AR(p) model, and whenever it is smaller its forecasting performance is better. Each of these five models can be used to forecast any number of desired periods ahead; we compare them over various forecasting horizons. We present results for the two sub-periods 1990M5–1994M4 and 1994M5–1998M4. The first sub-period was one when European countries were affected by recession. In the second sub-period, output growth was much less volatile. All our models are recursively estimated over the forecasting period. The number of lags is selected using the BIC criterion, recalculated at each stage of the out-of-sample forecasting process.

The choice of the RMSFE as the objective function in the comparison of the forecasting performance may not be optimal, although it is the most common choice in the literature. An alternative choice might consider the ability of the models to predict turning points (see, for example, Pesaran and Timmermann, (1992; Artis, Bladen-Hovell, Osborn, Smith, and Zhang, 1995; Clements and Smith, 1999). However, as work by Granger and Pesaran (2000) suggests, the choice of the objective function ultimately depends on the concerns of the forecast user. We assess the indicators from the perspective of somone who wants to forecast economic growth and does not place any particular weight on forecasting turning points or recessions.

17.3.2. Assessment of VAR models

The assessment of the naive model and the bivariate VARs is straightforward as described above. However, the treatment of the class of models represented by model 5 is much more complicated. There are many possible VARs which could be chosen from the indicator variables which the OECD uses and *a fortiori* from the extended data set. We do not take the view that a single correct VAR can be identified, but instead indicate the distribution of the performance of all possible VARs which could be constructed from the given data set. Thus we rank our VAR models in terms of their forecasting performance in the two sub-periods and the full assessment period. We establish the proportion of the VAR models which do better than the models which use the OECD leading indicator (models 3 and 4), as well as indicating how they compare with the autoregressive model. If a large proportion of VAR models performs better than models 3 and 4, then it is likely that either the method or the dataset used to construct the OECD leading indicator could be modified.

It is also of interest to investigate the robustness of the forecasting performance of the VAR models considered. We therefore evaluate the forecasting performance over two sub-periods. As an indicator of robustness, we compute a *transition probability matrix*. We define this as a matrix P with elements p_{ij}, $i, j = 1, 2, 3, 4$, where p_{ij} denotes the probability that a model whose RMSFE is in the j quartile of the empirical distribution of the RMSFEs during the first period will have an RMSFE in the i quartile during the second period. The reliability of the forecasting performance of VAR models could be assessed by studying whether or not the matrix P resembles a nondiagonal matrix or a diagonal one. Large off-diagonal elements imply that models which performed well in the first period do badly in the second period or vice versa. In such circumstances, researchers need to be sensitive to the structural changes in the economy which give rise to such effects.

17.3.3. Tests of predictive performance

We also use a formal statistical procedure to test the forecasting performance of the OECD leading indicator models (models 3 and 4) against the set of VAR models. This is provided by the test of predictive performance proposed by Diebold and Mariano (1995). The procedure is designed to test the null of equal predictive ability between two models by considering the mean of the differences of squared prediction errors of the two competing models. This mean, suitably normalized, has a standard normal distribution under the null. The test statistic is given by

$$S_{DM} = \frac{\bar{d}}{\sqrt{V(\bar{d})}} \xrightarrow{d} N(0, 1) \quad V(\bar{d}) = N^{-1}\left(\hat{\gamma}_0 + 2\sum_{i=1}^{n-1} \gamma_i\right),$$

where $\bar{d} = \frac{1}{N}\sum_{i=1}^{n}\hat{d}_i$, $\hat{d}_i = \hat{\eta}^2_{\text{Model } k,i} - \hat{\eta}^2_i$, $i = 1, \ldots, N$, $k = 3$ or 4, $\hat{\eta}_{\text{Model } k,i}$ are the prediction errors from models 3 or 4, $\hat{\eta}_i$ are the prediction errors from a VAR model, N is the number of prediction errors used, $\hat{\gamma}_i$, $i = 0, 1, \ldots, n - 1$ are the estimated autocovariances of the series of prediction error differences and n is the prediction horizon.[3] Harvey, Leybourne, and Newbold (1997) have proposed a small sample correction for the above test statistic: see also chapter 12 by Newbold and Harvey in this volume. The revised statistic is given by

$$S_{DM}^* = \left(\frac{N + 1 - 2n + N^{-1}n(n-1)}{N} \right) S_{DM}$$

and the critical values are taken from the t distribution with $N - 1$ degrees of freedom; we present the results of the revised statistics.[4] As explained above, there is large number of VAR models computed for our assessment of models 3 and 4. We report quantiles of the empirical distribution of the probability values of the predictive accuracy test. For a level of significance of 10 percent, values smaller than 0.05 imply that the performance of model 3 or 4, as relevant, is significantly better, and values larger than 0.95 that it is significantly worse. We present the results for the quartiles of our set of possible VARs ranked by RMSFE. Thus, if the figure in the third quartile is smaller than 0.05 this is evidence that the predictive accuracy of model 3 or 4 is significantly better than that of 75 percent of the VAR models. This would be evidence that the parameter restrictions implicit in the OECDs indicator system are a useful way of generating forecasts from the data they use. Conversely, a figure larger than 0.95 would indicate that the parameter restrictions may be inappropriate.

The above framework is similar to that suggested by Sullivan, Timmermann, and White (2000), Sullivan, Timmermann, and White (1999), and White (2000) regarding the effects of data snooping on the evaluation of forecasting performance when large numbers of models are considered. They argue that standard statistical tests do not account for model selection uncertainty since they assume that the model on which inference is carried out is known. When a large number of forecasting models is considered and compared to a benchmark model, pure chance can lead to some models performing significantly better than the benchmark in terms of forecasting over some period according to some predictive accuracy test. In other words, the actual rejection probability of the predictive accuracy test, under the null hypothesis of the benchmark model producing equally good forecasts as the alternative models, when such a search over models is carried out, is likely to be larger than the nominal rejection probability, because a maximum test statistic over the set of alternative models is considered rather than a single test statistic. White (2000) suggests a bootstrap procedure to correct for this. At this stage we do not consider this methodology in our work both because the computational cost of the bootstrap is prohibitive in our context and because evidence on the small sample properties of this methodology is lacking in the case when parameter estimation is involved. Nevertheless, this work suggests that the performance of the best performing VAR model is likely to be judged too favorably by the predictive accuracy test we consider; it may be more important to look at the performance of the median and quartiles.

17.4. THE DATA

For our first data set, we use a range of indicator variables as close as possible to that used by the OECD in its construction of "traditional" leading indicators.

Table 17.1 Variables used for each country[a]

	France	Germany	Italy	U.K.
Short interest rate				−3.40*
Real effective exchange rate	−2.82		−1.65	
Share price index	−2.50	−2.54		−1.31
Long-term bond yield		−1.90	−1.95	
Survey: production tendency	−2.72		−4.34*	−3.00
Survey: finished goods	−3.71*	−4.09*	−4.32*	−2.65
Survey: order book level		−3.80*	−4.18*	−2.67
New orders		−2.99	−3.26*	
New car registrations				−2.18
M1		−1.89	−1.42	
M3	0.07			
Labor cost		−0.78		
Business climate		−4.17*		

[a] ADF statistics are given in parentheses. Critical value: −3.15. Lag order is chosen using the BIC criterion. * indicates rejection of the null hypothesis of a unit root.

Details on the series used for each country in this chapter are given in table 17.1. More information on the data used by the OECD may be found in OECD (1987).

We estimate our models over the period up to 1990M4 with the start of the sample period varying from country to country depending on data availability. More specifically, the data for France and the U.K. start at 1978M4 and for Germany and Italy at 1975M4.

Our alternative data set is the set of variables used by Camba-Mendez, Kapetanios, Smith, and Weale (2001) in the construction of automatic leading indicators from a dynamic factor model. This data set includes a set of financial and expectational variables fuller than that used by OECD. It also includes the traditional leading variables, car registrations and housing activity and, for Germany, export activity. The presence or absence of any variable in the set used for each country reflects data availability rather than the outcome of any model selection process. The definition of the alternative data set is given in table 17.2.

17.5. EMPIRICAL RESULTS

17.5.1. The naive model

Our first results (table 17.3) show the performance of the naive model (model 2). For forecasts one month ahead this gives results better than any model except from perhaps the very best VARs. The RMSFE errors are between 70 percent and 77 percent of those found using more complicated autoregressive models. For

Table 17.2   Alternative data set[a]

	France	Germany	Italy	U.K.
Short interest rate	−2.60	−2.39	−2.88	−2.93
Real effective exchange rate	−3.52*			
Dwellings started/authorised	−2.23		1.57	
Share price index	−2.31	−2.54	−1.71	−2.32
Long bond – short rate	−3.74*	−2.36	−4.57*	−2.72
Long bond – German long rate	−2.90		−3.43*	−5.78*
Long bond – U.S. long rate	−3.78*	−2.38	−2.62	−2.34
Long bond – dividend yield				−3.93*
Survey: production tendency	−4.64*		−4.34*	
Survey: new orders		−2.99		−3.88*
Survey: industrial prospects			−3.32*	
Survey: order book level		−3.80*		
New car registrations	−3.27*	−2.66	−3.12	−2.62
Consumer confidence		−2.68		−2.68
Exports		−2.18		

[a] ADF statistics are given in parentheses. Critical value: −3.15. Lag order is chosen using the BIC criterion. * indicates rejection of the null hypothesis of a unit root.

forecasting two months ahead the performance is similar to that of the subsequent models, while for forecasts further ahead it is similar to, or only very slightly better than that of the autoregressive model (model 1). There are two striking aspects of these results. First of all, the excellent one-period result ought to be of interest to those concerned with very short-term forecasting. Second, the longer-term results suggest that, except in one or two cases, nothing is really gained and indeed something might be lost through careful choice of lag length in an AR model. Thus the results support the findings of Clements and Hendry (1999).

17.5.2.   OECD indicators and VARs using OECD indicator variables

We now move on to our comparisons between the VAR models constructed from the components of the leading indicator series and models 3 and 4 constructed using industrial output and the OECDs leading indicators.

Model 3 passes all the tests for all countries apart from France, for which the Granger causality test fails (that is, the null hypothesis is not rejected). Model 4 fails the test of Granger causality for all countries. This finding therefore casts considerable doubt on the claim that the OECD indicators have the lead which is claimed. In terms of explaining, rather than forecasting, the data, they do not make a statistically significant addition to the information already contained in the output series.

Table 17.3 RMSFE of naive model (model 2) relative to AR(p) model (model 1)[a]

		Period 1	Period 2	Total
FR	1	0.72	0.72	0.72
	2	0.96	0.92	0.93
	3	0.99	0.99	0.99
	4	0.99	1.01	1.00
	5	0.98	1.00	1.00
	6	0.98	1.00	1.00
	7	0.98	1.00	1.00
	8	0.98	1.00	1.00
GER	1	0.70	0.71	0.70
	2	0.96	0.94	0.95
	3	0.98	1.01	0.99
	4	0.98	1.00	0.99
	5	0.99	1.00	0.99
	6	0.98	1.00	0.99
	7	0.98	1.00	0.99
	8	0.98	1.00	0.99
IT	1	0.70	0.72	0.70
	2	0.98	1.01	0.99
	3	0.99	1.00	0.99
	4	0.99	1.01	1.00
	5	0.99	1.00	1.00
	6	1.00	1.00	1.00
	7	1.00	1.00	1.00
	8	1.00	1.00	1.00
U.K.	1	0.77	0.77	0.77
	2	0.98	0.96	0.97
	3	0.99	1.00	0.99
	4	0.99	1.00	1.00
	5	0.99	1.00	1.00
	6	0.99	0.99	1.00
	7	0.99	0.99	1.00
	8	0.99	0.99	1.00

[a] Period 1 = 90M4–94M4, Period 2 = 94M4–98M4, Total = 90M4–98M4.

At the same time a great majority of VAR models fail the Granger-causality test. For some countries where the number of indicator variables is small there are no acceptable VAR models as defined above. We therefore disregard this test and take into consideration the VAR models that fail it.[5]

Tables 17.4 and 17.6 present an analysis of the forecasting performance of the two OECD leading indicator models (3 and 4). The tables display the percentage of VAR models that perform better than these models, and the relative RMSFE of the OECD models with respect to the RMSFE of a AR(p) model used as a benchmark. The forecasting performance of both OECD models relative to the AR(p) model is certainly less than impressive. Comparing it with the performance generated from the naive model, it is difficult to argue that the OECD procedures add much at any forecast horizon, and they do much worse at the shortest horizon.

Despite this, the results show that model 3 performs well in a number of cases relative to VAR models. More specifically, the performance of this model is better than many of the VARs for longer horizons in the cases of France and for shorter horizons for Italy, Germany, and the U.K.. In a number of cases no VAR model can beat this model. Similar results hold for model 4. However, given the fact that the selection of this lag is exogenous to industrial output as reported above leads us to conclude that model 3 is more appropriate. These results suggest that the OECD's method of combining indicator variables imposes restrictions on VARs which help with forecasting performance, at least given the set of variables which they use.

Tables 17.5 and 17.7 present the results of the modified version of the Diebold–Mariano by Harvey, Leybourne, and Newbold (1997). As explained above, the empirical distribution of the probability values obtained by performing this test for all VAR models against models 3 and 4 are reported. The most prominent feature of the results is that whereas the null of equal predictive ability can in most cases be rejected when the worst-performing VAR is considered, the same null hypothesis cannot be rejected as often when the best-performing VAR is considered.

A detailed analysis of parameter constancy for both the OECD models was also carried out. Results for the Ploberger and Kramer (1992) parameter constancy test indicate that for all countries and both models the null hypothesis of parameter constancy cannot be rejected at the 5 percent significance level. However, for a number of cases and periods the null of the long-run parameter being equal to zero cannot be rejected, and in most cases the cointegration rank of the system, estimated using Johansen (1988), changes over the forecasting period. These results are not reported to save space.

The transition probability matrices in table 17.8 indicate that the performance of the VAR models is not robust over the two forecasting sub-periods. In most countries, the diagonal elements are smaller than the nondiagonal elements for most leads. For example, for Italy for lead 2 and the U.K. for leads 6 and 8 none of the models in the top quartile over the first period remains there over the second period. Also, for lead 8 for the U.K., 71 percent of those models in the top quartile in period 1 are in the bottom quartile for period 2. Given the small

Table 17.4   RMSFE performance of OECD leading indicator (model 3)

Lead	Models	Period 1[a]		Period 2		Period T	
		% VAR	Rel. RMSE	% VAR	Rel. RMSE	% VAR	Rel. RMSE
FR	1	68.750	1.028	23.077	1.000	43.750	1.006
	2	75.000	1.023	0.000	0.987	6.250	0.996
	3	12.500	0.989	15.385	0.999	6.250	0.992
	4	75.000	1.012	0.000	0.998	25.000	1.000
	5	12.500	0.998	0.000	0.998	6.250	0.994
	6	12.500	0.988	38.462	1.000	0.000	0.991
	7	6.250	0.992	0.000	0.993	0.000	0.985
	8	12.500	1.000	0.000	0.995	0.000	0.994
GER	1	29.204	0.996	58.163	1.052	28.182	1.017
	2	0.000	0.935	6.122	0.984	0.909	0.955
	3	5.310	0.954	57.143	1.045	5.455	0.988
	4	7.965	0.974	48.980	1.020	5.455	0.992
	5	12.389	0.979	55.102	1.036	22.727	1.004
	6	16.814	0.983	54.082	1.028	20.909	1.002
	7	15.929	0.985	63.265	1.047	24.545	1.006
	8	19.469	0.986	55.102	1.039	20.000	1.004
IT	1	0.000	0.960	13.158	0.968	0.000	0.956
	2	17.105	1.037	13.158	1.072	2.632	1.046
	3	64.474	1.009	92.105	1.026	65.789	1.013
	4	72.368	1.015	94.737	1.034	69.737	1.015
	5	43.421	1.013	94.737	1.036	42.105	1.011
	6	59.211	1.010	94.737	1.024	56.579	1.009
	7	53.947	1.016	86.842	1.023	51.316	1.013
	8	50.000	1.007	97.368	1.024	47.368	1.008
U.K.	1	67.857	1.098	22.222	1.041	47.273	1.080
	2	62.500	1.029	0.000	0.971	30.909	1.018
	3	48.214	1.009	13.333	1.011	27.273	1.011
	4	30.357	0.993	4.444	0.998	3.636	0.992
	5	35.714	0.991	17.778	1.000	9.091	0.993
	6	28.571	0.988	11.111	0.999	10.909	0.993
	7	48.214	1.003	22.222	1.001	18.182	1.002
	8	55.357	1.008	20.000	1.001	36.364	1.004

[a] Period 1 = 90M4–94M4, Period 2 = 94M4–98M4, Period T = 90M4–98M4. % VAR models performing better than model 3. Rel. RMSE refers to the relative RMSFE compared to the RMSFE of the AR(p) model.

Table 17.5 OECD leading indicator (model 3) predictive accuracy tests. Period 90M5–98M4

	Diebold–Mariano (corrected)				
	Min.	*1st quarter*	*Median*	*3rd quarter*	*Max.*
FR					
1 lead	0.002	0.041	0.381	0.586	0.805
2 leads	0.000	0.011	0.156	0.273	0.573
3 leads	0.017	0.063	0.212	0.223	0.551
4 leads	0.037	0.111	0.491	0.498	0.732
5 leads	0.027	0.066	0.302	0.320	0.535
6 leads	0.000	0.066	0.173	0.194	0.301
7 leads	0.007	0.094	0.156	0.179	0.301
8 leads	0.006	0.025	0.029	0.035	0.388
GER					
1 lead	0.002	0.087	0.241	0.514	0.846
2 leads	0.000	0.003	0.016	0.024	0.543
3 leads	0.000	0.030	0.147	0.301	0.851
4 leads	0.000	0.013	0.063	0.174	0.876
5 leads	0.002	0.098	0.198	0.485	0.918
6 leads	0.000	0.072	0.174	0.417	0.941
7 leads	0.000	0.128	0.231	0.484	0.957
8 leads	0.001	0.111	0.204	0.408	0.909
IT					
1 lead	0.000	0.009	0.030	0.060	0.270
2 leads	0.000	0.015	0.143	0.221	0.562
3 leads	0.000	0.025	0.905	0.990	1.000
4 leads	0.000	0.013	0.610	0.949	1.000
5 leads	0.000	0.046	0.435	0.669	0.860
6 leads	0.000	0.042	0.562	0.791	0.946
7 leads	0.000	0.085	0.587	0.807	0.938
8 leads	0.000	0.040	0.255	0.578	1.000
U.K.					
1 lead	0.001	0.103	0.484	0.771	0.993
2 leads	0.006	0.081	0.274	0.548	0.832
3 leads	0.004	0.078	0.165	0.508	0.986
4 leads	0.000	0.007	0.040	0.170	0.980
5 leads	0.000	0.047	0.176	0.282	0.826
6 leads	0.000	0.021	0.113	0.189	0.761
7 leads	0.000	0.074	0.236	0.398	0.813
8 leads	0.001	0.101	0.408	0.571	0.879

Table 17.6 RMSFE performance of OECD(-7) (model 4) leading indicator

Lead	Models	Period 1[a]		Period 2		Period T	
		% VAR	Rel. RMSE	% VAR	Rel. RMSE	% VAR	Rel. RMSE
FR	1	46.667	0.999	0.000	0.997	6.667	0.997
	2	46.667	1.001	23.077	1.004	26.667	1.002
	3	33.333	1.000	0.000	0.995	6.667	0.997
	4	33.333	1.000	69.231	1.001	53.333	1.000
	5	46.667	1.000	23.077	1.000	20.000	1.000
	6	20.000	1.000	53.846	1.000	13.333	1.000
	7	26.667	1.000	15.385	1.000	13.333	1.000
	8	33.333	1.000	61.538	1.000	33.333	1.000
GER	1	23.256	0.980	22.222	1.014	18.824	0.993
	2	10.465	0.992	1.389	0.972	2.353	0.982
	3	22.093	1.002	51.389	1.014	20.000	1.005
	4	51.163	1.006	27.778	1.002	28.235	1.003
	5	51.163	1.010	36.111	1.005	27.059	1.007
	6	46.512	1.002	44.444	1.013	31.765	1.007
	7	26.744	1.000	22.222	1.004	15.294	1.001
	8	50.000	1.002	18.056	1.005	24.706	1.003
IT	1	9.211	0.992	13.158	0.966	5.263	0.983
	2	23.684	1.040	13.158	1.071	14.474	1.052
	3	53.947	0.980	10.526	1.001	38.158	0.988
	4	18.421	0.999	23.684	0.998	27.632	1.000
	5	2.632	0.997	0.000	0.982	0.000	0.994
	6	59.211	1.010	0.000	0.983	44.737	1.003
	7	9.211	0.990	0.000	0.989	5.263	0.991
	8	3.947	0.998	0.000	0.992	6.579	0.996
U.K.	1	18.966	1.198	2.222	1.039	3.509	1.138
	2	46.552	1.050	2.222	0.986	15.789	1.022
	3	22.414	1.001	33.333	1.004	21.053	1.001
	4	17.241	1.009	24.444	0.994	12.281	1.006
	5	10.345	1.000	31.111	0.999	5.263	1.000
	6	18.966	0.990	22.222	0.999	12.281	0.995
	7	34.483	1.009	33.333	0.998	21.053	1.005
	8	43.103	1.010	35.556	1.002	26.316	1.007

[a] Period 1 = 90M4–94M4, Period 2 = 94M4–98M4, Period T = 90M4–98M4. % VAR models performing better than model 4. Rel. RMSE refers to the relative RMSFE compared to the RMSFE of the AR(p) model.

Table 17.7 Predictive accuracy tests for OECD(-7) (model 4) leading indicator. Period 90M5–98M4

	Diebold–Mariano (corrected)				
	Min.	*1st quarter*	*Median*	*3rd quarter*	*Max.*
FR					
1 lead	0.005	0.120	0.208	0.332	0.535
2 leads	0.000	0.007	0.051	0.088	0.965
3 leads	0.001	0.020	0.034	0.043	0.535
4 leads	0.091	0.222	0.550	0.673	0.919
5 leads	0.012	0.141	0.270	0.462	0.813
6 leads	0.054	0.143	0.228	0.282	0.986
7 leads	0.000	0.139	0.258	0.295	1.000
8 leads	0.001	0.020	0.181	0.593	0.848
GER					
1 lead	0.000	0.035	0.162	0.311	0.896
2 leads	0.000	0.002	0.009	0.033	0.852
3 leads	0.001	0.042	0.129	0.491	0.953
4 leads	0.000	0.061	0.170	0.515	0.959
5 leads	0.001	0.071	0.256	0.554	1.000
6 leads	0.001	0.100	0.281	0.683	0.981
7 leads	0.000	0.049	0.152	0.320	0.917
8 leads	0.000	0.099	0.185	0.471	0.937
IT					
1 lead	0.000	0.032	0.137	0.301	0.680
2 leads	0.000	0.030	0.174	0.340	0.808
3 leads	0.000	0.017	0.355	0.644	0.959
4 leads	0.000	0.026	0.371	0.486	0.911
5 leads	0.000	0.001	0.028	0.063	0.394
6 leads	0.000	0.039	0.404	0.694	0.860
7 leads	0.000	0.036	0.093	0.143	0.731
8 leads	0.000	0.038	0.073	0.195	0.534
U.K.					
1 lead	0.000	0.002	0.012	0.048	0.917
2 leads	0.001	0.035	0.116	0.309	0.644
3 leads	0.000	0.034	0.124	0.351	0.883
4 leads	0.000	0.010	0.056	0.155	0.991
5 leads	0.001	0.033	0.137	0.276	0.794
6 leads	0.000	0.046	0.133	0.298	0.920
7 leads	0.000	0.078	0.156	0.359	1.000
8 leads	0.000	0.065	0.205	0.514	1.000

Table 17.8   Transition probability matrices

	Quartiles[a]				Quartiles			
	1	2	3	4	1	2	3	4
				FR				
		Lead 2				Lead 6		
1	100.00	0.00	0.00	0.00	25.00	50.00	25.00	0.00
2	0.00	25.00	75.00	0.00	50.00	50.00	0.00	0.00
3	0.00	75.00	25.00	0.00	25.00	0.00	50.00	25.00
4	0.00	0.00	0.00	100.00	0.00	0.00	25.00	75.00
		Lead 4				Lead 8		
1	25.00	50.00	0.00	25.00	25.00	25.00	25.00	25.00
2	0.00	50.00	50.00	0.00	50.00	50.00	0.00	0.00
3	50.00	0.00	25.00	25.00	25.00	0.00	50.00	25.00
4	25.00	0.00	25.00	50.00	0.00	25.00	25.00	50.00
				GER				
		Lead 2				Lead 6		
1	10.71	25.00	42.86	20.69	32.14	39.29	14.29	13.79
2	53.57	14.29	14.29	17.24	17.86	28.57	39.29	13.79
3	10.71	32.14	25.00	31.03	21.43	17.86	17.86	41.38
4	25.00	28.57	17.86	31.03	28.57	14.29	28.57	31.03
		Lead 4				Lead 8		
1	25.00	50.00	21.43	3.45	10.71	57.14	17.86	13.79
2	28.57	28.57	17.86	24.14	32.14	21.43	21.43	24.14
3	25.00	7.14	25.00	41.38	28.57	10.71	35.71	24.14
4	21.43	14.29	35.71	31.03	28.57	10.71	25.00	37.93
				IT				
		Lead 2				Lead 6		
1	0.00	36.84	42.11	21.05	47.37	31.58	21.05	0.00
2	42.11	47.37	10.53	0.00	36.84	36.84	26.32	0.00
3	52.63	15.79	21.05	10.53	10.53	31.58	31.58	26.32
4	5.26	0.00	26.32	68.42	5.26	0.00	21.05	73.68
		Lead 4				Lead 8		
1	21.05	31.58	47.37	0.00	31.58	47.37	21.05	0.00
2	31.58	36.84	31.58	0.00	26.32	42.11	31.58	0.00
3	31.58	26.32	10.53	31.58	36.84	10.53	21.05	31.58
4	15.79	5.26	10.53	68.42	5.26	0.00	26.32	68.42

Table 17.8   (cont'd)

	Quartiles[a]				Quartiles			
	1	2	3	4	1	2	3	4

U.K.

	Lead 2				Lead 6			
1	21.43	35.71	28.57	14.29	0.00	42.86	35.71	21.43
2	28.57	21.43	21.43	28.57	28.57	28.57	35.71	7.14
3	35.71	28.57	14.29	21.43	35.71	7.14	7.14	50.00
4	14.29	14.29	35.71	35.71	35.71	21.43	21.43	21.43

	Lead 4				Lead 8			
1	7.14	50.00	28.57	14.29	0.00	50.00	35.71	14.29
2	21.43	28.57	28.57	21.43	0.00	35.71	35.71	28.57
3	21.43	7.14	35.71	35.71	28.57	7.14	14.29	50.00
4	50.00	14.29	7.14	28.57	71.43	7.14	14.29	7.14

[a] For a description of these matrices, see section 17.3.2. The best models are in the first quartile.

number of VAR models for France, no clear-cut conclusions should be read from the transition matrices. But in the Germany and U.K. cases, we can see that a good performance of a forecasting VAR in one sub-period is no guarantee of a good performance in the next sub-period. Only in Italy, where about 70 percent of the VARs which were in the bottom quartile in the first period are also there in the second period, do even poor VAR models show an element of consistency in their forecasting performance.

Finally, we also need to draw attention to the fact that most VAR models perform either as well or worse than the AR model, indicating that no added forecasting power results from the consideration of multivariate models. Furthermore, the forecasting performance of the VAR models using the underlying leading indicators is reasonably similar with different indicators as attested by the quartiles of the empirical distribution of the relative RMSFEs. The 25 percent, 50 percent and 75 percent quartiles of this distribution are 1.00, 1.01, and 1.12 for France, 1.03, 1.06, and 1.11 for Germany, 0.99, 1.00, and 1.17 for Italy, and 1.04, 1.08, and 1.22 for the U.K. over the whole forecasting period.

17.5.3.   VARs with a greater role for financial variables

Up to now, we have been using a new multivariate model evaluation strategy based on the investigation of a set of VAR models to determine the validity of models using the OECD composite leading indicator as a forecasting tool. Nevertheless, the investigation of the OECD leading indicator is conditional upon a given set of macroeconomic data chosen by the OECD. More specifically it is possible that the consideration of an alternative set of macroeconomic series used as possible leading indicators of economic activity might produce different results. This might indicate whether the chosen leading indicators are appropriate. To investigate this issue, we have used the indicators specified in table 17.2 which place greater emphasis on financial indicator series rather than variables like the money stock or labor costs, whose expectational role is less clear. The forecasting power of financial indicators and especially financial spreads has been documented by, among others, Bernanke (1990), Estrella and Hardouvelis (1991), Plosser and Rouwenhorst (1994), and Davis and Fagan (1997).

A repetition of the above forecasting evaluation exercise using the new set of variables to construct the set of VAR models leads to the results presented in table 17.9. The number of VAR models rises, since the new set has more variables. Again, VAR models of two to six variables are considered. Once again, for a great majority of VAR models the Granger-causality test fails, possibly indicating the unpredictable nature of industrial production.[6] We therefore again include the models where the causality test has failed in the analysis. The slight difference in the relative RMSE compared to table 17.4 for France and the U.K. reflects the changed sample for these countries, because data are now available since 1975M4. The results are revealing. The performance relative to the OECD leading indicator model 3 is much better. We now find that in most cases a high proportion of the VARs outperform this model, indicating that the new set of variables may provide a more potent forecasting tool.

This does not, of course, answer the question whether the performance of the OECD indicators would be enhanced if the data from which they are compiled were changed. But it does highlight the weakness of the OECD's exercise relative to what might be done. We finally note that once again the set of VAR models cannot beat in most cases the univariate AR model, with the exception of Italy, where a majority of the VAR models perform marginally better.

17.5.4. The effects of error-correction terms

Empirical evidence provided by authors such as Hoffman and Rasche (1996) and Clements and Hendry (1996) indicates that the introduction of an error correction term will not necessarily improve the forecasting performance of VAR models and it may even worsen it. Further, the theoretical results of Christoffersen and Diebold (1998) indicate that, at least when the loss function is RMSFE, including cointegration in the forecasting model will not significantly improve long-run forecasts. The crucial issue in terms of forecasting is imposing enough unit roots in the models. Underestimating the number of unit roots is worse than overestimating it.

To address this issue, we conducted a brief reexamination of the original exercise with the original and the alternative data set without investigating the cointegration properties of the VAR models; that is, no error-correction terms are included. The detailed results are available on request. Two conclusions, however, are prominent. First the absolute forecasting performance of models 3 and 4

Table 17.9 RMSFE performance of OECD leading indicator using alternative data set

		Period 1[a]		Period 2		Period T	
		% VAR	Rel. RMSE	% VAR	Rel. RMSE	% VAR	Rel. RMSE
FR	1	99.213	1.073	33.596	1.002	80.840	1.020
	2	13.386	1.007	53.543	1.005	24.934	1.003
	3	68.241	1.023	5.249	0.996	25.984	1.001
	4	91.601	1.033	86.352	1.011	80.052	1.011
	5	60.105	1.004	86.877	1.008	34.646	1.000
	6	70.604	1.013	83.465	1.008	44.619	1.001
	7	67.192	1.007	73.491	1.005	40.945	1.001
	8	76.115	1.009	92.126	1.012	58.530	1.001
GER	1	48.760	0.996	53.871	1.052	50.581	1.017
	2	0.000	0.935	3.871	0.984	0.291	0.955
	3	7.989	0.954	65.161	1.045	11.047	0.988
	4	19.008	0.974	43.226	1.020	13.081	0.992
	5	18.182	0.979	64.194	1.036	31.977	1.004
	6	22.314	0.983	57.742	1.028	29.360	1.002
	7	21.763	0.985	72.258	1.047	33.721	1.006
	8	28.099	0.986	67.742	1.039	35.756	1.004
IT	1	5.742	0.960	13.930	0.968	5.263	0.956
	2	49.761	1.037	24.876	1.072	34.928	1.046
	3	88.517	1.009	86.567	1.026	88.995	1.013
	4	86.603	1.015	96.517	1.034	83.254	1.015
	5	78.469	1.013	96.517	1.036	73.684	1.011
	6	74.163	1.010	96.020	1.024	71.292	1.009
	7	88.038	1.016	93.035	1.023	82.297	1.013
	8	62.201	1.007	87.065	1.024	63.158	1.008
U.K.	1	90.289	1.053	99.738	1.117	93.438	1.074
	2	86.877	1.009	70.866	1.016	82.940	1.006
	3	84.777	1.010	97.113	1.063	89.239	1.027
	4	83.202	1.013	98.425	1.060	89.239	1.029
	5	89.501	1.012	97.113	1.071	90.551	1.029
	6	88.714	1.004	98.163	1.078	91.339	1.025
	7	86.089	1.008	100.000	1.080	92.388	1.029
	8	82.940	1.010	98.163	1.068	87.139	1.025

[a] Period 1 = 90M4–94M4, Period 2 = 94M4–98M4, Period T = 90M4–98M4. % VAR models performing better than the OECD leading indicator model. Rel. RMSFE refers to the relative RMSFE compared to the RMSE of the AR(p) model.

is not greatly influenced because, in the recursive estimation, error-correction terms were found only rarely. On the other hand, the performance of the set of VAR models is influenced and deteriorates significantly relative to models 3 and 4 when error-correction terms are excluded. As a result, the latter beat a significant proportion of the VAR models for all forecasting horizons and countries. This effect is stronger for the alternative data set rather than the data set containing the variables used by the OECD in constructing its composite leading indicator. For example, we find that for the alternative data set and for horizons of 5–8 periods ahead, model 3 can beat all the models in the set of VAR models for France, Germany and the U.K. when error-correction effects are excluded from the latter, whereas results for VAR models incorporating error-correction indicate a much worse relative performance for models 3 and 4.

17.6. Conclusions

In this chapter, we have presented a strategy to assess the performance of composite leading indicators as tools used to forecast economic activity. Rather than assessing the performance of the leading indicator relative to a benchmark forecasting model, we propose a comparison of the effectiveness of the leading indicator against an appropriate set of VAR models. These models are built using the underlying economic variables used to construct the composite leading indicator. A number of criteria, including misspecification tests, may be used to select a subset of models from the set of all possible models.

We apply this strategy to an assessment of the OECD composite leading indicator as a tool for forecasting industrial production. A comparison with the forecasts produced from a range of VARs constructed from the variables used by the OECD suggests that the parameter restrictions implicit in the method used by the OECD to construct the indicators mean that models consisting of the indicator and the predicend outperform many of the unrestricted VARs which might be constructed from the data set. However, the performance is little better, and sometimes worse, than that of an autoregressive model and, in the very short term, much worse than that of a naive model, which simply assumes that the previous month's output growth rate will continue.

Some of the difficulty may arise from the variables which the OECD uses as indicators. We find, with an alternative set of indicator variables, that the performance of the VAR models relative to leading indicator models is much enhanced. This suggests that it may be possible to construct more satisfactory leading indicators using a better choice of variables.

Notes

1   The cointegrating vectors were estimated using the procedure of Johansen (1988). The number of cointegrating vectors was determined using Johansen's trace statistic.
2   Apart from the very important question of data revisions.
3   Note that for $n = 1$ only $\hat{\gamma}_0$ is used in the variance of $\bar{d}$.
4   The results of the original Diebold–Mariano test are available upon request.

5   At the beginning of the forecasting period, the following numbers of models fail the Granger-causality test: 27 out of 31 models for France, 130 out of 218 models for Germany, 108 out of 119 models for Italy, and 36 out of 62 models for the U.K.

6   At the beginning of the forecasting period, the following numbers of models fail the Granger-causality test: 377 out of 381 models for France, 156 out of 381 models for Germany, 274 out of 381 models for Italy, and 213 out of 381 models for the U.K.

References

Anderson, H.M. and F. Vahid (2000). Predicting the probability of a recession with nonlinear autoregressive leading indicator models. Monash University.

Artis, M., R. Bladen-Hovell, D. Osborn, G. Smith, and W. Zhang (1995). Turning point prediction for the U.K. using CSO leading indicators. *Oxford Economic Papers, 47*, 397–417.

Bernanke, B. (1990). On the predictive power of interest rates and interest rate spreads. *New England Economic Review (Federal Reserve Bank of Boston)*, 51–68.

Burns, A. and W. Mitchell (1946). *Measuring Business Cycles*. New York: National Bureau of Economic Research.

Camba-Mendez, G., G. Kapetanios, R.J. Smith, and M.R. Weale (2001). An automatic leading indicator model of economic activity. forecasting GDP growth for European countries. *Econometrics Journal, 4*, 556–90.

Christoffersen, P. and F. Diebold (1998). Co-integration and long-horizon forecasting. *Journal of Business and Economic Statistics, 16*, 450–8.

Clements, M.P. and D.F. Hendry (1996). Intercept corrections and structural change. *Journal of Applied Econometrics, 11*, 475–94.

Clements, M.P. and D.F. Hendry (1999). *Forecasting Non-Stationary Economic Series*. Cambridge, MA: MIT Press.

Clements, M.P. and J. Smith (1999). A Monte Carlo study of the forecasting performance of empirical SETAR models. *Journal of Applied Econometrics, 14*, 124–41.

Davis, E.P. and G. Fagan (1997). Are financial spreads useful indicators of of future inflation and output growth in EU countries? *Journal of Applied Econometrics, 12*, 701–14.

de Leeuw, F. (1991). Toward a theory of leading indicators. In K. Lahiri and G. Moore (eds.), *Leading Economic Indicators*. Cambridge: Cambridge University Press, 15–51.

Diebold, F.X. and R.S. Mariano (1995). Comparing predictive accuracy. *Journal of Business and Economic Statistics, 13*, 253–63.

Emerson, R.A. and D.F. Hendry (1996). An evaluation of forecasting using leading indicators. *Journal of Forecasting, 15*, 271–92.

Estrella, A. and G.A. Hardouvelis (1991). The term structure as a predictor of real economic activity. *Journal of Finance, 46*, 555–76.

Granger, C.W.J. and M.H. Pesaran (2000). Economic and statistical measures of forecast accuracy. *Journal of Forecasting*.

Hamilton, J.D. (1994). *Time Series Analysis*. Princeton University Press.

Harvey, D.I., S.J. Leybourne, and P. Newbold (1997). Testing the equality of prediction mean square errors. *International Journal of Forecasting, 13*, 273–81.

Hoffman, D.L. and R.H. Rasche (1996). Assessing forecast performance in a cointegrated system. *Journal of Applied Econometrics, 11*, 495–517.

Johansen, S. (1988). Statistical analysis of co-integration vectors. *Journal of Economic Dynamics and Control, 12*, 231–54.

Koopmans, T. (1947). Measurement without theory. *Review of Economics and Statistics, 29*, 161–72.

Lahiri, K. and G. Moore (1991). *Leading Economic Indicators*. Cambridge: Cambridge University Press.

Layton, A. (1991). Some Australian experience with leading indicators. In K. Lahiri and G. Moore (eds.), *Leading Economic Indicators*. Cambridge: Cambridge University Press, 211–30.

O'Dea, D.J. (1975). *Cyclical Indicators for the Postwar British Economy*. Cambridge University Press.

OECD (1987). *OECD Leading Indicators and Business Cycles in Member Countries: 1960–1985*. OECD.

Osborn, D. (1999). Leading indicators, nonlinear models and forecasts of U.K. macroeconomic time series. University of Manchester.

Pesaran, M.H. and A. Timmermann (1992). A simple nonparametric test of predictive performance. *Journal of Business and Economic Statistics*, 10, 461–5.

Ploberger, W. and W. Kramer (1992). The CUSUM test with OLS residuals. *Econometrica*, 60, 271–85.

Plosser, C.I. and K. Rouwenhorst (1994). International term structures and real economic growth. *Journal of Monetary Economics*, 33, 135–55.

Sullivan, R., A. Timmermann and H. White (1999). Data-snooping, technical trading rule performance and the bootstrap. *Journal of Finance*, 54, 1647–91.

Sullivan, R., A. Timmermann and H. White (2000). Dangers of data-driven inference: The case of calendar effects in stock returns. University of California, San Diego.

White, H. (2000). A reality check for data snooping. *Econometrica*, 68, 1097–1126.

CHAPTER EIGHTEEN

Unit-Root Versus Deterministic Representations of Seasonality for Forecasting

Denise R. Osborn

18.1. Introduction

Seasonality is an important feature of many economic time series. Indeed, examining the quarterly or monthly growth rates in real macroeconomic series over the postwar period, a number of studies have found that 50 percent or more of the variation can typically be "explained" by the quarter or month in which the data are observed: see, for example, Miron (1996, ch. 3) or Osborn (1990). Such measures should not be interpreted as necessarily implying that seasonality is fixed over time, but they do emphasize that patterns tend to repeat over successive years. Given the empirical importance which can be attached to seasonality, it is self-evident that its treatment will play a major role when forecasting quarterly or monthly economic time series.

Over the last 20 years, empirical workers in economics have paid a great deal of attention to the long-run properties of time series and, in particular, to whether such series are difference stationary or trend stationary. The vast bulk of this work has been conducted in a nonseasonal context, or at least the seasonality issue has been side-stepped by the use of seasonally-adjusted data. The seminal study of Nelson and Plosser (1982) adopted the statistical unit-root test of Dickey and Fuller (1979) and concluded that U.S. time series are generally integrated of order one, denoted $I(1)$, implying that first differences should be taken in order to render the series stationary. This unit-root analysis has been developed in many ways and applied in a wide variety of contexts, but the broad conclusion of Nelson and Plosser about the $I(1)$ nature of real economic time series remains widely accepted.

Seasonality does, however, raise a number of issues. Since seasonality is clearly related to the time of year, it may be argued that it is an intra-year phenomenon. As such, it is a type of short-run movement. Nevertheless, seasonality can itself exhibit a form of unit-root behavior and, therefore, may have long-run implications. Perhaps these long-run implications are best summarized by the phrase, often used in this context, that "summer can become winter." Put slightly differently, the presence of these seasonal unit roots implies that the long-run direction of intra-year movements are unpredictable. Unfortunately, economics itself has very little to say about the nature of seasonality, so the presence or not of seasonal unit roots is essentially a statistical question.

In a statistical context, two competing hypotheses relating to seasonality have attracted much recent attention. The first hypothesis states that the transformation required to induce stationarity in the time series is seasonal (that is, annual) differencing. This implies that conventional first differencing is not sufficient to remove the nonstationarity in the series because of seasonal unit roots. The underlying process is then often said to be seasonally integrated of order one, abbreviated as $SI(1)$. The second hypothesis is that, possibly after first differencing to remove a conventional unit root, the stochastic process is stationary around a constant underlying seasonal pattern. This case is termed deterministic seasonality. In contrast to the consensus on the unit-root properties of (real) nonseasonal series, there is no consensus in the literature as to which of these two competing possibilities generally provides a more adequate description of seasonal economic time series. There are, indeed, other contenders. In particular, dating back at least to the work of Box and Jenkins (1970), it is sometimes proposed that both first and seasonal differences may be required for stationarity. Due to these competing hypotheses and the lack of a consensus about seasonal integration, there is consequently no consensus about the appropriate differencing to be undertaken as a preliminary step in building a forecasting model for seasonal economic time series.

The purpose of this chapter is to examine, in a forecasting context, the issues concerned with seasonal unit-root models versus models with deterministic seasonality. Since our focus is forecasting, we do not attempt to review all the literature on testing for seasonal unit roots. We also restrict our attention to models where the parameters are constant over time, except possibly for one-off structural breaks. This restriction rules out the periodic class of models, where the coefficients change over the seasons of the year. This is to keep the amount of material covered within reasonable bounds. Periodic models are discussed extensively in Franses (1996) and, in a forecasting context, by Franses and Paap in chapter 19 of this volume.

The plan of this chapter is as follows. Section 18.2 outlines the competing models we consider, explaining how each is used for forecasting, the relationships between them and the role of structural breaks in a forecasting context. The selection between these competing models is typically based on prior testing for seasonal unit roots and hence, in section 18.3, we consider the principal seasonal unit-root tests employed. Against this background, section 18.4 then reviews the main published results on the use of seasonal unit-root models in forecasting. Some brief concluding remarks in section 18.5 complete the chapter.

18.2. THE COMPETING MODELS

To keep the discussion as straightforward as possible, we assume throughout this section that the series under analysis is quarterly. It should be emphasized, however, that the comments made can be generalized to the monthly case.

This section considers seasonal unit-root models, and models based on deterministic seasonality. These are examined in the first two subsections. After briefly outlining the properties in each case, we examine how each model is used to generate forecasts. A fuller analysis of the principal competing models can be found in Ghysels and Osborn (2001). The forecasts discussed are optimal in the sense that they minimize the theoretical mean square forecast error when the model (including the parameter values) is known. The classic reference on optimal linear forecasting is Whittle (1963), with many practical aspects discussed by Box and Jenkins (1970). Subsection 18.2.3 then explores the relationships between the models. All of this assumes that the underlying process is constant over time, but the final subsection considers the role of structural breaks.

18.2.1. Seasonal unit-root models

THE MODELS AND THEIR PROPERTIES

The simplest seasonal unit-root model is the quarterly seasonal random walk, which is

$$y_t = y_{t-4} + \varepsilon_t, \tag{18.1}$$

where ε_t is a zero-mean independent and identically distributed (*iid*) process with constant variance. In this case y_t is an integrated process, but it is not a conventional $I(1)$ process. One perspective on this is obtained by noting that the autoregressive operator of (1) is

$$1 - L^4 = (1 - L)(1 + L + L^2 + L^3)$$

$$= (1 - L)(1 + L)(1 + L^2)$$

$$= (1 - L)(1 + L)(1 \pm iL), \tag{18.2}$$

where L is the lag operator (so that $Ly_t = y_{t-1}$), and $i = \sqrt{-1}$. Thus, $\Delta_4 = 1 - L^4$ has four factors, namely the first difference $\Delta_1 = (1 - L)$, the half-year summation operator $1 + L$, and the complex factors $1 \pm iL$. All four of these factors are nonstationary, with the first implying the conventional unit root of 1: the second has the unit root -1 while the complex pair has the pair of unit roots $\pm i$; each of these roots has a modulus of unity.[1] Two features of this factorization are important. First, annual differencing will remove a conventional unit root because Δ_4 includes the factor Δ_1. Second, Δ_4 involves three additional unit roots ($-1, \pm i$) which are associated with seasonality. These latter three roots are known as seasonal unit roots. It should also be noted that the complex unit roots $\pm i$ cannot be separated: they must occur together as a pair in order that the resulting polynomial does not involve complex-valued coefficients.

The seasonal random walk process cannot be made stationary by first differencing, because such differencing leaves the nonstationary seasonal unit roots untouched. Thus, the seasonal random walk is not an $I(1)$ process. The appropriate stationarity-inducing transformation is seasonal differencing, since $\Delta_4 y_t = y_t - y_{t-4} = \varepsilon_t$ is stationary.[2] Thus, in the terminology of the Introduction, the seasonal random walk is $SI(1)$:

A second perspective on the seasonal random walk is obtained by noting that, for a specific quarter, the value involves only current and past disturbances which occurr(ed) in that quarter. To make this more specific, assume that y_1 relates to the first quarter of a year and that some specific t relates to a fourth-quarter observation. Then, substituting for lagged y in (1), it can be seen that

$$y_t = \varepsilon_t + \varepsilon_{t-4} + \ldots + \varepsilon_8 + \varepsilon_4, \qquad (18.3)$$

when we make the simplifying assumption that the starting value $y_0 = 0$. Thus, were we to consider only the observations $y_4, y_8, y_{12}, \ldots$ relating to the fourth quarter, then (18.3) implies that the process would be a conventional random walk. Analogously, considered in isolation, the first-quarter observations $y_1, y_5, y_9, \ldots$ constitute a random walk, as do those for the second and third quarters. These four random walks related to the four quarters are, however, independent of each other. This independence arises because the underlying disturbances ε_t are independent and each disturbance enters one (and only one) quarterly random walk process. The reason that "summer can become winter" is that these independent random walk processes for the four quarters of the year may move anywhere in relation to each other. Annual differencing removes the nonstationarity in the process, because the annual difference is the conventional first difference for each of these separate random walk processes.

The seasonal random walk can be generalized to include a constant term and stationary dynamics. The dynamics considered in practice are almost invariably of the autoregressive type, so that a more general $SI(1)$ process may be considered, where

$$\phi(L)\Delta_4 y_t = \gamma + \varepsilon_t, \qquad (18.4)$$

with all roots of the polynomial $\phi(L) = 1 - \phi_1 L - \ldots - \phi_p L^p$ outside the unit circle. All our comments relating to the nonstationarity of y_t in (18.1) apply also to this more general case. Thus, $y_t \sim SI(1)$ because all the nonstationary roots of Δ_4 are again present and, although the processes for the four quarters of the year are no longer independent, (18.4) implies that there are four separate underlying $I(1)$ processes with one of these relating to each of the four quarters of the year. The introduction of a nonzero constant γ introduces the same drift term into each of these integrated processes and hence $E(y_t)$ is trending over time, with the trend being identical over the four quarters.

Another point to be noted is that, at least theoretically, a series may contain some but not all of the seasonal unit roots implied by $1 - L^4$. For example, the stationarity-inducing transformation could be $1 - L^2$, implying (with quarterly data) that six-month differencing is the appropriate transformation to make the underlying process stationary. The factorization $1 - L^2 = (1 - L)(1 + L)$ shows that this process has the conventional unit root of 1 and the seasonal unit root of -1, but not the complex pair of unit roots $\pm i$. Such a process is intermediate between $I(1)$ and $SI(1)$, in the sense that it contains more unit roots than that implied by the former but less than that of the latter. These processes with only a subset of the seasonal unit roots are, however, relatively rarely used in practice.

One other important type of seasonal unit-root model should be mentioned. At least historically, both first and seasonal differences were often applied. Indeed, the so-called "airline model,"

$$\Delta_1\Delta_4 y_t = (1 - \theta_1 L)(1 - \theta_4 L^4)e_t, \tag{18.5}$$

was widely used, where e_t is a zero-mean *iid* disturbance with constant variance and the moving-average coefficients satisfy $-1 < \theta_1, \theta_4 < 1$. Box and Jenkins (1970) fitted a monthly version of this model to monthly data on airline passengers and for the following 10–20 years it was believed to provide a useful description for a wide range of seasonal time series. Indeed, Box et al. (1978) refer to this specification as being "a typical form of a seasonal nonstationary model that has been identified and used successfully in many economic time series." Although not based specifically on the airline model, the prominent method of seasonal adjustment based on the U.S. Bureau of the Census X-11 program also assumes implicitly that both first and seasonal differences are required to render the series stationary (Burridge and Wallis, 1984). Assuming autoregressive disturbances, we might consider the model

$$\phi^*(L)\Delta_1\Delta_4 y_t = e_t, \tag{18.6}$$

where we use $\phi^*(L)$ to distinguish the autoregressive polynomial here from that used in (18.4) above. The polynomial $\phi^*(L)$ is of order q and is assumed to have all roots outside the unit circle. If the airline model (18.5) is of interest, then $\phi^*(L)$ may be considered as an autoregressive approximation to the invertible moving average polynomial $(1 - \theta_1 L)(1 - \theta_4 L^4)$.

From the discussion of Δ_4 above, it is should be clear that the double-difference operator is $\Delta_1\Delta_4 = \Delta_1^2(1 + L)(1 + L^2)$, and hence that this operator includes two conventional first differences. Leaving aside the seasonal unit-root factors $1 + L$

and $1 + L^2$, such models imply that the series is integrated of order two, or $I(2)$. The double-difference model might, perhaps, then be dismissed on the grounds that the stylized fact of studies which consider unit roots in a nonseasonal context is that real economic time series are typically $I(1)$ and not $I(2)$. Nevertheless, practical problems associated with unit-root testing may make such a dismissal premature. Such issues are discussed in section 18.3.3, where we briefly revisit this question.

FORECASTING

If y_t is $SI(1)$, and hence it is modeled using $\Delta_4 y_t$, it is most natural to consider first forecasting the annual change in y_t. Assuming initially that the parameters of (18.4) are known, the one-step (that is, one-quarter) ahead forecast of $\Delta_4 y_{t+1}$, obtained using information available at time t, is

$$\Delta_4 \hat{y}_{t+1|t} = \gamma + \phi_1 \Delta_4 y_t + \ldots + \phi_p \Delta_4 y_{t-p+1}. \tag{18.7}$$

It will be noticed that here, and subsequently, our notation indicates the period being forecast (namely, $t + 1$ in this case) and the period up to which observations are available when this forecast is made (here t). In a practical sense, expression (18.7) can be obtained from (18.4) by writing out the lag polynomial in that expression explicitly in terms of lagged values of $\Delta_4 y$ and shifting all time subscripts forward by one, so that the left-hand side relates to time $t + 1$. Also note that the *iid* disturbance ε_{t+1} is unforecastable at time t and hence is set to its expected value of zero. Since all other terms are known, this disturbance is the only element giving rise to forecast inaccuracy one-step ahead. When forecasting more than one-quarter ahead, previously forecast values replace actual observations on the right-hand side of (18.4), so that forecasting proceeds recursively. Hence, for example, the two-quarter-ahead forecast of the annual growth rate at $t + 2$ is

$$\Delta_4 \hat{y}_{t+2|t} = \gamma + \phi_1 \Delta_4 \hat{y}_{t+1|t} + \phi_2 \Delta_4 y_t + \ldots + \phi_p \Delta_4 y_{t-p+2}, \tag{18.8}$$

which uses the one-step-ahead forecast $\Delta_4 \hat{y}_{t+1|t}$.

Forecasts of other transformations may also be of interest. In particular, using the identity $y_t = y_{t-4} + \Delta_4 y_t$, the forecast of the future level is obtained as

$$\hat{y}_{t+h|t} = y_{t+h-4} + \Delta_4 \hat{y}_{t+h|t} \quad h = 1, 2, 3, 4 \tag{18.9}$$

when forecasting up to one year ahead. In this case, only a forecast of the annual change from observed y_{t+h-4} is needed, and the accuracy of the forecast $\hat{y}_{t+h|t}$ is the same as that of $\Delta_4 \hat{y}_{t+h|t}$. Beyond a year, however, the forecast level has to be used in place of observed y_{t+h-4} on the right-hand side of (18.9). For example, to forecast two years ahead (horizon $h = 8$), $\hat{y}_{t+8|t} = \hat{y}_{t+4|t} + \Delta_4 \hat{y}_{t+8|t} = y_t + \Delta_4 \hat{y}_{t+4|t} + \Delta_4 \hat{y}_{t+8|t}$. If forecasts of future first differences are required, then these may be obtained from forecasts of the level. Thus, $\Delta_1 \hat{y}_{t+1|t} = \hat{y}_{t+1|t} - y_t$ and

$$\Delta_1 \hat{y}_{t+h|t} = \hat{y}_{t+h|t} - \hat{y}_{t+h-1|t} \quad h = 2, 3, \ldots \tag{18.10}$$

If the observed series does not contain all of the unit roots implied by annual differencing, then the logical implication is to forecast the series using the appropriate unit-root model. For example, if the roots 1 and -1 are present, then the required forecasts will be built up from forecasts of the six-month change in y_t, since the roots imply that the operator $(1 - L)(1 + L) = \Delta_2$ is required for stationarity. Other combinations of roots lead, however, to less intuitive models. For example, the presence of the conventional unit root together with the complex pair of roots $\pm i$ leads to the filter $(1 - L)(1 + L^2) = (1 - L + L^2)$, but a forecast of $(1 - L + L^2)y_t$ does not have a natural interpretation. Nevertheless, it is of course possible to derive any required forecasts based on this transformation.

In the case of the double-difference model of (18.6), any required forecasts are essentially based on forecasts of $\Delta_1\Delta_4 y$. Thus, in particular,

$$\Delta_1\Delta_4\hat{y}_{t+1|t} = \phi_1^*\Delta_1\Delta_4 y_t + \ldots + \phi_q^*\Delta_1\Delta_4 y_{t-q+1}. \tag{18.11}$$

The definition $\Delta_1\Delta_4 y_t = \Delta_1 y_t - \Delta_1 y_{t-4}$ implies that $\Delta_1 y_t = \Delta_1 y_{t-4} + \Delta_1\Delta_4 y_t$, so that the one-step-ahead forecast of the quarterly change is obtained as

$$\Delta_1\hat{y}_{t+1|t} = \Delta_1 y_{t-3} + \Delta_1\Delta_4\hat{y}_{t+1|t}. \tag{18.12}$$

Similarly, expressing the identity $\Delta_1\Delta_4 y_t = \Delta_4 y_t - \Delta_4 y_{t-1}$ as $\Delta_4 y_t = \Delta_4 y_{t-1} + \Delta_1\Delta_4 y_t$ yields the one-step-ahead forecast of the annual change as

$$\Delta_4\hat{y}_{t+1|t} = \Delta_4 y_t + \Delta_1\Delta_4\hat{y}_{t+1|t}. \tag{18.13}$$

The one-step-ahead forecast of the level y_{t+1} is then

$$\hat{y}_{t+1|t} = y_t + \Delta_1\hat{y}_{t+1|t}$$
$$= y_{t-3} + \Delta_4\hat{y}_{t+1|t}. \tag{18.14}$$

Once again, forecasts more than one step ahead are built up recursively using previously forecast values.

Although the description above discusses the use of the series being modeled as the basis of all forecasting, it might also be remarked that the required forecasts can be equivalently generated by rewriting the model in the form of the required forecasts. Taking the double-difference model with $q = 1$ as an example, assume

$$\Delta_1\Delta_4 y_t = \phi_1^*\Delta_1\Delta_4 y_{t-1} + \varepsilon_t.$$

Using the identity $\Delta_1\Delta_4 = 1 - L - L^4 + L^5$ yields

$$y_t - y_{t-1} - y_{t-4} + y_{t-5} = \phi_1^*(y_{t-1} - y_{t-2} - y_{t-5} + y_{t-6}) + \varepsilon_t,$$

which can be rewritten as an autoregressive model in y_t, where

$$y_t = (1 + \phi_1^*)y_{t-1} - \phi_1^* y_{t-2} + y_{t-4} - (1 + \phi_1^*)y_{t-5} + \phi_1^* y_{t-6} + \varepsilon_t.$$

If levels forecasts are required, this last equation can be used one step ahead to yield

$$\hat{y}_{t+1|t} = (1 + \phi_1^*)y_t - \phi_1^* y_{t-1} + y_{t-3} - (1 + \phi_1^*)y_{t-4} + \phi_1^* y_{t-5}. \qquad (18.15)$$

As usual, forecasts $\hat{y}_{t+h|t}$ can be obtained by using (18.15) recursively, with forecasts replacing unknown values on the right-hand side for $h > 1$. It is a matter of taste and convenience as to whether the forecasts required are built up from forecasts of $\Delta_1 \Delta_4 y_t$ or from (18.15).

18.2.2.   Models with deterministic seasonality

THE MODELS AND THEIR PROPERTIES

Since the presence of the conventional unit root of 1 is generally accepted for economic time series, our discussion of deterministic seasonality models also begins by making this assumption. In this case, the deterministic seasonality model has the form

$$\varphi(L)\Delta_1 y_t = \alpha_1 \delta_{1t} + \alpha_2 \delta_{2t} + \alpha_3 \delta_{3t} + \alpha_4 \delta_{4t} + u_t, \qquad (18.16)$$

where the disturbance u_t is assumed to be *iid* with mean zero and constant variance; δ_{it} for $i = 1, \ldots, 4$ are seasonal dummy variables which take the value one when the observation t falls in the quarter i and are otherwise zero. The use of seasonal dummy variables within regression models is prevalent in economics, where seasonality is often assumed to have the effect of shifting the dependent variable up or down in relation to the explanatory variables. In the context of (18.16), the rth-order polynomial $\varphi(L) = 1 - \varphi_1 L - \ldots - \varphi_r L^r$ is assumed to be stationary and hence to have all roots outside the unit circle. In order to capture stationary stochastic seasonality, $\varphi(L)$ may include important nonzero coefficients at the annual lags of 4, 8, etc.

The deterministic nature of seasonality in (18.16) is indicated by the fact that $E(\Delta_1 y_t) = E(\Delta_1 y_{t-4})$, but this mean varies with the quarter. For example, if $r = 1$ and t falls in quarter 1, then successively substituting for $\Delta_1 y_{t-j}$ ($j = 1, 2, 3$) yields

$$E(\Delta_1 y_t) = \frac{\alpha_1 + \varphi_1 \alpha_4 + \varphi_1^2 \alpha_3 + \varphi_1^3 \alpha_2}{1 - \varphi_1^4}, \qquad (18.17)$$

in which the role of each δ_i ($i = 1, 2, 3, 4$) is specific to t being in quarter 1. However, if the annual growth is of interest, then the identity $\Delta_4 y_t = \Delta_1 y_t + \Delta_1 y_{t-1} + \Delta_1 y_{t-2} + \Delta_1 y_{t-3}$ implies that $E(\Delta_4 y_t)$ is the sum of the four quarterly expected changes. For the case of general r, (18.16) implies

$$E(\Delta_4 y_t) = \frac{\alpha_1 + \alpha_2 + \alpha_3 + \alpha_4}{1 - \varphi_1 - \ldots - \varphi_r}, \qquad (18.18)$$

so that the expected annual growth is constant over t. This constant annual growth implies an underlying trend in the level y_t for the process (18.16), with this trend having the slope (18.18) when measured over a year.

In contrast to the four unit-root processes implicitly present in the seasonally integrated model, the model here contains only one unit-root process. This unit-root process implies that y_t will wander widely and smoothly over time, but in these meanderings y_t is linked to y_{t-1}. Put a different way, the change in y_t from one season to the next through (18.16) has a constant variance over time and hence the values for any two quarters cannot deviate "too far" from each other over time. Thus, unlike the seasonally integrated process, here "summer cannot become winter."

An alternative model to (18.16) for deterministic seasonality combines this with an underlying trend stationarity for y_t. In this case, the model contains no stochastic nonstationarity and has the form

$$\varphi^*(L)y_t = \alpha_1^*\delta_{1t} + \alpha_2^*\delta_{2t} + \alpha_3^*\delta_{3t} + \alpha_4^*\delta_{4t} + \beta t + v_t, \tag{18.19}$$

where the polynomial $\varphi^*(L)$ is of order s and has all roots outside the unit circle. The disturbance v_t is iid with zero mean and constant variance. The superscript $*$ is used here again to emphasize that the coefficients are not the same as those of the first-difference model with deterministic seasonality, (18.16). A linear trend term, βt, is included in (18.19) to account for the trend frequently encountered with economic time series. In this model the deviation $y_t - E(y_t)$ has a constant (and finite) variance for all t, so that y_t is not only linked to y_{t-1}, but also to its mean $E(y_t)$.

FORECASTING

Forecasting with the deterministic-seasonality model of (18.16) is straightforward. Once again assuming that the parameters are known, then the one-quarter-ahead forecast is

$$\Delta_1\hat{y}_{t+1|t} = \alpha_1\delta_{1,t+1} + \alpha_2\delta_{2,t+1} + \alpha_3\delta_{3,t+1} + \alpha_4\delta_{4,t+1} + \varphi_1\Delta_1 y_t + \ldots + \varphi_r\Delta_1 y_{t-r+1}. \tag{18.20}$$

Two steps ahead, the term $\Delta_1 y_{t+1}$ is not known, and it is replaced by $\Delta_1\hat{y}_{t+1|t}$ to obtain

$$\Delta_1\hat{y}_{t+2|t} = \alpha_1\delta_{1,t+2} + \alpha_2\delta_{2,t+2} + \alpha_3\delta_{3,t+2} + \alpha_4\delta_{4,t+2} + \varphi_1\Delta_1\hat{y}_{t+1|t}$$
$$+ \varphi_2\Delta_1 y_t + \ldots + \varphi_r\Delta_1 y_{t-r+2}. \tag{18.21}$$

In a similar way, forecasts of the quarter-to-quarter changes for longer horizons can be calculated recursively.

Forecasts of the future level y_{t+h} and/or the annual change $\Delta_4 y_{t+h}$ at the horizon h may also be required. At one step ahead, these can be obtained as

$$\hat{y}_{t+1|t} = y_t + \Delta_1\hat{y}_{t+1|t} \tag{18.22}$$

and

$$\Delta_4\hat{y}_{t+1|t} = \hat{y}_{t+1|t} - y_{t-3} \tag{18.23}$$

respectively. Two steps ahead, the level forecast is built up as

$$\hat{y}_{t+2|t} = \hat{y}_{t+1|t} + \Delta_1 \hat{y}_{t+2|t}$$
$$= y_t + \Delta_1 \hat{y}_{t+1|t} + \Delta_1 \hat{y}_{t+2|t}. \tag{18.24}$$

Similarly, at longer horizons, forecasts of the level are built up recursively. As in section 18.2.1, the levels forecasts can be equivalently obtained by deriving the levels representation of the model and employing this recursively. For horizons $h = 1, 2, 3, 4$, forecasts of the annual change can be obtained as $\Delta_4 \hat{y}_{t+h|t} = \hat{y}_{t+h|t} - \hat{y}_{t+h-4}$. At longer horizons, forecasts can be obtained either from the forecast levels or by accumulating quarter-to-quarter forecast changes, as

$$\Delta_4 \hat{y}_{t+h|t} = \hat{y}_{t+h|t} - \hat{y}_{t+h-4|t}$$
$$= \Delta_1 \hat{y}_{t+h|t} + \Delta_1 \hat{y}_{t+h-1|t} + \Delta_1 \hat{y}_{t+h-2|t} + \Delta_1 \hat{y}_{t+h-3|t}. \tag{18.25}$$

Thus, whichever particular forecast is required (quarter-to-quarter change, annual change or level of y), the forecast can be built up by forecasting future $\Delta_1 y_t$.

In the case of the trend-stationary plus deterministic-seasonality model of (18.19), forecasts are usually built up from the levels form because this is the form of the dependent variable. Thus, one-step-ahead forecasts for y are obtained as

$$\hat{y}_{t+1|t} = \alpha_1^* \delta_{1,t+1} + \alpha_2^* \delta_{2,t+1} + \alpha_3^* \delta_{3,t+1} + \alpha_4^* \delta_{4,t+1} + \beta(t+1) + \varphi_1^* y_t + \ldots + \varphi_s^* y_{t-s+1} \tag{18.26}$$

with forecasts for the quarter-to-quarter or annual changes, $\Delta_1 y_{t+1}$ or $\Delta_4 y_{t+1}$ respectively, obtained by subtracting the appropriate lagged y from this forecast. For forecasting more than one step ahead, previously forecast values are used. Two steps ahead, for example,

$$\hat{y}_{t+2|t} = \alpha_1^* \delta_{1,t+2} + \alpha_2^* \delta_{2,t+2} + \alpha_3^* \delta_{3,t+2} + \alpha_4^* \delta_{4,t+2} + \beta(t+2) + \varphi_1^* \hat{y}_{t+1|t}$$
$$+ \varphi_2^* y_t + \ldots + \varphi_s^* y_{t-s+2}. \tag{18.27}$$

Clearly, forecasts of the quarter-to-quarter or annual differences can be computed, if required, from these levels forecasts.

18.2.3. Relationships between models

Four principal forecasting models have been discussed above, namely the trend-stationary model with deterministic seasonality (18.19), the first-difference deterministic-seasonality model (18.16), the seasonal-difference model (18.4), and the double-difference model of (18.6). Although each has distinctive long-run implications about the nature of seasonal and/or nonseasonal movements, it is important to point out that the models are related to each other in a number of respects. Note first that all allow the possibility that y_t contains a deterministic linear trend. This trend is explicitly included as the term βt in the trend-stationary plus deterministic-seasonality model. As noted in the above discussion of the first-difference deterministic-seasonality model (18.16) and the seasonal-difference model (18.4), such a trend is allowed through the inclusion of intercept or seasonal dummy variable terms. Finally, the double-difference speci-fication of (18.6) implies that $E(\Delta_1\Delta_4 y_t) = 0$ and hence $E(\Delta_4 y_t) = E(\Delta_4 y_{t-1})$. Thus, this specification also allows a nonzero annual growth rate which is constant at $E(\Delta_4 y_t)$ for all t, giving rise to an underlying deterministic trend in $E(y_t)$.

Second, all models also allow the possibility that the deviations around the trend have means which depend on the season. This constant underlying sea-sonal pattern is explicitly allowed in both models with deterministic seasonality. For the seasonal-difference model, the implication that $E(\Delta_4 y_t)$ is constant over all t does not prevent $E(y_t)$, $E(y_{t-1})$, $E(y_{t-2})$, $E(y_{t-3})$ from exhibiting a seasonal pattern. For example, in the case of the seasonal random walk (1), $E(y_t) = E(y_{t-4})$ and ultimately a seasonal pattern in these expected values will be present if the pre-sample period "starting values" are such that $E(y_0)$, $E(y_{-1})$, $E(y_{-2})$, and $E(y_{-3})$ are not all equal. The same point holds for the double-difference model, where $E(\Delta_4 y_t)$ is constant over t.

Thus, the models in the previous two subsections have been specified to allow the same type of deterministic trend and seasonality components to be present. The models differ, therefore, only with respect to their stochastic properties. Focus-ing on seasonality, the key distinction of interest is whether the variation around the underlying seasonal pattern is nonstationary (the seasonally-integrated models) or stationary. If the former is true, the underlying seasonal pattern in $E(y_t)$ effectively becomes meaningless in the long run, because the observed values of y_t can wander far from their expected values.

One way to think of these models is that they represent a continuum of pos-sible stochastic specifications, ranging in orders of integration from the highest order, implied by the model using $\Delta_1\Delta_4$, to the model with stationary dynamic properties. However, the unit-root literature now recognizes that the data gener-ating process may lie "close" to the boundary of its class. If a general autoregressive operator $\varphi^*(L)$ is considered, the roots of this polynomial give rise to the order of integration. With all roots outside the unit circle, the appropriate model is that of (18.19). If, however, $\varphi^*(L) = (1 - L)\varphi(L)$, with all roots of $\varphi(L)$ outside the unit circle, then the first-difference model with deterministic seasonality is appropriate. Clearly, however, the former model will be "close" to the latter if the largest root of $\varphi^*(L)$ is "near" to, but strictly less than, 1. Similarly, a stationary polynomial $\varphi^*(L)$ may have coefficients[3] which make this model close to the seasonal-integration case of $\varphi^*(L) = (1 - L^4)\phi(L)$.

Practical questions follow from this discussion. If the different models can be close to each other, is it important to specify the order of integration for the series prior to building a forecasting model? If so, can the correct order of integration be established in a seasonal context using the sort of data generally available in economics? Are there practical advantages which point to a particular type of model being routinely used to forecast seasonal economic time series? We attempt to answer these questions in what follows. Indeed, our discussion of structural breaks in the next subsection throws some light on these issues.

18.2.4. The role of structural breaks

Clements and Hendry (1997) consider the possibility that seasonality is essentially of the deterministic type, but at some time τ this pattern alters. We can illustrate their arguments through a simple case of the deterministic model of (18.19) by assuming that the true process[4] is

$$y_t = \alpha_1^* \delta_{1t} + \alpha_2^* \delta_{2t} + \alpha_3^* \delta_{3t} + \alpha_4^* \delta_{4t} + \beta t$$
$$+ (\alpha_1^\dagger \delta_{1t} + \alpha_2^\dagger \delta_{2t} + \alpha_3^\dagger \delta_{3t} + \alpha_4^\dagger \delta_{4t}) I_t^\tau + v_t, \tag{18.28}$$

where I_t^τ is an indicator variable, which takes the value 1 for periods $t = \tau, \tau + 1$, ... and is zero for all t up to an including period $\tau - 1$. Prior to to time τ, the deterministic seasonal pattern for season i is given by $E(y_t) - \beta t = \alpha_i^*$, whereas from time τ onwards this pattern is $E(y_t) - \beta t = (\alpha_i^* + \alpha_i^\dagger)$. Much of the effect of this one-off change can be removed by taking annual differences, which yields

$$\Delta_4 y_t = 4\beta + (\alpha_1^\dagger \delta_{1t} + \alpha_2^\dagger \delta_{2t} + \alpha_3^\dagger \delta_{3t} + \alpha_4^\dagger \delta_{4t}) \Delta_4 I_t^\tau + v_t - v_{t-4}. \tag{18.29}$$

From the definition of I_t^τ, $\Delta_4 I_t^\tau = 1$ for $t = \tau, \ldots, \tau + 3$ and is zero otherwise. Since $E(\Delta_4 y_t)$ is constant at 4β for all time periods except for the four quarters $t = \tau, \ldots, \tau + 3$, then (18.29) effectively confines the effect of the structural change to "blips" relating to these four observations.

Irrespective of the horizon and prior to the structural change, the forecasts from (18.28) are $\hat{y}_t = \alpha_i^* + \beta t$ when the forecast for period t relates to season i. When forecasting a period $t \geq \tau$ and the structural change is not recognized, then the forecasts are biased by the amount of the structural change, namely $\alpha_i^\dagger$, because they are based on the wrong seasonal pattern. On the other hand, basing forecasts on the annual difference specification (18.4) involves a self-correction to such a structural change in the deterministic seasonal pattern. This is because the forecasts of the level are obtained by forecasting the annual change from the appropriate observed value and, as seen from (18.29), the effect of the structural change on these values is confined to four observations. Put more concretely, $\Delta_4 \hat{y}_{t+h|t} = 4\beta$ is unbiased for all t and h except when $t + h = \tau, \ldots, \tau + 3$. Therefore the level forecast $\hat{y}_{t+h|t} = 4\beta + y_{t+h-4}$ obtained using (18.29) for $h = 1, 2, 3, 4$ will be unbiased provided that $t + h - 4 \geq \tau$.

If the structural break occurs during the sample period, but is unmodeled, then the broad results carry over. Clearly, the structural break will affect the parameter estimates, but the effect on these estimates will be relatively slight if the break occurs toward the end of the sample period. Therefore, an inappropriate seasonal pattern will still be used when forecasting from the specification (18.19).

Clements and Hendry base their analysis directly on an annual-difference specification comparable to (18.29). There are, however, further practical complications which arise when this differenced specification is used for forecasting. The annual differencing results in the noninvertible seasonal moving average $v_t - v_{t-4}$ and it is appropriate to consider the impact of attempting to account for the autocorrelation this implies. As we have pointed out, in practice an autoregressive model is likely to be used and hence the approximating empirical model might be represented by

$$\hat{\phi}(L)\Delta_4 y_t = \hat{\gamma} + \hat{\varepsilon}_t \qquad (18.30)$$

which can be viewed as an estimated version of (18.4). In this case, the residuals $\hat{\varepsilon}_t$ approximate an *iid* disturbance sufficiently well for the researcher to conclude that the specification is an adequate description of the observed data. Because $\hat{\phi}(L)$ is specified to capture as much as possible of a noninvertible seasonal moving average, it would be anticipated that this polynomial will include large and positive annual lag coefficients. Ultimately, however, the model is misspecified and the noninvertible moving average cannot be fully captured by an autoregressive approximation (Box and Jenkins, 1970).

In any case, with an autoregressive approximation, the effects of the structural change on forecasts persist beyond $t = \tau + 3$ due to the presence of lagged dependent variables in (18.30). We have argued that the annual lag autoregressive coefficients may be especially important and, for simplicity, assume that $\hat{\phi}(L)$ contains only such lags and hence $\hat{\phi}(L) = 1 - \hat{\phi}_4 L^4 - \hat{\phi}_8 L^8 - \ldots - \hat{\phi}_p L^p$. Then, for example, the one-step-ahead annual change forecast made at $t = \tau + 3$ is

$$\Delta_4 \hat{y}_{\tau+4 \mid \tau+3} = \hat{\phi}_4 \Delta_4 y_\tau + \hat{\phi}_8 \Delta_4 y_{\tau-4} + \ldots + \hat{\phi}_p \Delta_4 y_{\tau+4-p} + \hat{\gamma}, \qquad (18.31)$$

which carries over effects of the structural change through $\hat{\phi}_4 \Delta_4 y_\tau$. Forecasts of the annual change more than one step ahead and of the levels will also be affected due to the recursive way in which such forecasts are calculated. Indeed, forecasts based on subsequent data will not be fully self-correcting for the structural break until all lagged $\Delta_4 y$ used in constructing the forecasts relate to periods subsequent to the structural break.

From their analysis, Clements and Hendry (1997) conclude that imposing seasonal unit roots and using a model based on $\Delta_4 y_t$ may improve accuracy even if the imposition is not warranted according to the outcomes of seasonal unit-root tests. We agree this may be so, with an important advantage of using forecasts $\hat{y}_{t+h \mid t} = \Delta_4 \hat{y}_{\tau+h \mid t} + y_{t+h-4}$ for $t + h - 4 \geq \tau$ being that y_{t+h-4} incorporates an "intercept correction" for the structural change. However, it is to be anticipated that it will be difficult to specify an adequate autoregressive model for $\Delta_4 y_t$ due to the effect of the noninvertible moving average. Whether the advantages outweigh the disadvantages depends partly on the frequency with which structural change occurs. Thus, it seems that the issue is largely an empirical one. Before turning to the empirical studies of seasonal unit-root models in forecasting, however, we consider seasonal unit-root tests in the next section.

18.3. TESTING SEASONAL INTEGRATION

The most widely applied test for seasonal integration is that of Hylleberg, Engle, Granger, and Yoo (1990), which (for obvious reasons) is often referred to as the HEGY test. Our discussion therefore focuses on this test.

18.3.1. HEGY and other tests

The HEGY test exploits the factorization of (18.2) to provide a test which considers separately the three unit roots 1, –1, and ±i. The form in which the HEGY test is typically applied is through the regression

$$\Delta_4 y_t = \pi_1 y_{t-1}^{(1)} + \pi_2 y_{t-1}^{(2)} + \pi_3 y_{t-2}^{(3)} + \pi_4 y_{t-1}^{(3)} + \sum_{i=1}^{p} \phi_i \Delta_4 y_{t-i} + \sum_{i=1}^{4} \alpha_i \delta_{it} + \beta t + \varepsilon_t, \qquad (18.32)$$

where

$$y_t^{(1)} = (1 + L + L^2 + L^3) y_t,$$

$$y_t^{(2)} = -(1 - L)(1 + L^2) y_t,$$

$$y_t^{(3)} = -(1 - L^2) y_t, \qquad (18.33)$$

the variables δ_{it} ($i = 1, 2, 3, 4$) are, as before, seasonal dummy variables, and it is assumed that $\varepsilon_t \sim iid(0, \sigma^2)$. The null hypothesis of the HEGY test is $y_t \sim SI(1)$ and under this null hypothesis $\pi_1 = \pi_2 = \pi_3 = \pi_4 = 0$. Although testing is usually confined to the coefficients π_i, under the null hypothesis the deterministic terms of (18.32) satisfy $\alpha_1 = \alpha_2 = \alpha_3 = \alpha_4 = \gamma$ and $\beta = 0$, so that the model becomes the $SI(1)$ process of (18.4).

Careful examination of the transformations defined in (18.33) indicates that each of these three variables is obtained by imposing two of the three factors of $\Delta_4 = (1 - L)(1 + L)(1 + L^2)$ on y_t. More specifically, the regressor $y_{t-1}^{(1)}$ is constructed by imposing the factors $(1 + L)$ and $(1 + L^2)$ on y_{t-1}, so that a test of the null hypothesis $\pi_1 = 0$ against the stationary alternative $\pi_1 < 0$ is a test of the remaining factor and hence is a conventional unit-root test. Indeed, one of the strong attractions of the HEGY approach is that (under the seasonal-integration null hypothesis) the t-ratio on the estimated coefficient $\hat{\pi}_1$ has the usual Dickey–Fuller unit-root distribution. This arises because the regressors $y_{t-1}^{(1)}$, $y_{t-1}^{(2)}$, $y_{t-2}^{(3)}$ and $y_{t-1}^{(3)}$ have the property of being asymptotically mutually orthogonal. Without going into technical details, this implies that when considering the distribution of the estimated coefficient for any one of these variables, the inclusion or exclusion of the others is (asymptotically) irrelevant.

In a similar way, $y_{t-1}^{(2)}$ is constructed by imposing the factors $(1 - L)$ and $(1 + L^2)$, and a test of $\pi_2 = 0$ is a test of the seasonal unit root of –1 implied by the factor $(1 + L)$. The stationary alternative here implies $\pi_2 < 0$. This hypothesis test can also be carried out using the Dickey–Fuller distribution.[5] Finally, $y_t^{(3)}$ imposes the factors of $(1 - L)$ and $(1 + L)$, so that this variable is used to test the factor $(1 + L^2)$ of Δ_4. Here, however, two coefficients are tested, with $\pi_3 = 0$ testing the unit coefficient on L^2 in this factor and $\pi_4 = 0$ testing the implied restriction that the coefficient on L is zero. Because both restrictions arise from the pair of roots ±i, it is common practice to test the joint null hypothesis $\pi_3 = \pi_4 = 0$ using an F-statistic as conventionally computed. Under the null hypothesis, however, the asymptotic distribution of the statistic does not follow the F-distribution; HEGY provide appropriate tables of critical values for this unit-root case.

Other tests for seasonal unit roots have been proposed in the literature. That of Osborn, Chui, Smith, and Birchenhall (1988), often known as OCSB, is sometimes used because it is explicitly designed to test (under the null hypothesis) the possibility that the double-difference model of (18.6) is appropriate against $SI(1)$ or $I(1)$ specifications under the alternative. As noted above in the discussion of the model (18.6), the implication of the OCSB null hypothesis is that the series contains two conventional unit roots in addition to the full set of seasonal unit roots. It might also be noted that another way of testing the same null hypothesis would to apply the HEGY test to the data after taking first differences.

18.3.2. Some extensions

Many subsequent papers by various authors have provided empirical applications and/or theoretical extensions to the HEGY analysis and three specific extensions are mentioned here. First, Beaulieu and Miron (1993) and Franses (1991) both generalize the approach to test for seasonal unit roots in monthly data. Their methods are, however, slightly different. That of Beaulieu and Miron is generally preferred because it yields asymptotic orthogonality for the transformed variables relating to the unit roots, as in the HEGY test. In this monthly context, the coefficients tested are $\pi_1, \ldots, \pi_{12}$, with π_1 relating to the nonseasonal root of 1 and $\pi_2, \ldots, \pi_{12}$ to the seasonal unit roots.

Second, in their quarterly context HEGY apply separate tests to the unit roots of 1, −1, and $\pm i$. The reason they adopt this approach is not only so that they can consider the roots separately, but also so that they can explicitly consider the alternative hypothesis of stationarity. Rejection using an F-type test of the null hypothesis $\pi_1 = \pi_2 = \pi_3 = \pi_4 = 0$ against the alternative that at least one of these coefficients is nonzero does not necessarily imply rejection in favor of stationarity. This is, first, because the true process may contain some but not all the unit roots tested; for example, the conventional unit-root restriction may be valid ($\pi_1 = 0$) but the seasonal unit roots may not be present. Second, an F-type test does not allow the one-sided alternatives for π_1, π_2, and π_3 which stationarity implies. Nevertheless, the HEGY approach needs to be applied with care, because if separate tests are undertaken for each of the unit roots at some given level of significance, the level of significance implied for the overall null hypothesis of seasonal integration is substantially more than the nominal level applied for each separate test. The importance of this in the monthly case is emphasized by Dickey (1993).

Joint testing allows the overall level of significance to be controlled, and Ghysels, Lee, and Noh (1994) provide critical values for tests[6] of $\pi_1 = \pi_2 = \pi_3 = \pi_4 = 0$ and also of $\pi_2 = \pi_3 = \pi_4 = 0$. The latter considers the seasonal unit roots as a group. Using a joint test of the seasonal unit roots together with the usual Dickey–Fuller test applied to π_1 allows four cases to be distinguished in this framework:

1   the series is seasonally integrated (do not reject either $\pi_1 = 0$ or $\pi_2 = \pi_3 = \pi_4 = 0$);
2   the series is integrated but not seasonally integrated (do not reject $\pi_1 = 0$, but reject $\pi_2 = \pi_3 = \pi_4 = 0$);
3   the series contains all seasonal unit roots but not the unit root of 1 (reject $\pi_1 = 0$, but not $\pi_2 = \pi_3 = \pi_4 = 0$);
4   the series is neither integrated nor does it contain the full set of seasonal unit roots (reject both $\pi_1 = 0$ and $\pi_2 = \pi_3 = \pi_4 = 0$).

This approach can, therefore, help to distinguish between true seasonal integration and deterministic seasonality.

Above, we discussed the role of structural breaks in forecasting. The third generalization of the HEGY test of interest to us is to allow for possible structural breaks in the deterministic seasonality model considered under the alternative hypothesis. Thus, this generalization tries to distinguish true seasonal unit roots from deterministic seasonality which has shifted over time. Here the approach of Franses and Vogelsang (1998), which permits the date of the break to be unknown, is attractive. Nevertheless, it should be borne in mind that such tests cannot help when the structural break occurs during the forecast period.

18.3.3.   Further practical issues

It will be noted that our HEGY-test regression specified in (18.32) includes seasonal dummy variable terms and a trend. There are two related reasons why these should be included. First, they allow the test regression to encompass the specifications of interest under the alternative hypothesis (Dickey, Bell, and Miller, 1986). Thus, by including these terms, we can test against either of the deterministic-seasonality specifications considered in section 18.2. Second, they ensure that the critical values used under the null hypothesis are invariant to the drift and the unobserved starting values for y (Smith and Taylor, 1998). If the HEGY test is to be applied to data after first differencing, this logic leads to the inclusion of seasonal dummy variables but no trend.

When the number of unit roots may be zero, one, or two, the literature stresses that the validity of sequentially testing the number of unit roots rests on beginning with the highest order of integration and testing down to lower orders (see Dickey and Pantula, 1987). Therefore, if the first plus seasonal-difference specification represents the highest order of integration tenable for seasonal data, then testing should begin with this as the initial null-hypothesis model. In practice, models with higher orders of integration than this are not used.

Another important practical issue is the order of augmentation to be employed, or in other words how the order p in (18.32) should be specified. Almost invariably, a data-based procedure is adopted, with the two alternatives being to specify this using a sequential "testing down" procedure from an initial high order or to use an information criterion (such as the Akaike or Schwarz Information Criterion).

Before turning to empirical applications of the HEGY approach in a forecasting context, one other important point should be noted. Monte Carlo studies by Ghysels, Lee, and Noh (1994) for quarterly data and by Rodrigues and Osborn

(1999) for monthly data indicate that the test may perform poorly in the presence of moving-average autocorrelation. For example, in the quarterly seasonally-integrated process

$$\Delta_4 y_t = \varepsilon_t - \theta_4 \varepsilon_{t-4}$$

with θ_4 less than, but "close" to, 1 approximate cancellation occurs between $\Delta_4 = 1 - L^4$ and the moving-average polynomial $1 - \theta_4 L^4$. As a result, for typical sample sizes used in applied work, the true seasonal integration null hypothesis can be rejected with a probability approaching 1. It might be argued that augmentation of the test regression with lagged $\Delta_4 y$ should help alleviate this problem. While augmentation does help, it is also the case that data-based procedures frequently fail to signal the need for any augmentation, so that in practical applications the problem remains; aspects of this are discussed by Taylor (1997) and by Rodrigues and Osborn (1999). Psaradakis (1997) proposes a pre-whitened version of the HEGY test designed to improve its performance in the presence of moving-average disturbances. This version of the HEGY test does not, however, appear to have been used to date in the context of specifying the order of integration for a forecasting model.

As documented by Schwert (1989) and many subsequent authors, the augmented Dickey–Fuller test performs poorly in the presence of a large positive first-order moving-average component; this is, of course, entirely analogous to the seasonal case just discussed. These considerations suggest that double-difference models, particularly those of the "airline model" type (see section 18.2.1), might be seriously considered for forecasting even if the differencing is rejected by unit-root tests as conventionally performed with autoregressive augmentation. Perhaps unfortunately, however, forecasts are generally computed using autoregressive dynamics and not moving-average ones.

18.4. EMPIRICAL STUDIES OF FORECAST ACCURACY

Having specified the order of integration to be used in the forecasting model, other aspects of model specification need to be addressed. It was noted in the preceding section that the HEGY seasonal unit-root test regression usually includes a trend and seasonal dummy variables for statistical reasons. When forecasts are to be computed, these arguments do not apply and the deterministic components (trend, seasonal dummy variables, constant) included are typically those specified for the respective models in section 18.2. Somewhat curiously, there appears to be no literature on the effect the inclusion of other deterministic variables may have on forecast accuracy in practice.

The autoregressive lag used in the forecasting model is typically specified separately from the lag order adopted for unit-root testing. The same procedure may, however, be used. The methods popular in practice are again those based on an information criterion or on a hypothesis testing approach. Almost invariably, parameter estimation is by the usual ordinary least squares technique.

Before turning to empirical studies of forecast accuracy, brief consideration should be made of how forecast accuracy is measured in this context. This is the purpose of the first subsection below, with empirical studies considered in the second.

18.4.1.   Measuring forecast accuracy

In practice, the empirical forecast mean-square error, or its square root, is generally used to measure forecast accuracy for a series of forecasts at a specific horizon h. For $h = 1$, and with m forecasts of y_t computed for periods $t + 1, t + 2, \ldots, t + m$, the forecast mean square error is defined as

$$\frac{1}{m} \sum_{i=1}^{m} (y_{t+i} - \hat{y}_{t+i|t+i-1})^2. \tag{18.34}$$

Corresponding definitions apply for different horizons and other transformations of y.

However, as our discussion in section 2 implies, for different purposes and in the context of a quarterly seasonal series, interest may centre on forecasts of y_t, on the annual change $\Delta_4 y_t$ or on the quarter-to-quarter change $\Delta_1 y_t$. Further, if the horizon h is relevant, it is also reasonable to assume that horizons $1, 2, \ldots, h - 1$ are also of interest. One problem with using forecast mean square error is that different models may yield the most accurate forecasts for different transformations of y or for different horizons. Clements and Hendry (1993) argue that, if a single forecasting model is to be selected, then a single measure of forecast accuracy should be used. They propose the use of the generalised forecast error second moment (GFESM). In the same way that the forecast mean square error (34) can be viewed as analogous to the sample variance of the forecast errors at horizon 1, the GFESM is analogous to the determinant of the covariance matrix of the forecast errors for y for all horizons from 1 to h. For $h = 1$, this is identical to the mean square forecast error. However, computed for $h > 1$, the measure effectively takes all horizons into account and all linear transformations of y. Thus, it is an appropriate general measure when the practitioner wishes to select a single forecasting model to be used for different purposes.

As acknowledged by Clements and Hendry (1993, 1997), if a particular transformation and horizon is of interest, then the usual mean square error should be preferred over the GFESM.

18.4.2.   Empirical studies

Although there are a large number of empirical studies which test for seasonal unit roots, few of these link the issue to that of post-sample forecast accuracy. Therefore, we have only a small number of studies to discuss explicitly here.

A relatively early study linking these is Franses (1991), who examines three monthly seasonal time series. These series are the natural logarithms of the airline passenger data of Box and Jenkins (1970), together with the index of industrial production and the number of new car registrations, both for the Netherlands. He obtains clear-cut results, in the sense that he finds that basing the specification of the forecasting model for y on the outcome of a HEGY-type seasonal unit-root test leads to improved accuracy. However, only two competing specifications are considered in this forecast comparison, with these adopting seasonal plus first-differences and first-differences with deterministic-seasonal effects. Thus, the trend-stationary plus deterministic-seasonality or, more importantly, the annual-difference model, are not included. Consequently, the generality of his conclusions is open to question.

A more comprehensive forecast comparison is undertaken by Osborn, Heravi, and Birchenhall (1999), or OHB. They consider all four specifications discussed in section 18.2, applying each to eight-monthly industry-level industrial production series for each of Germany, France, and the U.K. (usually after taking logarithms). Their prior seasonal unit-root tests point, in the vast majority of cases, to the use of models with first differences plus deterministic seasonality; that is, to a monthly version of (18.16). In other words, the conclusion on the nature of seasonality is that it is of the deterministic form, after the removal of the conventional unit root by differencing. It might be noted that they use the approach, outlined in section 18.3.2, that treats the seasonal unit roots as a group with a separate test of the unit root of 1. Thus, they do not attempt to determine whether a series might contain some but not the complete set of seasonal unit roots. One important qualification to their unit-root testing is that they have a relatively short sample period available (less than 15 years).

OHB consider separately forecast horizons up to one year and examine forecasts of the month-on-month change and the level of the series, with forecast accuracy measured by the root mean square forecast error. Nothwithstanding the rejection of seasonal unit roots, the model based on the annual difference $\Delta_{12}y_t$ produces the most accurate forecasts overall, especially when forecasting the level of the series. In general, the second-best specification is the first-differences plus dummies specification, namely the model supported by the seasonal unit-root test results. Over the two-year post-sample period considered, they find that substantial improvements in the accuracy of the forecasts from this model can be obtained by reestimation as each new observation becomes available. Despite this improvement, however, it generally remains inferior to the annual-difference model. The other two specifications generally yield much less accurate forecasts for these series.

Although they do not quote the overall GFESM measure of forecast accuracy to a one-year horizon, it is reasonable to conclude from the results of OHB that the annual-difference model would emerge best on this criterion. Nevertheless, when forecasting month-to-month changes, the first-difference plus seasonal-dummies model (with reestimation) is generally the best forecasting model for series which have very strong and unchanging seasonal patterns in the sense that seasonal dummy variables "explain" 90 percent or more of the monthly variation.

The arguments of Clements and Hendry (1997) in favor of using an annual-difference specification for forecasting, even when this is not supported by seasonal unit test results, has been rehearsed in section 18.2 above. They empirically test their hypothesis by examining two quarterly seasonal series, namely those for Norwegian income and U.K. consumers' expenditure. The HEGY test results for Norwegian income point to the presence of a unit root of 1, and possibly the seasonal unit root -1, but do not support the seasonal integration null hypothesis overall. Although conclusions on the presence or otherwise of specific unit roots differ over sub-periods, seasonal integration is generally supported for U.K. consumers' expenditure. It is, however, worth remarking that, in common with many other studies, these authors do not quote an overall test statistic for the seasonal integration null hypothesis. Despite the different outcomes of the unit-root tests, for both series forecast accuracy is improved by imposing the full set of unit roots through the use of annual differences, compared with specifications where no unit roots or a subset of the unit roots of (18.2) are imposed. In contrast to the findings of OHB, relatively small gains are obtained by sequentially updating estimated coefficients for the deterministic seasonality model of (18.16). At least part of the explanation for this last finding might be that Clements and Hendry have more years of data with which to estimate the coefficients of seasonal dummy variables prior to commencing forecasting.

Paap, Franses, and Hoek (1997) focus on forecasting in conjunction with possible structural breaks during the sample period. Once again the series used relate to quarterly consumption, in this case real total consumption in Sweden, the U.K., and the U.S. Here the HEGY test applied as in (18.32) points to the use of annual differences, $\Delta_4 y_t$, in each case. The forecast comparison is with a model in first differences allowing for structural breaks in the seasonal means, with the break point $t = \tau$ estimated from the data. This latter model generally produces more accurate forecasts, as measured by GFESM, for the U.S. and the U.K. consumption series. This leads the authors to advocate that prior seasonal unit-root testing should allow the possibility of structural breaks in the seasonal intercepts during the sample period. As they acknowledge, and as we note above, such testing cannot assist if the structural break occurs during the post-sample forecast period. Hence, they conclude that modeling using annual differences may yield more accurate forecasts in practice if structural breaks are not rare events.

Although we shall not go into details, readers should note that the analysis of univariate seasonal unit roots has been extended to consider seasonal cointegration. Reimers (1997) provides an empirical forecast comparison using the seasonal cointegration approach and the more usual cointegration (nonseasonal) methodology applied with the inclusion of seasonal intercepts. The data are quarterly Norwegian real income and real consumption. Using root mean square forecast error for the separate series at different horizons, the seasonal cointegration model generally yields less accurate forecasts at horizons up to a year, but is more accurate at longer horizons. Another seasonal cointegration study is that of Kunst and Franses (1998). The particular interest in this study is the role of intercepts for forecast accuracy in these models, but the authors are unable to draw any general conclusions.

18.5. CONCLUDING REMARKS

This chapter has considered issues related to seasonal modeling and forecasting. Seasonal unit roots and deterministic models of seasonality have been explained, including details of how these models are used to generate forecast values. The key feature of forecast generation is that any forecasts required (for the level, annual difference or period-to-period change) can be built up from forecasts of the variable modeled. Therefore, the question of the type of differencing to be employed for modeling, with the related issue of seasonal unit roots versus deterministic models of seasonality, is a fundamental issue for forecasting. Following this, the popular HEGY test for seasonal unit roots has been explained, including some practical issues which arise in its implementation. Finally, the results of empirical studies of forecast accuracy have been reviewed.

Unfortunately, there have been too few empirical studies to draw very strong conclusions about the extent to which prior seasonal unit-root testing assists forecast accuracy. The treatment of seasonality in the context of possible cointegration among series is even less clear. Nevertheless, the recent literature concerned with univariate models appears to have a large measure of agreement, namely that the practitioner should lean toward the use of annual differencing when building a model for forecasting seasonal economic time series up to one or two years ahead, even when the seasonal integration null hypothesis is not supported by the results of seasonal unit-root tests. However, given the known poor performance of such seasonal unit-root tests in the presence of seasonal integration with moving-average disturbances (see section 18.3.3), it is unclear whether the forecasting result should be attributed to the robustness of the seasonal difference specification to structural breaks (as argued by Clements and Hendry, 1997), to the over-rejection of the seasonal integration null hypothesis when this hypothesis is true, or to some other cause.

There are, however, some important qualifications to be stated. First, in forecasting period-to-period movements, including one-step-ahead forecasting, there is some evidence in the results of Osborn et al. (1999) that deterministic-seasonality models may perform better than annual-difference ones, and this is especially true for series which exhibit very strong deterministic seasonality. This is, perhaps, not surprising. It is in period-to-period (that is, month-to-month or quarter-to-quarter, as appropriate) changes that seasonal movements are most marked and hence it is here that any deterministic effects may be expected to show most strongly. Second, modeling structural change in the deterministic-seasonality model may improve its forecast performance. Once again, this finding is unsurprising, but it points against the automatic use of a standard HEGY seasonal unit-root test.

Third, and perhaps most importantly, the range of series examined in the empirical studies has been relatively narrow, with real consumption, income, and production series being the focus of interest to date. These series have been selected by the authors of the studies partly because they exhibit strong seasonal patterns. It remains to be verified whether the general recommendation for the use of annual differences will carry over to less strongly seasonal series.

In summary, the current recommendation for the choice of a single model for forecasting seasonal economic time series up to a year ahead is that the annual difference specification should be the default choice. Nevertheless, the nature of seasonality is worth careful attention, using seasonal unit-root tests (possibly allowing for structural breaks) as part of the toolkit for such an examination.

Acknowledgments

I am grateful to Mike Clements and David Hendry for their constructive comments and careful proof-reading of the first version of this chapter.

Notes

1 The complex number $a + bi$ has modulus, or absolute value, $\sqrt{a^2 + b^2}$.
2 Technically, to define an integrated process we require that the stochastic part of the differenced process is invertible as well as stationary. These requirements are satisfied in this case as $\Delta_4 y_t = \varepsilon_t$ is *iid*.
3 In all these cases, the appropriate deterministic terms of the models in sections 18.2.1 and 18.2.2 are also understood to be included in the differenced specification.
4 In fact, Clements and Hendry consider a more general specification of the deterministic component to allow trending seasonals. This specification is not, however, in the class of models we consider and hence we restrict our attention to the seasonal intercept case.
5 Dickey and Fuller (1979) note that the distribution of the test statistic for a unit root of -1 has a mirror image property compared with that for the root of 1. By construction of $y_{t-1}^{(2)}$ in the HEGY test regression, the mirror image is taken into account by the minus sign and therefore the t-ratio on $\hat{\pi}_2$ has the usual Dickey–Fuller distribution.
6 Analogous critical values for the monthly case are given by Taylor (1998).

References

Beaulieu, J.J. and J.A. Miron (1993). Seasonal unit roots in aggregate U.S. data. *Journal of Econometrics*, 55, 305–28.

Box, G.E.P., S.C. Hillmer, and G.C. Tiao (1978). Analysis and modeling of seasonal time series. (1978) *Seasonal Analysis of Economic Time Series*, ed. Zellner, A. Washington, D.C.: Bureau of the Census, pp. 309–34.

Box, G.E.P. and G.M. Jenkins (1970). *Time Series Analysis, Forecasting and Control*. San Francisco: Holden-Day.

Burridge, P. and K.F. Wallis (1984). Unobserved-components models for seasonal adjustment filters. *Journal of Business and Economic Statistics*, 2, 350–9.

Clements, M.P. and D.F. Hendry (1993). On the limitations of comparing mean squared forecast errors. *Journal of Forecasting*, 14, 617–37 (with discussion).

Clements, M.P. and D.F. Hendry (1997). An empirical study of seasonal unit roots in forecasting. *International Journal of Forecasting*, 13, 341–55.

Dickey, D.A. (1993). Discussion: seasonal unit roots in aggregate U.S. data. *Journal of Econometrics*, 55, 329–31.

Dickey, D.A., W.R. Bell, and R.B. Miller (1986). Unit roots in time series models: tests and implications. *The American Statistician*, 40, 12–26.

Dickey, D.A. and W.A. Fuller (1979). Distribution of the estimators for autoregressive time series with a unit root. *Journal of the American Statistical Association*, 74, 427–31.

Dickey, D.A. and S.G. Pantula (1987). Determining the order of differencing in auto-regressive processes. *Journal of Business and Economic Statistics*, 5, 455–61.

Franses, P.H. (1991). Seasonality, non-stationarity and the forecasting of monthly time series. *International Journal of Forecasting*, 7, 199–208.

Franses, P.H. (1996). *Periodicity and Stochastic Trends in Economic Time Series*. Oxford: Oxford University Press.

Franses, P.H. and T.J. Vogelsang (1998). On seasonal cycles, unit roots, and mean shifts. *Review of Economics and Statistics*, 80, 231–40.

Ghysels, E., H.S. Lee, and J. Noh (1994). Testing for unit roots in seasonal time series: some theoretical extensions and a Monte Carlo investigation. *Journal of Econometrics*, 62, 415–42.

Ghysels, E. and D.R. Osborn (2001). *The Econometric Analysis of Seasonal Time Series*. Cambridge: Cambridge University Press.

Hylleberg, S., R.F. Engle, C.W.J. Granger, and B.S. Yoo (1990). Seasonal integration and cointegration. *Journal of Econometrics*, 44, 215–38.

Kunst, R.M. and P.H. Franses (1998). The impact of seasonal constants on forecasting seasonally cointegrated time series. *Journal of Forecasting*, 17, 109–24.

Miron, J.A. (1996). *The Economics of Seasonal Cycles*. Cambridge, MA: MIT Press.

Nelson, C.R. and C. Plosser (1982). Trends and random walks in macroeconomic time series: some evidence and implications. *Journal of Monetary Economics*, 10, 139–62.

Osborn, D.R. (1990). A survey of seasonality in U.K. macroeconomic variables. *International Journal of Forecasting*, 6, 327–36.

Osborn, D.R., A.P.L. Chui, J.P. Smith, and C.R. Birchenhall (1988). Seasonality and the order of integration for consumption. *Oxford Bulletin of Economics and Statistics*, 50, 361–77.

Osborn, D.R., S. Heravi, and C.R. Birchenhall (1999). Seasonal unit roots and forecasts of two-digit European industrial production. *International Journal of Forecasting*, 15, 27–47.

Paap, R., P.H. Franses, and H. Hoek, Mean Shifts (1997). Unit roots and forecasting seasonal time series. *International Journal of Forecasting*, 13, 357–68.

Psaradakis, Z. (1997). Testing for unit roots in time series with nearly deterministic seasonal variation. *Econometric Reviews*, 16, 421–39.

Reimers, H.-E. (1997). Forecasting of seasonal cointegrated processes. *International Journal of Forecasting*, 13, 369–80.

Rodrigues, P.M.M. and D.R. Osborn (1999). Performance of seasonal unit root tests for monthly data. *Journal of Applied Statistics*, 26, 985–1004.

Schwert, G.W. (1989). Tests for unit roots: a Monte Carlo investigation. *Journal of Business and Economic Statistics*, 7, 147–59.

Smith, R.J. and A.M.R. Taylor (1998). Additional critical values and asymptotic representations for seasonal unit root tests. *Journal of Econometrics*, 85, 269–88.

Taylor, A.M.R. (1997). On the practical problems of computing seasonal unit root tests. *International Journal of Forecasting*, 13, 307–18.

Taylor, A.M.R. (1998). Testing for unit roots in monthly data. *Journal of Time Series Analysis*, 19, 349–68.

Whittle, P. (1963). *Prediction and Regulation by Linear Least-Squares Methods*. London: English Universities Press.

CHAPTER NINETEEN

Forecasting with Periodic Autoregressive Time-Series Models

Philip Hans Franses and Richard Paap

19.1. INTRODUCTION

There are various approaches to modeling and forecasting (seasonally unadjusted) seasonal time series. Franses (1996c) provides a recent survey. One approach builds on the work of Box and Jenkins (1970) and relies on moving-average models for double-differenced time series (so-called seasonal ARIMA [SARIMA] models). Another approach assumes that seasonal time series can be decomposed into trend, cycle, seasonal, and irregular components (see Harvey, 1989). Reduced forms of the resultant models have many similarities with the afore-mentioned SARIMA models. A third approach questions the use of the double-differencing filter in SARIMA models and mainly addresses the issue of how many unit roots should be imposed in autoregressive models: see Hylleberg, Engle, Granger, and Yoo (1990, HEGY), and chapter 18 of this volume by Denise Osborn. Finally, a fourth approach assumes that seasonal variation is best described by allowing the parameters in an autoregression to vary with the seasons; that is, the so-called periodic autoregression [PAR]. Of course, one may want to consider periodic ARMA models, but this is rarely done in practice. Periodic autoregressions have been frequently used in environmental and hydrological studies – see Franses (1996b) for a summary of early references – but were introduced into the economic literature by Osborn (1988) and Osborn and Smith (1989). The latter study focused on out-of-sample forecasting of quarterly U.K.

consumption series. Since that study, the literature on periodic models has developed substantially, and in this chapter we will highlight some of these issues in more detail. Specifically, we will address unit roots and deterministic terms and how they should be incorporated in a PAR model. There have been several studies on evaluating forecasts from PAR models – see Novales and Flores de Fruto (1997), Wells (1997), Herwartz (1997), Herwartz (1999), and Franses and Paap (1996) – and they yield mixed results. The novelty of this chapter is that we take explicit account of a proper inclusion of deterministic terms in our PAR models and that we use encompassing tests to formally evaluate forecast performance. Following the seminal study by Osborn and Smith (1989), we will also consider various U.K. consumption series.

In section 19.2, we first discuss several preliminaries on PAR models, like representation, estimation, unit roots, and deterministic terms. In section 19.3, we discuss out-of-sample forecasting. In section 19.4, we consider PAR models for forecasting several quarterly U.K. consumption series. In section 19.5, we conclude this chapter with some remarks.

19.2. PRELIMINARIES

In this section, we give a brief overview of periodic autoregressions. The discussion draws heavily on material covered in detail in Franses (1996a), Franses (1996b), Boswijk and Franses (1996), Boswijk, Franses, and Haldrup (1997), Franses and Paap (1994), Franses and Paap (1996), and Paap and Franses (1999). In section 19.2.1, we consider representation and estimation. Section 19.2.2 deals with unit roots and periodic integration. To save notation, we consider models without intercepts and trends in these two sections. As these are very relevant in practice, we dedicate section 19.2.3 to that issue.

19.2.1. Representation and parameter estimation

Consider a univariate time series y_t which is observed quarterly for N years; that is, $t = 1, 2, \ldots, n = 4N$. A periodic autoregressive model of order p [PAR(p)] for y_t can be written as

$$y_t = \phi_{1,s} y_{t-1} + \ldots + \phi_{p,s} y_{t-p} + \varepsilon_t, \tag{19.1}$$

or $\tilde{\phi}_{p,s}(L) y_t = \varepsilon_t$, where L is the usual lag operator, and where $\phi_{1,s}$ through $\phi_{p,s}$ are autoregressive parameters, which may take different values across the seasons $s = 1, 2, 3, 4$. The disturbance ε_t is assumed to be a standard white-noise process with constant variance σ^2. Of course, this assumption may be relaxed by allowing for different variances σ_s^2 in each season.

The periodic process described by model (19.1) is nonstationary, as the variance and autocovariances are time-varying within the year. For some purposes, a more convenient representation of a PAR(p) process is given by rewriting it in a time-invariant form. As the PAR(p) model considers different AR(p) models for different seasons, it seems natural to rewrite it as a model for annual observations: see also Gladyshev (1961), Tiao and Grupe (1980), Osborn (1991), and Lütkepohl (1993). In general, the PAR(p) process in (19.1) can be rewritten as an AR(P) model for the four-dimensional vector process $\mathbf{Y}_T = (Y_{1,T}, Y_{2,T}, Y_{3,T}, Y_{4,T})'$, $T = 1, 2, \ldots, N$, where $Y_{s,T}$ is the observation in season s in year T, $s = 1, 2, 3, 4$, and where $P = 1 + [(p - 1)/4]$, where [·] denotes the integer function. The corresponding vector autoregressive [VAR] model is given by

$$\mathbf{\Phi}_0 \mathbf{Y}_T = \mathbf{\Phi}_1 \mathbf{Y}_{T-1} + \ldots + \mathbf{\Phi}_P \mathbf{Y}_{T-P} + \varepsilon_T, \tag{19.2}$$

where $\varepsilon_T = (\varepsilon_{1,T}, \varepsilon_{2,T}, \varepsilon_{3,T}, \varepsilon_{4,T})'$, and $\varepsilon_{s,T}$ is the value of the error process ε in season s in year T. The $\mathbf{\Phi}_0$, $\mathbf{\Phi}_1$ to $\mathbf{\Phi}_P$ are (4×4) parameter matrices with elements

$$\mathbf{\Phi}_0(i, j) = 1 \qquad i = j,$$
$$= 0 \qquad j > i,$$
$$= -\phi_{i-j,i} \qquad j < i,$$
$$\mathbf{\Phi}_k(i, j) = \phi_{i+4k-j,i}, \tag{19.3}$$

for $i = 1, 2, 3, 4$, $j = 1, 2, 3, 4$ and $k = 1, 2, \ldots, P$. The lower triangularity of $\mathbf{\Phi}_0$ shows that (19.2) is in fact a recursive set of equations.

As an example, consider the PAR(2) model

$$y_t = \phi_{1,s} y_{t-1} + \phi_{2,s} y_{t-2} + \varepsilon_t, \tag{19.4}$$

which can be written as

$$\mathbf{\Phi}_0 \mathbf{Y}_T = \mathbf{\Phi}_1 \mathbf{Y}_{T-1} + \varepsilon_T, \tag{19.5}$$

with

$$\mathbf{\Phi}_0 = \begin{pmatrix} 1 & 0 & 0 & 0 \\ -\phi_{1,2} & 1 & 0 & 0 \\ -\phi_{2,3} & -\phi_{1,3} & 1 & 0 \\ 0 & -\phi_{2,4} & -\phi_{1,4} & 1 \end{pmatrix} \quad \text{and} \quad \mathbf{\Phi}_1 = \begin{pmatrix} 0 & 0 & \phi_{2,1} & \phi_{1,1} \\ 0 & 0 & 0 & \phi_{2,2} \\ 0 & 0 & 0 & 0 \\ 0 & 0 & 0 & 0 \end{pmatrix}. \tag{19.6}$$

In order to avoid confusion with multivariate time-series models, one often refers to models like (19.5) as the vector of quarters [VQ] representation. Notice from (19.5) and (19.6) that one can also write a nonperiodic AR model in a VQ representation.

There are two useful versions of (19.2) for the analysis of unit roots and for forecasting. The first is given by simply pre-multiplying (19.2) by $\mathbf{\Phi}_0^{-1}$; that is,

$$\mathbf{Y}_T = \mathbf{\Phi}_0^{-1} \mathbf{\Phi}_1 \mathbf{Y}_{T-1} + \ldots + \mathbf{\Phi}_0^{-1} \mathbf{\Phi}_P \mathbf{Y}_{T-P} + \mathbf{\Phi}_0^{-1} \varepsilon_T, \tag{19.7}$$

which amounts to a genuine VAR(P) for $\mathbf{Y}_T$. When $\varepsilon_T \sim N(0, \sigma^2 I_4)$, it follows that $\Phi_0^{-1}\varepsilon_T \sim N(0, \sigma^2 \Phi_0^{-1}(\Phi_0^{-1})')$. It is easy to see that Φ_0^{-1} for any PAR process is also a lower triangular matrix. For example, for the PAR(2) model in (19.5) it can be found that

$$
\Phi_0^{-1} = \begin{pmatrix}
1 & 0 & 0 & 0 \\
\phi_{1,2} & 1 & 0 & 0 \\
\phi_{1,2}\phi_{1,3} + \phi_{2,3} & \phi_{1,3} & 1 & 0 \\
\phi_{1,2}\phi_{1,3}\phi_{1,4} + \phi_{1,2}\phi_{2,4} + \phi_{2,3}\phi_{1,4} & \phi_{1,3}\phi_{1,4} + \phi_{2,4} & \phi_{1,4} & 1
\end{pmatrix}.
\tag{19.8}
$$

This implies that the first two columns of $\Phi_0^{-1}\Phi_1$ contain only zeros; that is,

$$
\Phi_0^{-1}\Phi_1 = \begin{pmatrix}
0 & 0 & \phi_{2,1} & \phi_{1,1} \\
0 & 0 & \phi_{1,2}\phi_{2,1} & \phi_{1,2}\phi_{1,1} + \phi_{2,2} \\
0 & 0 & (\phi_{1,2}\phi_{1,3} + \phi_{2,3})\phi_{2,1} & \phi_{1,1}\phi_{1,2}\phi_{1,3} + \phi_{1,1}\phi_{2,3} + \phi_{1,3}\phi_{2,2} \\
0 & 0 & (\phi_{1,2}\phi_{1,3}\phi_{1,4} + \phi_{1,2}\phi_{2,4} + \phi_{2,3}\phi_{1,4})\phi_{2,1} & (\phi_{1,2}\phi_{1,3}\phi_{1,4} + \phi_{1,2}\phi_{2,4} + \phi_{2,3}\phi_{1,4})\phi_{1,1}
\end{pmatrix},
\tag{19.9}
$$

displaying that $\mathbf{Y}_T$ depends only on the third and fourth quarters in $\mathbf{Y}_{T-1}$.

A second version of (19.2) is based on the possibility of decomposing a pth order polynomial $\tilde{\psi}_p(L)$ with at least k real roots as $\tilde{\psi}_{p-k}(L)(1 - \psi_k L) \ldots (1 - \psi_1 L)$. Hence, it can be useful to rewrite (19.2) as

$$
[\tilde{\Psi}_{p-k}(L)\Psi_k(L) \ldots \Psi_1(L)]\mathbf{Y}_T = \varepsilon_T,
\tag{19.10}
$$

where the $\Psi_i(L)$, $i = 1, \ldots, k$ are (4×4) matrices with elements that are first-order polynomials in L and $\tilde{\Psi}_{p-k}(L)$ is a matrix polynomial of order $(p - k)$. An example is again given by the PAR(2) process in (19.5), which can be written as

$$
\Psi_2(L)\Psi_1(L)\mathbf{Y}_T = \varepsilon_T,
\tag{19.11}
$$

with

$$
\Psi_2(L) = \begin{pmatrix}
1 & 0 & 0 & -\beta_1 L \\
-\beta_2 & 1 & 0 & 0 \\
0 & -\beta_3 & 1 & 0 \\
0 & 0 & -\beta_4 & 1
\end{pmatrix}, \quad
\Psi_1(L) = \begin{pmatrix}
1 & 0 & 0 & -\alpha_1 L \\
-\alpha_2 & 1 & 0 & 0 \\
0 & -\alpha_3 & 1 & 0 \\
0 & 0 & -\alpha_4 & 1
\end{pmatrix},
\tag{19.12}
$$

such that (19.4) becomes

$$
(1 - \beta_s L)(1 - \alpha_s L)y_t = \varepsilon_t.
\tag{19.13}
$$

This expression equals

$$y_t - \alpha_s y_{t-1} = \beta_s(y_{t-1} - \alpha_{s-1} y_{t-2}) + \varepsilon_t, \tag{19.14}$$

as the backward shift operator L also operates on α_s; that is, $L\alpha_s = \alpha_{s-1}$ for all $s = 1$, 2, 3, 4 and with $\alpha_0 = \alpha_4$.

Parameter estimation

To estimate the parameters in a PAR model, we use seasonal dummy variables $D_{s,t}$ which are equal to 1 if t corresponds to season s, and zero elsewhere. The parameters of the PAR(p) model in (19.1) can be estimated by considering the regression model

$$y_t = \sum_{s=1}^{4} \phi_{1,s} D_{s,t} y_{t-1} + \ldots + \sum_{s=1}^{4} \phi_{p,s} D_{s,t} y_{t-p} + \varepsilon_t. \tag{19.15}$$

Under normality of the error process ε_t and with fixed starting values, the maximum likelihood [ML] estimators of the parameters $\phi_{i,s}$, $i = 1, 2, \ldots, p$ and $s = 1, 2, 3, 4$, are obtained from ordinary least squares [OLS] estimation of (19.15). For alternative estimation methods and asymptotic results, see Pagano (1978) and Troutman (1979). Notice that the available sample for estimating the periodic parameters is in fact $N = n/4$, that is, the number of observations can be small.

Once the parameters in a PAR(p) process have been estimated, an important next step involves testing for periodic variation in the autoregressive parameters. Boswijk and Franses (1996) show that the likelihood-ratio test for the null hypothesis,

$$H_0 : \phi_{i,s} = \phi_i \quad \text{for } s = 1, 2, 3, 4 \text{ and } i = 1, 2, \ldots, p, \tag{19.16}$$

has an asymptotic $\chi^2(3p)$ distribution, whether the y_t series has unit roots or not. We denote by F_{per} the F-version of this test. An important implication of this result is that (19.15) can be estimated for the y_t series itself; that is, there is no need to *a priori* difference the y_t series to remove stochastic trends when one wants to test for periodicity. This suggests that, for practical purposes, it seems most convenient to start with estimating the model in (19.15) and testing the null given by (19.16). In a second step one may then test for unit roots in periodic or nonperiodic models depending on the outcome of the test. An additional advantage is that this sequence of steps allows the possibility of having a periodic differencing filter, which is useful in case of periodic integration. We address this issue in more detail in the next subsection.

Order selection

To determine the order p of a periodic autoregression, Franses and Paap (1994) recommend using the BIC in combination with diagnostic tests of residual autocorrelation. As we are dealing with periodic time-series models, it seems sensible to opt for an LM test for periodic serial correlation in the residuals. This test corresponds to a standard F-test for the significance of the ρ_s parameters in the following auxiliary regression:

$$\hat{\varepsilon}_t = \sum_{s=1}^{4} \gamma_{1,s} D_{s,t} y_{t-1} + \ldots + \sum_{s-1}^{4} \gamma_{p,s} D_{s,t} y_{t-p} + \sum_{s=1}^{4} \rho_s D_{s,t} \hat{\varepsilon}_{t-1} + \eta_t, \qquad (19.17)$$

where $\hat{\varepsilon}_t$ are the estimated residuals of (19.15) (see Franses, 1993). Of course, one may also consider the nonperiodic version, where one imposes in (19.17) that $\rho_s = \rho$ for all s. Finally, standard tests for normality and ARCH effects can also be applied.

19.2.2.   Unit roots and periodic integration

To analyze the presence of stochastic trends in y_t we consider the solutions to the characteristic equation of (19.2); that is, the solutions to

$$|\Phi_0 - \Phi_1 z - \ldots - \Phi_p z^P| = 0. \qquad (19.18)$$

When k solutions to (19.18) are on the unit circle, the $\mathbf{Y}_T$ process, and also the y_t process, has k unit roots. Notice that the number of unit roots in y_t equals that in $\mathbf{Y}_T$, and that, for example, no additional unit roots are introduced in the multivariate representation. We illustrate this with several examples.

As a first example, consider the PAR(2) process in (19.4) for which the characteristic equation is

$$|\Phi_0 - \Phi_1 z| = \begin{vmatrix} 1 & 0 & -\phi_{2,1}z & -\phi_{1,1}z \\ -\phi_{1,2} & 1 & 0 & -\phi_{2,2}z \\ -\phi_{2,3} & -\phi_{1,3} & 1 & 0 \\ 0 & -\phi_{2,4} & -\phi_{4,1} & 1 \end{vmatrix} = 0, \qquad (19.19)$$

which becomes

$$1 - (\phi_{2,2}\phi_{1,3}\phi_{1,4} + \phi_{2,2}\phi_{2,4} + \phi_{2,1}\phi_{1,2}\phi_{1,3} + \phi_{2,1}\phi_{2,3} + \phi_{1,1}\phi_{1,2}\phi_{1,3}\phi_{1,4}$$
$$+ \phi_{1,1}\phi_{1,2}\phi_{2,4} + \phi_{1,1}\phi_{1,4}\phi_{2,3})z + \phi_{2,1}\phi_{2,2}\phi_{2,3}\phi_{2,4}z^2 = 0. \qquad (19.20)$$

Hence, when the nonlinear parameter restriction

$$\phi_{2,2}\phi_{1,3}\phi_{1,4} + \phi_{2,2}\phi_{2,4} + \phi_{2,1}\phi_{1,2}\phi_{1,3} + \phi_{2,1}\phi_{2,3} + \phi_{1,1}\phi_{1,2}\phi_{1,3}\phi_{1,4} + \phi_{1,1}\phi_{1,2}\phi_{2,4}$$
$$+ \phi_{1,1}\phi_{1,4}\phi_{2,3} - \phi_{2,1}\phi_{2,2}\phi_{2,3}\phi_{2,4} = 1 \qquad (19.21)$$

is imposed on the parameters, the PAR(2) model contains a single unit root.

When (19.19) yields two real-valued solutions, one can also analyze the characteristic equation

$$|\Psi_2(z)\Psi_1(z)| = 0. \qquad (19.22)$$

It is easy to see that this equation equals

$$(1 - \beta_1\beta_2\beta_3\beta_4 z)(1 - \alpha_1\alpha_2\alpha_3\alpha_4 z) = 0, \tag{19.23}$$

and hence that the PAR(2) model has one unit root when either $\beta_1\beta_2\beta_3\beta_4 = 1$ or $\alpha_1\alpha_2\alpha_3\alpha_4 = 1$, and has at most two unit roots when both products equal unity. Obviously, the maximum number of unity solutions to the characteristic equation of a PAR(p) process is equal to p.

The expression (19.23) shows that one may need to consider a periodic differencing filter to remove the stochastic trend. Consider the simple PAR(1) model

$$y_t = \alpha_s y_{t-1} + \varepsilon_t, \tag{19.24}$$

which can be written as (19.5) with

$$\Phi_0 = \begin{pmatrix} 1 & 0 & 0 & 0 \\ -\alpha_2 & 1 & 0 & 0 \\ 0 & -\alpha_3 & 1 & 0 \\ 0 & 0 & -\alpha_4 & 1 \end{pmatrix} \quad \text{and} \quad \Phi_1 = \begin{pmatrix} 0 & 0 & 0 & \alpha_1 \\ 0 & 0 & 0 & 0 \\ 0 & 0 & 0 & 0 \\ 0 & 0 & 0 & 0 \end{pmatrix}. \tag{19.25}$$

The characteristic equation is

$$|\Phi_0 - \Phi_1 z| = (1 - \alpha_1\alpha_2\alpha_3\alpha_4 z) = 0, \tag{19.26}$$

and hence the PAR(1) process has a unit root when $\alpha_1\alpha_2\alpha_3\alpha_4 = 1$. In case one or more α_s values are unequal to α – that is, when $\alpha_s \neq \alpha$ for all s, and $\alpha_1\alpha_2\alpha_3\alpha_4 = 1$ – the y_t process is said to be periodically integrated of order 1 [PI(1)]. Periodic integration of order 2 can similarly be defined in terms of the α_s and β_s parameters in the PAR(2) process using (19.23). The concept of periodic integration was first defined in Osborn (1988).

As the periodic AR(1) process nests the model $y_t = \alpha y_{t-1} + \varepsilon_t$, it is obvious that a unit root in a PAR(1) process implies a unit root in the nonperiodic AR(1) process. The characteristic equation is then $(1 - \alpha^4 z) = 0$. Hence, when $\alpha = 1$, the Y_T process has a single unit root. Also, when $\alpha = -1$, the process Y_T has a unit root. The first case corresponds to the simple random walk process, that is, the case where y_t has a nonseasonal unit root, while the second case corresponds to the case where y_t has a seasonal unit root (see Hylleberg, Engle, Granger, and Yoo, 1990). In other words, both the nonseasonal and the seasonal unit-root process are nested within the PAR(1) process. This suggests a simple testing strategy; that is, first investigating the presence of a unit root by testing whether $\alpha_1\alpha_2\alpha_3\alpha_4 = 1$, and second to test whether $\alpha_s = 1$ or $\alpha_s = -1$ for all s. Boswijk and Franses (1996) show that, given $\alpha_1\alpha_2\alpha_3\alpha_4 = 1$, these latter tests are $\chi^2(3)$ distributed. See also Boswijk, Franses, and Haldrup (1997) for testing for so-called seasonal unit roots along a similar line.

TESTING FOR PERIODIC INTEGRATION

To test for periodic integration in the PAR(p) model (19.1), Boswijk and Franses (1996) consider a likelihood-ratio [LR] test. The test statistic equals

$$LR_{PI} = n[\ln (SSR_0) - \ln (SSR_a)], \tag{19.27}$$

where SSR_0 and SSR_a denote the sum of the squared residuals of the estimated PAR(p) model under the restriction of periodic integration and without this restriction, respectively. The latter can be obtained directly from the estimated residuals of the regression model (19.15). To obtain the residuals under the null, one has to estimate the PAR(p) model under the nonlinear restriction of periodic integration using nonlinear least squares [NLS]. As this restriction may be complicated in higher-order PAR models, it is more convenient to consider the generalization of (14) to a PAR(p) model; that is,

$$(y_t - \alpha_s y_{t-1}) = \sum_{i=1}^{p-1} \beta_{i,s}(y_{t-i} - \alpha_{s-i} y_{t-1-i}) + \varepsilon_t, \tag{19.28}$$

with $\alpha_{s-4k} = \alpha_s$ and where the restriction of periodic integration is simply $\alpha_1\alpha_2\alpha_3\alpha_4 - 1$. Again, this model can be estimated by NLS.

The asymptotic distribution of the LR test statistic (19.27) under periodic integration is the same as the asymptotic distribution of the square of the standard unit-root t-test of Dickey and Fuller (1979): see Boswijk and Franses (1996). The critical values are given in the first row of table 15.1 of Johansen (1995). It is also possible to consider a one-sided test by taking the square root of (19.27). The sign of the resulting statistic is negative if all roots of the characteristic equation (19.18) are outside the unit circle and positive in all other cases. Under the null hypothesis, this test statistic has the same distribution as the τ statistic of Fuller (1976).

Similar to the standard Dickey–Fuller case, the asymptotic distribution of the test statistic depends on the presence of deterministic terms in the test equation. In the next subsection, we discuss the role of intercepts and trends in periodic autoregressions and the appropriate asymptotic distribution of LR statistic for periodic integration for different specifications. This discussion is particularly relevant, as a trend will dominate out-of-sample forecast patterns.

19.2.3. Intercepts and trends

So far, the periodic models did not include any deterministic terms. Seasonal intercepts and seasonal linear trends can be added to (19.1) as

$$y_t = \mu_s + \tau_s T_t + \phi_{1,s} y_{t-1} + \ldots + \phi_{p,s} y_{t-p} + \varepsilon_t, \tag{19.29}$$

where $T_t = [(t - 1)/4] + 1$ represents an annual linear deterministic trend and μ_s and $\tau_s, s = 1, 2, 3, 4$ are seasonal dummy and trend parameters. In general, unrestricted periodic processes like (19.29) can generate data with diverging seasonal trends, which may not be plausible in all practical cases. Common seasonal linear deterministic trends require parameter restrictions on seasonal trend parameters τ_s. Note that the simple restriction $\tau_1 = \tau_2 = \tau_3 = \tau_4$ does not correspond to common seasonal trends, because the τ_s parameters are a function of trend parameters and the periodic autoregressive parameters.

PERIODIC TREND-STATIONARITY

To analyze the role of the linear trend under periodic trend-stationarity, we rewrite (19.29) as

$$(y_t - \mu_s^* - \tau_s^* T_t) = \sum_{i=1}^{p} \phi_{i,s}(y_{t-i} - \mu_{s-i}^* - \tau_{s-i}^* T_{t-i}) + \varepsilon_t, \tag{19.30}$$

where μ_s^* and τ_s^* are nonlinear functions of the μ_s, τ_s and $\phi_{i,s}$ parameters and where $\mu_{s-4k}^* = \mu_s^*$ and $\tau_{s-4k}^* = \tau_s^*$. This model can easily be estimated using NLS. The restriction for common linear seasonal deterministic trends is given by $\tau_1^* = \tau_2^* = \tau_3^* = \tau_4^*$. This restriction can be tested with a standard likelihood-ratio test, which is $\chi^2(3)$ distributed. The restriction for the absence of linear deterministic trends is simply $\tau_1^* = \tau_2^* = \tau_3^* = \tau_4^* = 0$.

PERIODIC INTEGRATION

The presence of a linear deterministic trend in an autoregression for y_t with an imposed unit root corresponds to the presence of quadratic trend in y_t. Likewise, the inclusion of linear deterministic trends in a periodically integrated autoregression [PIAR] assumes the presence of seasonal quadratic trends in y_t. To discuss the role of trends in a PIAR we distinguish three cases: the presence of no quadratic trends [NQT], common (seasonal) linear trends [CLT], and no linear trends [NLT].

To discuss these three cases, it is convenient to write (19.29) using (19.28) as

$$(y_t - \alpha_s y_{t-1} - \mu_s^{**} - \tau_s^{**} T_t) = \sum_{i=1}^{p-1} \beta_{i,s}(y_{t-i} - \alpha_{s-i} y_{t-1-i} - \mu_{s-i}^{**} - \tau_{s-i}^{**} T_{t-i}) + \varepsilon_t \tag{19.31}$$

with $\alpha_1 \alpha_2 \alpha_3 \alpha_4 = 1$ and where μ_s^{**}, τ_s^{**} and $\beta_{i,s}$ are again nonlinear functions of μ_s, τ_s, and $\phi_{i,s}$, and $\mu_{s-4k}^{**} = \mu_s^{**}$ and $\tau_{s-4k}^{**} = \tau_s^{**}$. Note that it is not possible to write (19.29) like (19.30) under the restriction of periodic integration. To analyze the role of the deterministic terms, it is convenient to write (19.31) in VQ representation. The restrictions on the deterministic elements follow from applying Granger's representation theorem to this VQ representation: see Paap and Franses (1999) for a complete derivation.

For example, it follows that the restriction for NQT in y_t corresponds to

$$\tau_1^{**} + \alpha_1 \alpha_3 \alpha_4 \tau_2^{**} + \alpha_1 \alpha_4 \tau_3^{**} + \alpha_1 \tau_4^{**} = 0, \tag{19.32}$$

or to the trivial solution $\tau_1^{**} = \tau_2^{**} = \tau_3^{**} = \tau_4^{**} = 0$. To obtain CLT in y_t, one has to impose the four restrictions

$$\tau_s^{**} = (1 - \alpha_s)d \quad \text{for } s = 1, 2, 3, 4, \tag{19.33}$$

where d is given by

$$d = \mu_4^{**} + \alpha_4\mu_3^{**} + \alpha_3\alpha_4\mu_2^{**} + \alpha_2\alpha_3\alpha_4\mu_1^{**}. \tag{19.34}$$

Finally, the restriction for the absence of linear deterministic trends [NLT] in y_t is given by

$$\mu_4^{**} + \alpha_4\mu_3^{**} + \alpha_3\alpha_4\mu_2^{**} + \alpha_2\alpha_3\alpha_4\mu_1^{**} = 0 \quad \text{and} \quad \tau_1^{**} = \tau_2^{**} = \tau_3^{**} = \tau_4^{**} = 0. \tag{19.35}$$

Of course, a special case is the trivial solution $\mu_s^{**} = \tau_s^{**} = 0$ for all s.

All restrictions can be tested with standard likelihood-ratio tests. Under the restriction of periodic integration, these tests are asymptotically $\chi^2(v)$ distributed, where v denotes the number of restrictions. Finally, these restrictions are also valid in nonperiodic AR models or PAR models for the first differences of a time series.

**DETERMINISTIC COMPONENTS AND
TESTING FOR PERIODIC INTEGRATION**

The inclusion of deterministic components in the test equation for periodic integration changes the asymptotic distribution of the LR statistic. If one includes only seasonal dummies, the percentiles of the asymptotic distribution of the statistic are tabulated in the first row of table A.2 of Johansen and Juselius (1990). If one also includes seasonal linear deterministic trends, the asymptotic distribution is given by the square of the τ_τ statistic of Fuller (1976). As this asymptotic distribution has virtually no mass on the positive part of the line, one can simply take the square of the corresponding critical values of the τ_τ statistic. Obviously, the asymptotic distributions of the one-sided LR statistics are the same as the asymptotic distributions of the τ_μ and τ_τ statistics of Fuller (1976).

Finally, it is also possible to perform a joint test of periodic integration and the absence of quadratic (or linear) trends. For example, one may test jointly for the presence of periodic integration and the absence of quadratic trends; that is, restriction (19.32) using a LR test. Hence, one compares specification (19.29) with (19.31) under the restriction (19.32). The asymptotic distribution of this joint test is tabulated in the first row of table 15.4 of Johansen (1995). Likewise, one may test with a LR test, under the restriction that $\tau_1 = \tau_2 = \tau_3 = \tau_4$, for the presence of periodic integration and for the absence of linear deterministic trends (19.35). The asymptotic distribution of this joint test is tabulated in the first row of table 15.2 of Johansen (1995). In the empirical section below, we will apply the various tests.

19.3. FORECASTING

Once the parameters in the PAR models have been estimated, and appropriate parameter restrictions for unit roots and deterministic terms have been imposed, one can use the resultant model for out-of-sample forecasting. In this section, we first consider generating forecasts, and then briefly turn to their evaluation.

POINT AND INTERVAL FORECASTS

Forecasting with PAR models proceeds roughly in the same way as with standard AR models: see Franses (1996a) for an extensive discussion. To illustrate this, we consider the PAR(1) model in (19.24). The one-step-ahead forecast made at $t = n$ is simply

$$\hat{y}_{n+1} = E_n[y_{n+1}] = E_n[\alpha_s y_n + \varepsilon_{n+1}] = \alpha_s y_n, \tag{19.36}$$

where we assume that time $n + 1$ corresponds to season s. The forecast error $y_{n+1} - \hat{y}_{n+1}$ is ε_{n+1} and hence the variance of the one-step-ahead forecast equals σ^2. Likewise, we can construct the two-, three-, and four-steps-ahead forecasts, which equal

$$\hat{y}_{n+2} = E_n[y_{n+2}] = E[\alpha_{s+1}\alpha_s y_n + \varepsilon_{n+2} + \alpha_{s+1}\varepsilon_n] = \alpha_{s+1}\alpha_s y_n,$$

$$\hat{y}_{n+3} = E_n[y_{n+3}] = E_n[\alpha_{s+2}y_{n+2} + \varepsilon_{n+1}] = \alpha_{s+2}\alpha_{s+1}\alpha_s y_n,$$

$$\hat{y}_{n+4} = E_n[y_{n+4}] = E_n[\alpha_{s+3}y_{n+3} + \varepsilon_{n+3}] = \alpha_{s+3}\alpha_{s+2}\alpha_{s+1}\alpha_s y_n. \tag{19.37}$$

In case of periodic integration the four-steps-ahead forecast simplifies to $\hat{y}_{n+4} = y_n$. Note that the expressions for the forecasts depend on the season in which you start to forecast.

The forecast errors are

$$\hat{y}_{n+2} - y_{n+2} = \varepsilon_{n+2} + \alpha_{s+1}\varepsilon_{n+1},$$

$$\hat{y}_{n+3} - y_{n+3} = \varepsilon_{n+3} + \alpha_{s+2}\varepsilon_{n+2} + \alpha_{s+2}\alpha_{s+1}\varepsilon_{n+1},$$

$$\hat{y}_{n+4} - y_{n+4} = \varepsilon_{n+4} + \alpha_{s+3}\varepsilon_{n+3} + \alpha_{s+3}\alpha_{s+2}\varepsilon_{n+2} + \alpha_{s+3}\alpha_{s+2}\alpha_{s+1}\varepsilon_{n+1}, \tag{19.38}$$

and hence the variances of the forecast errors equal $\sigma^2(1 + \alpha_{s+1}^2)$, $\sigma^2(1 + \alpha_{s+2}^2 + \alpha_{s+2}^2\alpha_{s+1}^2)$ and $\sigma^2(1 + \alpha_{s+3}^2 + \alpha_{s+3}^2\alpha_{s+2}^2 + \alpha_{s+3}^2\alpha_{s+2}^2\alpha_{s+1}^2)$, respectively. These forecast error variances also depend on the season in which one generates forecasts. The variances can be used to construct forecast intervals in the standard way.

In general, it is more convenient to use the VQ representation to compute forecasts and forecast-error variances. Forecasts can then be generated along the same lines as for VAR models (see Lütkepohl, 1993). Consider again the PAR(1) model in (19.24). The VQ representation is given by (19.5) and (19.25). The forecasts made at $t = n = 4N$ for the next year (the forecasting origin is quarter 4) using the VQ representation are given by

$$\hat{\mathbf{Y}}_{N+1} = E[\mathbf{Y}_{N+1}] = E[\mathbf{\Phi}_0^{-1}\mathbf{\Phi}_1\mathbf{Y}_N + \mathbf{\Phi}_0^{-1}\varepsilon_{N+1}] = \mathbf{\Phi}_0^{-1}\mathbf{\Phi}_1\mathbf{Y}_N. \tag{19.39}$$

The forecast errors equal $\hat{\mathbf{Y}}_N - \mathbf{Y}_N = \mathbf{\Phi}_0^{-1}\varepsilon_{N+1}$ and hence the covariance matrix of the forecast errors is simply $\sigma^2(\mathbf{\Phi}_0^{-1}(\mathbf{\Phi}_0^{-1})')$. It is easy to show that the diagonal elements of this matrix correspond to the forecast error variances derived above.

Likewise, the forecast for two years ahead, that is five to eight steps ahead for the quarterly series y_t, is given by

$$\hat{\mathbf{Y}}_{N+2} = E[\mathbf{Y}_{N+2}] = E[(\mathbf{\Phi}_0^{-1}\mathbf{\Phi}_1)^2\mathbf{Y}_N + \mathbf{\Phi}_0^{-1}\varepsilon_{N+2} + (\mathbf{\Phi}_0^{-1}\mathbf{\Phi}_1)\mathbf{\Phi}_0^{-1}\varepsilon_{N+1}]$$

$$= (\mathbf{\Phi}_0^{-1}\mathbf{\Phi}_1)^2\mathbf{Y}_N, \tag{19.40}$$

where the corresponding covariance matrix for the forecast errors is given by

$$\sigma^2(\mathbf{\Phi}_0^{-1}(\mathbf{\Phi}_0^{-1})' + (\mathbf{\Phi}_0^{-1}\mathbf{\Phi}_1\mathbf{\Phi}_0^{-1})(\mathbf{\Phi}_0^{-1}\mathbf{\Phi}_1\mathbf{\Phi}_0^{-1})'). \tag{19.41}$$

The covariances between one-year-ahead and two-year-ahead forecasts follow directly from $E[(\hat{\mathbf{Y}}_{N+2} - \mathbf{Y}_{N+2})(\hat{\mathbf{Y}}_{N+1} - \mathbf{Y}_{N+1})'] = \sigma^2(\mathbf{\Phi}_0^{-1}\mathbf{\Phi}_1\mathbf{\Phi}_0^{-1}(\mathbf{\Phi}_0^{-1})')$.

Multi-year-ahead forecasts can be generated in a similar way. Note that if the series is periodically integrated, it can be shown that the matrix $(\mathbf{\Phi}_0^{-1}\mathbf{\Phi}_1)$ is idempotent, which may simplify the expressions for the forecasts and forecast error covariances. For instance, it follows from (19.40) that the two-years-ahead forecasts for $\mathbf{Y}_T$ generated by a PIAR(1) model without deterministic elements is equal to the one-year-ahead forecast. This implies that forecasts from a PIAR(1) model are the same as those of the seasonally integrated model $\Delta_4 y_t = y_t - y_{t-4} = u_t$, where u_t is white noise.

EVALUATING FORECASTS

To compare forecasts generated by PAR models with forecasts from alternative periodic or nonperiodic models, one can consider the familiar Root Mean Squared Prediction Error [RMSPE]. One may also opt for an encompassing test. In brief, one then estimates the following regression equation for the generated forecasts:

$$(\hat{y}_{n+h} - y_{n+h}) = \gamma(\hat{y}_{n+h} - \tilde{y}_{n+h}) + \eta_{n+h}, \tag{19.42}$$

where $\tilde{y}_{n+h}$ is the forecast generated by a competing model – see Clements and Hendry (1993), Harvey, Leybourne, and Newbold (1998), and also chapter 12 of this volume, by Newbold and Harvey. If $\gamma = 0$, the forecasts $\hat{y}_{n+h}$ encompass forecasts generated by the competing model $\tilde{y}_{n+h}$. This restriction can be tested using a standard F-test. As the h-step-ahead forecast errors of the (PAR) models are seasonal heteroskedastic and correlated over time, we correct the standard errors for heteroskedasticity and autocorrelation in the error term using the method of Newey and West (1987).

19.4. EMPIRICAL ILLUSTRATION

Our data concern nondurable consumption in the United Kingdom on food, alcohol, clothing, energy, other goods, services, and total nondurable consumption (which does not include services). The sample ranges from 1955.I–1994.IV. We use the sample 1955.I–1988.IV for model construction and estimation, and we reserve the period 1989.I–1994.IV for out-of-sample forecasting. All series are log

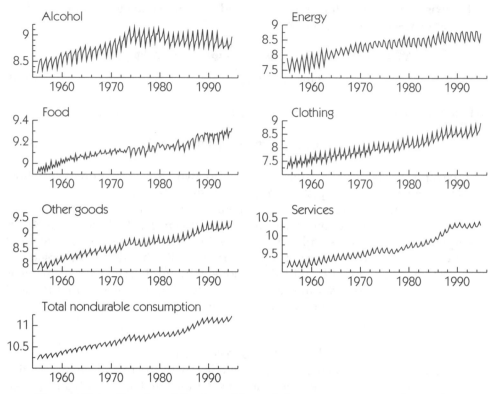

Figure 19.1   Graphs of the logarithm of the seven consumption series

transformed. Graphs of the series appear in figure 19.1. In section 19.4.1, we test for periodicity in the series and construct PAR models. In section 19.4.2, we estimate nonperiodic models for the series that turn out to be periodic, as we aim to evaluate these relative to the PAR models in our forecasting exercise. In section 19.4.3, we compare forecasts generated by the various models.

19.4.1.   Periodic models

We construct periodic autoregressions with seasonal dummies and seasonal trends for the seven series under consideration. In the first step we determine the appropriate lag order of the PAR models. This lag order is determined using the BIC criterion in combination with LM tests for (periodic) serial correlation. The estimated lag orders of the PAR models are given in the second column of table 19.1. For these lag orders, the PAR models pass diagnostic tests for first, and first- to fourth-order serial correlation, and ARCH effects in the residuals. The third column of table 19.1 shows the F_{per}-statistics that the autoregressive parameters are the same over the seasons. For three out of seven series, this restriction cannot be rejected at the 5 percent level of significance. As the main focus of this chapter concerns periodic models, we will not consider these series any further.

Table 19.1 Specification tests in PAR models for the seven nondurable consumption series

Series	Order	F_{per}	LR_{PI}	LR_{NQT}	$LR_{\tau=0}$	LR_{CLT}	$LR_{\Delta 1}$	Final model
Alcohol	2	2.97***	4.70	0.09	33.13***	10.32**	4.94	$\Delta_1 PAR(1)$, NQT
Energy	4	3.11***	0.04	0.06	12.84**	4.39	28.94***	PIAR(4), CLT
Food	3	1.67						nonperiodic
Clothing	2	2.29**	4.87	2.19	14.30***	4.85	82.93***	PIAR(2), CLT
Other	5	1.19						nonperiodic
Services	5	1.55						nonperiodic
Total	1	7.26***	6.32	0.20	30.36***	70.00***	21.59***	PIAR(2), NQT

Note: The cells contain the values of various F- and LR test statistics. ***, ** ,* denote significant at 1, 5, 10%, respectively.

For the other four periodic time series, we proceed with testing for the presence of periodic integration. The fourth column of table 19.1 shows the outcomes of the LR_{PI} test for the presence of periodic integration. None of the LR_{PI} statistics is significant at the 5 percent level of significance, if we compare the results with the squares of the percentiles of the asymptotic distribution of the τ_τ statistic of Fuller (1976). A joint test for periodic integration and the absence of quadratic trends (not reported here) gave the same conclusion. As the remaining roots of the characteristic equation (19.18) are far outside the unit circle, we do not consider tests for multiple unit roots.

The next step in our model selection strategy concerns testing for restrictions on the deterministic components in the periodically integrated autoregressions. The fifth column of table 19.1 shows the outcomes of the LR test for the absence of a quadratic trend (19.32). If we compare the outcomes with the percentiles of a $\chi^2(1)$ distribution, we conclude that this restriction cannot be rejected for any of the series. The stronger condition $\tau_1 = \tau_2 = \tau_3 = \tau_4 = 0$ is clearly rejected for all series, as can be seen from the sixth column of the table (this test statistic is asymptotically $\chi^2(4)$). The seventh column shows the results of the LR test statistic for the restriction of common linear deterministic trends given in (19.33) in an unrestricted PIAR model. If we compare the results with the percentiles of the $\chi^2(4)$ distribution, we conclude that this restriction is only rejected for the alcohol series.

Given the restrictions on the deterministic terms indicated by the above test results, we then compute an LR test of whether $\alpha_1 = \alpha_2 = \alpha_3 = \alpha_4 = 1$ and hence whether the periodic differencing filter $(1 - \alpha_s L)$ can be simplified to the nonperiodic filter $\Delta_1 = (1 - L)$ to obtain stationarity. If this is the case, we end up with a periodic autoregression for the first differences of the time series. Column 8 of table 19.1 displays the test results. If we compare the results with the percentiles of the $\chi^2(3)$ distribution, we conclude that the restriction is only valid for the alcohol series. A LR test whether the seasonal differencing filter $(1 + L)$ is appropriate $(\alpha_1 = \alpha_2 = \alpha_3 = \alpha_4 = -1)$ is not considered here as the estimated α_s parameters are all close to 1 (and hence far from -1).

In the final column of table 19.1 we present the model suggested by the sequence of tests. For the alcohol series, we have a PAR model in first differences with no quadratic trend, for clothing and energy we have a PIAR model with a common linear deterministic trend, while for total nondurable consumption we have a PIAR model without quadratic trends.

19.4.2. Nonperiodic models

As competing models for our four periodic autoregressions, we consider two nonperiodic models, which roughly correspond to the alternative approaches discussed in the introduction. First, we consider autoregressive models resulting from tests for the presence of (seasonal) unit roots. Second, we consider SARIMA models for the four series, which usually amount to the so-called airline model.

To construct nonperiodic autoregressions for alcohol, energy, clothing, and total consumption, we first test for the presence of (seasonal) unit roots using the commonly applied version of the HEGY test equation of Hylleberg, Engle, Granger, and Yoo (1990); that is,

$$\Delta_4 y_t = \sum_{s=1}^{4}\mu_s + \tau t + \pi_1(1 + L + L^2 + L^3)y_{t-1} + \pi_2(-1 + l - L^2 + L^3)y_{t-1}$$
$$+ (\pi_3 + \pi_4 L)(1 + L^2)y_{t-1} + \sum_{i=1}^{k}\theta_i\Delta_4 y_{t-i} + \varepsilon_t, \tag{19.43}$$

where $\Delta_4 y_t = (1 - L^4)y_t = y_t - y_{t-4}$. The presence of a nonseasonal root of unity corresponds to the restriction $\pi_1 = 0$. This can be tested with a t-test. The presence of the three seasonal unit roots, -1, i, and $-i$ corresponds to the restriction $\pi_2 = \pi_3 = \pi_4 = 0$, which can be tested with an F-test. Critical values of these tests can be found in Hylleberg, Engle, Granger, and Yoo (1990) and Ghysels, Lee, and Noh (1994).

Table 19.2 shows the results of the tests for unit roots in a nonperiodic autoregression. The second column shows the lags that are included in the test equation (19.43). These lags are determined using a similar approach as that taken for the periodic models. The third column of this table shows the t-test for $\pi_1 = 0$. This test statistic is not significant at the 5 percent level of significance for all four variables and hence we cannot reject the presence of a nonseasonal unit root. The

Table 19.2 HEGY tests in nonperiodic AR models

Series	Lags	$t(\pi_1)$	$F(\pi_2, \pi_3, \pi_4)$	Final model
Alcohol	1	−1.05	6.08**	Δ_1, AR(4), SD
Energy	0	−1.04	12.76***	Δ_1, AR(3), SD
Clothing	1	−1.80	7.11**	Δ_1, AR(4), SD
Total	1,4,5	−2.68	1.16	Δ_4, AR(5), const

Note: In the final column we give the selected AR order for the appropriately differenced series and whether this model contains seasonal dummies [SD]. ***, **, * denote significant at 1, 5, 10%, respectively.

Table 19.3 Encompassing tests

Series	PAR/AR	AR/PAR	PAR/AIR	AIR/PAR
Alcohol	8.42***	16.91***	11.04***	20.43***
Energy	0.04	0.70	0.05	19.96***
Clothing	0.28	14.34***	0.26	8.57***
Total	0.82	1.82**	0.25	74.99***

Note: Wald test statistics for the significance of the fitted values of the second model added to the first model. ***, **, * denote significant at 1, 5, 10%, respectively.

test results for the presence of the three seasonal unit roots are given in the fourth column of table 19.2. The presence of these seasonal unit roots is rejected for alcohol, energy, and clothing series and hence we arrive at an autoregressive model for the first differences of these series with seasonal dummies. For total consumption, we cannot reject the presence of seasonal unit roots and we end up with an autoregressive model for the fourth differences of the series. The last column of the table displays the finally selected models.

The second type of nonperiodic time-series models we consider in our forecasting comparison is the airline (AIR) model, where one imposes the differencing filter $\Delta_1\Delta_4$ for the series. Using the standard model selection strategy, we find that the model

$$\Delta_1\Delta_4 y_t = (1 - \theta L)(1 - \lambda L^4)\varepsilon_t \tag{19.44}$$

is adequate for alcohol, energy, and total consumption. For the clothing series, we replace (19.44) by a moving-average model of order 5, where we impose the MA(2) and MA(3) parameters to equal zero.

Before we turn to out-of-sample forecasting, we first have a brief look at the in-sample performance of the preferred periodic and nonperiodic models using encompassing-type tests. For this purpose we use the nonnested testing framework advocated in Franses and McAleer (1997); that is, we add the fit of model A to model B (upon appropriate differencing) and see if this new variable has explanatory power using a Wald test. The results in table 19.3 indicate that for the alcohol series all three models encompass each other, while for the other three series it is seen that the periodic model encompasses the nonperiodic models.

19.4.3. Forecast comparison

In this subsection, we report on the performance of the three models in out-of-sample forecasting. We consider one-, four-, and eight-step-ahead forecasting for y_t in table 19.4. We consider similar forecasts for each of the quarters separately in table 19.5. In table 19.6 we consider forecasting $\Delta_1 y_t$ and $\Delta_4 y_t$, as this may be relevant in practice even though this transformation does not match with most models.

Table 19.4 RMSPEs and encompassing tests for forecasts of y_t generated by the three models. The forecasting sample is 1989.I–1994.IV

Series	Horizon	RMSPE × 100			Encompassing tests[1]			
		PAR	AR	Airline	$F_{PAR/AR}$	$F_{AR/PAR}$	$F_{PAR/Air}$	$F_{Air/PAR}$
	1	4.38	3.22	3.23	5.72**	3.30*	7.50**	4.91**
Alcohol	4	3.85	4.04	3.66	0.09	3.61*	5.81**	1.06
	8	5.61	8.16	6.57	1.37	19.89**	1.23	14.95***
	1	3.81	4.70	4.08	0.09	12.04***	4.27*	9.35***
Energy	4	3.15	4.04	3.77	3.72*	15.57***	0.42	9.27***
	8	3.84	6.12	5.21	14.33***	50.29***	0.31	14.17***
	1	3.32	2.60	3.15	58.13***	12.11**	29.58***	2.03
Clothing	4	3.39	3.30	3.67	1.14	2.70	3.13*	14.13***
	8	6.05	6.00	6.53	0.14	0.65	4.22*	14.05***
	1	2.14	1.21	1.25	62.43***	1.54	96.12***	3.16*
Total	4	1.92	1.74	1.63	6.60**	0.98	10.80***	3.12*
	8	3.85	3.60	3.92	4.97**	0.68	8.58**	9.15***

[1] $F_{A,B}$ denotes a F-type statistic for the null hypothesis that forecasts generated by model A encompass forecasts generated by model B. Standard errors are corrected for heteroskedasticity and autocorrelation using Newey and West (1987). ***, **, * denote significant at 1, 5, 10%, respectively.

Table 19.5 Forecasting rank per quarter[1] for y_t based on the RMSPE. The forecasting sample is 1989.I–1994.IV

Series	Horizon	PAR quarter				AR quarter				Airline quarter			
		I	II	III	IV	I	II	III	IV	I	II	III	IV
	1	3	3	1	3	1	2	3	2	2	1	2	1
Alcohol	4	3	1	1	2	2	3	3	3	1	2	2	1
	8	1	1	1	1	3	3	3	2	2	2	2	3
	1	1	2	2	2	3	1	3	1	2	3	1	3
Energy	4	1	1	1	1	3	3	3	2	2	2	2	3
	8	1	1	1	1	3	3	3	2	2	2	2	3
	1	1	3	2	2	2	2	1	1	3	1	3	3
Clothing	4	1	3	1	2	2	1	3	1	3	2	2	3
	8	2	1	1	2	1	3	2	1	3	2	3	3
	1	2	3	3	2	1	2	2	1	3	1	1	3
Total	4	3	2	3	3	2	1	2	2	1	3	1	1
	8	2	1	3	3	1	2	2	1	3	3	1	2
Average rank		1.8	1.8	1.7	2.0	2.0	2.2	2.5	1.6	2.3	2.0	1.8	2.4

[1] Rank 1 corresponds to the smallest RMSPE for the corresponding quarter, while rank 3 corresponds to the largest RMSPE.

The results in table 19.4 for the RMSPE criterion show that in 4 of the 12 cases the PAR model yields the smallest value (with three of the four for energy), while this occurs for the HEGY-AR and airline model in six and two cases, respectively. For the energy series, the PAR model outperforms the other models on all three horizons. In case the PAR model does not produce the best forecasts, the average difference in RMSPE between the PAR model and the best performing model is 0.46. For the AR-HEGY and the airline model, this average difference equals 1.18 and 0.50, respectively. This shows that the PAR model still performs reasonably well if it is not the best forecasting model. This is however not the case for the AR-HEGY model.

The forecast encompassing test results in the second panel of table 19.4 indicate that in 2 (out of the 12) cases the forecasts generated by the PAR and the HEGY-AR models encompass each other (four- and eight-step-ahead clothing). In most other cases forecasts generated by the PAR model do not encompass forecasts generated by the AR-HEGY model and vice versa. The PAR model is encompassed by the AR-HEGY model in three cases (one-, four-, and eight-step-ahead total nondurable consumption) and the HEGY-AR model is only encompassed three times by the PAR model. The PAR model encompasses the airline model three times, while it is encompassed by that model two times. Hence, there is no clear picture on to which model encompasses the other.

In table 19.5, we present the ranks (based on RMSPE) of the three models for each quarter. We observe mixed results, although the PAR model seems most useful for the alcohol and energy series. The last row of the table gives the average rank across the 12 different forecasting runs (four variables, three horizons). Clearly, the PAR model obtains the lowest rank for quarters 1, 2, and 3, while the HEGY-AR models give the most accurate forecast for quarter 4. The airline model does not seem to give useful forecasts.

Table 19.6 displays the RMSPEs for forecasts of $\Delta_1 y_t$ and $\Delta_4 y_t$, which may sometimes be of interest in practice. In the first panel for $\Delta_1 y_t$, we observe that even

Table 19.6 RMSPE for forecasting quarterly and annual growth rates ($\Delta_1 y_t$ and $\Delta_4 y_t$) for 1989.I–1990.IV

Series H	Horizon	Quarterly growth rates			Annual growth rates		
		PAR	AR	Airline	PAR	AR	Airline
Alcohol	4	5.55	3.69	3.49	3.85	4.04	3.66
	8	6.09	5.67	6.53	3.79	4.71	4.55
Energy	4	3.74	4.14	4.03	3.15	4.04	3.77
	8	4.28	4.66	4.29	3.84	4.37	4.09
Clothing	4	3.31	2.91	3.34	3.39	3.30	3.67
	8	3.32	3.78	3.67	3.49	3.49	3.71
Total	4	1.88	0.98	1.01	1.92	1.74	1.63
	8	1.78	1.18	1.23	2.06	1.97	2.44

Table 19.7 Gain in RMSPE from imposing restrictions on deterministic elements for the PAR models

Series	Horizon	y_t	Δy_t	$\Delta_4 y_t$
Alcohol	1	−0.02	−0.02	−0.02
	4	0.02	0.01	0.02
	8	0.09	0.01	0.01
Energy	1	0.99	0.99	0.99
	4	0.53	1.01	0.53
	8	1.41	1.11	0.49
Clothing	1	0.33	0.33	0.33
	4	0.70	0.26	0.69
	8	1.87	0.24	0.72
Total	1	−0.02	−0.02	−0.02
	4	−0.30	−0.03	−0.30
	8	−0.70	−0.05	−0.29

Note: Decrease in RMSPE for forecasts generated by models with restrictions on the deterministic elements and by models without restrictions.

though the Δ_1 transformation appears relevant for the alcohol, energy, and clothing series, the corresponding forecasts are outperformed by PAR models (three times) and airline models (once). For total consumption, we notice that the HEGY-AR model is best for four- and eight-step-ahead forecasts. From the second panel of table 19.6, dealing with forecasts for the annual growth rates, we observe that the PAR model beats alternative models in four of the eight cases.

Finally, in table 19.7 we report on the differences between the performance of the periodic models (with unit root restrictions imposed if indicated earlier) without and with the proper restrictions on the deterministic terms (see also table 19.1). From this table we observe that trend restrictions yield better forecasts for energy and clothing (all horizons), alcohol (four and eight steps ahead), but not for total consumption. In most of the 12 forecast runs, however, it seems that imposing proper restrictions on the deterministic terms, leads to better forecasts.

In sum, it seems that a carefully constructed PAR model, when proper account is taken of unit roots and deterministic terms, often yields better forecasts than those generated from HEGY-AR and airline models.

19.5. Concluding Remarks

In the last few years, periodic time-series models have become increasingly popular for describing and forecasting univariate seasonal time series. In this chapter, we have discussed some important aspects of these models, and we have evaluated their forecasting performance. We showed that when the PAR models are properly specified; that is, when proper care is taken of unit roots and deterministic trends, they tend to outperform popular alternative models.

A next important step on the research agenda concerns the forecasting properties of multivariate PAR models. These models are considerably more complicated to specify and analyze with respect to unit roots and deterministic terms. It is therefore of importance to examine if these efforts result in more accurate forecasts.

Acknowledgments

We thank the editors for their helpful comments and Jeremy Smith for his help with collecting the data. The second author thanks the Netherlands Organisation for Scientific Research (N.W.O.) for their financial support.

References

Boswijk, H. and P. Franses (1996). Unit roots in periodic autoregressions. *Journal of Time Series Analysis*, 17, 221–45.

Boswijk, H., P. Franses, and N. Haldrup (1997). Multiple unit roots in periodic autoregression. *Journal of Econometrics*, 80, 167–93.

Box, G. and G. Jenkins (1970). *Time Series Analysis: Forecasting and Control*. San Francisco: Holden-Day.

Clements, M. and D. Hendry (1993). On the limitations of comparing mean squared forecast errors. *Journal of Forecasting*, 12, 617–37.

Dickey, D. and W. Fuller (1979). Distribution of estimators for autoregressive time series with a unit root. *Journal of the American Statistical Association*, 74, 427–31.

Franses, P. (1993). Periodically integrated subset autoregressions for Dutch industrial production and money stock. *Journal of Forecasting*, 12, 601–13.

Franses, P. (1996a). Multi-step forecast error variances for periodically integrated time series. *Journal of Forecasting*, 15, 83–95.

Franses, P. (1996b). *Periodicity and Stochastic Trends in Economic Time Series*. Oxford: Oxford University Press.

Franses, P. (1996c). Recent advances in modeling seasonality. *Journal of Economic Surveys*, 10, 299–345.

Franses, P. and M. McAleer (1997). Testing nested and non-nested periodically integrated autoregressive models. *Communication in Statistics: Theory and Methods*, 26, 1461–75.

Franses, P. and R. Paap (1994). Model selection in periodic autoregressions. *Oxford Bulletin of Economics and Statistics*, 56, 421–39.

Franses, P. and R. Paap (1996). Periodic integration: further results on model selection and forecasting. *Statistical Papers*, 37, 33–52.

Fuller, W. (1976). *Introduction to Statistical Time Series*. New York: John Wiley.

Ghysels, E., H. Lee and J. Noh (1994). Testing for unit roots in seasonal time series. *Journal of Econometrics*, 62, 415–42.

Gladyshev, E. (1961). Periodically correlated random sequences. *Soviet Mathematics*, 2, 385–8.

Harvey, A. (1989). *Forecasting Structural Time Series and the Kalman Filter*. Cambridge: Cambridge University Press.

Harvey, D., S. Leybourne, and P. Newbold (1998). Tests for forecast encompassing. *Journal of Business & Economic Statistics*, 16, 254–59.

Herwartz, H. (1997). Performance of periodic error correction models in forecasting consumption data. *International Journal of Forecasting*, 13, 421–31.

Herwartz, H. (1999). Performance of periodic time series models in forecasting. *Empirical Economics*, 24, 271–301.

Hylleberg, S., R. Engle, C. Granger, and B. Yoo (1990). Seasonal integration and cointegration. *Journal of Econometrics*, 44, 215–38.

Johansen, S. (1995). *Likelihood-Based Inference in Cointegrated Vector Autoregressive Models.* Oxford: Oxford University Press.

Johansen, S. and K. Juselius (1990). Maximum likelihood estimation and inference on cointegration – with applications to the demand for money. *Oxford Bulletin of Economics and Statistics*, 52, 169–210.

Lütkepohl, H. (1993). *Introduction to Multiple Time Series Analysis*, 2nd edn. Berlin: Springer-Verlag.

Newey, W. and K. West (1987). A simple positive semi-definite, heteroskedasticity and autocorrelation consistent covariance matrix. *Econometrica*, 55, 703–8.

Novales, A. and R. Flores de Fruto (1997). Forecasting with periodic models: a comparison with time invariant coefficient models. *International Journal of Forecasting*, 13, 393–405.

Osborn, D. (1988). Seasonality and habit persistence in a life cycle model of consumption. *Journal of Applied Econometrics*, 3, 255–66.

Osborn, D. (1991). The implications of periodically varying coefficients for seasonal time-series processes. *Journal of Econometrics*, 48, 373–84.

Osborn, D. and J. Smith (1989). The performance of periodic autoregressive models in forecasting seasonal U.K. consumption. *Journal of Business & Economic Statistics*, 7, 117–27.

Paap, R. and P. Franses (1999). On trends and constants in periodic autoregressions. *Econometric Reviews*, 18, 271–86.

Pagano, M. (1978). On periodic and multiple autoregressions. *The Annals of Statistics*, 6, 1310–17.

Tiao, G. and M. Grupe (1980). Hidden periodic autoregressive-moving average models in time series data. *Biometrika*, 67, 365–73.

Troutman, B. (1979). Some results in periodic autoregressions. *Biometrika*, 66, 219–28.

Wells, J. (1997). Modelling seasonal patterns and long-run trends in U.S. time series. *International Journal of Forecasting*, 13, 405–18.

Nonlinear Models and Forecasting

Ruey S. Tsay

20.1. INTRODUCTION

The focus of this chapter is on a univariate time series, x_t, which, for simplicity, is observed at equally-spaced time intervals. We denote the observations by $\{x_t\}_{t=1}^{n}$, where n is the sample size. The time series x_t is said to be *linear* if it can be written as

$$x_t = c + \sum_{i=0}^{\infty} \psi_i a_{t-i},$$

(20.1)

where c is a constant, $\psi_0 = 1$, ψ_i are real numbers, and $\{a_t\}$ is a sequence of independent and identically distributed (iid) random variables with a well-defined distribution function. We assume that the distribution of a_t is continuous and $E(a_t) = 0$. In many cases, we further assume that $\sigma_a^2 = \text{var}\,(a_t)$ is finite, or even stronger, that a_t is Gaussian. If $\sigma_a^2 \sum_{i=1}^{\infty} \psi_i^2 < \infty$, then x_t is weakly stationary. That is, the first two moments of x_t are time-invariant. Any process that does not satisfy the condition of (20.1) is said to be nonlinear. Our definition of linearity is for a purely stochastic process. It can be extended to include time series with a deterministic component such as $x_t = \beta t + a_t$. Because the deterministic component is often handled differently from the stochastic component, we shall focus on purely stochastic processes.

To better understand the development of nonlinear models, it is informative to write the model of x_t in terms of its conditional moments. Let F_{t-1} be the σ-field generated by available information at time $t - 1$ (inclusive). Typically, F_{t-1} denotes the σ-field generated by $\{x_{t-1}, x_{t-2}, \dots\}$ or $\{a_{t-1}, a_{t-2}, \dots\}$. The conditional mean and variance of x_t given F_{t-1} are

$$\mu_t = E(x_t \mid F_{t-1}) = f(F_{t-1}), \tag{20.2}$$

$$\sigma_t^2 \equiv h_t = V(x_t \mid F_{t-1}), \tag{20.3}$$

where the notation h_t is commonly used in the econometric literature. For the linear series x_t in (20.1), μ_t is a linear function of elements of F_{t-1} and $\sigma_t^2 = \sigma_a^2$, which is time-invariant. The development of nonlinear models involves extensions of equations (20.2) and (20.3).

One extension to nonlinearity, which originates mainly from the econometric literature and focuses on analysis of financial time series, is to modify equation (20.3) by allowing the conditional variance to evolve over time. Well-known examples here are the autoregressive conditional heteroskedastic (ARCH) model of Engle (1982) and the generalized ARCH (GARCH) model of Bollerslev (1986). The basic idea of these models is to parameterize σ_t^2 as a simple, yet flexible, positive linear function of elements of F_{t-1}. These models are further extended to various linear and nonlinear volatility models. Another extension to nonlinearity, which is mainly in the statistical literature and focuses on modeling physical and environmental time series, is to modify the conditional mean equation in (20.2). Examples of such an extension include the bilinear models of Granger and Andersen (1978), the threshold autoregressive (TAR) model of Tong (1978), the state-dependent model of Priestley (1980), the Markov switching model of Hamilton (1989), etc. The basic idea underlying this approach is to let the conditional mean μ_t evolve over time according to some simple parametric nonlinear function. Finally, there are extensions to nonlinearity by making use of the recent advances in computing facilities and methods. Examples of such extensions include the nonlinear state-space modeling of Carlin, Polson, and Stoffer (1992), the functional-coefficient autoregressive (FAR) model of Chen and Tsay (1993a), the nonlinear additive autoregressive (NAAR) model of Chen and Tsay (1993b), and the multivariate adaptive regression spline (MARS) of Lewis and Stevens (1991). The basic idea of these extensions is either to use simulation methods to describe the evolution of the conditional distribution of x_t or to use data-driven methods to explore nonlinear features of the series. Details of these nonlinear extensions will be discussed in section 20.2.

Apart from the development of various nonlinear models, there is substantial interest in studying test statistics that can discriminate linear series from nonlinear ones. Both parametric and nonparametric tests are now available. Most parametric tests employ either the Lagrange multiplier or likelihood ratio statistics. Nonparametric tests depend either on higher-order spectra of x_t or the concept of dimension correlation developed for chaotic time series. We shall review some nonlinearity tests in section 20.3.

The application of nonlinear models is less studied in the literature. Contributions of nonlinear models in forecasting are discussed only in recent years. Several factors contribute to this lack of progress. First, there exist no commercially available statistical packages that can handle various nonlinear models. Second, no generally agreed upon methods are available to judge the real contributions of nonlinear models over linear ones. This is particularly so in forecasting because evaluation of forecasting accuracy depends on forecasting origin, forecasting horizon, as well as the way in which forecasts are used. There are, however, some general guidelines that can be used to build a nonlinear model. These guidelines are given in section 20.4. In section 20.5, we shall discuss methods commonly used to produce nonlinear forecasts and to measure forecasting performance. Section 20.6 illustrates applications of nonlinear models by analyzing some real examples.

20.2. NONLINEAR MODELS

In this section, we briefly discuss some nonlinear models and give some references that may be useful to those who are interested in the models.

20.2.1. Volatility models

Volatility plays an important role in pricing options of a security. By volatility, we mean the conditional variance σ_t^2 of x_t in (20.3). There are two basic types of volatility models. The first type of model uses an exact function to describe the evolution of σ_t^2 over time such as a GARCH model. The second type of model incorporates a stochastic element into the conditional variance equation in (20.3) and these are called stochastic volatility models.

GARCH MODEL
A time series x_t follows a pure GARCH(r, s) model if $\mu_t = 0$ and

$$x_t = \sqrt{h_t}\varepsilon_t, \quad h_t = \alpha_0 + \sum_{i=1}^{r} \alpha_i x_{t-i}^2 + \sum_{j=1}^{s} \beta_j h_{t-j}, \tag{20.4}$$

where $\{\varepsilon_t\}$ is a sequence of iid random variables with mean 0 and variance 1.0, $\alpha_0 > 0$, $\alpha_i \geq 0$, $\beta_j \geq 0$, and $\sum_{i=1}^{\max(r,s)}(\alpha_i + \beta_i) < 1$. Here it is understood that $\alpha_i = 0$ for $i > r$ and $\beta_j = 0$ for $j > s$. The latter constraint on $\alpha_i + \beta_j$ implies that the unconditional variance of x_t is finite, whereas its conditional variance $\sigma_t^2 = h_t$ evolves over time (see Bollerslev, 1986). In practice, ε_t is often assumed to be a standard normal or Student's t distribution. Equation (20.4) reduces to a pure ARCH(r) model if $s = 0$.

For those who are familiar with the autoregressive moving-average (ARMA) model of Box, Jenkins, and Reinsel (1994), it is easier to understand properties of GARCH models by using the following representation. Let $\eta_t = x_t^2 - h_t$. The GARCH model can be written as

$$x_t^2 = \alpha_0 + \sum_{i=1}^{\max(r,s)} (\alpha_i + \beta_i)x_{t-i}^2 + \eta_t - \sum_{j=1}^{s} \beta_j \eta_{t-j}. \tag{20.5}$$

It is easy to check that $\{\eta_t\}$ is a martingale difference series; that is, $E(\eta_t) = 0$ and Cov $(\eta_t, \eta_{t-j}) = 0$ for $j \geq 1$. However, $\{\eta_t\}$ is in general not an iid sequence. Thus, a

GARCH model can be regarded as an application of the ARMA idea to the squared series x_t^2. It is then clear that

$$E(x_t^2) = \frac{\alpha_0}{1 - \sum_{i=1}^{\max(r,s)}(\alpha_i + \beta_i)},$$

provided that the denominator of the above fraction is positive.

   The strengths and weaknesses of GARCH models can easily be seen by focusing on the simplest GARCH(1, 1) model with

$$h_t = \alpha_0 + \alpha_1 x_{t-1}^2 + \beta_1 h_{t-1}, \quad 0 \le \alpha_1, \beta_1 \le 1, \quad (\alpha_1 + \beta_1) < 1. \tag{20.6}$$

First, a large x_{t-1}^2 or h_{t-1} gives rise to a large h_t. This means that a large x_{t-1}^2 tends to be followed by another large x_t^2, creating the well-known behavior of volatility clustering in the finance literature. Second, it can be shown that if $1 - 2\alpha_1^2 - (\alpha_1 + \beta_1)^2 > 0$, then

$$\frac{E(x_t^4)}{[E(x_t^2)]^2} = \frac{3[1 - (\alpha_1 + \beta_1)^2]}{1 - (\alpha_1 + \beta_1)^2 - 2\alpha_1^2} > 3.$$

Consequently, the tail distribution of a GARCH(1, 1) process is heavier than that of a normal distribution. Heavy-tailed behavior is commonly observed in financial time series. Third, the model provides a simple parametric form that can be used to describe the evolution of volatility.

   Turn to weaknesses. First, the model does not separate positive x_{t-1} from negative ones. This is in conflict with behavior of many return series of financial assets. Second, the model is rather restrictive. In particular, it often fails to adjust quickly to an isolated big value in x_{t-1}^2. Third, recent empirical studies of high-frequency financial time series indicate that the tail behavior of GARCH models remains too short, even using Student-t innovations.

   The literature on ARCH and GARCH models is enormous. See Bollerslev, Chou, and Kroner (1992) and Bollerslev, Engle, and Nelson (1994) and the references therein.

EXPONENTIAL GARCH MODEL

To overcome some weaknesses of GARCH models in handling financial time series, Nelson (1991) proposes the exponential GARCH (EGARCH) model. In particular, to allow for asymmetric effects between positive and negative asset returns, he considers the weighted innovation

$$g(\varepsilon_t) = \theta\varepsilon_t + \gamma[|\varepsilon_t| - E(|\varepsilon_t|)], \tag{20.7}$$

where θ and γ are real constants. Both ε_t and $|\varepsilon_t| - E(|\varepsilon_t|)$ are zero-mean iid sequences. Thus, $E[g(\varepsilon_t)] = 0$. The asymmetry of $g(\varepsilon_t)$ can easily be seen by rewriting it as

$$g(\varepsilon_t) = \begin{cases} (\theta + \gamma)\varepsilon_t - \gamma E(|\varepsilon_t|) & \text{if } \varepsilon_t \geq 0, \\ (\theta - \gamma)\varepsilon_t - \gamma E(|\varepsilon_t|) & \text{if } \varepsilon_t < 0. \end{cases}$$

An EGARCH(r, s) model can then be written as

$$x_t = \sqrt{h_t}\,\varepsilon_t, \quad \ln(h_t) = \frac{\alpha}{1 - \delta_1 B - \ldots - \delta_r B^r} + \frac{1 + \beta_1 B + \ldots + \beta_s B^s}{1 - \delta_1 B - \ldots - \delta_r B^r} g(\varepsilon_{t-1}), \tag{20.8}$$

where α is a constant, B is the back-shift (or lag) operator such that $Bg(\varepsilon_t) = g(\varepsilon_{t-1})$ and $1 + \beta_1 B + \ldots + \beta_s B^s$ and $1 - \delta_1 B - \ldots - \delta_r B^r$ are polynomials with all zeros outside the unit circle and have no common factors. Again, equation (20.8) uses the usual ARMA parameterization to describe the evolution of the conditional variance of x_t, and some properties of the EGARCH model can be obtained in a similar manner as that of GARCH models. For instance, the unconditional mean of $\ln(h_t)$ is $\alpha/(1 - \delta_1 - \ldots - \delta_r)$. However, it differs from the GARCH model in several ways. First, it uses logged conditional variance to relax the positiveness constraint of model coefficients. Second, the use of $g(\varepsilon_t)$ enables the model to respond asymmetrically to positive and negative lagged values of x_t. Some further properties of the EGARCH model can be found in Nelson (1991).

To better understand the EGARCH model, let us consider the simple EGARCH(1, 0) model

$$x_t = \sqrt{h_t}\,\varepsilon_t, \quad (1 - \delta B)\ln(h_t) = \alpha + g(\varepsilon_{t-1}), \tag{20.9}$$

where $\varepsilon_t's$ are iid standard normal and the subscript of δ is omitted. In this case, $E(|\varepsilon_t|) = \sqrt{2/\pi}$ and the model for $\ln(h_t)$ becomes

$$1 - \delta B \ln(h_t) = \begin{cases} \alpha_0 + (\theta + \gamma)\varepsilon_{t-1} & \text{if } \varepsilon_{t-1} \geq 0, \\ \alpha_0 + (\theta - \gamma)\varepsilon_{t-1} & \text{if } \varepsilon_{t-1} < 0, \end{cases} \tag{20.10}$$

where $\alpha_0 = \alpha - \sqrt{\frac{2}{\pi}}\gamma$. This is a nonlinear function similar to that of the TAR model of Tong (1978), which will be discussed later. It suffices to say that for this simple EGARCH model the conditional variance evolves in a nonlinear manner depending on the sign of x_{t-1}. Specifically, we have

$$h_t = h_{t-1}^{\delta} \exp(\alpha_0) \begin{cases} \exp\left[(\theta + \gamma)\dfrac{x_{t-1}}{\sqrt{h_{t-1}}}\right] & \text{if } x_{t-1} \geq 0, \\[4mm] \exp\left[(\theta - \gamma)\dfrac{x_{t-1}}{\sqrt{h_{t-1}}}\right] & \text{if } x_{t-1} < 0. \end{cases}$$

The coefficients $(\theta + \gamma)$ and $(\theta - \gamma)$ show the asymmetry in response to positive and negative x_{t-1}. Cao and Tsay (1992) use nonlinear models, including EGARCH models, to obtain multi-step-ahead volatility forecasts.

CHARMA MODEL

Many other models have been proposed in the literature to describe the evolution of conditional variance σ_t^2 in (20.3). We mention a model called the conditional heteroskedastic ARMA (CHARMA) model that uses random coefficients to produce conditional heteroskedasticity; see Tsay (1987). The CHARMA model is not the same as the GARCH model, but the two models have similar second-order conditional properties. The CHARMA model can be generalized to the multivariate case in a rather parsimonious manner. A simple CHARMA model is defined as

$$x_t = \sqrt{h_t}\, \varepsilon_t \equiv a_t, \quad \delta_t(B)a_t = \eta_t, \tag{20.11}$$

where η_t's are iid $N(0, \sigma_\eta^2)$ and $\delta_t(B) = 1 - \delta_{1,t}B - \ldots - \delta_{r,t}B^r$ is a purely random coefficient polynomial in B. The random coefficient vector $\delta_t = (\delta_{1,t}, \ldots, \delta_{r,t})'$ is a sequence of iid random vectors with mean zero and nonnegative definite covariance matrix Σ. In addition, $\{\delta_t\}$ is independent of $\{a_t\}$. For $r > 0$, the conditional variance of x_t in (20.11) is

$$h_t = \sigma_\eta^2 + (a_{t-1}, \ldots, a_{t-r})\Sigma(a_{t-1}, \ldots, a_{t-r})',$$

which is equivalent to that of an ARCH(r) model if Σ is a diagonal matrix. Because Σ is a covariance matrix, it is nonnegative definite and, hence, $h_t \geq \sigma_\eta^2 > 0$. An obvious difference between ARCH and CHARMA models is that the latter uses cross-products of the lagged values of x_t in the variance equation. Higher-order properties of CHARMA models are harder than those of GARCH models.

RANDOM COEFFICIENT AUTOREGRESSIVE (RCA) MODEL

In the literature, the RCA model is introduced to account for variability among different subjects under study, similar to panel data analysis in econometrics and hierarchical models in statistics. We classify the RCA model as a conditional heteroskedastic model, but historically it is used to obtain a better description of the conditional mean equation of the process by allowing for the parameters to evolve over time. A time series x_t is said to follow a RCA(p) model if it satisfies

$$x_t = c + \sum_{i=1}^{p}(\phi_i + \delta_{it})x_{t-i} + a_t, \tag{20.12}$$

where p is a positive integer, $\{\delta_t\} = \{(\delta_{1t}, \ldots, \delta_{pt})'\}$ is a sequence of independent random vectors with mean zero and covariance matrix Σ_δ, and $\{\delta_t\}$ is independent of $\{a_t\}$. See Nicholls and Quinn (1982) for further discussions of the model. The conditional mean and variance of the RCA model in (20.12) are

$$\mu_t = E(x_t \mid F_{t-1}) = \sum_{i=1}^{p} \phi_i x_{t-i},$$

$$\sigma_t^2 = h_t = \sigma_a^2 + (x_{t-1}, \ldots, x_{t-p})\Sigma_\delta(x_{t-1}, \ldots, x_{t-p})',$$

which is similar to that of a CHARMA model.

STOCHASTIC VOLATILITY MODEL

An alternative approach to describe the evolution of volatility is to introduce an innovation to the conditional variance equation of x_t: see Melino and Turnbull (1990), Harvey, Ruiz, and Shephard (1994), and Jacquier, Polson, and Rossi (1994). The resulting model is referred to as a stochastic volatility (SV) model. Similar to EGARCH models, to ensure positiveness of the conditional variance, SV models use ln (h_t) instead of h_t. A simple SV model is defined as

$$x_t = \sqrt{h_t}\,\varepsilon_t, \quad (1 - \delta_1 B - \ldots - \delta_r B^r)\ln(h_t) = \alpha + v_t, \tag{20.13}$$

where ε_t's are iid $N(0, 1)$, v_t's are iid $N(0, \sigma_v^2)$, $\{\varepsilon_t\}$ and $\{v_t\}$ are independent, α is a constant, and all zeros of the polynomial $1 - \sum_{i=1}^{r}\delta_i B^i$ are outside the unit circle. Introducing the innovation v_t makes the SV model more flexible in describing the evolution of h_t, but it also increases the difficulty in parameter estimation. A quasi-likelihood or Monte Carlo method is needed to estimate a SV model.

The appendices of Jacquier, Polson, and Rossi (1994) provide some properties of the SV model when $r = 1$. For instance, with $r = 1$, we have

$$\ln(h_t) \sim N\left(\frac{\alpha}{1 - \delta_1}, \frac{\sigma_v^2}{1 - \delta_1^2}\right) \equiv N(\mu_h, \sigma_h^2),$$

and $E(x_t^2) = \exp[\mu_h + 1/(2\sigma_h^2)]$, $E(x_t^4) = 3\exp[2\mu_h + 2\sigma_h^2]$, and corr $(x_t^2, x_{t-i}^2) = [\exp(\sigma_h^2\delta_1^i) - 1]/[3\exp(\sigma_h^2) - 1]$.

LONG-MEMORY STOCHASTIC VOLATILITY MODEL

More recently, the SV model has been further extended to allow for long memory in volatility, using the idea of fractional difference. A process is said to have long memory if its autocorrelation function decays at a hyperbolic, instead of an exponential, rate as the lag increases. The extension to long memory in volatility study is motivated by the fact that the autocorrelation function of the squared or absolute-value series of an asset return often decays slowly, even though the return series itself has no serial correlation; see Ding, Granger, and Engle (1993). A simple long-memory stochastic volatility (LMSV) model can be written as

$$x_t = \sqrt{h_t}\varepsilon_t, \quad \sqrt{h_t} = \sigma\exp(u_t/2), \quad (1 - B)^d u_t = \eta_t, \tag{20.14}$$

where $\sigma > 0$, ε_t's are iid $N(0, 1)$, η_t's are iid $N(0, \sigma_\eta^2)$ and independent of ε_t, and $0 < d < 0.5$. For such a model, we have

$$\ln (x_t^2) = \ln (\sigma^2) + u_t + \ln (\varepsilon_t^2)$$
$$= [\ln (\sigma^2) + E(\ln \varepsilon_t^2)] + u_t + [\ln (\varepsilon_t^2) - E(\ln \varepsilon_t^2)]$$
$$\equiv \mu + u_t + e_t.$$

Thus, the $\ln (x_t^2)$ series is a Gaussian long-memory signal plus a non-Gaussian white noise; see Breidt, Crato, and de Lima (1998). For applications, Ray and Tsay (2000) study common long-memory components in daily stock volatilities of groups of companies classified by various characteristics. They found that companies in the same industrial or business sector tend to have more common long-memory components; for example, big U.S. national banks and financial institutions.

In addition to applications in pricing options, volatility models are also useful in interval forecasts. These models can be used to predict the conditional variances of forecast errors and hence to construct interval forecasts. In applications where conditional heteroskedasticity is present, for example analysis of financial time series, such interval forecasts should fare better than those based on the unconditional variances of forecast errors. Chapter 22 by Mills in this volume discusses forecasting financial variables.

20.2.2.   Models with nonlinear conditional mean

Turn to nonlinear models that are developed by generalizing the conditional mean equation in (20.2). There are many such models some of which can be found in Tong (1990). Our goal here is to introduce some of the models that are commonly used in the literature.

BILINEAR MODEL

Using Taylor series expansion, linear models are simply the first-order approximations to equation (20.2). A natural extension is then to employ the second-order terms in the expansion to improve model approximation. This is the basic idea of bilinear models, which can be defined as

$$x_t = c + \sum_{i=1}^{p} \phi_i x_{t-i} - \sum_{j=1}^{q} \theta_j a_{t-j} + \sum_{i=1}^{r} \sum_{j=1}^{s} \beta_{ij} x_{t-i} a_{t-j} + a_t, \qquad (20.15)$$

where p, q, r, and s are nonnegative integers. This model was introduced by Granger and Andersen (1978) and has been widely investigated. Subba Rao and Gabr (1984) discuss properties and some applications of the model, and Liu and Brockwell (1988) study general bilinear models. Properties of bilinear models such as stationarity conditions are often derived by (a) putting the model in a state-space form and (b) using the state transition equation to express the state as a product of past innovations and random coefficient vectors.

THRESHOLD AUTOREGRESSIVE (TAR) MODEL

This model is motivated by several nonlinear characteristics commonly observed in practice, such as asymmetry in declining and rising patterns of a process. It uses piecewise linear models to obtain a better approximation of the conditional mean equation. However, unlike the traditional piecewise linear model that allows for model changes to occur in the "time" space, the TAR model uses threshold space to improve linear approximation. A time series x_t is said to follow a k-regime self-exciting TAR (SETAR) model with threshold variable x_{t-d} if it satisfies

$$(1 - \phi_1^{(j)}B - \ldots - \phi_p^{(j)}B^p)x_t = c^{(j)} + a_t^{(j)}, \quad \text{if } r_{j-1} \leq x_{t-d} < r_j, \quad j = 1, \ldots, k, \quad (20.16)$$

where k and d are positive integers, the r_i's are real numbers such that $-\infty = r_0 < r_1 < \ldots < r_{k-1} < r_k = \infty$, the superscript (j) is used to denote parameters in the jth regime, and $\{a_t^{(j)}\}$ are iid sequences with mean 0 and variance σ_j^2 and are mutually independent for different j. The parameter d is referred to as the delay parameter, and r_j's as thresholds. Here it is understood that at least one of the parameters is different for different regimes; otherwise, the number of regimes can be reduced. Equation (20.16) says that a SETAR model is a piecewise linear AR model in the threshold space. Thus, it is similar to the usual piecewise linear models available in regression analysis. The latter, however, is piecewise linear in time. The SETAR model is nonlinear provided that $k > 1$.

To appreciate the contributions of SETAR models, let us consider a simple two-regime AR(1) model:

$$r_t = \begin{cases} -1.5x_{t-1} + a_t & \text{if } x_{t-1} < 0, \\ 0.5x_{t-1} + a_t & \text{if } x_{t-1} \geq 0, \end{cases} \quad (20.17)$$

where a_t's are iid $N(0, 1)$. Figure 20.1 shows the time plot of a simulated series of x_t with 200 observations. A horizontal line of zero is added to the plot, which illustrates several characteristics of SETAR models. First, despite the coefficient -1.5 in the first regime, the process x_t is geometrically ergodic and stationary. In fact, the necessary and sufficient condition for model (20.17) to be geometrically ergodic is $\phi_1^{(1)} < 1$, $\phi_1^{(2)} < 1$ and $\phi_1^{(1)}\phi_1^{(2)} < 1$; see Petruccelli and Woolford (1984) and Chen and Tsay (1991). Second, the series exhibits asymmetric increasing and decreasing patterns. If x_{t-1} is negative, then x_t tends to switch to a positive value due to the negative and explosive coefficient -1.5. On the other hand, when x_{t-1} is positive, it tends to take multiple time indices for x_t to reduce to a negative value. Consequently, the time plot of x_t shows that regime 2 has more observations than regime 1 and the series contains large upward jumps when it becomes negative. The series is therefore not time-reversible. Third, the model contains no constant terms, but $E(x_t)$ is not zero. The sample mean of the particular realization is 0.705 with a standard deviation 0.081. In fact, $E(x_t)$ is a weighted average of the conditional means of the two regimes, which are nonzero. The weight for each regime is simply the probability that x_t is in that regime under its stationary distribution. It is also clear from the discussion that for a SETAR model to have zero mean, nonzero constant terms in some of the regimes are needed. This is very different from a stationary linear model, for which a nonzero constant implies nonzero mean for the series.

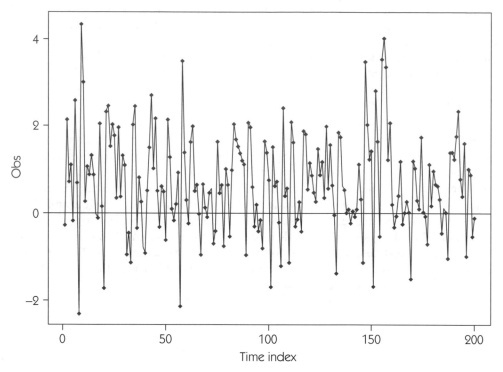

Figure 20.1   Time plot of a simulated two-regime TAR(1) series

Properties of general SETAR models are hard to obtain, but some of them can be found in Tong (1990), Chan (1993), Chan and Tsay (1998), and the references therein. In recent years, there is increasing interest in TAR models and their applications: see, for instance, Hansen (1997), Tsay (1998) and Montgomery, Zarnowitz, Tsay, and Tiao (1998). A testing and modeling procedure for univariate SETAR models is proposed in Tsay (1989).

The SETAR model in (20.16) can be generalized by using a threshold variable z_t that is measurable with respect to F_{t-1}. The main requirements are that z_t is stationary with a continuous distribution function over a compact subset of the real line and that z_{t-d} is known at time t. Such a generalized model is referred to as an open-loop TAR model.

SMOOTH TRANSITION AR (STAR) MODEL

A criticism of the SETAR model is that its conditional mean equation is not continuous. The thresholds r_j's are the discontinuity points of the conditional mean function μ_t. In response to this criticism, smooth TAR models have been proposed; see Chan and Tong (1986) and Teräsvirta (1994), and the references therein. Chapter 21 by Lundbergh and Teräsvirta in this volume provides a review. A time series x_t is said to follow a two-regime STAR(p) model if it satisfies

$$x_t = c_0 + \sum_{i=1}^{p} \phi_{0,i} x_{t-i} + F\left(\frac{x_{t-d} - r}{s}\right)\left(c_1 + \sum_{i=1}^{p} \phi_{1,i} x_{t-i}\right) + a_t, \tag{20.18}$$

where d is the delay parameter, r and s are parameters representing the location and scale parameters of model transition, and $F(.)$ is a smooth transition function. In practice, $F(.)$ often assumes one of the three forms, namely logistic, exponential, or a cumulative distribution function. From equation (20.18), the conditional mean of a STAR model is a weighted linear combination between the following two equations:

$$\mu_{1t} = c_0 + \sum_{i=1}^{p} \phi_{0,i} x_{t-i},$$

$$\mu_{2t} = (c_0 + c_1) + \sum_{i=1}^{p} (\phi_{0,i} + \phi_{1,i}) x_{t-i}.$$

The weights are determined in a continuous manner by $F(\frac{x_{t-d} - r}{s})$. The above two equations also determine the properties of a STAR model. For instance, a prerequisite for the stationarity of a STAR model is that all zeros of both AR polynomials are outside the unit circle. An advantage of the STAR model is that the conditional mean function is differentiable. However, empirical experience shows that the STAR models are hard to estimate. In particular, most empirical studies show that standard errors of estimates of r and s are often large, resulting in t-ratios for estimates of r and s about 1.0; see Teräsvirta (1994). This uncertainty leads to complications in interpreting an estimated STAR model, but see chapter 21 by Lundbergh and Teräsvirta in this volume.

MARKOV SWITCHING MODEL

Using ideas similar to TAR models, but emphasizing aperiodic transition between various states of an economy, Hamilton (1989) proposes the Markov switching autoregressive (MSA) model. Here the transition is driven by a hidden two-state Markov chain. A time series x_t follows a MSA model if it satisfies

$$x_t = \begin{cases} c_1 + \sum_{i=1}^{p} \phi_{1,i} x_{t-i} + a_{1t} & \text{if } s_t = 1, \\ c_2 + \sum_{i=1}^{p} \phi_{2,i} x_{t-i} + a_{2t} & \text{if } s_t = 2, \end{cases} \tag{20.19}$$

where s_t assumes values in $\{1, 2\}$ and is a first-order Markov chain with transition probabilities

$$P(s_t = 2 \mid s_{t-1} = 1) = w_1, \ P(s_t = 1 \mid s_{t-1} = 2) = w_2.$$

The innovation series $\{a_{1t}\}$ and $\{a_{2t}\}$ are sequences of iid random variables with mean zero and finite variance and are independent of each other. A small w_i means that the model tends to stay longer in state i.

From the definition, a MSA model uses a hidden Markov chain to govern the transition from one conditional mean function to another. This is different from that of a SETAR model, for which the transition is determined by a particular lagged variable. Consequently, a SETAR model uses a deterministic scheme to govern the model transition, whereas a MSA model uses a stochastic scheme. In practice, this implies that one is never certain about which state x_t belongs to in a MSA model. On the other hand, as long as x_{t-d} is observed, the regime of x_t is known in a SETAR model. This difference has important practical implications in forecasting. For instance, forecasts of a MSA model are always a linear combination of forecasts produced by submodels of individual states. But those of a SETAR model only come from a single regime provided that x_{t-d} is observed. The forecasts of a SETAR model also become a linear combination of forecasts obtained from individual regimes when the forecast horizon exceeds d. In applications, MSA models are often estimated using the EM algorithm (Hamilton, 1989). McCulloch and Tsay (1994) consider a Markov Chain Monte Carlo (MCMC) method to estimate a general MSA model.

McCulloch and Tsay (1993) generalize the MSA model in (20.19) by letting the transition probabilities w_1 and w_2 be logistic (or probit) functions of some explanatory variables available at time $t - 1$. Chen, McCulloch, and Tsay (1997) uses the idea of Markov switching as a tool to perform model comparison and selection between nonnested nonlinear time-series models; for example, comparing bilinear and SETAR models. Each competing model is represented by a state. This approach to model selection is a generalization of the odds-ratio commonly used in Bayesian analysis.

FUNCTIONAL COEFFICIENT AR MODEL

Recent advances in nonparametric techniques enable researchers to relax parametric constraints in proposing nonlinear models. In some cases, nonparametric methods are used in a preliminary study to help select a parametric nonlinear model. This is the approach taken by Chen and Tsay (1993a) in proposing the functional-coefficient autoregressive (FAR) model that can be written as

$$x_t = f_1(X_{t-1})x_{t-1} + \ldots + f_p(X_{t-1})x_{t-p} + a_t, \tag{20.20}$$

where $X_{t-1} = (x_{t-1}, \ldots, x_{t-k})'$ is a vector of lagged values of x_t. If necessary, one can further include other explanatory variables that are available at time $t - 1$ into X_{t-1}. The functions $f_i(.)$ of (20.20) are assumed to be continuous (even twice differentiable) almost surely with respect to their arguments. Most of the nonlinear models discussed before are special cases of the FAR model.

In applications, one can use nonparametric methods such as kernel regression or local linear regression to estimate the functional coefficients $f_i(.)$, especially when the dimension of X_{t-1} is low; for example, X_{t-1} is a scalar. Cai, Fan, and Yao (1999) use a local linear regression method to estimate $f_i(.)$ and show that substantial improvements in one-step-ahead forecasts can be achieved by using FAR models.

NONLINEAR ADDITIVE AR MODEL

A major difficulty in applying nonparametric methods to nonlinear time-series analysis is the "curse of dimensionality." Consider a general nonlinear AR(p) process $x_t = f(x_{t-1}, \ldots, x_{t-p}) + a_t$. A direct application of nonparametric methods to estimate $f(.)$ would require p-dimensional smoothing, which is hard to do when p is large, especially if the number of data points is not large. A simple, yet effective way to overcome this difficulty is to entertain an additive model that only requires lower-dimensional smoothing. A time series x_t follows a nonlinear additive AR (NAAR) model if

$$x_t = f_0(t) + \sum_{i=1}^{p} f_i(x_{t-i}) + a_t, \qquad (20.21)$$

where $f_i(\cdot)$s are continuous functions almost surely. Because each function $f_i(.)$ has a single argument, it can be estimated nonparametrically using one-dimensional smoothing techniques and, hence, avoids the curse of dimensionality. In applications, an iterative estimation method, that estimates $f_i(.)$ nonparametrically conditioned on estimates of $f_j(.)$ for all $j \neq i$, is used to estimate a NAAR model. See Chen and Tsay (1993b) for further details and examples of NAAR models.

The additivity assumption is rather restrictive and needs to be examined carefully in application. Chen, Liu, and Tsay (1995) consider test statistics for checking the additivity assumption.

NONLINEAR STATE-SPACE MODEL

Making using of recent advances in MCMC methods (Gelfand and Smith, 1987), Carlin, Polson, and Stoffer (1992) propose a Monte Carlo approach to nonlinear state-space modeling. The model considered is

$$S_t = f_t(S_{t-1}) + u_t, \; x_t = g_t(S_t) + v_t, \qquad (20.22)$$

where S_t is the state vector, $f_t(.)$ and $g_t(.)$ are known functions depending on some unknown parameters, $\{u_t\}$ is a sequence of iid multivariate random vectors with mean zero and nonnegative definite covariance matrix Σ_u, $\{v_t\}$ is a sequence of iid random variables with mean zero and variance σ_v^2, and $\{u_t\}$ is independent of $\{v_t\}$. Monte Carlo techniques are employed to handle the nonlinear evolution of the state transition equation, because the whole conditional distribution function of S_t given S_{t-1} is needed for a nonlinear system. Other numerical smoothing methods for nonlinear time series analysis have been considered by Kitagawa (1998) and the references therein.

MCMC methods (or computing-intensive numerical methods) are powerful tools for nonlinear time-series analysis. Their potential has not been fully explored. However, the assumption of knowing $f_t(.)$ and $g_t(.)$ in model (20.22) may hinder practical use of the proposed method. A possible solution to overcome this limitation is to use nonparametric methods such as the analyses considered in FAR and NAAR models to specify $f_i(.)$ and $g_i(.)$ before using nonlinear state-space models.

20.3. NONLINEARITY TESTS

In this section, we discuss some nonlinearity tests available in the literature that have decent power against the nonlinear models considered in section 20.2. The tests discussed include both parametric and nonparametric statistics. The Ljung–Box statistics of squared residuals, the bispectral test, and the BDS test belong to nonparametric methods. The RESET test (Ramsey 1969), the F-tests (Tsay 1986; Tsay 1989), and other Lagrange multiplier and likelihood ratio tests depend on parametric functions. Because nonlinearity may occur in so many ways, there exists no single test that dominates others in detecting nonlinearity.

For a time series y_t, either an observed series or a residual series, with data points $\{y_t\}_{t=1}^n$, define the lag-ℓ sample autocorrelation function as

$$\hat{\rho}_\ell(y_t) = \frac{\sum_{t=\ell+1}^n(y_t - \bar{y})(y_{t-\ell} - \bar{y})}{\sum_{i=1}^n(y_t - \bar{y})^2},$$

where $\bar{y} = \sum_{t=1}^n y_t/n$ is the sample mean of y_t.

20.3.1. Nonparametric tests

Some of the nonlinearity tests are designed to check for possible violation in quadratic forms of the underlying time series. Under the null hypothesis of linearity, the residuals of a properly specified linear model should be independent. Any violation of independence in residuals indicates inadequacy of the entertained model, including the linearity assumption. This is the basic idea behind various nonlinearity tests. We review some of these tests and discuss their strengths and weaknesses.

Q-STATISTIC OF SQUARED RESIDUALS

McLeod and Li (1983) apply the Ljung–Box statistics to the squared residuals of an ARMA(p, q) model to check for model inadequacy. The test statistic is

$$Q(m) = n(n + 2) \sum_{i=1}^m \frac{\hat{\rho}_i^2(r_t^2)}{n - i}, \tag{20.23}$$

where m is a properly chosen number of autocorrelations used in the test and r_t denotes the residual series. If the entertained linear model is adequate, $Q(m)$ is asymptotically a chi-square random variable with $m - p - q$ degrees of freedom. The Q-statistics are available in many time-series packages. They are particularly useful in detecting conditional heteroskedasticity of x_t. In fact, the Lagrange multiplier test statistic of Engle (1982) for ARCH models is closely related to the Q-statistics. In essence, Engle considers the linear regression

$$r_t^2 = \beta_0 + \sum_{i=1}^{m} \beta_i r_{t-i}^2 + e_t, \quad t = m + 1, \ldots, n,$$

where r_t is a residual series of x_t, e_t denotes the error term, and the null hypothesis is $H_o : \beta_1 = \ldots = \beta_m = 0$. The test statistic is then the usual F-ratio in linear regression analysis. Under the assumption of no conditional heteroskedasticity, the F-ratio follows an F-distribution with degrees of freedom m and $n - 2m - 1$. Asymptotically, this F-statistic has a chi-square distribution with m degrees of freedom.

BISPECTRAL TEST

This test can be used to test for linearity as well as Gaussianity. It depends on the result that a properly normalized bispectrum of a linear time series is constant over all frequencies and that the constant is zero under normality. Details of the test can be found in Priestley (1988) and Hinich (1982). Limited experience shows that the bispectral test has decent power when the sample size is large.

BDS STATISTIC

Brock, Dechert, and Scheinkman (1987) propose a test statistic, commonly referred to as the BDS test, to detect the iid assumption of a time series. The statistic is, therefore, different from other test statistics discussed, because the latter mainly focus on either the second- or third-order properties of x_t. The basic idea of the BDS test is to make use of "correlation integral" popular in chaotic time-series analysis. Interested readers are referred to Hsieh (1989) and Brock, Hsieh, and Lebaron (1991) for theory and applications of the BDS test.

20.3.2. Parametric tests

Turning to parametric tests, we consider the RESET test of Ramsey (1969) and its generalizations. We also discuss some test statistics for detecting threshold nonlinearity.

THE RESET TEST

Ramsey (1969) proposes a specification test for linear least squares regression analysis. The test is referred to as a RESET test and is readily applicable to linear AR models. Consider the linear AR(p) model

$$x_t = X_{t-1}' \phi + a_t, \tag{20.24}$$

where $X_{t-1} = (1, x_{t-1}, \ldots, x_{t-p})'$. The first step of the RESET test is to obtain the least squares estimate $\hat{\phi}$ of (20.24), compute the fit $\hat{x}_t = X_{t-1}' \hat{\phi}$, the residual $\hat{a}_t = x_t - \hat{x}_t$, and the sum of squared residuals $SSR_0 = \sum_{t=p+1}^{n} \hat{a}_t^2$, where n is the sample size. In the second step, consider the linear regression

$$\hat{a}_t = X'_{t-1}\alpha_1 + M'_{t-1}\alpha_2 + v_t, \tag{20.25}$$

where $M_{t-1} = (\hat{x}_t^2, \ldots, \hat{x}_t^{s+1})'$ for some $s \geq 1$, and compute the least squares residuals $\hat{v}_t = \hat{a}_t - X'_{t-1}\hat{\alpha}_1 - M'_{t-1}\hat{\alpha}_2$ and the sum of squared residuals $SSR_1 = \sum_{t=p+1}^{n}\hat{v}_t^2$. Because $\hat{x}_t^k$ for $k = 2, \ldots, s + 1$ tend to be highly correlated with X_{t-1} and among themselves, principal components of $\hat{x}_t^k$ that are not collinear with X_{t-1} are often used in this step. In any case, the basic idea of the RESET test is that if the linear AR(p) model in (20.24) is adequate, then α_1 and α_2 of equation (20.25) should be zero. This can be tested by the usual F-statistic of equation (20.25), given by

$$F = \frac{(SSR_0 - SSR_1)/g}{SSR_1/(n - p - g)} \quad \text{with} \quad g = s + p + 1 \tag{20.26}$$

which, under the linearity assumption, has an F-distribution with degrees of freedom g and $n - p - g$.

Kennan (1985) proposes a nonlinearity test that uses $\hat{x}_t^2$ only and modifies the second step to avoid multicollinearity between $\hat{x}_t^2$ and X_{t-1}. Specifically, the linear regression (20.25) is divided into two steps. In step 2(a), one removes linear dependence of $\hat{x}_t^2$ on X_{t-1} by fitting the regression

$$\hat{x}_t^2 = X'_{t-1}\beta + u_t$$

and obtaining the residual $\hat{u}_t = \hat{x}_t^2 - X_{t-1}\hat{\beta}$. In step 2(b), consider the linear regression

$$\hat{a}_t = \hat{u}_t\alpha + v_t,$$

and obtain the sum of squared residuals $SSR_1 = \sum_{t=p+1}^{n}(\hat{a}_t - \hat{u}_t\hat{\alpha})^2 = \sum_{t=p+1}^{n}\hat{v}_t^2$ to test the null hypothesis $\alpha = 0$.

TSAY'S TEST

To improve the power of Kennan's and RESET tests, Tsay (1986) uses a different choice of the regressor M_{t-1}. Specifically, he suggests using $M_{t-1} = vech(X_{t-1}X'_{t-1})$, where $vech$ denotes a half-stacking vector of the matrix $X_{t-1}X'_{t-1}$ using elements on and below the diagonal only. The dimension of M_{t-1} is then $p(p + 1)/2$. In practice, the test is simply the usual partial F-statistic for testing $\alpha = 0$ in the linear least squares regression

$$x_t = X'_{t-1}\phi + M'_{t-1}\alpha + e_t,$$

where e_t denotes the error term. Under the linearity assumption, the partial F-statistic follows a F-distribution with degrees of freedom g and $n - p - g - 1$, where $g = p(p + 1)/2$. Luukkonen, Saikkonen, and Teräsvirta (1988) further extend the test by augmenting M_{t-1} with cubic terms x_{t-i}^3 for $i = 1, \ldots, p$.

THRESHOLD TEST

When the alternative model under study is a SETAR model, one can derive specific test statistics to increase detecting power. One of the specific tests is the likelihood ratio statistic. This test, however, encounters the difficulty of undefined parameters under the null hypothesis of linearity. Another specific test seeks to transform testing threshold nonlinearity into detecting model changes. It is then interesting to discuss the differences between these two specific tests.

To simplify the discussion, let us consider the simple case that the alternative is a two-regime SETAR model with given threshold variable x_{t-d}. The null hypothesis is H_o: x_t follows the linear AR(p) model

$$x_t = \phi_0 + \sum_{i=1}^{p} \phi_i x_{t-i} + a_t,$$ (20.27)

whereas the alternative hypothesis is H_a: x_t follows the SETAR model

$$x_t = \begin{cases} \phi_0^{(1)} + \sum_{i=1}^{P} \phi_i^{(1)} x_{t-i} + a_{1t} & \text{if } x_{t-d} < r_1, \\ \phi_0^{(2)} + \sum_{i=1}^{P} \phi_i^{(2)} x_{t-i} + a_{2t} & \text{if } x_{t-d} \geq r_1, \end{cases}$$ (20.28)

where r_1 is the threshold. For a given realization $\{x_t\}_{t=1}^{n}$ and assuming normality, let $l_0(\hat{\phi}, \hat{\sigma}_a^2)$ be the log-likelihood function evaluated at the maximum likelihood estimates of $\phi = (\phi_0, \ldots, \phi_p)'$ and σ_a^2. This is easy to compute. The likelihood function under the alternative is also easy to compute if the threshold r_1 is given. Let $l_1(r_1; \hat{\phi}_1, \hat{\sigma}_1^2; \hat{\phi}_2, \hat{\sigma}_2^2)$ be the log-likelihood function evaluated at the maximum likelihood estimates of $\phi_i = (\phi_0^{(i)}, \ldots, \phi_p^{(i)})'$ and σ_i^2, conditioned on knowing the threshold r_1. The log-likelihood ratio $l(r_1)$ defined as

$$l(r_1) = l_1(r_1; \hat{\phi}_1, \hat{\sigma}_1^2; \hat{\phi}_2, \hat{\sigma}_2^2) - l_0(\hat{\phi}, \hat{\sigma}_a^2),$$

is then a function of the threshold r_1, which is unknown. Furthermore, under the null hypothesis, there is no threshold and r_1 is not defined. For this reason, the asymptotic distribution of the likelihood ratio is rather different from that of the usual test. See Chan (1991) for critical values of the test. A common approach is to use $l_{max} = \sup_{v < r_1 < u} l(r_1)$ as the test statistic, where v and u are pre-specified lower and upper bounds of the threshold. See Davis (1987) and Andrews and Ploberger (1994) for further discussion on hypothesis testing involving a undefined parameter under the null hypothesis. Simulation is often used to obtain empirical critical values of the test statistic l_{max}, which depends on the choices of v and u. An average of $l(r_1)$ over $r_1 \in [v, u]$ is also considered by Andrews and Ploberger as a test statistic.

Tsay (1989) makes use of arranged autoregression and recursive estimation to derive an alternative test for threshold nonlinearity. The arranged autoregression seeks to transfer the SETAR model in the alternative hypothesis H_a into a model change problem with the threshold r_1 serving as the change point. To see this, the

SETAR model in (20.28) says that x_t follows essentially two linear models depending on whether $x_{t-d} < r_1$ or $x_{t-d} \geq r_1$. For a realization $\{x_t\}_{t=1}^{n}$, x_{t-d} can assume values $\{x_1, \ldots, x_{n-d}\}$. Let $x_{(1)} \leq x_{(2)} \leq \ldots \leq x_{(n-d)}$ be the ordered statistics of $\{x_t\}_{t=1}^{n-d}$. The SETAR model can then be written as

$$x_{(j)+d} = \beta_0 + \sum_{i=1}^{p} \beta_i x_{(j)+d-i} + a_{(j)+d}, \quad j = 1, \ldots, n - d, \qquad (20.29)$$

where $\beta_i = \phi_i^{(1)}$ if $x_{(j)} < r_1$ and $\beta_i = \phi_i^{(2)}$ if $x_{(j)} \geq r_1$. Consequently, the threshold r_1 is a change point for the linear regression in (20.29), and we refer to equation (20.29) as an arranged autoregression (in increasing order of the threshold x_{t-d}).

Note that the arranged autoregression in (20.29) does not alter the dynamic dependence of x_t on x_{t-i} for $i = 1, \ldots, p$, because $x_{(j)+d}$ still depends on $x_{(j)+d-i}$ for $i = 1, \ldots, p$. What is done is simply to present the SETAR model in the threshold space instead of in the time space. That is, the equation with a smaller x_{t-d} appears before that with a larger x_{t-d}.

The threshold test of Tsay (1989) is obtained as follows:

- Step 1: Fit the equation (20.29) using $j = 1, \ldots, m$, where m is a pre-specified positive integer; for example, 30. Denote the least squares estimates of β_i by $\hat{\beta}_{i,m}$, where m denotes the number of data points used in estimation.
- Step 2: Compute the predictive residual

$$\hat{a}_{(m+1)+d} = x_{(m+1)+d} - \hat{\beta}_{0,m} - \sum_{i=1}^{p} \hat{\beta}_{i,m} x_{(m+1)+d-i}$$

and its standard error. Let $\hat{e}_{(m+1)+d}$ be the standardized predictive residual.
- Step 3: Use the recursive least squares method to update the least squares estimates to $\hat{\beta}_{i,m+1}$ by incorporating the new data point $x_{(m+1)+d}$.
- Step 4: Repeat steps 2 and 3 until all data points are processed.
- Step 5: Consider the linear regression of the standardized predictive residual

$$\hat{e}_{(m+j)+d} = \alpha_0 + \sum_{i=1}^{p} \alpha_i x_{(m+j)+d-i} + v_t, \quad j = 1, \ldots, n - d - m \qquad (20.30)$$

and compute the usual F-statistic for testing $\alpha_i = 0$ in (20.30) for $i = 0, \ldots, p$. Under the null hypothesis that x_t follows a linear AR(p) model, the F-ratio has a limiting F-distribution with degrees of freedom $p + 1$ and $n - d - m - p$.

We refer to the above F-test test as a TAR test. The idea behind the test is that under the null hypothesis there is no model change in the arranged autoregression in (20.29), so that the standardized predictive residuals should be close to iid with mean zero and variance 1. In this case, they should have no correlations with the regressors $x_{(m+j)+d-i}$. For further details including formulae for a recursive least squares method and a simulation study on the performance of the TAR test, see Tsay (1989).

The above F-test avoids the problem of nuisance parameters encountered by the likelihood ratio test. It does not require knowing the threshold r_1. In fact, it does not depend on knowing that there is only a single threshold in the model. On the other hand, the F-test is not as powerful as the likelihood ratio test if the model is indeed a two-regime SETAR model with a known innovation distribution.

20.4. MODELING

Nonlinear time-series modeling necessarily involves subjective judgment. However, there are some general guidelines to follow. It starts with building an adequate linear model on which nonlinearity tests are based. For financial time series, the Ljung–Box statistics and Engle's test are commonly used to detect conditional heteroskedasticity. For general series, other tests of section 20.3 apply. If nonlinearity is statistically significant, then one chooses a class of nonlinear models to entertain. The selection here may depend on the experience of the analyst and the substantive matter of the problem under study.

For volatility models, the order of an ARCH process can often be determined by checking the partial autocorrelation function of the squared series. For GARCH and EGARCH models, only lower orders such as (1, 1), (1, 2) and (2, 1) are considered in most applications. Higher-order models are hard to estimate and understand. For TAR models, one may use the procedures given in Tong (1990) and Tsay (1989, 1998) to build an adequate model. When the sample size is sufficiently large, one may apply nonparametric techniques to explore the nonlinear feature of the data and choose a proper nonlinear model accordingly (see Chen and Tsay, 1991; Cai, Fan, and Yao, 1999). The MARS procedure of Lewis and Stevens (1991) can also be used to explore the dynamic structure of the data.

Finally, information criteria such as Akaike information criterion (Akaike, 1974) and the generalized odd-ratios in Chen, McCulloch, and Tsay (1997) can be used to discriminate between competing nonlinear models. The chosen model should be carefully checked before it is used for prediction.

20.5. FORECASTING

Unlike the linear model, in many cases there exist no closed-form formulae to compute forecasts of nonlinear models when the forecast horizon is greater than 1. Thus, we use parametric bootstraps to compute nonlinear forecasts. Here it is understood that the model used in forecasting has been rigorously checked and is judged to be adequate for the series under study. By a model, we mean the dynamic structure and innovational distributions. In some cases, we may treat the estimated parameters as given.

20.5.1. Parametric bootstrap

Let T be the forecast origin and ℓ be the forecast horizon ($\ell > 0$). That is, we are at time index T and interested in forecasting $x_{T+\ell}$. The parametric bootstrap considered computes realizations $x_{T+1}, \ldots, X_{T+\ell}$ sequentially by (a) drawing a new innovation from the proper innovation distribution of the model and (b) computing x_{T+i} using the model, the data, and previous forecasts $x_{T+1}, \ldots, x_{T+i-1}$. This results in a realization for $x_{T+\ell}$. The procedure is repeated M times to obtain M realizations of $x_{T+\ell}$ denoted by $\{x_{T+\ell}^{(j)}\}_{j=1}^{M}$. The point forecast of $x_{T+\ell}$ is then the sample average of $x_{T+\ell}^{(j)}$. Let the forecast be $x_T(\ell)$. We used $M = 3,000$ in some applications and the results seem fine.

The realizations $\{x_{T+\ell}^{(j)}\}_{j=1}^{M}$ can also be used to obtain an empirical distribution of $x_{T+\ell}$. We shall make use of this empirical distribution later to evaluate forecasting performance.

20.5.2. Forecasting evaluation

There are many ways to evaluate the forecasting performance of a model, ranging from directional measures through magnitude measures to distributional measures. A directional measure considers the future direction (up or down) implied by the model. Predicting that tomorrow's S&P 500 index will go up or down is an example of directional forecasts that are of practical interest. Predicting the year-end value of the daily S&P 500 index belongs to the case of magnitude measure. Finally, assessing the likelihood that the daily S&P 500 index will go up 10 percent or more between now and the year end requires knowing the future conditional probability distribution of the index. Evaluating the accuracy of such an assessment needs a distributional measure.

In practice, the available data set is divided into two subsamples. The first subsample of the data is used to build a nonlinear model and the second subsample is used to evaluate the forecasting performance of the model. We refer to the two subsamples of data as estimation and forecasting subsamples. In some studies, a rolling forecasting procedure is used in which a new data point is moved from the forecasting subsample into the estimation subsample as the forecast origin advances. In what follows, we briefly discuss some measures of forecasting performance that are commonly used in the literature. Keep in mind, however, that there exists no widely accepted single measure to compare models. A utility function based on the objective of the forecast might be needed in order to better understand the comparison.

DIRECTIONAL MEASURE

A typical measure here is to use a 2×2 contingency table that summarizes the numbers of "hits" and "misses" of the model in predicting ups and downs of $x_{T+\ell}$ in the forecasting subsample. Specifically, the contingency table is given as

Actual	Predicted		
	up	down	
up	m_{11}	m_{12}	m_{10}
down	m_{21}	m_{22}	m_{20}
	m_{01}	m_{02}	m

where m is the total number of ℓ-step-ahead forecasts in the forecasting subsample, m_{11} is the number of "hits" in predicting upward movements, m_{21} is the number of "misses" in predicting downward movements, etc. Larger values in m_{11} and m_{22} indicate better forecasts. The test statistic

$$\chi^2 = \sum_{i=1}^{2} \sum_{j=1}^{2} \frac{\left(m_{ij} - \frac{m_{i0} m_{0j}}{m} \right)^2}{\frac{m_{i0} m_{0i}}{m}}$$

can then be used to evaluate the performance of the model. Under some mild conditions, χ^2 has an asymptotic chi-square distribution with one degree of freedom. For further discussion of this measure, see Dahl and Hylleberg (1999).

MAGNITUDE MEASURE

Three statistics are commonly used to measure the performance of point forecasts. They are the mean squared error (MSE), mean absolute deviation (MAD), and mean absolute percentage error (MAPE). For ℓ-step-ahead forecasts, these measures are defined as

$$MSE(\ell) = \frac{1}{m} \sum_{j=0}^{m-1} [x_{T+\ell+j} - x_{T+j}(\ell)]^2, \tag{20.31}$$

$$MAD(\ell) = \frac{1}{m} \sum_{j=0}^{m-1} |x_{T+\ell+j} - x_{T+j}(\ell)|, \tag{20.32}$$

$$MAPE(\ell) = \frac{1}{m} \sum_{j=0}^{m-1} \left| \frac{x_{T+j}(\ell)}{x_{T+j+\ell}} - 1 \right|, \tag{20.33}$$

where m is the number of ℓ-step-ahead forecasts available in the forecasting subsample. In applications, one often chooses one of the above three measures and the model with the smallest magnitude on that measure is regarded as the best ℓ-step-ahead forecasting model. It is possible that different ℓ may result in selecting different models. The measures also have other limitations in model comparison: see, for instance, Clements and Hendry (1993).

DISTRIBUTIONAL MEASURE

Practitioners recently began to assess forecasting performance of a model using its predictive distributions. Strictly speaking, predictive distributions incorporate parameter uncertainty in forecasts. We shall call it a conditional predictive distribution if the parameters are treated as fixed. The empirical distribution of $x_{T+\ell}$ obtained by the parametric bootstrap above is a conditional predictive distribution: see Dawid (1984) and Rosenblatt (1952) for more discussions. Let $u_T(\ell)$ be the percentile of the observed $x_{T+\ell}$ in the above empirical distribution. We then have a set of m percentiles $\{u_{T+j}(\ell)\}_{j=0}^{m-1}$, where again m is the number of ℓ-step-ahead forecasts in the forecasting subsample. If the model entertained is adequate, $\{u_{T+j}(\ell)\}$ should be a random sample from the uniform distribution on $[0, 1]$. For a sufficiently large m, one can compute the Kolmogorov–Smirnov statistic of $\{u_{T+j}(\ell)\}$ with respect to uniform $[0, 1]$. The statistic can be used both for model checking and for forecasting comparison.

20.6. EXAMPLES

In this section, we illustrate nonlinear time series-models by analyzing two real examples.

Example 1

Consider the quarterly U.S. civilian unemployment rate, seasonally adjusted, from 1948 to 1993. This series was analyzed in detail by Montgomery, Zarnowitz, Tsay, and Tiao (1998), which is referred to as MZTT in the sequel. We repeat some of the analyses here, especially that related to nonlinear models. Figure 20.2 shows the time plot of the data. Well-known characteristics of the series include that (a) it tends to move countercyclically with U.S. business cycles and (b) the rate rises quickly, but decays slowly. The latter characteristic suggests that the dynamic structure of the series is nonlinear.

Denote the series by x_t and define $\Delta x_t = x_t - x_{t-1}$. The linear model

$$(1 - 0.31B^4)(1 - 0.65B)\Delta x_t = (1 - 0.78B^4)a_t, \quad \hat{\sigma}_a^2 = 0.090 \qquad (20.34)$$

was built by MZTT. The standard errors of the three coefficients are 0.11, 0.06, and 0.07 respectively. This is a seasonal model even though the data were seasonally adjusted. It indicates that the seasonal adjustment procedure used did not successfully remove the seasonality. This model is used as a benchmark model for forecasting comparison.

To test for nonlinearity, we apply some of the nonlinearity tests of section 20.3 with an AR(5) model for the differenced series Δx_t. The results are given in table 20.1. All of the tests reject the linearity assumption. In fact, the linearity assumption is rejected for all AR(p) models we applied, where $p = 2, \ldots, 10$.

Using a modeling procedure similar to that of Tsay (1989), MZTT build the following TAR model for the Δx_t series:

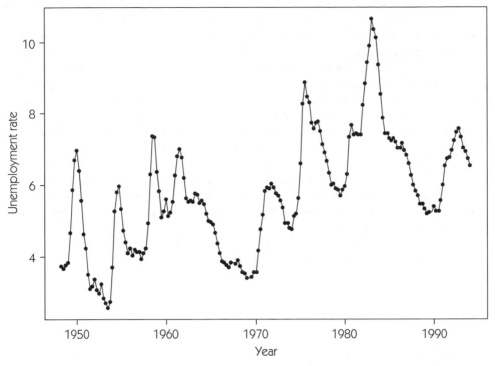

Figure 20.2 Time plot of U.S. quarterly unemployment rate
(seasonally adjusted): 1948–1993

Table 20.1 Nonlinearity test for the series of changes in U.S. quarterly unemployment rate: 1948.II–1993.IV

Type	Tsay	LST	TAR(1)	TAR(2)	TAR(3)	TAR(4)
Test	2.80	2.83	2.41	2.16	2.84	2.98
p-value	0.0007	0.0002	0.0298	0.0500	0.0121	0.0088

Note: An AR(5) model was used in the tests, where LST denotes the test of Luukkonen, et al. (1988) and TAR(d) means threshold test with delay d.

$$\Delta x_t = \begin{cases} 0.01 + 0.73\Delta x_{t-1} + 0.10\Delta x_{t-2} + a_{1t} & \text{if } \Delta x_{t-2} \leq 0.1, \\ 0.18 + 0.80\Delta x_{t-1} - 0.56\Delta x_{t-2} + a_{2t} & \text{otherwise.} \end{cases} \qquad (20.35)$$

The sample variances of a_{1t} and a_{2t} are 0.76 and 0.165 respectively, the standard errors of the three coefficients of regime 1 are 0.03, 0.10, and 0.12 respectively, and those of regime 2 are 0.09, 0.1, and 0.16. This model says that the change in the U.S. quarterly unemployment rate, Δx_t, behaves as a piecewise linear model in the reference space of $x_{t-2} - x_{t-3}$ with threshold 0.1. Intuitively, the model implies that the dynamics of unemployment act differently depending on the recent change in the unemployment rate. In the first regime, the unemployment rate has had either a decrease or a minor increase. Here the economy should be stable, and essentially the change in the rate follows a simple AR(1) model, because lag-2 coefficient is insignificant. In the second regime, there is a substantial jump in the unemployment rate (0.1 or larger). This typically corresponds to the contraction phase in the business cycle. It is also the period during which government interventions and industrial restructuring are likely to occur. Here Δx_t follows an AR(2) model with a positive constant, indicating an upward trend in x_t. The AR(2) polynomial contains two complex characteristic roots, which indicate possible cyclical behavior in Δx_t. Consequently, the chance of having a turning point in x_t increases, suggesting that the period of large increases in x_t should be short. This implies that the contraction phases in the U.S. economy tend to be shorter than the expansion phases.

Applying the MCMC method of McCulloch and Tsay (1994), MZTT obtain the Markov switching model for Δx_t:

$$\Delta x_t = \begin{cases} -0.07 + 0.38\Delta x_{t-1} - 0.05\Delta x_{t-2} + \varepsilon_{1t} & \text{if } s_t = 1, \\ 0.16 + 0.86\Delta x_{t-1} - 0.38\Delta x_{t-2} + \varepsilon_{2t} & \text{if } s_t = 2. \end{cases} \qquad (20.36)$$

The conditional means of Δx_t are -0.10 for $s_t = 1$ and 0.31 for $s_t = 2$. Thus, the first state represents the expansionary periods in the economy, and the second state represents the contractions. The sample variances of ε_{1t} and ε_{2t} are 0.031 and 0.192 respectively. The standard errors of the three parameters in state $s_t = 1$ are 0.03, 0.14, and 0.11 and those of state $s_t = 2$ are 0.04, 0.13, and 0.14 respectively. The state transition probabilities are $P(s_t = 2 \mid s_{t-1} = 1) = 0.084(0.060)$ and $P(s_t = 1 \mid s_{t-1} = 2) = 0.126(0.053)$, where the number in parentheses is the corresponding standard error. This model implies that in the second state, the unemployment rate x_t has an upward trend with an AR(2) polynomial possessing complex characteristic roots. This feature of the model is similar to the second regime of the TAR model in (20.35). In the first state, the unemployment rate x_t has a slightly decreasing trend with a much weaker autoregressive structure.

FORECASTING PERFORMANCE

A rolling procedure was used by MZTT to forecast the unemployment rate x_t. The procedure works as follows:

1   Begin with forecast origin $T = 83$, corresponding to 1968.II which was used in the literature to monitor performance of various econometric models in forecasting unemployment rate. Estimate the linear, TAR, and MSA models using the data from 1948.I to the forecast origin (inclusive).
2   Perform one-quarter- to five-quarter-ahead forecasts and compute the forecast errors of each model. Forecasts of nonlinear models used are computed by using the parametric bootstrap method of section 20.5.

Table 20.2 Out-of-sample forecast comparison between linear, TAR and MSA models for the U.S. quarterly unemployment rate

Model	Relative MSE of forecast					Mean of forecast errors				
	1-step	2-step	3-step	4-step	5-step	1-step	2-step	3-step	4-step	5-step
					(a) Overall comparison					
Linear	1.00	1.00	1.00	1.00	1.00	0.03	0.09	0.17	0.25	0.33
TAR	1.00	1.04	0.99	0.98	1.03	−0.1	−0.02	−0.03	−0.03	−0.01
MSA	1.19	1.39	1.40	1.45	1.61	0.00	−0.02	−0.04	−0.07	−0.12
MSE	0.08	0.31	0.67	1.13	1.54					
					(b) Forecast origins in economic contractions					
Linear	1.00	1.00	1.00	1.00	1.00	0.31	0.68	1.08	1.41	1.38
TAR	0.85	0.91	0.83	0.72	0.72	0.24	0.56	0.87	1.01	0.86
MSA	0.97	1.03	0.96	0.86	1.02	0.20	0.41	0.57	0.52	0.14
MSE	0.22	0.97	2.14	3.38	3.46					
					(c) Forecast origins in economic expansions					
Linear	1.00	1.00	1.00	1.00	1.00	−0.01	0.00	0.03	0.08	0.17
TAR	1.06	1.13	1.10	1.15	1.17	−0.05	−0.11	−0.17	−0.19	−0.14
MSA	1.31	1.64	1.73	1.84	1.87	−0.03	−0.08	−0.13	−0.17	−0.16
MSE	0.06	0.21	0.45	0.78	1.24					

Note: The starting forecast origin is 1968.II, where the row marked by "MSE" shows the MSE of the benchmark linear model.

3 Advance the forecast origin by one and repeat the estimation and forecasting processes until all data are employed.
4 Use MSE and mean forecast error to compare performance of the models.

Table 20.2 shows the relative MSE of forecasts and mean forecast errors for the linear model in (20.34), the TAR model in (20.35), and the MSA model in (20.36), using the linear model as a benchmark. The comparisons are based on overall performance as well as on the status of the U.S. economy at the forecast origin. From the table, we make the following observations:

1 For the overall comparison, the TAR model and the linear model are very close in MSE, but the TAR model has smaller biases. On the other hand, the MSA model has the highest MSE, but smallest biases.
2 For forecast origins in economic contractions, the TAR model shows improvements over the linear model both in MSE and bias. The MSA model also shows some improvement over the linear model, but the improvement is not as large as that of the TAR model.

3   For forecast origins in economic expansions, the linear model outperforms
    both nonlinear models.

The results suggest that the contributions of nonlinear models over linear ones in
forecasting the U.S. quarterly unemployment rate are mainly in the periods when
the U.S. economy is in contractions. This is not surprising, because as mentioned
before it is during the economic contractions that government interventions and
industrial restructuring are most likely to occur. These external events could
introduce nonlinearity in the U.S. unemployment rate. Intuitively, such improvements seem important, because it is during the contractions that people pay more
attention to economic forecasts.

Example 2

In this example, we consider the growth rate of U.S. quarterly real gross national
product (GNP) from 1947.II to 1991.I; that is,

$$x_t = \ln (X_t) - \ln (X_{t-1})$$

where X_t is the U.S. quarterly real GNP, seasonally adjusted and obtained from
Citibase database. This series was analyzed by Tiao and Tsay (1994), on which
our report is based (see also Potter, 1995). Figure 20.3 shows the time plot of the
U.S. GNP growth rate. The horizontal line denotes the zero growth rate.
    If linear models are employed, the AR(2) model

$$x_t = 0.0041 + 0.33x_{t-1} + 0.13x_{t-2} + a_t, \quad \hat{\sigma}_a = 0.00986, \tag{20.37}$$

fits the data well, where the standard errors of the parameters are 0.001, 0.075,
and 0.076 respectively. The Ljung–Box statistic of residuals gives $Q(12) = 10.1$,
indicating no serial correlation in the residuals. Using the AR(2) model, we apply
the threshold nonlinearity test to the series. The results are given in table 20.3.
The test finds significant nonlinearity when the delay is $d = 2$.
    After building a two-regime TAR model for x_t, Tiao and Tsay (1994) further
modified the model to obtain the four-regime TAR model

$$x_t = \begin{cases} -0.015 - 1.076x_{t-1} + \varepsilon_{1,t} & \text{Regime I} \\ -0.006 + 0.630x_{t-1} - 0.756x_{t-2} + \varepsilon_{2,t} & \text{Regime II} \\ 0.006 + 0.438x_{t-1} + \varepsilon_{3t} & \text{Regime III} \\ 0.004 + 0.443x_{t-1} + \varepsilon_{4t} & \text{Regime IV} \end{cases} \tag{20.38}$$

where the regimes are defined as follows:

• Regime I: $x_{t-1} \leq x_{t-2} \leq 0$. This regime denotes a recession period in which the
  economy changed from contraction to an even worse one.

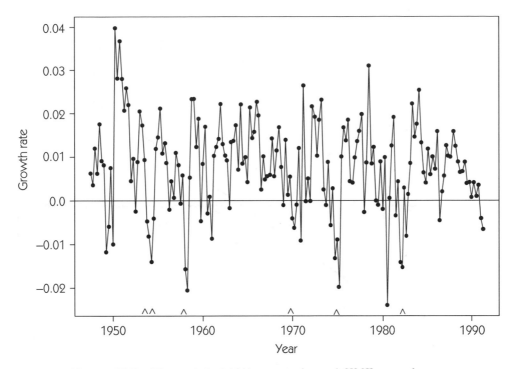

Figure 20.3 Time plot of U.S. quarterly real GNP growth rate (seasonally adjusted): 1947.II–1991.I, where a mark at the bottom denotes data points in regime 1 of a TAR model

Table 20.3 Threshold nonlinearity tests of the growth rate of the U.S. quarterly real GNP, seasonally adjusted

d	1	2	3	4	5	6
Test	0.37	3.16	2.55	2.65	1.70	1.80
p-value	0.778	0.026	0.058	0.051	0.169	0.150

- Regime II: $x_{t-1} > x_{t-2}$ but $x_{t-2} \leq 0$. Here the economy was in contraction, but improving.
- Regime III: $x_{t-1} \leq x_{t-2}$ but $x_{t-2} > 0$. This regime corresponds to a period in which the economy was reasonable, but declining.
- Regime IV: $x_{t-1} > x_{t-2} > 0$. This is an expansion period in which the economy was reasonable and became stronger.

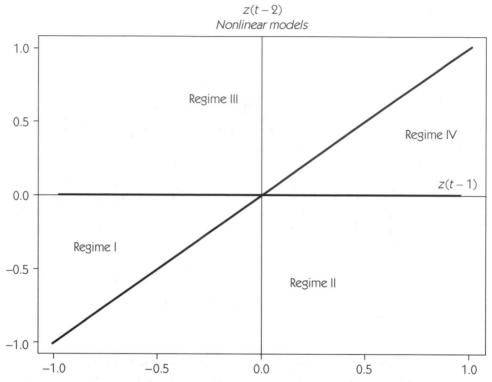

Figure 20.4   Regimes of the TAR model in (20.38) for the growth rate of
the U.S. quarterly real GNP

Figure 20.4 shows the regime classification. In model (20.38), all the parameters
have a t-ratio greater than 2.0 in modulus except for the constant terms in
regimes II and IV, for which the t-ratios are -1.35 and 1.32, respectively. The
residual standard errors of regimes I to IV are 0.0062, 0.0132, 0.0094, and 0.0082,
respectively. The numbers of data points in each regime are 6, 31, 79, and 58,
respectively. Given the history of the U.S. economy, it is not surprising to see that
regime I has only six data points. These points are marked by a "hat" on the
bottom of figure 20.3. It is of particular interest to see the negatively explosive
nature of the submodel in regime I, which indicates that the economy usually
recovers quickly from a recession period. See the marked points in figure 20.3
that exhibit a "negative-down-up" pattern for all but one occasion. Figure 20.5
shows some out-of-sample forecast comparison between the four-regime TAR
model in (20.38) and the linear model in (20.37). The comparison is divided
based on the regime of a forecast origin. The left panel of figure 20.5 is for MSE
and the right panel is for ratio of MSE. Clearly, the main contribution of nonlinear
model lies in the forecasts of regime I, where the improvements are substantial
for one- to four-quarter-ahead forecasts. This example, again, demonstrates that

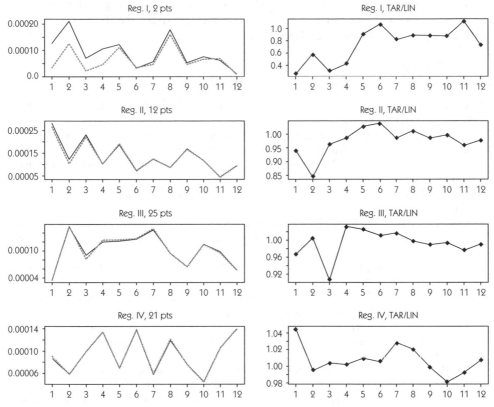

Figure 20.5 Out-of-sample forecast comparison between linear and TAR models for the growth rate of the U.S. quarterly real GNP. The left panel contains mean squared error (MSE) of forecasts and the right panel is ratio of MSE. The horizontal axis is the forecast horizon

proper use of nonlinear models can improve forecasting accuracy for some forecast origins. Clements and Smith (1997) come to similar conclusions on the gains to forecasting the U.S. GNP coming from the recession regime. Clements and Krolzig (1998) discuss extensively the forecasting performance of SETAR and MSA models for the U.S. GNP series.

20.7. CONCLUSION

In this chapter, we discussed some nonlinear models commonly used in the literature for univariate time-series analysis. Nonlinearity may occur in the conditional mean and/or the conditional variance of the series. We also reviewed some parametric and nonparametric nonlinearity tests. A parametric bootstrap method is used to obtain multi-step-ahead forecasts of nonlinear models. Finally, we discussed various criteria for evaluating the forecasting performance of a nonlinear model and demonstrated the modeling of nonlinear time series by analyzing two real examples. The nonlinear models used are found to improve forecasting accuracy under certain conditions.

References

Akaike, H. (1974). A new look at the statistical model identification. *IEEE Transactions on Automatic Control, AC-19*, 716–23.

Andrews, D.W.K. and W. Ploberger (1994). Optimal tests when a nuisance parameter is present only under the alternative. *Econometrica, 62*, 1383–1414.

Bollerslev, T. (1986). Generalized autoregressive conditional heteroskedasticity. *Journal of Econometrics, 31*, 307–27.

Bollerslev, T., R.Y. Chou, and K.F. Kroner (1992). ARCH modeling in finance. *Journal of Econometrics, 52*, 5–59.

Bollerslev, T., R.F. Engle, and D.B. Nelson (1994). ARCH models. In R.F. Engle and D. McFadden (eds.), *The Handbook of Econometrics*, Vol. 4. Amsterdem: North-Holland, 2959–3038.

Box, G.E.P., G.M. Jenkins, and G.C. Reinsel (1994). *Time Series Analysis: Forecasting and Control*, 3rd edn. Englewood Cliffs, N.J.: Prentice-Hall.

Breidt, F.J., N. Crato, and P. de Lima (1998). On the detection and estimation of long memory in stochastic volatility. *Journal of Econometrics, 83*, 325–48.

Brock, W., W.D. Dechert, and J. Scheinkman (1987). A test for independence based on the correlation dimension. Working paper, Department of Economics, University of Wisconsin, Madison.

Brock, W., D.A. Hsieh, and B. LeBaron (1991). *Nonlinear Dynamics, Chaos and Instability: Statistical Theory and Economic Evidence*. Cambridge, MA: MIT Press.

Cai, Z., J. Fan and Q. Yao (1999). Functional-coefficient regression models for nonlinear time series. Working paper, University of North Carolina, Charlotte.

Cao, C. and R.S. Tsay (1992). Nonlinear time series analysis of stock volatilities. *Journal of Applied Econometrics, 7*, s165–85.

Carlin, B.P., N.G. Polson, and D.S. Stoffer (1992). A Monte Carlo approach to nonnormal and nonlinear state apace modeling. *Journal of the American Statistical Association, 87*, 493–500.

Chan, K.S. (1991). Percentage points of likelihood ratio tests for threshold autoregression. *Journal of the Royal Statistical Society, Series B, 53*, 691–6.

Chan, K.S. (1993). Consistency and limiting distribution of the least squares estimator of a continuous autoregressive model. *The Annals of Statistics, 21*, 520–33.

Chan, K.S. and H. Tong (1986). On estimating thresholds in autoregressive models. *Journal of Time Series Analysis, 7*, 179–90.

Chan, K.S. and R.S. Tsay (1998). Limiting properties of the conditional least squares estimator of a continuous TAR model. *Biometrika, 85*, 413–26.

Chen, R., J. Liu and R.S. Tsay (1995). Additivity tests for nonlinear autoregressive models. *Biometrika, 82*, 369–83.

Chen, C.W.S., R.E. McCulloch, and R.S. Tsay (1997). A unified approach to estimating and modeling univariate linear and nonlinear time series. *Statistica Sinica, 7*, 451–72.

Chen, R. and R.S. Tsay (1991). On the ergodicity of TAR(1) processes. *Annals of Applied Probability, 1*, 613–34.

Chen, R. and R.S. Tsay (1993a). Functional-coefficient autoregressive models. *Journal of the American Statistical Association, 88*, 298–308.

Chen, R. and R.S. Tsay (1993b). Nonlinear additive ARX models. *Journal of the American Statistical Association*, 88, 955–67.

Clements, M.P. and D.F. Hendry (1993). On the limitations of comparing mean square forecast errors. *Journal of Forecasting*, 12, 617–37.

Clements, M.P. and H.M. Krolzig (1998). A comparison of the forecast performance of Markov-switching and threshold autoregressive models of U.S. GNP. *Econometrics Journal*, 1, 47–75.

Clements, M.P. and J. Smith (1997). The performance of alternative forecasting methods for SETAR models. *International Journal of Forecasting*, 13, 463–75.

Dahl, C.M. and S. Hylleberg (1999). Specifying nonlinear econometric models by flexible regression models and relative forecast performance. Working paper, Department of Economics, University of Aarhus, Denmark.

Davis, R.B. (1987). Hypothesis testing when a nuisance parameter is present only under the alternative. *Biometrika*, 74, 33–43.

Dawid, A.P. (1984). Statistical theory: the prequential approach. *Journal of the Royal Statistical Society, Series A*, 147, 278–92.

Ding, Z., C.W.J. Granger and R.F. Engle (1993). A long memory property of stock returns and a new model. *Journal of Empirical Finance*, 1, 83–106.

Engle, R.F. (1982). Autoregressive conditional heteroskedasticity with estimates of the variance of United Kingdom inflations. *Econometrica*, 50, 987–1007.

Gelfand, A.E. and A.F.M. Smith (1990). Sampling-based approaches to calculating marginal densities. *Journal of the American Statistical Association*, 85, 398–409.

Granger, C.W.J. and A.P. Andersen (1978). *An Introduction to Bilinear Time Series Models*. Gottingen: Vandenhoek and Ruprecht.

Hamilton, J.D. (1989). A New approach to the economic analysis of nonstationary time series and the business cycle. *Econometrica*, 57, 357–84.

Hansen, B.E. (1997). Inference in TAR models. *Studies in Nonlinear Dynamics and Econometrics*, 1, 119–31.

Harvey, A.C., E. Ruiz, and N. Shephard (1994). Multivariate stochastic variance models. *Review of Economic Studies*, 61, 247–64.

Hinich, M. (1982). Testing for Gaussianity and linearity of a stationary time series. *Journal of Time Series Analysis*, 3, 169–76.

Hsieh, D.A. (1989). Testing for nonlinear dependence in daily foreign exchange rates. *Journal of Business*, 62 339–68.

Jacquier, E., N.G. Polson, and P. Rossi (1994). Bayesian analysis of stochastic volatility models (with discussion). *Journal of Business & Economic Statistics*, 12, 371–417.

Kennan, D.M. (1985). A Tukey non-additivity-type test for time series nonlinearity. *Biometrika*, 72, 39–44.

Kitagawa, G. (1998). A self-organizing state space model. *Journal of the American Statistical Association*, 93, 1203–15.

Lewis, P.A.W. and J.G. Stevens (1991). Nonlinear modeling of time series using multivariate adaptive regression spline (MARS). *Journal of the American Statistical Association*, 86, 864–77.

Liu, J. and P.J. Brockwell (1988). On the general bilinear time-series model. *Journal of Applied Probability*, 25, 553–64.

Luukkonen, R., P. Saikkonen, and T. Teräsvirta (1988). Testing linearity against smooth transition autoregressive models. *Biometrika*, 75, 491–99.

McCulloch, R.E. and R.S. Tsay (1993). Bayesian inference and prediction for mean and variance shifts in autoregressive time series. *Journal of the American Statistical Association*, 88, 968–78.

McCulloch, R.E. and R.S. Tsay (1994). Statistical inference of macroeconomic time series via Markov switching models. *Journal of Time Series Analysis*, 15, 523–39.

McLeod, A.I. and W.K. Li (1983). Diagnostic checking ARMA time series models using squared-residual autocorrelations. *Journal of Time Series Analysis*, 4, 269–73.

Melino, A. and S.M. Turnbull (1990). Pricing foreign currency options with stochastic volatility. *Journal of Econometrics*, 45, 239–65.

Montgomery, A.L., V. Zarnowitz, R.S. Tsay, and G.C. Tiao (1998). Forecasting the U.S. unemployment rate. *Journal of the American Statistical Association*, 93, 478–93.

Nelson, D.B. (1991). Conditional heteroskedasticity in asset returns: a new approach. *Econometrica*, 59, 347–70.

Nicholls, D.F. and B.D. Quinn (1982). *Random Coefficient Autoregressive Models: An Introduction*. Lecture Notes in Statistics, 11. Springer-Verlag: New York.

Petruccelli, J. and S.W. Woolford (1984). A threshold AR(1) model. *Journal of Applied Probability*, 21, 270–86.

Potter, S.M. (1995). A nonlinear approach to U.S. GNP. *Journal of Applied Econometrics*, 10, 109–25.

Priestley, M.B. (1980). State-dependent models: a general approach to nonlinear time series analysis. *Journal of Time Series Analysis*, 1, 47–71.

Priestley, M.B. (1988). *Non-linear and Non-stationary Time Series Analysis*. London: Academic Press.

Ramsey, J.B. (1969). Tests for specification errors in classical linear least squares regression analysis. *Journal of the Royal Statistical Society, Series B*, 31, 350–71.

Ray, B.K. and R.S. Tsay (2000). Long-range dependence in daily stock volatilities. *Journal of Business & Economic Statistics*, 18, 254–62.

Rosenblatt, M. (1952). Remarks on a multivariate transformation. *Annals of Mathematical Statistics*, 23, 470–2.

Subba Rao, T. and M.M. Gabr (1984). *An Introduction to Bispectral Analysis and Bilinear Time Series Models*. Lecture Notes in Statistics, 24. New York: Springer-Verlag.

Teräsvirta, T. (1994). Specification, estimation, and evaluation of smooth transition autoregressive models. *Journal of the American Statistical Association*, 89, 208–18.

Tiao, G.C. and R.S. Tsay (1994). Some advances in nonlinear and adaptive modeling in time series. *Journal of Forecasting*, 13, 109–31.

Tong, H. (1978). On a threshold model. In C.H. Chen (ed.), *Pattern Recognition and Signal Processing*. Amsterdam: Sijhoff & Noordhoff.

Tong, H. (1990). *Non-Linear Time Series: A Dynamical System Approach*. Oxford: Oxford University Press.

Tsay, R.S. (1986). Nonlinearity tests for time series. *Biometrika*, 73, 461–6.

Tsay, R.S. (1987). Conditional heteroskedastic time series models. *Journal of the American Statistical Association*, 82, 590–604.

Tsay, R.S. (1989). Testing and modeling threshold autoregressive processes. *Journal of the American Statistical Association*, 84, 231–40.

Tsay, R.S. (1998). Testing and modeling multivariate threshold models. *Journal of the American Statistical Association*, 93, 1188–202.

CHAPTER TWENTY-ONE

Forecasting with Smooth Transition Autoregressive Models

Stefan Lundbergh and Timo Teräsvirta

21.1. Introduction

Forecasting with a nonlinear model is numerically more complicated than carrying out a similar exercise with a linear model. This makes it worthwhile to discuss forecasting from nonlinear models in more detail. In this chapter, we consider forecasting with a special type of nonlinear model, the so-called smooth transition autoregressive (STAR) model: chapter 20 in this volume by Tsay discusses other types of nonlinear model. The idea of smooth transition in the form it appears here can be traced back to Bacon and Watts (1971). For the history and applications of the STAR model to economic time series see, for example, Granger and Teräsvirta (1993) or Teräsvirta (1994). The STAR model nests a linear autoregressive model, and the extra parameters give the model added flexibility, which may be useful in econometric modeling and forecasting. Much of what will be said in this chapter generalizes to the case where we have a smooth transition regression model with regressors that are strongly exogenous for their coefficients.

At the moment there do not exist very many examples of forecasting with STAR models in the econometrics or time series literature. Teräsvirta and Anderson (1992) forecast quarterly OECD industrial production series with these models. The results were mixed: in some cases the STAR model yielded slightly better one-quarter-ahead forecasts than the linear model, but in other cases the situation was the reverse. Forecasters who have forecast with other nonlinear models have obtained similar results. A conclusion of the authors was that the results of comparing forecasts from a linear and a nonlinear model probably depend on how "nonlinear" the forecast period is. Recently, Sarantis (1999) modeled nonlinearities in real effective exchange rates for ten major industrialized countries with STAR models. A set of out-of-sample forecast experiments indicated that the STAR model yielded more accurate forecasts than a pure random walk. On the other hand, it did not perform any better than a linear autoregressive model. The STAR model did outperform another nonlinear model, a hidden Markov model with a switching intercept parameterized as in Hamilton (1989). It is worth pointing out that these forecast comparisons are based on point forecasts. We shall argue below that the real value of forecasts from nonlinear models may well lie in forecast densities, whose shape may offer important information to policy-makers.

We begin this chapter by defining a STAR model and briefly discussing its properties. We also mention a systematic approach to STAR modeling proposed in the literature. The idea is to first specify the model, estimate its parameters and, finally, evaluate the estimated model. After a short presentation of the modeling cycle, we turn to forecasting. First, we show how to obtain multi-period forecasts numerically from STAR models. Next, we highlight some of the issues emerging in STAR forecasting with a simulation experiment. This includes a discussion of ways of reporting forecasts and forecast densities that result from the numerical forecasting procedure. Finally, we illustrate with an example in which two quarterly unemployment series modeled in Skalin and Teräsvirta (2002) are forecast up to nine quarters ahead with logistic STAR models.

21.2. STAR Model

21.2.1. Definition

The smooth transition autoregressive model is defined as follows:

$$y_t = \phi' \mathbf{w}_t + (\theta' \mathbf{w}_t) G_k^L(\gamma, \mathbf{c}; s_t) + \varepsilon_t, \tag{21.1}$$

where $\{\varepsilon_t\}$ is a sequence of normal $(0, \sigma^2)$ independent errors, $\phi = (\phi_0, \dots, \phi_p)'$ and $\theta = (\theta_0, \dots, \theta_p)'$ are $(p + 1) \times 1$ parameter vectors; $\mathbf{w}_t = (1, y_{t-1}, \dots, y_{t-p})'$ is the vector of consisting of an intercept and the first p lags of y_t. Furthermore, the transition function is

$$G_k^L(\gamma, c; s_t) = (1 + \exp\{-\gamma \prod_{i=1}^{k}(s_t - c_i)\})^{-1}, \tag{21.2}$$

where $\gamma > 0$ and $c_1 \leq \dots \leq c_k$ are identifying restrictions. This model is called the logistic STAR model of order k (LSTAR(k)) model. The transition variable s_t is either a weakly stationary stochastic variable or a deterministic function of time, t. A common case considered here is that $s_t = y_{t-d}$, $d > 0$. In the application of

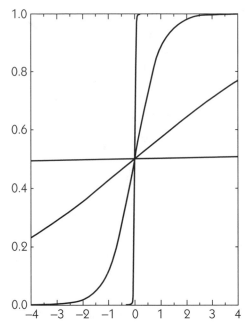

Figure 21.1   Graphs of the logistic transition function (21.2) with $k = 1$
for $\gamma = 0.01$, 3, 20, and 50. The graph corresponding to the lowest value of
γ lies closest to the line $G_1^L = 1/2$

section 21.4.2, however, $s_t = \Delta_4 y_{t-d}$. The slope or smoothness parameter γ controls
the slope of the transition function (21.2). For example, if $k = 1$ and $\gamma \to \infty$ then
(21.2) becomes a step function and the STAR model (21.1) a threshold autoregressive (TAR) model with two regimes. Note that if $\gamma \to 0$ the model becomes
linear as (21.2) becomes a constant.

The most common cases in practice are $k = 1$ and $k = 2$ in (21.2). In the former
case, illustrated in figure 21.1, the transition function increases monotonically
from zero to unity with s_t. The LSTAR(1) model may thus be applied, for example, to modeling asymmetric business cycles because the dynamics of the model
are different in the expansion from the recession. In the latter case, depicted in
figure 21.2, the transition function is symmetric about its minimum at $(c_1 + c_2)/2$
and approaches unity as $s_t \to \pm\infty$. The minimum lies between zero and $1/2$. It
equals $1/2$ if $c_1 = c_2$ and approaches zero as $\gamma \to \infty$ while $c_1 < c_2$. This is clearly
seen from figure 21.2. The dynamics of the LSTAR(2) model are therefore similar
both for high and low values of the transition variable and different in the middle.
Note that if $k = 2$ and $c_1 = c_2$ then (21.2) may be replaced by

$$G^E(\gamma, \mathbf{c}; s_t) = 1 - \exp\{-\gamma(s_t - c)^2\}. \qquad (21.3)$$

The STAR model (21.1) with (21.3) is called the exponential STAR (ESTAR) model
and has the property that the minimum value of the transition function equals

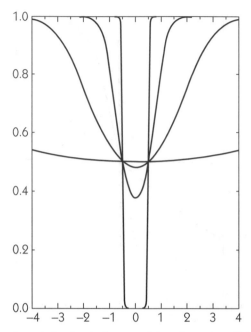

Figure 21.2 Graphs of the logistic transition function (21.2) with k = 2 for
γ = 0.01, 3, 20, and 50. The graph corresponding to the lowest value of
γ lies closest to the line $G_2^L = 1/2$

zero; see figure 21.3. This is often convenient when interpreting the estimated model, which is the main reason for preferring the ESTAR model to the LSTAR(2) one. Note, however, that the exponential transition function degenerates to constant 1 except for $s_t = c$ as $\gamma \to \infty$, which is an argument in favor of using the logistic function with $k = 2$. Other choices of transition function are possible. The cumulative distribution function of the normal distribution (Chan and Tong, 1986) and the hyperbolic tangent function (Bacon and Watts, 1971) are among those proposed for the purpose. We just have to assume that the transition function is bounded, continuous, and at least twice differentiable with respect to its parameters everywhere in the sample space.

Equation (21.1) may also be written as follows:

$$y_t = \phi(s_t)'\mathbf{w}_t + \varepsilon_t, \tag{21.4}$$

where $\phi(s_t) = \phi + G(\gamma, c; s_t)\theta$. From (21.4) it is seen that the STAR model may be interpreted as a linear AR model with time-varying parameters. We may call the STAR model "locally linear" in the sense that for a fixed value of s_t, (21.4) is linear. When $s_t = t$, the coefficients of the AR model evolve deterministically over time. The STAR model may thus display locally-explosive behavior (the roots of the polynomial $1 - \sum_{j=1}^{p}[\phi_j + G_k^L(\gamma, c; s_t)\theta_j]z^j$ lie inside the unit circle for some s_t) but

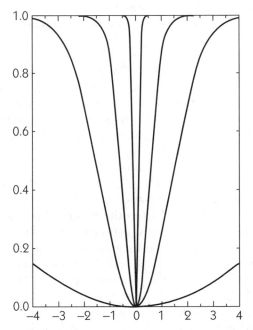

Figure 21.3 Graphs of the logistic transition function (21.3) for $\gamma = 0.01$, 3, 20, and 50. The graph corresponding to the lowest value of γ lies closest to the horizontal axis $G^E = 0$

still be globally stable. This property may help in modeling economic time series with sudden movements and asymmetric behavior.

21.2.2. Modeling cycle

GENERAL

Modeling time series in an organized fashion becomes an important issue when the model is not completely determined by theory. This is often the situation in univariate modeling. Box and Jenkins (1970) devised a modeling cycle for the specification, estimation, and evaluation of the family of linear ARMA or ARIMA models. Similar cycles have been proposed for nonlinear models: see Tsay (1989) and Tsay (1998) for the families of univariate and multivariate TAR models. There exists a modeling cycle for STAR models as well. The most recent description of this cycle can be found in Teräsvirta (1998); for earlier accounts, see Teräsvirta (1994) and Granger and Teräsvirta (1993). The cycle consists of the specification, estimation, and evaluation stages. The specification stage may include the choice of the type of the LSTAR model (order k) and the specification of the lag structure. This stage usually already requires estimation of STAR models. The parameter estimation can be carried out by nonlinear least squares, which is equivalent to conditional maximum likelihood when we assume normality as in section 21.2.1. At the evaluation stage the model is subjected to a number of misspecification tests and other checks to ensure its adequacy and feasibility. We discuss these stages below.

SPECIFICATION

It can be seen from equation (21.1) that a linear AR(p) model is nested in the logistic STAR model. As mentioned above, the STAR model is linear if $\gamma = 0$. The possibility that the series has in fact been generated by a linear model must not be overlooked. Since linear models are easier to apply and forecast from than most nonlinear ones, our first task is to test linearity against STAR. A possible null hypothesis is $H_0 : \gamma = 0$ and the alternative $H_1 : \gamma > 0$. This choice makes a statistical problem easily visible: model (21.1) is only identified under the alternative. Under H_0, both θ and c are nuisance parameters such that no information about their values can be obtained from the observed series. As a consequence, the parameters cannot be consistently estimated and the standard asymptotic distribution theory for the classical test statistics does not work. The first discussion of this problem appeared in Davies (1977). For a recent overview and solutions, see Hansen (1996). To solve the problem we follow Luukkonen, Saikkonen, and Teräsvirta (1988) and expand the transition function into a Taylor series around the null point $\gamma = 0$. To illustrate, we choose G_1^L and its third-order expansion. Substituting this expansion for the transition function in (21.1) yields, after merging terms and reparameterizing,

$$y_t = \beta_1' \mathbf{w}_t + \beta_2' \tilde{\mathbf{w}}_t y_{t-d} + \beta_3' \tilde{\mathbf{w}}_t y_{t-d}^2 + \beta_4' \tilde{\mathbf{w}}_t y_{t-d}^3 + \varepsilon_t^* \tag{21.5}$$

where $\tilde{\mathbf{w}}_t = (y_{t-1}, \ldots, y_{t-p})'$, $\beta_1 = (\beta_{10}, \beta_{11}, \ldots, \beta_{1p})'$, $\beta_j = (\beta_{j1}, \ldots, \beta_{jp})'$, $j = 2, 3, 4$, and $\varepsilon_t^* = \varepsilon_t + R_3(\gamma, c; y_{t-d}) \theta' \mathbf{w}_t$, the term $R_3(\gamma, c; y_{t-d})$ being the remainder from the expansion. Every element $\beta_{ji} = \gamma \tilde{\beta}_{ji}$, $\tilde{\beta}_{ji} \neq 0$, for $i = 1, \ldots, p$; $j = 2, 3, 4$. Note, furthermore, that under H_0 $\varepsilon_t^* = \varepsilon_t$. Thus testing the original hypothesis can be done within (5) by applying the Lagrange Multiplier principle. The new null hypothesis is $H_0' : \beta_2 = \beta_3 = \beta_4 = 0$. Assuming $E(\varepsilon_t^8) < \infty$, the standard LM statistic has an asymptotic χ^2 distribution with $3p$ degrees of freedom under the null hypothesis. The auxiliary regression based on the third-order Taylor expansion has power against both $k = 1$ and $k = 2$. For a detailed derivation of the test, see Luukkonen, Saikkonen, and Teräsvirta (1988) or Teräsvirta (1994). It is advisable to use an F-version of the test if the sample size is small. In that situation, the F-test has better size properties, when the dimension of the null hypothesis H_0' is large, than the asymptotic χ^2 test.

In the above, we have assumed that the delay parameter d is known. In practice, it has to be determined from the data. We may combine our linearity test and the determination of d. This is done as follows. First define a set $\mathcal{D} = \{1, 2, \ldots, d_o\}$ of possible values of the delay parameter. Carry out the test for each of them. Choose the value in $\mathcal{D}$ that minimizes the p-value of the test, if the value is sufficiently low for the null hypothesis to be rejected. If no individual test rejects, accept linearity. The motivation of this strategy is given in Teräsvirta (1994).

In practice we have to first determine the maximum lag p in our test equation (21.5). This can be done by applying an appropriate model selection criterion such as AIC to the null model, which is a linear AR(p) model. As autocorrelation in the errors may cause size distortion (Teräsvirta, 1994), it is useful to check that the selected AR model has uncorrelated errors. The Ljung–Box statistic may be used for the purpose.

It may be argued that when this test and selection procedure is applied, the significance level of the linearity test is not under the model builder's control. This is true, but the linearity tests are used here as a model specification device rather than as a strict test. If linearity is erroneously rejected this mistake will most likely show up at the estimation or evaluation stages of the modeling cycle. If the main interest lies not in modeling but in testing theory – that is, testing a linear specification against a STAR one – the auxiliary regression may be modified as in Luukkonen, Saikkonen, and Teräsvirta (1988) to correspond to the case where we only assume that $d \in \mathcal{D}$ when carrying out the test.

If we restrict ourselves to cases $k = 1$ and $k = 2$, a choice between them may be made at the specification stage by testing a sequence of hypotheses within the auxiliary regression (21.5). This is described in Teräsvirta (1994) or Teräsvirta (1998). Another possibility is to estimate both an LSTAR(1) and an LSTAR(2) model and postpone the final choice to the evaluation stage. As estimating a STAR model is no longer a time-consuming affair, this may be a feasible alternative.

Testing linearity and determining the delay d are carried out using the auxiliary regression (21.5). The specification also includes determining the lag structure in (21.1). This is best done by selecting a maximum lag (the lag selected for the linear AR model for testing linearity is often a reasonable choice, at least if it exceeds one), estimating the LSTAR model with this maximum lag, then eliminating insignificant lags from the linear and nonlinear part of the equation (21.1). Here it should be noted that, in addition to the standard restrictions $\phi_i = 0$ and $\theta_j = 0$, the exclusion restriction $\phi_j = -\theta_j$ is a feasible alternative. It makes the combined parameter $\phi_j + \theta_j G$ approach zero as $G \to 1$. The restriction $\phi_j = 0$ has the same effect as $G \to 0$. Some experimenting may thus be necessary to find the appropriate restrictions. In some cases, these become evident from the estimates of the unrestricted model.

ESTIMATION

The estimation of the parameters of the LSTAR(k) model (21.1) is carried out by conditional maximum likelihood. We assume that the model satisfies the assumptions and regularity conditions MLE.1–MLE.7 in Wooldridge (1994), without actually verifying them here. The conditions guarantee the consistency and asymptotic normality of the parameter estimators. They imply, among other things, that $\{y_t\}$ is weakly stationary and geometrically ergodic. The estimation can be carried out by using a suitable iterative estimation algorithm. For a useful review, see Hendry (1995, Appendix A5). Many of the algorithms normally lead to the same estimates but may yield rather different estimates of the Hessian matrix which is required for the inference. Thus the Newton–Raphson algorithm is in principle an excellent choice. However, in addition to analytic second derivatives it requires starting from values that already are rather close to the optimal ones. The BFGS algorithm based on numerical derivatives has also turned out to be a reasonable choice in practice.

The starting-values are an important issue. First, the location parameter γ is not scale invariant, which makes it difficult to find a good starting-value for it. Replacing the transition function (21.2) by

$$G_k^L(\gamma, \mathbf{c}; s_t) = (1 + \exp\{-\gamma \prod_{i=1}^{k}(s_t - c_i)/\hat{\sigma}(s)^k\})^{-1},$$

where $\hat{\sigma}(s)$ is a sample standard deviation of s_t that makes γ approximately scale-free. Note that if γ and c are fixed in (21.1), then the STAR model is linear in parameters. This suggests constructing a grid for γ and the elements of c. The remaining parameters are estimated conditionally on every parameter combination in the grid by linear least squares. The parameter estimates of the combination with the lowest sum of squared residuals constitute the desired starting-values.

We shall not discuss potential numerical problems in the estimation. Difficulties may sometimes be expected if γ is very large. This is due to the fact that the transition function is close to a step function ($k = 1$) or "a step and a reverse" ($k = 2$): for more information about this, see, for example, Bates and Watts (1988, p. 87), Teräsvirta (1994), or Teräsvirta (1998).

EVALUATION BY MISSPECIFICATION TESTS

After estimating the parameters of a STAR model it is necessary to evaluate the model. Misspecification tests play an important role in doing that. The validity of the assumptions underlying the estimation have to be tested carefully. Homoskedasticity and no serial error correlation and parameter stability are among them. When we are dealing with a family of nonlinear models, it is also of interest to know whether or not the estimated model adequately characterizes the nonlinearity present in the series. The null hypothesis of no remaining nonlinearity should thus also be tested.

Testing homoskedasticity of errors against conditional heteroskedasticity is carried out exactly as outlined in Engle (1982). The STAR structure of the conditional mean does not affect the test. The assumption $E\varepsilon_t^4 < \infty$ is required for the asymptotic theory to work. The other tests may be characterized by including an additive component in (21.1) such that

$$y_t = \phi'\mathbf{w}_t + (\theta'\mathbf{w}_t)G_k^L(\gamma, \mathbf{c}; s_t) + A(\mathbf{w}_t, \mathbf{w}_{t-1}, \ldots, \mathbf{w}_{t-p}; \psi) + \varepsilon_t, \qquad (21.6)$$

where ψ is a parameter vector and $\varepsilon_t \sim \text{nid}(0, \sigma^2)$. Under the null hypothesis, $A \equiv 0$. If we test the null of no error autocorrelation,

$$A(\mathbf{w}_t, \mathbf{w}_{t-1}, \ldots, \mathbf{w}_{t-p}; \psi) = \alpha'\mathbf{v}_t,$$

where $\alpha = (\alpha_1, \ldots, \alpha_m)'$ and $\mathbf{v}_t = (\mathbf{u}_{t-1}, \ldots, \mathbf{u}_{t-m})'$ with $u_t = y_t - \phi'\mathbf{w}_t + (\theta'\mathbf{w}_t)G_k(\gamma, \mathbf{c}; s_t)$. The null hypothesis is $\alpha = \mathbf{0}$. As to parameter constancy, it is natural to test the hypothesis in the smooth transition spirit by allowing the parameters to change smoothly over time under the alternative. Generalize (21.1) to

$$y_t = \phi(t)'\mathbf{w}_t + \theta(t)'\mathbf{w}_t G_k^L(\gamma, \mathbf{c}; s_t) + \varepsilon_t,$$

where the time-varying coefficient vectors have the form $\phi(t) = \phi_0 + \phi_1 H_\ell^L(\gamma_1, c_1; t)$ and $\theta(t) = \theta_0 + \theta_1 H_\ell^L(\gamma_1, c_1; t)$ with $H_\ell^L(\gamma_1, c_1; t) = (1 + \exp\{-\gamma_1 \Pi_{i=1}^\ell (t - c_{li})\})^{-1}$, $\gamma_1 > 0$ and $c_{11} \le \ldots \le c_{1\ell}$. This yields

$$A(\mathbf{w}_t, \mathbf{w}_{t-1}, \ldots, \mathbf{w}_{t-p}; \psi) = \phi_1'\mathbf{w}_t H_\ell^L(\gamma_1, c_1; t) + \theta_1'\mathbf{w}_t G_k^L(\gamma, c; s_t) H_\ell^L(\gamma_1, c_1; t).$$

The null hypothesis is $\gamma_1 = 0$ and the alternative $\gamma_1 > 0$. When $k = 1$ in the transition function H_ℓ^L and $\gamma_1 \to \infty$, then the model has a single structural break. This alternative, very popular among econometricians, thus appears as a special case in this more general setting. The test is based on an approximation of $H_\ell^L(\gamma_1, c_1; t)$ by a Taylor series expansion to circumvent the identification problem present even here.

The null of no additive nonlinearity may be tested by assuming $A(\mathbf{w}_t, \mathbf{w}_{t-1}, \ldots, \mathbf{w}_{t-p}; \psi) = \pi'\mathbf{w}_t \mathbf{G}_n(\gamma_2, c_2; r_t)$ in (21.6) where $\pi = (\pi_0, \pi_1, \ldots, \pi_p)'$ and r_t is another transition variable. The null hypothesis $\gamma_2 = 0$ is tested against $\gamma_2 > 0$. Even here, the ensuing identification problem is solved by replacing the transition function by its Taylor series expansion. Derivation of the tests and the asymptotic distribution theory are discussed in detail in Eitrheim and Teräsvirta (1996) and Teräsvirta (1998).

If at least one misspecification test rejects, the model-builder should reconsider the specification. One possibility is carry out a new specification search. Another one is to conclude that the family of STAR models does not provide a good characterization of the series. Yet another one is to estimate the alternative model and retain that, at least if it passes the new misspecification tests. There is at least one case where that may be a sensible alternative. If the series contains seasonality, which is often the case in the analysis of economic time series, then it is very common that the seasonal pattern changes slowly over time. The reasons include slowly changing institutions and, for instance in production series, technological change. Augmenting an LSTAR(k) model by deterministically changing coefficients instead of trying to respecify it may then be a good alternative. The question then is what to do when forecasting with the model. Should the value of H_ℓ^L be frozen to where it is at the end of the observation period or should it be predicted as well? The latter would mean extrapolating its values into the future and using the extrapolated values in forecasting. In some other cases the answer is quite clear. If a model contains a linear trend, then the trend is always extrapolated and the extrapolated values used in forecasting. The same is obviously true when the trend is nonlinear and parameterized as a STAR component, as in Leybourne, Newbold, and Vougas (1998). It may be less clear if we consider extrapolating changes in seasonality. Rahiala and Teräsvirta (1993) were in this situation, but in their case the transition function had already practically reached its final value of unity at the end of the observed series.

Evaluation by extrapolation

It is difficult to draw conclusions on the stationarity of an estimated STAR model from its estimated coefficients. Nevertheless, from the forecasting point of view it would be important to know whether or not the estimated model is stable. An explosive model may only be applied in very short-term forecasting. When the forecasting horizon increases the model becomes useless rapidly. A necessary condition for stability is discussed in Granger and Teräsvirta (1993). Consider model (21.1) without noise. Extrapolate this "skeleton" (Tong, 1990) from different starting-values. The necessary condition for stability is that the sequence of extrapolated values always converges to a single point called the stable stationary point. Note, however, that this point need not be unique. If an estimated STAR model satisfies this condition, one may repeat the same exercise with noise added. In fact, this has a few things in common with actual forecasting with STAR models, to which we now turn.

21.3. Forecasting with STAR Models

21.3.1. General procedure

The STAR model is a nonlinear model, which makes multi-period forecasting from them more complicated than from linear models. In forecasting a single period ahead there is no difference between STAR and linear AR models. We shall first discuss the general procedure for obtaining multi-period forecasts. Our exposition closely follows that in Granger and Teräsvirta (1993).

Consider the nonlinear univariate model

$$y_t = g(\mathbf{w}_t; \psi) + \varepsilon_t, \tag{21.7}$$

where ψ is the parameter vector and $\{\varepsilon_t\}$ is a sequence of independent, identically distributed errors. In the logistic STAR case,

$$g(\mathbf{w}_t; \psi) = \phi'\mathbf{w}_t + (\theta'\mathbf{w}_t)G_k^L(\gamma, \mathbf{c}; s_t). \tag{21.8}$$

From (21.7) it follows that $E(y_{t+1} | \mathcal{I}_t) = g(\mathbf{w}_{t+1}; \psi)$, which is the unbiased forecast of y_{t+1} made at time t given the past information $\mathcal{I}_t$ up until that time. In the case, the relevant information is contained in $\mathbf{w}_{t+1} = (1, y_t, y_{t-1}, \ldots, y_{t-(p-1)})'$. We denote this forecast $y_{t+1|t}^f$. Forecasting two periods ahead is not as easy, because obtaining $E(y_{t+2} | \mathcal{I}_t)$ is more complicated. We have

$$y_{t+2|t}^f = E(y_{t+2} | \mathcal{I}_t) = E\{[g(\mathbf{w}_{t+2}^f; \psi) + \varepsilon_{t+2}] | \mathcal{I}_t\} = E\{g(\mathbf{w}_{t+2}^f; \psi) | \mathcal{I}_t\}, \tag{21.9}$$

where $\mathbf{w}_{t+2}^f = (1, y_{t+1|t}^f + \varepsilon_{t+1}, y_t, \ldots, y_{t-(p-2)})'$. The exact expression for (21.9) is

$$y_{t+2|t}^f = E\{g(\mathbf{w}_{t+2}^f; \psi) | \mathcal{I}_t\} = \int_{-\infty}^{\infty} g(\mathbf{w}_{t+2}^f; \psi) d\Phi(z), \tag{21.10}$$

where $\Phi(z)$ is the cumulative distribution function of ε_{t+1}. Obtaining the forecast would require numerical integration, and multiple integration would be encountered for longer time horizons. As an example, in an LSTAR(1) model with the maximum lag $p = 1$ and delay $d = 1$ (21.10) has the form

$$
y^f_{t+2|t} = \int_{-\infty}^{\infty} [\phi_0 + \phi_1(y^f_{t+1|t} + z) + (\theta_0 + \theta_1(y^f_{t+1|t} + z))
$$

$$
\times (1 + \exp\{-\gamma(y^f_{t+1|t} + z - c_1)\})^{-1}]d\Phi(z)
$$

$$
= \phi_0 + \phi_1 y^f_{t+1|t}
$$

$$
+ \int_{-\infty}^{\infty} [(\theta_0 + \theta_1(y^f_{t+1|t} + z)(1 + \exp\{-\gamma(y^f_{t+1|t} + z - c_1)\})^{-1}]d\Phi(z), \quad (21.11)
$$

where $y^f_{t+1|t} = \phi_0 + \phi_1 y_t + (\theta_0 + \theta_1 y_t)(1 + \exp\{-\gamma(y_t - c_1)\})^{-1}$. Numerical integration of (21.11) is not very complicated, but, as noticed above, the dimension of the integral grows with the forecast horizon. Thus it would be computationally more feasible to obtain the forecasts recursively without numerical integration. A simple way would be to ignore the error term ε_{t+1} and just use the skeleton. Granger and Teräsvirta (1993) called this the naive method:

(i)   Naive: $y^{fn}_{t+2|t} = g(\mathbf{w}^{fn}_{t+2}; \psi)$ where $\mathbf{w}^{fn}_{t+2} = (1, y^f_{t+1|t}, y_t, \dots, y_{t-(p-2)})'$. This is equivalent to extrapolating with the skeleton. In the above LSTAR(1) case,

$$
y^{fn}_{t+2|t} = \phi_0 + \phi_1 y^f_{t+1|t} + (\theta_0 + \theta_1 y^f_{t+1|t})(1 + \exp\{-\gamma(y^f_{t+1|t} - c_1)\})^{-1}.
$$

Extrapolating this way is simple, but in view of equation (21.10) it leads to biased forecasts. Another way is to simulate: this is called Monte Carlo in Granger and Teräsvirta (1993).

(ii) Monte Carlo: $y^{fm}_{t+2|t} = (1/M)\sum_{m=1}^{M} g(\mathbf{w}^f_{t+2,m}; \psi)$ where each of the M values of ε_{t+1} in $\mathbf{w}^f_{t+2,m}$ is drawn independently from the error distribution of (21.1). By the weak law of large numbers, the forecast is asymptotically unbiased as $M \to \infty$. In the LSTAR(1) case,

$$
y^{fm}_{t+2|t} \approx \phi_0 + \phi_1 y^f_{t+1|t} \tag{21.12}
$$

$$
+ (1/M) \sum_{m=1}^{M} (\theta_0 + \theta_1(y^f_{t+1|t} + \varepsilon^{(m)}_{t+1}))(1 + \exp\{-\gamma(y^f_{t+1|t} + \varepsilon^{(m)}_{t+1}) - c_1)\})^{-1}.
$$

Finally, if we do not want to rely on the error distribution we have assumed for parameter estimation we may apply resampling to obtain the forecast. This is the bootstrap method:

(iii)   Bootstrap: $y_{t+2|t}^{fb} = (1/B)\sum_{b=1}^{B} g(\mathbf{w}_{t+2,b}^{f}; \psi)$ where each of the B values of ε_{t+1} in $\mathbf{w}_{t+2,b}^{f}$ is drawn independently from the set of the residuals of the estimated model with replacement.

An advantage of these numerical approximations to the true expectations is that they automatically give a number (M or B) of point forecasts for each period to be predicted. In fact, what is available is a forecast density, and interval forecasts may be constructed on the basis of them. In so doing, one has to remember that the interval forecasts obtained this way do not account for sampling uncertainty and the intervals are therefore somewhat too narrow. Sampling uncertainty may be accounted for by numerical techniques. Suppose $\hat{\psi}$ is a consistent and (after rescaling) asymptotically normal estimator with a positive definite covariance matrix of the parameter vector ψ in (21.7). The forecasts obtained by any of the above techniques are based on the estimate $\hat{\psi}$. We can draw a random sample of size R, say, from the large-sample distribution of the estimator $\hat{\psi}$ and obtain R sets of new estimates. Plugging those into (21.7) gives R new models. By repeating the procedure (ii) or (iii) for each of these leads to RM or RB forecasts. The interval forecasts based on these predictions now accommodate the sampling uncertainty.

This approach is quite computer-intensive. In the case of STAR models it also requires plenty of human resources. We cannot always exclude the possibility that some of the R models are unstable, and instability in turn would mess up the forecasts. Every model thus has to be checked for stability, which requires human control and an even greater amount of computational resources. In the application of section 21.4.2, we choose to ignore the sampling uncertainty.

21.3.2.   Estimating and representing forecast densities

When we generate multi-period forecasts with Monte Carlo and bootstrap procedures we have a whole set of forecasts for each time period. A density forecast for each of these periods may be obtained as follows. First arrange the individual forecasts for a given time period in ascending order. Represent this empirical distribution as a histogram and smooth it to obtain an estimate of the density of the forecast. Various smoothing techniques exist, the most popular of them being kernel estimation and spline smoothing. These are discussed, for example, in Silverman (1986) or Härdle (1990, ch. 3).

In practical work it is helpful to represent these densities by graphs. STAR model density forecasts may well be multimodal. If we want to stress this property, we may graph the densities for each time period; for a recent application, see Matzner-Lober, Gannoun, and De Gooijer (1998). Another idea is to compute and graph so-called highest-density regions. This is a compact way of representing these densities for a number of forecast periods simultaneously. Hyndman (1996) shows how to do that. Hyndman (1995) discusses the use of highest-density regions in representing forecasts and provides an example of a bimodal density forecast. The $100\alpha\%$ highest-density region is estimated as follows. Let x be a continuous random variable with probability density $f(x)$. The highest-density region $HDR_\alpha(x) = \{x : f(x) \geq f_\alpha\}$ where $f_\alpha > 0$ is such that the probability of a given x having a density that at least equals f_α is α. Any point x belonging to a highest-density region has a higher density than any point outside this region. If the density is multi-modal, then a given highest-density region may consist of disjoint subsets of points, depending on α.

Wallis (1999), see also Tay and Wallis, chapter 3 of this book, considers another way of graphing density forecasts called the fan chart. The graph opens up like a fan as the forecast horizon increases. The idea is to compute $100\alpha\%$ prediction intervals $PI_\alpha(x) = \{x : \Pr[a < x < b] = \alpha\}$ from the density forecast and represent 10 percent, 20 percent, ..., 90 percent, say, intervals for forecasts with different shades of color, the color getting lighter as the interval is widens. As such prediction intervals are not unique, choosing one depends on the loss function of the user. One possibility is to choose a and b such that $f(a) = f(b) = f_\alpha$. Wallis (1999) shows that this choice may be derived from an all-or-nothing loss function: no loss if the observed value lands in the interval and a positive constant loss if it lies outside. The requirement that the prediction interval have the shortest possible length also leads to $f(a) = f(b)$. Note that we may want to allow the interval to consist of a number of disjoint sub-intervals while imposing the shortest possible length requirement. In that case the resulting prediction interval equals the highest-density region discussed above. We may call the corresponding unbroken interval the equal density interval.

Another way of defining the prediction interval is to let the tail probabilities be equal:

$$PI_a(x) = \{x : \Pr[x < a] = \Pr[x > b] = 1 - \alpha/2, \, a < b\}.$$

A loss function yielding this choice is linear: there is no loss if the observed value lies in the interval, and the loss is a linear function of the distance between the nearest endpoint of the interval and the realization if the latter lies outside the interval. When $\alpha \to 0$, this prediction interval shrinks to the median of the density forecast. This is the prediction interval we shall use in the application of section 21.4.2. The equal density interval shrinks to the mode of the density. Examples of these intervals and fan graphs will be given in the next section.

21.4. EXAMPLES

21.4.1. Simulated example

In this section, we discuss the forecasting power of an LSTAR model through a simulated example. Of course, the results cannot therefore be generalized to the whole family of STAR models, but the main purpose of the simulation study is to highlight some issues in forecasting with STAR models. A recurring argument is that, in practice, a nonlinear model hardly forecasts better than a linear one. This seems to be the case even if the nonlinear model seems to fit better in-sample than the linear one built on the same information set. Thus it is natural to compare forecasts from a STAR model to those from a linear one.

The LSTAR model we use to generate the data is defined as follows:

$$y_t = -0.19 + 0.38[1 + \exp(-10y_{t-1})]^{-1} + 0.9y_{t-1} + 0.4u_t \qquad (21.13)$$

where $\{u_t\}$ is a sequence of independent normally distributed random numbers with zero mean and unit variance. A total of 1,000,000 observations is generated with this data-generating process (DGP). In this special case where only the intercept is time-varying the DGP may also be interpreted as a special case of single hidden-layer feedforward artificial neural network (ANN) model; see, for example, Granger and Teräsvirta (1993, p. 105), for a definition of such a model.

The forecasting experiment is set up in the following way. From our time series of one million observations, we randomly choose a subset of 6,282 observations. Taking each of these observations as the last observation in a subseries of 1,000 observations we estimate the parameters of the LSTAR model by nonlinear least squares. We also estimate the parameters of two linear models. The first is a linear first-order autoregressive (AR) model for y_t. The second is a linear first-order autoregressive model for Δy_t: we call this an autoregressive integrated (ARI) model. The rationale for the ARI model is that if we take those 1,000 observations and test the unit-root hypothesis it is most often not rejected at the 5 percent significance level. This is not a general feature of data generated by an LSTAR model but it happens for model (21.13). In fact, this model shares some dynamic properties with the simple nonlinear time-series model in Granger and Teräsvirta (1999).

Having done this, we generate forecasts from each nonlinear model by simulation as discussed in the previous section. We also do this under the assumption that we know the parameters of the LSTAR model. This gives us an idea of how much the fact that the parameters have to be estimated affects the forecast accuracy. Furthermore, we generate the corresponding forecasts from the two linear autoregressive models. To compare the accuracy of the forecasts we use the Relative Efficiency (RE) measure that Mincer and Zarnowitz (1969) proposed. It is defined as the ratio of the Mean Square Forecast Error (MSFE) of the model under consideration and its benchmark. We use the linear autoregressive models as the benchmark. A value of RE greater or equal to unity indicates that the benchmark model provides more accurate models than the nonlinear LSTAR model.

Figure 21.4 contains the RE based on 6,282 forecast simulations with the linear AR models as the benchmark. It is seen that when the linear AR model is used as the benchmark the relative forecast accuracy of the LSTAR model is steadily improved up until ten periods ahead, after which it stabilizes. With 1,000 observations, having to estimate the parameters does not make things much worse compared to the hypothetical case where they are known. The situation is unchanged when the ARI model is used as a benchmark. The corresponding RE graph is not reproduced here. Furthermore, if the median forecast or the mode of the forecast density obtained from the estimated forecast density are used as the nonlinear point forecast, the situation does not change very much.

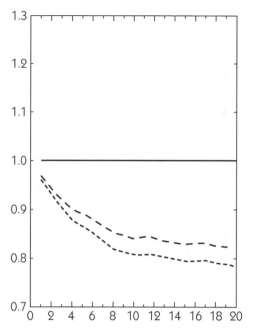

Figure 21.4 Relative Efficiency (RE) of the mean forecasts from the LSTAR model (21.13) based on 6,282 randomly chosen forecast samples when the linear AR model serves as the benchmark model. Dashed lines represent the case where the parameters of the LSTAR model are estimated, the short dashed lines the case where they are known

It is often argued that the nonlinear model forecasts better than the linear one only when one forecasts "nonlinear observations"; that is, a sequence of observations whose behavior cannot be explained in a satisfactory fashion without a nonlinear model. This possibility was mentioned in the Introduction. Recently, Montgomery, Zarnowitz, Tsay, and Tiao (1998) found that the nonlinear threshold autoregressive and the Markov-switching autoregressive (Lindgren, 1978) model outperformed the AR model during periods of rapidly increasing unemployment but not elsewhere. In our case, we define our "nonlinear observations" to be those which correspond to large changes in the value of the transition function. A large change is defined to occur when the change of the transition function of the LSTAR model exceeds 0.2 in absolute value. There are exactly 6,282 such observations out of one million in our simulated time series, so that such a large change is already a rare event. We choose every such observation to be the last observation in one of our subseries, which leads to 6,282 subseries. As before, we estimate our models and generate our forecasts using those subseries.

Figure 21.5 contains the RE up to 20 periods ahead when the AR model is the benchmark. It is seen that now the advantage of knowing the parameters is

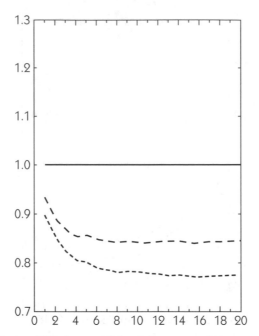

Figure 21.5   Relative Efficiency (RE) of the mean forecasts from the LSTAR model (21.13) based on 6,282 forecast samples whose last observation represents a large change and the linear AR model is the benchmark model. Dashed lines represent the case where the parameters of the LSTAR model are estimated, the short dashed lines the case where they are known

clearly greater than in the previous case with randomly-chosen series. It seems that estimating the parameters of the LSTAR model sufficiently accurately may not be easy if there is not much information available about the nonlinearity in the sample (large changes in the transition function were a rare event). Besides, the RE values stabilize already after six periods or so. From figure 21.6 we see that the situation changes dramatically when the ARI model is the benchmark. When the parameters of the LSTAR model are estimated (the realistic case), the model loses its predictive edge after 13 periods into the future, and the overall gain from using the LSTAR model for forecasting is much smaller than in the previous simulation. This may appear surprising at first, but Clements and Hendry (1999, ch. 5) offer a plausible explanation. They argue that first differences are a useful device in forecasting in case of structural breaks in levels, because the model adapts quickly to a new situation even if it is misspecified. Here we do not have structural breaks, but rapid shifts in levels are typical for our simulated STAR model. These may resemble structural breaks, for example, changes in the intercept of a model defined in levels. Flexibility inherent in first difference models is an asset when a large shift in the series occurs at the beginning of the forecasting period.

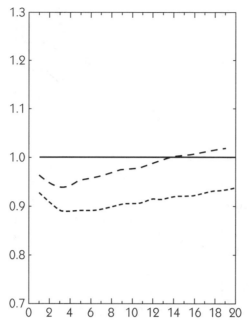

Figure 21.6 Relative Efficiency (RE) of the mean forecasts from the LSTAR model (21.13) based on 6,282 forecast samples whose last observation represents a large change and the linear ARI model is the benchmark model. Dashed lines represent the case where the parameters of the LSTAR model are estimated, the short dashed lines the case where they are known

When forecasting with nonlinear models one may also think of using either the median or mode of the forecast density as the point forecast. Figure 21.7 shows the evolution of the RE in the ARI case when the mode of the forecast density is used for the purpose. It appears that the nonlinear forecasts are off the track very quickly. It should be noted, however, that the mode forecast is not an optimal one when the loss function is quadratic. The RE is based on the quadratic loss function and may therefore be used for comparing mean forecasts. When forecasting with nonlinear models, this is an important distinction. It may also be pointed out that the RE, when the median is used as the point forecast from the LSTAR model, lies between those based on the mean and the mode forecasts, respectively.

The lessons from this experiment may be summed up as follows. First, there exist STAR models with which one forecasts consistently better than with linear models. Second, a part of the theoretical predictive edge of the STAR model may vanish when the parameters are estimated, and this may still happen at sample sizes that may already be considered unrealistically large in macroeconometric applications. Third, when the stationary STAR model depicts "near unit-root behavior," a misspecified linear model based on first differences may become a

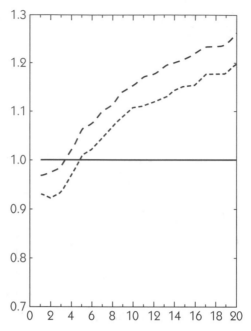

Figure 21.7 Relative Efficiency (RE) of the mode forecasts from the LSTAR model (21.13) based on 6,282 forecast samples whose last observation represents a large change and the linear ARI model is the benchmark model. Dashed lines represent the case where the parameters of the LSTAR model are estimated, the short dashed lines the case where they are known

close competitor to the nonlinear model. Moreover, in our experiment this happens when the observations to be predicted show "nonlinear behavior," which is in some sense atypical. Finally, when comparing point forecasts other than mean forecasts from nonlinear models with forecasts from linear models the choice of the loss function becomes very important.

21.4.2. Empirical example

In this section, we consider an application to Danish and Australian quarterly unemployment series. Many unemployment rates seem asymmetric in the sense that the rate may go up rather sharply and then decrease more slowly. Skalin and Teräsvirta (2002) have modeled such series with LSTAR models that are able to characterize asymmetric behavior. A typical LSTAR model of this kind may be defined as follows:

$$\Delta y_t = -\alpha y_{t-1} + \phi' \mathbf{w}_t + \psi_1' \mathbf{d}_t + (\theta' \mathbf{w}_t + \psi_2' \mathbf{d}_t) G_1^L(\gamma, \mathbf{c}; \Delta_4 y_{t-d}) + \varepsilon_t, \qquad (21.14)$$

Table 21.1 Percentiles of the forecast densities of the Australian unemployment rates 1996(1)–1998(1) obtained using both an AR model and an LSTAR model of type (21.14). Compare with Figures 21.8 and 21.9

Horizon quarter	Forecasts						True values observed
	AR			LSTAR			
	25%	50%	75%	25%	50%	75%	
1996(1)	8.7	9.2	9.7	8.5	9.0	9.5	9.2
1996(2)	7.8	8.6	9.4	7.7	8.5	9.3	8.3
1996(3)	7.6	8.7	9.7	7.4	8.5	9.6	8.4
1996(4)	7.4	8.9	10.2	7.2	8.5	9.9	8.4
1997(1)	8.1	9.9	11.6	8.0	9.4	10.8	9.4
1997(2)	7.3	9.3	11.1	7.4	8.8	10.2	8.5
1997(3)	7.0	9.2	11.2	7.3	8.7	10.1	8.4
1997(4)	7.0	9.3	11.5	7.3	8.6	10.1	8.0
1998(1)	7.7	10.2	12.5	8.2	9.6	10.0	8.9

where $\mathbf{w}_t = (1, \Delta y_{t-1}, \ldots, \Delta y_{t-p})'$, $\mathbf{d}_t = (d_{1t}, d_{2t}, d_{3t})'$ is a vector of seasonal dummy variables, $\alpha > 0$, and the transition function is defined as in (21.2). Note that model (21.14) is in levels if $\alpha \neq 0$. The transition variable is a four-quarter difference because possible intra-year nonlinearities are not our concern. The estimated equations and interpretations can be found in Skalin and Teräsvirta (2002). These series show unit-root behavior: testing the unit-root hypothesis with the standard augmented Dickey–Fuller test does not lead to rejecting the null hypothesis at conventional significance levels.

The estimation period of Skalin and Teräsvirta for these two models ends in 1995. We forecast the two series nine quarters ahead starting from 1996(1) and compare the forecasts with the corresponding nine new observations that have meanwhile become available. We also forecast the same period with an AR model for Δy_t augmented with seasonal dummies. The results are given in tables 21.1 and 21.2. For Denmark, the LSTAR model forecasts the slow downward movement better than the AR model. In the Australian case, both models forecast reasonably well, the nonlinear model somewhat better than the linear one. (As the forecast horizon is not the same for all forecasts, the standard Diebold–Mariano test (Diebold and Mariano, 1995) for comparing the accuracy of forecasts is not available here.) The 50 percent equal tails interval forecasts from the STAR models contain the true values for all periods in both cases. The mode and median point forecasts differ from the means, because the forecast densities are not symmetric.

Table 21.2 Percentiles of the forecast densities of the Danish unemployment rates 1996(1)–1998(1) obtained using both an AR model and an LSTAR model of type (21.14). Compare with Figures 21.10 and 21.11

Horizon quarter	Forecasts						True values observed
	AR			LSTAR			
	25%	50%	75%	25%	50%	75%	
1996(1)	9.1	9.9	10.6	8.9	9.7	10.4	9.9
1996(2)	7.3	8.7	10.0	7.1	8.7	9.9	8.6
1996(3)	7.0	8.8	10.6	6.6	8.6	10.3	8.6
1996(4)	6.5	8.6	10.7	5.6	8.1	10.4	7.8
1997(1)	7.1	9.8	12.4	5.7	8.6	10.3	8.8
1997(2)	5.6	8.8	11.8	4.2	7.5	10.9	7.7
1997(3)	5.3	9.0	12.2	3.9	7.4	11.0	7.7
1997(4)	5.3	9.0	12.5	3.2	6.9	10.8	6.9
1998(1)	6.0	10.1	14.0	3.4	7.2	11.2	7.7

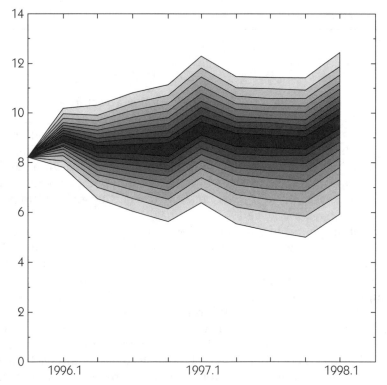

Figure 21.8 The fan graphs for forecast densities of the Australian unemployment rates 1996(1)–1998(1) obtained from LSTAR models of type (21.14) reported in Skalin and Teräsvirta (2002). The largest interval represents 90% of the estimated forecast density

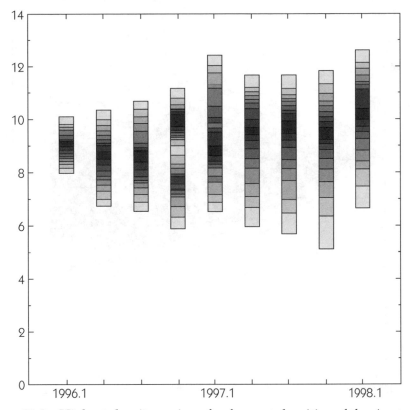

Figure 21.9 Highest-density regions for forecast densities of the Australian unemployment rates 1996(1)–1998(1) obtained from LSTAR models of type (21.14) reported in Skalin and Teräsvirta (2002). The largest interval represents 90% of the estimated forecast density

The asymmetry is clearly visible in the fan charts and highest-density regions for the forecasts in figures 21.8–21.11. For the Australian unemployment rate, the graph of the highest-density regions in figure 21.9 also shows that the densities are bimodal for forecasts four and five quarters ahead. As to the forecasts of the Danish unemployment, the fan chart in figure 21.10 indicates much greater predictive uncertainty than is the case for the Australian forecasts. While the point forecasts from an LSTAR model evaluated in MSE terms may not be more accurate than those from a linear model, the advantage of forecasts from nonlinear models may lie in this asymmetry. Asymmetric forecast densities may convey important information to decision-makers. In the present case the message is that while the unemployment rate may well decrease in the future, an even faster decrease than foreseen (point forecasts) is less likely than a slowdown or even another upturn. Such information is not available to those relying on forecasts from linear models. Those forecasts have symmetric forecast densities.

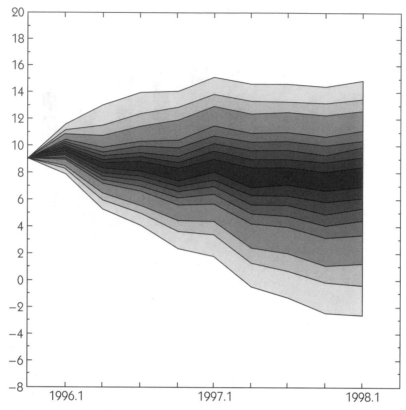

Figure 21.10   The fan graphs for forecast densities of the Danish unemployment rates 1996(1)–1998(1) obtained from LSTAR models of type (21.14) reported in Skalin and Teräsvirta (2002). The largest interval represents 90% of the estimated forecast density

If we accept the idea that the forecast densities contain useful information then, instead of comparing point forecasts, the focus could be on comparing forecast densities. Clements and Smith (2000) recently compared linear and nonlinear forecasts of the seasonally adjusted U.S. GNP and unemployment series. The point forecasts from nonlinear models considered were not better than those from linear ones. On the other hand, the nonlinear density forecasts were more accurate than those obtained from linear models. These comparisons did not include STAR models, but the results are suggestive anyway. Density forecasts are surveyed by Tay and Wallis in chapter 3 of this book.

21.5.   CONCLUSIONS

We have seen that forecasting with STAR models is somewhat more complicated than forecasting with linear models. As a reward, the forecaster obtains forecast

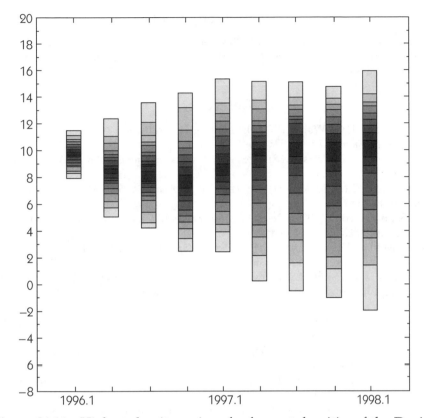

Figure 21.11 Highest-density regions for forecast densities of the Danish unemployment rates 1996(1)–1998(1) obtained from LSTAR models of type (21.14) reported in Skalin and Teräsvirta (2002). The largest interval represents 90% of the estimated forecast density

densities that contain considerably more information than mere point forecasts. Reporting these densities in practical work therefore seems worthwhile, and this chapter contains examples of ways of doing that in a compact and illustrative fashion.

The simulation results in the chapter show that mean forecasts from a correctly specified STAR model can be more accurate than their counterparts from a misspecified linear model. This should not come as a surprise. The results also indicate, however, that the nonlinear model may not have always a predictive edge where it may be expected to, namely in forecasting "nonlinear observations." On the other hand, it is no doubt possible to construct STAR models which, at least in simulation studies, have this property. As a whole, we may conclude that STAR models offer an interesting alternative in modeling and forecasting economic time series, and that more work is needed to fully understand their potential in economic forecasting.

Acknowledgments

The first author thanks the Tore Browaldh's Foundation for financial support. The work of the second author has been supported in part by the Swedish Council for Research in the Humanities and Social Sciences.

References

Bacon, D.W. and D.G. Watts (1971). Estimating the transition between two intersecting straight lines. *Biometrika*, 58, 525–34.

Bates, D.M. and D.G. Watts (1988). *Nonlinear Regression Analysis and its Applications*. New York: John Wiley.

Box, G.E.P. and G.M. Jenkins (1970). *Time Series Analysis, Forecasting and Control*. San Francisco: Holden-Day.

Chan, K.S. and H. Tong (1986). On estimating thresholds in autoregressive models. *Journal of Time Series Analysis*, 7, 178–90.

Clements, M.P. and D.F. Hendry (1999). *Forecasting Non-Stationary Economic Time Series. The Zeuthen Lectures on Economic Forecasting*. Cambridge, MA: MIT Press.

Clements, M.P. and J. Smith (2000). Evaluating the forecast densities of linear and nonlinear models: Applications to output growth and unemployment. *Journal of Forecasting*, 19, 255–76.

Davies, R. (1977). Hypothesis testing when a nuisance parameter is present only under the alternative. *Biometrika*, 64, 247–54.

Diebold, F.X. and R.S. Mariano (1995). Comparing predictive accuracy. *Journal of Business and Economic Statistics*, 13, 253–63.

Eitrheim, Ø. and T. Teräsvirta (1996). Testing the adequacy of smooth transition autoregressive models. *Journal of Econometrics*, 74, 59–75.

Engle, R.F. (1982). Autoregressive conditional heteroscedasticity with estimates of the variance of United Kingdom inflation. *Econometrica*, 50, 987–1007.

Granger, C.W.J. and T. Teräsvirta (1993). *Modeling Nonlinear Economic Relationships*. Oxford: Oxford University Press.

Granger, C.W.J. and T. Teräsvirta (1999). A simple nonlinear time series model with misleading linear properties. *Economics Letters*, 62, 161–5.

Hamilton, J.D. (1989). A new approach to the economic analysis of nonstationary time series and the business cycle. *Econometrica*, 57, 357–84.

Hansen, B.E. (1996). Inference when a nuisance parameter is not identified under the null hypothesis. *Econometrica*, 64, 413–30.

Härdle, W. (1990). *Applied Nonparametric Regression*. Cambridge: Cambridge University Press.

Hendry, D.F. (1995). *Dynamic Econometrics*. Oxford: Oxford University Press.

Hyndman, R.J. (1995). Computing and graphing highest density regions. *American Statistician*, 50, 120–6.

Hyndman, R.J. (1996). Highest-density forecast regions for nonlinear and non-normal time series models. *Journal of Forecasting*, 14, 431–41.

Leybourne, S.J., P. Newbold and D. Vougas (1998). Unit roots and smooth transitions. *Journal of Time Series Analysis*, 19, 83–97.

Lindgren, G. (1978). Markov regime models for mixed distributions and switching regressions. *Scandinavian Journal of Statistics*, 5, 81–91.

Luukkonen, R., P. Saikkonen, and T. Teräsvirta (1988). Testing linearity against smooth transition autoregressive models. *Biometrika*, 75, 491–99.

Matzner-Løber, E., A. Gannoun, and J.G. De Gooijer (1998). Nonparametric forecasting: A comparison of three kernel-based methods. *Communications in Statistics, Theory and Methods*, 27, 1593–617.

Mincer, J. and V. Zarnowitz (1969). The evaluation of economic forecasts. In J. Mincer (ed.), *Economic Forecasts and Expectations*. New York: National Bureau of Economic Research.

Montgomery, A.L., V. Zarnowitz, R.S. Tsay, and G.C. Tiao (1998). Forecasting the U.S. uneployment rate. *Journal of the American Statistical Association*, 93, 478–93.

Rahiala, M. and T. Teräsvirta (1993). Business survey data in forecasting the output of Swedish and Finnish metal and engineering industries: a Kalman Filter approach. *Journal of Forecasting*, 12, 255–71.

Sarantis, N. (1999). Modeling nonlinearities in real effective exchange rates. *Journal of International Money and Finance*, 18, 27–45.

Silverman, B.W. (1986). *Density Estimation for Statistics and Data Analysis*. London: Chapman and Hall.

Skalin, J. and T. Teräsvirta (2002). Modelling asymmetries and moving equilibria in unemployment rates. *Macroeconomic Dynamics*, 6 (forthcoming).

Teräsvirta, T. (1994). Specification, estimation, and evaluation of smooth transition autoregressive models. *Journal of the American Statistical Association*, 89, 208–18.

Teräsvirta, T. (1998). Modelling economic relationships with smooth transition regressions. In A. Ullah and D.E.A. Giles (eds.), *Handbook of Applied Economic Statistics*. New York: Dekker, 507–52.

Teräsvirta, T. and H.M. Anderson (1992). Characterizing nonlinearities in business cycles with smooth transition autoregressive models. *Journal of Applied Econometrics*, 7, S119–36.

Tong, H. (1990). *Nonlinear Time Series. A Dynamical System Approach*. Oxford: Oxford University Press.

Tsay, R.S. (1989). Testing and modeling threshold autoregressive processes. *Journal of the American Statistical Association*, 84, 231–40.

Tsay, R.S. (1998). Testing and modeling multivariate threshold models. *Journal of the Americal Statistical Association*, 93, 1188–202.

Wallis, K.F. (1999). Asymmetric density forecasts of inflation and the Bank of England's fan chart. *National Institute Economic Review*, 168, 106–12.

Wooldridge, J.M. (1994). Estimation and inference for dependent processes. In R.F. Engle and D.L. McFadden (eds.), *Handbook of Econometrics*, Vol. 4. Amsterdam: Elsevier, 2638–737.

CHAPTER TWENTY-TWO

Forecasting Financial Variables

Terence C. Mills

22.1. INTRODUCTION AND HISTORICAL PERSPECTIVE

The predictability of financial markets has engaged the attention of both market professionals and academic economists for many years, but has also attracted the interest of numerous "amateur" investors, whether gifted or otherwise. The benefits of being able to accurately forecast movements in financial markets are aptly demonstrated by the example presented by Andrew Lo (1997), who contrasted the returns from investing $1 in January 1926 in one-month U.S. Treasury bills with that of investing $1 at the same time in the S&P 500 stock market index. If the proceeds were reinvested each month, then the $1 investment in Treasury bills would have grown to $14 by December 1996, while the same investment in the S&P 500 would have been worth $1,371. But the greater returns obtained from investing in the stock rather than the bond market is not the point of the example, for suppose that at the start of each month the investor was able to forecast correctly which of these two investments would yield a higher return for that month, and acted on this forecast by switching the running total of his investment into the higher-yielding asset. Ignoring transaction costs, such a "perfect foresight" investment strategy would have been worth $2,296,183,456 by December 1996. Obviously, few, if any, investors have perfect foresight, but Lo's point was that even a modest ability to forecast financial asset returns would have been handsomely rewarded, for it does not take a large fraction of $2 billion plus to beat $1,371.

Detailed analysis of financial markets began in earnest in the 1920s in the United States, and a thriving industry was soon in operation, although this did not prevent many practitioners (and indeed academics, most notably Irving Fisher) from failing to forecast the 1929 Crash (see the reflections of Samuelson, 1987). These analysts focused on the study of past price movements and patterns using the information provided by charts of the price history, which led to them being called *chartists*, although the subject now often goes under the name *technical analysis*. Chartists typically regard price movements as falling into three classes. The primary trend is the main direction in which the market carries out its "search for the 'right' price"; these trend movements usually last for more than a year and sometimes for much longer periods. Secondary trends zig-zag up and down across the axis of the primary trend; these are the directions in which the market seeks the right price for periods of at least several weeks and perhaps many months. Finally, tertiary trends wander across the axis of the secondary trends and endure for a day or two and at most for a few weeks.

Long-term investors read charts to decide on the direction of the primary trend and to determine, as early as possible, if it changes. Speculators and short-term investors, on the other hand, attempt to determine whether tertiary and secondary trends have changed. The "art" of chartism is thus to identify trend changes by assessing whether certain price patterns, regarded by chartists as having prophetic significance, in the sense that they are believed regularly to precede trend changes, have occurred or, indeed, are occurring. There are many chartist patterns, of varying degrees of complexity, and going by such evocative terms as "gaps," "flags," "pennants," "symmetrical triangles," "rising wedges," "resistance lines," "reflecting barriers," and, perhaps the most celebrated of all, the "head-and-shoulders." An extended discussion of these may be found in, for example, Stewart (1986) and a formal empirical examination of the head-and-shoulders rule is conducted by Chang and Osler (1998). Malkiel (1999) continues to provide a trenchant critique of chartism.

Technical analysis has, in recent years, evolved further in the sense that attempts have been made to provide a theoretical underpinning to what, on the face of it, is a purely descriptive forecasting technique. Plummer (1989), for example, invokes the psychology of crowd behavior and the mathematics of spirals, notably limit cycles and Fibonacci Sequences, to provide what he regards as a formal underpinning to technical analysis.

Even while this "eyeball" examination of past price patterns for possible prophetic significance was becoming standard practice for investment analysts, academics had begun to analyse financial price series using statistical techniques. Kendall (1953) found that *changes* in financial prices behaved nearly as if they had been generated by a suitably designed roulette wheel for which each outcome was statistically independent of past outcomes and for which the probabilities of occurrence were reasonably stable through time. This has the implication that, once the investor accumulates enough evidence to make good estimates of the probabilities of different outcomes of the wheel, his forecasts can be based only on those probabilities, and he need pay no attention to the pattern of recent spins. Such spins are relevant to forecasting only insofar as they contribute to more precise estimates of probabilities – in gambling terms, Kendall's roulette wheel "has no memory."

Similar conclusions had, in fact, been reached long before Kendall's study, notably by Working (1934), who had focused on the related characteristic of financial prices, that they resemble cumulations of purely random changes. Further impetus to research on price forecastability was provided by the publication of the papers by Roberts (1959) and Osborne (1959). The former presents a largely heuristic argument for why successive price changes should be independent, while the latter develops the proposition that it is not the actual price changes but the logarithmic price changes which are independent of each other. With the auxiliary assumption that the logarithmic changes themselves are normally distributed, this implies that prices are generated as Brownian motion.

The stimulation provided by these papers was such that numerous articles appeared over the next few years investigating the hypothesis that price changes (or logarithmic price changes) are independent, a hypothesis that came to be termed the random walk model, in recognition of the similarity of the evolution of a price series to the random stagger of a drunk. Indeed, the term "random walk" is believed to have first been used in an exchange of correspondence appearing in *Nature* in 1905 (see Pearson and Rayleigh, 1905), which was concerned with the optimal search strategy for finding a drunk who had been left in the middle of a field. The solution is to start exactly where the drunk had been placed, as that point is an unbiased estimate of the drunk's future position, since he will presumably stagger along in an unpredictable and random fashion. This example illustrates the crucial property of a random walk: if prices follow a random walk, then the optimal forecast of *any* future price, made using the information contained in past prices, is simply today's price. Any patterns observed in the past have thus occurred by chance, and will therefore have zero probability of ever occurring again.

Why, though, should people be fooled into seeing patterns in series that are no more than accumulations of random numbers, as must technical analysts under the random walk hypothesis? This self-deception seems to be because there is a tendency to ascribe to *sums* of independent random variables behavior which is typical of the individual random variables themselves. Indeed, Working noted precisely all the "chartist" effects in his artificially generated random walks. Hence, if price changes are indeed random, the price level, which is the sum of the changes, will be expected to be random as well, although it will, in fact, be highly correlated with past price levels. Conversely, when patterns are observed in the levels, successive price changes will be expected to be related. This counter-intuitive result is, in fact, a consequence of the *first arc sine law* of probability and is typical of many problems involving the cumulation of chance fluctuations.

These ideas are illustrated by four representative financial series. Figure 22.1 shows monthly levels and changes of the U.K. Treasury bill rate from 1952 to 1998. Figure 22.2 shows weekly levels and changes of the dollar/sterling exchange rate from 1972 to 1998. Figure 22.3 shows daily levels and changes (that is, returns) of the logarithms of the FTSE 100 stock market index from 1984 to 1998. Figure 22.4 shows levels and changes of the dollar/sterling exchange rate observed at 30 minute intervals during 1996. The series are chosen to represent various types of financial assets observed at different observation intervals over alternative time periods. All show patterns and trends in their levels, but all appear to be essentially random in their changes, in apparent confirmation of the random walk model. This conclusion is too simple, however, for predictabilities

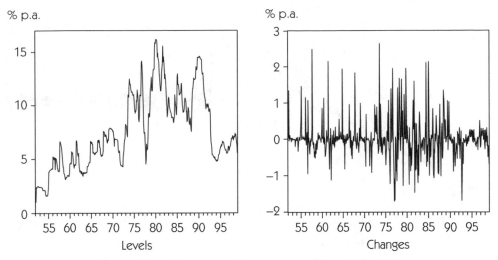

Figure 22.1 Treasury Bill rate, monthly, 1952–1998

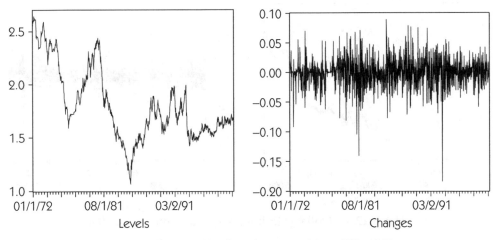

Figure 22.2 Dollar/sterling, weekly, 1972–1998

can be uncovered in these series of changes, but they only emerge when various extensions of the random walk model are considered, and this is the theme of the next section.

22.2. RANDOM WALKS, ARIMA MODELS, AND MARTINGALES

The most natural way to state formally the random walk model is as

$$P_t = P_{t-1} + a_t, \tag{22.1}$$

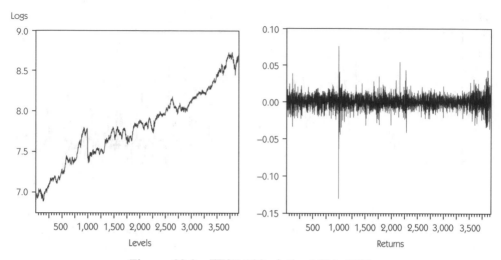

Figure 22.3   FTSE 100, daily, 1984–1998

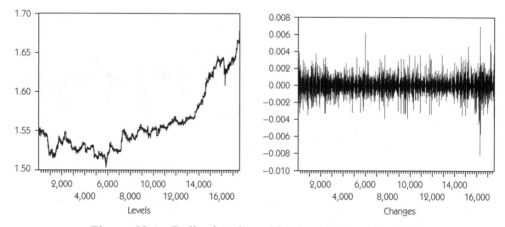

Figure 22.4   Dollar/sterling, 30-minute intervals, 1996

where P_t is the price observed at the beginning of time t and a_t is an error term which has zero mean and whose values are independent of each other: we refer to this as being white noise. The price change, $\Delta P_t = P_t - P_{t-1}$, is thus simply a_t and hence is independent of past price changes. Note that, by successive backward substitution in (22.1), we can write the current price as the cumulation of all past errors, that is, as

$$P_t = \sum_{i=1}^{t} a_i,$$

so that the random walk model implies that prices are indeed generated by Working's "cumulation of purely random changes." Osborne's model of Brownian motion implies that equation (22.1) holds for the logarithms of P_t and, further, that a_t is drawn from a zero mean normal distribution having constant variance.

Most of the early papers in this area are contained in the collection of Cootner (1964), while Granger and Morgenstern (1970) provide a detailed development and empirical examination of the random walk model and various of its refinements. Amazingly, much of this work had been anticipated by the French mathematician Louis Bachelier (1900, English translation in Cootner, 1964) in a remarkable Ph.D thesis in which he developed an elaborate mathematical theory of speculative prices, which he then tested on the pricing of French government bonds, finding that such prices were consistent with the random walk model. What made the thesis even more remarkable was that it also developed many of the mathematical properties of Brownian motion which had been thought to have first been derived some years later in the physical sciences, particularly by Einstein. Yet, as Mandelbrot (1989) remarks, Bachelier had great difficulty in even getting himself a university appointment, let alone getting his theories disseminated throughout the academic community.

It should be emphasized that the random walk model is only a hypothesis about how financial prices move. One way it can be tested is by examining the autocorrelation properties of the price changes, while another way is suggested by the implied behavior of longer differences of P_t. If we denote the variance of ΔP_t as $E(a_t^2) = \sigma^2$, then the variance of

$$\Delta_k P_t = P_t - P_{t-k} = \sum_{i=0}^{k-1} \Delta P_{t-i}$$

must be $k\sigma^2$ under the random walk assumptions. Thus the variance of price changes must increase one-for-one with the differencing interval under the random walk hypothesis. For example, two-week price changes must have a variance twice that of one-week changes; the variance of four-week price changes must be exactly twice the variance of two-week changes; and so on. For details of the variety of procedures available for testing the random walk hypothesis, see, for example, Mills (1999, ch. 3).

If the random walk hypothesis is rejected then, since (22.1) can be viewed as a particular model within the autoregressive-integrated-moving average (ARIMA) class, models of this type can be fitted using standard techniques and these can then be used to forecast P_t (see Mills, 1999, ch. 2, for details).

During the 1960s much research was also carried out on the theoretical foundations of financial markets, leading to the development of the theory of efficient capital markets. As LeRoy (1989) discusses, this led to some serious questions being raised about the random walk hypothesis as a *theoretical* model of financial markets. It is the assumption in (22.1) that price changes are independent that is the problem here, for it was found to be too restrictive to be generated within a reasonably broad class of optimizing models. Independence rules out not only any dependence of the conditional expectation of ΔP_t on past values of ΔP, but also any dependence involving higher conditional moments, such as the conditional variance of ΔP_t. Relaxing the assumption of independence to that of ΔP_t being *uncorrelated* with past values leads to P_t following a *martingale* process. The

Table 22.1   Forecastability of changes and squared changes

Treasury bill rate, monthly changes

k	1	10	20	50
r	0.080	0.080	0.097	0.125
r^2	0.014	0.025	0.021	0.026
$|r|$	0.052	0.104	0.110	0.133

Dollar/sterling, weekly changes

k	1	10	20	50
r	0.001	0.001	0.004	−0.005
r^2	0.012	0.020	0.034	0.030
$|r|$	0.036	0.079	0.082	0.085

FTSE 100, daily returns

k	1	10	20	50
r	0.006	0.010	0.015	0.020
r^2	0.329	0.345	0.348	0.351
$|r|$	0.067	0.123	0.128	0.132

Dollar/sterling, 30 minute changes

k	1	10	20	50
R	0.017	0.018	0.019	0.019
r^2	0.106	0.120	0.122	0.129
$|r|$	0.099	0.149	0.152	0.157

Note: r denotes the change in levels (log levels for returns), r^2 the square of these changes, and $|r|$ the absolute value. The cells of each block provide $\bar{R}^2$ statistics calculated from autoregressions of order k.

importance of this distinction is that financial series are known to go through both protracted quiet periods and protracted periods of turbulence, as is clearly seen in the plots of the changes in figures 22.1–22.4. This type of behavior could be modeled by a process in which successive conditional variances of ΔP_t (but *not* successive levels) are positively autocorrelated: such a specification is consistent with a martingale, but not with the more restrictive random walk.

How well do these models fit the four series? Table 22.1 presents some evidence concerning the forecastability of the changes of each of the series, showing $\bar{R}^2$ statistics calculated from autoregressions of increasing order (for the daily FTSE 100 *logarithmic* changes are used, which equate to returns). If the random walk model is appropriate, then both the changes and squared changes should have $\bar{R}^2$ statistics which are essentially equal to zero, whereas the martingale model would allow the squared changes (which are proxies for the conditional variances) to have significant statistics. Although all the $\bar{R}^2$ statistics are statistically significant at the 5 percent level, both the 30 minute and weekly changes of the dollar/sterling rate are essentially unforecastable, as are the daily returns of the FTSE 100. There is some evidence, however, that monthly changes in the Treasury bill rate are forecastable. Squared 30 minute changes in the dollar/ sterling rate and squared daily returns of the FTSE 100 are also forecastable, but the squared weekly changes in the dollar/sterling rate and the squared monthly changes in the Treasury bill rate are much less so. Thus the results indicate that forecastability of changes increases with sampling interval, while forecastability of squared changes (that is, conditional variances) tends to decrease with sampling interval, findings that are common to many studies (for example, Baillie and Bollerslev, 1989a).

22.3. FORECASTING VOLATILITY

Given this evidence of martingale-like behavior in many financial series, forecasts of conditional variances, usually referred to as volatility, are of great interest to financial analysts, particularly as such measures are essential inputs into option pricing formulae such as Black–Scholes (see, for example, Jorion, 1995). Several methods of estimating volatility are regularly used, perhaps the simplest being a moving average of past variances (see Kroner, Kneafsey, and Claessens, 1995). Let r_t be either the change or the logarithmic change in an asset price, that is, $r_t = \Delta P_t$: we refer to this as the return at time t. The moving-average forecast of volatility at time t, using the n most recent observations, is thus

$$\hat{\sigma}^2_{n,t} = n^{-1}\sum_{j=t-n}^{t-1}(r_j - \bar{r}_{n,t-1})^2 \quad \bar{r}_{n,t-1} = n^{-1}\sum_{j=t-n}^{t-1}r_j.$$

A more popular method is to use one of the autoregressive conditional heteroskedasticity (ARCH) class of models (see Mills, 1999, ch. 4, for a textbook development). The basis for the ARCH model is to write r_t as a product process

$$r_t = \mu_t + U_t\sigma_t,$$

where U_t is a standardised process, that is, it is an independent, identically distributed random variable having a zero mean and unit variance. σ^2_t is the conditional variance of the return at time t and may be expressed as

$$\sigma^2_t = V(r_t\,|\,r_{t-1}, r_{t-2}, \ldots) = V(\varepsilon_t\,|\,r_{t-1}, r_{t-2}, \ldots),$$

where

$$\varepsilon_t = r_t - E(r_t | r_{t-1}, r_{t-2}, \ldots) = r_t - \mu_t = U_t \sigma_t$$

is the error made in forecasting r_t based on the conditional mean process μ_t, which may, for example, be a function of the past history of returns or it may contain other variables as well. The GARCH(1, 1) model allows σ_t^2 to depend linearly on the previous squared forecasting error and the previous value of σ_t^2:

$$\sigma_t^2 = \alpha_0 + \alpha_1 \varepsilon_{t-1}^2 + \beta_1 \sigma_{t-1}^2.$$

This model, for which α_0, α_1, and β_1 must all be nonnegative to ensure that σ_t^2 is always nonnegative, has been found to provide a good fit to the conditional variance of many financial time series. Forecasts of future volatility are easily computed. The forecast of σ_{t+h}^2, made at time t, is given by

$$\hat{\sigma}_t^2(h) = \alpha_0 (\textstyle\sum_{k=0}^{h-1}(\alpha_1 + \beta_1)^k) + \sigma_t^2(\alpha_1 + \beta_1)^h.$$

The unconditional variance will exist if $\alpha_1 + \beta_1 < 1$ and is given by $\sigma^2 = \alpha_0/(1 - \alpha_1 - \beta_1)$: $\hat{\sigma}_t^2(h)$ will then converge to this value as h increases. If $\alpha_1 + \beta_1 = 1$, then the unconditional variance does not exist and

$$\hat{\sigma}_t^2(h) = h\alpha_0 + \sigma_t^2, \qquad (22.2)$$

which tends to infinity as h increases. If this is the case, then we have an integrated GARCH, or IGARCH(1, 1), model. It is often the case with financial series that the estimated values of α_1 and β_1 sum to a value that is close to unity, so that shocks to the conditional variance are persistent in the sense that they remain important for all future forecasts.

More general GARCH models and a large variety of ARCH-type models, along with methods of estimation and tests for the presence of ARCH, are discussed in Mills (1999, ch. 4), while a model that is closely related to the IGARCH(1, 1) is the *stochastic volatility* (SV) model, which defines the conditional variance equation to be

$$\log(\sigma_t^2) = \gamma_0 + \gamma_1 \log(\sigma_{t-1}^2) + \eta_t.$$

Typically, γ_1 is found to be close to unity, so that $\log(\sigma_t^2)$ is effectively a random walk. In such cases the fit of the SV model, and hence the forecasts of volatility, will be similar to those of the IGARCH(1, 1) model.

A third approach to forecasting volatility is to derive the volatility implied by solving the Black and Scholes option pricing model for the case when the option price equals the market price. While this "market-based" method is certainly attractive, computation of the volatilities can be rather complicated (see Jorion, 1995).

We shall concentrate on GARCH model-based forecasts of volatility. Significant ARCH effects were found in all four of our example series and, with the

Table 22.2 GARCH model estimates

	Treasury bill	Weekly $/£	FTSE	30 min $/£
Constant	–	–	0.00053	–
			(0.00013)	
r_{t-1}	0.358	0.052	0.080	−0.169
	(0.048)	(0.032)	(0.017)	(0.012)
r_{t-2}	–	–	–	−0.052
				(0.011)
r_{t-10}	–	–	0.041	–
			(0.020)	
α_0	0.206	0.717*	0.027*	0.249
	(0.038)	(0.318)	(0.007)	(0.030)
α_1	0.336	0.136	0.082	0.258
	(0.081)	(0.032)	(0.017)	(0.017)
β_1	−0.110	0.835	0.887	0.713
	(0.054)	(0.038)	(0.018)	(0.016)
$\alpha_1 + \beta_1$	0.226	0.971	0.969	0.971
T	562	1407	3903	17566
R^2	0.077	0.001	0.009	0.016

* Denotes that the estimates are scaled by 10^4. Heteroskedasticity consistent standard errors are shown in parentheses.

conditional mean μ_t being specified to be an autoregression, GARCH(1, 1) processes were then fitted, the estimated models being reported in table 22.2. For the monthly changes in the Treasury bill rate, an AR(1) model was adequate for the conditional mean, so that h-step-ahead forecasts of the *level* of the rate, P_t, are given by

$$P_t(1) = P_t \qquad + 0.358(P_t - P_{t-1}), \qquad\qquad h = 1,$$

$$P_t(2) = P_t(1) \qquad + 0.358(P_t(1) - P_t), \qquad\qquad h = 2,$$

$$P_t(h) = P_t(h - 1) + 0.358(P_t(h - 1) - P_t(h - 2)), \quad h \geq 3.$$

Forecasts of the *conditional variance* are given by

$$\hat{\sigma}^2(h) = 0.206(\textstyle\sum_{k=0}^{h-1}0.226^k) + \sigma_t^2(0.226^h),$$

which will converge to $\sigma^2 = 0.206/(1 - 0.226) = 0.266$.

Similar models are found for the weekly dollar/sterling rate. For $h \geq 3$, h-step-ahead forecasts of the level are given by

$$P_t(h) = P_t(h-1) + 0.052(P_t(h-1) - P_t(h-2)),$$

while forecasts of the conditional variance are given by

$$\hat{\sigma}^2(h) = (0.717 \times 10^{-4})(\textstyle\sum_{k=0}^{h-1} 0.971^k) + \sigma_t^2(0.971^h).$$

As the dollar/sterling exchange rate is "closer" to a martingale, with the coefficient of r_{t-1} being small and not particularly significant, the forecast of next week's exchange rate is almost identical to this week's observed rate, within only a small weight given to the current change (or momentum) in the rate. In contrast, the forecast of next month's Treasury bill rate adjusts this month's rate quite substantially for the current momentum in the rate.

On the other hand, forecasts of the future volatility of the Treasury bill rate converge much quicker to the unconditional variance (as powers of 0.226) than do future volatility forecasts of the exchange rate, which converge as powers of 0.971.

Forecasts of the level of the daily (logarithmic) level of the FTSE 100 and the 30 minute dollar/sterling exchange rate incorporate longer memory (in terms of observation frequency). Such forecasts are given by, for sufficiently large h,

$$P_t(h) = 0.00053 + P_t(h-1) + 0.080(P_t(h-1) - P_t(h-2))$$
$$+ 0.041(P_t(h-10) - P_t(h-11))$$

and

$$P_t(h) = P_t(h-1) - 0.169(P_t(h-1) - P_t(h-2)) - 0.052(P_t(h-2) - P_t(h-3)),$$

respectively. The forecasts for the FTSE 100 contain a constant, to incorporate the upward drift in the series observed in figure 22.3, and also place a small, but significant, weight on the return lagged ten trading days, reflecting a "seasonal" pattern. The 30 minute exchange rate is negatively related to changes in the rate observed half an hour and one hour previously. Both conditional variance forecasting equations, however, are virtually identical to that for the weekly exchange rate, since $\hat{\alpha}_1 + \hat{\beta}_1$ is approximately 0.97 in all three cases, the equations differing only in the variance scaling parameter $\hat{\alpha}_0$.

One-step-ahead forecasts of conditional standard deviations, that is, $\hat{\sigma}_t(1)$, are shown in figures 22.5–22.8, from which the stylized fact of ARCH processes, that of periods of tranquility interspersed with bouts of turbulence, is clearly observed. The volatility persistence of the Treasury bill rate is also seen to be substantially less than that of the other three series. Note also that, in all four cases, the martingale assumption can be rejected, since lagged changes are found to be important for forecasting future levels of the series.

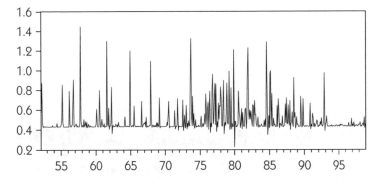

Figure 22.5 One-step-ahead conditional standard deviations:
Treasury bill rate

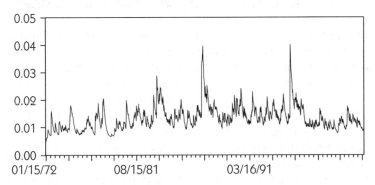

Figure 22.6 One-step-ahead conditional standard deviations:
dollar/sterling changes

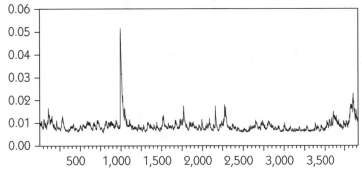

Figure 22.7 One-step-ahead conditional standard deviations:
FTSE 100

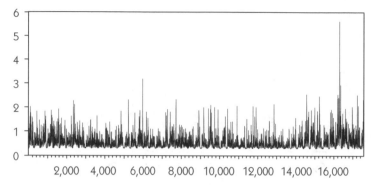

Figure 22.8 One-step-ahead conditional standard deviations:
dollar/sterling, changes, 30-minute intervals, 1996

22.4. LONG MEMORY, FAT TAILS, AND FORECASTING EXTREME EVENTS

An important departure from the martingale assumption that is often argued to
be a feature of financial time series is that of *long memory* or *long-range dependence*.
This is the phenomenon whereby past observations are nontrivially correlated
with observations in the distant future, even as the time span between the observations increases. The typical model for the conditional mean discussed in
previous sections assumes that the level of the series is an integrated process of
order one; that is, it is $I(1)$, so that the first differences are $I(0)$, and therefore
stationary. In general, the level of the series may be $I(d)$ and so require differencing
d times to become stationary.

For the random walk (22.1), and indeed for any $I(1)$ process, the autocorrelations
of the level, P_t, will be given approximately by $\rho_j = c(1 - \delta j)$, where δ is a small
positive number and $c > 0$. Consequently, the ρ_j will decline at a linear rate. On the
other hand, if there is any correlation between successive first differences, ΔP_t, then
the size of these autocorrelations will decline at an exponential rate: $|\rho_j| \leq c\delta^{-j}$.

Long memory is a feature of a class of models that relax the assumption that
the differencing parameter, d, must be integer. For any real $d > -1$, we may make
use of the binomial series expansion to write

$$\Delta^d x_t = 1 - dx_{t-1} + \frac{d(d-1)}{2!}x_{t-2} - \frac{d(d-1)(d-2)}{3!}x_{t-3} + \ldots + (-1)^j\frac{d!}{j!(d-j)!}x_{t-j} + \ldots$$

$$(22.3)$$

The *fractional white noise* process may then be defined as

$$\Delta^d x_t = a_t.$$

For noninteger values of d, it can be shown that the autocorrelations of x_t are
given by $\rho_j = \Gamma j^{2d-1}$, where Γ is the ratio of two gamma functions, so that the

autocorrelations exhibit a *hyperbolic* decay, the speed of which depends upon d (see, for example, Baillie, 1996). Thus the decay in the autocorrelations is slower than for the random walk that occurs when $d = 1$, but faster than for the stationary series with $d = 0$. For $d < 0.5$, x_t is still stationary, but for $d \geq 0.5$ x_t has an infinite variance and hence is nonstationary, although Robinson (1994) refers to it as being "less nonstationary" than an $I(1)$ process. For typical financial time series, x_t will actually be the change in the (logarithmic) price level, that is, $x_t = r_t = \Delta P_t$, so what is being examined here is whether *returns* exhibit long-memory, a question that has been asked since the original research of Mandelbrot (1972). For a recent polemical restatement of his position, see Mandelbrot (1997), and for reviews of the empirical evidence and methods of testing for long memory and of estimating d, see Baillie (1996) and Lo (1997).

The natural extension of the fractional white-noise process is the AR-Fractionally Integrated-MA (ARFIMA) process, and such models have also been used to model long memory in volatility by Baillie, Bollerslev, and Mikkelson (1996) and Bollerslev and Mikkelsen (1996).

Forecasting from ARFIMA processes requires the use of the formulae provided by Peiris and Perera (1988). For example, for the ARFIMA(1, d, 0) process

$$\Delta^d x_t = y_t, \; y_t = \phi y_{t-1} + a_t$$

one-step-ahead forecasts are given by

$$x_t(1) = dx_t - \frac{d(d-1)}{2!} x_{t-1} + \frac{d(d-1)(d-2)}{3!} x_{t-2} - \ldots + \phi a_t + \phi^2 a_{t-1} + \ldots,$$

where, by convention, we assume that $x_0 = x_{-1} = \ldots = a_0 = a_{-1} = \ldots = 0$.

The fractional-differencing parameter d was estimated using the procedure proposed by Geweke and Porter-Hudak (1983) for the differences of each of our four series and also for the squared and absolute differences. For the Treasury bill rate the estimates of d were 0.03, 0.08, and 0.10, respectively. Since the standard error associated with these estimates is approximately 0.13, no evidence of long memory is thus found for any of these transformations. For the weekly exchange rate, the estimates of d were 0.18, 0.23, and 0.39, with standard errors now of 0.10, while for the 30 minute exchange rate the estimates were 0.01, 0.13, and 0.24, with standard errors 0.04. Finally, the daily FTSE 100 returns produced estimates of d of 0.02, 0.17, and 0.36, with standard errors 0.06. Thus there appears to be no evidence of long memory in the differences (returns) of any of the three series, but significant evidence for the squares and absolute values. These results are consistent both with the statistics provided in table 22.1 and with the findings of Ding, Granger, and Engle (1993), Ding and Granger (1996), Granger, Ding, and Spear (1997), and Mills (1997) for a wide variety of financial time series observed at intervals of a week or less and for other power transformations of returns. Taken together, these imply that nonlinear models have potential forecasting ability.

Associated with long memory in power transformations of returns is a second "stylized fact" of financial returns – that their (marginal) distributions are "fat-tailed" and more highly peaked than a normal distribution (and are often skewed, although we shall not emphasize this latter feature here). This stylized fact was first emphasized by Mandelbrot (1963), who proposed using the stable class of distributions to model financial returns: see McCulloch (1996) for a recent survey of this very large literature. A property of the stable distribution is that it has an infinite variance, which, if true, would throw a great deal of statistical analysis of financial time series into question. More recently, attention has focused on determining the actual shape of the tails of returns distributions; in particular, on estimating the *tail index*, denoted ζ and defined for a random variable x to be the value such that $E(|x|^k) < \infty$ for all $0 \le k < \zeta$. If $\zeta < 2$, then the variance of x is infinite and x can be characterized as being generated by a stable distribution. If $\zeta \ge 2$, the variance of x is finite, but the distribution is not necessarily normal and may thus still have fat tails: for example, it may be Student's t, in which case ζ defines the degrees of freedom. Distributions such as the normal (and power exponential) possess all moments and for these ζ is infinite and they may be described as being thin-tailed.

The tail index may be estimated by a variety of methods (see, for example, Mills, 1999, ch. 5). Using the technique proposed by Loretan and Phillips (1994), and concentrating on the left-hand tail of the returns distributions for expository purposes, ζ was estimated to be 4.69 for the Treasury bill rate, 3.30 for the weekly exchange rate, 2.04 for the FTSE 100, and 2.28 for the 30 minute exchange rate. In all four cases, the variance of the returns is therefore finite, although highly fat-tailed. However, McCulloch (1997) argues that this method of estimating the tail index can provide an upwardly biased estimate of ζ when the distribution really is stable, so perhaps the inference regarding the FTSE 100 should be treated with some degree of caution.

Given an estimate of the tail index, extreme return levels that are only rarely exceeded can be established by extrapolating the distribution outside of the observed sample, and this can be useful for analyzing "safety first" portfolio selection strategies (see Jansen and de Vries, 1991). Using the formulae provided in Mills (1999, ch. 5.3), then, although the largest observed monthly fall in the Treasury bill rate during the period 1952 to 1998 was 1.71 percentage points, we calculate that there is a 0.6 percent chance of a monthly fall of two percentage points in any one year; that is, once in every 167 years is the Treasury bill rate likely to drop by two percentage points in a month. Similarly, although the largest weekly fall in the dollar/sterling exchange rate observed during the period 1972 to 1998 is 17 cents, there is a 1.2 percent chance of a weekly fall of 20 cents in any one year; that is, once in every 83 years is the exchange rate likely to drop by 20 cents in a week. For the FTSE 100, we find that there is an 8.4 percent chance of a 20 percent daily fall in the index in any one year, so that once in every 12 years is the FTSE 100 likely to drop by 20 percent (the largest observed fall of 13.1 percent was on Black Monday, October 19, 1987). Finally, there is a 1 percent chance of a 0.026 cent fall in the exchange rate during a 30 minute period in any one week.

22.5. NONLINEAR MODELS, NEURAL NETWORKS, AND CHAOS

Granger, Spear and Ding (2000) and Mills (1996a, 1997a) investigate the distributional properties of absolute returns, the usefulness of such a transformation for measuring risk being discussed in Granger and Ding (1995). They find that absolute returns for a wide variety of financial series tend to have an exponential marginal distribution, especially after the trimming of outliers. This has the implication that linear regressions of absolute returns on lagged absolute returns may have some forecasting power, and the results presented in table 22.1 for absolute returns suggest that this is indeed the case.

Several more complicated nonlinear models have been proposed for forecasting returns, and a review of these may be found in Mills (1999, ch. 4). We will focus on two, related, classes of models here: regime switching models and artificial neural networks, as these have proved the most popular. The Markov chain switching regime model popularized by Hamilton (1990) and Engle (1994) can be written, in its simplest form, as

$$r_t = \begin{cases} \mu_0 + \varepsilon_t & \text{if } S_t = 0, \\ \mu_1 + \varepsilon_t & \text{if } S_t = 1, \end{cases}$$

where S_t is a state variable determining the mean of r_t, whose value is thus conditional upon which regime the tth observation falls into. The conditional probabilities determining the evolution of the regimes are $P(S_t = i \mid S_{t-1} = i) = p_{ii}$ and $P(S_t = j \mid S_{t-1} = i) = 1 - p_{ii}$, $i, j = 0, 1$. An equivalent formulation is

$$r_t = \alpha_0 + \alpha_1 S_t + \varepsilon_t,$$

where $\alpha_0 = \mu_0$ and $\alpha_1 = \mu_1 - \mu_0$. It can be shown that S_t is generated by the process

$$S_t = (1 - p_{11}) + (p_{00} + p_{11} - 1)S_{t-1} + v_t$$

The innovation v_t is heteroskedastic and, although uncorrelated with lagged values of S_t, is not independent of them. One-step-ahead forecasts then require a forecast of the regime at time $t + 1$, $\hat{S}_t(1)$, and this requires use of the EM algorithm outlined in Hamilton (1990) to obtain the required conditional probabilities. Although simple, the model does allow for a wide range of nonlinear behavior. For example, asymmetry in the two regimes can be characterized by μ_0 being large and positive and p_{00} being small, so that upward moves are short and sharp, and μ_1 being negative and small and p_{11} being large, so that downward moves are drawn out and gradual. If r_t is completely independent of the previous state, then we have a random walk (strictly a martingale) in the levels with $p_{00} = 1 - p_{11}$; alternatively, the idea of there being "long swings" in the series can be represented by μ_0 and μ_1 being opposite in sign and p_{00} and p_{11} both being large.

This model was fitted to the Treasury bill rate, leading to the following set of parameter estimates:

$$\hat{\mu}_0 = 0.057 \quad \hat{\mu}_1 = -0.023,$$

$$\hat{p}_{00} = 0.705 \quad \hat{p}_{11} = 0.813,$$

$$\hat{\sigma}_0^2 = 0.681 \quad \hat{\sigma}_1^2 = 0.020,$$

where $\hat{\sigma}_0^2$ and $\hat{\sigma}_1^2$ are estimates of the variances attached to the two regimes. Thus regime 0 is associated with a 0.06 percentage point monthly rise in the rate and regime 1 with 0.02 percentage point fall. These estimates also show that the movements in the Treasury bill rate are characterized by moderately long swings, since the point estimates of p_{00} and p_{11} are both in excess of 0.7. The expected length of stay in regime 0 (an upswing) is given by $(1 - p_{00})^{-1} = 3.4$ months, while that for regime 1 is $(1 - p_{11})^{-1} = 5.4$ months. An upswing is associated with much greater volatility than a downswing, given the difference in the two estimated variances. The random walk hypothesis is clearly rejected, and forecasts of the future state are given by $S_t(1) = 0.187 + 0.518S_t$, so that one-step-ahead forecasts of the level of the Treasury bill rate are given by

$$P_t(1) = P_t + 0.042 - 0.041S_t.$$

The Markov approach assumes that the process can shift randomly and abruptly from one regime to the other. An alternative is to consider a process in which the regime transition occurs in a smooth fashion. This can be done by considering *smooth transition* autoregressive (STAR) models, a popular example of which is the *logistic* STAR (LSTAR) process. Noting that we have already fitted an AR(1)-GARCH(1, 1) to the weekly changes in the dollar/sterling exchange rate, then an LSTAR(1) model for the conditional mean is defined as

$$r_t = (\pi_1 + \pi_2 S_t(\gamma, c, r_{t-d}))r_{t-1} + \varepsilon_t,$$

where

$$S_t(\gamma, c, r_{t-d}) = (1 + \exp(-\gamma(r_{t-d} - c)))^{-1}$$

is the logistic function and is known as the smooth transition, in which c is the threshold between regimes and γ measures the speed of adjustment from one regime to the other. For a given value of the delay parameter d, the model can be estimated by nonlinear least squares. (For methods of testing for the presence of and specifying STAR processes, see Teräsvirta (1994). Lundbergh and Teräsvirta in chapter 21 of this volume discuss STAR models.)

Because there is considerable evidence that nonlinear models, although fitting better than linear models within-sample, nevertheless often produce worse out-of-sample forecasts (see, for example, Dacco and Satchell, 1999), we estimated

AR(1) and LSTAR(1) models for a sample period that omitted the 1998 observations, leaving these for out-of-sample forecasting. The delay was set at $d = 1$, and GARCH(1, 1) models were fitted to each error process. As these were very similar to each other and, indeed, similar to the full-sample estimates reported in table 22.2, we concentrate here on the models for the conditional mean, which were estimated as, respectively,

$$r_t = 0.060 r_{t-1} + \varepsilon_t$$
$$(0.032)$$

and

$$r_t = \left(\begin{array}{c} 0.124 - 0.238 S_t(645, 0.031, r_{t-1}) \\ (0.042) \quad (0.079) \end{array} \right) r_{t-1} + \varepsilon_t.$$

The smooth transition is seen to be significant and, consequently, the in-sample RMSE is slightly smaller than that from the linear model, 0.0241 to 0.0242. The parameters of the logistic function imply a rapid transition from one regime to the other ($\hat{\gamma}$ is large), with the threshold estimated to be at $\hat{c} = 0.031$ (that is, 3 cents). The out-of-sample RMSE from the LSTAR model is, however, 6.2 percent smaller than that from the linear model, showing that, in this case, a nonlinear model offers a better out-of-sample forecasting performance.

A related class of nonlinear models are artificial neural networks (ANNs). These are flexible functional forms whose development was motivated by the way the brain processes information, although the use of the word "artificial" recognizes that these models represent at best an approximation of the brain's behavior. With the development of high-speed computing, ANNs have become popular methods of forecasting financial time series, although some of the extravagent claims that have been made concerning their success is probably a consequence of ineffective validation of the technique (see the survey by Adya and Collopy, 1998), while their transparency has been effectively masked by an inpenetrable jargon (for a particularly sceptical reaction to ANNs, see Chatfield, 1993). In fact, ANNs are closely related to STAR processes: for example, a simple ANN can be written as

$$r_t = \pi_1 r_{t-1} + \pi_2 S_t(\gamma, c, r_{t-1}) + \varepsilon_t. \tag{22.4}$$

The logistic function $S_t(\gamma, c, r_{t-1})$ is here known as a *hidden layer*. Generalizations include the addition of further lags, additional logistic functions to allow for more hidden layers, the inclusion of multi-layers, for example, $S_t(\gamma, c, S_t(r_{t-1}))$, and alternative nonlinear functions.

Estimation of the simple ANN in (22.4) produced

$$r_t = 0.122 r_{t-1} - 0.017 S_t(202, 0.041, r_{t-1})$$
$$(0.045) \quad (0.008)$$

with an in-sample RMSE of 0.2410, slightly smaller than either the linear or LSTAR alternatives. The out-of-sample RMSE was slightly larger than the LSTAR model but still 6.1 percent smaller than the linear model.

The nonlinear processes that have been introduced so far all have in common the aim of modeling *stochastic* nonlinearities. This would seem a natural approach to take, but recently a literature has developed that considers the question of whether time series could have been generated, at least in part, by nonlinear *deterministic* laws of motion. This literature has been prompted by findings in the natural sciences of completely deterministic processes that generate behavior which looks random under statistical tests: processes that are termed "deterministic" or "white chaos." A popular example is the deterministic function

$$x_t = 4x_{t-1}(1 - x_{t-1}) = 4x_{t-1} - 4x_{t-1}^2,$$

which produces a series having the same autocorrelation properties as white noise, hence the term white chaos. Are such models useful in finance? Brock (1988) considers some models of equilibrium asset pricing that might lead to chaos and complex dynamics: the idea that there should be no arbitrage profits in financial equilibrium is linked with the theory of economic growth to show how dynamics in the "dividend" process are transmitted through the equilibrating mechanism to equilibrium asset prices. These dynamics can be linear, nonlinear, or chaotic, depending on the constraints imposed on the models. Apart from this, there have only been a few attempts to build theoretical financial models from chaotic foundations (for example, Huang and Day, 1993; Wen, 1996). Furthermore, there has been little empirical evidence of chaotic dynamics uncovered in financial time series, although, as we have seen, much evidence of other types of stochastic nonlinearities (for a particularly skeptical view concerning the presence of chaos in economic data, see Granger, 1991).

22.6. Trading Rules, Directional Forecasts, and Forecast Evaluation

As mentioned in the introductory section, technical analysts study the past history of price series to forecast future prices. However, it is misleading to think that all of their techniques are "exotic," informal, and impossible to test rigorously. Many of them can, in fact, be expressed as linear combinations of past prices or returns, and we refer to these as *technical indicators* or *trading rules*. For example, a simple rule provides a *sell signal* at time t if $MA_t(n) < MA_t(m)$, where

$$MA_t(q) = q^{-1}\Sigma_{i=0}^{q-1}P_{t-i}, \quad q = n, m, \quad n < m;$$

that is, if a short moving average of current and past prices is below a long moving average then a fall in price is forecast, so that a decision to sell is signalled. Typical values for (n, m) are (1, 150) and (5, 200): see, for example, Mills (1997b). More detailed trading rules that can be expressed as linear combinations of prices or returns are set out in Acar (1998). Note that trading rules do not provide an h-step-ahead point forecast, but a one-step-ahead trading signal. In general, if the trading rule is written as $F_t = f(P_t, P_{t-1}, \dots)$, then the rule produces the binary stochastic process B_t, defined as

$$\text{sell: } B_t = -1 \quad \text{iff} \quad F_t < 0,$$

$$\text{buy: } B_t = +1 \quad \text{iff} \quad F_t \geq 0.$$

B_t is completely defined by the rule and only in the trivial case of a buy (sell) and hold strategy is it deterministic, taking the value +1 (−1) irrespective of the underlying price process.

The study of the binary process B_t is of limited interest for trading purposes. What is important is the returns process implied by the decision rule. Denoting the return at time t made by applying the rule F_{t-1} as R_t, then

$$R_t = B_{t-1} r_t = \begin{cases} -r_t & \text{if} \quad B_{t-1} = -1, \\ +r_t & \text{if} \quad B_{t-1} = +1. \end{cases}$$

Trading rules and, indeed, other forecasting models, should therefore be evaluated by their implied returns or profits (net of trading costs if these can be calculated) – a view that has been argued in a more general context by Leitch and Tanner (1991, 1995), who suggest that there is little relationship between profit measures and summary error measures such as RMSE, an implication of which is that a squared error cost function may not be appropriate, and hence least squares estimation sub-optimal, in these situations. The use of asymmetric cost functions, particularly in the context of financial forecasting, has been proposed by Stockman (1987), and the theory of optimal forecasting under asymmetric loss is developed in Christoffersen and Diebold (1996, 1997).

Alternative methods of evaluating *directional* forecasts of this type have been developed by Pesaran and Timmermann (1992) and Stekler (1994), and have been applied to the foreign exchange market by Satchell and Timmermann (1995). Methods of evaluating volatility forecasts are discussed in Taylor (1999).

As an example of the use of trading rules and directional forecasts, the moving average rule with $n = 5$ and $m = 200$ was used to produce trading signals for the daily FTSE 100 series and cumulative profits were compared to those obtained from a buy and hold strategy. The (5, 200) rule produced a return of 46 percent compared with a buy and hold return of 165 percent: the much greater return from the latter strategy (even greater if transaction costs are taken into account) being a consequence of the upward trend in the index during this period and being consistent with the results reported in Mills (1997b). There were 24.7 percent sell signals and, on defining a trade to occur when $\Delta B_t \neq 0$, application of the rule leads to 52 trades (1.4 percent of the effective sample). As a second example, a (1, 20) rule was applied to the weekly dollar/sterling exchange rate. Now the trading rule produces a 142 percent return compared to a loss of 45 percent for a buy and hold strategy – the exchange rate has fairly long swings which the trading rule can take advantage of to produce much larger returns than buy and hold, which makes a loss because of the overall depreciation of sterling during the sample period. Here there were 52.45 percent sell signals and 123 (8.9 percent) trades.

22.7. Predicting Long Horizon Returns and Forecasting High-Frequency Price Changes

A feature peculiar to financial time series is that, because of the wide range of frequencies for which data is available, distinct techniques have evolved for forecasting over long and very short time horizons. Focusing first on the former, Fama and French (1988) and Poterba and Summers (1988) were the first to consider the predictability of stock market returns over long time horizons. Fama and French considered a particularly simple model. The k-period return may be defined in terms of the one-period return r_t and the (logarithmic) price P_t:

$$r_{t,k} = \sum_{i=0}^{k-1} r_{t+i} = \Delta_k P_t = P_t - P_{t-k}.$$

Suppose that P_t is the sum of a random walk, z_t, and a stationary component, u_t:

$$P_t = z_t + u_t,$$

$$z_t = z_{t-1} + \mu + \eta_t,$$

where the stationary component is an AR(1) process,

$$u_t = \phi u_{t-1} + a_t,$$

so that η_t and a_t are independent white noises. If ϕ is close to one, u_t will exhibit slow "mean reversion." Fama and French show that the slope coefficients from the regression of $r_{t,k}$ on $r_{t-k,k}$ – that is, the current k-period return on the previous *nonoverlapping* k-period return – will then form a U-shaped pattern as k increases, starting at around 0 for short horizons, becoming more negative as k increases and the mean reversion of the stationary component exerts its influence, before finally moving back toward 0 as the variance of the random walk innovation begins to dominate at long horizons.

Using this model on annual stock return data for the U.S., Fama and French estimate that 25–45 percent of the variation of 3–5 year stock returns is predictable from past returns, the higher value being found for portfolios of small firms. Poterba and Summers use the same intuition to construct tests of mean reversion using variance ratio statistics, although their focus was not primarily on the predictability of returns.

At the other extreme of the frequency range, Engle and Russell (1997, 1998; see also Engle, 2000) consider how to model the arrival of price quotes in the foreign exchange market. Such quotes inherently arrive in irregular time intervals, but there are difficulties with the natural inclination of choosing some fixed interval and aggregating the information within each interval: choosing too short an interval will mean that most data points will be zero, thus introducing a form of heteroskedasticity, while if too long an interval is chosen features of the data will be smoothed and potentially hidden. Engle and Russell thus introduce the *autoregressive conditional duration* model, a type of dependent Poisson process, which predicts how long it will be until prices change; that is, it measures the expected time per unit price change, rather than the usual expected price change per unit time. They also show how the model can be interpreted to give measures of volatility.

22.8. CALENDAR EFFECTS AND OTHER ANOMALIES

One form of predictability that has created a good deal of interest in recent years is the presence of calendar effects and other anomalies. To date, researchers have found evidence of a January effect, in which stock returns in this month are exceptionally large when compared to the returns observed for other months; a weekend effect, in which Monday mean returns are negative rather than positive as for all other weekdays; a holiday effect, showing a much larger mean return for the day before holidays; a turn-of-the-month effect, in which the four-day return around the turn of a month is *greater* than the average total monthly return; an intramonth effect, in which the return over the first half of a month is significantly larger than the return over the second half; and a variety of intraday effects.

Early reviews of these anomalies are Thaler (1987a,b), while Mills and Coutts (1995) provide a more recent survey and additional evidence. A wide range of statistical techniques have been employed to detect such anomalies and to use them for forecasting. Taylor (1986, pp. 41–4) discusses some of the techniques and the interested reader is recommended to examine both this and further papers cited in the above references. Whilst the analysis of anomalies dominated much of the 1980s research in empirical finance, it has become less popular in recent years and, indeed, the difficulties for statistical inference of "data-snooping" has led some researchers, notably Sullivan, Timmermann, and White (2001), to seriously question the significance, and by implication the forecasting performance, of the calendar effects found in stock returns.

22.9. USING OTHER VARIABLES TO FORECAST RETURNS

The variety of models that have so far been introduced all investigate whether past returns are useful in forecasting future returns. Although the martingale assumption would preclude the use of other variables, there is no empirical reason, of course, why such variables should not be used in conjunction with past returns and many of the econometric issues involved in the building of multivariate models are outlined in detail in Mills (1999, ch. 6). We will concentrate here on reviewing some of the approaches that have been taken to forecast returns within a single equation regression framework (see also Granger, 1992).

A popular approach when attempting to forecast high-frequency (for example, daily) returns is to include as an additional regressor in the conditional mean equation the conditional variance (or standard deviation) obtained from a GARCH equation, thus leading to the GARCH-in-Mean (GARCH-M) model proposed by Engle, Lilien, and Robins (1987). Unfortunately, we could find no evidence in favor of including either of these conditional volatility measures in the conditional mean equations of the models of table 22.2. An alternative variable that is often used when modeling daily stock returns and volatility is trading volume, although only the contemporaneous volume is typically included and no forecasting is carried out (see, for example, Campbell, Grossman, and Wang, 1992; Gallant, Hsieh, and Tauchen, 1992; Hiemstra and Jones, 1994). Brooks (1998) has conducted a forecasting exercise using volatility and volume measures from the New York Stock Exchange and found that only very modest improvements were brought about by the inclusion of lagged volume measures, and augmenting our models for the FTSE 100 returns and squared returns with similar volume measures produced results that were consistent with this.

A richer selection of variables are available with monthly data. Concentrating on forecasting monthly stock returns (often it is returns in excess of a risk-free rate that are modeled), then several financial variables that have proved useful are the dividend yield associated with the index being analyzed, the gilt-equity yield ratio, inflation, and various interest rates. Finance theory also suggests that in markets with risk averse agents, stock returns should vary with the state of the business cycle (Balvers, Cosimano, and MacDonald, 1990). Consequently, the growth of industrial production and the money supply are often included in such models. Pesaran and Timmermann (1994, 1995) argue that, in constructing regression models to predict returns based on these variables, it is very important to build models in "real time," using only data that is available to the investor at any given time period, so that genuine *ex ante* forecasts are made and the benefits of hindsight are avoided. They therefore champion the use of recursive regression strategies and also emphasize forecast evaluation based on profits from a well defined trading strategy, as we have discussed above. Qi and Maddala (1999) extend this approach by using ANNs to incorporate nonlinearities between stock returns and the predicting variables.

There have also been various models constructed to forecast returns on other financial assets using wider information sets. Attempts have often been made to forecast exchange rate returns using fundamentals such as monetary and macroeconomic variables, but with little consistent success, although evidence is beginning to accrue that, just as in the case of stock returns, long-horizon predictability of exchange rates is quite substantial (see, for example, Mark, 1995).

22.10. USING EQUILIBRIUM RELATIONSHIPS TO FORECAST RETURNS

The models discussed above all attempt to predict the returns of a financial asset, which are typically stationary, by other stationary time series, usually the growth rates or changes of financial or macroeconomic variables. It is possible, however, that there may be long-run, equilibrium, relationships linking the asset price *level* with the levels of these variables, so that one or more cointegrating relationships hold. If this is the case then, via Granger's Representation Theorem (Engle and Granger, 1987), the lagged equilibrium error (or error correction) should be useful in forecasting the returns of the asset. Several examples of this may be found in the literature. The Capital Asset Pricing Model (CAPM) posits that the return on the *i*th asset or small portfolio, $r_{i,t}$, is linearly related to the return on the overall market portfolio, $r_{m,t}$:

$$r_{i,t} = \beta r_{m,t} + a_t, \tag{22.5}$$

where a_t is assumed to be white noise and β is known as the "investment beta," measuring the sensitivity of the return on the asset to variation in the returns on the market portfolio. Using the definitions $r_{i,t} = \Delta P_{i,t}$ and $r_{m,t} = \Delta P_{m,t}$, where $P_{i,t}$ and $P_{m,t}$ are the respective logarithmic price levels, summing over time gives (with $P_{i,0} = P_{m,0} = 0$)

$$P_{i,t} = \beta P_{m,t} + \varepsilon_t,$$

where $\varepsilon_t = \sum_{j=1}^{t} a_j$ must be $I(1)$, so that cointegration *cannot* occur between $P_{i,t}$ and $P_{m,t}$ under the CAPM. However, if there *is* cointegration between the price levels, then there must exist a stationary linear combination $P_{i,t} - \theta P_{m,t}$, whose lagged value should be included in (22.5), thus defining the equilibrium correction model

$$\Delta P_{i,t} = \beta \Delta P_{m,t} + \phi(P_{i,t-1} - \theta P_{m,t-1}) + a_t,$$

which has the implication that the past history of asset and market prices are useful in forecasting current returns of the asset. Models of this type are analyzed in Mills (1996b), where it is shown that cointegration between individual stock prices and the market index is by no means unusual and hence equilibrium-correction models are potentially useful for forecasting individual stock returns.

When analyzing the stock market as a whole, many investment professionals in the U.K. monitor the behavior of the gilt-equity yield ratio, believing that large deviations of this ratio from its "normal," or equilibrium, level will produce corrections in the gilt and stock markets. Defining P_t and D_t to be the logarithms of the price and dividend indices, respectively, and G_t to be the yield on gilt-edged stock, then this ratio can be written as

$$G_t - (D_t - P_t) = \alpha + u_t,$$

where α is the equilibrium level of the ratio and u_t is thus the current equilibrium error. Rewriting this as

$$P_t - D_t + G_t = \alpha + u_t \tag{22.6}$$

reveals that, for this ratio to maintain the assumption of an equilibrium relationship, u_t must be stationary and $P_t - D_t + G_t - \alpha$ must therefore be a stationary linear combination and hence a cointegrating relationship. Lagged values of this combination must therefore be useful in forecasting returns, along with past dividend growth, ΔD_{t-i}, and gilt yield changes, ΔG_{t-i}. Mills (1991, 1999) finds evidence of cointegration between P_t, D_t, and G_t for the U.K. and, moreover, cointegration coefficients insignificantly different from 1, −1, and 1 as predicted by (22.6), leading to the construction of equilibrium correction models to forecast stock market returns (see also Clare, Thomas, and Wickens, 1994).

Other examples of cointegration have been found in modeling the term structure of interest rates and in analyzing sets of foreign exchange rates (Baillie and Bollerslev, 1989b, 1994). This latter application also uses the ideas of multiple cointegrating vectors and the possibility of fractional cointegration. The econometric analysis of such extensions, along with several varieties of nonlinear cointegration, is developed in Mills (1999, chs. 7 and 8) and such models are now becoming very popular in forecasting financial time series.

22.11.   FUTURE TRENDS IN FORECASTING FINANCIAL TIME SERIES

Forecasting future trends in the empirical analysis of financial time series is probably just as difficult as forecasting the series themselves. What is clear is that increasing, and virtually costless, computer power, along with more sophisticated software, will lead to greater reliance on nonlinear models and computer-intensive evaluation techniques such as resampling methods like the bootstrap (see Mills, 1997b). Neural networks will continue to increase in popularity, and applications already include the pricing of options, which require forecasts of volatility (Lo and Wang, 1995; Anders, Korn, and Schmitt, 1998), and the evaluation of more complex trading rules (Gençay and Stengos, 1998). Multivariate techniques using both linear and nonlinear cointegration formulations should also become more widespread.

References

Acar, E. (1998). Expected returns of directional forecasters. In E. Acar and S.E. Satchell, (eds.), *Advanced Trading Rules*. Oxford: Butterworth-Heinemann, 51–80.

Adya, M. and F. Collopy (1998). How effective are neural networks at forecasting and prediction? A review and evaluation. *Journal of Forecasting*, 17, 481–95.

Anders, U., O. Korn and C. Schmitt (1998). Improving the pricing of options: a neural network approach. *Journal of Forecasting*, 17, 369–88.

Bachelier, L. (1900). Théorie de la spéculation. *Annales de l'Ecole Normale Superieure*, Series 3, 17, 21–86.

Baillie, R.T. (1996). Long memory processes and fractional integration in econometrics. *Journal of Econometrics*, 73, 5–59.

Baillie, R.T. and T. Bollerslev (1989a). The message in daily exchange rates: a conditional variance tale. *Journal of Business and Economic Statistics*, 7, 297–305.

Baillie, R.T. and T. Bollerslev (1989b). Common stochastic trends in a system of exchange rates. *Journal of Finance*, 44, 167–81.

Baillie, R.T. and T. Bollerslev (1994). Cointegration, fractional cointegration, and exchange rate dynamics. *Journal of Finance*, 49, 737–43.

Baillie, R.T., T. Bollerslev, and H.-O. Mikkelsen (1996). Fractionally integrated generalised autoregressive conditional heteroskedasticity. *Journal of Econometrics*, 74, 3–30.

Balvers, R.J., T.F. Cosimano, and B. MacDonald (1990). Predicting stock returns in an efficient market. *Journal of Finance*, 45, 1109–28.

Bollerslev, T. and H.-O. Mikkelson (1996). Modeling and pricing long memory in stock market volatility. *Journal of Econometrics*, 73, 151–84.

Brock, W.A. (1988). Nonlinearity and complex dynamics in economics and finance. In P. Anderson, K. Arrow, and D. Pines (eds.), *The Economy as an Evolving Complex System.* Reading, MA: SFI Studies in the Sciences of Complexity, 77–97.

Brooks, C. (1998). Predicting stock index volatility: Can market volume help? *Journal of Forecasting*, 17, 59–80.

Campbell, J.Y., S.J. Grossman, and J. Wang (1993). Trading volume and serial correlation in stock returns. *Quarterly Journal of Economics*, 108, 905–39.

Cootner, P.A. (ed.) (1964). *The Random Character of Stock Market Prices.* Cambridge, MA: MIT Press.

Chang, P.H.K. and C.L. Osler (1998). Is more always better? Head-and-shoulders and filter rules in foreign exchange markets. In E. Acar and S.E. Satchell (eds.), *Advanced Trading Rules.* Oxford: Butterworth-Heinemann, 127–42.

Chatfield, C. (1993). Editorial: Neural networks – forecasting breakthrough or passing fad? *International Journal of Forecasting*, 9, 1–3.

Christoffersen, P.F. and F.X. Diebold (1996). Further results on forecasting and model selection under asymmetric loss. *Journal of Applied Econometrics*, 11, 561–72.

Christoffersen, P.F. and F.X. Diebold (1997). Optimal prediction under asymmetric loss. *Econometric Theory*, 13, 808–17.

Clare, A.D., S.H. Thomas, and M.R. Wickens (1994). Is the gilt–equity yield ratio useful for predicting U.K. stock returns? *Economic Journal*, 104, 303–16.

Dacco, R. and S. Satchell (1999). Why do regime-switching models forecast so badly? *Journal of Forecasting*, 18, 1–16.

Ding, Z. and C.W.J. Granger (1996). Modeling volatility persistence of speculative returns: a new approach. *Journal of Econometrics*, 73, 185–215.

Ding, Z., C.W.J. Granger, and R.F. Engle (1993). A long memory property of stock market returns and a new model. *Journal of Empirical Finance*, 1, 83–106.

Engle, C. (1994). Can the Markov model forecast exchange rates? *Journal of International Economics*, 36, 151–65.

Engle, R.F. (2000). The econometrics of ultra-high-frequency data. *Econometrica*, 68, 1–22,

Engle, R.F. and C.W.J. Granger (1987). Cointegration and error correction: representation, estimation and testing. *Econometrica*, 55, 251–76.

Engle, R.F., D.M. Lilien, and R.P. Robbins (1987). Estimating time varying risk premia in the term structure: the ARCH-M model. *Econometrica*, 55, 391–408.

Engle, R.F. and J.E. Russell (1997). Forecasting the frequency of changes in quoted foreign exchange prices with the autoregressive conditional duration model. *Journal of Empirical Finance*, 4, 187–212.

Engle, R.F. and J.E. Russell (1998). Autoregressive conditional duration: a new model for irregularly spaced transaction data. *Econometrica*, 66, 1127–62.

Fama, E.F. and K.R. French (1988). Permanent and temporary components of stock prices. *Journal of Political Economy*, 96, 246–73.

Gallant, A.R., D.A. Hsieh, and G. Tauchen (1992). Stock prices and volume. *Review of Financial Studies*, 5, 199–242.

Gençay, R. and T. Stengos (1998). Moving average rules, volume and the predictability of security returns with feedforward networks. *Journal of Forecasting*, 17, 401–14.

Geweke, J. and S. Porter-Hudak (1983). The estimation and application of long memory time series models. *Journal of Time Series Analysis*, 1, 15–29.

Granger, C.W.J. (1991). Developments in the nonlinear analysis of economic series. *Scandinavian Journal of Economics*, 93, 263–76.

Granger, C.W.J. (1992). Forecasting stock market prices: Lessons for forecasters. *International Journal of Forecasting*, 8, 3–13.

Granger, C.W.J., S. Spear, and Z. Ding (2000). Stylized facts on the temporal and distributional properties of absolute returns. In W.-S. Chan, W.K. Li, and H. Tong (eds), *Statistics and Finance: An Interface*. London: Imperial College Press, 97–120.

Granger, C.W.J. and O. Morgenstern (1970). *Predictability of Stock Market Prices*. Lexington, MA: Heath.

Hamilton, J.D. (1990). Analysis of time series subject to changes in regime. *Journal of Econometrics*, 45, 39–70.

Hiemstra, C. and J.D. Jones (1994). Testing for linear and nonlinear Granger causality in the stock price–volume relationship. *Journal of Finance*, 49, 1639–64.

Huang, W.H. and R.H. Day (1993). Chaotically switching bear and bull markets: the derivation of stock price distributions from behavioural rules. In P. Chen and R.H. Day (eds.), *Nonlinear Dynamics and Evolutionary Economics*. Cambridge, MA: MIT Press.

Jansen, D.W. and C.G. de Vries (1991). On the frequency of large stock returns: putting booms and busts into perspective. *Review of Economics and Statistics*, 73, 18–24.

Jorion, P. (1995). Predicting volatility in the foreign exchange market. *Journal of Finance*, 50, 507–28.

Kendall, M.J. (1953). The analysis of economic time series, part 1: prices. *Journal of the Royal Statistical Society, Series A*, 96, 11–25.

Kroner, K.F., K.P. Kneafsey, and S. Claessens (1995). Forecasting volatility in commodity markets. *Journal of Forecasting*, 14, 77–95.

Leitch, G. and J.E. Tanner (1991). Economic forecast evaluation: profits versus the conventional error measures. *American Economic Review*, 81, 580–90.

Leitch, G. and J.E. Tanner (1995). Professional economic forecasts: are they worth the cost? *Journal of Forecasting*, 14, 143–57.

LeRoy, S.F. (1989). Efficient capital markets and martingales. *Journal of Economic Literature*, 27, 1583–621.

Lo, A.W. (1997). Fat tails, long memory, and the stock market since the 1960s. *Economic Notes*, 26, 213–46.

Lo, A.W. and J. Wang (1995). Implementing option pricing models when asset returns are predictable. *Journal of Finance*, 50, 87–129.

Loretan, M. and P.C.B. Phillips (1994). Testing the covariance stationarity of heavy-tailed time series. An overview of the theory with applications to several financial datasets. *Journal of Empirical Finance*, 1, 211–48.

McCulloch, J.H. (1996). Financial applications of stable distributions. In G.S. Maddala and C.R. Rao (eds.), *Handbook of Statistics, Vol. 14: Statistical Methods in Finance*. Amsterdam: Elsevier Science, 393–425.

McCulloch, J.H. (1997). Measuring tail thickness to estimate the stable index α: a critique. *Journal of Business and Economic Statistics*, 15, 74–81.

Malkiel, B.G. (1999). *A Random Walk Down Wall Street*. New York: Norton.

Mandelbrot, B.B. (1963). New methods of statistical economics. *Journal of Political Economy*, 71, 421–40.

Mandelbrot, B.B. (1972). Statistical methodology for nonperiodic cycles: from the covariance to R/S analysis. *Annals of Economic and Social Measurement*, 1/3, 259–90.

Mandelbrot, B.B. (1989). Louis Bachelier. In J. Eatwell, M. Milgate, and P. Newman (eds.), *The New Palgrave: Finance*. London: Macmillan, 86–8.

Mandelbrot, B.B. (1997). Three fractal models in finance: discontinuity, concentration, risk. *Economic Notes*, 26, 171–221.

Mark, N.C. (1995). Exchange rates and fundamentals: Evidence on long-horizon predictability. *American Economic Review*, 85, 201–18.

Mills, T.C. (1991). Equity prices, dividends and gilt yields in the U.K.: cointegration, error correction and "confidence." *Scottish Journal of Political Economy*, 38, 242–55.

Mills, T.C. (1996a). Nonlinear forecasting of financial time series: an overview and some new models. *Journal of Forecasting*, 15, 127–35.

Mills, T.C. (1996b). The econometrics of the "market model": cointegration, error correction and exogeneity. *International Journal of Finance and Economics*, 1, 275–86.

Mills, T.C. (1997a). Stylized facts on the temporal and distributional properties of daily FT-SE returns. *Applied Financial Economics*, 7, 599–604.

Mills, T.C. (1997b). Technical analysis and the London Stock Exchange: testing trading rules using the FT30. *International Journal of Finance and Economics*, 2, 319–31.

Mills, T.C. (1999). *The Econometric Modeling of Financial Time Series*, 2nd edn. Cambridge: Cambridge University Press.

Mills, T.C. and J.A. Coutts (1995). Anomalies and calendar affects in the new FT-SE indices. *European Journal of Finance*, 1, 79–93.

Pearson, K. and Lord Rayleigh (1905). The problem of the random walk. *Nature*, 72, 294, 318, 342.

Peiris, M.S. and B.J.C. Perera (1988). On prediction with fractionally differenced ARMA models. *Journal of Time Series Analysis*, 9, 215–20.

Pesaran, M.H. and A. Timmermann (1992). A simple nonparametric test of predictive performance. *Journal of Business and Economic Statistics*, 10, 461–5.

Pesaran, M.H. and A. Timmermann (1994). Forecasting stock returns: an examination of stock market trading in the presence of trading costs. *Journal of Forecasting*, 13, 335–367.

Pesaran, M.H. and A. Timmermann (1995). Predictability of stock returns: robustness and economic significance. *Journal of Finance*, 50, 1201–28.

Plummer, T. (1989). *Forecasting Financial Markets: The Truth Behind Technical Analysis*. London: Kogan Page.

Poterba, J.M. and L.H. Summers (1988). Mean reversion in stock prices: Evidence and implications. *Journal of Financial Economics*, 22, 27–59.

Qi, M. and G.S. Maddala (1999). Economic factors and the stock market: a new perspective. *Journal of Forecasting*, 18, 151–66.

Robinson, P.M. (1994). Time series with strong dependence. In C.A. Sims (ed.), *Advances in Econometrics: Sixth World Congress*, Vol. 1. Cambridge: Cambridge University Press, 47–95.

Samuelson, P.A. (1987). Paradise lost and refound: the Harvard ABC barometers. *Journal of Portfolio Management*, 4, 4–9.

Satchell, S.E. and A. Timmermann (1995). An assessment of the economic value of nonlinear foreign exchange rate forecasts. *Journal of Forecasting*, 14, 477–97.

Stekler, H.O. (1994). Are economic forecasts valuable? *Journal of Forecasting*, 13, 495–505.

Stewart, T.H. (1986). *How Charts Can Make You Money: Technical Analysis for Investors*. Cambridge: Woodhead-Faulkner.

Stockman, A.C. (1987). Economic theory and exchange rates. *International Journal of Forecasting*, 3, 3–15.

Sullivan, R., A. Timmermann and H. White (2001). Dangers of data mining: the case of calendar effects in stock returns. *Journal of Econometrics*, 105, 249–86.

Taylor, J.W. (1999). Evaluating volatility and interval forecasts. *Journal of Forecasting*, 18, 111–28.

Taylor, S.J. (1986). *Modeling Financial Time Series*. New York: John Wiley.

Teräsvirta, T. (1994). Specification, estimation, and evaluation of smooth transition autoregressive models. *Journal of the American Statistical Association*, 89, 208–18.

Thaler, R. (1987a). The January effect. *Journal of Economic Perspectives*, 1(1), 197–201.

Thaler, R. (1987b). Seasonal movements in security prices II: weekend, holiday, turn of the month, and intraday effects. *Journal of Economic Perspectives*, 1(2), 169–77.

Wen, K. (1996). Continuous-time chaos in stock market dynamics. In W.A. Barnett, A.P. Kirman, and M. Salmon (eds.), *Nonlinear Dynamics and Economics*. Cambridge: Cambridge University Press, 133–159.

Working, H. (1934). A random-difference series for use in the analysis of time series. *Journal of the American Statistical Association*, 29, 11–24.

CHAPTER TWENTY-THREE

Explaining Forecast Failure in Macroeconomics

Michael P. Clements and David F. Hendry

23.1. Introduction

Confidence in model-based macroeconomic forecasting has been punctured periodically by episodes of serious predictive failure. In the U.K., recent examples include the poor performance in forecasting the consumer boom of the late 1980s, and the depth and duration of the recession in the early 1990s. But these are merely the latest examples in a long catalog of failures, with noteworthy antecedents including the under-prediction of postwar consumption (see, for example, Spanos, 1989) and the 1974–5 and 1979–81 recessions (Wallis (1989) discusses the forecasting record of the major U.K. model-based forecasting teams during these two periods).

The problem with forecasting is that it is difficult to foretell what will come to pass. Modern "capitalist" economies are exceedingly complex, with the macro-aggregates that are observed being the outcomes of myriad interrelated decisions and actions taken by large numbers of heterogeneous agents with conflicting objectives. Such economies both evolve, and are subject to sudden shifts precipitated by institutional, political, social, financial, legal, and technological change. Examples of changing "institutional arrangements" relevant to the U.K. include membership of the European Union and privatization; political changes include the right/left swings of politics and the Gulf War; social changes include the consequences of the "welfare state" and its dismemberment; financial and legal changes with important economic repercussions include the abolition of exchange controls, the introduction of interest-bearing checking accounts, and the removal of mortgage rationing, the last two following the Banking Act of 1984 and the

Building Societies Act of 1986; and technological change is pandemic. These also interact, as with family organization following divorce-law changes, improved birth-control technology, and greater equality for women. Moreover, it is hard to envision what, and how large, the consequences of such changes will be, and how rapidy they will come to pass: apparently minor items of legislation can have major repercussions.

Forecasting *models* are just that, and empirically, the extent of misspecification of any given model for the process generating the data is unknown, but probably large. The data series used may be inaccurate, are prone to revision, and are often provided after a nonnegligible delay. Since an imperfect tool is being used to forecast a complicated and changing process, it is perhaps hardly surprising that forecasts sometimes go badly awry. Formally, we define forecast failure as a significant deterioration in forecast performance relative to the anticipated outcome.

In this chapter, we consider the causes of forecast failure.[1] As the above (partial) catalog of episodes of forecast failure makes plain, periods of forecast failure and economic turbulence often go hand in glove, so it is natural to identify structural breaks and regime shifts as primary causes of forecast failure. What is less obvious is that it is possible to narrow down the types of structural change that result in forecast failure, and show that many of the factors commonly held to be important, such as misspecified models, play only a peripheral role.

The structure of this chapter is as follows. In the next section, we present a taxonomy of possible sources of forecast error in a stationary dynamic system. In section 23.3, we consider the primary sources of forecast errors in a vector equilibrium-correction system. Both analyses suggest that deterministic shifts are the main source of systematic forecast failure, and we discuss possible causes of these shifts. Section 23.4 considers the possible sources of forecast failure in more detail: these include misspecification of stochastic components in stationary and nonstationary processes (section 23.4.1), misspecification of deterministic components (section 23.4.1), as well as breaks in misspecified models (section 23.4.2); estimation uncertainty (section 23.4.3); model uncertainty (section 23.4.4); and forecast-origin uncertainty (section 23.4.5). Finally, section 23.5 concludes.

23.2. A TAXONOMY OF SOURCES OF FORECAST ERROR

The structure of our inquiry into the sources of forecast failure has the following form. We specify a data generation process (DGP), and a model thereof, then delineate the possible mistakes that might induce forecast failure. For this approach to be useful in terms of delivering relevant conclusions about empirical forecasting, we require that the DGP adequately captures the appropriate aspects of the real world to be forecast, and that realistic assumptions are made about the forecasting models. Over the last 15 years, a consensus has emerged that the economy can be approximated by a system of integrated variables, subject to restrictions implied by cointegration, perturbed by periodic nonconstancies.[2] This is the form of DGP that underlies our analysis. The forecasting model is often formulated in accordance with some theoretical notions, but will be misspecified to an unknown extent for the DGP, particularly when the economy is evolving. While theory often serves as a guide, the model will also typically have been selected by some empirical criteria (raising concerns about model-selection effects – see section 23.4.4), and the parameters will have been estimated (possibly inconsistently) from (probably inaccurate) observations. Any or all of these mistakes might precipitate either poor, or significantly bad, forecasts.

To motivate the form of the taxonomy, forecasting models can be thought of as having three distinct components: deterministic terms (such as intercepts and trends) with known future values; observed stochastic variables (those which the model seeks to characterize) with unknown future values; and unobserved errors with unknown values (past, present, and future). Each element is in principle susceptible to many types of mistake: for example, they could be inaccurately measured, misspecified, incorrectly estimated, or change in unanticipated ways. Thus, at least $4 \times 3 = 12$ types of mistake could be made, but the following taxonomy is selective, and focuses on mistakes relating to the first two components; namely, deterministic and stochastic terms.

We first derive a taxonomy of forecast errors for a stationary vector autoregression, and then relate these sources of possible error to the parameters of an integrated-cointegrated system (henceforth, abbreviated to its acronym VEqCM, for vector equilibrium-correction model). For notational convenience, we assume a first-order process. Thus, the DGP for the n-dimensional vector process $\{y_t\}$ is given by

$$\mathbf{y}_t = \phi + \mathbf{\Pi}\mathbf{y}_{t-1} + \varepsilon_t \quad \text{with} \quad \varepsilon_t \sim \mathsf{IN}_n[\mathbf{0}, \mathbf{\Omega}_\varepsilon]. \tag{23.1}$$

The notation $\mathsf{IN}_n[\mathbf{0}, \sigma_\varepsilon^2]$, denotes a multivariate independent (I), normal (N) distribution with a mean of zero ($\mathsf{E}[\varepsilon_t] = \mathbf{0}$) and a positive-definite variance matrix $\mathsf{V}[\varepsilon_t] = \mathbf{\Omega}_\varepsilon$: since these are constant parameters, an identical distribution holds at every point in time. The eigenvalues of $\mathbf{\Pi}$ all lie inside the unit circle (so that the process is stationary, and being nonintegrated, we denote this by I(0)). Thus, we can calculate the unconditional mean of $\mathbf{y}_t$ from

$$\mathsf{E}[\mathbf{y}_t] = \phi + \mathbf{\Pi}\mathsf{E}[\mathbf{y}_{t-1}] \tag{23.2}$$

yielding

$$\mathsf{E}[\mathbf{y}_t] = (\mathbf{I}_n - \mathbf{\Pi})^{-1}\phi = \varphi, \tag{23.3}$$

so $\mathsf{E}[\mathbf{y}_s] = \varphi$ for all s. Then the mean-adjusted form of (23.1) is

$$\mathbf{y}_t - \varphi = \mathbf{\Pi}(\mathbf{y}_{t-1} - \varphi) + \varepsilon_t. \tag{23.4}$$

Given the information set $\{\mathbf{y}_t, t = 1, \ldots, T\}$, and the knowledge that the system is linear with one lag, using estimated parameters ("^"s on parameters denote estimates, and on random variables, forecasts), the h-step-ahead forecasts, $\hat{\mathbf{y}}_{T+h|T}$, at forecast origin T for horizons $h = 1, \ldots, H$ are obtained from (23.4) by iterating on

$$\hat{\mathbf{y}}_{T+h|T} - \hat{\varphi} = \hat{\mathbf{\Pi}}(\hat{\mathbf{y}}_{T+h-1|T} - \hat{\varphi}),$$

to give

$$\hat{\mathbf{y}}_{T+h|T} = \hat{\varphi} + \hat{\mathbf{\Pi}}^h(\hat{\mathbf{y}}_T - \hat{\varphi}), \tag{23.5}$$

where $\hat{\varphi} = (\mathbf{I}_n - \hat{\mathbf{\Pi}})^{-1}\hat{\phi}$. In this simple system, the h-step-ahead forecast equals the estimated equilibrium mean, plus the deviation therefrom at the estimated forecast origin $(\hat{\mathbf{y}}_T)$, scaled by the hth power of the dynamic matrix. Although the forecast origin $\hat{\mathbf{y}}_T$ is uncertain, we assume $\mathsf{E}[\hat{\mathbf{y}}_T | \mathbf{y}_T] = \mathbf{y}_T$ so $\hat{\mathbf{y}}_T$ provides an unbiased estimate of the forecast origin. By using (23.5), we do not assume that the forecaster knows the DGP (23.1), because we allow for the possibility that the parameter estimates are inconsistent, reflecting any extent of model misspecification. For example, elements of $\hat{\mathbf{\Pi}}$ might be restricted to zero (dynamic misspecification); the wrong variables might be used in the various equations, or the intercepts suppressed despite $\phi \neq \mathbf{0}$. A subscript p on a parameter will denote the $\text{plim}_{T\to\infty}$ (under constant parameters) of the corresponding estimate.

Because the system is dynamic, the impacts of breaks differ with the time-lapse since the break. Thus, after a structural break, the system becomes nonstationary in that its first and second moments are not constant, but change every period. We consider the case when a single permanent break occurs just after a forecast announcement. Consequently, but unknown to the forecaster, at time T, the parameters $(\phi : \mathbf{\Pi})$ change to $(\phi^* : \mathbf{\Pi}^*)$ where $\mathbf{\Pi}^*$ still has all its eigenvalues inside the unit circle. Thus, from $T + 1$ onwards, the data are generated by

$$\mathbf{y}_{T+h} = \phi^* + \mathbf{\Pi}^*\mathbf{y}_{T+h-1} + \varepsilon_{T+h}, \quad h = 1, \ldots \tag{23.6}$$

While the properties of $\{\varepsilon_{T+h}\}$ are not explicitly altered, we do not preclude changes in their distribution, serial correlation, or variance. Letting $\phi^* = (\mathbf{I}_n - \mathbf{\Pi}^*)\varphi^*$:

$$\mathbf{y}_{T+h} - \varphi^* = \mathbf{\Pi}^*(\mathbf{y}_{T+h-1} - \varphi^*) + \varepsilon_{T+h}$$

$$= (\mathbf{\Pi}^*)^h(\mathbf{y}_T - \varphi^*) + \sum_{i=0}^{h-1}(\mathbf{\Pi}^*)^i\varepsilon_{T+h-i}. \tag{23.7}$$

The future outcomes, as a deviation from the new equilibrium, are the appropriate powers of the new dynamic matrix, times the deviation at the forecast origin, but measured from the *new* equilibrium, plus the accumulated "discounted" future errors.

From (23.5) and (23.7), the h-step-ahead forecast errors $\hat{\varepsilon}_{T+h|T} = \mathbf{y}_{T+h} - \hat{\mathbf{y}}_{T+h|T}$ are (letting $\mathbf{u}_{T+h} = \sum_{i=0}^{h-1}(\mathbf{\Pi}^*)^i\varepsilon_{T+h-i}$)

$$\hat{\varepsilon}_{T+h|T} = \varphi^* - \hat{\varphi} + (\mathbf{\Pi}^*)^h(\mathbf{y}_T - \varphi^*) - \hat{\mathbf{\Pi}}^h(\hat{\mathbf{y}}_T - \hat{\varphi}) + \mathbf{u}_{T+h}. \tag{23.8}$$

Table 23.1 Forecast-error taxonomy

$$
\begin{aligned}
\hat{\varepsilon}_{T+h\,|\,T} \simeq\ & ((\mathbf{\Pi}^{*})^{h} - \mathbf{\Pi}^{h})(\mathbf{y}_{T} - \varphi) && (ia) && \text{slope change} \\
& + (\mathbf{I}_{n} - (\mathbf{\Pi}^{*})^{h})(\varphi^{*} - \varphi) && (ib) && \text{equilibrium-mean change} \\
& + (\mathbf{\Pi}^{h} - \mathbf{\Pi}_{p}^{h})(\mathbf{y}_{T} - \varphi) && (iia) && \text{slope misspecification} \\
& + (\mathbf{I}_{n} - \mathbf{\Pi}_{p}^{h})(\varphi - \varphi_{p}) && (iib) && \text{equilibrium-mean misspecification} \\
& - \mathbf{F}_{h}\delta_{\Pi}^{\nu} && (iiia) && \text{slope estimation} \\
& - (\mathbf{I}_{n} - \mathbf{\Pi}_{p}^{h})\delta_{\varphi} && (iiib) && \text{equilibrium-mean estimation} \\
& - (\mathbf{\Pi}_{p}^{h} + \mathbf{C}_{h})\delta_{y} && (iv) && \text{forecast origin uncertainty} \\
& + \sum_{i=0}^{h-1} (\mathbf{\Pi}^{*})^{i}\varepsilon_{T+h-i} && (v) && \text{error accumulation}
\end{aligned}
$$

We now rearrange (23.8) into interpretable factors, which can be analyzed separately without much loss, despite ignoring some interaction terms. Deviations between sample estimates and the population values of model parameters are denoted by $\delta_{\varphi} = \hat{\varphi} - \varphi_{p}$, where $\varphi_{p} = (\mathbf{I}_{n} - \mathbf{\Pi}_{p})^{-1}\phi_{p}$, and $\delta_{\Pi} = \hat{\mathbf{\Pi}} - \mathbf{\Pi}_{p}$, with $(\hat{\mathbf{y}}_{T} - \mathbf{y}_{T}) = \delta_{y}$. To obtain a clearer interpretation of the various sources of forecast errors, we ignore all powers and cross-products in the δ's for parameters (these are generally of a smaller order of magnitude than the terms retained), but retain terms involving parameters interacting with the forecast origin. Section 23.6 details the derivation, and defines the $\mathbf{C}_{h}$ and $\mathbf{F}_{h}$ matrices used in this taxonomy.

Table 23.1 combines the possible sources of forecast errors that arise from the decompositions. Five main sources are distinguished, but because of their central role below, we analyze deterministic terms and dynamics separately. Before proceeding, we note those sources of error that are not being considered. We do not directly address forecast errors emanating from the effects involving ε_{t}: a change in their mean is equivalent to a change in φ; a change in their variance could induce forecast failure, since interval forecasts calculated from the past fit of the model would be incorrect; and the model errors could be predictable (for example, serially correlated) as a result of misspecification of $\mathbf{\Pi}$. Consequently, some of these sources of forecast error will be picked up elsewhere in our taxonomy. We consider every potential effect of the deterministic and stochastic components, φ and $\mathbf{\Pi}$: change, misspecification, and estimation uncertainty. The contribution of forecast-origin uncertainty is also noted in the table: this can be viewed as mis-measurement of $\mathbf{y}_{T}$. Finally, the taxonomy allows for the chosen model to be misspecified for the DGP, but assumes the model is "pre-specified," in the sense that the taxonomy does not capture model uncertainty, or "overfitting" effects that arise from the model being selected from the data. Recently, these effects have been stressed by a number of authors (for example, Draper, 1995), and are discussed by us in section 23.4.4.

Section 23.4 considers the rows relating to misspecification and estimation in some detail. Here we provide a brief overview. Consider taking the unconditional expectation of each row of table 23.1 in turn. All rows must vanish other than rows (*ib*) and (*iib*), so that these two terms alone induce biases.[3] The remaining rows only affect the precision of the forecasts (that is, forecast-error variances), but do not cause the central tendency of the forecast errors to differ from zero. So, systematic forecast-error biases will result when either the "equilibrium mean", φ, is nonconstant, $(\varphi^* - \varphi) \neq \mathbf{0}$, or is misspecified, $(\varphi - \varphi_p) \neq \mathbf{0}$.

First consider $(\varphi - \varphi_p)$. Almost all estimation methods ensure that residuals have zero means in-sample, so provided that φ has remained constant in-sample, this term is zero by construction. However, if φ has previously altered, and that earlier shift has not been modeled, then φ_p will be a weighted average of the different in-sample values, and hence will not equal the end-of-sample value φ. One advantage of developing models that are congruent in-sample, even when the objective is forecasting, is to minimize such effects.

Second, when $\varphi^* \neq \varphi$ a systematic bias results: since $(\mathbf{\Pi}^*)^h \to \mathbf{0}$ as h $\to \infty$, the term (*ib*) is increasing in h, and eventually rises to the full effect of $(\varphi^* - \varphi)$. Consequently, direct or induced shifts in the model's equilibrium means relative to those of the data can lead to serious forecast biases. Moreover, such effects do not die out as the horizon increases, but converge to the full impact of the shift. By way of contrast, changes in the dynamics, and dynamic parameter misspecifications, are both multiplied by the mean-zero term $(\mathbf{y}_T - \varphi)$, so vanish on average: indeed, they would have no effect whatever on the forecast errors if the forecast origin equalled the equilibrium mean. Conversely, the larger the disequilibrium is at the time of any shift in the dynamics, the larger is the resulting impact.

The variance effects in the taxonomy result mainly from parameter estimation ((*iiia*) and (*iiib*)) and the variances of the cumulated errors (*v*) (assumed independent over time):

$$V[\mathbf{u}_{T+h}] = \sum_{i=0}^{h-1} (\mathbf{\Pi}^*)^i \mathbf{\Omega}_\varepsilon (\mathbf{\Pi}^*)^{i\prime}. \tag{23.9}$$

The parameter estimation terms are of order T^{-1} (under stationarity) so vanish as the sample gets large, and have been derived, *inter alia*, by Schmidt (1974) and Baillie (1979b) under the assumption of a correct system specification (see also Chong and Hendry, 1986; Doornik and Hendry, 2001). In section 23.4.3, we note the correction terms for an AR(1), and give an empirical example which indicates that the component from parameter estimation may often be small relative to (23.9) (when this is not the case, as in for example, Marquez and Ericsson (1993) – who report large increases in forecast-error variances from adding the effects of parameter uncertainty to a Monte Carlo simulation – any or all of nonlinearities, high-dimensionality, inappropriate estimation methods, or near nonstationarity may be operating: see section 23.4.3).

23.3. An I(1) Data Generation Process

The taxonomy and analysis in section 23.2 suggest that shifts in "equilibrium means" may be chiefly responsible for systematic forecast failure; that is, the realization of a run of large forecast errors of the same sign. We wish to find the counterparts of the equilibrium means of the stationary VAR in the VEqCM. Fortunately, this is straightforward.

Let $\mathbf{x}_t$ be an $n \times 1$ vector of time-series variables satisfying the first-order dynamic linear system for $t = 1, 2, \ldots, T$:

$$\mathbf{x}_t = \mathbf{Y}\mathbf{x}_{t-1} + \tau + \mathbf{v}_t, \tag{23.10}$$

where $\mathbf{v}_t \sim \mathsf{IN}_n[\mathbf{0}, \mathbf{\Omega}_v]$. In (23.10), the initial value $\mathbf{x}_0$ is fixed, $\mathbf{Y}$ is an $n \times n$ matrix of coefficients, and τ an $n \times 1$ vector of intercepts. The change from $\{\mathbf{y}_t\}$ to $\{\mathbf{x}_t\}$ high-lights that we are now allowing for nonstationarity: specifically, that $\mathbf{x}_t \sim I(1)$. When the integrated variables are also cointegrated, say with cointegrating rank r, (23.10) can be reparameterized as

$$\Delta\mathbf{x}_t = \mathbf{\Phi}\mathbf{x}_{t-1} + \tau + \mathbf{v}_t, \tag{23.11}$$

where $\mathbf{\Phi} = \mathbf{Y} - \mathbf{I}_n = \alpha\beta'$ and α and β are $n \times r$ of rank $r < n$. Hence

$$\Delta\mathbf{x}_t = \alpha\beta'\mathbf{x}_{t-1} + \tau + \mathbf{v}_t. \tag{23.12}$$

Let $\alpha_\perp, \beta_\perp$ be $n \times (n - r)$ matrices orthogonal to α, β respectively, so $\alpha'_\perp\alpha = \mathbf{0}, \beta'_\perp\beta = \mathbf{0}$; then (23.10) is not $I(2)$ if $\alpha'_\perp\beta_\perp$ has rank $(n - r)$, which we assume, as well as requiring sufficient restrictions to ensure uniqueness in α and β. Note that, for example, the matrix $\mathbf{I}_n - \alpha(\alpha'\alpha)^{-1}\alpha'$ annihilates α.

Let the expectation of $\Delta\mathbf{x}_t$ be γ $(n \times 1)$, which defines the unconditional growth in the system, and let $\mathsf{E}[\beta'\mathbf{x}_t] = \mu$, which is $r \times 1$, then from (23.12) on premultiplying by β':

$$\mathsf{E}[\beta'\mathbf{x}_t] = (\mathbf{I}_r + \beta'\alpha)\mathsf{E}[\beta'\mathbf{x}_{t-1}] + \beta'\tau = \mu,$$

so that when $\beta'\alpha$ is nonsingular (so the system is indeed $I(1)$), then $\mu = -(\beta'\alpha)^{-1}\beta'\tau$, and hence

$$\mathsf{E}[\Delta\mathbf{x}_t] = \mathsf{E}[\alpha\beta'\mathbf{x}_{t-1} + \tau + \mathbf{v}_t] = \alpha\mathsf{E}[\beta'\mathbf{x}_{t-1}] + \tau$$
$$= [\mathbf{I}_n - \alpha(\beta'\alpha)^{-1}\beta']\tau = \mathbf{K}\tau = \gamma. \tag{23.13}$$

Thus, $\tau = \gamma - \alpha\mu$ (see Johansen and Juselius, 1990). The matrix $\mathbf{K}$ is nonsymmetric but idempotent with $\beta'\mathbf{K} = \mathbf{0}'$ and $\mathbf{K}\alpha = \mathbf{0}$, so $\mathbf{Y}\mathbf{K} = \mathbf{K}$ and $\beta'\gamma = \mathbf{0}$. Consequently, the DGP can be written as

$$\Delta\mathbf{x}_t = \gamma + \alpha(\beta'\mathbf{x}_{t-1} - \mu) + \mathbf{v}_t. \tag{23.14}$$

The equilibrium means in the VEqCM formulation (23.14) are the underlying growth rate, $\mathsf{E}[\Delta\mathbf{x}_t] = \gamma$ and the means of the cointegrating relations, $\mathsf{E}[\beta'\mathbf{x}_{t-1}] = \mu$. Thus, we expect unmodeled shifts in μ and γ to be the prime sources of forecast failure in systems that can be represented by VEqCMs.

23.3.1.   Forecast-error biases and variances in three models

To examine the impact of deterministic shifts in econometric forecasting, we consider the relative susceptibility of three different forecasting devices to shifts in the equilibrium means and growth rates. The first model is the VEqCM itself, which matches the DGP (23.14), but will not coincide with the DGP in the forecast period after a structural change. The second model is a VAR in the differences of the variables (denoted DV):

$$\Delta \mathbf{x}_t = \gamma + \xi_t, \tag{23.15}$$

so is correctly specified only when $\alpha = 0$ in (23.14), in which case $\xi_t = \mathbf{v}_t$. Otherwise, it is misspecified by omitting the cointegrating vectors, and hence omits causal information. The third "model" we examine is a DV in the differences of the variables (DDV), defined by

$$\Delta^2 \mathbf{x}_t = \zeta_t \quad \text{or} \quad \mathbf{x}_t = \mathbf{x}_{t-1} + \Delta \mathbf{x}_{t-1} + \zeta_t. \tag{23.16}$$

These models are convenient for analytic calculations, and can be generalized to allow for longer lags, other deterministic terms, etc., to match empirical work.

The unconditional biases of the one- and two-step-ahead forecasts from the three contending models are reported in tables 23.2 (pre-break forecasting) and 23.3 (post-break forecasting). The symbols $\nabla_\alpha = \alpha^* - \alpha$, etc., and $\mathbf{B} = \mathbf{I}_r + \mathbf{\Lambda} = \beta'\alpha$ where $\mathbf{\Lambda} = \mathbf{I}_r + \beta'\alpha$.

The various methods perform about equally badly when forecasting before a break that occurs over the forecast horizon, whereas the biases are much smaller for DDV if the break has happened before the forecast is made, albeit that this is not taken into account in the forecast. Since DV and DDV are "noncausal" forecasting devices, we see that noncausal information can dominate causal when forecasting in the face of deterministic shifts.

Table 23.2 One and two steps pre-break

	VEqCM	DV	DDV
		One-step forecasts	
$\mu \to \mu^*$	$-\alpha\nabla_\mu$	$-\alpha\nabla_\mu$	$-\alpha\nabla_\mu$
$\gamma \to \gamma^*$	∇_γ	∇_γ	∇_γ
$\alpha \to \alpha^*$	0	0	0
		Two-step forecasts	
$\mu \to \mu^*$	$-\alpha\mathbf{B}\nabla_\mu$	$-\alpha\mathbf{B}\nabla_\mu$	$-\alpha\mathbf{B}\nabla_\mu$
$\gamma \to \gamma^*$	$2\nabla_\gamma$	$2\nabla_\gamma$	$2\nabla_\gamma$
$\alpha \to \alpha^*$	0	0	0

Table 23.3 One and two steps post-break

	VEqCM	DV	DDV
		One-step forecasts	
$\mu \to \mu^*$	$-\alpha\nabla_\mu$	$-\alpha\Lambda\nabla_\mu$	$-\alpha\beta'\alpha\nabla_\mu$
$\gamma \to \gamma^*$	∇_γ	∇_γ	0
$\alpha \to \alpha^*$	0	0	0
		Two-step forecasts	
$\mu \to \mu^*$	$-\alpha\mathbf{B}\nabla_\mu$	$-\alpha\Lambda\mathbf{B}\nabla_\mu$	$-\alpha(\mathbf{I}_r + \mathbf{B})\beta'\alpha\nabla_\mu$
$\gamma \to \gamma^*$	$2\nabla_\gamma$	$2\nabla_\gamma$	0
$\alpha \to \alpha^*$	0	0	0

Table 23.4 One-step unconditional variances

$T \to T+1$	VEqCM	DV	DDV
$\alpha = 0$	0	0	$\mathbf{\Omega}_v$
$\alpha = \alpha^*$	0	$\alpha\mathbf{V}\alpha'$	$\mathbf{H}\mathbf{\Omega}_v\mathbf{H}' + \mathbf{AVA}'$
$\alpha \neq \alpha^*$	$\nabla_\alpha\mathbf{V}\nabla'_\alpha$	$\alpha^*\mathbf{V}\alpha^{*'}$	$\mathbf{H}^*\mathbf{\Omega}_v\mathbf{H}^{*'} + \mathbf{A}^*\mathbf{VA}^{*'}$

$T+1 \to T+2$	VEqCM	DV	DDV
$\alpha = 0$	0	0	$\mathbf{\Omega}_v$
$\alpha = \alpha^*$	0	$\alpha\mathbf{V}\alpha'$	$\mathbf{H}\mathbf{\Omega}_v\mathbf{H}' + \mathbf{AVA}'$
$\alpha \neq \alpha^*$	$\nabla_\alpha\mathbf{V}^*\nabla'_\alpha$	$\alpha^*\mathbf{V}^*\alpha^{*'}$	$\mathbf{H}^*\mathbf{\Omega}_v\mathbf{H}^{*'} + \alpha^*\beta'\alpha^*\mathbf{V}\alpha^{*'}\beta\alpha^{*'}$

Note: Here and in the text, $\alpha = 0$ implicitly implies $\alpha^* = 0$.

Table 23.4 shows the excess in the one-step variances over $\mathbf{\Omega}_v$, for various values of α, the parameter change that most affects the variances, where $\mathbf{A}^* = \alpha^*\Lambda - \alpha$ and $\mathbf{H}^* = \mathbf{I}_n - \alpha^*\beta'$.

The unstarred matrices replace any starred parameter with its unstarred value: thus, $\mathbf{A} = \alpha\Lambda - \alpha = \alpha(\beta'\alpha)$. The pattern is clear, and the only exception is the DDV when $\alpha \neq \alpha^*$, although the fact that $\mathbf{V}^* = \Lambda^*\mathbf{V}\Lambda^{*'} + \beta'\mathbf{\Omega}_v\beta$ allows considerable rearrangement without altering the substance.

Next, table 23.5 records the excess in the two-step variances over $\mathbf{\Omega}_v$, where $\mathbf{C}^* = \alpha^*(\mathbf{I}_r + \Lambda^*)$, $\mathbf{D}^* = \mathbf{C}^* - \mathbf{C}$, $\mathbf{F}^* = \mathbf{C}^*\Lambda - 2\alpha$, and $\mathbf{G}^* = \mathbf{C}^*\beta' - 2\mathbf{I}_n$. As before, $\mathbf{C} = \alpha(\mathbf{I}_r + \Lambda)$, so $\mathbf{D} = 0$, and $\mathbf{F} = \alpha(\beta'\alpha)(2\mathbf{I}_r + \Lambda)$ and $\mathbf{G} = \alpha\beta'(2\mathbf{I}_n + \alpha\beta') - 2\mathbf{I}_n$, where $\mathbf{F}^{**} = \mathbf{C}^*\Lambda^* - 2\alpha^*$.

Table 23.5 Two-step unconditional variances

$T \to T + 2$	VEqCM	DV	DDV
$\alpha = 0$	$\boldsymbol{\Omega}_v$	$\boldsymbol{\Omega}_v$	$5\boldsymbol{\Omega}_v$
$\alpha = \alpha^*$	$\mathbf{Y}\boldsymbol{\Omega}_v\mathbf{Y}'$	$\mathbf{Y}\boldsymbol{\Omega}_v\mathbf{Y}' + \mathbf{CVC}'$	$\mathbf{Y}\boldsymbol{\Omega}_v\mathbf{Y}' + \mathbf{G}\boldsymbol{\Omega}_v\mathbf{G}' + \mathbf{FVF}'$
$\alpha \neq \alpha^*$	$\mathbf{Y}^*\boldsymbol{\Omega}_v\mathbf{Y}^{*'} + \mathbf{D}^*\mathbf{V}\mathbf{D}^{*'}$	$\mathbf{Y}^*\boldsymbol{\Omega}_v\mathbf{Y}^{*'} + \mathbf{C}^*\mathbf{V}\mathbf{C}^{*'}$	$\mathbf{Y}^*\boldsymbol{\Omega}_v\mathbf{Y}^{*'} + \mathbf{G}^*\boldsymbol{\Omega}_v\mathbf{G}^{*'} + \mathbf{F}^*\mathbf{VF}^{*'}$

$T + 1 \to T + 3$	VEqCM	DV	DDV
$\alpha = 0$	$\boldsymbol{\Omega}_v$	$\boldsymbol{\Omega}_v$	$5\boldsymbol{\Omega}_v$
$\alpha = \alpha^*$	$\mathbf{Y}\boldsymbol{\Omega}_v\mathbf{Y}'$	$\mathbf{Y}\boldsymbol{\Omega}_v\mathbf{Y}' + \mathbf{CVC}'$	$\mathbf{Y}\boldsymbol{\Omega}_v\mathbf{Y}' + \mathbf{G}\boldsymbol{\Omega}_v\mathbf{G}' + \mathbf{FVF}'$
$\alpha \neq \alpha^*$	$\mathbf{Y}^*\boldsymbol{\Omega}_v\mathbf{Y}^{*'} + \mathbf{D}^*\mathbf{V}^*\mathbf{D}^{*'}$	$\mathbf{Y}^*\boldsymbol{\Omega}_v\mathbf{Y}^{*'} + \mathbf{C}^*\mathbf{V}^*\mathbf{C}^{*'}$	$\mathbf{Y}^*\boldsymbol{\Omega}_v\mathbf{Y}^{*'} + \mathbf{G}^*\boldsymbol{\Omega}_v\mathbf{G}^{*'} + \mathbf{F}^{**}\mathbf{VF}^{**'}$

The pattern is similar to the one-step outcomes, although the values are larger, and the formulae more complicated: the rapid increase in the DDV variance is especially noticeable.[4] When forecasting before a break, therefore, all three models are susceptible to forecast failure, and there is little to choose between them, although the VEqCM has the smallest variance component when it is correctly specified and no break occurs. When forecasting after a break, the DDV has the greatest robustness to a deterministic shift, but the largest and most rapidly-increasing forecast-error variances in general. The DV lies between, depending on which deterministic terms change.

The longer the multi-step horizon for evaluation, the less well the DDV, and probably the DV should perform, partly from their variance terms, and also because as the horizon lengthens, so does the likelihood that most breaks will be after the forecast was made, a case in which these models offer no gains. Conversely, the shorter the horizon, for a sequence of horizons, the more likely some breaks will precede forecasting, and consequently, DDV and DV may outperform the VEqCM, even when it is correctly specified in-sample.

This behavior is precisely what was observed by Eitrheim, Husebø, and Nymoen (1999) in their study of the forecasting performance of the Norges Bank model. Over the longest (12-quarter) evaluation horizon, the Bank's model performed well, followed by a DV modeled to be congruent: the equivalent of the DDV did worst. But over sequences of three four-period divisions of the same evaluation data, the DDV did best more often than any other method: also see chapter 16.

23.3.2. Deterministic terms and changes therein

Given the preeminence attributed to the equilibrium means above, it is of interest to consider the nature of deterministic terms in more detail. The parameters μ and γ are treated as "autonomous" in our analysis, but potentially subject to shifts in their values. Possible examples of equilibrium means are the savings ratio and the velocity of circulation (in determining consumers' expenditure and money demand, respectively).

Since all the parameters of the DGP depend on economic agents' decision rules, changes in parameter values could be viewed as arising from changed decision rules, or deriving from changes in unmodeled variables. One way of conceptualizing the analysis is to note that, between the actual DGP of the economy (generating many billions of outcomes) and the forecasting model (for a small number of aggregate variables), lies a "local DGP" of the variables being modeled – denoted the LDGP (see Bontemps and Mizon, 2001). The LDGP is the generating mechanism entailed by marginalizing the DGP with respect to all unmodeled variables. Viewing the VEqCM in (23.14) as the LDGP, then changes in its autonomous growth rates and equilibrium means proxy the impact from unmodeled nonstationary influences in the DGP. For example, a change in legislation permitting interest payments on checking accounts will induce a jump in the interest rate on such deposits from zero, and by making checking accounts more attractive, result in a shift in the equilibrium mean of holdings in models that do not include a measure of the own rate of interest.

Growth rates of real variables depend on such factors as R&D, technical progress, discoveries, and innovations, as well as investment in human and physical capital. The VEqCM model class is not well suited to modeling growth-rate changes, since the growth in the system comes about from the term γ, which is itself left unexplained. One might imagine adding variables to model γ, but this would occasion new γs in their equations, and so on, if growth is to occur. Nevertheless, the correspondence between the LDGP and DGP is assumed to be close enough to allow an analysis of forecasting based on the assumption that the VEqCM represents the DGP. Of course, this assumption can be checked by whether our analysis based on the VEqCM and models thereof is useful for explaining empirical outcomes.

23.4. OTHER SOURCES OF FORECAST FAILURE

Our focus remains on explaining forecast failure in multivariate equilibrium-correction models. We first consider the role of model misspecification in forecast failure (section 23.4.1), separately discussing misspecification of stochastic components (corresponding to (*iia*) in table 23.1), then deterministic (*iib*). Then we investigate breaks in misspecified models in section 23.4.2 ((*ia*) and (*ib*)), before considering estimation uncertainty in section 23.4.3 ((*iiia*) and (*iiib*)). The problem of "overfitting" or model selection is the subject of section 23.4.4. Finally, we discuss the impact of forecast origin mis-measurement in section 23.4.5 ((*iv*)).

23.4.1. Model misspecification

In the absence of parameter nonconstancies, model misspecification always reduces forecast accuracy, where we refer to pre-forecasting misspecifications (after an unanticipated break, the model is bound to be misspecified). The forecast-error taxonomy delineates effects from both stochastic and deterministic misspecification, so we consider each in turn. Shifts in, or misspecifications of, equilibrium means appear to have the most pernicious influence on forecast failure, and can be "imported" from one equation to another via model misspecification (see section 23.4.2).

Model misspecification is distinct from model uncertainty. Model misspecification arises when we use the wrong model, so that, in the notation of section 23.2, $\varphi_p \neq \varphi$ or $\Pi_p \neq \Pi$. Model uncertainty is not explicitly identified in the taxonomy, but refers to uncertainty concerning the model "structure" when that is selected on the basis of the data, and the implications of assessing the uncertainty surrounding the forecasts relative to when the structure is pre-specified, or known (see, for example, Chatfield, 1995; Draper, 1995). This is related to a problem sometimes known as "overfitting." However, recent results on structured approaches to econometric modeling suggest a much more sanguine view of data-based modeling than previously prevalent (see for example, Hendry and Krolzig, 1999; Hoover and Perez, 1999; Krolzig and Hendry, 2001), so the model selection problem outlined in section 23.4.4 may also transpire to be peripheral to explaining forecast failure.

Misspecification of stochastic components

In a stationary world, least squares estimated models are consistent for their associated conditional expectations (when second moments exist), so forecasts on average attain their expected accuracy unconditionally (see, for example, Miller, 1978; Hendry, 1979). Reconsider the I(0) VAR in (23.17), where before the break:

$$\mathbf{y}_t - \varphi = \Pi(\mathbf{y}_{t-1} - \varphi) + \varepsilon_t \quad \text{with} \quad \varepsilon_t \sim \mathsf{IN}_n[0, \Omega_\varepsilon]. \tag{23.17}$$

Provided that $\{\mathbf{y}_t\}$ is, and remains, stationary, then (23.17) is isomorphic to the mean-zero representation

$$\mathbf{w}_t = \psi + \Pi\mathbf{w}_{t-1} + \varepsilon_t, \tag{23.18}$$

where $\mathbf{w}_t = \mathbf{y}_t - \varphi$, and $\psi = 0$. Omitting any set of $\{w_{j,t-1}\}$ in any of the equations will not bias the forecasts, because we are omitting zero-mean terms. The fit will be inferior to the correctly specified representation, but the resulting model will on average forecast according to its in-sample operating characteristics. Thus, tests of forecast failure that compare the in-sample fit of the model to the out-of-sample forecast performance will not reject – there will be no indication of forecast failure. In fact, forecasts from misspecified models may be more or less accurate than those from the estimated DGP, depending on the precision with which parameters are estimated – since invalid zero restrictions on coefficients that are close to zero can improve forecast accuracy: see Clements and Hendry, 1998, ch. 12) – and on the horizon (see Clements and Hendry, 1998, ch. 11).

The same logic holds for the initial formulation in (23.17), despite the equilibrium mean being unknown. Some simple analyses will serve to illustrate these claims. Let the DGP comprise two blocks:

$$\begin{pmatrix} \mathbf{y}_{1,t} \\ \mathbf{y}_{2,t} \end{pmatrix} = \begin{pmatrix} \phi_1 \\ \phi_2 \end{pmatrix} + \begin{pmatrix} \mathbf{\Pi}_{11} & \mathbf{\Pi}_{12} \\ 0 & \mathbf{\Pi}_{22} \end{pmatrix} \begin{pmatrix} \mathbf{y}_{1,t-1} \\ \mathbf{y}_{2,t-1} \end{pmatrix} + \begin{pmatrix} \varepsilon_{1,t} \\ \varepsilon_{2,t} \end{pmatrix},$$ (23.19)

where only the first block is modeled. The model of $\mathbf{y}_{1,t}$ is misspecified by omitting $\mathbf{y}_{2,t-1}$. Setting $\mathbf{\Pi}_{21} = 0$ in the DGP is only to simplify the algebra, and is inconsequential for the one-step analysis below. However, it could be a crucial restriction in other settings, such as conditional multi-step forecasts. We will need the following expressions for the unconditional moments of $\{\mathbf{y}_t\}$:

$$\mathsf{E}[\mathbf{y}_t] = \varphi = (\mathbf{I}_n - \mathbf{\Pi})^{-1}\phi,$$

$$\mathsf{E}[(\mathbf{y}_t - \varphi)(\mathbf{y}_t - \varphi)'] = \mathbf{M} = \mathbf{\Omega}_\varepsilon + \mathbf{\Pi}\mathbf{M}\mathbf{\Pi}',$$

$$\mathsf{E}[(\mathbf{y}_t - \varphi)(\mathbf{y}_{t-1} - \varphi)'] = \mathbf{\Pi}\mathbf{M}.$$ (23.20)

Given the DGP (23.19), the model to be used for forecasting is obtained by reduction as

$$\mathbf{y}_{1,t} = \phi_1 + \mathbf{\Pi}_{11}\mathbf{y}_{1,t\;1} + \mathbf{\Pi}_{12}\mathbf{y}_{2,t\;1} + \varepsilon_{1,t}$$

$$= (\phi_1 + \mathbf{\Pi}_{12}\rho) + (\mathbf{\Pi}_{11} + \mathbf{\Pi}_{12}\mathbf{\Psi}_{11})\mathbf{y}_{1,t-1} + (\mathbf{\Pi}_{12}\mathbf{u}_{2,t-1} + \varepsilon_{1,t})$$

$$= \delta_1 + \mathbf{\Gamma}_{11}\mathbf{y}_{1,t-1} + \mathbf{v}_{1,t},$$ (23.21)

and letting $\mathbf{\Psi}_{11} = \mathbf{M}_{21}\mathbf{M}_{11}^{-1}$:

$$\mathbf{y}_{2,t} = \rho + \mathbf{\Psi}_{11}\mathbf{y}_{1,t} + \mathbf{u}_{2,t},$$ (23.22)

on enforcing $\mathsf{E}[\mathbf{y}_{1,t}\mathbf{u}_{2,t}'] = 0$, so that

$$\rho = \mathsf{E}[\mathbf{y}_{2,t} - \mathbf{\Psi}_{11}\mathbf{y}_{1,t}] = \varphi_2 - \mathbf{\Psi}_{11}\varphi_1 = (-\mathbf{\Psi}_{11} : \mathbf{I}_{n_2})(\mathbf{I}_n - \mathbf{\Pi})^{-1}\phi.$$ (23.23)

Despite the misspecification, the model given by the last row of (23.21) is well defined, and its error variance in any forecast period will on average match that in-sample. Importantly, the entailed equilibrium mean from

$$\mathbf{y}_{1,t} = \delta_1 + \mathbf{\Gamma}_{11}\mathbf{y}_{1,t-1} + \mathbf{v}_{1,t},$$ (23.24)

remains φ_1. From (23.21) and the middle expression in (23.23),

$$\delta_1 = \phi_1 + \mathbf{\Pi}_{12}\rho = \phi_1 - \mathbf{\Pi}_{12}\mathbf{\Psi}_{11}\varphi_1 + \mathbf{\Pi}_{12}\varphi_2.$$

From the first line of (23.20), ϕ is given by

$$
\begin{pmatrix} \mathbf{I}_{n_1} - \mathbf{\Pi}_{11} & -\mathbf{\Pi}_{12} \\ 0 & \mathbf{I}_{n_2} - \mathbf{\Pi}_{22} \end{pmatrix} \begin{pmatrix} \varphi_1 \\ \varphi_2 \end{pmatrix} = \begin{pmatrix} (\mathbf{I}_{n_1} - \mathbf{\Pi}_{11})\varphi_1 - \mathbf{\Pi}_{12}\varphi_2 \\ (\mathbf{I}_{n_2} - \mathbf{\Pi}_{22})\varphi_2 \end{pmatrix},
$$

and hence

$$
\begin{aligned}
\delta_1 &= (\mathbf{I}_{n_1} - \mathbf{\Pi}_{11})\varphi_1 - \mathbf{\Pi}_{12}\varphi_2 - \mathbf{\Pi}_{12}\mathbf{\Psi}_{11}\varphi_1 + \mathbf{\Pi}_{12}\varphi_2 \\
&= (\mathbf{I}_{n_1} - \mathbf{\Pi}_{11} - \mathbf{\Pi}_{12}\mathbf{\Psi}_{11})\varphi_1 \\
&= (\mathbf{I}_{n_1} - \mathbf{\Gamma}_{11})\varphi_1.
\end{aligned}
\tag{23.25}
$$

Substituting (23.25) into (23.24):

$$
\mathbf{y}_{1,t} - \varphi_1 = \mathbf{\Gamma}_{11}(\mathbf{y}_{1,t-1} - \varphi_1) + \mathbf{v}_{1,t},
$$

as required: the mean-zero case implications still hold.

Thus, model misspecification *per se* cannot account for forecast failure, because the model's out-of-sample forecast performance will be consistent with what would have been expected based on how well the model fits the historical data. However, an exception arises to the extent that inconsistent standard errors are used to judge forecast accuracy, as we now discuss (or, if deterministic terms are misspecified, see below). Corsi, Pollock, and Prakken (1982) find that residual autocorrelation, perhaps induced by other misspecifications, leads to excess rejection on parameter-constancy tests. For example, untreated positive residual autocorrelation can downward bias estimated standard errors which thereby induces excess rejections on constancy tests. In practice, an investigator is likely to add extra lags of $\mathbf{y}_1$ to remove any residual autocorrelation. This strategy will make the model congruent (see, for example, Hendry, 1995) although it remains misspecified. But by having innovation residuals, excess rejections in parameter constancy tests will not occur.

Conversely, model misspecification is *necessary* for forecast failure, because otherwise the model coincides with the LDGP at all points in time, so never fails. This is consistent with the result in Clements and Hendry (1998) that causal variables will always dominate in forecasting when the model coincides with the DGP (or that DGP is stationary), but need not do so when the model is misspecified for a DGP that is subject to deterministic shifts.

Stochastic misspecification in nonstationary processes

An example will illustrate that stochastic misspecification need not cause forecast failure even in nonstationary processes. We refer to a study of two contending models of nonstationarity in Clements and Hendry (2001). The models are difference stationary (DS) and trend stationary (TS) models. The stochastic-trend model treats the variable $\{y_t\}$ as integrated of order one, $y_t \sim I(1)$, as in the random walk with drift:

$$y_t = y_{t-1} + \mu + \varepsilon_t \quad \text{where} \quad \varepsilon_t \underset{a}{\sim} \text{IN}[0, \sigma_\varepsilon^2], \tag{23.26}$$

where $\underset{a}{\sim}$ denotes "is assumed to be distributed as." The TS model is ostensibly quite different, whereby $\{y_t\}$ is stationary about a deterministic function of time, here taken to be a simple linear trend:

$$y_t = \phi + \gamma t + u_t \quad \text{where} \quad u_t \underset{a}{\sim} \text{IN}[0, \sigma_u^2]. \tag{23.27}$$

Both these models can be viewed as special cases of the basic "structural time series" class of models of Harvey (1989). Ignoring cyclical and seasonal components, the structural time-series model can be written as

$$y_t = v_t + \xi_t, \tag{23.28}$$

where

$$v_t = v_{t-1} + \mu_{t-1} + \eta_t,$$
$$\mu_t = \mu_{t-1} + \zeta_t, \tag{23.29}$$

and the disturbance terms η_t, ζ_t and ξ_t are zero-mean, uncorrelated white noise, with variances given by σ_η^2, σ_ζ^2, and σ_ξ^2. The interpretation of this model is that v_t is the (unobserved) trend component of the time series, and ξ_t is the irregular component. η_t affects the level of the trend, and ζ_t allows its slope to change.

Suppose now that $\sigma_\zeta^2 = 0$. Then, from (23.29), $\Delta v_t = \mu + \eta_t$, so that differencing (23.28) and substituting gives

$$\Delta y_t = \mu + \eta_t + \Delta \xi_t,$$

which is the same as (23.26) when $v_t = \eta_t + \Delta \xi_t$, but now $\{v_t\}$ cannot be IID unless $\sigma_\xi^2 = 0$. Thus, the DS model is a structural time-series model in which there is no "irregular" component (i.e., no measurement error), and the "slope" does not change. The TS model can be obtained as a special case of the structural time-series model by setting $\sigma_\eta^2 = \sigma_\zeta^2 = 0$, so that (23.29) becomes

$$v_t = v_{t-1} + \mu = v_0 + \mu t. \tag{23.30}$$

Equation (23.30) indicates that the trend has a constant "slope" ($\sigma_\zeta^2 = 0$), and the "level" is not subject to stochastic shocks ($\sigma_\eta^2 = 0$). Substituting into (23.28) results in

$$y_t = v_0 + \mu t + \xi_t,$$

which is identical to (23.27) when $v_0 = \phi$, $\mu = \gamma$ and $\xi_t = u_t$. Thus, the trend-stationary model is a limiting case of the structural time-series model in which the level and the slope of the trend component are constant over time.

Some macroeconomists have argued that important theoretical issues turn on whether real GDP is generated by (23.26) or (23.27): see, for example, Campbell and Perron (1991), for a survey. If shocks are permanent (as in (23.26)) then – possibly orchestrated by the government – they can permanently affect the level of real output in the economy. Conversely, (23.27) suggests that shocks can only cause short-run fluctuations from an essentially predetermined path.

These two models would appear to have radically different implications for forecastability. If the DS model is correct, then forecast-error variances grow linearly in the forecast horizon, but if the TS model is correct, the forecast-error variance is simply the variance of the shock. However, on a test for forecast failure, neither model is quite as likely to be rejected as one might anticipate when the other is the actual data-generating mechanism.

Heuristically, first consider a DS model predictor of the TS process. It is simple to derive the h-step error (ignoring estimation uncertainty for simplicity), noting that γ is the value of μ that minimizes the DS model expected in-sample sum of squares (see Clements and Hendry (2001), for details), so that we set $\mu = \gamma$ in the DS model forecast function. Then,

$$e_{DS,T+h} = y_{T+h} - y_{DS,T+h} = \phi + \gamma(T + h) + u_{T+h} - (\mu h + y_T) = u_{T+h} - u_T, \quad (23.31)$$

which delivers an unconditional expected squared forecast error $2\sigma_u^2$. This is comparable to the DS model in-sample error variance, since from (23.27) and (23.26),

$$\varepsilon_t = \gamma - \mu + \Delta u_t = \Delta u_t, \quad (23.32)$$

which implies that

$$\sigma_\varepsilon^2 = \mathsf{E}_{TS}[\varepsilon_t^2] = 2\sigma_u^2, \quad (23.33)$$

where the subscript on the expectations operator denotes that we are taking expectations under the TS DGP. Thus, the expected squared forecast error and the in-sample model fit are the same.

Now, we reverse the DGP and model, and find a somewhat different outcome. The value of $\{\phi, \gamma\}$ that minimizes the in-sample prediction error for the TS model is $\{y_0, \mu\}$, so the forecast error with known parameters is (as $y_T = \mu T + \sum_{i=1}^{T}\varepsilon_i + y_0$)

$$e_{TS,T+h} = \mu h + y_T + \sum_{i=0}^{h-1}\varepsilon_{T+h-i} - \mu(T + h) - y_0 = \sum_{i=0}^{T+h-1}\varepsilon_{T+h-i}, \quad (23.34)$$

so

$$\mathsf{E}_{DS}[e_{TS,T+h}^2] = (h + T)\sigma_\varepsilon^2. \quad (23.35)$$

To obtain the corresponding in-sample fit of the model, notice that from (23.27) and (23.26),

$$u_t = y_0 - \phi + (\mu - \gamma)t + \sum_{i=0}^{t}\varepsilon_i = \sum_{i=0}^{t}\varepsilon_i, \quad (23.36)$$

so that the population variance of the TS-model disturbance will be heteroskedastic, $\sigma_{u,t}^2 = \sigma_\varepsilon^2 t$. On average over the sample, $\bar{\sigma}_u^2 = T^{-1}\sum_{t=1}^{T}\sigma_\varepsilon^2 t = \frac{1}{2}\sigma_\varepsilon^2(T+1)$, so the expected squared forecast errors are about double the in-sample (see the 16 percent rejection rate on the forecast failure test recorded below). The intuition follows from (23.36): since the error variances in (23.27) are growing over time when the DGP is a DS process, the error-of-fit is initially small relative to the forecast errors, providing some detectability. Of course, the manifest residual autocorrelation in (23.27) would be a simpler diagnostic here, but in empirical research, where the actual DGP is vastly more complicated, need not be so noticeable.

We term the choice of the DS model for a TS DGP (and vice versa) a stochastic (rather than a deterministic) misspecification, because, as shown above, the model's forecasts are unbiased (cf., section 23.4.1). That is, the expected value of the model's forecast function is indistinguishable at all horizons from that of the actual process.

Simulation experiments with the DS and TS DGPs "calibrated" on the log of U.K. Net National Income over 1870–1993 (data from Friedman and Schwartz, 1982; Attfield, Demery, and Duck, 1995) reinforce this conclusion. Neither model is a congruent representation of that data, but the estimates of the parameters so obtained (including the error variances) are taken as "typical" values for the DGPs in a Monte Carlo. Data are simulated from each of the two DGPs assuming independently-distributed Gaussian disturbances, with the estimated error variances. For the simulated data from the DS DGP, the first-period value is always equal to the 1870 historical value. We considered sample sizes (T) from 20 to 200 in steps of 1, with an additional "forecast-period" observation in each case. For the simulated data (whether from the DS or TS DGP) both models are estimated on the first T observations and used to forecast the $T + 1$ observation. For the DS model, the single parameter, μ, is estimated, and for the TS, the pair $\{\phi, \gamma\}$. The adequacy of each model from a forecasting perspective is gauged by the following test for forecast failure, calculated on each of $R = 100,000$ replications of the Monte Carlo:

$$\hat{Q} = \frac{\hat{v}_{T+1|T}^2}{\mathsf{V}[\hat{v}_{T+1|T}]},$$

where $\hat{v}_{T+1|T}$ is the conditional one-step-ahead forecast error with estimated variance $\mathsf{V}[\hat{v}_{T+1|T}]$. The statistic $\hat{Q}$ is implemented as

$$\hat{Q} = \frac{\hat{v}_{T+1|T}^2}{\dfrac{T+p}{T}\hat{\sigma}_v^2} \sim \mathsf{F}_{T-p}^1, \tag{23.37}$$

where p is the number of regressors (one for the DS model, two for the TS model). Thus, the test statistic compares the squared error made over the forecast period with an estimate of the expected forecast-error variance (based on the estimated in-sample error variance). When the model is the DGP, and the disturbances are normal white noise, because the numerator depends on post-sample errors, and the denominator on within-sample, they are independently distributed. As both are exactly χ^2 scaled by their respective degrees of freedom, the outcome is a central F under the null. $\hat{Q}$ would appear to be a reasonable metric for judging forecast failure (or success).

Letting F_s^{ij} denote the test statistic value recorded on replication s of the Monte Carlo, where i and j refer to the model and DGP respectively (both either DS or TS), and F_α^i is an α-level critical value (depending on the model i, and not the DGP j), then the estimated rejection frequencies ($\tilde{r}$) are given by:

$$\tilde{r}^{ij} = R^{-1} \sum_{s=1}^{R} 1_{(F_s^{ij} > F_\alpha^i)},$$

where $1_{()}$ is the indicator function ($1_{(x>y)} = 1$ if $x > y$, and zero otherwise). Actual and nominal test size coincide when $r^{ii} = \alpha$.

We used the conventional $\alpha = 0.05$, and found that $\tilde{r}^{ii} \simeq \alpha$ for both i, so that there was no evidence against actual and nominal test size coinciding for all T: neither model is rejected excessively when it is the DGP. However, for the DS model of the TS DGP ($i = $ DS, $j = $ TS), the test was also approximately equal to its nominal size, while the rejection frequencies for the TS model of the DS DGP were around one sixth (so around 85 percent to 95 percent of the time, no failure was detected in these two misspecifications).

In short, "forecast success" is consistent with model misspecifications that could have important policy implications. A comparison of the forecast performance of the two models (on MSFE, say) would clearly delineate between these two models – see the comparisons in Clements and Hendry (2001)) – but now the information set has been enlarged to include rival models' performance. The point is that the forecast performance of a model in isolation, without recourse to additional information, need not depend on the model being correctly specified. Logically, model (stochastic) misspecification *alone* does not cause forecast failure, because the model's out-of-sample forecast performance will (on average) be consistent with what would have been expected based on how well the model fitted the historical data. An exception was noted above, when inconsistent standard errors were used to judge forecast accuracy. This arises in the above example, because the TS model errors for the DS DGP are approximately partial sums of the DS process disturbances, and so are highly positively autocorrelated. Corsi, Pollock, and Prakken (1982) find that untreated positive residual autocorrelation can downward bias estimated standard errors, and thereby induce excess rejections on parameter-constancy (and thus forecast-failure) tests. In our example, the TS model is rejected one sixth of the time (when the DGP is a DS process) for this reason.

MISSPECIFICATION OF DETERMINISTIC COMPONENTS

An example of deterministic misspecification arises when we consider (23.27) along with a simplified version of (23.26). Suppose the TS process is the DGP, whereas the model is now

$$y_t = \mu + \varepsilon_t \quad \text{where} \quad \varepsilon_t \underset{a}{\sim} \text{IN}[0, \sigma_\varepsilon^2], \tag{23.38}$$

which corresponds to a deterministic misspecification of omitting the trend. To simplify the analysis, we set $\phi = 0$, so the pseudo-true value of $\mu = \gamma T/2$. The h-step forecast error is

$$e_{S,T+h} = y_{T+h} - y_{S,T+h} = \gamma(T + h) + u_{T+h} - \gamma\frac{T}{2} = \gamma\left(\frac{T}{2} + h\right) + u_{T+h}. \qquad (23.39)$$

The "S" subscript denotes the stationary, constant-mean model. Systematic forecast errors will result, and will be increasing in T and h. The unconditional expected squared forecast error is

$$\mathsf{E}_{TS}[e_{S,T+h}^2] = \sigma_u^2 + \gamma^2\left(h^2 + \frac{T^2}{4} + Th\right). \qquad (23.40)$$

To compare this to the S model in-sample error variance, note that

$$\varepsilon_t = \gamma t - \gamma\frac{T}{2} + u_t, \qquad (23.41)$$

which implies that $\sigma_{\varepsilon,t}^2 = \gamma^2(t - T/2)^2 + \sigma_u^2$. On average over the sample, $\bar{\sigma}_\varepsilon^2 = T^{-1}\sum_{t=1}^T \sigma_{\varepsilon,t}^2$, so that

$$\bar{\sigma}_\varepsilon^2 = T^{-1}\sum_{t=1}^T\left(\gamma^2\left(t^2 - Tt + \frac{T^2}{2}\right) + \sigma_u^2\right)$$

$$= \sigma_u^2 + \gamma^2\left(\frac{(T+1)(2T+1)}{6} + \frac{T^2}{4} - \frac{T(T+1)}{2}\right)$$

$$\simeq \sigma_u^2 + \frac{\gamma^2 T^2}{12}. \qquad (23.42)$$

Even for $h = 1$, the dominant term in (23.40) $(T^2/4)$ exceeds that in the in-sample expression (23.42) by a factor of three, so that the disparity between the out-of-sample and in-sample "fits" suggests that forecast failure will be marked. The S model is said to be deterministically misspecified for the TS model because the forecasts of the S model are biased at all forecast horizons.

In effect, there is an ever-increasing deterministic shift between the model and the data due to the omitted trend, so the outcome is similar to a trend break.

23.4.2.   Breaks in misspecified models

In practice, model misspecification may work in conjunction with structural breaks to cause forecast failure. Consider the following deterministic change. Let the

$n_2 \times 1$ intercept ϕ_2 of the second block in (23.19) change at T_1 to ϕ_2^*, so that after T_1,

$$E[\mathbf{y}_t \mid T > T_1] = (\mathbf{I}_n - \mathbf{\Pi})^{-1}\phi^* = \varphi^*,$$

the second moments around φ^* remaining constant. Letting $\rho^* = (-\mathbf{\Psi}_{11} : \mathbf{I}_{n_2})(\mathbf{I}_n - \mathbf{\Pi})^{-1}\phi$, the analogous equation to (23.22) becomes

$$\mathbf{y}_{2,t} = \rho^* + \mathbf{\Psi}_{11}\mathbf{y}_{1,t} + \mathbf{u}_{2,t}.$$

Thus, after T_1, as in (23.21),

$$\mathbf{y}_{1,t} = \delta_1^* + \mathbf{\Gamma}_{11}\mathbf{y}_{1,t-1} + \mathbf{v}_{1,t}. \qquad (23.43)$$

The under-specified $\mathbf{y}_{1,t}$ equation will now mis-forecast, although the correctly specified version that includes $\mathbf{y}_{2,t-1}$ would not. Here the source of failure is indirect, resulting from a deterministic change elsewhere in the system (in the equation for $\mathbf{y}_{2,t}$), which is "imported" into the forecasting equation for $\mathbf{y}_{1t}$ via the model misspecification.

We could summarize these findings overall as: "forecast failure out, needs changed conditions in," although this can be at several steps removed from the "equation of interest." Of course, if the entire system was used to generate multi-step forecasts, but the change in ϕ_2 was not known, forecast failure would also be directly observed.

23.4.3. Estimation uncertainty

The forecast-error taxonomy (table 23.1) revealed that parameter-estimation uncertainty enters both through intercepts and slopes, and could potentially be an important source of forecast error. A failure to allow for parameter estimation uncertainty may lead to interval forecasts being too narrow (so that the actual coverage is less than the nominal), but the effect of estimation uncertainty is of order T^{-1}, and a variety of techniques can be used to make the requisite adjustments to interval forecasts (see, for example, Chatfield, 1993). However, estimation uncertainty may operate indirectly via, for example, high degrees of collinearity of the regressors, or in conjunction with a lack of parsimony. We will not treat these here, except to note that in the absence of parameter nonconstancies, neither by itself will generate forecast failure. For a detailed treatment, see Clements and Hendry (1998, ch. 12), especially section 12.6. In this section, we consider the role of estimation uncertainty in model simulation, but before doing that, we present some standard analyses of the impact of estimation uncertainty on forecasts.

As an example, consider the AR(1) model

$$y_t = \mu + \rho y_{t-1} + \varepsilon_t, \quad \varepsilon_t \sim \text{ID}\,[0, \sigma_\varepsilon^2].$$

For known parameters, the h-step-ahead forecast is obtained by backward iteration of $y_{T+h} = \mu + \rho y_{T+h-1}$, so denoting that by $\tilde{y}_{T+h|T}$,

$$\tilde{y}_{T+h|T} = \mu(1 - \rho^h)(1 - \rho)^{-1} + \rho^h y_T. \qquad (23.44)$$

This is the conditional mean of y_{T+h} given y_T. In the stationary case, ρ^h tends to zero as h increases, and the forecast converges to the unconditional mean $\mu/(1 - \rho)$. The actual value of y_{T+h} is

$$y_{T+h} = \mu(1 - \rho^h)(1 - \rho)^{-1} + \rho^h y_T + \sum_{i=0}^{h-1} \rho^i v_{T+h-i}, \qquad (23.45)$$

so the multi-period forecast-error variance (for known parameters) is

$$V[e_{T+h|T}] = V[y_{T+h} \mid y_T] = \sigma_v^2 \frac{(1 - \rho^{2h})}{(1 - \rho^2)}, \qquad (23.46)$$

where $e_{T+h|T} = y_{T+h} - \tilde{y}_{T+h|T}$.

When parameters are not known but have to be estimated, (23.44) becomes

$$\hat{y}_{T+h|T} = \hat{\mu}(1 - \hat{\rho}^h)(1 - \hat{\rho})^{-1} + \hat{\rho}^h y_T, \qquad (23.47)$$

and hence

$$\hat{e}_{T+h|T} = \sum_{i=0}^{h-1} (\mu\rho^i - \hat{\mu}\hat{\rho}^i) + (\rho^h - \hat{\rho}^h)y_T + \sum_{i=0}^{h-1} \rho^i v_{T+h-i}. \qquad (23.48)$$

In section 23.7, we show that $V[\hat{e}_{T+h} \mid y_T]$ can be approximated by

$$V[\hat{e}_{T+h|T} \mid y_T] = \sigma_v^2 \frac{(1 - \rho^{2h})}{(1 - \rho^2)} + \mathbf{d}'V[\hat{\theta}]\mathbf{d}, \qquad (23.49)$$

where

$$\mathbf{d}' = \left(\frac{(1 - \rho^h)}{(1 - \rho)} : \left\{ \mu \frac{[1 - h\rho^{h-1}(1 - \rho) - \rho^h]}{(1 - \rho)^2} + h\rho^{h-1}y_T \right\} \right).$$

When $V[\hat{\theta}]$ is the asymptotic variance of the estimated parameters, (23.49) is sometimes known as the approximate forecast-error variance (or MSFE, more generally), as distinct from either the asymptotic MSFE (no parameter-estimation uncertainty, so that the second term in (23.49) is zero), or the exact MSFE. As Ericsson and Marquez (1998) note, there are four reasons why the approximate MSFE will differ from the exact. The first we have already mentioned: the finite-sample variance of the estimated parameters will differ from the asymptotic (namely the approximation in (23.63) in appendix B). Also, the estimated parameters (and powers thereof) are biased in finite samples, but not asymptotically; a first-order Taylor series expansion for $\hat{\rho}^h$ is used (see section 23.7); and y_T is conditioned on, rather than being treated as stochastic. The exact MSFE could be obtained by numerical integration.

From (23.49), it is apparent that because $V[\hat{\theta}]$ is $O(T^{-1})$, then so is the second term in (23.49) that accounts for the effect of parameter estimation uncertainty. Moreover, the in-sample and out-of-sample fits will be similar in the presence of parameter estimation uncertainty, so in the absence of any changes in the underlying DGP, forecast failure tests are unlikely to detect any problems.

We illustrate, with an empirical example, the impact on computed interval forecasts of adding parameter variances to the variances arising from the innovation errors. Consider a four-dimensional system of nominal M1 (M), total final expenditure (I), its implicit deflator (P), and the opportunity cost of holding money (R_n). We generate VAR and VEqCM multi-step forecasts over 1985(3)–1986(2) from an estimation sample of 1978(3)–1985(2) (both periods deliberately shortened to allow some discrimination), for ($m - p$, Δp, i, R_n) (lower case denotes logs).[5] Figures 23.1 and 23.2 show the resulting forecasts, with the bars based on the innovation errors only, and bands showing the overall 95 percent interval forecasts once parameter-estimation variances are included. There are distinct

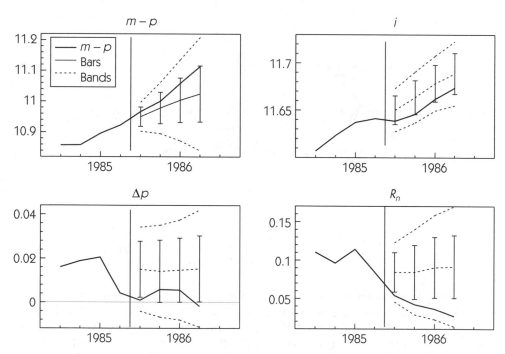

Figure 23.1 Forecasts and 95% prediction bars and bands for the monetary VAR

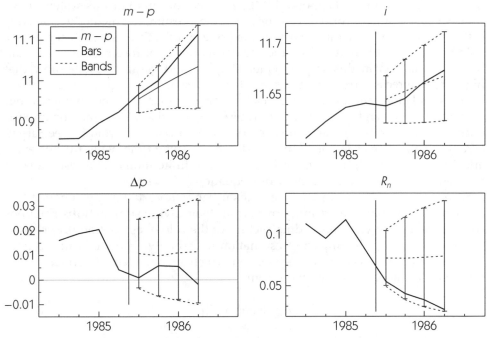

Figure 23.2 Forecasts and 95% prediction bars and bands for the monetary VEqCM

differences between the bands and bars for the VAR (which has 12 parameters in every equation for $T = 28$), but virtually none in the VEqCM, which was obtained as a valid reduction of the VAR. In systems of this sort, only when the model is highly over-parameterized, and the sample small (relative to the number of regressors), might we expect parameter estimation uncertainty to have much effect on the actual coverage levels of interval forecasts, at least until long horizons are considered (see for example, Stock, 1996).

MACROECONOMETRIC MODELS AND SIMULATION

A number of studies, such as, Fair (1980, 1984), suggest that parameter-estimation uncertainty is a significant source of forecast-error uncertainty in large-scale macroeconometric models. These studies attempt, via simulation of the model, to assess the quantitative importance of factors such as the equation disturbances, and uncertainty surrounding the exogenous variables, as well as that due to estimating the model parameters. Ericsson and Marquez (1998) also explore this issue in a large, practical forecasting system. Both suggest important impacts from parameter estimation. However, there are at least two ways in which the impact of estimation uncertainty may be over-stated.

The first follows from the use of estimation methods for which the second moments of the estimators do not exist. Sargan (1964) shows that while full-information maximum likelihood (FIML) estimates of simultaneous systems have finite second moments for reduced-form parameter estimates, methods which directly estimate the "structural" coefficients (for example, three-stage least squares: 3SLS) may not. This may inflate the second moments of forecasts derived from models estimated in this way. Hoque, Magnus, and Pesaran (1988) show that high-order forecast-error moments need not exist in autoregressive processes. Thus, simulation studies that used estimation methods with no moments, but reported (say) mean forecast biases or MSFEs, would likely overstate the importance of parameter estimation as an explanation of forecast uncertainty (see Sargan (1982), on the properties of Monte Carlo studies when moments do not exist, and Maasoumi (1978), for a method of ensuring finite moments in estimates of parameters derived from simultaneous equations).

Second, measuring estimation and disturbance uncertainty by independent drawings of the parameters and errors from their own (estimated) distributions could give a somewhat misleading picture of the role of estimation uncertainty. Consider assessing the impact of estimation uncertainty on forecast uncertainty by generating forecasts from a system in which independent drawings for an estimated parameter $\hat{\theta}$ were made from

$$\theta_j \sim IN_k[\hat{\theta}, V[\hat{\theta}]]. \tag{23.50}$$

and simply "plugged in" to generate forecasts. In dynamic or simultaneous systems, drawings from (23.50) may yield eigenvalues very close to, on, or occasionally outside, the unit circle, when the eigenvalues of $\hat{\theta}$ are well within the unit circle. In the latter cases, the integration–cointegration properties of the model may be altered, and the forecasts so generated may have radically different properties: but this is not a "pure" parameter uncertainty effect. To assess the impact of parameter-estimation uncertainty alone requires reestimating the model each time data are generated. Any desired restrictions on the cointegrating rank could then be imposed to ensure that the forecasts have their anticipated time-series properties. When, as in the case alluded to above, we are simulating data from an estimated model on time-series data, it may be sensible to bias-correct $\hat{\theta}$ before simulating data, and to make a commensurate bias-correction to the estimates of θ obtained on each of the simulated time paths. Kilian (1998) details how this can be done, in the context of generating impulse–response functions, to ensure that the bias-corrected parameter estimates are not pushed into the nonstationary region of the parameter space.

23.4.4. Model uncertainty or "overfitting"

The issue in this section is that models are typically selected by a data-based search over a (possibly large) number of alternative specifications, as distinct from the model being misspecified for the DGP. This "uncertainty" over the specification is not typically allowed for in the calculation of, for example, interval forecasts, so that in practice, such intervals might turn out to be too narrow.

Thus, forecasts generated from models selected in this way might tend to be less precise than anticipated. Recently, these effects have been stressed by a number of authors in the statistics literature (for example, Chatfield, 1995; Draper, 1995), and have also been a source of concern in the econometrics literature. How to allow for estimation uncertainty was discussed in section 23.4.3, but it is less clear how to allow for the impact on forecast uncertainty of data-based search: Draper suggests a Bayesian approach that averages over models.

That model uncertainty is almost always present is, of course, correct. Models are specified and fitted to data, and then forecasts are made – usually without taking in to account the model-selection strategy. But is this neglect important for assessing forecast uncertainty? Although the answer must be context specific, and dependent on the selection algorithm, there is evidence based on simple simulation experiments that downplays its importance. This could always be overturned in a specific instance, but we do not think selection is of critical importance in a stationary, constant-parameter world, as we now discuss.

We first consider reasons why model selection might matter. A large literature on "pre-testing" shows that model selection usually leads to biased parameter estimates (see, for example, Judge and Bock, 1978). For example, Chatfield (1995, section 2.4, example 4) considers the AR(1) DGP, $y_t = \rho y_{t-1} + \varepsilon_t$, with $\varepsilon_t \sim \text{IN}[0, 1]$, where $\rho = 0.4$ for a sample of $T = 30$. The pre-test estimator can be viewed as the average across a model-selection strategy where the two models are an AR(1) (when $\hat{\rho}$ is significant) and an AR(0) (when $\hat{\rho}$ is insignificant). Chatfield found the Monte Carlo estimate of ρ, conditional on $\hat{\rho}$ being significant, exceeded 0.5, whereas unconditional estimates are usually biased downwards. Given that such model-selection strategies lead to biased coefficient estimates, in-sample estimates of equation standard errors are also likely to be biased. Because these affect interval forecasts (and are often the only constituent for one-step intervals), then such intervals are likely to be biased in turn.

However, against this argument, consider the following "thought experiment" Monte Carlo. On iteration j data is simulated from the true model, say an ARMA(1, 1). Two models, say, an AR(1) and an MA(2) are estimated, and some model-selection strategy is used to select between them (for example, AIC or BIC). The chosen model is then used to forecast values of the series, interval forecasts calculated, and a forecast-failure test carried out that compares the in-sample fit to the out-of-sample squared errors (this example may be expanded to any number of models, and the logic remains the same). Over the replications of the Monte Carlo, are we likely to obtain an excessive number of forecast-failure test rejections? We have already established that stochastic misspecification need not lead to excess rejections, so on each replication of the Monte Carlo, it would not seem to matter which of the models we choose, since for each, the expected rejection rate equals the nominal size of the forecast-failure test.

This presents an apparent paradox: model selection seems irrelevant, yet the "quality" of the resulting forecasts should depend on that of the model. The resolution is that on any iteration of the Monte Carlo, a model-selection strategy (based on in-sample fit) is likely to choose the model where the estimated equation standard error under-estimates the true standard error, and that is the model for which the forecast-failure test is most likely to reject. This is one route by which model-selection strategies may under-estimate forecast uncertainty, and thus lead to over-rejections on tests of forecast failure. The larger the pool of models searched over, the larger such an effect might be.

Model selection and pre-test effects are complex phenomena, particularly in high-dimensional systems where there are parameter nonconstancies. Clements and Hendry (2002) consider a number of simulation experiments designed to explore the implications of pre-testing and model selection on the finding of forecast failure, and conclude that concerns may have been exaggerated. Moreover, we doubt that studies which address the issue by counting up the number of times "wrong" models are chosen in simulation studies, or by assessing the size of pre-test biases in coefficient estimates, offer many insights for forecasting. In particular, as noted above, biased estimation does not entail biased forecasts for symmetrically distributed errors, so any remaining problems concern understating the width of interval forecasts, which is not a "first-order" mistake in the context of economic forecasting. Contrast that last difficulty, for example, with the next problem – which can readily generate first-order forecast errors.

23.4.5.   Forecast origin mis-measurement

A poor assessment of the state of the economy at the time a forecast is made may impart an important source of error. The frequency with which preliminary data are subsequently revised suggests that forecasts may often be conditioned on data measured with a substantial degree of error. In practice, forecasts will be conditioned on information of varying degrees of reliability, spanning several periods (see, for example, Wallis, Andrews, Fisher, Longbottom, and Whitley, 1986). Typically, several "estimates" are released (such as the preliminary, or provisional, followed by revised figures), before the "final" data are made available. Gallo (1996) described an approach which eschews all but the final data as "purist," compared to the "naive" approach which treats all published data as if it were "true." He treats the estimates that become available as forecasts of the "true" value based on different information sets. If later estimates do not fully encapsulate all the information in earlier ones, then the potential for pooling arises to extract a better "signal" of the initial state of the economy from the noisy observations. Thus, survey information would appear to have a useful role in providing estimates of forecast-origin values. Howrey (1978) considered predicting final values from preliminary ones, then using those updates where final values were not available: see Harvey, McKenzie, Blake, and Desai (1983) and Boucelham and Teräsvirta (1990) for applications. Rahiala and Teräsvirta (1993) used a similar idea to extract a first estimate of quarterly industrial production from business survey data and forecast the next quarter. Clements and Hendry (1998, ch. 8) considered pooling preliminary estimates and model predictions of the initial state. Nevertheless, unless the forecast-origin values are systematically biased for the underlying state of the economy, "on average" this putative source of forecast failure will only have variance effects.

23.5. Conclusion

Forecast failure has occurred sufficiently frequently in macroeconomics that "economic forecasting" has come to have some of the same connotations as "military intelligence." We have sought to delineate the potential sources of such failure, and from among the possible contenders, ascertain those which are the most salient explanations. The outcome is perhaps surprising: unmodeled shifts in the deterministic components of models, howsoever these arise, are the primary cause of forecast failure, and other potential explanations (such as stochastic misspecification, inconsistent parameter estimates, etc.) appear to play a secondary role. Thus, forecast failure is not so much due to poor models, badly estimated from inaccurate data – although obviously none of those helps – as to unanticipated shifts occurring in nonstationary economies: in an important sense, unpredicted "economic earthquakes" are to blame. Of course, that does not make the forecasts any better, nor the policies contingent on them, but it does point to a way ahead.

Without anticipating the unpredictable, little can be done about deterministic shifts that occur after forecasts are announced. However, some models and methods are more robust to breaks that have occurred recently, and these will experience less systematic failure. While far from optimal, even avoiding systematic failure would be a distinct improvement over the past track record.

Appendix A: Taxonomy derivations for table 23.1

First, we use the approximation:

$$\hat{\Pi}^h = (\Pi_p + \delta_\Pi)^h \simeq \Pi_p^h + \sum_{i=0}^{h-1} \Pi_p^i \delta_\Pi \Pi_p^{h-i-1} \doteq \Pi_p^h + C_h. \tag{23.51}$$

Let $(\cdot)^v$ denote a vectorizing operator which stacks the columns of an $m \times n$ matrix $\mathbf{A}$ in an $mn \times 1$ vector $\mathbf{a}$, after which $(\mathbf{a})^v = \mathbf{a}$. Also, let $\otimes$ be the associated Kronecker product, so that when $\mathbf{B}$ is $p \times q$, then $\mathbf{A} \otimes \mathbf{B}$ is an $mp \times nq$ matrix of the form $\{b_{ij}\mathbf{A}\}$. Consequently, when $\mathbf{ABC}$ is defined,

$$(\mathbf{ABC})^v = (\mathbf{A} \otimes \mathbf{C}')\mathbf{B}^v.$$

Using these, from (23.51),

$$C_h(\mathbf{y}_T - \varphi_p) = (C_h(\mathbf{y}_T - \varphi_p))^v$$

$$= \left(\sum_{i=0}^{h-1} \Pi_p^i \otimes (\mathbf{y}_T - \varphi_p)' \Pi_p^{h-i-1'} \right) \delta_\Pi^v$$

$$\doteq \mathbf{F}_h \delta_\Pi^v. \tag{23.52}$$

To highlight components due to different effects (parameter change, estimation inconsistency, and estimation uncertainty), we decompose the term $(\mathbf{\Pi}^*)^h(\mathbf{y}_T - \varphi^*)$ in (23.8) into

$$(\mathbf{\Pi}^*)^h(\mathbf{y}_T - \varphi^*) = (\mathbf{\Pi}^*)^h(\mathbf{y}_T - \varphi) + (\mathbf{\Pi}^*)^h(\varphi - \varphi^*),$$

whereas $\hat{\mathbf{\Pi}}^h(\hat{\mathbf{y}}_T - \hat{\varphi})$ equals

$$(\mathbf{\Pi}_p^h + \mathbf{C}_h)(\delta_y - (\hat{\varphi} - \varphi_p) + (\mathbf{y}_T - \varphi) - (\varphi_p - \varphi))$$

$$= (\mathbf{\Pi}_p^h + \mathbf{C}_h)\delta_y - (\mathbf{\Pi}_p^h + \mathbf{C}_h)\delta_\varphi + (\mathbf{\Pi}_p^h + \mathbf{C}_h)(\mathbf{y}_T - \varphi_p)$$

$$= (\mathbf{\Pi}_p^h + \mathbf{C}_h)\delta_y - (\mathbf{\Pi}_p^h + \mathbf{C}_h)\delta_\varphi + \mathbf{F}_h\delta_\Pi^v + \mathbf{\Pi}_p^h(\mathbf{y}_T - \varphi) - \mathbf{\Pi}_p^h(\varphi_p - \varphi).$$

Thus, $(\mathbf{\Pi}^*)^h(\mathbf{y}_T - \varphi^*) - \hat{\mathbf{\Pi}}^h(\hat{\mathbf{y}}_T - \hat{\varphi})$ yields

$$((\mathbf{\Pi}^*)^h - \mathbf{\Pi}_p^h)(\mathbf{y}_T - \varphi) - \mathbf{F}_h\delta_\Pi^v - (\mathbf{\Pi}_p^h + \mathbf{C}_h)\delta_y - (\mathbf{\Pi}^*)^h(\varphi^* - \varphi)$$

$$+ \mathbf{\Pi}_p^h(\varphi_p - \varphi) + (\mathbf{\Pi}_p^h + \mathbf{C}_h)\delta_\varphi. \tag{23.53}$$

The interaction $\mathbf{C}_h\delta_\varphi$ is like a "covariance," but is omitted from the table. Hence (23.53) becomes

$$((\mathbf{\Pi}^*)^h - \mathbf{\Pi}^h)(\mathbf{y}_T - \varphi) + (\mathbf{\Pi}^h - \mathbf{\Pi}_p^h)(\mathbf{y}_T - \varphi)$$

$$- (\mathbf{\Pi}^*)^h(\varphi^* - \varphi) + \mathbf{\Pi}_p^h(\varphi_p - \varphi) - (\mathbf{\Pi}_p^h + \mathbf{C}_h)\delta_y - \mathbf{F}_h\delta_\Pi^v + \mathbf{\Pi}_p^h\delta_\varphi.$$

The first and third rows have expectations of zero, so the second row collects the "noncentral" terms.

Finally, for the term $\varphi^* - \hat{\varphi}$ in (23.8), we have (on the same principle)

$$(\varphi^* - \varphi) + (\varphi - \varphi_p) - \delta_\varphi.$$

Appendix B: Approximating powers of estimates

We use a number of approximations to obtain tractable expressions for variances of powers of estimated parameters, following Schmidt (1977), Baillie (1979b), Baillie (1979a), and Chong and Hendry (1986): see Ericsson and Marquez (1989, 1998) and Campos (1992) for good expositions and unifying treatments. We consider the stationary AR(1) model

$$y_t = \mu + \rho y_{t-1} + v_t \quad v_t \sim \text{IN}[0, \sigma_v^2],$$

where estimation is by OLS. Let

$$\hat{\rho} = \rho + \delta, \tag{23.54}$$

where δ is $O_p(1/\sqrt{T})$, so that powers of δ are asymptotically negligible. Then the first approximation is

$$\hat{\rho}^h = (\rho + \delta)^h \simeq \rho^h + h\delta\rho^{h-1} = \rho^h + h\rho^{h-1}(\hat{\rho} - \rho). \qquad (23.55)$$

Consequently,

$$\mathsf{E}[\hat{\rho}^h] \simeq \rho^h + h\rho^{h-1}\mathsf{E}[\hat{\rho} - \rho] \simeq \rho^h,$$

by the approximation that $\mathsf{E}[\hat{\rho} - \rho] = 0$. Higher-order approximations can be calculated if needed. Next,

$$\mathsf{V}[(\hat{\rho}^h - \rho^h)] \simeq \mathsf{V}[h\rho^{h-1}(\hat{\rho} - \rho)] = h^2\rho^{2(h-1)}\mathsf{V}[\hat{\rho}]. \qquad (23.56)$$

This result also follows from the usual formula for a nonlinear estimation function:

$$\mathsf{V}[\hat{\rho}^h] \simeq \frac{\partial\rho^h}{\partial\rho}\mathsf{V}[\hat{\rho}]\frac{\partial\rho^h}{\partial\rho}. \qquad (23.57)$$

Further,

$$\mu\rho^j - \hat{\mu}\hat{\rho}^j = \rho^j(\mu - \hat{\mu}) + \mu(\rho^j - \hat{\rho}^j) - (\mu - \hat{\mu})(\rho^j - \hat{\rho}^j), \qquad (23.58)$$

where the final term is negligible relative to the first two as $T \to \infty$. The second main approximation comes in ignoring that term, so that from (23.55),

$$\sum_{j=0}^{h-1}(\mu\rho^j - \hat{\mu}\hat{\rho}^j) \simeq (\mu - \hat{\mu})\sum_{j=0}^{h-1}\rho^j + \mu(\rho - \hat{\rho})\sum_{j=0}^{h-1}j\rho^{j-1}$$

$$= (\mu - \hat{\mu})\frac{(1 - \rho^h)}{(1 - \rho)} + (\rho - \hat{\rho})\mu\frac{(1 - h\rho^{h-1}(1 - \rho) - \rho^h)}{(1 - \rho)^2}$$

$$= (\theta - \hat{\theta})'\mathbf{b}, \qquad (23.59)$$

say, where

$$\mathbf{b}' = \left[\frac{(1 - \rho^h)}{(1 - \rho)} : \mu\frac{[1 - h\rho^{h-1}(1 - \rho) - \rho^h]}{(1 - \rho)^2}\right].$$

Then,

$$\mathsf{E}\left[\left\{\sum_{j=0}^{h-1}(\mu\rho^j - \hat{\mu}\hat{\rho}^j)\right\}^2\right] = \mathbf{b}'\mathsf{V}[\hat{\theta}]\mathbf{b}. \qquad (23.60)$$

Finally, using (23.55) and (23.59),

$$\mathsf{E}\left[\left\{\sum_{j=0}^{h-1}(\mu\rho^j - \hat{\mu}\hat{\rho}^j)\right\}(\rho^h - \hat{\rho}^h)\right]y_T = h\rho^{h-1}\mathbf{b}'\mathsf{E}[(\theta - \hat{\theta})(\rho - \hat{\rho})]y_T \quad (23.61)$$

$$= h\rho^{h-1}\mathbf{b}'\mathsf{V}[\hat{\theta}]\mathbf{s}y_T,$$

where $\mathbf{s}' = (0 : 1)$. Letting $h\rho^{h-1}y_T\mathbf{s} = \mathbf{c}$ and $\mathbf{d} = \mathbf{b} + \mathbf{c}$, then

$$\mathsf{V}[\hat{e}_{T+h}|y_T] = \sigma_v^2\frac{1 - \rho^{2h}}{1 - \rho^2} + \mathbf{d}'\mathsf{V}[\hat{\theta}]\mathbf{d}, \quad (23.62)$$

where

$$\mathsf{V}[\hat{\theta}] = \mathsf{V}\begin{bmatrix}\hat{\mu}\\\hat{\rho}\end{bmatrix} = \sigma_v^2\mathsf{E}\begin{bmatrix}T & \Sigma_{t=1}^T y_{t-1}\\\Sigma_{t=1}^T y_{t-1} & \Sigma_{t=1}^T y_{t-1}^2\end{bmatrix}^{-1}$$

$$\simeq T^{-1}\begin{bmatrix}\sigma_v^2 + \mu^2(1 + \rho)(1 - \rho)^{-1} & -\mu(1 + \rho)\\-\mu(1 + \rho) & (1 - \rho)^2\end{bmatrix} \quad (23.63)$$

is the asymptotic covariance matrix of the estimated parameters.

Notes

1 This chapter draws on our joint work over the last decade on economic forecasting. Our two-volume set, Clements and Hendry (1998) *Forecasting Economic Time Series*, CUP, and Clements and Hendry (1999) *Forecasting Non-stationary Economic Time Series*, MIT, provide a unified treatment.
2 On integration and cointegration, some seminal references are Nelson and Plosser (1982), Engle and Granger (1987), and Johansen (1988).
3 We assume finite-sample estimation biases are small enough that they can be ignored. Forecasts may be approximately unbiased even though parameter estimates are not: see, for example, Hendry and Trivedi (1972) and Clements and Hendry (1998, chs. 5 and 6).
4 For the DV and DDV models, the formulae programmed for the forecast-error variances in most software assumes that the errors are serially uncorrelated, and can be seriously misleading when the DGP departs from the assumed model.
5 These models were developed by Hendry and Doornik (1994).

References

Attfield, C.L.F., D. Demery, and N.W. Duck (1995). Estimating the U.K. demand for money function: a test of two approaches. Mimeo, Economics Department, University of Bristol.

Baillie, R.T. (1979a). The asymptotic mean squared error of multi-step prediction from the regression model with autoregressive errors. *Journal of the American Statistical Association*, 74, 175–84.

Baillie, R.T. (1979b). Asymptotic prediction mean squared error for vector autoregressive models. *Biometrika*, 66, 675–78.

Bontemps, C. and G.E. Mizon (2001). Congruence and encompassing. In B.P. Stigum (ed.), *Econometrics and the Philosophy of Economics*. Cambridge, MA: MIT Press, forthcoming.

Boucelham, J. and T. Teräsvirta (1990). Use of preliminary values in forecasting industrial production. *International Journal of Forecasting*, 6, 463–8.

Campbell, J.Y. and P. Perron (1991). Pitfalls and opportunities: What macroeconomists should know about unit roots. In O.J. Blanchard and S. Fischer (eds.), *NBER Macroeconomics Annual 1991*. Cambridge, MA: MIT Press.

Campos, J. (1992). Confidence intervals for linear combinations of forecasts from dynamic econometric models. *Journal of Policy Modeling*, 14, 535–60.

Chatfield, C. (1993). Calculating interval forecasts. *Journal of Business and Economic Statistics*, 11, 121–35.

Chatfield, C. (1995). Model uncertainty, data mining and statistical inference. *Journal of the Royal Statistical Society, A*, 158, 419–66 (with discussion).

Chong, Y.Y. and D.F. Hendry (1986). Econometric evaluation of linear macro-economic models. *Review of Economic Studies*, 53, 671–90. Reprinted in Granger, C.W.J. (ed.) (1990). *Modelling Economic Series*. Oxford: Clarendon Press.

Clements, M.P. and D.F. Hendry (1998). *Forecasting Economic Time Series*. Cambridge: Cambridge University Press.

Clements, M.P. and D.F. Hendry (1999). *Forecasting Non-Stationary Economic Time Series*. Cambridge, MA.: MIT Press.

Clements, M.P. and D.F. Hendry (2001). Forecasting with difference-stationary and trend-stationary models. *Econometrics Journal*, 4, S1–19.

Clements, M.P. and D.F. Hendry (2002). Modelling methodology and forecast failure. *The Econometrics Journal*, forthcoming.

Corsi, P., R.E. Pollock, and J.C. Prakken (1982). The Chow test in the presence of serially correlated errors. In G.C. Chow and P. Corsi (eds.), *Evaluating the Reliability of Macro-Economic Models*. New York: John Wiley.

Doornik, J.A. and D.F. Hendry (2001). *Modelling Dynamic Systems using PcFive 10*. London: Timberlake Consultants Press.

Draper, D. (1995). Assessment and propagation of model uncertainty. *Journal of the Royal Statistical Society, B* 57, 45–97. With discussion.

Eitrheim, Ø., T.A. Husebø, and R. Nymoen (1999). Equilibrium-correction versus differencing in macroeconometric forecasting. *Economic Modelling*, 16, 515–44.

Engle, R.F. and C.W.J. Granger (1987). Cointegration and error correction: representation, estimation and testing. *Econometrica*, 55, 251–76.

Ericsson, N.R. and J.R. Marquez (1989). Exact and approximate multi-period mean-square forecast errors for dynamic econometric models. International Finance Discussion Paper 348, Federal Reserve Board.

Ericsson, N.R. and J.R. Marquez (1998). A framework for economic forecasting. *Econometrics Journal*, 1, C228–66.

Fair, R.C. (1980). Estimating the expected predictive accuracy of econometric models. *International Economic Review*, 21, 355–78.

Fair, R.C. (1984). *Specification, Estimation, and Analysis of Macroeconometric Models*. Cambridge, MA: Harvard University Press.

Friedman, M. and A.J. Schwartz (1982). *Monetary Trends in the United States and the United Kingdom: Their Relation to Income, Prices, and Interest Rates, 1867–1975*. Chicago: University of Chicago Press.

Gallo, G.M. (1996). Forecast uncertainty reduction in nonlinear models. *Journal of Italian Statistical Soceity*, 5, 73–98.

Harvey, A.C. (1989). *Forecasting, Structural Time Series Models and the Kalman Filter*. Cambridge: Cambridge University Press.

Harvey, A.C., C.R. McKenzie, D.P.C. Blake, and M.J. Desai (1983). Irregular data revisions. In A. Zellner (ed.), *Applied Time Series Analysis of Economic Data*. Washington, D.C.: Bureau of the Census.

Hendry, D.F. (1979). The behavior of inconsistent instrumental variables estimators in dynamic systems with autocorrelated errors. *Journal of Econometrics*, 9, 295–314.

Hendry, D.F. (1995). *Dynamic Econometrics*. Oxford: Oxford University Press.

Hendry, D.F. and J.A. Doornik (1994). Modelling linear dynamic econometric systems. *Scottish Journal of Political Economy*, 41, 1–33.

Hendry, D.F. and H.-M. Krolzig (1999). Improving on "Data mining reconsidered" by K.D. Hoover and S.J. Perez. *Econometrics Journal*, 2, 41–58.

Hendry, D.F. and P.K. Trivedi (1972). Maximum likelihood estimation of difference equations with movingaverage errors: a simulation study. *Review of Economic Studies*, 32, 117–45.

Hoover, K.D. and S.J. Perez (1999). Data mining reconsidered: encompassing and the general-to-specific approach to specification search. *Econometrics Journal*, 2, 1–25.

Hoque, A., J.R. Magnus, and B. Pesaran (1988). The exact multi-period mean-square forecast error for the first-order autoregressive model. *Journal of Econometrics*, 39, 327–46.

Howrey, E.P. (1978). The use of preliminary data in econometric forecasting. *Review of Economics and Statistics*, 60, 193–200.

Johansen, S. (1988). Statistical analysis of cointegration vectors. *Journal of Economic Dynamics and Control*, 12, 231–254. Reprinted in R.F. Engle and C.W.J. Granger (eds.) (1991). *Long-Run Economic Relationships*. Oxford: Oxford University Press, 131–52.

Johansen, S. and K. Juselius (1990). Maximum likelihood estimation and inference on cointegration – with application to the demand for money. *Oxford Bulletin of Economics and Statistics*, 52, 169–210.

Judge, G.G. and M.E. Bock (1978). *The Statistical Implications of Pre-Test and Stein-Rule Estimators in Econometrics*. Amsterdam: North Holland.

Kilian, L. (1998). Small-sample confidence intervals for impulse response functions. *The Review of Economics and Statistics*, 80, 218–30.

Krolzig, H.-M. and D.F. Hendry (2001). Computer automation of general-to-specific model selection procedures. *Journal of Economic Dynamics and Control*, 25, 831–66.

Maasoumi, E. (1978). A modified Stein-like estimator for the reduced form coefficients of simultaneous equations. *Econometrica*, 46, 695–704.

Marquez, J.R. and N.R. Ericsson (1993). Evaluating forecasts of the U.S. trade balance. In R. Bryant, P. Hooper, and C.L. Mann (eds.), *Evaluating Policy Regimes: New Research in Empirical Macroeconomics*. Washington, D.C.: Brookings Institution, 671–732.

Miller, P.J. (1978). Forecasting with econometric methods: A comment. *Journal of Business*, 51, 579–86.

Nelson, C.R. and C.I. Plosser (1982). Trends and random walks in macroeconomic time series: some evidence and implications. *Journal of Monetary Economics*, 10, 139–62.

Rahiala, M. and T. Teräsvirta (1993). Business survey data in forecasting the output of Swedish and Finnish metal and engineering industries. *Journal of Forecasting*, 12, 255–71.

Sargan, J.D. (1964). Three-stage least-squares and full maximum likelihood estimates. *Econometrica*, 32, 77–81. Reprinted in J.D. Sargan (1988). *Contributions to Econometrics*, Vol. 1. Cambridge: Cambridge University Press, 118–23.

Sargan, J.D. (1982). On Monte Carlo estimates of moments that are infinite. In R.L. Basmann and G.F. Rhodes (eds.), *Advances in Econometrics: A Research Annual*, Vol. 1. Greenwich, CT: Jai Press, 267–99.

Schmidt, P. (1974). The asymptotic distribution of forecasts in the dynamic simulation of an econometric model. *Econometrica*, 42, 303–9.

Schmidt, P. (1977). Some small sample evidence on the distribution of dynamic simulation forecasts. *Econometrica*, 45, 97–105.

Spanos, A. (1989). Early empirical findings on the consumption function, stylized facts or fiction: a retrospective view. *Oxford Economic Papers*, 41, 150–69.

Stock, J.H. (1996). VAR, error correction and pre-test forecasts at long horizons. *Oxford Bulletin of Economics and Statistics*, 58, 685–701.

Wallis, K.F. (1989). Macroeconomic forecasting: a survey. *Economic Journal*, 99, 28–61.

Wallis, K.F., M.J. Andrews, P.G. Fisher, J. Longbottom, and J.D. Whitley (1986). *Models of the U.K. Economy: A Third Review by the ESRC Macroeconomic Modelling Bureau*. Oxford: Oxford University Press.

Author Index

Subject Index